TH**I**NK
SOCIAL PSYCHOLOGY

KIMBERLEY J. DUFF
Cerritos College

Allyn & Bacon

Boston   Columbus   Indianapolis   New York   San Francisco   Upper Saddle River
Amsterdam   Cape Town   Dubai   London   Madrid   Milan   Munich   Paris   Montreal   Toronto
Delhi   Mexico City   Sao Paulo   Sydney   Hong Kong   Seoul   Singapore   Taipei   Tokyo

Editorial Director: Craig Campanella
Editor in Chief: Jessica Mosher
Senior Sponsoring Editor: Amber Mackey
Editorial Assistant: Jackie Moya
Director of Marketing: Brandy Dawson
Executive Marketing Manager: Jeanette Koskinas
Marketing Assistant: Shauna Fishweicher
Senior Production Project Manager: Patrick Cash-Peterson
Manufacturing Buyer: Debbie Rossi

Manager, Design Development: John Christiana
Interior Design: Kathy Mrozek and John Christiana
Cover Design: John Christiana
Photo Researcher: Noami Kornhauser
Full-Service Project Management: Staci Wolfson, Darrell Walker, Matt Skalka, Russ Hall, and Michael Egolf/Words & Numbers
Composition: Words & Numbers
Printer/Binder: LSC Communications
Cover Printer: LSC Communications

> To all of my current and past students: You continue
> to influence my thinking and my teaching.
> Finally, to my husband who helped me to "sway in
> the breeze" while chaos reigned.

Library of Congress Cataloging-in-Publication Data

Duff, Kimberley, 1969
  Think social psychology / Kimberley Duff. -- 1st ed.
      p. cm.
  Includes bibliographical references and index.
  ISBN-13: 978-0-205-01354-8 (student ed. : alk. paper)
  ISBN-10: 0-205-01354-6 (student ed. : alk. paper)
  ISBN-13: 978-0-205-05533-3 (exam copy : alk. paper)
  ISBN-10: 0-205-05533-8 (exam copy : alk. paper)
  1. Social psychology. I. Title.

HM1033.D84 2012
302--dc22

                                2010050676

20 2023

Allyn & Bacon
is an imprint of

www.pearsonhighered.com

Exam Copy: ISBN-10:   0-205-05533-8
                  ISBN-13:   978-0-205-05533-3

Student Edition: ISBN-10:   0-205-01354-6
                  ISBN-13:   978-0-205-01354-8

BRIEF CONTENTS

CONTENTS

ACKNOWLEDGMENTS

I sincerely appreciate the quality of feedback from all of the reviewers: Claudette Jackson (McLennan Community College), William Goggin (University of Southern Mississippi), Darla Rocha (San Jacinto College North Campus), Nathan Arbuckle (The Ohio State University), Luis Vega (California State University, Bakersfield), Suzanne Kieffer (University of Houston), Elizabeth Rhodes (Florida International University), Kimberly Fairchild (Manhattan College), and Kari Terzino (Iowa State University). Your insightful reviews contributed to shaping the final product.

Thank you to Jessica Mosher for being the driving force behind this textbook. Susan Hartman, I am once again honored to work with you on such a fun project. My thanks to Jeff Marshall, for all of your feedback. Amber Mackey, your guidance and mentoring along the way kept me sane, and I have thoroughly enjoyed our correspondence. And of course, Paige Clunie, whom I relied on throughout. Thank you to my assistant, Jessie Osuna, for your help in researching articles for this text.

Thank you to the Marketing Team at Pearson for their dedication to this project: Jeanette Koskinas, Nicole Kunzmann, and Shauna Fishweicher.

A special thanks to the production team at Pearson, for their commitment to bringing this book to life visually: Liz Napolitano, Patrick Cash-Peterson, John Christiana, and Naomi Kornhauser.

The members of the Words & Numbers team were outstanding to work with. Staci Wolfson, your ability to conceptualize from idea to reality was essential, and I will miss your Friday e-mails. My gratitude to Salimah Perkins for her guidance. And to the many individuals who worked behind the scenes, thank you for your efforts to bring this vision to life: Michael Egolf, Darrell Walker, Matt Skalka, Adam Noll, Russ Hall, and Ashley Johnson.

Kimberley Duff
Cerritos College

KIMBERLEY J. DUFF received her PhD in Social Psychology at the University of Illinois at Chicago. She is currently a professor of psychology at Cerritos Community College in California, where she is passionate about teaching and helping her students succeed. Every year, she teaches over 600 students in Social Psychology, Introductory Psychology (both online and in traditional classrooms) and a Research Methods laboratory course. At Cerritos College, she has twice been recognized for her teaching and mentoring of students with the Outstanding Faculty Award and the Outstanding Advisor of the Year Award. More recently, the American Psychological Association's Society for the Teaching of Psychology honored her with the Wayne Weiten Teaching Excellence Award. She has given presentations on teaching methods at the American Psychological Association, NITOP (National Institute for the Teaching of Psychology) and Western Psychological Association annual conventions.

Kimberley has conducted research on spontaneous attributions, racial and social stereotypes, the benefits of tutorials on learning, and the impact of podcasting in the classroom. She also mentors her students in original psychological research that many of them present at psychological conferences, and she serves as a mentor for graduate students in the Teaching Assistant Program. To capture the success of her students' accomplishments, Kimberley developed a mentoring Web site for psychology students found at www.cerritos.edu/kduff/map. She serves as a co-advisor for the Cerritos College Psychology Club and Psi Beta chapter, which has been recognized three times with the national Outstanding Chapter of the Year Award under her guidance. Additionally, she has authored and developed multimedia content for a top-selling Introductory Psychology textbook.

WHAT IS SOCIAL PSYCHOLOGY?

WHAT IS SOCIAL PSYCHOLOGY?
WHAT ARE THE ROOTS OF SOCIAL PSYCHOLOGY?
WHAT ARE THE DIFFERENT PERSPECTIVES OF SOCIAL PSYCHOLOGY?
IS SOCIAL PSYCHOLOGY JUST COMMON SENSE?

In 1968,

Jane Elliott, a teacher from Riceville, Iowa, demonstrated the arbitrary nature of prejudice by initiating a polarizing activity with her third-grade students. Elliott's activity was prompted by the assassination of Martin Luther King, Jr. Unsure of how to explain what King stood for and why he was killed to her young students, Elliott decided to teach her students, all of whom were white, what it is like to be discriminated against. Elliott divided her students into two groups, those with blue eyes and those with brown eyes. The blue-eyed group, or Blues, was designated the superior group, and the brown-eyed group, or Browns, was designated the inferior group. As the inferior group, the Browns were told that they were less intelligent and less important than their fellow students, and Elliott constantly belittled them. Eventually, the Blues joined in on the discriminatory behavior, making judgments against and showing hatred toward those in the inferior group. The next day, Elliott reversed the experiment, making the Browns the superior group, and the brown-eyed students expressed the same prejudicial behavior (Tozer, Violas, & Senese, 1993).

How much of a role do prejudice and bigotry play in your life? Have you ever been the victim of prejudice or bigotry, or have you ever been the perpetrator of this behavior? If you are a member of a minority group, you may have sometimes felt unjustly judged by other members of society. If you are a member of a majority group, you may have acted superior to a member of a minority group. As a society, we are programmed to assume that the divide that instigates bigotry between minority and majority groups is based on race, gender, or other socially significant factors (e.g., white versus black, men versus women, or gay versus straight). Our social norms support this idea, but social psychologists argue that discrimination is based on factors that are purely arbitrary and meaningless, such as height, hair color, or even shoe size. These kinds of seemingly insignificant factors can instigate discrimination just as easily as skin color or sex. Elliott's experiment highlights just how random and powerful prejudice can be. The Blues were quick to embody their initial superiority, while the Browns readily accepted their inferiority.

While Elliott's activity was simply a demonstration rather than an experiment in discrimination (and used methods that are ethically questionable—something that social psychologists have also had to deal with), it does expose the irrational nature of discrimination. Prejudice and bigotry can take their place in the long list of concepts that are widely misunderstood. Social psychologists seek to examine and analyze these types of concepts so that we can begin to understand the motivation and reasoning behind our behavior.

CHAPTER **01**

What Is Social Psychology?

What possessed explorers hundreds of years ago to leave their home countries to sail across virtually unknown seas? Why were members of the U.S. space program so eager to launch themselves into uncharted areas beyond the reach of Earth? If you were a psychologist, you might say that the possibility of locating new resources and the novelty of being the first to discover something was the motivation.

If you were a sociologist, you might say that humans are curious by nature, and that their interest in the unknown drove them to seek out uncharted territories. If you were a social psychologist, however, you might say that the motivation came from the individual cultures of the explorers. Christopher Columbus set out on his expedition because the people of Spain desired to gain political and economic power in Europe by discovering new trade routes. Neil Armstrong and the rest of the Apollo 11 crew were fulfilling the United States' desire to flaunt its capabilities in science and exploration and to secure its status as a superpower in the industrial world.

No explanation is right or wrong; they simply emerge from different schools of thought. Psychology, sociology, and social psychology can be viewed as existing on a continuum, with psychology at one end, sociology at the other, and social psychology somewhere in between. Sociologists focus on the entire group, or the societal level, while social psychologists are interested in the interaction of the individual person and the given situation. The focus of social psychology can be described as having three main facets: social perception, social influence, and social interaction. Additionally, social psychologists apply their research to help understand and address issues in other fields such as law, business, and health.

Social perception is the process through which individuals form impressions of others and interpret information about them. For example, when we see a person driving a flashy sports car, we may think that the driver has a lot of money and is successful in life. **Social influence** is the process through which other people affect an individual's thoughts or actions. A person may experience social influence when deciding what profession to pursue. For example, an individual may choose to become a doctor not just because she is interested in medicine, but also because her parent is a doctor. Or the choice could be influenced by the fact that in our society, medicine is viewed as a noble profession, and the individual wishes to be respected by others. Social influence results from social interaction. Social interaction refers to the relationship between two or more individuals. This is the basis of analysis for social psychologists, who strive to understand and explain how the thoughts, feelings, and behaviors of individuals are influenced by the actual, imagined, or implied presence of others (Allport, 1954).

Much like social psychology complements and interacts with the disciplines of sociology, it also intersects with a number of other subdivisions of the umbrella field of psychology. For instance, both social and personality psychologists study the behaviors, thoughts, and feelings of individuals. Personality psychologists seek to

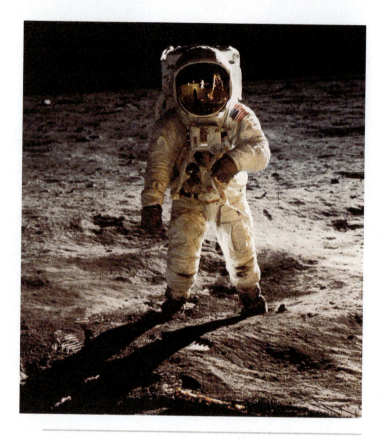

∧
∧ Social factors can influence many different
∧ types of behavior, **even a journey to the moon.**

understand what distinguishes one personality from another; social psychology complements that by taking into account situational factors.

Similarly, while cognitive psychologists examine mental processes, like thinking, reasoning, remembering, and learning, social psychologists can strengthen their findings by considering how the social world impacts thought processes. And clinical psychologists, who study mental disorders, can benefit from social psychological research that may help explain how situational and social factors can contribute to and affect mental health.

What Are the Roots of Social Psychology?

Social psychology is a fairly young discipline that did not distinguish itself within the field of psychology until the 20th century. In fact, in 1979, Dorwin Cartwright stated that approximately "90 percent of all social psychologists who have ever lived are alive at the present time" (Cartwright, 1979). While the activities that define concepts such as social interaction and social influence have been

<<< **Social perception causes us to think that people who** wear glasses are more intelligent than those who don't.

present for as long as there have been humans on Earth, a strong platform on which to study these concepts did not exist until the development of Western culture. Some might even pinpoint it to the development of modern American culture. When introducing social psychology to a new generation of American graduate students in 1954, psychologist Gordon Allport stated, "While the roots of social psychology lie in the intellectual soil of the whole Western tradition, its present flowering is recognized to be characteristically an American phenomenon" (Farr, 1996).

One of the earliest formal studies in social psychology occurred at the end of the 19th century. In 1898, Norman Triplett, a professor at Indiana University, conducted a study that asked the question, "What happens

when individuals join together with other individuals?" As a fan of bicycling, Triplett noticed that competitive cyclists performed better during races than during solo rides. He timed their unpaced rides, only an effort to lower previously established times, and compared them to paced rides against other contestants (Triplett, 1898).

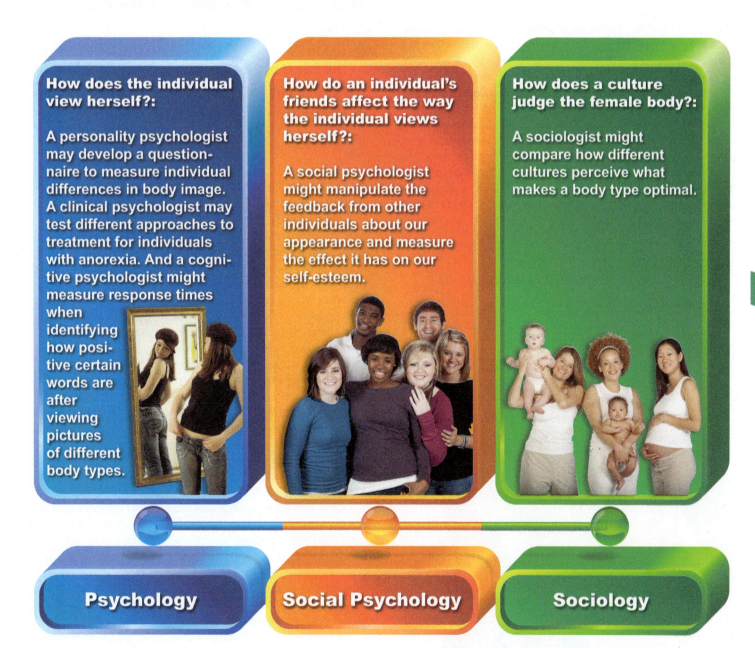

How does the individual view herself?:

A personality psychologist may develop a questionnaire to measure individual differences in body image. A clinical psychologist may test different approaches to treatment for individuals with anorexia. And a cognitive psychologist might measure response times when identifying how positive certain words are after viewing pictures of different body types.

How do an individual's friends affect the way the individual views herself?:

A social psychologist might manipulate the feedback from other individuals about our appearance and measure the effect it has on our self-esteem.

How does a culture judge the female body?:

A sociologist might compare how different cultures perceive what makes a body type optimal.

Psychology   **Social Psychology**   **Sociology**

∧
∧ **Teen Body Image Issues on the Method of Thinking Spectrum.** Psychology, sociology, and social psychology can be viewed as existing on a continuum, with psychology at one end, sociology at the other, and social psychology somewhere in between. But it doesn't have to be one or another; an interdisciplinary approach merging two or all three can be taken as well.

SOCIAL FACILITATION the enhancement of a well-learned performance when another person is present

SOCIAL LOAFING a phenomenon that occurs when individuals make less of an effort when attempting to achieve a particular goal as a group than they would if they were attempting to achieve the goal on their own

To understand how pace keeping and competition among others affect an individual's performance, Triplett arranged a study that measured the performance of 40 children while playing a simple game. The results of the study suggested that the children performed better when playing in pairs than when playing alone. This study, considered to be the first published study in social psychology, documented the concept of **social facilitation**, or the enhancement of performance when another person is present. You may feel the effects of social facilitation in your academic life. For example, your instructor asks you to complete a task that you are well skilled at, such as reading a paragraph in a foreign language, and you perform better in class than if you were alone.

While the concept of social facilitation has been supported in studies beyond Triplett's studies, at the time, it was at odds with an earlier study that involved performance evaluation. In 1883, French professor Max Ringelmann conducted a study (although it was not published until 1913) from which he concluded that an individual's performance actually gets worse in the presence of others. Ringelmann asked a group of individuals to tug on a rope both individually and as a team. He found that the

The phenomenon of social facilitation would
∨
∨ cause this athlete to lift more weight in
∨ front of a crowd than he would alone.

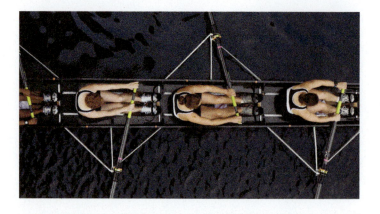

∧
∧ According to the concept of social loafing,
∧ the presence of others may cause these
rowers to put forth less of an effort when working as a team than they would if they were working individually.

participants pulled harder when working as individuals than as a team. In fact, he found that the larger the group, the weaker the individual effort.

On the surface, Ringelmann's and Triplett's studies seem to be at odds, but when examined closely, one can see that the results actually highlight two different patterns of human behavior. In the bicycle study, the contribution of each individual member could not be identified, but in the rope study, each individual's contribution was not discernible, meaning that each individual's effort, or lack thereof, would not be noticed by the spectators.

Ringelmann's study illustrated the concept of **social loafing**, a phenomenon that occurs when individuals make less of an effort when attempting to achieve a goal as a group than they would if they were attempting to achieve the goal on their own. You may have had first-hand experience with social loafing if you have worked on a group project for class and one member of the group doesn't pull his or her weight. You might refer to this type of social loafer as a slacker. Social loafing can apply to more than just the individual. A subgroup that is part of a larger unit can participate in social loafing. This can occur in the corporate world when one department does not make an adequate contribution to the success of a company and leaves other departments to pick up the slack.

Other early social psychologists had profound impacts on the field. When people began to recognize social prejudice in the 1930s, researchers Katz and Braly gave shape to the idea of stereotypes as social psychologists study them now. After asking 100 Princeton University graduates to list five characteristics of 10 different racial and ethnic groups, Katz and Braly found that the subjects developed ideas about each group without having necessarily had any contact with members of these groups (Katz & Braly, 1933).

Another example of a landmark study is Richard LaPiere's empirical study of the discrepancies between individuals' attitudes and behaviors. LaPiere traveled around the country with a Chinese couple. Visiting over 350 restaurants and hotels, the couple was rejected entry just once. When surveyed after the trip, however, 92 percent of the businesses who answered the questions reported they would not accept Chinese individuals (LaPiere, 1934). The topic of the relationship between attitudes and behaviors became a mainstay among the topics social psychologists continue to study.

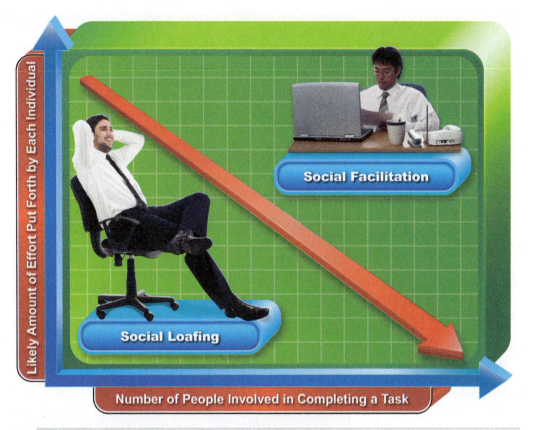

Likely Amount of Effort Put Forth by Each Individual

Social Facilitation

Social Loafing

Number of People Involved in Completing a Task

∧
∧
∧ **Social Loafing vs. Social Facilitation.** Accountability is a major factor in determining **if a person will be a loafer or a facilitator, as illustrated here.** But if the task is important, loafing is diminished, and if we are good at it, we will likely perform well. **These factors can eclipse accountability.**

SOCIAL PSYCHOLOGY IN THE 20TH CENTURY

By the start of the 20th century, social psychology had begun to establish itself as an independent discipline through the development of a separate curriculum and the formation of a specialized organization. A major milestone in the development of social psychology curriculum was the publishing of textbooks. The first two textbooks on the subject of social psychology were published in 1908, one by sociologist Edward Ross and the other by psychologist William McDougall, titled *Social Psychology* and *Introduction to Social Psychology*,

>>> Social psychologists address important social issues by working with refugees, or internally displaced persons (IDPs), to help them deal with the stress of being forced to migrate from their homes and communities (Porter & Haslam, 2005).

respectively. Both works laid the groundwork for further study in the field. In 1924, psychologist Floyd Allport created a second version of *Social Psychology* that was heavily based on experimental research studies. Unlike McDougall's ideas, which focused on instinct as the main driver of behavior, many of the theories Allport established in his text focused on external influences (Katz, 1979). This contradiction helped bring a new depth and a new way of thinking to the field of social psychology. The *Handbook of Social Psychology*, now in its fifth edition, was first published in 1935 and is considered the quintessential reference guide for the field of social psychology.

In 1936, Gordon Allport, Floyd's younger brother, and other social psychologists formed the Society for the Psychological Study of Social Issues (SPSSI) in an effort to bring together a national group of socially minded psychologists to address social and economic issues, applying social psychological research to social issues and public policy. The organization established a mission to utilize theory and practice to focus on social problems of the group, the community, and the nation. Since its formation, the SPSSI has had a significant impact on the discipline of psychology and on society as a whole. Its publication, the *Journal of Social Issues*, has published research that has changed the way psychologists and other concerned members of society understand human behavior. The organization strives to inform public policy and encourages public education through its research and advocacy efforts. Today, SPSSI has grown into an international group of more than 3,000 psychologists, allied scientists, students, and other

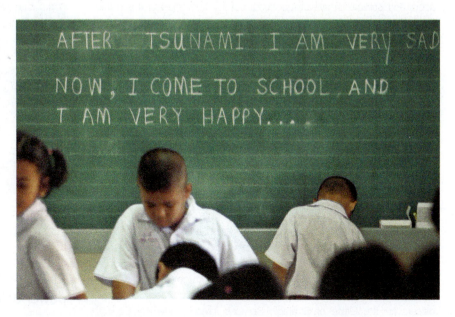

AFTER TSUNAMI I AM VERY SAD

NOW, I COME TO SCHOOL AND I AM VERY HAPPY....

Table 1.1: Topics in Social Psychology

Social Perception: Understanding How We View Ourselves and Others	• Why do we worry more about having safe flights than having safe car rides? (See Chapter 3) • What impact does culture have on the way you see yourself? (See Chapter 4) • How can you tell when someone is lying to you? (See Chapter 5)
Social Influence: Understanding How We Influence One Another	• Why do your attitudes sometimes disagree with your actions? (See Chapter 6) • Why are we more likely to say yes when we are already in a good mood? (See Chapter 7) • How far would you go to obey someone? (See Chapter 8) • How does competition affect performance? (See Chapter 9)
Social Interaction: Understanding Why We Interact the Ways We Do With Others	• Is racial prejudice on the decline? (See Chapter 10) • What impact does testosterone have on aggression? (See Chapter 11) • Do opposites really attract? (See Chapter 12) • Why does helping make you feel good? (See Chapter 13)

academics who share a common interest in research on the psychological facets of important social issues (Society for the Psychological Study of Social Issues, 2010). Journals in social psychology include *Basic and Applied Social Psychology*, *Journal of Applied Social Psychology*, *Journal of Experimental Social Psychology*, *Journal of Personality*, *Journal of Personality and Social Psychology*, *Journal of Social Psychology*, *Personality and Social Psychology Bulletin*, *Social Cognition*, *Social Psychology Quarterly*, and many others in which social psychologists publish research on a vast area of topics such as those noted in Table 1.1.

The Impact of World War II

As social psychology moved into a more modern form during the mid-20th century, global events began to have a major influence on the development of the academic discipline. World War I had a significant impact on the social and political climate of the world, but it was World War II and the Nazis' occupation of Europe that completely changed the structure and direction of social psychology. In fact, Cartwright stated in his 1979 article for *Social Psychology Quarterly*, "If I were required to name the one person who has had the greatest impact upon the field, it would have to be Adolf Hitler" (Cartwright, 1979).

How could one person have such a significant impact on an entire academic field? The rise of fascism brought about by Hitler and the Nazi regime created a strong anti-Semitic and anti-intellectual environment in several of Europe's academic institutions. This forced several of the continent's leading social scientists, such as Kurt Lewin, Fritz Heider, and Solomon Asch, to migrate to the United States to escape persecution.

When the United States entered World War II, it took advantage of its wealth of native and immigrant social psychologists. As the United States watched countries and cultures willingly convert to a fascist form of thinking, government officials looked to social psychology to answer their questions about human behavior and the power of political propaganda. Social psychologists used their knowledge and results from government-funded research to develop several wartime programs, including the selection of officers for the Office of Strategic Services, precursor to the Central

Intelligence Agency (CIA), and the manipulation of enemy confidence and morale. The budding respect for the science behind social psychology and its useful application in solving real-world problems that occurred during World War II confirmed the beliefs of influential social psychologist Kurt Lewin, who is credited with the adage, "No research without action, and no action without research" (Ash, 1992). Lewin pioneered what is today called the *interactionist perspective*, combining internal factors (from personality psychology) and external factors (from social psychology). Lewin and his colleagues conducted research on leadership style (Lewin, Lippitt, & White, 1939). They found when groups of boys worked under three different types of leaders—autocratic, democratic, or laissez-faire—that they performed the best when they had a democratic leader.

> " No research without action, **and no action without research.**
> —Kurt Lewin "

Conformity had been a subject of research even before Hitler and World War II gave it a new relevance. In 1936, Turkish social psychologist Muzafer Sherif (further discussed in Chapter 8) was the first researcher to

∧ Adolf Hitler's ability to manipulate the values of thousands of Germans **generated many questions about human behavior and the power of propaganda.**

take the complex idea of social influence and apply a scientific method to it. Using the idea of *autokinetic effect*, the illusion that a stationary pinpoint of light in a dark room appears to move, Sherif asked subjects to estimate how far it moved. When accompanied by other participants in the room, the subjects altered their estimations, increasing or decreasing them to get them to most closely resemble the guesses of their counterparts (Sherif, 1936).

In the postwar era, social psychology research became an integral part of understanding how certain social changes could take place, specifically the widespread acceptance of Nazi ideology by Germans and other European citizens. Following World War II, there was an explosion of many of the theories that now make up the core of social psychology. For instance, Solomon Asch (1951) showed that people were readily willing to agree to a clearly wrong answer provided by the majority, and later, Stanley Milgram (1963) illustrated how people would compromise their personal values in the interest of obedience. The powerful concept of social influence will be discussed in greater detail in Chapter 8.

Leon Festinger further took these ideas about conformity and developed his theory of cognitive dissonance (1957), the idea that our attitudes are often at odds with our behaviors (see Chapter 6). He also developed social comparison theory (1954), a theory to explain how people perceive themselves in terms of others (see Chapter 4). Another building block of

BASIC RESEARCH IN SOCIAL PSYCHOLOGY the fundamental ideas behind behavior and cognitive processes

APPLIED RESEARCH IN SOCIAL PSYCHOLOGY the use of the ideas of social psychology to address issues in other fields

social psychology, attribution theory, developed by Fritz Heider (1958), examined how and why people explain their own behaviors and the behaviors of others (further discussed in Chapter 5). Using these basic theories of Sherif, Asch, Milgram, Festinger, and Heider, social psychologists today continue to expound upon these ideas and generate new questions and theories from them.

While social psychological research, both **basic** (the fundamental ideas behind behavior and cognitive processes) and **applied** (the use of the ideas of social psychology to address issues in other fields) flourished, so did debate. One debate centered on the use of laboratory research, which many argued was artificial and limited to applications outside the laboratory and outside the United States, where research primarily existed during this time. The advantages and disadvantages of laboratory and non-laboratory research will be discussed in depth in Chapter 2. The second debate, over research ethics (which will also be elaborated in Chapter 2), became a hot

ACTION LEARNING

Practicing What We Preach

Kurt Lewin, the father of modern social psychology, coined the term "action research" a half-century ago to describe research that is conducted with the goal of solving social problems. Lewin was interested in discovering how to get individuals to act in ways that are beneficial both to them and to society as a whole. Unlike the majority of his professional peers, Lewin was less interested in "pure research" that has no implication for practical application and more interested in research that encourages action learning, which he felt would lead to a better understanding of human behavior and a more considerate and peaceful world. He is credited with stating, "Research that produces nothing but books will not suffice" (Lewin, 1948).

Lewin found that the encouragement of actions is more effective when people make public commitments to them. For example, in one of his experiments on the power of public commitment, Lewin attempted to convince people to switch from eating white bread to eating wheat bread. When participants were asked to make a public commitment, such as raising their hands or verbally announcing that they intended to serve only wheat bread in their homes, they displayed a stronger commitment to the change.

Lewin's idea of action learning inspired a new generation of social psychologists who

aim to make the world a better place through research. Dacher Keltner, a psychologist from the University of California, Berkeley, used research to develop the GreaterGood Web site (www.greatergood.com), designed to promote the study and development of human happiness, compassion, and prosocial behavior through the delivery of scientific and educational resources. The GreaterGood Web site translates social psychology research on compassion and cooperation for a broad audience of educators, health care providers, government officials, and concerned citizens by offering resources that can help people learn how to forgive, apologize, and express gratitude, along with several other behaviors.

The GreaterGood Web site shows that experimental findings from social psychology are powerful tools for promoting a more compassionate and cooperative society because its resources, which are derived from research, can benefit the individual user as well as society as a whole. For example, a review of research on forgiveness encourages individuals to consider how the new field of remedial justice offers an alternative to the traditional legal justice system (Social Psychology Network, 2010). Lewin's concept of action learning has inspired other projects that use research to promote activities, such as reconciliation between conflicting nations and the reduction of youth violence.

Now that you know how social psychology can benefit the individual and society—take

action! Think about the issues that affect the students on your campus, for example, campus safety. Create a program that can decrease crime on your campus.

What will you learn from this action project?

1. Learn what makes students on your campus feel unsafe, and identify elements that can help deter crime on campus.
2. Understand the motivation behind the crimes that occur on campus.
3. Get firsthand knowledge of the benefits of applying the concepts of social psychology.

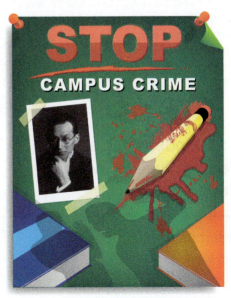

SOCIOCULTURAL PERSPECTIVE a perspective that focuses on the relationship between social behavior and culture

EVOLUTIONARY PERSPECTIVE a perspective that focuses on the physical and biological predispositions that result in human survival

topic during this time as well. Due to studies like Milgram's obedience study, in which individuals were ordered to administer what they believed were potentially lethal electric shocks to another individual, and which you will learn more about later, there are stringent ethical guidelines in place today to protect the rights of participants.

During the mid-1950s and 1960s, research turned to topics dealing with social relations and interactions like stereotyping and prejudice. The foundation of social psychology was further built upon by psychologists like Gordon Allport (see Chapter 10), who developed the Scale of Prejudice (1954); Latane and Darley (see Chapter 13), who researched altruism and prosocial behavior (1969); and Clark and Clark (1947), whose work later impacted the Supreme Court's 1954 decision to desegregate schools. Aggression and attraction also took a front seat during this period in social psychology, and these topics will be covered in Chapters 11 and 12, respectively.

During the 1970s and 1980s, a cognitive revolution impacted psychology as a whole, and this included social psychology. Festinger's theory of cognitive dissonance (1957) was central to this, and researchers Kahneman and Tversky (1973, 1974, 1982) developed the idea of different *heuristics*, or mental shortcuts, that people unintentionally take to make sense of the world around them. Kahneman and Tversky's findings will be covered in Chapter 3. These ideas changed the approach researchers took to studying topics like stereotyping, personal relationships, and helping behaviors, among other ideas. Today, many researchers take a social-cognitive approach to understanding behavior.

It is important to remember that social psychology is primarily considered to be a Western-dominated discipline. In fact, 75–90 percent of social psychologists live in North America (Smith & Bond, 1993). However, during the 1990s, research by social psychologists in other cultures began to take on more prominence, and the impact of culture became a closely investigated subject (Triandis, 1994). For instance, social psychology is greatly impacted by the idea of *individualistic cultures*, or those that focus on independent individuals, like that of the United States; and the idea of *collectivist cultures*, or those that emphasize the individual in relation to his or her connectedness to those surrounding him or her. You will learn more about individualism and collectivism at the cultural level in Chapter 4.

>>> **Modern Social Perspectives on Why People Steal.** While each perspective takes a different approach, **they can work together to address the same issues.**

^^^ An evolutionary psychologist might say that we find a muscular build to be attractive because muscles are viewed as a sign of virility, **and humans have a natural desire to reproduce.**

What Are the Different Perspectives of Social Psychology?

All psychologists use the scientific method in their research, but since there is no one single perspective that can explain all human behavior or thinking, they may use several different theoretical approaches when testing hypotheses. Modern social psychological perspectives maintain that prior learning experiences and intrapsychic forces (e.g., the unconscious), as well as social and cultural context, shape human behavior and mental processes. The **sociocultural perspective** focuses on the relationship between social behavior and culture. This perspective is important because it highlights the fact that human behavior is not only influenced by an individual's close companions, but also by the culture in which the individual lives. For example, the children in the blue-eye/brown-eye experiment described in the chapter opener showed signs of prejudice as a result of the influence of their teacher and classmates, as well as the intolerant culture of their small town.

The **evolutionary perspective** takes a slightly different approach by focus-

Sociocultural Perspective: People steal because our culture appreciates objects more than people.

Evolutionary Perspective: People steal because gaining certain objects, even if through stealing, improves a person's ability to survive.

Social Learning Perspective: A person steals because he learned through example that stealing is an acceptable behavior.

Social Cognitive Perspective: A person steals because he simply doesn't believe it is wrong.

ing on the biological bases for universal mental characteristics that all humans share. Psychologists who follow the evolutionary perspective are interested in explaining general mental strategies and characteristics, such as how we attract members of the opposite sex, why we lie, why we like to play sports, and other similar concepts. The evolutionary perspective involves principles that are derived from evolutionary biology and Charles Darwin's principle of natural selection, and it focuses on the physical and biological predispositions that result in human survival (Boyd & Richerson, 1985). **Natural selection** is the process by which individuals with certain characteristics are more frequently represented in subsequent generations as a result of being better adapted to their environments. The evolutionary perspective would answer the question, "Why do we lie?" by claiming that lying somehow aided in our ancestors' survival, and over time, the characteristic of lying became so widely represented that it is now common in our society.

The **social cognitive perspective** and the **social learning perspective** accept and expand on conditioning principles, which assume direct correlations between learning and behavior. The social cognitive perspective builds on behavioral theories and demonstrates that an individual's cognitive process influences and is influenced by behavioral associations. The social learning perspective stresses the particular power of learning through social rewards and punishments.

A key theory to many of social psychology's core concepts, Albert Bandura's (1977) social learning theory argues that, in addition to learning through consequences in our environment, people also learn from each

NATURAL SELECTION the process whereby individuals with certain characteristics are more frequently represented in subsequent generations as the result of being better adapted for their environment

SOCIAL COGNITIVE PERSPECTIVE a perspective that builds on behavioral theories and demonstrates that an individual's cognitive process influences and is influenced by behavioral associations

SOCIAL LEARNING PERSPECTIVE a perspective that stresses the particular power of learning through social reinforcements and punishments

other. This is called *observational learning*, when people are influenced by watching the modeled behaviors of others.

SOCIAL PSYCHOLOGY AND OTHER DISCIPLINES

Social psychologists do not work alone in their field. Economists, business leaders, and even neuroscientists help to guide and also benefit from the work of social psychologists. Because social psychologists are interested in what motivates particular behavior such as purchasing items, economists may team up with social psychologists to better understand the spending habits of certain populations. Similarly, business leaders may enlist the help of social psychologists to better understand and manage the behavior of their employees. Social loafing, for example, may be a problem that a company hopes to minimize. Social psychologists can help the

Health Care
Some people will conform to the popular opinion of what is healthy even if they feel otherwise.

Business
Some employees will conform to a company's standards even if they go against their personal standards.

Solomon Asch's Conformity Experiment

Consumer Science
Some consumers will purchase items that are popular even if they do not completely meet their needs.

Government
Some voters will agree with policies that are popular even if they go against their personal views.

∧
∧ **Social Psychology and Other Fields.** Social psychologists can work with individuals from other disciplines to perform research that is mutually beneficial.

> **Social psychologists do not work alone in their field. Economists, business leaders, and even neuroscientists help to guide and also benefit from the work of social psychologists.**

company change how it assesses the accountability of employees. Conversely, individuals from these various disciplines can assist social psychologists by creating tools and platforms for research.

Neuroscientists have helped social psychologists literally look into the minds of humans through the development of magnetic resonance imaging (MRI) and positron emission tomography (PET) scans. These tools allow social psychologists, and neuroscientists, to observe brain activity when a study participant thinks about or engages in certain behavior, such as solving a problem or engaging in stereotyping. There is an emerging field called *social neuroscience*, which integrates the study of physiological mechanisms with social psychological perspectives (Cacioppo et al., 2007). The possibilities for social psychology to interact with other fields and industries are endless.

Is Social Psychology Just Common Sense?

As you were reading about Elliott's blue-eye/brown-eye experiment in the introduction to this chapter, you may not have been surprised that the children demonstrated prejudicial behavior. In fact, you may have even predicted the outcome. This reaction is not exclusive to Elliott's activity; it occurs in several major social psychology experiments.

For example, Asch's classic conformity experiment, mentioned earlier, also has seemingly predictable results. Asch administered a verbal vision test to a group of actual participants and several confederate participants (to see what the test looked like, see Chapter 8). The **confederates**, or the individuals who are part of the research team and are placed in the experiment to play a particular role, were asked to answer select questions incorrectly, even when the correct answer was obvious, to see if the participants would conform to the majority opinion. The results of the study showed that 37 percent of

>>> **In love, do "opposites attract"** or do "birds of a feather flock together"?

the time, participants conformed to the wrong answer. Asch concluded that people conformed to what was obviously wrong because they were afraid of being ridiculed and wanted to fit in with the group (Asch, 1956). Does this conclusion seem obvious to you? Did you predict the results of this experiment before they were disclosed? You may answer yes to these questions because you already know that people want to fit in—it's common sense. But if common sense tells us all the answers to questions such as these, what need is there for social psychology?

Common sense is our natural understanding of things. We sometimes assume that social psychology is common sense because the subject matter is often personal and familiar. We believe that we are naturally knowledgeable about human behavior, but many of our common beliefs have been disproved by social psychologists. For example, the idea that "opposites attract" is believed by many, but a 2005 study published in the *Journal of Personality and Social Psychology* concluded that married couples were more likely to be similar in terms of religious beliefs, political attitudes, and values than randomly paired couples (de Vries, 2005). The study also found that married couples who showed similar personality traits in terms of anxiety and avoidance, agreeableness, and conscientiousness were more satisfied and happy in their marriages than the couples who did not show similar personality traits. The findings support the old adage that "birds of a feather flock together" rather than "opposites attract."

Psychologists cannot rely on common sense because they must base their conclusions on evidence that is acquired through careful and deliberate study. Through such studies, psychologists form theories that predict behavior before it occurs. When people use their common sense, they make "predictions" after the behavior occurs. This type of prediction occurs due to a phenomenon that psychologists call **hindsight bias**, or the tendency to think that you knew that something would occur all along. For instance, did you find yourself saying that you knew Barack Obama would win the 2008 presidential election especially if you had been planning all along to vote for him?

Although beliefs developed through common sense are often the result of good judgment, they can also generate ambiguous and conflicting explanations for behavior. Let's say you have a friend who is madly in love with her boyfriend. As she prepares to leave for a study-abroad program in Paris, she becomes worried about her ability to maintain her relationship with her boyfriend, who will be waiting for her at home. You reassure her that her relationship will overcome the distance because you believe that "absence makes the heart grow fonder." After two months abroad, however, your friend tells you that she's fallen in love with an artist named Pierre and wants to stay in France. You think, "I knew this was going to happen. After all, Paris is a romantic city, and when a person is out of sight, he is out of mind." If your friend's relationship survived the separation, then you probably would have said, "I told you so" and never doubted your original judgment.

DOESN'T EVERYONE AGREE WITH US?

Have you ever judged someone by claiming she has no common sense? As in, "Emma is book smart, but she has no common sense." As a child, your parents may have questioned your common sense after you did something foolish, such as crossing the street without looking. You didn't ignore your common sense when engaging in this behavior; at the time, you and your parents had different senses of danger. Common sense is a subjective concept, which makes it problematic to rely on common sense to explain behavior. What one person believes to be common sense might not fall in line with another person's belief. This is because common sense assumptions are usually based on personal observation and experience rather than solid evidence, and therefore bias becomes a factor.

> "Common sense is a subjective concept, which makes it problematic to rely on common sense to explain behavior."

For example, it's common knowledge that men are more authoritative than women, right? You might believe that if you grew up in a male-dominated household, but you might think quite differently if women were the authority figures in your upbringing. A person's values, principles, and tendencies can create bias in his or her perception of how broadly these beliefs are held (Ross, Greene, & House, 1977).

The False Consensus Effect

The assumption that everyone shares the same opinion as oneself occurs as the result of the **false consensus effect**. The false consensus effect increases when situations permit **differential construal**, or the act of judging circumstances differently (Gilovich, 1990). For example, you may think that everyone knows it is unprofessional to wear flip-flops in the workplace, but that is in reality a matter of opinion, not a matter of fact. Multiple parties can construe the idea of what is considered "professional" differently. False consensus can be problematic in activities such as creating public policy. If elected officials or committees assume that the majority of constituents are in favor of strong regulations on issues such as gun control, they could pass legislation that does not actually represent the desires of the public.

HOW DO YOU MINIMIZE BIAS?

Hindsight bias and the false consensus effect are two ways in which false conclusions can be derived through biased actions or thoughts. But sometimes, the conclusion itself can create biased actions or thoughts. Let's say you just moved to a new town and are looking to make new friends. You read a recent article in a major newspaper that cited a study that concluded that people who wear colorful clothing tend to be friendlier than people who wear neutral tones. As you mingle with people at a local event, you realize that the study was right—the people you met who were wearing colorful clothing were significantly friendlier than those in muted clothing. What you might not have realized is that by reading only the conclusion of the study, you created a bias that may have subconsciously caused you to demonstrate behavior that helped to confirm your thoughts. For example, you may have been more relaxed around the people who were wearing

>>> **If you are against the death penalty, then you may believe most people are as well.** But if you support it, you may overestimate how many people also support it.

CONFEDERATE an individual who is part of the research team and is placed in the experiment to play a particular role

HINDSIGHT BIAS the tendency to think that one knew that something would occur all along

FALSE CONSENSUS EFFECT a phenomenon that causes individuals to assume that everyone shares the same opinion they do

DIFFERENTIAL CONSTRUAL the act of judging circumstances differently

CONFIRMATION BIAS the tendency to notice information that confirms one's beliefs and to ignore information that disconfirms one's beliefs

SCIENTIFIC METHOD an approach to thinking that involves using systematic observations, measurements, and experiments to assess information

colorful clothing because you assumed that they were sociable, thereby making it easier to have a friendly conversation. This tendency to notice information that confirms one's beliefs and to ignore information that disconfirms one's beliefs is called **confirmation bias**.

How do social psychologists eliminate these biases when conducting their research? The answer to that question is complex because there is no way to completely remove bias from processes that humans administer. But social psychologists strive to minimize bias through the use of the scientific method. The **scientific method** is an approach to thinking that uses systematic observations, measurements, and experiments to assess information. It is used by other members of the scientific community such as chemists, physicists, biologists, and other psychologists to minimize bias and reduce errors. As you move forward in this course, you will need to apply the scientific method to your everyday thinking. We will discuss the scientific method in more detail in Chapter 2.

Social psychology is not just of interest to neuroscientists, other scientists, and people in the medical field. Understanding human behavior, and particularly how it relates to social and cultural aspects, can be beneficial to almost any field. So it is safe to say that the young field of social psychology will continue to grow and mature as it becomes increasingly useful and relevant to our modern world. As we continue our journey into learning about social psychology, we will explore many of these ideas in detail.

01

• Review

Summary

WHAT IS SOCIAL PSYCHOLOGY? p. 4

• While psychology is the study of an individual's behavior, and sociology is the study of cultural behaviors, social psychology combines the two. Social psychology approaches discussing individual behaviors within the context of the individual's environment and culture, as well as many other factors. Concepts that are integral to the study of social psychology include social perception, social influence, and social interaction.

WHAT ARE THE DIFFERENT PERSPECTIVES OF SOCIAL PSYCHOLOGY? p. 10

• The four main perspectives that social psychologists may take are the sociocultural perspective, the evolutionary perspective, the social learning perspective, and the social cognitive perspective.

• The sociocultural perspective focuses on the relationship between social behavior and culture. The evolutionary perspective emphasizes the biological bases for universal mental characteristics that all humans share. The social cognitive perspective builds on behavioral theories and demonstrates how an individual's cognitive process influences and is influenced by behavioral associations. And the social learning perspective stresses that social rewards and punishments are responsible for the way people act.

IS SOCIAL PSYCHOLOGY JUST COMMON SENSE? p. 12

• Common sense is our natural understanding of things. We sometimes assume that social psychology is common sense because the subject matter is often personal and familiar. We believe that we are naturally knowledgeable about human behavior, but many of our common beliefs have been disproved by social psychologists.

• Social psychologists cannot rely on common sense because they must base their conclusions on evidence that is achieved through careful and deliberate study. In these studies, social psychologists form theories that predict behavior before it occurs. Avoiding relying on common sense helps researchers avoid bias.

WHAT ARE THE ROOTS OF SOCIAL PSYCHOLOGY? p. 4

• Social psychology is a relatively new discipline within the larger field of general psychology. Two of the earliest formal studies in social psychology were Norman Triplett's social facilitation experiment and Max Ringelmann's social loafing study.

• Soon after, social psychology textbooks began to be published, and the Society for the Psychological Study of Social Issues (SPSSI) was established. Social psychology studies became particularly prominent in the wake of World War II, when people questioned how someone like Adolf Hitler was able to exert his influence over so many.

Key Terms

applied research in social psychology the use of the ideas of social psychology to address issues in other fields 9

basic research in social psychology the fundamental ideas behind behavior and cognitive processes 9

confederate an individual who is part of the research team and is placed in the experiment to play a particular role 12

confirmation bias the tendency to notice information that confirms one's beliefs and to ignore information that disconfirms one's beliefs 13

differential construal the act of judging circumstances differently 13

evolutionary perspective a perspective that focuses on the physical and biological predispositions that result in human survival 10

false consensus effect a phenomenon that causes individuals to assume that everyone shares the same opinion they do 13

hindsight bias the tendency to think that one knew that something would occur all along 12

natural selection the process whereby individuals with certain characteristics are more frequently represented in subsequent generations as the result of being better adapted for their environment 11

scientific method an approach to thinking that involves using systematic observations, measurements, and experiments to assess information 13

social cognitive perspective a perspective that builds on behavioral theories and demonstrates that an individual's cognitive process influences and is influenced by behavioral associations 11

social facilitation the enhancement of a well-learned performance when another person is present 6

social influence the process through which other people affect an individual's thoughts or actions 4

social learning perspective a perspective that stresses the particular power of learning through social reinforcements and punishments 11

social loafing a phenomenon that occurs when individuals make less of an effort when attempting to achieve a particular goal as a group than they would if they were attempting to achieve the goal on their own 6

social perception the process through which individuals form impressions of others and interpret information about them 4

sociocultural perspective a perspective that focuses on the relationship between social behavior and culture 10

Test Your Understanding

MULTIPLE CHOICE

1. Which individuals are interested in the interaction of the person and situation?
   - a. behavioral psychologists
   - b. sociologists
   - c. social psychologists
   - d. social workers

2. Which is an example of social influence?
   - a. seeing a person in a military uniform and assuming he is trustworthy
   - b. eating only seafood that is sustainable to help the environment
   - c. taking a fashion design class in an attempt to meet girls
   - d. buying the same cell phone as your friend

3. What historic event was a precursor to the development of social psychology?
   - a. the damage done by the Nazis during World War II
   - b. the Industrial Revolution
   - c. the Harlem Renaissance
   - d. the start of the Golden Age in Europe

4. Which is an example of social loafing?
   - a. finishing a race with a personal best time
   - b. doing extra credit to raise your grade in class
   - c. forgetting to turn in a research paper
   - d. putting forth a minimal effort on a group project, in which every student will receive the same grade

5. What was a major milestone in the development of social psychology?
   - a. the formation of organizations
   - b. the development of field-specific textbooks
   - c. the migration of psychologists to Europe
   - d. the invention of the radio

6. Who do some think is the individual who had the greatest influence on social psychology?
   - a. Theodore Roosevelt
   - b. Martin Luther King, Jr.
   - c. Adolf Hitler
   - d. Sigmund Freud

7. Which social psychologist developed the theory of cognitive dissonance?
   - a. Milgram
   - b. Festinger
   - c. Asch
   - d. LaPiere

8. Which of the following is NOT a reason why common sense is unreliable?
   - a. It is a subjective concept.
   - b. It can be obstructed by hindsight bias.
   - c. It is used to make predictions before events occur.
   - d. It is not based on scientific research.

9. Which social psychology perspective focuses on the relationship between social behavior and culture?
   - a. evolutionary perspective
   - b. sociocultural perspective
   - c. cognitive learning perspective
   - d. social learning perspective

10. How might a member of congress use social psychology to improve his or her political campaign?
    - a. impressing constituents with a large vocabulary
    - b. using common sense to figure out what the people want
    - c. making voting machines easier to use
    - d. using research to find out what makes a candidate likable

ESSAY RESPONSE

1. Explain how a psychologist, a sociologist, and a social psychologist might approach an explanation of the mass shooting that occurred at Virginia Tech in 2007.

2. Have you ever been guilty of social loafing? Explain how you rationalized your lack of effort.

3. Explain why social psychology can apply to areas not involving science or psychology. Use an example from your own life where social psychology may apply.

4. Think about Jane Elliott's blue-eye/brown-eye experiment. What role might confirmation bias have had in this activity?

5. Examine the problem of student debt from a sociocultural perspective. How does the relationship between social behavior and culture affect students' finances?

APPLY IT!

Based on what you have learned about social psychology as a discipline, think about why it would be important to educate your campus or community about social psychological research. Prepare a two-page argument in which you try to convince students of the importance of taking a social psychology class and what they could learn from it that would impact their daily lives.

Remember to check www.thinkspot.com for additional information, downloadable flashcards, and other helpful resources.

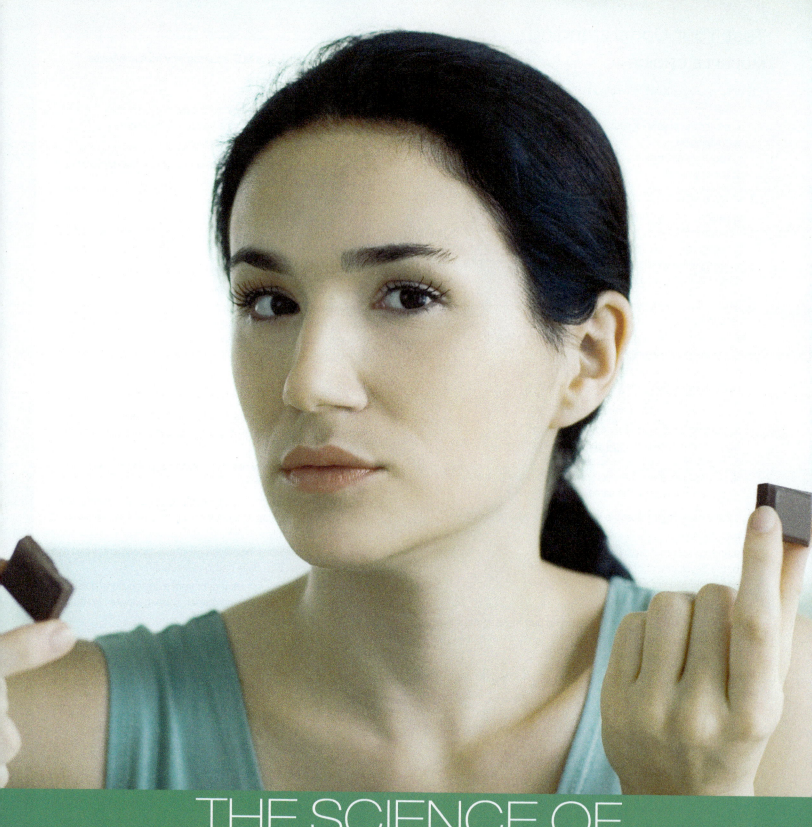

THE SCIENCE OF
SOCIAL PSYCHOLOGY

Have you

ever wondered why you think about things the way you do? It seems as if thoughts float in and out of our heads effortlessly. But are they ever easy to control?

When your stomach is tied up in knots days before an important exam, what do you tell yourself? "Just try not to think about it." When you're in a restaurant and you can smell the french fries, but you're trying to lose a few pounds, what do you tell yourself? "Just try not to think about it." Everyone has tried to shut out certain thoughts at some point. However, is there any merit to this strategy? Sometimes, it seems trying to block out those fries is not only futile, but also counterproductive. Why?

This is where research comes in. It helps us more accurately evaluate and attempt to explain our thought processes. For instance, when it comes to thought suppression, social psychologists have applied research methods to examine these and other questions. Researchers have found that, in general, being told not to think of something means your mind becomes inundated with thoughts of that particular thing (Wenzlaff & Wegner, 2000). The "something" can be almost anything. In one investigation, a researcher found that participants were likely to eat more chocolate if they had been actively trying not to think about it (Erskine, 2008). In another study, stereotypical thoughts persisted more frequently in the minds of those subjects who had been actively trying to inhibit them (Macrae, Bodenhausen, Milne, & Jetten, 1994).

What this tells us is that the science of social psychology helps us objectively examine our thoughts and behaviors, and this is done through research. This chapter will help you recognize the importance of psychological research, understand the research process and techniques, and learn how to apply research results to your daily life.

CHAPTER **02**

How Can Research Methods Impact You Every Day?

Thought suppression is just one area that social psychological research can attempt to explain and understand. Why do you like what you like? Why do you dislike other things? This is another example of questions social psychologists may try to answer. A study published in the *Journal of Applied Social Psychology* investigated the role of ingratiation on tipping habits in restaurants. The study observed two servers and 94 dining couples at one restaurant. The servers either complimented or did not compliment the couples on their meal selections. Results showed that complimented couples gave their waiters significantly higher tips than those who did not receive compliments, indicating that the complimentary servers were better liked (Seiter, 2007).

Understanding research can help you critically evaluate information that is presented to you within your culture. Once you achieve this level of comprehension, you can make well-informed decisions in all aspects of your life. Every day, we struggle to make the right choices. Although this process is difficult, in general, we would all like to think that we choose the option that makes us the happiest. But that's not always the case.

Harvard psychologist Daniel Gilbert argues that our brains regularly misjudge what makes us happy. In his book *Stumbling on Happiness*, he explains that people often think they can accurately determine the outcome of their actions, guaranteeing a positive result. But most decisions in life involve subjective, rather than objective, variables of what we stand to gain and how valuable that gain is, and most people are terrible at estimating these variables (Gilbert, 2006).

The way people estimate odds is typically influenced by past experiences rather than facts, skewing their estimates. For example, if a person was asked to estimate the odds of contracting the H1N1 virus, the "swine flu" that reached pandemic status in 2009, and he or she recently watched a news program that featured a report on an outbreak at a local school, then that person

∧∧∧ Advertisements for temporary price cuts **create a false sense of value for consumers.**

>>> **When purchasing luxury items,** consumers often associate high price with high quality, **resulting in an overestimated value.**

might guess the odds are three in five. Conversely, a person who has read or heard very little about the H1N1 virus might estimate the odds to be one in 50. According to the Centers for Disease Control and Prevention (CDC), the actual odds of contracting the H1N1 virus are three in 10.

Estimating value also proves challenging for most people. Gilbert cites the use of advertisements such as temporary price cuts or clearance sales at retail outlets as prime examples of value inflation. For instance, a consumer may see a Blu-ray disc player marked down from $199 to $125 and one with an original price of $125. She may assume the marked-down appliance has a higher value simply because at one time it held a higher price. Gilbert explains that people are often preoccupied with past value rather than focusing on possible value.

Gilbert's theories point to one main flaw in human decision making: We underestimate the odds of our current gains and overestimate our future value (Gilbert, 2006). By learning to interpret information with facts rather than feelings, people can avoid this pitfall and, in turn, make better decisions in their personal, professional, and academic lives. Imagine you want to purchase a new car. Wouldn't it be best if that decision were influenced by objective data rather than flashy media messages? Or imagine you are stuck on a multiple-choice test question in one of your classes. Wouldn't you be most likely to get the question right if you analyzed each option with facts rather than gut feelings?

COMMON SENSE DOES NOT HOLD TRUE

The first step to understanding the importance of psychological research is to realize that it is more than just common sense. Many people assume

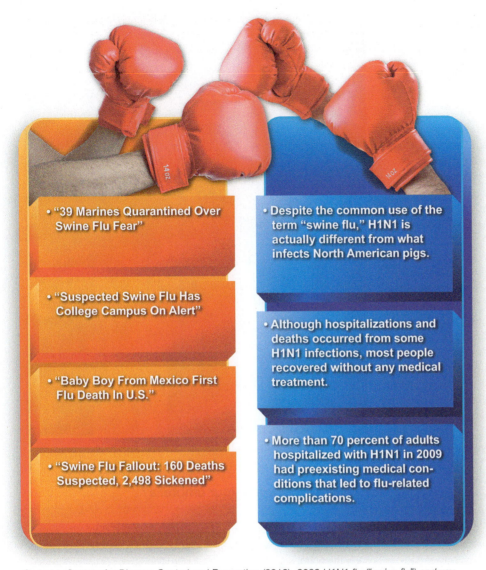

- "39 Marines Quarantined Over Swine Flu Fear"
- "Suspected Swine Flu Has College Campus On Alert"
- "Baby Boy From Mexico First Flu Death In U.S."
- "Swine Flu Fallout: 160 Deaths Suspected, 2,498 Sickened"

- Despite the common use of the term "swine flu," H1N1 is actually different from what infects North American pigs.
- Although hospitalizations and deaths occurred from some H1N1 infections, most people recovered without any medical treatment.
- More than 70 percent of adults hospitalized with H1N1 in 2009 had preexisting medical conditions that led to flu-related complications.

Sources: Centers for Disease Control and Prevention (2010). *2009 H1N1 flu ("swine flu") and you.* Retrieved May 14, 2010, from http://www.cdc.gov/h1n1flu/qa.htm.
Wayland, M. (2009). Today's swine flu headlines. *NBC San Diego.* Retrieved May 14, 2010, from http://www.nbcsandiego.com/news/local-beat/New-Today-on-Swine-Flu.html.

<<< **Thinking Critically about H1N1.** To attract readers and viewers, the media often use misleading sensationalism, as in the case of 2009's H1N1 virus outbreak.

true if the bonus undermines intrinsic motivation (Amabile, Hennessey, & Grossman, 1986).

Although following our intuition can lead us to false conclusions, it can still hold value. It's not necessary to read a fire safety study to know that you shouldn't put a candle next to a set of loose curtains. Common sense is enough to tell you this combination is hazardous. However, it may not clue you into the fact that smoking cigarettes in your home can be equally dangerous. But a 2008 study by the National Fire Protection Association reveals that smoking is the leading cause of civilian home fire deaths, showing how research informs our ideas about how the world works (National Fire Protection Association, 2008).

USING RESEARCH IN YOUR OWN LIFE

Common sense is developed from past experiences. Even when we fail to stop an unfavorable event from happening, we tend to think the events were inevitable. For example, when the housing market crashed in 2008, some financial experts—and even some regular citizens—said they saw it coming and predicted it. Hindsight bias is the tendency to view events that have already occurred as more predictable than they were before they took place (Fischhoff, 2007). This tendency gives way to the classic adage, "Hindsight is 20/20," meaning the warning signs that were blurred before an occurrence seem crystal clear after it. Most people have experienced this phenomenon at some time in their lives.

that researchers who study human behavior reach conclusions that ordinary people already know. It's true that several psychological studies support ideas that are commonly known to most people, but many of them demonstrate how some knowledge is not so common. For example, many people assume that women fall in love faster than men, but research suggests this assumption is false. In reality, men tend to fall in love faster than women. Women typically hang onto baggage from past relationships and approach new ones more slowly and with more caution than men (Alexander, 2006). It may seem intuitive that giving an employee a bonus will help boost performance, but research has shown the opposite to be

>>> Today, many consider it common sense to wear a seatbelt while riding in a car, but that wasn't the case 50 years ago. Research from the National Highway Traffic Safety Administration has made it common knowledge that seatbelts save lives.

THEORY a general framework for understanding a concept that allows us to describe, explain, and predict behavior

RESEARCH QUESTION the query that is the first step in the research process

After a teacher issues a pop quiz to your class, have you ever thought to yourself, "I knew this was going to happen?" You suddenly remember your teacher mentioning that certain information would be helpful in the "future." Your hindsight bias has led you to believe that you predicted the quiz, but if you actually knew that it was going to happen, you would have been able to prepare yourself. Have you ever gotten stranded in the rain, kicking yourself for not bringing an umbrella when you just *knew* it would rain?

A phenomenon such as hindsight bias can cause errors in the way we recall and explain information. This is not because what we believe to be common knowledge is necessarily wrong, but because it is always easier to describe what *has* happened than what *will* happen (Slovic & Fischhoff, 1977). Psychological research is our most adequate resource for predicting what will happen, but even the most thorough research cannot guarantee that certain events or behaviors will occur (Slovic & Fischhoff, 1977). The Nobel Prize winning physicist Niels Bohr once quipped, "Prediction is very difficult, especially if it's about the future." This statement is true for even the most intuitive or well-informed people. To avoid this, social psychologists state their predictions before they put them to the test.

Another cause of failed assumptions is a phenomenon called the false consensus effect, which is the tendency to overestimate the extent to which others share our beliefs and behaviors. This usually occurs in contained environments, which can range from a small group of friends to an entire country. If you lived in Chicago, Illinois, during the 2008 presidential election, you probably assumed Senator Barack Obama would win by a landslide. After all, his posters were everywhere, local news programs followed his every move, and the majority of people around you planned to vote for him. However, if you lived in Phoenix, Arizona, at this time, you probably thought your state's Senator, John McCain, had just as good a shot at winning for similar reasons. The false consensus effect can potentially have dangerous consequences, as it can lead individuals to think certain actions are "normal," when in fact they can be abnormal and potentially harmful to their health or well-being.

A 1988 study by Suls, Wan, and Sanders determined that in a sample group of college-aged males, individuals who behave in unhealthy or undesirable ways tend to overestimate the actual number of others who behave in a similar manner. On the other hand, individuals who do not participate in unhealthy or undesirable ways tend to underestimate the number of people who also abstain from this behavior. The false consensus effect can create an artificial sense of normalcy around possibly dangerous behaviors, like excessive alcohol consumption on college campuses. A male student who drinks four to five times a week, sometimes in excess of six drinks per day, may think that this behavior is "normal" for a college student and, therefore, not a threat to his health. His

∧
∧ If you knew it was going to rain, **why**
∧ **didn't you bring your umbrella?**

like-minded friends, combined with media outlets that glamorize excessive drinking, probably support this false consensus, which is not necessarily the norm.

So, how does one avoid hindsight bias and the false consensus effect? Because these are common results of human behavior, it is difficult to avoid these ways of thinking completely, but understanding the value of research is the first step toward becoming a critical thinker who uses scientifically supported facts rather than intuition to make a decision. Consider what the chapter opener illustrated about the shortcomings of thought suppression. This information could prompt you to think of another technique to keep a diet on track or to limit any thoughts of stereotyping. As we explore the steps of the research process in the next section, think about other ways you can apply research to your everyday life.

>>> **A person who comes from a family that eats large portions of food may be under the false assumption that a half-pound burger is only one serving of meat.** In reality, four ounces of meat is considered one serving.

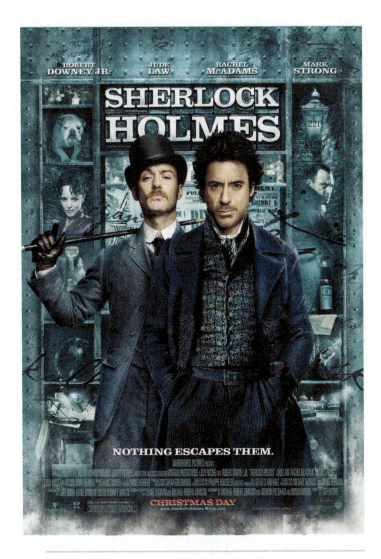

^
^ **To be good researchers,** psychologists
^ have to put their detective skills to use.

How Do Social Psychologists Find the Truth?

To understand how social psychologists test their ideas, think less Sigmund Freud and more Sherlock Holmes. Social psychologists gather evidence to answer a question just as detectives gather evidence to solve crimes. To be confident in their conclusions, good detectives want to collect as much evidence as possible. Usually, the strongest evidence takes the form of physical support such as DNA and fingerprints and testimonies such as eyewitness accounts and alibis. Similarly, to confidently answer a question about behavior and mental processes, psychological researchers collect information from many different sources and multiple methods such as self-report measures, naturalistic observation, surveys, correlations, or experimental design. Each type of method is able to answer a different type of question, and each has its advantages and limitations. Therefore, like a detective, a researcher must collect as much evidence as possible to best understand a behavior using multiple sources and methods.

STEPS IN THE RESEARCH PROCESS

So, what prompts a psychologist to start the research process? Again, like a detective, a psychologist may wonder why or how an event, trend, or behavior in society happened. He may ponder questions both simple and complicated, from "Why do companies use celebrities to market products?" to "How do others' expectations of us change our own behaviors?" Before a psychologist begins looking for evidence, she may have already developed a **theory**, or a general framework for understanding a concept that allows us to describe, explain, and predict behavior. A theory is a framework that ties together existing ideas from which we can make and test predictions about future events or behaviors. It explains a set of observations and is considered to be better as more data are collected to support its predictions. Good theories will attempt to explain behavior, generate a testable model, and use multiple methods. For instance, social learning theory suggests that aggression is learned from others (Bandura, 1977). Researchers can expand upon this theory to attempt to explain other behavioral patterns, and these ideas can be tested in a multitude of ways.

What question or theory do you have about human behavior? Your query can be crafted into a **research question**, the first step in the research process. Anything from firsthand observations to recent news stories may inspire research questions. For example, in 2009, a 15-year-old California teenager was sexually assaulted and beaten by multiple assailants outside a high school homecoming dance in front of a crowd of 20 people. Some onlookers laughed and took pictures, and others just observed in silence. None of the witnesses attempted to stop—or even report—the crime (Chen, 2009). Many wondered why. For psychologists, the resulting research question in such a situation is, "How does a large group influence an individual's reaction to a crime?"

Once a research question is formed, the next step in the research process is to scour the preexisting, relevant research literature. Doing so provides background information on the topic, giving an understanding of the broader context of the research as well as the limits of the topic. Before starting a search, scientists identify the relevant key words. For example, in the instance of the behavior during the California crime, useful key words might include "group," "influence," "helping behavior," and "crime." Looking for these key words in journal articles and books published by other scientists can yield useful materials. Remember, although Wikipedia and personal blogs and Web sites may be easy to use, the information is not always accurate, nor has it

^
^ **Psychologists refer to the lack of help people**
^ provide when witnessing a crime as
"bystander apathy."

PEER REVIEW a process by which experts in the field review and comment on each other's work

HYPOTHESIS a proposed explanation that can be either supported or disproven with statistics or observations

VARIABLES stimuli or characteristics that can take on different values, such as level of attraction or age

OPERATIONAL DEFINITION a definition that assigns one or more specific operational conditions to an event and then identifies how those conditions should be measured

VALID when a variable measures what it is supposed to measure

RELIABLE consistent measurement

SAMPLE selection of who or what will be tested in the research process

REPLICATION the process of repeating a study to verify effects, usually with a different sample of participants

undergone **peer review** (the process by which experts in the field review and comment on each other's work), so it is therefore not considered reliable.

This material can be used to form a testable hypothesis. A **hypothesis** is a proposed explanation that can be either supported or disproven with statistics. It must be testable with **variables**, stimuli or characteristics that can take on different values, and must be capable of being falsified. This doesn't mean that it is false, but rather that the data don't support it. For instance, a psychic may not actually be able to read your mind. But unless she admits to those shortcomings, you have no way of disproving her claim.

Applying an **operational definition**, or a definition that assigns one or more specific operational conditions to an event and then identifies how those conditions should be measured, can make a variable specific. An example of a hypothesis in need of tweaking would be, "Good design makes people better at navigating a Web site." Because "good design" and "better at navigating" are vague and abstract, it is impossible to

∧ ∧ ∧ **What is considered** attractive in one culture may not be seen as attractive in another culture.

empirically support or deny that a person becomes a better Web navigator due solely to the site design. A better version of this hypothesis would be "People are better able to navigate a Web site that has a horizontal navigation bar instead of a vertical one" (Wu, 2007). In this example, a researcher may identify speed of navigation as an operational condition and use a timer to measure quantitatively how quickly the test subjects can navigate different Web sites. It is important that operational definitions are **valid**, meaning they measure what they are supposed to measure, and **reliable**, meaning the results are consistent measurements (Robinson, 2007). Validity and reliability are vital in a hypothesis so that one's desire to support a theory does not lead to manipulation of the facts of research. As American physicist David Douglass said, "If the facts are contrary to any predictions, then the hypothesis is wrong, no matter how appealing."

Once a testable hypothesis is formed, it is time to propose a study. To do this, the researcher must determine the best method to collect data for the hypothesis. This includes choosing the **sample**, or who or what subjects will be tested, and describing the reasons for testing this particular group.

Every year, *People Magazine* puts out its list of the sexiest men alive. Similarly, *Esquire* publishes its list of sexiest women alive. Past recipients of this title, such as Johnny Depp and Jessica Biel, are generally viewed as attractive, but "sexie*st*" man or woman alive? Says who? The opinion of a few magazine editors is probably not the same as that of every person in the world, especially because studies have shown that what people view as

<<< It is difficult to build a testable hypothesis around a vague idea like "good design," because such a concept is subjective, not objective.

<<< In American culture, shaking hands when greeting someone is expected, but in Japanese culture, bowing is the generally accepted greeting.

attractive varies across cultures. African Americans and Hispanics tend to find women with shapely figures more attractive, while Caucasians and Asians are drawn to women with slim figures (Fox, 1997).

This highlights the fact that for an experiment to be valid, it is imperative that researchers take into consideration cultural variables and examine whether they hold up across different cultures. For instance, one study shows that Japanese individuals do not show the same level of conformity as American subjects (Frager, 1970). But this can be explained by the different relationships the subjects have with their respective groups (Bond & Smith, 1996). The subtle impacts of culture cannot be ignored.

REPLICATION

When it comes to research processes, replication can be used to apply the basic findings of one study to another. **Replication** describes the process of repeating a study to verify effects, usually with a different sample of participants to determine whether the findings of the original are applicable to other variables. For example, researchers who want to study the effects of violent cartoons on school-aged girls might use the same operational definitions and data collection methods as a previous study on the effects of violent cartoons on school-aged boys. In some cases, researchers may perform an

exact replication of a previous experiment to strengthen the reliability of the original findings (King, 1995).

Anyone can use the scientific method to solve a problem. For example, in the book *The Scientist in the Crib: What Early Learning Tells Us About the Mind*, Alison Gopnik and her colleagues describe research showing how infants generate and test theories about their environments (Gopnik, Meltzoff, & Kuhl, 1999). You probably do this, too, without even realizing it. You might try different ways to jump-start your car if it's being difficult on a frosty morning. Or think about if you received a C on an important exam. If you used the scientific method as a way of thinking, you would try to generate explanations why you received this grade. You may hypothesize that you didn't study enough.

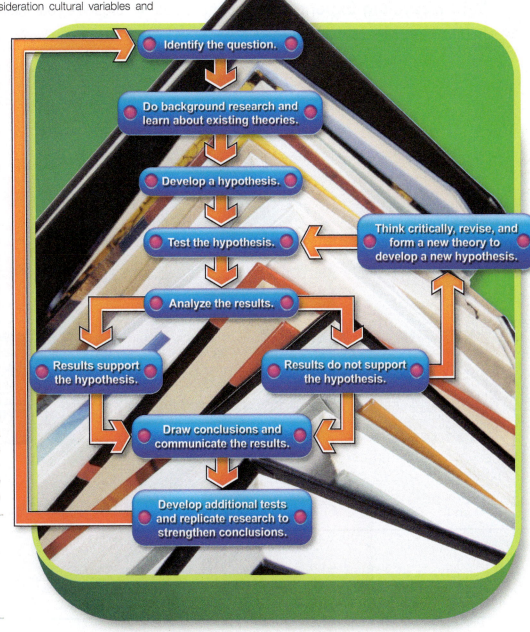

>>> **The Scientific Method.** The scientific research process is a cyclical one.

Research, Replication, and Recycling

Social psychologists cannot just rely on common sense; they must put their ideas to the test. You might think that littering in public places is a rare occurrence or that only certain types of people litter. Previous research has suggested, however, that the situation may have a powerful impact on our behavior. Our environment can impact our likelihood of engaging in destructive acts (Zimbardo, 1969) or littering (for a review, see Cialdini, 2003).

One study showed that when participants find a flier on their cars, 38 percent litter by throwing it on the ground, and individuals are more likely to do so when their current environment is already littered. But when a member of the research team, a *confederate*, models the desirable behavior of throwing away the trash or putting recyclables in their appropriate receptacles, only 4 percent of the observed subjects litter (Cialdini, Reno, & Kallgren, 1990).

Replication is key to validating your research findings. Would you find the same type of results in your campus environment? Select a public environment to observe littering behavior and take note of the individuals' behaviors. Model throwing away or recycling the trash, and monitor how that affects the subjects you're observing. Are your observa-

tions similar or different from past research? How could you develop this project into a true experiment? Share your findings and the overall experience with your classmates and friends. Once you see the impact that your behavior can have on others, you should be more aware of your own recycling and littering behavior.

What will you learn from this action project?

1. Discover how to develop a research project.
2. Learn the importance of replication in scientific research.
3. Prevent littering and encourage eco-friendly behavior.

∨∨∨ Your Recycling Experiment. Use this visual to **organize your ideas** about your action learning project.

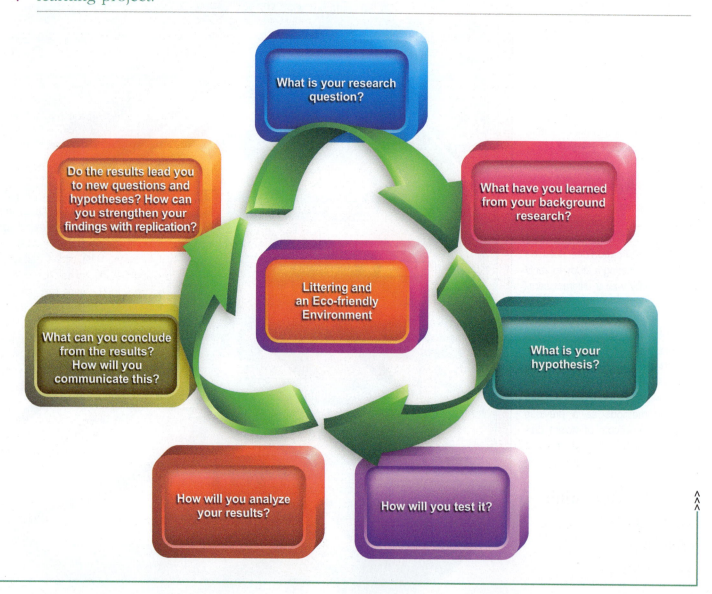

- What is your research question?
- What have you learned from your background research?
- Littering and an Eco-friendly Environment
- What is your hypothesis?
- How will you test it?
- How will you analyze your results?
- What can you conclude from the results? How will you communicate this?
- Do the results lead you to new questions and hypotheses? How can you strengthen your findings with replication?

But what if you studied every day for the last two weeks? You would revise your hypothesis. Maybe the exam did not address what you studied, maybe it wasn't graded accurately, or maybe you were anxious. You might test your hypothesis by visiting your instructor during office hours to surmise what factors led to your unsatisfactory grade.

DESCRIPTIVE RESEARCH research used to obtain information regarding the current status of a population or phenomena to describe the who, what, when, where, and how questions with respect to variables or conditions in a situation

NATURALISTIC OBSERVATION research that involves watching behavior in a real-world setting

What Can Descriptive Methods Show Us?

In this chapter, we have described the standard steps in the research process, but it is important to remember that there is not just one methodology. Techniques used in research can vary depending on the research question, how feasible it is to study a particular behavior, and even on potential resources. No method is perfect; each has advantages and limitations. However, if multiple studies using a wide range of methodologies all generate similar results, we can be more confident in our conclusions and develop a better understanding of the behavior we are studying.

Using descriptive methods of research is a common practice in psychology. **Descriptive research** is used to obtain information regarding the current status of a population or phenomena to describe the who, what, when, where, and how questions with respect to variables or conditions in a situation. For example, descriptive research can help psychologists determine whether boys are more susceptible to peer pressure than girls, or to learn about adults' most common reactions to work-related stress. Descriptive research involves a range of methods from observations to case studies (Key, 1997). The common thread among all descriptive methods is that their purpose is to describe a phenomenon or the relationship of two or more variables. In this section, we will discuss the different descriptive methods researchers use to test their hypotheses.

OBSERVATION

Let's say you want to learn about dancing, but not about how to do the cha-cha or the waltz. Instead, you want to learn about the social impacts of dancing. How often do people dance? Do children dance more than adults? What makes people want to dance? You could answer these questions by passing a survey that asks about dancing behavior to 50 people. Although this method might offer some interesting answers, it may not provide the most accurate data. The individuals who fill out the survey may be unaware of how often they dance or not be able to accurately describe what makes them dance. The survey data is useful for getting a self-report of what individuals think; however, it may not accurately reflect the behavior that is taking place. Observation is a more appropriate research method for this particular subject because it allows researchers to use their own eyes and ears to gather information instead of relying on the opinions of test subjects, which can be skewed by bias.

Observation can occur in a contained environment or in the real world. A contained environment, like a laboratory, is useful when certain variables must be consistent (Evans & Rooney, 2008). For instance, a researcher may put study participants in a contrived party situation to examine how three alcoholic drinks impact the participants' willingness to dance. But even if the atmosphere is realistic, some elements of the manufactured situation could alter the way the participants feel and behave, thus damaging the validity of the study. In this situation, a naturalistic observation might be most appropriate.

Naturalistic observation involves watching behavior in a real-world setting. Observations can be collected with video or audio recordings or with old-fashioned paper and pencil. To observe the dancing behaviors of a group of people, one could attend a wedding or a birthday party and take note of the relevant whos, whats, and whys.

In a naturalistic study, sometimes it is not the people but the environment that can give researchers valuable results. One study sought to determine the popularity of certain exhibits at the Museum of Science and Industry in Chicago. Instead of observing and counting the number of people who approached each exhibit, researchers observed the wear on the tiles leading to each exhibit. Through this method of observation, it could be determined that exhibits with significant deterioration on the surrounding tile experience more foot traffic than those with

<<< **Like animals, it is sometimes best to** observe human beings in their natural environment.

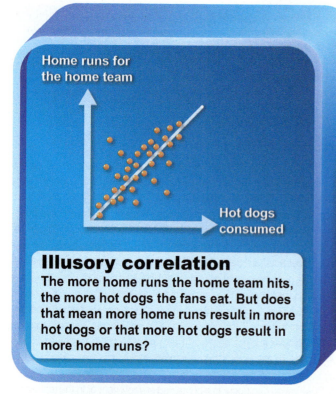

Illusory correlation

The more home runs the home team hits, the more hot dogs the fans eat. But does that mean more home runs result in more hot dogs or that more hot dogs result in more home runs?

Negative correlation

The fewer home runs the home team hits, the shorter and less interesting the ball game is.

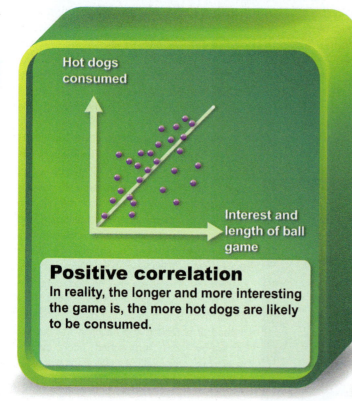

Positive correlation

In reality, the longer and more interesting the game is, the more hot dogs are likely to be consumed.

No correlation

There is no relationship between the number of fans in the home team colors and the number of home runs for the home team.

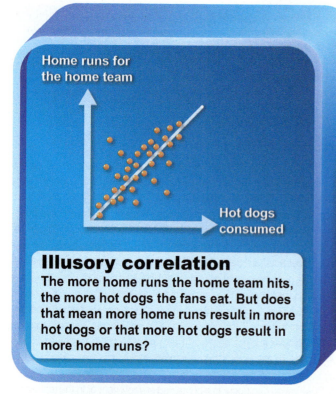

Types of Correlations. Did hot dog sales cause more home runs or vice versa? Or, more likely, is there a third variable that affects each of the other two? Correlations indicate a relationship between two variables, but it's not necessarily a causal one.

minimal wear and tear on the surrounding tile (Webb, Campbell, Schwartz, & Sechrest, 1966). This type of naturalistic observation allows researchers to gather months' worth of data in a short amount of time.

SELF-REPORT AND SURVEY MEASURES

After purchasing an item online, have you ever received a survey asking you to evaluate your online shopping experience? Or has a server at a restaurant offered a comment card along with your dinner bill? If you filled out these documents or similar forms, then you participated in a method of research referred to as the self-report method. The **self-report or survey method** is a form of data collection in which participants are asked to rate or describe their own behaviors or mental states (e.g., I am satisfied, I am unsatisfied, I have no opinion). This type of method is typically conducted in the form of interviews or questionnaires.

ARCHIVAL STUDIES

Archival studies entail culling information from existing records ranging from magazine articles to Web site analytics. The appeal of archival research is that researchers can look at data from an extended period, knowing that they will not inadvertently influence the implications. For example, a researcher looking to define the differences between American and European standards of beauty may analyze what is represented in American and European magazines over an extended period.

CORRELATIONS

Have you ever wondered if your bad luck with finding a date is related to your poor fashion sense, or if your unsatisfactory grades are connected to your lack of sleep? Data from descriptive studies may lead researchers to notice correlations. **Correlational research**, often the first level of investigation, aims to explore if there is a relationship between two variables. For example, a correlational study might find that there is a relationship between poor sleeping habits and lower grades, but that doesn't mean that poor sleeping habits necessarily cause unsatisfactory grades.

One example of correlational research that was done without the manipulation of any variables is Feldman, Weller, Zagoory-Sharon, and

∧
∧ Age and sex **are two variables that are often**
∧ **present in a matched sample.**

SELF-REPORT/SURVEY METHOD a form of data collection in which participants are asked to rate or describe their own behavior or mental state

ARCHIVAL STUDIES research that entails culling information from existing records ranging from magazine articles to Web site analytics

CORRELATIONAL RESEARCH research in which researchers do not manipulate variables but observe whether there is a relationship between two variables

THIRD VARIABLE any other factor that could be responsible for the observed effect

MATCHED SAMPLES DESIGN research design in which two or more groups of individuals are identical, or matching, in terms of the third variable

Levine's 2007 study on the role of the hormone oxytocin in mother–infant bonding. They found a positive correlation between oxytocin levels in the mothers and their bonding behaviors, like affectionate touch and attachment-related thoughts. These findings, combined with others, have encouraged some individuals to name oxytocin the "love drug" or "liquid trust." The fact that there is an established relationship between oxytocin and the desire to love or trust may change the way the hormone is used for therapeutic measures in the medical field and in social situations (Childs, 2008).

Limitations and Advantages of Correlation

Correlations can be very useful for determining whether two or more variables are connected, but there are definitive limitations to the conclusions that can be drawn from the findings of a correlational study. One of the most common errant conclusions of a correlational study is that one element of the relationship causes the other (e.g., oxytocin causes a person to trust another more easily). But correlation does not automatically indicate causation. Two variables can be connected without having a cause-and-effect relationship. For example, there may be a correlation between men who wear blue socks and men who hold high-paying jobs, but that does not mean that wearing blue socks will earn a man a higher salary.

In the correlation between sleeping habits and grades mentioned earlier, there is no manipulation of variables, so it is impossible to conclude that one thing indeed caused the other. People who neglect their sleep may also neglect their studies because they are busy playing video games or hanging out with friends, and those may be the actual culprits to blame for the poor grades.

Two reasons why it is difficult to draw a causal inference from correlational studies are the third variable problem and the problem of direction. The first suggests that there is a **third variable**, any other factor that could be responsible for the observed effect. For example, when we hear that there is a correlation between aggression and watching television, a possible third variable might be lack of supervision. When children are left unsupervised, they may watch more aggressive television.

To avoid the third variable, researchers might choose study participants through the use of matched samples. A **matched samples design** is a research design in which two or more groups of individuals are identical, or matching, in terms of the third variable. For example, in a study linking sleep to academic success, researchers may want to choose subjects who commit a similar amount of time to their academic studies. It wouldn't make sense to compare a person who studies 40 hours a week to a person who only studies five hours a week. This is just one of the scientific safeguards that researchers can use to try to ensure their research is valid and objective.

The problem of direction is like the chicken and the egg riddle: How do we know which came first? In a correlation, it is unknown which variable preceded the other. Did watching a lot of television lead to aggressive behavior? Or was the child already aggressive, leading her to watch more television?

But just because correlational research doesn't identify the exact cause of an event or behavior doesn't mean that it can't offer useful and interesting information. We can still make predictions based around the strength of a correlation. For example, if credit score has a positive correlation with a person's job performance, then hiring employers would be able to predict which candidates will perform best in a given job. Still, it is important to remember that because the relationship between credit scores and job performance isn't necessarily a cause-and-effect one, it should not be the sole consideration of what causes job performance.

Distinguishing correlation from causation can be difficult, and the news media only makes it harder by reinforcing the blurry line with misleading headlines. Consider the following headline from *Good Morning America*: "Recession causes increase in teen dating violence." The headline suggests a failing economy causes teens in relationships to be more violent with each other, implying that Rob, a sophomore in high school, is so upset about the economy that he takes his anger out on his girlfriend. Although possible, this scenario is unlikely. The body of the article explains that nearly half of all teens whose families have experienced economic problems in the past year report having witnessed their parents abusing each other. The teens then emulate that abusive behavior in their own relationships (Sintay & Ibanga, 2009). There could be multiple factors involved here and the correlational design does not allow us

to isolate what is the causal factor, but this sentence as a headline doesn't grab you like the first one does. Next time you see a headline that claims to establish a relationship between two variables, read with caution and think critically. If the study is based only on correlational data, then you'll know that the headline is simply implying a relationship.

What Do Experimental Methods Have to Say?

Although descriptive methods of research often provide valuable data, many studies benefit from experimental methods. **Experimental research** attempts to control all the factors (like a potential third variable) that may affect the results of an experiment. Controlling these factors allows the researcher to identify the exact cause of an event or behavior and, therefore, predict future events or behaviors. In middle school, you may have built a mini-volcano and been asked if more vinegar or more baking soda would get you the better "eruption." You might hypothesize that twice as much baking soda as vinegar gets you the best reaction, and you'd go about experimenting with different amounts of baking soda. You might conclude that more baking soda gives you the best eruption.

This ability to identify cause and effect is what separates experimental methods from descriptive methods that show correlations. Once Paul Zak established a relationship between oxytocin and trust in data found from measuring oxytocin levels after monetary transfers (Zak, Kurzban, & Matzner, 2005), he proceeded with experimental research to isolate the cause. To identify the actual causation of the trusting feeling that people get from oxytocin, Zak conducted an experiment in which he controlled the amount of oxytocin participants were given and measured their generosity to strangers. His results showed that an artificial increase in oxytocin hormone levels in a participant's body caused 80 percent of participants to be more generous to a stranger than when oxytocin hormones were at a natural level (Claremont Graduate University, 2010). Because Zak was able to control the level of the oxytocin, he was able to take his conclusions beyond the correlation, and he established that oxytocin was a potential cause for the increased feelings of trust. Taken together, the correlation and experiment complement one another and strengthen the conclusions about the role of oxytocin in bonding.

We often use the word "experiment" casually. You might say you are conducting an "experiment" when you hold off mentioning that your anniversary is coming up because you want to see if your significant other remembers the date. In psychology, an experiment has very specific components: the manipulation of the variable hypothesized to be the cause, the independent variable, and random assignment of participants to experimental conditions.

In social psychology, experiments can take place in the laboratory and also in the field. Field experiments, similar to naturalistic observation, are considered to be high in **external validity**, which is the extent to which results apply to a general population. Lab experiments cater more toward **internal validity**, which is focused on a particular experiment and, therefore, better for

Study says lots of candy can lead to violence

<<< Media **headlines can** falsely **imply causation.**

examining potential cause-and-effect relationships. There is usually a trade-off with internal and external validity; if you increase one, you usually decrease the other. Lab experiments can be high in internal validity because the researcher has more control, but because the lab setting may be artificial, the external validity is lower. In contrast, research conducted in natural settings are higher in external validity, but once you leave the lab, you may compromise internal validity.

INDEPENDENT AND DEPENDENT VARIABLES

A study cannot be an experiment without the manipulation of an independent variable. An **independent variable** is the variable the experimenter has control over and can alter. A **dependent variable** is the variable the experimenter does not control, and it is used to measure whether the change in the independent variable has had an effect. In Zak's experiment, the independent variable was the level of oxytocin

> **"** An easy way to remember the difference between these two variables is to remember that **the dependent variable relies (or depends) on the level of independent variable, or what was manipulated. "**

given to the test subjects. Therefore, the dependent variable were the participants' subsequent levels of generosity to strangers. The group that gets the main treatment or manipulation—in this case, the oxytocin—is called the **experimental group**. The group that doesn't, and can be used for comparisons, is called the **control group**.

You may conduct experiments with dependent and independent variables in your everyday life. When cooking, you may experiment by adding crushed garlic to your pasta sauce to see if it improves the taste. In this example, the amount of garlic is the independent variable, and the dependent variable is the level of taste in the sauce after you are finished cooking. An easy way to remember the difference between these two variables is to remember that the dependent variable relies (or depends) on the level of the independent variable, or what was manipulated. Or think of the independent variable as the cause and the dependent variable as the effect.

RANDOM ASSIGNMENT

The second component of a true experiment is **random assignment**. Random assignment is a required technique in an experiment to be able to infer cause and effect; every participant has any equal chance of being assigned to any group in the experiment. Stanford Prison Experiment, a simulated study

>>> **Experiments involve** manipulating variables to test a hypothesis.

INDEPENDENT VARIABLE the variable the experimenter has control over and can alter

DEPENDENT VARIABLE the variable the experimenter does not control that is used to measure whether the change in the independent variable has an effect

EXPERIMENTAL GROUP in an experiment, the group that gets the main treatment or manipulation

CONTROL GROUP the group that does not get the main treatment in an experiment, but is used as a baseline to compare results with the experimental group

RANDOM ASSIGNMENT a required technique in an experiment to be able to infer cause and effect; every participant has any equal chance of being assigned to any group in the experiment

of the psychological impacts of incarceration, is a classic example of the importance of random assignment. To conduct this study, experimenters gathered a group of 24 voluntary male college students from the Stanford area. After preliminary examinations, all participants were deemed healthy, intelligent, and with normal dispositions. Half of the group was randomly labeled guards, while the rest were prisoners. The prisoners were brought in police cars to a simulated but realistic jail. They were handcuffed and blindfolded at the time of arrival. Each prisoner was systematically searched, stripped naked, and sprayed with a liquid that seemed to be a disinfectant, simulating the humiliation that real prisoners experience in real prisons. Prisoners were also assigned uniforms and placed in chains.

The guards were given no specific training on how to perform their duties. They were free, within limits, to do whatever they believed was necessary to maintain order in the prison system. They received clubs, uniforms, and special sunglasses to create a "tough guy" image. Standard prison activities such as roll call, punishment with push-ups, and set eating, drinking, chores, and bathroom use times were enforced. Less than 36 hours into the experiment, the first prisoner began to suffer from acute emotional disturbance, disorganized thinking, and uncontrollable crying. Similar emotional breakdowns occurred with other prisoners, as well as some aggressive and defiant behavior (Zimbardo, 1971). The results of this

	Type of Method	What is it?	Advantages and Limitations	Example Studies	Type of Question
Descriptive Methods	Naturalistic Observation	Watching behavior in an actual, real-world setting	• Able to generalize findings (external validity) • Difficult to draw cause-and-effect inferences (internal validity)	The speed of life is more fast-paced in places like Western Europe than in economically less-developed countries like Mexico or Brazil (Levine & Norenzayan, 1999).	How do individuals behave in their naturally occurring environment?
	Self-Report/ Survey	Data collection in which participants are asked to rate or describe their own behavior or mental state	• Rich source of data from the individual • Individuals may not be fully honest in responses	In the late 1960s, college students reported that it was more important to develop a meaningful philosophy of life than it was to be wealthy. However, college students in the 1990s reported the opposite (Astin, 1998).	How do people think about their own attitudes, beliefs, and behaviors?
	Archival Studies	Examining what existing materials over time imply	• Researchers have no effect on collection of data • Available data may be incomplete	Research examines the ideal body type of Miss America winners and Playboy playmates over several decades (Singh, 1993).	What do historical trends tell us?
Experimental Methods	Laboratory Experiment	Experiments with controlled variables in a controlled environment	• Ability to identify cause of behavior • May be artificial, and researchers unable to manipulate all variables	People are less likely to report that there is smoke coming into a room they are working in if they are in a room with other people than they are if they are in the room alone (Latane & Darley, 1968).	Did the variable that was manipulated cause a change in the measured behavior?
	Field Experiment	Experiments with controlled variables in an uncontrolled environment	• Allows cause-and-effect conclusions, and behavior may be more natural • Less control than in a laboratory experiment	Children dressed in Halloween costumes who could not be identified took more pieces of candy than children who shared their names (Diener, Fraser, Beaman, & Kelem, 1976).	Did the variable that was manipulated cause a change in the measured behavior?

∧
∧
∧ **Research Methodologies at a Glance.** Social psychologists use multiple methodologies to support or deny their findings. Each method has its advantages and limitations, so the more methods used, the better.

experiment highlighted the emotional strain that imprisonment has on an individual. The fact that this group was picked through random assignment showed that imprisonment can have adverse effects on average individuals, not just hardened criminals. Random assignment made it so that each group contained the same types of individuals, making the results more reliable. Had the groups been sorted according to particular traits, the results could have been skewed.

CONFOUNDS

In order for an experiment to be considered valid, the independent variable must be the only differentiating factor in the experimental group and the control group. If there is an additional difference in the groups, then it is impossible to know whether it was the independent variable that forced an effect on the dependent variable. Psychologists refer to any difference other than the levels of the independent variable between the experimental group and the control group to be a confounding variable, or **confound**.

> **CONFOUND** any difference other than the levels of the independent variable between the experimental group and the control group
>
> **PARTICIPANT BIAS** bias that occurs when a participant's suspicions, expectations, or assumptions about the study influence the result

Participant Bias

Researchers can do their best to control every aspect of an experiment, but when dealing with human beings, it can be difficult to control everything, so researchers must plan for some things to go wrong. **Participant bias** occurs when a participant's suspicions, expectations, or assumptions about the study influence the results. For instance, if one of Erskine's participants in the thought-suppression study suspected that the researchers were measuring the amount of chocolate she would eat, she may try to control it to avoid "falling for the trick." This type of participant can skew the results of a study and create unreliable results.

∨
∨ **The Experimental Method.** Experiments can be compared to cooking. Is your pasta sauce
∨ bland? Change up the recipe!

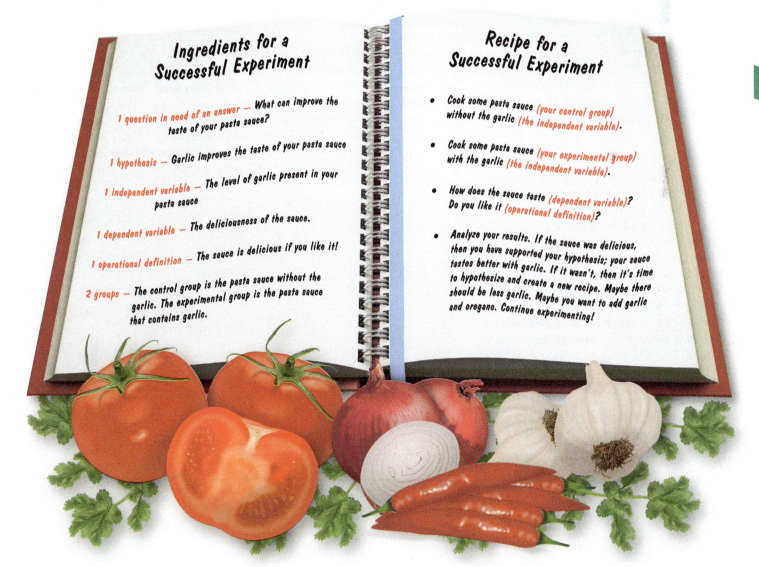

Ingredients for a Successful Experiment

1 question in need of an answer — What can improve the taste of your pasta sauce?

1 hypothesis — Garlic improves the taste of your pasta sauce

1 independent variable — The level of garlic present in your pasta sauce

1 dependent variable — The deliciousness of the sauce.

1 operational definition — The sauce is delicious if you like it!

2 groups — The control group is the pasta sauce without the garlic. The experimental group is the pasta sauce that contains garlic.

Recipe for a Successful Experiment

• Cook some pasta sauce (your control group) without the garlic (the independent variable).

• Cook some pasta sauce (your experimental group) with the garlic (the independent variable).

• How does the sauce taste (dependent variable)? Do you like it (operational definition)?

• Analyze your results. If the sauce was delicious, then you have supported your hypothesis; your sauce tastes better with garlic. If it wasn't, then it's time to hypothesize and create a new recipe. Maybe there should be less garlic. Maybe you want to add garlic and oregano. Continue experimenting!

Another issue that complicates the interpretation of the results is the **placebo effect**. The placebo effect refers to a measurable or observable improvement in health or behavior that is not attributed to medication or any other treatment given. In Latin, "placebo" means "I shall please," and in layman's terms, it means "fake." You may have heard of a sugar pill. This is a type of pill made up of sugar, saline, or some other inactive substance that produces an effect that is similar to what would be expected from an active drug. In some cases, a sugar pill can have the same results as an active pill. Researchers from the University of British Columbia discovered through a study that in patients with Parkinson's disease, a placebo could produce the same results—a significant increase in dopamine in the brain—as actual pharmaceuticals. Researchers concluded that dopamine release is connected to the expectation of reward, which in this case is the anticipation of therapeutic benefits (Graham, 2001). The placebo effect makes the job of the researcher more difficult, but as in this example, the effects can sometimes be beneficial.

Single-Blind Study

Conducting a single-blind study is one way to avoid the placebo effect. In a **single-blind study**, two groups of participants are not told whether they are given the real treatment or the sugar pill, and, therefore, do not know in which group they are. It is important to include the placebo in this study, so that lack of the active treatment cannot be detected. Imagine you are in a smoking cessation study and you are told that only one of the two study groups is going to be given a pill that is supposed to suppress cravings. If your group takes a pill while the other group receives nothing, there is no question as to which group is getting active treatment. But with one group taking the actual pill and the other the sugar pill, the participants are "blind" to whether they are receiving actual treatment.

A single-blind study reduces the participant's expectations and, therefore, reduces the placebo effect,

>>> **A placebo effect indicates the** importance of perception and the brain's role in maintaining health.

but it still leaves room for bias—from the individual administering the study in this instance. Administrators may inadvertently but subtly change their behaviors toward participants if they know who is receiving the real treatment, which may affect a participant's interpretation of treatment. Or the researcher may subconsciously show bias in his or her evaluation of results in an effort to reach the desired conclusion.

This potential confound is referred to as **experimenter bias**, and it was the subject of a study conducted by Robert Rosenthal and Lenore Jacobson in 1968. The study team asked a group of teachers to administer an intelligence test called "The Harvard Test of Inflected Acquisitions" and told them that this test could determine intelligence quotients (IQs) as well as identify those students who will thrive in future grades. Before the next school year, the teachers received the names of the students with the "highest test results," but these names were simply chosen at random by Rosenthal and Jacobson. By the next year, those students who were designated as likely to excel in academics showed better test results on the same intelligence test and higher reading scores. Teachers even believed the behavior of these students was better than during the previous year. Rosenthal and Jacobson concluded that these changes in the students' behaviors and academic performances were the result of a self-fulfilling prophecy imposed by the teachers. Because the teachers were told the students had potential, they unintentionally spent more time with the students designated as "intelligent" and were even friendlier than before. As a result of this change in behavior from the teachers, the students felt more capable and performed accordingly (Rosenthal & Jacobson, 1968).

Double-Blind Study

Participant bias and experimenter bias can both be avoided through a double-blind study. In a **double-blind study**, neither the experimenter nor the participant knows which group is experimental and which is control. The double-blind study is considered the gold standard in research because it supplies the most reliable results without the threat of bias from either party. However, it might not always be possible to conduct a double-blind study. Although the process can be complicated,

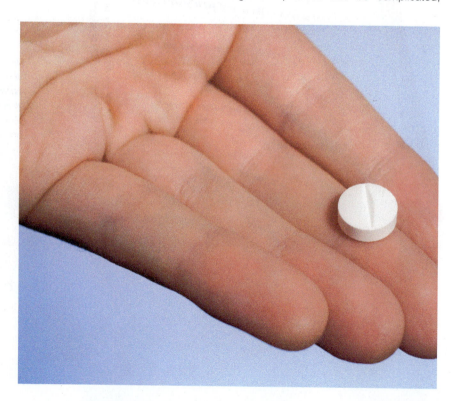

researchers may be able to employ this technique to guard against unintentionally tampering with the results.

ETHICS

Consider research conducted by social psychologists, and think about if you would have wanted to participate: Participants have been asked to sing the national anthem out loud, to steal money from an office drawer, to write statements about politicians with which they don't agree, to lie, and many other peculiar situations. In 1963, Dr. Stanley Milgram conducted what is now a classic study of obedience, using **deception**, or providing participants with false or incomplete information. He gave study participants what they believed to be a machine designed to give electric shocks to someone they couldn't see, but could hear, on the other side of a wall. Every time the person on the other side of the wall answered a question incorrectly, the participant was instructed to administer increasingly dangerous shocks. The participants could hear cries of pain on

> An understanding of research methods will assist you **as you explore different topics that social psychologists study.**

the other side, and eventually silence, but the majority of participants persisted in obeying the researcher and giving shocks—even at the maximum levels—to the person on the other side (Milgram, 1963). The person on the other side wasn't actually receiving shocks, and the participants had a **debriefing** following the experiment, that is, they were given a full explanation of the hypothesis being tested, procedures used to deceive participants, and the reasons for the deception. But given the guidelines we have in place today, would it be likely that this study would be allowed? How would you feel if you had participated? Was it ethical? Researchers continue to disagree.

The National Commission for the Protection of Human Subjects of Biomedical and Behavioral Research outlined three basic ethical principles in its Belmont Report. These influenced the American Psychological Association and include beneficence, autonomy, and justice. Beneficence requires that researchers do no harm by maximizing the potential benefits to the participant and minimizing the possible harm. Autonomy refers to having respect for the participants, and doing so by using informed consent. At the beginning of a study, the researcher should provide participants with enough detail about the study, including risks and benefits, so that the potential subjects can decide with their eyes open whether they would like to participate. Finally, justice demands

DECEPTION providing participants with false or incomplete information

DEBRIEFING procedure of giving participants a full explanation of the hypothesis being tested, procedures used to deceive participants, and the reasons for the deception

INSTITUTIONAL REVIEW BOARD (IRB) a committee that has been established to approve and oversee research that involves human and nonhuman animal subjects

INFORMED CONSENT when subjects are told at the beginning of a study as much information as possible about the participation in the study to determine if they would like to be involved

that the benefits and burdens of the research be fairly distributed (National Commission for the Protection of Human Subjects of Biomedical and Behavioral Research, 1974).

Institutions in which scientific research is conducted are required to have **institutional review boards** (IRBs) that evaluate proposed research to ensure that research meets the three ethical guidelines for both human and nonhuman participation. To maintain the integrity of a research study though, it is sometimes necessary to deceive study participants. For instance, if testing whether participants know the difference between an authentic piece of art and an amateur replication, they shouldn't already know which piece is the phony.

Milgram used deception in his obedience study by allowing participants to believe they were physically harming another person when in reality they weren't. When deception is used, subjects must be told at the beginning of a study as much information as possible about the participation in the study to determine if they would like to be involved. This is called **informed consent**. Participants do not need to know which information is omitted or changed—just that 100 percent of the details involved in the study are not disclosed. Participants will be debriefed on the complete details of the study after the study is complete.

Once data are collected, the results can be analyzed and developed into a conclusion. The conclusion of a study must answer the initial research question and support or deny a hypothesis. While analyzing results, researchers must note areas where further research may be necessary or the limitations of the process. If results indicate major flaws in the original hypothesis or theory, the researcher may choose to revise it and begin the research process again.

An understanding of research methods will assist you as you explore different topics that social psychologists study. Importantly, taking this course and gaining knowledge of research methodology will help you become a better consumer of information in your everyday decisions, ability to think critically, and capability to evaluate real-world problems (VanderStoep & Shaughnessy, 1997).

<<< Researchers do not have to divulge every detail of a study, **but they do need to inform patients if they will not be given complete information.**

Review

Summary

HOW CAN RESEARCH METHODS IMPACT YOU EVERY DAY? p. 18

• Research methods can help us better understand why we think and behave the way we do. This helps us think more effectively and critically evaluate and process the information we confront every day.

• The ability to think critically is the first step in making better decisions about everything from which products to buy to how to answer a question on an exam. Separating common sense, hindsight bias, and the false consensus effect from a scientific way of thinking can lead you to make the most effective choices.

HOW DO SOCIAL PSYCHOLOGISTS FIND THE TRUTH? p. 21

• Like detectives, social psychologists gather evidence to answer questions, test theories, and come to a conclusion. To do this, researchers pose a question, research theories, develop a hypothesis, and test it using variables with operational definitions, samples, and replication. Once they draw a conclusion, the cycle begins again.

• When conducting research, social psychologists must consider ethics and culture. Because study participants are often human beings, informed consent and debriefing must be a part of the process.

WHAT CAN DESCRIPTIVE METHODS SHOW US? p. 25

• Descriptive methods answer the who, what, when, where, and how questions about a particular phenomenon to describe it or to establish a relationship between two or more variables.

• These methods include naturalistic observation, self-report or survey data, and other methods such as archival research. It is important to remember, however, that data showing correlations do not establish cause-and-effect relationships, but instead allow for the researcher to make educated predictions.

WHAT DO EXPERIMENTAL METHODS HAVE TO SAY? p. 28

• Experimental methods differ from descriptive ones in that researchers attempt to control all factors that may affect the results. These methods can support or deny an existence of a cause-and-effect relationship.

• Independent and dependent variables are used to conduct experimental methods. Researchers will take measures like random assignment, single- and double-blind studies, and the use of placebos to take into account confounds and participant and experimenter bias that could alter the results.

Key Terms

archival studies research that entails culling information from existing records ranging from magazine articles to Web site analytics *27*

confound any difference other than the levels of the independent variable between the experimental group and the control group *31*

control group the group that does not get the main treatment in an experiment, but is used as a baseline to compare results with the experimental group *29*

correlational research research in which researchers do not manipulate variables but observe whether there is a relationship between two variables *27*

debriefing procedure of giving participants a full explanation of the hypothesis being tested, procedures used to deceive participants, and the reasons for the deception *33*

deception providing participants with false or incomplete information *33*

dependent variable the variable the experimenter does not control that is used to measure whether the change in the independent variable has an effect *29*

descriptive research research used to obtain information regarding the current status of a population or phenomena to describe the who,

what, when, where, and how questions with respect to variables or conditions in a situation *25*

double-blind study study in which neither the experimenter nor the participant knows which group is experimental and which is control *32*

experimental group in an experiment, the group that gets the main treatment or manipulation *29*

experimental research research that attempts to control all the factors (like a potential third variable) that may affect the results of an experiment *28*

experimenter bias bias exhibited by the experiment administrator in inadvertently but subtly changing his behavior toward participants because of knowledge of which group is control and which group is experimental; this also occurs when the researcher subconsciously shows bias in his or her evaluation of results in an effort to reach the desired conclusion *32*

external validity the extent to which results apply to a general population *28*

hypothesis a proposed explanation that can be either supported or disproven with statistics or observations *22*

independent variable the variable the experimenter has control over and can alter *29*

informed consent when subjects are told at the beginning of a study as much information as

possible about the participation in the study to determine if they would like to be involved *33*

institutional review board (IRB) a committee that has been established to approve and oversee research that involves human and nonhuman animal subjects *33*

internal validity the ability to infer cause and effect; that the variable was manipulated was the only factor to change across conditions and so was what led to the observed effect *28*

matched samples design research design in which two or more groups of individuals are identical, or matching, in terms of the third variable *27*

naturalistic observation research that involves watching behavior in a real-world setting *25*

operational definition a definition that assigns one or more specific operational conditions to an event and then identifies how those conditions should be measured *22*

participant bias bias that occurs when a participant's suspicions, expectations, or assumptions about the study influence the result *31*

peer review a process by which experts in the field review and comment on each other's work *22*

placebo effect a measurable or observable improvement in health or behavior that is not attributed to medication or any other treatment given *32*

random assignment a required technique in an experiment to be able to infer cause and effect; every participant has any equal chance of being assigned to any group in the experiment *29*

reliable consistent measurements *22*

replication repeating a study to verify effects, usually with a different sample of participants *23*

research question the query that is the first step in the research process *21*

sample selection of who or what will be tested in the research process *22*

self-report/survey method a form of data collection in which participants are asked to rate or describe their own behavior or mental state *27*

single-blind study study in which two groups of participants are not told whether they are given the real treatment or the placebo and, therefore, do not know in which group they are *32*

theory a general framework for understanding a concept that allows us to describe, explain, and predict behavior *21*

third variable any other factor that could be responsible for the observed effect *27*

valid when a variable measures what it is supposed to measure *22*

variables stimuli or characteristics that can take on different values, such as level of attraction or age *22*

Test Your Understanding

MULTIPLE CHOICE

1. Which psychological researcher is responsible for a controversial study on obedience?
   a. Sigmund Freud
   b. Paul Zak
   c. Stanley Milgram
   d. Daniel Gilbert

2. Which is an example of hindsight bias?
   a. knowing that putting a candle near a loose set of curtains is dangerous
   b. thinking you knew it was going to rain after it did
   c. assuming more expensive wine tastes better than cheaper wine
   d. overestimating the amount of people who shared your belief that Barack Obama would win the 2008 presidential election

3. Which key word is unlikely to help you if you're researching bystander apathy?
   a. obedience
   b. group
   c. crime
   d. influence

4. What makes a hypothesis untestable?
   a. a variable that has an operational definition
   b. a variable that is reliable and valid
   c. a variable that is subjective
   d. a variable that is objective

5. Which is not one of the three basic ethical principles established in the Belmont Report?
   a. justice
   b. integrity
   c. beneficence
   d. autonomy

6. Which would not be an example of a good source for doing research?
   a. an encyclopedia
   b. an online peer-reviewed journal
   c. a newspaper
   d. wikipedia

7. What is an example of a cause-and-effect relationship wrongly assumed from a correlation?
   a. The more home runs a home team hits at a ball game, the more hot dogs are consumed.
   b. The more home runs a home team hits at a ball game, the longer the game lasts.
   c. The longer a ball game lasts, the more hot dog fans eat.
   d. The more exciting a ball game is, the likelier people are to attend and stay.

8. Which group of participants receives the main manipulation or treatment?
   a. the control group
   b. the matched sample group
   c. the experimental group
   d. none of the above

9. What aspect of an experiment is considered a confound?
   a. the independent variable
   b. matched samples
   c. a third variable
   d. external validity

10. Which technique eliminates experimenter bias?
    a. placebo effect
    b. single-blind study
    c. correlational study
    d. double-blind study

ESSAY RESPONSE

1. Using Paul Zak's work as an example, explain the differences between descriptive research and experimental research.
2. Why is the false consensus effect potentially dangerous? Give an example of when this could be the case.
3. Provide an example of a hypothesis in need of improvement. Alter it to make it testable and explain the difference.
4. Describe the role of an institutional review board.
5. Explain the differences between naturalistic observation and the observation that takes place in a laboratory. What are the advantages and disadvantages of each?

APPLY IT!

Find a newspaper article that implies causation from a correlational study. What does the study actually explain? How is the article misleading?

ANSWERS: 1. c; 2. b; 3. a; 4. c; 5. b; 6. d; 7. a; 8. c; 9. c; 10. d

Remember to check www.thinkspot.com for additional information, downloadable flashcards, and other helpful resources.

THINK READINGS

NATURE

Most People Are Not WEIRD

By JOSEPH HENRICH, STEVEN J. HEINE and ARA NORENZAYAN

Published: July 1, 2010

From what you learned in Chapters 1 and 2 about the development of social psychology and the process of setting up experiments, why do you think people from "WEIRD" societies are the most commonly used participants?

Much research on human behaviour and psychology assumes that everyone shares most fundamental cognitive and affective processes, and that findings from one population apply across the board. A growing body of evidence suggests that this is not the case.

Experimental findings from several disciplines indicate considerable variation among human populations in diverse domains, such as visual perception, analytic reasoning, fairness, cooperation, memory and the heritability of IQ[1,2]. This is in line with what anthropologists have long suggested: that people from Western, educated, industrialized, rich and democratic (WEIRD) societies—and particularly American undergraduates—are some of the most psychologically unusual people on Earth[1].

So the fact that the vast majority of studies use WEIRD participants presents a challenge to the understanding of human psychology and behaviour. A 2008 survey of the top psychology journals found that 96% of subjects were from Western industrialized countries—which house just 12% of the world's population[3]. Strange, then, that research articles routinely assume that their results are broadly representative, rarely adding even a cautionary footnote on how far their findings can be generalized.

The evidence that basic cognitive and motivational processes vary across populations has become increasingly difficult to ignore. For example, many studies have shown that Americans, Canadians and western Europeans rely on analytical reasoning strategies—which separate objects from their contexts and rely on rules to explain and predict behaviour—substantially more than non-Westerners. Research also indicates that Americans use analytical thinking more than, say, Europeans. By contrast, Asians tend to reason holistically, for example by considering people's behaviour in terms of their situation[1]. Yet many long-standing theories of how humans perceive, categorize and remember emphasize the centrality of analytical thought.

It is a similar story with social behaviour related to fairness and equality. Here, researchers often use one-shot economic experiments such as the ultimatum game, in which a player decides how much of a fixed amount to offer a second player, who can then accept or reject this proposal. If the second player rejects it, neither player gets anything. Participants from industrialized societies tend to divide the money equally, and reject low offers. People from non-industrialized societies behave differently, especially in the smallest-scale nonmarket societies such as

[1]Henrich, J., Heine, S. J. & Norenzayan, A. Behav. Brain Sci. doi:10.1017/ S0140525X0999152X (2010).
[2]Henrich, J., Heine, S. J. & Norenzayan, A. Behav. Brain Sci. doi: 10.1017/ S0140525X10000725 (2010).
[3]Arnett, J. Am. Psychol. 63, 602–614 (2008).

NATURE, Vol. 466, Page 29 Copyright 2010 Macmillan Publishers Limited

Throughout this book, you will learn about the differences between individualist and collectivist cultures. Individualist cultures, like that of the United States, approach each person in the context of himself or herself, unconnected to anyone else. Collectivist cultures, like that of many Asian countries, approach each person in the context of his or her relationships to those surrounding him or her.

foragers in Africa and horticulturalists in South America, where people are neither inclined to make equal offers nor to punish those who make low offers[4].

Recent developments in evolutionary biology, neuroscience and related fields suggest that these differences stem from the way in which populations have adapted to diverse culturally constructed environments. Amazonian groups, such as the Piraha, whose languages do not include numerals above three, are worse at distinguishing large quantities digitally than groups using extensive counting systems, but are similar in their ability to approximate quantities. This suggests the kind of counting system people grow up with influences how they think about integers[1].

Costly generalizations

Using study participants from one unusual population could have important practical consequences. For example, economists have been developing theories of decision-making incorporating insights from psychology and social science—such as how to set wages—and examining how these might translate - into policy[5]. Researchers and policy-makers should recognize that populations vary considerably in the extent to which they display certain biases, patterns and preferences in economic decisions, such as those related to optimism[1]. Such differences can, for example, affect the way that experienced investors make decisions about the stock market[6].

We offer four suggestions to help put theories of human behaviour and psychology on a firmer empirical footing. First, editors and reviewers should push researchers to support any generalizations with evidence. Second, granting agencies, reviewers and editors should give researchers credit for comparing diverse and inconvenient subject pools. Third, granting agencies should prioritize cross-disciplinary, cross-cultural research. Fourth, researchers must strive to evaluate how their findings apply to other populations. There are several low-cost ways to approach this in the short term: one is to select a few judiciously chosen populations that provide a 'tough test' of universality in some domain, such as societies with limited counting systems for testing theories about numerical cognition[1,2].

A crucial longer-term goal is to establish a set of principles that researchers can use to distinguish variable from universal aspects of psychology. Establishing such principles will remain difficult until behavioural scientists develop interdisciplinary, international research networks for long-term studies on diverse populations using an array of methods, from experimental techniques and ethnography to brain-imaging and biomarkers.

Recognizing the full extent of human diversity does not mean giving up on the quest to understand human nature. To the contrary, this recognition illuminates a journey into human nature that is more exciting, more complex, and ultimately more consequential than has previously been suspected ∎

Joseph Henrich, Steven J. Heine and Ara Norenzayan are in the Department of Psychology, University of British Columbia, Vancouver, British Columbia V6T 1Z4, Canada. Joseph Henrich is also in the Department of Economics.
e-mail: joseph.henrich@gmail.com

[4]Henrich, J. et al. Science 327, 1480–1484 (2010).
[5]Foote, C. L., Goette, L. & Meier, S. Policymaking Insights from Behavioral Economics (Federal Reserve Bank of Boston, 2009).
[6]Ji, L. J., Zhang, Z. Y. & Guo, T. Y. J. Behav. Decis. Making 21, 399–413 (2008).

This statement is an illustration of why the concept of random sampling that you learned about in Chapter 2 is so vital to our analysis of the results of any experiment. Think about what would happen if the federal government made all its decisions based on the cognitive processes of only people from Montana. Then think about how such a process could affect the world on a global scale.

How would you ensure a diverse participant sample when utilizing each of the methods discussed in Chapter 2?

Evaluate these four suggestions. Do you think they will solve the problem discussed in this article? Do you have any suggestions to add based on what you learned in Chapter 2?

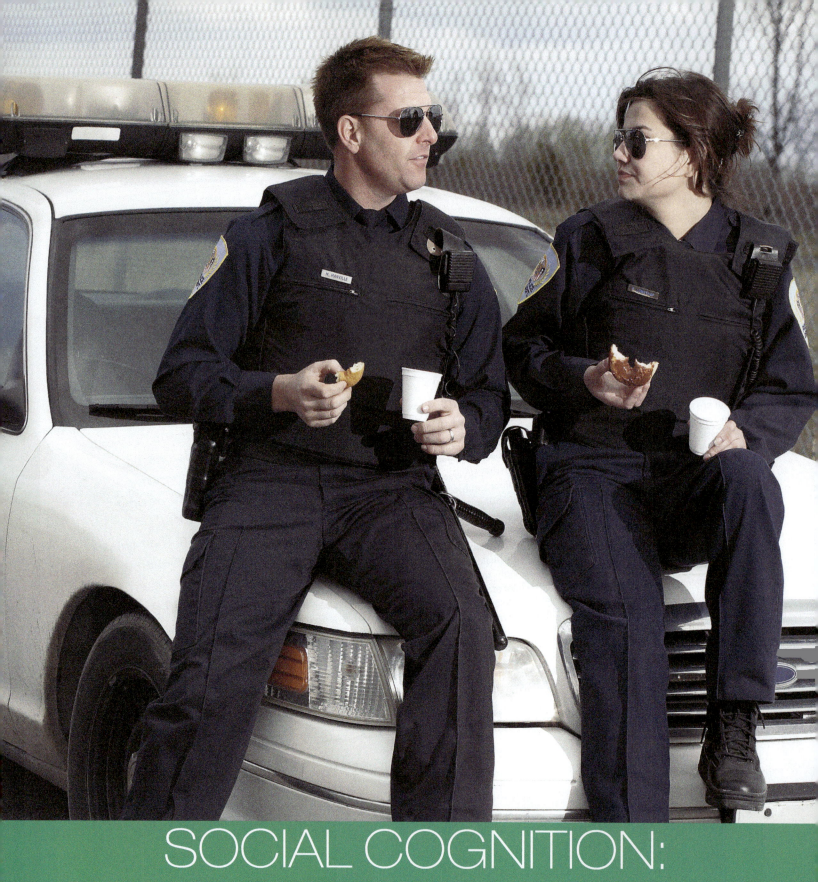

SOCIAL COGNITION:
THINKING ABOUT THE SOCIAL WORLD

HOW DO SCHEMAS GUIDE THE WAY YOU THINK ABOUT THE WORLD AROUND YOU? **HOW** EFFECTIVE ARE MENTAL SHORTCUTS? **WHAT** ARE OTHER SOURCES OF BIAS IN SOCIAL COGNITION?

Having

just pulled off a successful heist, three black-clad bank robbers hop into the getaway car. "Move it!" their leader yells to the woman behind the wheel, and she floors it, peeling out of the parking lot. She drives faster and faster down Main Street, shocked that there are no cops in sight. Nervously, the two robbers in the back look over their shoulders. The police officers must be on to them! Any second, they'll hear the sirens and see the flashing lights.

As the car picks up speed, the law-breaking foursome blows past a diner. They can barely make out a figure sitting at the counter. It's a police officer. With a steaming cup of coffee at his elbow, he tears into a pink-frosted donut, completely oblivious to the gang of bad guys speeding their way to freedom.

In the darkened movie theater, the audience erupts into laugher. It's inevitable, really. Think of all the times you've seen a similar scenario played out on TV or in a movie—it always gets at least a chuckle, doesn't it? Somehow, we've all collectively come to associate police officers with donuts and coffee.

In fact, you can probably think of a time you've noticed (and maybe even pointed out to your friends) police officers eating donuts. Have you paid the same attention to the times you've seen a police officer without a donut in his hand? Probably not, because looking for these instances takes more controlled and effortful cognitive processing.

Our brains don't always have the resources to devote to such a level of processing. To help save time and mental energy, we rely on mental shortcuts such as this police officer–donut connection. Sometimes this results in accurate judgments, but often it leads us to biased thoughts. These collections of information, including our knowledge and expectations for a particular stimulus, are called schemas, and they are just one of the ways your brain attempts to bring order to and understand the world around you and your place in it.

CHAPTER **03**

How Do Schemas Guide the Way You Think About the World Around You?

Schemas are automatically created cognitive frameworks that help guide the way we think about and understand the world around us. Think of a schema as all of the information that you have about a particular concept. This schema continues to help guide your processing of future information efficiently.

Consider what happens when you go to the movies. You buy your ticket at the counter (or take one look at the long line and decide to buy a ticket using your smartphone instead). You buy popcorn and a drink at a separate concessions counter, and before you can go to your seat in the theater, you hand your ticket to a theater employee who tears it in half and waves you on. You know once you're in the theater, you'll sit through some commercials and then some movie trailers before watching the movie you came to see. If you went to the movies in a new city that you had never been to before, you would still know exactly what to do, because you have a schema that guides the experience of going to the movies.

Schemas can exist for people, places, events, or any other stimulus that you might encounter in the social world. Of course, as helpful as schemas are for organizing information accurately and efficiently, they can also result in errors in thinking or remembering information. Schemas affect what we notice, seek out, and remember; when you encounter something that doesn't fit a schema, it could lead to such a processing error. Have you ever gone to the movies and noticed a long line at the ticket counter, while several of those automated ticket kiosks sat unused? Many people fail to notice them, even though using the kiosks could save them 10 minutes in line, simply because they haven't yet been fully incorporated into their schema for going to the movies.

Schemas are created through experience. As you encounter similar experiences, people, social roles, and so on, you develop schemas for those things. After going to the movies a few times, you have the process down and have a pretty robust schema for that experience. Think about the donut-eating police officer from the beginning of this chapter. What kind of effect do you think the media have on the creation of schemas?

Once they are in place, schemas are activated through a stimulus. You go to the movies and the schema for going to the movies is activated, or **primed**. You go to the doctor's office, and your expectations for the experience and for the behavior of your doctor are activated. Most of the time, these behaviors are carried out more or less involuntarily. Activated schemas affect what we notice, actively seek out, and remember. We often notice and remember information that is in line with the schema that has already been developed. We are also less likely to notice information that is inconsistent with our schema. This reliance on schemas makes it easier for us to organize information, but it can also invite a few problems.

According to the confirmation bias, activated schemas affect how we process incoming information. It stays activated until there is an opportunity for expression of the behaviors associated with that schema. How do you feel after going to see a horror movie? Maybe you look over your shoulder a few times as you go to your car. Maybe the road seems just a little darker, and you wouldn't be surprised if someone jumped out in front of the car. Maybe you turn on every light in your home as you get ready for bed. You feel nervous, no matter how many times you tell yourself, "It was only a movie."

Once a schema has been activated, it will color how subsequent information is interpreted. If you just had an experience that activated your schema for being in a dangerous situation or feeling fearful, you're more likely to perceive the experiences that follow that one in a similar way. Schemas can dramatically affect our thinking, even when we're removed from the initial stimuli that activated them.

Higgins, Rholes, and Jones (1977) first demonstrated the impact of priming on how we form impressions of other individuals. As part of a first task, participants read word lists such as "brave, adventurous, independent" or "reckless, foolish, careless."

In what participants thought was a separate experiment, they were then asked to read about an individual who climbed mountains and sailed across the Atlantic Ocean. The types of words that participants had previously been exposed to colored their perceptions of this individual. All the participants read the same description, but if they had read the list of positive words, they formed a more positive impression of the target individual than if they had read the list of negative words.

Stereotypes, which we will discuss in detail shortly, are an example of a type of schema. The recent use of a stereotype, even in an unrelated situation, can actually carry over to influence a person's interpretation of behaviors and interactions. This activation of stereotypes can affect the behavior of the individual holding the view, sometimes in unexpected ways. When participants in a study by John Bargh and his colleagues (Bargh, Chen & Burrows, 1996) had stereotypes for the elderly primed through a scrambled sentence exercise (involving words like *careful*, *wise*, *helpless*, and other terms sometimes associated with older people), they actually took on traits associated with those stereotypes themselves. Specifically, after the exercise, the participants walked more slowly down the hallway than those who had not had the stereotype primed. None of the participants believed that the words in the list had any impact on their actions, nor did they identify any of the words as being relevant to a stereotype of the elderly. This serves to make another important point about schemas and stereotypes—they're often shaped and activated without you ever knowing it!

> "The recent use of a stereotype, even in an unrelated situation, **can actually carry over to influence a person's interpretation of behaviors and interactions.**"

THE TROUBLE WITH SCHEMAS

If we encounter something that doesn't match up with the schema for a particular stimulus, we either filter it out or mentally file it away as the "exception that proves the rule." Your brain wants sensory information within your schemas to be consistent, because this makes it much easier for your brain to process and retrieve the information. Of course, this filtering out of valid information simply because it's not consistent with a developed schema is just one of the ways in which schemas can distort the way we view the world.

Stereotyping

Once it's been formed, a schema can be hard to change. The tendency for a schema to remain intact even when it comes up against discrediting information is called the **perseverance effect**. This plays a large role in one type of schema previously mentioned—the **stereotype**, in which the characteristics of someone or something are generalized according to preconceived notions about the group to which that person or thing seems to belong.

Imagine your friend was set up on a blind date. You meet her for coffee the next day to get the rundown. She simply can't stop gushing about him. He was funny, charming, and athletic. "I thought this date was

going to be snoozeville," she admits, "but he's really not like all of those other dull math majors!"

Rather than acknowledge that her schema for math majors may be incomplete or incorrect, your friend has, instead, filed this example as a subcategory of "math major," the previously mentioned exception that proves her stereotype. She continues thinking that all other math majors are dull, whereas this particular one is just different. We will revisit the idea of schemas when we discuss stereotypes and subtyping in Chapter 10.

Behavior linked to the schema is expressed, and subconscious expectations are activated. You know exactly what's going to happen, from approaching the counter to placing the order, to picking up your drink.

Experience develops and strengthens a schema. Your first trip to Starbucks, with so many options and a specific ordering process, might have been overwhelming. Now that you've learned the ropes, you know what to do.

What if they get your order wrong? What if the cashier forgets your change? If something doesn't fit your schema, you'll either ignore it or file it away as an unusual occurrence.

The person, situation, etc., are encountered, priming the schema. The next time you go to Starbucks, and each time after that, your previously gained knowledge will be activated once you enter.

A Schema for Starbucks. Schemas are developed and verified through experience.

SELF-FULFILLING PROPHECY a prediction that causes itself to come true

SELECTIVE FILTERING paying more attention to sensory information that fits a given schema, at the same time filtering out information that is inconsistent

AUTOMATIC PROCESSING the processing of information "on the fly," using schemas as shortcuts

CONTROLLED PROCESSING a type of mental processing that takes purposeful thought and effort as decisions or courses of action are weighed carefully

Self-Fulfilling Prophecy

Related to the issue of stereotyping is the fact that schemas can also lead to what Robert Merton (1948) termed **self-fulfilling prophecies**, predictions that cause themselves to come true. Numerous studies have found that the stronger and more developed the schema is, the more attention we pay to sensory information and traits that fit that schema. At the same time, our minds automatically filter out traits and information that are not consistent with the schema (Allen, Sherman, Conrey, & Stroessner, 2009). In paying more attention to information that fits a given schema, it seems that the schema is confirmed as correct (no matter how much discrediting information we have to filter out to make that confirmation!).

This **selective filtering** can lead to self-fulfilling prophecies in another way. Because schemas include set expectations for experiences, we tend to unconsciously mold our behavior to those expectations. Imagine you have to go into a store you hate. Your schema for that store includes expectations that it is crowded and that the employees there are unhelpful and rude. Because of this, you dread going in, but it's the only local place that carries your favorite brand of ice cream.

Before you even set foot in the door, you have set yourself up to have a terrible experience in the store. Your nerves might already be on edge, a small amount of clutter at the end of an aisle could lead you to break out in a cold sweat, and you're more likely to judge a store employee as being rude if she does so much as fail to smile as soon as you approach her. You might even behave in the way you criticize the employees for behaving. Your own attitude going in, guided by your schema for this store, has helped ensure that you have the terrible experience you anticipated. Can you override this experience by controlling your schemata?

Self-fulfilling prophecies can have pretty serious consequences, as demonstrated in a study by Robert Rosenthal and Lenore Jacobson

(1968). They visited a public elementary school, telling teachers that a test called the Harvard Test of Inflected Acquisition would accurately predict which of their students would be "growth spurters." Of course, there is no such test, and the researchers picked these star pupils at random. The study showed that the teachers' expectations served as a self-fulfilling prophecy. After all, the only differences between the students were in the minds of the teachers. Sure enough, at the end of the school year, when the students were given an intelligence test, the children who had been targeted as "growth spurters" and, therefore, held to higher expectations by their teachers showed a significantly greater intellectual gain than their classmates did.

This same concept of self-fulfilling prophecies can also be easily applied to real-world events. Think of a stock-market crash. News starts trickling in that things are getting bad, people panic and start selling off their stocks, and what happens? It *does* get bad, and depositors don't even realize that it's their own panicked withdrawals and sales that cause the collapse. Now, the Internet can play a major role in these panic-driven, self-fulfilling prophecies. In 2008, an online rumor claimed that Apple CEO Steve Jobs had suffered a massive heart attack. As word spread, a curious thing happened—Apple's stock dropped more than 2 percent to hit a 17-month low. Why? Jobs is perceived to be irreplaceable as the head of Apple. People assume that, without him, the company would suffer greatly. After seeing what happened after the false story, though, some of the harm to the company might result from a self-fulfilling prophecy created out of panic (Thomasch & Paul, 2008).

AUTOMATIC VERSUS CONTROLLED PROCESSING

The problems that arise from relying on schemas to organize the social world often come from the distinction between automatic and controlled processing. **Automatic processing** is just what it sounds like. We process information "on the fly," effortlessly making use of those schemas and mental shortcuts without conscious awareness. **Controlled processing**, on the other hand, takes careful thought and effort. It comes into play when decisions or courses of action must be carefully weighed before a judgment is reached.

Scientists have discovered that these two types of processing, though they might be used during the same experiences, seem to be housed in different areas of the brain. Researchers think that automatic processing, which is more emotion driven, occurs for the most part in the

>>> **Before even going through the gate, you've decided the food's going to be too expensive,** the lines are going to be too long, and it's just going to be too hot outside. **This could lead to a self-fulfilling prophecy,** as you'll tend to ignore anything that doesn't fit your negative schema for a trip to the amusement park.

limbic system, thought to be critical to emotional processing. In one study, limbic structures were activated when subjects were offered the choice of immediate reward (Cohen, 2005).

> "Scientists have discovered that these two types of processing, though they might be used during the same experiences, **seem to be housed in different areas of the brain.**"

It also seems that the **amygdala**, a small structure found in the medial temporal lobe of the brain, is involved in automatic processing. This structure has been linked to emotional learning and fear conditioning—both of which, as you might assume, are strongly related to automatic processing. Consider automatic race bias—unconscious judgments made on a basis of perceived race. In studies of this bias using subliminal display of photographs, behavioral measures associated with such bias correlated with amygdala activation (Cunningham, Johnson, Gatenby, Gore, & Banaji, 2003). The researchers went a step further to show that the amygdala does not play a role in controlled processing. People with damage to the amygdala show problems with automatic responses in fear conditioning but are able to successfully demonstrate controlled processing (Cunningham et al., 2003).

Controlled processing, which calls for much more mental work than does automatic processing, appears to involve parts of the **prefrontal cortex**. The prefrontal cortex plays a role in higher-order thinking and evaluation. Patients with damage to the prefrontal cortex demonstrate difficulty in controlled processing. Though it plays a major role in controlled processing, the prefrontal cortex is thought to play somewhat of a part in automatic processing, too (Cunningham et al., 2003).

Because of the enormous amount of information with which we come into contact every day, we must rely on automatic processing much of the time. If we didn't, we might not get past picking out what to wear or choosing what to have for breakfast in the morning! If a situation fits into a schema, the schema is used even when evaluating new situations. For example, if you meet someone new, you might rely on a schema for that "type" of person in making a quick decision as to whether or not you like him or her. Most of the time we are on "automatic pilot," but we can engage in effortful, conscious processing when necessary.

Sometimes, though, we are forced out of this automatic processing. If a new experience doesn't fit into any of our schemas, we must think more carefully and logically. Consider this: Your schema for visiting a restaurant most likely involves being told how much money you are expected to pay for each item on the menu. In 2010, the former CEO of Panera Bread Co. opened the St. Louis Bread Company Cares Café. Following the model of One World Everybody Eats Café, a restaurant in Salt Lake City, Utah, the St. Louis Bread Company Cares Café operates under a pay-what-you-will premise. Visitors to the restaurant are informed of the suggested "funding level" for each item on the menu, but it's up to each patron what to pay. If a person can't afford the suggested price, he or she may volunteer in the restaurant in order to "pay" for the food that was ordered (Volkman, 2010).

Now, how might going into the St. Louis Bread Company Cares Café force you out of automatic processing and into controlled processing? Rather than having someone tell you how much you owe and handing over cash or your credit card, you actually have to think about how much you will pay. Will you pay the suggested price? More? Less? The Associated Press reported shortly after the restaurant opened that 60 to 70 percent of patrons pay the full suggested amount, 15 percent pay more, and 15 percent pay less or nothing at all. They also said that many people report feeling quite confused when they encounter the restaurant's unique business model (Leonard, 2010). It would seem that this new café has become quite the experiment in challenging schemata!

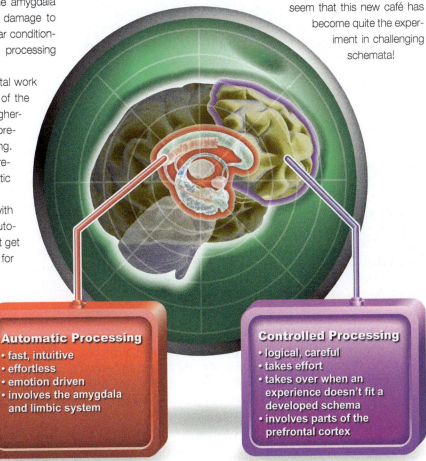

Automatic Processing
- fast, intuitive
- effortless
- emotion driven
- involves the amygdala and limbic system

Controlled Processing
- logical, careful
- takes effort
- takes over when an experience doesn't fit a developed schema
- involves parts of the prefrontal cortex

Automatic Versus Controlled Processing. Automatic processing is effortless, while controlled processing takes mental work.

HEURISTICS simple rules that reduce mental effort and allow us to make decisions or judgments quickly

AVAILABILITY HEURISTIC a rule used to estimate the likelihood of a given occurrence based on how easily one can recall an example of that occurrence

A similar method has been tested by several rock bands in the past few years. In 2007, British rock band Radiohead released their album *In Rainbows* online, allowing fans to pay as much—or as little—as they wished to download the album. Of course, it created a huge buzz, especially once it was revealed that many fans were still willing to pay "normal" prices for the music. Other bands, such as Oasis and Jamiroquai followed with announcements that they would be using similar models for upcoming albums (Wallop & Cockcroft, 2007). Could this lead to a shift in our schemas for buying music?

How Effective Are Mental Shortcuts?

Imagine your friend has asked you to drive him to the airport. After you help him unload his bags from the car, you give him a hug and say, "Have a safe flight!" Why is it so common for people to wish others a safe flight? If you ask people if they are more likely to be in an airplane crash or a car accident, most people are likely to pick the former, even though you are far more likely to be in a car accident. Statistically speaking, there's about a 1,000 times greater chance of a person being killed in a car accident than in an airplane crash (Bailey, 2006). In fact, it would be more fitting for your friend to wish you a safe drive home from the airport than for you to wish him a safe flight!

> "Though the statistics tell us otherwise, we continue to worry more about getting on a plane than about getting in our cars.

Though the statistics tell us otherwise, we continue to worry more about getting on a plane than about getting in our cars. This can be explained by taking a look at **heuristics**, simple rules that reduce mental effort and allow us to make decisions or judgments quickly. Here, we'll discuss four of the heuristics, first described by Israeli psychologists Amos Tversky and Daniel Kahneman in the 1970s: availability, representativeness, anchoring and adjusting, and framing. They're definitely use-

>>> At a restaurant where patrons decide **how much to pay for a meal,** controlled processing might have to **take over for the usual automatic processing.**

ful in cutting down on decision-making time, but each invites bias that can affect the outcomes of those decisions.

THE AVAILABILITY HEURISTIC

Consider the letter *R* and all the words in which it appears. Do you think the letter *R* most often holds the first position within those words, or the third position? What do you think is the ratio for those two options?

Tversky and Kahneman (1973) used this question in a study to illustrate the **availability heuristic**. Participants were given the same question about five consonants in the English language: *K, L, N, R,* and *V.* Among 152 subjects, 105 answered that these consonants were more often found in the first position, while only 47 answered that they were more often found in the third position. Overall, participants estimated that the ratio of first-position appearances to third-position appearances was 2-to-1. In fact, all of the consonants listed appear more frequently as third letters than as first letters within words.

Tversky and Kahneman (1973) described the availability heuristic as the rule used to estimate the likelihood of a given occurrence based on how easily one can recall an example of that occurrence. What does that have to do with all of those people wrongly determining that those five consonants are more often the first rather than the third letter in words? It's far easier to think of a list of words that begin with *K* or *N* than it is to think of a list of words that have one of those letters in the third position within the word. Using the shortcut of the availability heuristic, the participants followed this easy recall to the conclusion that more words must start with these letters.

We often use the availability heuristic in efforts to protect ourselves. After the terrorist attacks of September 11, 2001, air travel drastically declined. Even though terrorist attacks in the United States were rare, the constant media coverage of the events of September 11 and the fact that the attacks were fresh in people's minds made this example of a terrorist attack very easy to recall. The situation, therefore, presented a prime example of the use of the availability heuristic. People avoided travel by air because it *seemed* more likely that a terrorist attack could occur.

This, however, can have unintended—and perhaps tragic—consequences. In a 2004 study, German researcher Gerd Gigerenzer found that more Americans died in car crashes during the last three months of 2001 than in the four hijacked planes combined. Gigerenzer described terrorist attacks as dread risks, events that are low in probability but have high consequences. People fear dread risks and seek to avoid them. He concluded that the fear of this particular dread risk, so fresh in people's minds after the September 11 attacks, led to more people

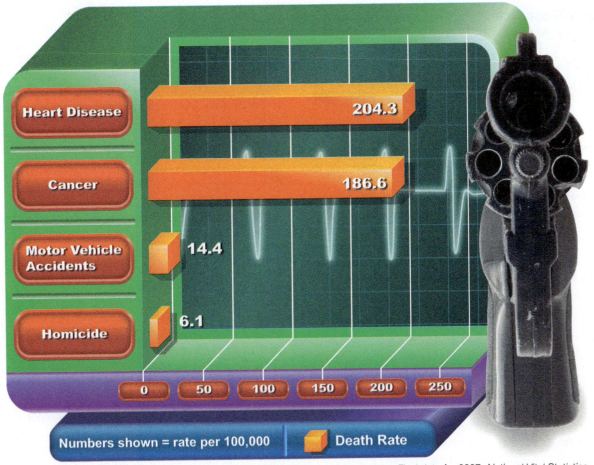

Heart Disease				204.3	
Cancer			186.6		
Motor Vehicle Accidents	14.4				
Homicide	6.1				
	0	50	100	150	200	250

Numbers shown = rate per 100,000   ▮ Death Rate

Source: Jiaquan, X., Kochanek, K. D., Murphy, S. L., & Tejada-Vera, B. (2010). Deaths: Final data for 2007. *National Vital Statistics Reports, 58*(19).

∧∧∧ **Death and the Availability Heuristic.** **Even though people are more likely to die** *of heart disease than homicide, the availability heuristic creates* **a far greater fear** **of the latter cause.**

traveling by car despite the fact that it is far more likely that one will die in a car accident than in a terrorist attack.

In this case, the use of the availability heuristic may have, according to Gigerenzer (2004a), cost lives. In the end, he attributes 350 deaths to the increase in car travel in the last three months of 2001. In fact, he counts these deaths as a second toll of "unnoticed" lives lost to the September 11 attacks.

Once you know about the availability heuristic, it's actually pretty easy to use it to influence decision making. In their book *Nudge*, Richard H. Thaler and Cass R. Sunstein (2008) point out that people can be "nudged" toward a particular decision using this heuristic. If you want to increase the fear of a bad outcome, remind them of a related scenario in which everything went wrong. If you want to make people feel more

confident about a decision, remind them of a related scenario in which things went well.

Let's say you're at the convenience store with your sister, and she mentions she might buy a lottery ticket. Here's where this exercise comes into play. Remind her of the last three times she bought one and didn't

>>> Whether or not you hit the button **to** **purchase the ticket could depend on what kind of** **outcome**—positive or negative—comes more easily to mind.

win a thing—that she spent the whole rest of the evening complaining about throwing money away. With this on her mind, she is more likely to decide that she'll skip buying a ticket this time.

What if, however, you remind her of the one time she won $50 and how excited she was? With this more positive scenario called up, she is more willing to hand over the price of the ticket, confident that she might get lucky again. Making use of the availability heuristic involves the ease with which we can call various events or outcomes to mind. Of course, your newfound powers of the availability heuristic should be used only for good!

THE REPRESENTATIVENESS HEURISTIC

Imagine you've received an e-mail from your friend Sarah. The subject line is "Go out Friday night?" Sarah's always been really quiet and mellow. In school, she could be found under a tree with a book between classes, and she's never been big on crowds. So what do you think Sarah wants to do—check out a singer/songwriter at a coffee shop downtown, or go out to a nightclub and dance all night?

When you use the **representativeness heuristic**, you estimate the likelihood of an event based on how well it fits with your expectations of a model for that event (often, a stereotype). As Tversky and Kahneman (1974) described it, you're deciding the probability that object A belongs to category B, that event A is a result of process B, that process A will result in event B—all based on how closely A seems to represent B. In the above example, Sarah's personality (A) more closely fits going to a coffee shop (B). So, when you open the e-mail, you might be pretty shocked to find Sarah asking if you want to join her in dancing the night away. The representativeness heuristic can be useful in sizing up new situations, but it's most certainly susceptible to error.

While useful, the representativeness heuristic can cause misperceptions. Given a sequence of coin tosses, people expect the string of heads

and tails to match what they conceive of as "random." On the other hand, given an actual random string of events, people often seek to find patterns where there are none. Flip a coin three times. If it comes up heads every time, you might be surprised or think that something is up with the coin. If you flip a coin many times, though, it wouldn't be odd to see three heads in a row; however, isolating those three flips and coming up heads every time does not match up with our notion of what is random, and so we feel it cannot *be* random.

The same trap of misperceiving random sequences as somehow ordered is illustrated in the "hot hand" seen in basketball games. Fans tend to believe that a player is "on fire"—that he is more likely to make a basket following a hit rather than a miss on the previous shot. Of course, when the records are analyzed, it's shown that streaks are a misperception and that sequences of hit shots really are random (Gilovich, Vallone, & Tversky, 1985). The differences in these two heuristics are summarized in Table 3.1.

Base Rate Fallacy

Suppose you meet your friend's new girlfriend, Erin, for the first time. You strike up a conversation with her and find she's very passionate about feminist issues and politics. Now, suppose you had to guess Erin's major. Is she more likely to be a gender studies major or a math major? Based on your brief encounter with Erin, you might guess that she is a gender studies major. That might fit, but you would be forgetting an important part of the puzzle. There are far more math majors than gender studies majors at your university, so it is actually more likely that Erin is a math major.

Base rate refers to how common a behavior or characteristic is. When we use the representativeness heuristic to draw a conclusion without considering the base rate, this is an example of **base rate fallacy**. When deciding whether Erin is more likely to be a gender studies major or a math major, you cannot take into account only how similar she is to other members of the available categories. You must also consider the base rate, and there is a very low base rate for gender studies majors at your school.

Let's say you're given a description of a person. This person is either an engineer or a lawyer. You're told that there are 100 descriptions total, half of which are of engineers and half of which are for lawyers. Based on this information, what would you say is the likelihood that the description you've been given is of a lawyer? Would the content of the description affect your judgment? The answer seems kind of obvious, right? There is a 50 percent chance that the description you have is of a lawyer.

Table 3.1: The Availability and Representativeness Heuristics

Heuristic	Definition	Example	Downside
Availability	a rule used to estimate the likelihood of a given occurrence based on how easily one can recall an example of that occurrence	Fearing air travel more after the events of Sept. 11	Giving more weight to the scarier, more vivid occurrences without fearing other, more likely instances
Representativeness	a rule used to estimate the likelihood of an event based on how well it fits with your expectations of a model for that event	Thinking that Jen is a librarian because she wears glasses and is considered to be an introvert	Ignoring other important information

Source: Based on Gigerenzer, G. (2004b). Fast and frugal heuristics: The tools of bounded rationality. In D. Koehler & N. Harvey (Eds.), *Blackwell handbook of judgment and decision making* (pp. 62–88). Oxford, UK: Blackwell.

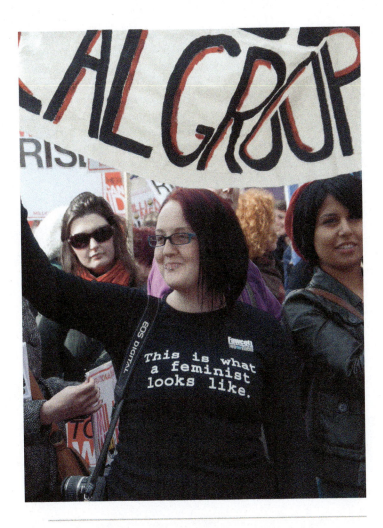

subjects correctly determined the probability that a random person was an engineer to be 70 percent (Tversky & Kahneman, 1974).

When the researchers added a description—even one with absolutely no guiding information—this logical thinking went out the window. For example, Tversky and Kahneman gave subjects the following description:

> Dick is a 30-year-old man. He is married with no children. A man of high ability and high motivation, he promises to be quite successful in his field. He is well liked by his colleagues.

Tversky and Kahneman (1974) intended for this description to contain no information relative to the lawyer or engineer question. The probability that Dick is an engineer should be equal to the given proportion of engineers in the group (70 percent or 30 percent, depending upon the group to which the subject belonged), right? Subjects ignored this fact and judged that there was a 50/50 chance of Dick being an engineer, thereby committing a base rate fallacy.

THE ANCHORING AND ADJUSTMENT HEURISTIC

It's your big chance. You've been jumping up and down and yelling all through the taping, and you've finally heard the words you want to hear: "Come on down!" Soon, you find yourself face-to-face with one of your favorite games, the "Bonus Game" on *The Price is Right*. Four prizes are lined up, each with an incorrect price tag attached. Your challenge? To go down the line and determine whether the actual price of each item is higher or lower than the number shown.

As you begin to play, do you just start blindly guessing, hoping you'll end up with a correct answer? Of course not. There's a system to playing this game. The incorrect price displayed for each item gives you a point from which to start your estimation of the actual price. You know *about* how much each item should cost, relative to the incorrect tags. Mentally, you take the information you do know (the incorrect price) and adjust until you've reached a satisfactory answer. When you do this, you

∧ **Gender studies major or math major?** When we
∧ fail to take into account how common a
behavior or characteristic is, **we run the risk of
committing *base rate fallacy*.**

Tversky and Kahneman (1974) put the representativeness heuristic (and its drawbacks) to the test in a study using the same setup. They gave subjects personality descriptions of several individuals, supposedly sampled from 100 engineers and lawyers. Divided into two groups, the subjects were asked to assign the label "lawyer" or "engineer" to each description. In the first group, subjects were told that there were 70 engineers and 30 lawyers. In the second, they were told that there were 70 lawyers and 30 engineers.

The odds that any one description is of a lawyer would be much higher in the second group, right? For every seven lawyers, there should be three engineers—and the reverse would be true for the first group. So, did the subjects take their knowledge of these ratios into account when categorizing the descriptions?

Surprisingly, no. Both groups of subjects produced the very same probability judgments. Rather than pay attention to the base rate of engineers and lawyers in the sample, they evaluated the descriptions based on the degree to which they fit their stereotypes of engineers and lawyers. They did, however, use the base rates correctly when they weren't provided with descriptions. For example, the first group of

∧ Higher or lower? Contestants on *The Price*
∧ *is Right* **must make use of the anchoring and**
∧ **adjustment heuristic to win.**

ANCHORING AND ADJUSTMENT HEURISTIC a heuristic in which we use a number as a starting point on which to anchor our judgment

are using the **anchoring and adjustment heuristic**, in which known information is used as a starting point from which revisions are made until an answer is reached.

In the "Bonus Game" example, the incorrect price is your anchor. As you consider what the actual price must be, you are making adjustments. This heuristic, first described by Tversky and Kahneman in 1974, does of course have its problems. For one, there is the problem of insufficient adjustment. In one study, when people used self-generated anchor values, they tended to stop adjusting once a reasonable value was reached. Basically, once they reached an answer that was "good enough," they stopped working toward finding a more accurate answer (Epley & Gilovich, 2006).

In another study, Tversky and Kahneman (1974) asked subjects to estimate percentages such as that of African countries in the United Nations. For each question, a number between zero and 100 was determined by spinning a wheel (this, of course, became the anchor). The subjects were asked to decide whether that random number was higher or lower than the anchor and then to estimate the percentage by moving upward or downward from the anchor. The median estimates of the percentage of African countries in the UN were 25 percent for subjects who had an anchor of 10, and 45 percent for subjects with 65 as an anchor. The researchers determined that anchors, even when they are arbitrary, have major impact on the final adjusted answer.

Thaler and Sunstein (2008) also demonstrated this odd effect of arbitrary anchors influencing the outcome of a question in an experiment they conducted with their students. Each student was asked to take the last three digits of his or her phone number, add 200 to that number, and then write down the result. Then, the students were asked when they thought Attila the Hun sacked Europe in relation to the numbers they came up with using their phone numbers. Each student determined whether the target date was higher or lower than the created number.

Of course, Attila the Hun's actions have nothing to do with arbitrary numbers created by adding 200 to part of a phone number. The year in which he sacked Europe was 411. When Thaler and Sunstein conducted this experiment, however, they discovered that students who started out with higher anchor numbers ended up with answers more than 300 years later than those who started with low anchor numbers.

Anchors can also affect your mood or your outlook in life. In one study (Thaler & Sunstein, 2008), college students were asked a two-part question: How happy are you? How often are you dating? Asked in that order, the questions didn't seem to correlate to one another (the correlation was .11). When the researchers switched the questions, though, it was a different story. Suddenly, the correlation went up to .62. With the dating question as an anchor, the answer to the question about students' happiness was adjusted accordingly. Students were suddenly given a frame of reference for their happiness. They might have thought "I'm not dating . . . and I'm not happy" (or the reverse). Given an anchor for the question of their happiness, their emotional states became dependent upon that anchor.

THE FRAMING HEURISTIC

Imagine your doctor wants you to try a new medication. He says there is a 75 percent success rate. You decide that it sounds like it's worth a try and accept the prescription. Now, imagine the same scenario, only your doctor tells you that the drug has a 25 percent failure rate. Would this change the decision you make?

Looking at both scenarios together like this, you might say, "No, it's the same thing." Consider this, though: Researchers have found on several occasions that the presentation of a product can greatly influence your decision about that product. There's a reason that ground beef is labeled "75 percent lean" instead of "25 percent fat." Presenting a negative attribute of a consumer product invites negative associations.

Subjects asked to evaluate beef reacted more favorably to that which was labeled in terms of percent-lean and more unfavorably to beef labeled in terms of percent-fat, even though the two percentages refer to

>>> You might be less likely to buy this candy if it prominently displayed **the percent of artificial flavorings used to make it—even if that percentage were low.**

the very same ratio between lean and fat (Levin & Gaeth, 1988). When you base a conclusion about a situation or item on the framework in which it is presented, you are using the **framing heuristic**.

What Are Other Sources of Bias in Social Cognition?

We like to think that we are incredibly logical beings. When we think about making decisions, we picture ourselves carefully weighing all aspects of a situation and making informed decisions, but that's not always the case, is it? Think about the mental energy that must be devoted to making such careful decisions. Now, think about using that mental energy for every single decision you make throughout your daily life. It would be exhausting, not to mention completely inefficient!

Of course, the fact that we can't make every decision according to a perfect model and must instead rely on shortcuts such as schemas and heuristics can sometimes cause trouble. Using these shortcuts invites bias. This results in certain "tilts" in social cognition that can lead us to serious error as we depart from rational thought in favor of easily accessed shortcuts.

One of these possible tilts is the **illusion of control** (Langer, 1982; Thompson, 1999). This is the perception that uncontrollable events are somehow controllable, and that one can influence events that actually depend upon chance. This illusion can be used to explain gambling behaviors. In one study, people were either assigned a lottery number or were invited to choose a number. Then, participants were asked if they would sell their tickets. Those who chose their own numbers demanded four times as much money as those who had been assigned random numbers. In a second study concerning a game of chance, it was found that people bet significantly more money against an opponent who seemed nervous and awkward than when faced with a confident person (Langer, 1975). Even though the outcome of these games depended entirely upon chance, people found ways to feel they had control.

NEGATIVITY BIAS

Imagine you're taking a date to a new restaurant for the first time. Everything is going wonderfully. The food is fantastic, the servers have been attentive, and the conversation has been flowing easily. Then something happens. Perhaps the server is a little late coming with the bill, or the couple one table over starts talking a little too loudly. It's just one thing, but it's enough to ruin the whole experience. This is an illustration of **negativity bias** (Fiske, 1980; Rozin & Royzman, 2001).

Negative information tends to stick out in our minds. We focus on it and are more sensitive to it. We are more likely to notice and remember negative information than positive information. Research shows that negative information has a stronger influence over our evaluation of people and situations than does positive information. This is most evident in impression formation. One study, in which participants evaluated positive and negative descriptions of people, showed that negative traits are given greater weight than positive ones (Ito, Larsen, Smith, & Cacioppo, 1998).

Is there any value to (often subconsciously) focusing on the negative? Some say yes. From an evolutionary point of view, this negativity bias makes perfect sense. If we are wired to protect ourselves from danger, it follows that we would pay more attention to potential warning signs than to positive information. For example, did you know that we

FRAMING HEURISTIC a rule that guides decision making based on the framework in which a situation or item is presented

ILLUSION OF CONTROL the perception of uncontrollable events as being controllable

NEGATIVITY BIAS the tendency for people to be more sensitive to and more likely to notice and remember negative information, which then influences the evaluation of people and situations

seem to be much faster and better at identifying negative facial expressions than we are at identifying positive facial expressions? This research supports the idea that we must be able to respond to negative stimuli, and so we are more likely to filter out the positive (Ohman, Lundqvist, & Karolinska, 2001).

THE OPTIMISTIC BIAS

It's a sunny day in May, and just about every member of the college community has gathered for the graduation ceremony. Those years of hard work, of endless papers, and tough exams, have finally paid off. The graduating students are surrounded by beaming family members. Onstage, one of the most popular professors is positioned behind the podium and is speaking about how proud she is of all the students in front of her. As they listen, are the graduates thinking about the discouraging job market and the difficulty of finding a job? Are they thinking about the potential struggle of paying off student loans? Of course not! They are caught up in the excitement of the day and the promise of future possibilities.

In our lives, we generally expect things to turn out well for us, despite any statistics or figures that might demonstrate the likelihood of the contrary. We expect that bad things are more likely to happen to

∧ ∧ ∧ **You've had a great evening,** but then you get stuck in traffic on the way home, and suddenly the whole night is ruined. **This attitude may be a downer,** but is there an evolutionary reason for it?

OPTIMISTIC BIAS the belief that bad things will happen to other people and that an individual is more likely to experience good things in life

OVERCONFIDENCE BARRIER a state of having more confidence in one's judgment or control over a situation than is really justified

COUNTERFACTUAL THINKING the tendency to imagine alternative outcomes for an event

other people and that we will experience mostly good things. This "rose-colored glasses" view is the flipside of the negativity bias and is called the **optimistic bias** (Armor & Taylor, 2002). Research has shown that most people believe they are less likely than others to experience negative events and more likely to experience positive ones. When you think about the future, you probably think about what will make you happy—about the plans and goals you have for your life.

It doesn't really sound bad, does it? You'd think it would be considered healthy to assume positive outcomes in your life. Of course, in many ways it is, but the optimistic bias does have its drawbacks. One of these is the **overconfidence barrier**, which describes a state of having more confidence in our judgments or control over a situation than is really justified.

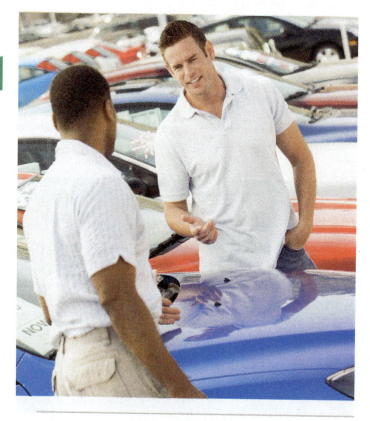

∧
∧ **Is he thinking about the possibility of losing his**
∧ **job or one of his children being ill?** Chances are, he's hit the overconfidence barrier and believes his financial situation will always be secure enough that he can make the car payments.

Sure, it's good to be confident, but this overconfidence barrier can lead to some pretty serious consequences. For example, overconfidence in one's financial situation could lead a person to take on more debt than he can handle, believing that he'll be able to pay it off in the future. Because of the overconfidence barrier, he doesn't account for the possibility that he may lose his job or become seriously ill, instead thinking that everything will be just fine. In Chapter 4, we will further discuss some of the downsides of overconfidence in social interactions.

COUNTERFACTUAL THINKING

It's the moment you've been dreading. Exam grades are coming back, and you don't think you're going to like what you see. Unfortunately, it turns out that you're right. As you stare at the "72 percent" in front of you, the very first thought that pops into your head is "If only I had spent more time studying, I would have gotten a much higher grade." This kind of thinking, called **counterfactual thinking**, happens automatically. It is defined as the tendency to imagine alternative outcomes for an event and comes into play especially when something bad has happened. This counterfactual thinking can have a dramatic effect on a person's emotional reaction to an event or situation.

Many times, counterfactual thinking has a negative effect on your mood. If you imagined a better outcome for an event (like getting a 97 on that exam instead of a 72), you could end up feeling pretty bad about your performance, or envious of those classmates who got better grades. These imagined outcomes in which things turn out better are called *upward counterfactuals* (Roese, 1997). And when do you think you are more likely to be upset—when you receive a 75 percent or a 79 percent? Although you might expect that you would be most upset by the lower score, Medvec and Savitsky (1997) found that individuals on the borderline of a grade (i.e., 79 percent) report being more upset, because it is easier to imagine getting a B if they got a 79 percent rather than a 75 percent.

Sometimes, though, counterfactual thinking can actually help you feel *better* about a situation. If you compare a real-life outcome with something less desirable, then counterfactual thinking can actually lighten your mood. Picture seeing that 72 percent on your exam again. Only this time, imagine that you felt completely confused when you were taking the test and thought you were going to completely bomb it. In this situation, you'd engage in counterfactual thinking more along the lines of "it could have been worse," which might actually make you feel better about the real event. This imagined worse alternative is called a *downward counterfactual* (Roese, 1997).

Researchers have demonstrated the dramatic emotional difference between upward and downward counterfactuals, using Olympic medalists as their subjects. For any given event, do you think the bronze or silver medalist is happier with the outcome? You might think it would be the silver medalist, because he or she reached a higher level of achievement. As illustrated by a 1995 study (Husted, Madey, & Gilovich, 1995), however, it turns out that the opposite is generally the case. For silver medalists, the most convincing counterfactual scenario is having won gold. This upward counterfactual leads them to feel less satisfied than bronze medalists, for whom the easiest alternative to picture is usually finishing without a medal.

Counterfactual thinking is often used to assign blame in a situation. If Karen was supposed to take care of buying flood insurance for her family business but dropped the ball, what happens when the building floods? Is it Karen's fault that the flood occurred? Sometimes, that's where our minds automatically go. We see a causal relationship where there is none, saying something like, "Of course, if Karen had taken care of the insurance, this probably never would have happened." As irrational as it is, the mind may actually create an alternative outcome in which Karen's buying flood insurance (or not buying it) is related to the likelihood of the building flooding.

The phenomenon of counterfactual thinking also explains why we get so upset when we hear stories in which people are in the "wrong place at the wrong time." We've all heard stories of situations like the flight attendant who switches schedules with a friend, only to end up on a plane that crashes; or the man who leaves for work an hour earlier than usual, only to be involved in a car accident. Here, the imagined alternatives in which the subject of the story never goes through his or her ordeal are even easier to call up, since they are what was "supposed to happen."

It might not be immediately obvious, but counterfactual thinking can actually be useful. Imagining what "could have been" can help us better plan and prepare for similar experiences in the future. Maybe getting that 72 percent, but feeling you could have gotten an A if you had devoted more time to studying, leads you to set aside more time to prepare for the next test. By imagining what could have been, you can picture achieving it and, therefore, set a plan to make it happen.

Marketing and Counterfactual Thinking

It's a hot summer day. "Mom! We're bored!" comes the call from two miserable-looking kids slumped on the living room sofa. The day seems to drag on, Mom is getting irritated, and she just doesn't know what to do. As she yells at the kids to get out of the house and find something to

do, a helpful, booming voice comes from nowhere, reminding Mom that she could have easily combated the mid-summer blues. All she had to do was take the kids to the circus!

Suddenly, there's a fake flashback in which we see how different things could have been. The kids are laughing, Mom's smiling, and, in the background, an elephant pulls off a clown's hat. See how much happier the family could have been, if only they'd bought tickets to the circus?

Watch television for a half hour, and you'll see plenty of examples of counterfactual thinking being used to sell you things. You'd get a date so easily, if only you'd use the right deodorant. Your dinner guests would have had so much fun, if only you'd served them the right brand of pasta. Advertising seems to have been built on how easy it is for us to picture alternative outcomes, as well as on harnessing our emotional responses to counterfactual thinking.

The Effect of Mood on Cognition

The way we use heuristics—and even the way we think—has much to do with mood. When you're in a good mood, annoying little

∧
∧ Between the bronze and silver medalists, who is happier? The
∧ answer might actually surprise you—it's due to the difference
between upward and downward counterfactuals.

things just don't bother you as much, do they? Negative experiences just roll off, you're more willing to give people the benefit of the doubt, and the day seems to go pretty well. This is explained by **mood congruence effects**—the fact that we are more likely to remember positive information when in a positive mood, and negative information when in a negative mood (Bower, 1987; Myers, 2000; Forgas, Bower, & Kranitz, 1984).

This isn't the only way in which mood affects the way we think. It can also influence what specific information is retrieved from memory, due to an effect called **mood dependent memory** (Eich, Macauley, & Ryan, 1994). This refers to the fact that what we remember when in a given mood is influenced in part by what was learned when previously in that mood. Do you get nervous when you take exams? Do you feel like you forget everything, only to remember it all hours later when you're just relaxing? Think about your state of mind when you study—if you are calm when you study, the principle of mood dependent me-

mory tells us you're more likely to recall the information you studied when you're feeling calm. If you are a person who gets nervous when you take a test, you might actually remember more of the test material if you study when you're feeling nervous!

Is a good mood always a good thing? That's a ridiculous question, right? Of course it is! This isn't always the case, though. It turns out that when you're in a good mood, you're more likely to rely on heuristics, more likely to use stereotypes, and (as we'll explore in Chapter 7) more easily persuaded. It might sound strange, but it makes sense—think back to what you learned about automatic versus controlled processing.

When we are faced with a difficult task or something unfamiliar, our brains work harder. Otherwise, we tend to rely on the autopilot setting of automatic processing. When you are in a good mood, you're just not motivated to use effort to evaluate incoming information. Instead, the tendency is to rely on heuristics and other shortcuts so as not to distract from our mood state (Wegener & Petty, 1994).

∧ ∧ ∧ **If she doesn't get the part,** she'll probably engage in counterfactual thinking, imagining how things could have been different—**if only she hadn't stumbled over that line, or had been more confident shaking hands with the director.** This thinking actually can end up being good for her, **if she uses it to prepare herself for her next audition.**

Action Learning: Hyping It Up

Social cognition isn't just about our own social experiences. The same biases that affect our personal interactions also play a major role in the way we learn about events around the world. Turn on the news, and you're likely to hear plenty of sensational reports about negative subjects, but how much of it is an accurate portrayal of what's going on in the world? One researcher found that, in a one-week period, 66 percent of headlining stories on major news networks' Web sites were about negative subjects (Caldwell, 2005). This, he argued, might lead people to believe that the United States is not a safe place to live. When he matched the media's focus on murder, rapes, and kidnappings up against figures from the Bureau of Justice Statistics, he found that violent crime rates were actually at a three-decade low in 2005 (Caldwell). So why are we inundated with stories of horrible crimes? What is at play here?

For years, researchers have studied how bias affects the way stories are reported and the ways in which the public responds. Arguing that the public depends on news media for reliable information, researchers have pressed for more responsible reporting. In one study, it was found that the news media significantly distorts the prevalence of and risk factors for the leading causes of death (Frost, Frank, & Maibach, 1997). Some causes—such as tobacco use—were underrepresented, while others—including car accidents—were vastly overrepresented. It was found that homicide, which was ranked the 11th most frequent cause of death, received the same amount of news coverage as the number one cause, heart disease.

So what's the big deal? Well, think about the availability heuristic. If we see something popping up on the news frequently, we believe that it's a reflection of what's going on in the real world. If homicide gets just as much attention as heart disease, our view of how likely we are to be murdered starts to become distorted. Statistically, you are far less likely to be a victim of homicide than of heart disease, but watching the news, you might become fearful that you could easily become a victim.

Throughout this chapter, you've considered how heuristics and other sources of bias influence our social interactions. Now, you will discover how they affect our relationship with media. Think about a news story that is currently creating controversy. Find two different media outlets in which the story is being reported but described differently. Using what you have learned in this chapter, identify the ways in which bias shows up in the reporting. What effect does the bias in each of the two reports have? Who or what does the bias seem to benefit?

Then, rewrite the story so that it is more objective. Share what you have learned with your classmates and friends. Discuss the possible effects of heuristics and other sources of bias on our perception. How does an awareness of these sources of bias make you a better consumer of information?

What will you learn from this action project?

1. Identify heuristics and other sources of bias used in the media.
2. Isolate the objective facts from a news story.
3. Encourage more responsible consumption of media.

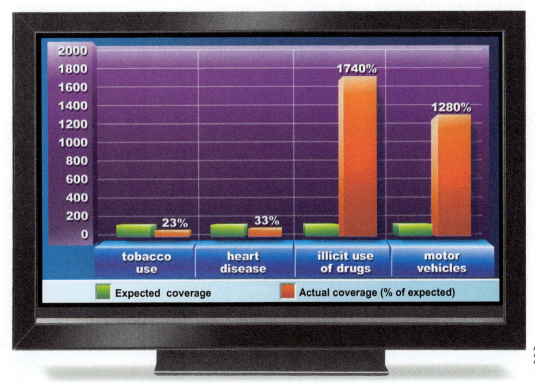

>>> Coverage of Leading Causes of Death. The news media significantly distorts the prevalence of leading causes of death. How does this reveal bias in the media? What effect does this have on the public?

Source: Frost, K., Frank, E., & Maibach, E. (1997). Relative risk in the news media: A qualification of misrepresentation. *American Journal of Public Health, 87*(5), 842–845.

Review

Summary

HOW DO SCHEMAS GUIDE THE WAY YOU THINK ABOUT THE WORLD AROUND YOU? p. 40

- Schemas are automatically created cognitive frameworks that help guide the way we think about and understand the world around us. They are created through experience as you encounter similar people, processes, social roles, occupations, and so on. Once in place, they are activated through a stimulus and trigger behavior and expectations.

- The tendency to ignore sensory information that doesn't fit with a schema is just one of the problems associated with schemas. Stereotypes, which are a form of schema, can lead to bias in our social interactions. Selective filtering can lead to self-fulfilling prophecies, in which we unconsciously mold our behaviors to fit expectations. These problems come from the brain's tendency to favor automatic over controlled processing.

HOW EFFECTIVE ARE MENTAL SHORTCUTS? p. 44

- Heuristics reduce mental effort and allow us to make quick decisions. The availability heuristic allows us to estimate the likelihood that something will happen based on how easily we can recall examples of that event. The anchoring and adjustment heuristic involves starting with a supposed given and working toward a solution from there. Basing a decision on the framework in which it is presented is referred to as using the framing heuristic.

- We use the representativeness heuristic to determine how well a given person or event will fit into a certain category. This heuristic is subject to base rate fallacy, which occurs when we draw a conclusion without taking into account how common a behavior or event truly is.

WHAT ARE OTHER SOURCES OF BIAS IN SOCIAL COGNITION? p. 49

- Though we like to think we are logical beings, this isn't really the case. Our minds favor automatic shortcuts, and this can lead to bias. Negative information tends to have stronger influence than does positive information, leading to a negativity bias in social cognition. On the flip side, the optimistic bias can lead us to believe we are unlikely to experience bad events in life.

- Counterfactual thinking, in which we imagine alternative outcomes for events, can have a strong effect on your emotional reaction to given events. Depending on whether the imagined alternative is better or worse than the real-life event, counterfactual thinking can darken or lighten your mood. Advertisers use this strong emotional connection to the "what-if" to influence our decisions as consumers.

Key Terms

amygdala a small structure found in the medial temporal lobe of the brain's limbic system that is involved in automatic processing and emotion 43

anchoring and adjustment heuristic a heuristic in which we use a number as a starting point on which to anchor our judgment 48

automatic processing the processing of information "on the fly," using schemas as shortcuts 42

availability heuristic a rule used to estimate the likelihood of a given occurrence based on how easily one can recall an example of that occurrence 44

base rate fallacy an erroneous conclusion reached when the representativeness heuristic is used to draw a conclusion without considering the base rate 46

controlled processing a type of mental processing that takes purposeful thought and effort as decisions or courses of action are weighed carefully 42

counterfactual thinking the tendency to imagine alternative outcomes for an event 50

framing heuristic a rule that guides decision making based on the framework in which a situation or item is presented 49

heuristics simple rules that reduce mental effort and allow us to make decisions or judgments quickly 44

illusion of control the perception of uncontrollable events as being controllable 49

limbic system the area of the brain thought to be crucial to emotional processing and memory 43

mood congruence effect the fact that we are more likely to remember positive information when in a positive mood, and negative information when in a negative mood 51

mood dependent memory the fact that the mood that we are in when we learn information may serve as a retrieval cue when we try to remember that information 51

negativity bias the tendency for people to be more sensitive to and more likely to notice and remember negative information, which then influences the evaluation of people and situations 49

optimistic bias the belief that bad things will happen to other people and that an individual is more likely to experience good things in life 50

overconfidence barrier a state of having more confidence in one's judgment or control over a situation than is really justified 50

perseverance effect the tendency for a schema to remain intact, even when it comes up against discrediting information 41

prefrontal cortex the part of the brain that plays a role in higher-order thinking, including judgment, decision making, and evaluation 43

prime to activate a schema through a stimulus 40

representativeness heuristic a rule used to estimate the likelihood of an event based on how well it fits with your expectations of a model for that event 46

schema an automatically created cognitive framework that helps guide the way we think about and understand the society around us 40

selective filtering paying more attention to sensory information that fits a given schema, at the same time filtering out information that is inconsistent 42

self-fulfilling prophecy a prediction that causes itself to come true 42

stereotype a type of schema in which we apply generalized information to an individual based on the group to which he or she belongs 41

Test Your Understanding

MULTIPLE CHOICE

1. Schemas exist for
   a. people.
   b. processes.
   c. situations
   d. all of the above.

2. The tendency for a schema to remain intact even when it comes up against discrediting information is called
   a. a stereotype.
   b. priming.
   c. the perseverance effect.
   d. selective filtering.

3. Scientists believe automatic processing involves the
   a. amygdala only.
   b. prefrontal cortex only.
   c. prefrontal cortex and amygdala.
   d. limbic system and amygdala.

4. Controlled processing is activated when
   a. you must make a decision quickly.
   b. a new experience doesn't fit an existing schema.
   c. your brain is tired.
   d. None of these are correct.

5. The concept of heuristics was first described by
   a. Tversky and Kahneman.
   b. Gerd Gigerenzer.
   c. Thaler and Sunstein.
   d. Sparrow and Wegner.

6. Which is an example of the availability heuristic?
   a. choosing a different route to work because yesterday your friend got a flat tire on your usual route
   b. guessing that your friend's new boyfriend isn't very intelligent because he works at Burger King
   c. forgetting the year your parents got married, but figuring it out using your birth date as a starting point
   d. being thrown off by an automated ticket machine at the movies because you weren't expecting it to be there

7. Which is an example of the representativeness heuristic?
   a. assuming that Oliver is Californian, because he is tan and likes to surf
   b. thinking that Janice can't be a librarian because she is female

   c. deciding that Dan is a good student because he has a GPA of 3.85
   d. thinking about Charlene because you just saw her walk by

8. Upward counterfactuals tend to have a _____ effect on mood.
   a. positive
   b. negative
   c. negligible
   d. short-term

9. Which is an example of a downward counterfactual?
   a. betting an 88 percent on a test and imagining how you could have gotten an A
   b. being more likely to buy ice cream that is labeled "90 percent fat free" than ice cream that is labeled "10 percent fat"
   c. being passed up for a promotion at work and imagining that you could be without a job
   d. having a terrible time at a party in part because you expected it would be a negative experience

10. Research on bias in the news media has found that
    a. news outlets tend to emphasize negative stories.
    b. headline stories contain factual errors 40 percent of the time.
    c. the media is biased strongly toward Democrats.
    d. heart disease is emphasized as the leading cause of death.

ESSAY RESPONSE

1. Explain how schemas are developed and how they affect how we process incoming information. Include an example in your response.
2. Provide an example of a self-fulfilling prophecy. How do you think the outcome could be altered? What kind of processing would that require?
3. Choose one of the heuristics. Define it, and provide an example of a situation demonstrating the use of that heuristic.
4. Describe how base rate fallacy leads to cognitive error.
5. What is the difference between upward and downward counterfactuals? What effect does each have on a person's emotional response to an event?

APPLY IT!

Make a point of watching several television commercials. Identify where upward and downward counterfactuals are being used. What do you think is the intended emotional effect of each instance?

ANSWERS: 1. d; 2. c; 3. d; 4. b; 5. a; 6. a; 7. b; 8. b; 9. c; 10. a

Remember to check www.thinkspot.com for additional information, downloadable flashcards, and other helpful resources.

facebook

Facebook helps you connect and share with the people in your life.

THE SELF: WHO AM I AND HOW DO OTHER INDIVIDUALS SEE ME?

WHAT IS SELF-CONCEPT, AND WHERE DOES IT COME FROM?
IN WHAT WAYS DOES OUR NEED FOR SELF-ESTEEM MOTIVATE OUR ACTIONS?
HOW DO WE PRESENT OURSELVES TO OTHERS?

Imagine

being asked to explain who you are—that is, how you define yourself—while responding to questions at a job interview, while eating dinner with your significant other's parents for the first time, while writing in your journal or diary and asking the question of yourself, and while having a heart-to-heart conversation with your mother or father. Think about four or five things you would say in each situation. Don't consider the question for too long; just respond with whatever comes to mind.

There are many ways to answer the question about your identity, and the way you respond will probably depend on the situation, who's asking the question, and even life circumstances that are influencing you at the time. From a cultural background, I, Kimberley Duff, am of Scottish heritage but I was born in England, and I am an American citizen. But usually, when people ask, I just say I am from California, where I currently live. I was raised in Great Britain and emigrated to the United States when I was 11. I never realized I had an accent or that I was "different" until my family moved to the States. All of a sudden, I was a girl from England with an accent. Among my American friends, the way I dressed, the music I listened to, and my attitudes were all considered part of my Britishness. What was interesting, however, is that my British family perceived me as being very American because I had picked up habits and attitudes from my American peers. It was hard to define my concept of self, because sometimes it depended on the situation or with whom I was interacting.

Think about the ways your own self-description changes based on the previously mentioned scenarios. How much do your responses differ from one another? What factors do you think play the strongest roles in your self-descriptions? Which description of yourself do you think is the most accurate? The following chapter may help you begin to answer some of these questions. It will guide you to discovering the various factors that impact your sense of identity and the way you present yourself to others. You will learn how sometimes these presentations and perceptions can be deceiving, and how certain things about you might be more revealing than you would guess.

CHAPTER **04**

What Is Self-Concept, and Where Does It Come From?

For each of us, our sense of self is affected by culture, by personal factors (such as gender or motivations), and by social factors (the way we see ourselves in relation to others) that we will explore in this chapter. If you play several sports well and like to be physically active, you may think of yourself as an athlete. If you are the only one among your family members or friends who plays sports, you are even more likely to include "athlete" as part of your sense of identity because your athleticism is something that sets you apart from the people around you.

Your **self-concept**, your mental representation or overall sense of "you," is made up of all the various beliefs you hold about yourself. When asked to describe yourself, you can probably identify traits like "outgoing," "smart," and "funny" that describe you and even identify roles that make up part of your self-concept like "student," "big brother," "best friend," or "musician." Each of these beliefs about an aspect of your identity is a **self-schema** that helps organize the processing of information related to yourself. Self-schemata are like puzzle pieces that fit together to create your overall self-concept (Markus, 1977). Of course, certain schemata will be more significant to you than others, just as different schemata take on different levels of importance for different people. For example, fashion is an important self-schema for some people. They think of themselves, and like others to think of them, as stylish dressers. For fashion schematics, everyday situations involving clothing, such as walking past a row of clothing boutiques, watching an episode of *What Not to Wear* on TV, or even noticing how other people around them are dressed, will trigger thoughts about the self. They may think, "Am I wearing the right clothes for the occasion? Are other people here better dressed than I am? Is there a fashion trend I'm missing out on?" On the other hand, there are many people for whom this is not the case; fashion doesn't play an important role in their lives, and they don't connect it with their thoughts about themselves.

Our individual schemata also take on different levels of importance in different situations. We all have private selves and public selves. For example, you probably find that you have certain traits that become more pronounced when you're among close friends or family than when you're in the company of casual acquaintances. Our self-concepts are complicated and somewhat fluid. They evolve with life experience and can change in relation to environment, circumstances, mood, and social situation.

Sometimes major events, such as relationship breakups, can alter self-concepts. In a study of undergraduates at Northwestern University, researchers found that romantic partners come to shape one another's identities through the sharing of activities, social groups, and goals (Slotter, Gardner, & Finkel, 2009). After a breakup, participants reported a disrupted self-concept, leading to confusion and emotional distress.

Whether you realize it or not, much of your self-concept is shaped by your relationships with other people. Sociologist Charles H. Cooley (1902) coined the term *looking-glass self* for the way other people act as a mirror in which we perceive ourselves. To expand on this idea, George Herbert Mead (1934) further theorized that our self-concept is not based on how others actually see us, but on how we imagine they do. Researchers have also theorized that the self is relational and that relationships with important people in our lives significantly impact the way we act and how we evaluate and define ourselves (Andersen & Chen, 2002). The way we believe others see us, which impacts the way we see ourselves, can have an important effect on our ability to succeed.

One recent study found that when children saw their future selves as being in careers dependent on college education (law or medicine, for instance), rather than being in degree-independent careers (like pop music or sports), they performed better in school, an area consistent with their future selves (Destin & Oyserman, 2010). Having a well-developed sense of self can lead to stronger **self-efficacy**. Self-efficacy refers to a person's belief in her ability to overcome challenges and achieve certain goals. The concept of self-efficacy was central to psychologist Albert Bandura's research (1977), in which he found that people with high levels of self-efficacy approach difficult tasks as challenges they can master, rather than as threats they should avoid. Other recent studies have confirmed that when we have a positive sense of self-efficacy, we are more likely to achieve our goals (Lent, Brown, & Larkin, 1984; Zimmerman, Bandura, & Martinez-Pons, 1992; Pajares, 1996; Schunk, 1995). One found that teens with higher perceived self-efficacy were more likely to achieve personal health goals, like regular exercise, than teens with poor perceived self-efficacy (Luszczynska et al., 2010).

∧
∧ **We all have different selves that**
∧ **we project in different situations.**
Celebrity gossip magazines and tabloids attract readers by promising to deliver glimpses **into both the public and private lives of today's big stars.**

PHYSIOLOGICAL INFLUENCES

So where do our self-concepts come from? While our self-concepts can be shaped by a variety of outside factors, our abilities to form self-concepts are rooted in the brain itself. When people experience major brain injuries, for instance, their self-concepts may be altered or completely destroyed. Take the case of Clive Wearing,

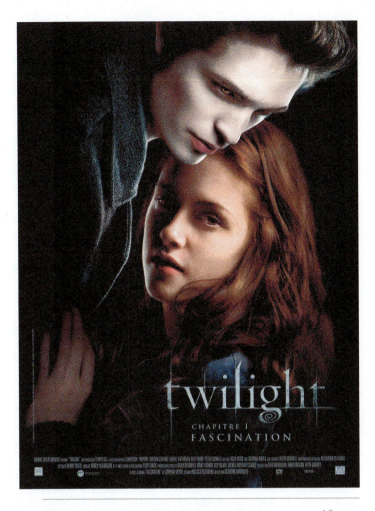

∧
∧ **Our significant relationships shape** our self-
∧ concepts to a large degree.

who, in 1985, contracted herpes encephalitis, an infection of the brain that not only erased nearly all of his past memories, but also prevented him from forming new memories that lasted beyond several seconds by almost completely destroying the hippocampus, a structure of the brain implicated in memory (Sacks, 2007). After the infection, Wearing, who had been a professional musician with a detailed knowledge of composers and musical scores, couldn't name more than a handful of composers and didn't recognize the names of songs he once knew. He couldn't remember the names of his daughter or his wife, the places he had traveled, or most of the things he once cared about. Surprisingly, however, he was still able to play music, he could recognize his wife by sight, and he could perform many everyday tasks. But, without memory to give these things a meaningful context, Wearing had completely lost his sense of self.

As we learn new information or skills, the synapses in our brains record and store information. If the synapses become unable to record information, as in Wearing's case, we no longer have a biological method of forming memories (Shors & Matzel, 1997). The way we think about ourselves, our beliefs about what others think of us, and our knowledge about how we respond to different situations are mostly learned through experience and stored in memory. In his 2002 book, *Synaptic Self: How Our Brains Become Who We Are*, Joseph LeDoux posits that memory is the glue that enables each of us to have a coherent self-concept.

> "The way we think about ourselves, our beliefs about what others think of us, and our knowledge about how we respond to different situations are mostly learned through experience and stored in memory."

Brain imaging technologies have shown that certain parts of our brains are activated when we're thinking about ourselves (Craik, Moroz, Moscovitch, Stuss, Winocur, Tulving, & Kapur, 1999; Gusnard, Akbudak, Shulman, & Raichle, 2001). For instance, researchers found that certain portions of the brain that became active when observers were shown unflattering photographs of themselves were not activated when the subjects of the study looked at unflattering photographs of other people (Morita et al., 2008). Though research is continuing to develop in this area, it is becoming clear that the self occupies a unique part of the brain and that trauma to the brain can transform who we are.

Although the roots of self-concept are housed in the brain, many psychologists believe that self-recognition—the ability, when standing in front of a mirror, to recognize the reflection as one's own—shows the influence of social relations in developing the self-concept (Boysen & Himes, 1999).

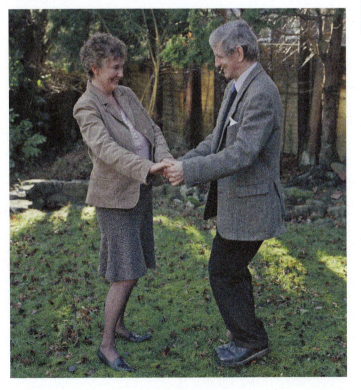

∧ Clive Wearing keeps journals in which he
∧ records his thoughts about himself. **Without**
∧
**memory as a "glue," these thoughts consist only of
statements like "I am awake" or "fully conscious."**

∧
∧ **Gallup's experiments with chimpanzees**
∧ **suggest** that self-concept begins with self-recognition.

In one classic experiment, Gordon Gallup placed a full-length mirror outside chimpanzee cages to determine whether the chimps were able to recognize themselves in the reflection (Gallup, 1977). At first, they displayed social behaviors, reacting as if the reflection was another chimpanzee, but after several days, they began to respond in self-oriented ways, such as using the mirror for grooming.

To further support his findings, Gallup replicated the experiment by anesthetizing the chimps and placing a spot of red dye on their foreheads. Without the mirror, the chimpanzees seemed unaware of the marks, but when they saw their reflections, they responded by reaching up to touch the red dots on their own faces. Interestingly, the test only worked on chimpanzees that had been raised in social environments. Those that had been raised in isolation were not able to recognize their reflections in the mirror, suggesting that the self's relationship to others is an important part of the development of self-concept.

SOCIAL INFLUENCES

The chapter opener highlights how at different times and in different contexts, our self-perceptions will shift. Some ways of thinking about yourself may even seem to contradict others. So which "you" is the truest you, and how do you know? In fact, there isn't one self-concept that defines you more accurately than others. Each of our selves reflects a part of who we are.

Our sense of self is connected to others (Chen, Boucher, & Tapias, 2006). According to **social identity theory**, the development of our identities is connected to particular social groups (Tajfel & Turner, 1986). On the continuum between personal identity and social identity, we may, at one extreme, focus only on the attributes of personal identity that set us apart from other members in a social group. For instance, you may characterize yourself as adventurous or artistic because you see yourself as being more adventurous or more artistic than some of your friends and acquaintances. Of course, these perceptions will change depending on the group to which you are comparing yourself. Within your family, you might see yourself as "the chef" because you are a better cook than anyone else. However, if you started going to culinary school, you might view yourself as an amateur cook relative to your instructors and peers. Group membership results in a categorization of an ingroup—a group that we consider ourselves to be a part of—and an outgroup—a group that we do not belong to that is separate from our ingroup (Tajfel & Turner, 1986). As soon as we categorize groups into an ingroup and an outgroup, we engage in an "us versus them" mentality, favoring the ingroup as one way to bolster our self-concept.

At the other extreme of the identity continuum, the social end, we identify ourselves in terms of the traits we share with a certain group that is different from other groups. Think, for instance, of my own example in the chapter opener, when I said that when I was growing up, I thought of myself as British when I was among other Americans because I shared "British" traits and an accent that set me apart from my American friends. However, after living in America for so long, my ingroup became other Americans, as I have assimilated to my new culture. According to social identity theory, we can develop different group identities and associate with new groups.

Gender is another social identity. If you are male, you might think of yourself in terms of the characteristics you see yourself sharing with other men. You would not see yourself as possessing traits associated with being feminine, further reinforcing your masculine identity and setting you apart from females.

Where you place yourself on the personal-versus-social identity continuum may at times be situational. However, a large body of research also suggests that culture largely dictates a tendency toward one or the other end of the spectrum. In Western cultures like that of the United States, people tend to emphasize **individualism**, focusing on the self as independent of others and placing more importance on individual, rather than collective, goals. People are encouraged to "stand out from the crowd" and to discover and embrace the attributes that make them unique. The common American expression, "The squeaky wheel gets the grease" illustrates this idea. Individualism thrives off the typical American standards of urbanism, wealth, and mass media (Triandis, 1994).

Many non-Western cultures, on the other hand, emphasize **collectivism** and focus on the self as interdependent and defined by the connectedness of people to one another—and not just any group of people, but the individuals closest to them, like family members and friends (Brewer & Chen, 2007; Kitayama & Markus, 1995). An individual's talents and opinions are considered to be of secondary importance to his or her membership to various groups. A common expression in Japan is "the nail that sticks up gets pounded down" (Markus & Kitayama, 1991). But just as nothing is black and white, no culture is homogeneously individualist or collectivist. Instead, there are varying degrees of both among every culture's members (Oyserman et al., 2002).

Kuhn and McPartland's (1954) **Twenty Statements Test (TST)** has become a popular method of identifying differences in self-perception (Bond & Cheung, 1983; Rhee, Uleman, Lee, & Roman, 1995). The test highlights the contents of an individual's self-perception by asking him or her to write 20 statements in response to the question, "Who am I?" One study found that American students responding to the TST were more likely to cite trait descriptions, while Chinese students were more likely to cite group affiliations (Trafimow, Triandis, & Goto, 1991). While the TST demonstrates that social groups play a powerful role in shaping our self-concepts, research has shown that personal influences play an important part as well.

PERSONAL INFLUENCES

What was the last decision you made? How did you make it? Whether it was something major (*Should I accept this summer internship, or look for a summer job that pays?*) or something fairly insignificant (*Do I want sushi or a sandwich for lunch?*), you probably had a process for making your choice. Did you carefully consider the pros and cons, or did you "go with your gut"? How did you feel after you made your decision? Were you satisfied with your choice? It may surprise you to know that research has shown that when we make choices based on our gut instincts, rather than on careful reflection about our preferences, we are generally happier with the outcome (Gilbert & Ebert, 2002). This has to do with the process of introspection, the results of which are not always as accurate as we'd like to believe. In this next section, we will consider how this and other personal factors influence our self-concepts.

SOCIAL IDENTITY THEORY a theory in which we develop our identity from our group memberships

INDIVIDUALISM at the cultural level, focus on the self as independent from others and defining individual goals over the collective

COLLECTIVISM a cultural focus on the self as interdependent and defined by the connectedness of people to one another, in particular, the people closest to them

TWENTY STATEMENTS TEST (TST) a measure of self-concept that asks individuals to self-report "who am I?"

INTROSPECTION the process of thinking about your own thoughts

Introspection

Self-help books often advise us to look inward when facing a challenge or difficult decision, concentrating on our thoughts and feelings until we understand our inner states. After all, no one knows you as well as you know yourself, right?

This process of **introspection**, or thinking about your own thoughts, is not as helpful as conventional wisdom would lead us to believe. In fact, some research suggests the process can lead us astray more often

∧
∧ **Independent and interdependent view of self.** Western cultures emphasize the independent self, which focuses on individuals' unique attributes, while non-Western cultures tend to emphasize the interdependent self, placing value on each person's connectedness to others (Markus & Kitayama, 1991).

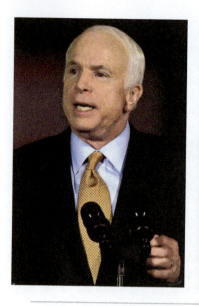

∧
∧ **Which candidate did you guess would feel happier six**
∧ **months down the road?** According to studies, it may
not be as easy as you think to predict.

than not. In a number of studies, when people were asked to analyze their reasons for holding particular attitudes, their stated attitudes were *less* likely to match up with their actual behaviors. This shows that we are not always good at predicting or understanding our feelings (Wilson, 1990; Wilson & Schooler, 2008). This is also why we are likely to make better decisions based on instinct than when we engage in analysis. When students ranked their preferences for a number of college courses, the students who analyzed the reasons for their preferences before ranking the courses were less likely to agree with expert opinion than students who responded to the questionnaire directly (Wilson & Schooler, 2008).

We are also less in touch with our "inner selves" when it comes to predicting the impacts that certain events will have on our feelings and attitudes. Think about your dream job, car, and house. If someone suddenly handed you all of those things today, how do you think you would feel five years from now? Chances are pretty high that you wouldn't feel as happy then as you might guess right now. This is because our attempts at **affective forecasting**, predicting the impact future events will have on our overall emotional states, are usually inaccurate.

We tend to overestimate the intensity and duration of our emotional responses (Wilson & Gilbert, 2005). For instance, Daniel Gilbert and his colleagues asked college students to predict how

they would feel two months into the future if their girlfriends or boyfriends broke up with them (Gilbert et al., 1998). Participants guessed that they would be unhappy for a long time, but in reality, students who had been through a breakup two months earlier did *not* report being as unhappy as they had predicted; in fact, they were generally just as happy as students who had not been through the same experience.

When Our Selves Don't Match

At some point, we all have wished we could act differently or be different than we actually are; we all have *ideal selves* that don't correspond exactly to our *actual selves* (Higgins, 1987; Markus & Nurius, 1986). Maybe, for instance, you wish you were more confident, more physically fit, or better at telling jokes. According to **self-discrepancy theory**, our concepts of self are influenced by how close our actual selves are to the selves we would like to be (Higgins, 1987). If you perceive a large gap between your actual and ideal selves, then you will generally have a more negative self-image. For example, if you think of yourself as an A student, and then you get a C grade on an exam or paper, you are likely to feel worse about it than a student who already perceives himself as a C student and receives the same grade.

However, some researchers argue that we are not always aware of the discrepancy between our actual and ideal selves, but if we experience heightened **self-awareness**, we will be motivated to change our behaviors to match our personal standards. Have you ever seen a video of yourself giving a speech, performance, or presentation? Did it reveal tics or other flaws of which you hadn't been aware? Often, people record themselves in these situations so that they will be able to improve their performance in the future. Looking in a mirror, standing in front of a crowd, and listening to a recording of your voice are all ways to increase self-awareness. In a classic study, a bowl of candy was left on a researcher's front porch on Halloween with a request that each trick-or-treater take just one piece (Beaman et al., 1979). Results showed that when a full-length mirror was placed behind the bowl, only 12 percent of children took more than one piece of candy, as opposed to the 34 percent

>>> **Self-Discrepancy Theory.** When we perceive our actual selves to be closer to our ideal selves, we have a more positive self-concept than when we perceive a large gap between the actual and the ideal.

who took more than one piece without the mirror in which to see themselves (Beaman et al., 1979). In a more recent study, researchers found that employees chipped in more cash for coffee in an office break room when a picture of a pair of eyes was placed over the donations box than when the box had other images over it (Bateson, Nettle, & Roberts, 2006).

An increase in self-awareness can lead people to match their behaviors to their attitudes. Conversely, it can result in an individual's desire to escape self-awareness. In a study by Hull and Young (1983), individuals who were given negative feedback about their IQs tended to drink more wine at a tasting following the receipt of feedback than those who were given positive feedback, indicating a desire to escape the unpleasant feelings associated with the negative feedback (Hull & Young, 1983). A number of other studies have produced similar results, supporting the idea that it is common for people to use alcohol as a way to escape self-awareness.

Roy Baumeister (1991) argues that binge eating, suicide, and even watching television can serve to decrease self-awareness. To examine if individuals would escape from self-awareness, Moskalenko and Heine (2003) manipulated the type of feedback that individuals would receive about their level of intelligence. After measuring participants' actual and

ideal selves, they found that individuals who received negative feedback about an IQ test they had taken spent more time watching television in the laboratory than those who received positive feedback.

What Does Our Behavior Say About Ourselves?

Have you ever noticed that you make assumptions about other people's attitudes and preferences based on the behavior patterns you

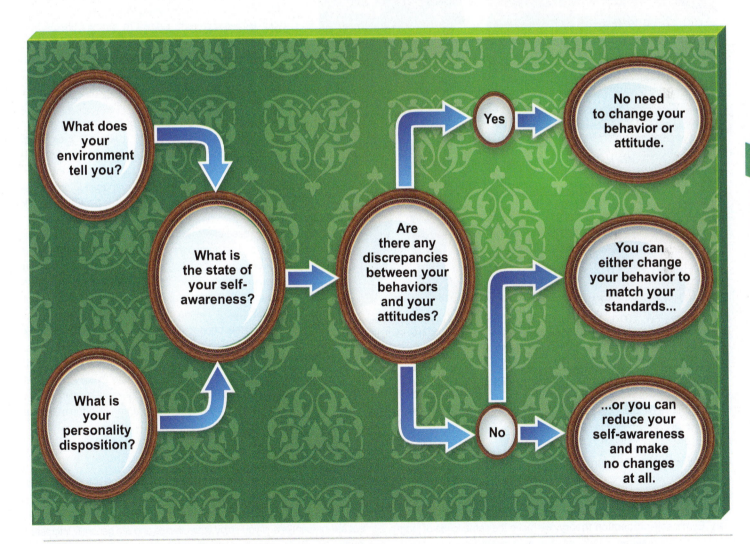

∧∧ **Self-Awareness Theory and Discrepancies.** Increased self-awareness makes people conscious of the gap between their actual and ideal selves, which in turn may cause them to modify their behavior to bring it more in line with their ideals. On the other hand, the situation might also lead people to try to escape self-awareness.

1	Clergy
2	Physical Therapists
3	Firefighters
4	Education Administrators
5	Painters, Sculptors, and Related
6	Teachers
7	Authors
8	Psychologists
9	Special Education Teachers
10	Operating Engineers

Source: Smith, T.W. (2007). Job satisfaction in the United States. *NORC/University of Chicago.* Retrieved July 19, 2010, from http://www.norc.org/NR/rdonlyres/2874B40B-7C50-4F67-A6B2-26BD3B06EA04/0/JobSatisfactionintheUnitedStates.pdf.

Most Satisfying Jobs in the United States. What about these careers might be intrinsically motivating?

actually really enjoy the music and that your previous opinion of jazz was founded on a lack of exposure. This positive experience can shift your own self-perception and turn you into a lifelong fan of the music.

Are we happy because we smile, or do we smile because we are happy? Similar to self-perception theory, the **facial feedback hypothesis** states that our facial movements can impact the emotions we experience. According to this hypothesis, smiling, even when you don't feel like it, can help improve your mood. So there is some truth in the common advice to "just smile—you'll feel better," as smiling can lead to more positive emotions. In the first study to test this, James Laird (1974) attached electrodes to individuals' faces and gave them instructions to either smile or frown while they were watching cartoons. When people were instructed to smile, they rated the cartoons as funnier than when they viewed cartoons while frowning. Try this technique yourself and see if changing your expression from a smile to a frown affects how you feel.

What if we could not change our facial expressions? Would we still experience a change in emotion? Recent research suggests that impairment of facial movement may be an obstacle (Havas et al., 2010). When individuals were given Botox treatments that impaired their abilities to frown, it actually took them longer to emotionally process a series of angry and sad statements they were asked to read. Participants with impaired facial movement lost their response to emotions. What is the mechanism behind the facial feedback hypothesis?

Some researchers, including Laird, argue that it works as a form of self-perception, and that we infer our mood state from our behavior (i.e., if I'm smiling, it must be because I am happy). Other researchers (Izard, 1990; Zajonc, 1993) argue that facial expressions bring about a physiological change in the brain and that is responsible for the change in emotion. The facial feedback hypothesis even extends to other nonverbal gestures, such as a shrug of the shoulder or a nod of the head. In fact, Briñol and Petty (2003) found that if you can get audience members to shake their head affirmatively, then they will be more likely to agree with the message the speaker is presenting.

notice? If your roommate turns you down every time you invite him to go get pizza with you, you might assume that he doesn't like pizza. (On the other hand, if he turns you down every time you ask him to do anything with you, you might assume he doesn't like *you*.) According to Daryl Bem's **self-perception theory**, we make the same kinds of judgments about ourselves based on our own behavior (Bem, 1972). According to self-perception theory, if we are unsure of the attitudes we hold, we look to our behavior and use that to make inferences about our attitudes, much like an outside observer. For example, growing up, you may never have been exposed to much jazz music, and as a result, a dislike of jazz has become a part of your self-concept. However, if a friend convinced you to attend a jazz show, you may find that you

Motivation

Think about the subject area you have chosen to study. What were your reasons for choosing this major or concentration? Motivation—the force that drives us to complete a task or achieve a goal—also plays a part in our self-perceptions. If you enjoy your classes and are generally interested in your academic major, this is probably because your choice to pursue this major was an **intrinsically motivated** one. When we take a certain action because we enjoy it, we are likely to engage more fully and with greater curiosity and pleasure.

By the same token, **extrinsically motivated** actions—those that we perform in response to an external pressure or obligation, to avoid punishment, or to achieve some outside benefit (money, success, recognition, etc.)—can have negative consequences for our overall sense of well-being and happiness if they dominate our experience (Sheldon, 2005). Interestingly, the National Opinion Research Center at the University of Chicago reports that the 10 happiest groups of workers in the United States, individuals who report being "very satisfied" with their careers, include clergy members, artists, firefighters, and psychologists (Smith, 2007). None of these occupations are necessarily high paying or typically considered "prestigious." But benefits are intrinsic, including things like helping people or creating something original. This supports the idea that we prefer to engage in activities when our reasons for doing so are internally triggered.

> "If compensation for a task is a surprise, people are more likely to derive satisfaction **from it because they still believe they are engaging in the task for its own sake.**"

In one study of the impact of motivation on behavior, Mark Lepper and his colleagues asked children at a nursery school to create drawings with magic markers—a task the children already had an intrinsic motivation to complete (Lepper et al., 1973). One group of children was asked to draw a picture for the researcher and was promised and given a reward upon completion of the task. A second group was asked to draw a picture but was not promised or given a reward. In the final group, the children were asked to draw pictures and then were given surprise rewards when the drawings were all completed. The next day, the researchers recorded the amount of time all of the children in the class devoted to drawing when they were allowed to freely choose an activity. They found that children from the first group, who received an external reward for the task, only spent 8.6 percent of their free time on drawing, while children in the second and third groups devoted 16.7 percent and 18.1 percent of their time respectively to the activity. They concluded that when people engage in a task knowing that they will receive a reward, they no longer feel like they are performing the task for its own sake. This phenomenon, known as overjustification, causes people to lose interest in a task when the motivation is apparently extrinsic. If compensation for a task is a surprise, people are more likely to derive satisfaction from it because they still believe they are engaging in the task for its own sake.

Motivations can also be influenced by culture. Iyengar and Lepper (2000) found that white American children, coming from a cultural background in which individualism is highly valued, showed the greatest motivation to perform when they engaged in tasks they had chosen for themselves. By contrast, Asian American children, coming from cultural backgrounds in which interdependence is highly valued, were more motivated to engage in tasks that were chosen for them by trusted authority figures or peers. In one of their studies, Iyengar and Lepper (2000) asked white American children and Asian American children to complete an anagrams task. In each group, some of the children were allowed to choose a task from among several categories, while others were told their mothers had made the choice for them. The researchers found that the white children performed better when they were allowed to make a personal choice, whereas the Asian children performed significantly better when they believed their mothers had made the choice for them.

In What Ways Does Our Need for Self-Esteem Motivate Our Actions?

How do you feel about yourself? Your **self-esteem** encompasses your own attitudes about yourself, from the way you look to your intelligence, to your physical abilities and more. Although self-esteem is a mostly stable construct, it can fluctuate on a moment's notice in response to our social environment. What remains present, however, is an innate human need to feel good about ourselves.

Morris Rosenberg (1965) developed a self-esteem scale to measure these feelings among individuals. It exists of 10 statements indicative of how one feels about oneself overall, and the statements can be rated on

According to Iyengar and Lepper (2000), someone from a Western culture might apologize if she orders the same menu item as others in her group because choosing from a menu is motivated by one's concept of individuality. **By contrast, in Asian cultures, ordering from the menu could be a group decision motivated by a desire to show belongingness.**

a four-point scale from strongly agree to strongly disagree. Because the need for high self-esteem is such a powerful and inherent factor in our lives, it seems to have a direct effect on our overall happiness and perhaps our successes throughout life.

However, Roy Baumeister and his colleagues (2003) found that while positive self-esteem is correlated with positive performance in school and work, high degrees of popularity, and good physical health, it's just that—a correlation. A cause cannot necessarily be inferred, as explained in Chapter 2's discussion of correlations. Jennifer Crocker and Lora Park (2004) and others (Taylor & Brown, 1988) have shown that there can be a downside to pursuing an increase in self-esteem. They argued that trying hard to maintain and boost self-esteem can cause anxiety and can cause people to avoid activities that may end in failure, to neglect others, and to struggle with stress-induced health problems.

The relentless need for positive self-esteem can cause us to sometimes ignore criticism or to justify our actions when we might condemn the same actions in other people. Moreover, in many cases, we aren't even aware of our biased thinking about ourselves in relation to others. Of course, there are times when we *do* feel inferior to others, when we think someone else is smarter, better-liked, or more attractive than we are (Leary, 1998, 2004, 2007; Zuckerman & Jost, 2001). And there are some individuals who do legitimately struggle with self-esteem. However, in general, self-esteem as a motivating factor behind our actions is more prevalent than most people realize (Leary, 2004, 2007; Tesser, 1988).

MEMORY BIAS

Have you ever had the experience of discussing a common memory with a family member only to find out that she remembers the event differently? Maybe you were certain that it snowed on your birthday two years ago, but your mother insists that it didn't snow at all that year. It is no secret that memory is unreliable. In fact, distorting some memories to come out slightly in your favor is one trick your brain may play on you to help maintain a positive self-esteem. Multiple studies have found that when remembering past choices, we tend to attribute positive features to options we selected and negative features to options we decided against (Mather, Shafir, & Johnson, 2000; Henkel & Mather, 2007). For example, when individuals were asked to make a choice between two different job candidates, each of whom had about the same number of positive and negative attributes, participants were more likely later on to remember more positive qualities about the candidate they selected and to assign more negative qualities to the one they rejected (Mather & Johnson, 2000).

ACTION LEARNING

Maintaining a Positive Self-Concept

Maintaining a positive self-concept is the key to succeeding at our goals and experiencing overall well-being throughout our lives. Individuals who have stable, high self-esteem experience positive emotions more consistently than those with poor self-concepts. Additionally, they have a lower chance of depression (Tennen & Affleck, 1993). Where goals are concerned, it should come as no surprise that people who believe in themselves and their abilities have a higher chance of accomplishing what they set out to do (Parker et al., 2010). When we experience self-doubt and think poorly of our attributes and abilities, on the other hand, we are likely to fail (Crocker, 2002; Crocker & Luhtanen, 2003; Kernis, 2003).

This is an example of a self-fulfilling prophecy, or coming to embody others' preconceived images of ourselves. For example, a student whose teacher thinks she is a poor performer will come to share this belief, and as a result, the student is more likely to fail (Jussim, 1986). On the other hand, if we have a positive self-view, we are likely to live up to our expectations. Researchers found that if an individual thinks of himself or herself as a likeable person, others are apt to like him or her (Stinson et al., 2009). In their study of undergraduates at a large university, they found that students with positive self-concepts were more likely to behave warmly when meeting a group of new acquaintances, and the group, in turn, was more likely to accept those students who behaved this way.

With this in mind, you can appreciate why it is important for people to take steps to maintain a positive self-concept. Design a public service announcement using social psychological principles to demonstrate how to maintain a positive view of the self. Think about how your self-concept is defined and provide an example to your audience of where your self-concept comes from and of what it is composed. Select two ideas from this chapter and show how they impact the self-concept. Finally, share at least one technique that can be used to improve an individual's self-concept.

What will you learn from this action project?

1. Identify ways social psychologists think about the self.
2. Discover the real impacts our behaviors, attitudes, and biases have on self-concept.
3. Learn how to develop and help others develop a positive self-concept.

>>> **Nicknamed "King James,"** LeBron James exhibits high self-esteem.

SELF-SERVING BIASES

In her research on human motivation, psychologist Carol Dweck has found that individuals who hold a fixed theory of intelligence—that is, those who believe their intelligence is something that can't be altered—are less likely to take certain kinds of risks because they think failure will reflect poorly on their innate abilities. By contrast, individuals with a growth-based theory of their intelligence, that is, those who believe that by challenging themselves they can increase their intelligence, are more likely to set goals and face challenges that will help them grow intellectually (Dweck, 1999).

With her colleague Claudia Mueller, Dweck performed a study in which researchers praised children's high performance on test questions by linking the children's success to their intelligence (Mueller & Dweck, 1998). When this happened, the children were more likely to respond negatively to setbacks because they believed that confusion or failure was due to an uncontrollable lack of intelligence. By the same token, children with a fixed view of their intelligence were less motivated to take on challenges because they were afraid that failure would invalidate their abilities and confirm their deficiencies. However, children who were praised for their effort, rather than their intelligence, were more likely to recover quickly after failure because they attributed setbacks to a temporary lapse in effort, rather than a failure of intelligence. Because they attributed their success to variable factors, these children were also more likely to enjoy and seek out challenging tasks.

Attribution, or deciding who or what is responsible for the outcome of a situation, is another way we cope with failure and respond to success in order to maintain self-esteem (Heider, 1958). Sometimes, Heider argues, it is clear whether the outcome of a situation is due to a person's innate abilities or whether it can be attributed to her level of effort. The 4-foot fifth grader who can't make a slam dunk when he plays basketball, for instance, doesn't fail because he didn't try hard enough, but because he is too short to reach the basket. In many cases, however, the causes of an event are unclear. Heider (1958) explained that in ambiguous situations, "the person's own needs or wishes determine the attribution." In other words, our bias leads us to choose an explanation that will make us feel better about ourselves. We will further consider attributions for other individuals' behaviors in Chapter 5.

Self-Serving Attribution

Imagine you meet up with a friend after class on the day he is expecting to get his graded biology exam back. When you ask him how he did, he tells you that he got a D but then quickly goes on to explain that the teacher's assistant graded some of the questions unfairly. Also, he was feeling sick on the day he took the test, *and* he had just had a fight with his girlfriend before going to class that day. So clearly he was not in the right frame of mind to perform well.

You may have heard similar explanations—or offered similar explanations—for poor test results in the past. The **self-serving attribution**, a tendency to see ourselves in a favorable way leads us to make attributions for our behavior that favor the self. A self-serving attribution is a self-protection strategy in which we are likely to believe that external factors like unfair grading or a difficult environment are responsible for situations in which we perform poorly (Campbell & Sedikides, 1999). By the same token, in situations when we succeed, we tend to attribute the outcome to internal qualities, like intelligence or skill. If your friend did well on the test, he might be likely to tell you he tends to be a good test taker or that biology is his best subject.

Other studies have found that therapists tend to blame the client or the situation, rather than their own abilities, when a client terminates his

> **ATTRIBUTION** deciding who or what is responsible for the outcome of a situation; another way we cope with failure and respond to success in order to maintain self-esteem
>
> **SELF-SERVING ATTRIBUTION** a self-protection strategy in which we are likely to believe that external factors are responsible for situations in which we perform poorly

or her therapy sessions prematurely (Murdock et al., 2010). Drivers involved in car accidents tend to attribute the accident to external factors (like road conditions), while observers and passengers tend to attribute the accident to both internal and external factors (Bordel et al., 2007). And when group projects turn out well, individual group members are likely to cite their own efforts as a factor, whereas when the projects turn out poorly, they are likely to blame others in the group (Fast & Tiedens, 2010).

False Consensus

When young adult smokers were asked to estimate the percentage of those in their age group who also smoked, the respondents overestimated the proportion of others who smoked by an average of 20 percent (Cunningham & Selby, 2007). In another study conducted during a water conservation crisis, when a shower ban was put in place for several days, those who ignored the ban and showered anyway were highly likely to overestimate the number of others who also disregarded the ban (Monin & Norton, 2003). Both of these studies demonstrate the false consensus effect discussed in Chapter 2. When we do something we feel guilty

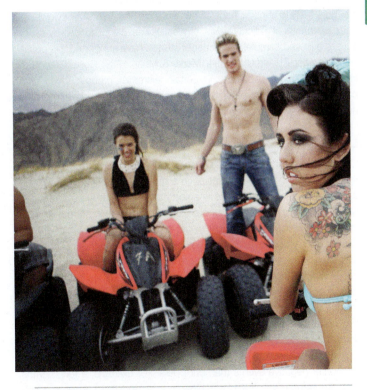

∧∧∧ **In which case do you think the false consensus effect is due to our self-esteem need, and** in which might it be more likely the result, as Dawes argues, of the company we keep?

UNREALISTIC OPTIMISM when we tend to imagine that the outcomes of situations will be better for us than for other people

SOCIAL COMPARISON THEORY a theory wherein we compare ourselves to others in different situations because there is no given standard against which to measure our abilities and opinions

DOWNWARD SOCIAL COMPARISON the process of comparing yourself to someone who is less capable or worse off than you are

BIRGING "basking in reflected glory," a strategy by which we reinforce our positive self-concepts by identifying ourselves with successful others

CORFING "cutting off reflective failure," a strategy by which we try to disassociate ourselves from others who have failed or behaved poorly

SELF-HANDICAPPING a process that involves setting up an obstacle before engaging in a task as a way to give ourselves a ready-made excuse in case we don't perform well

INGRATIATION a way of controlling others' impressions of us through flattery

about or when we fail at a task, we often choose to protect our self-esteem or justify our actions by assuming that others have done the same thing. We are also likely to overestimate consensus when it comes to our opinions, especially those opinions we hold on controversial issues. For instance, research has shown that when we hold prejudiced attitudes, we are more likely to assume that a significant number of people share these feelings, making it so we do not appear to ourselves to be prejudiced in relation to others (Watt & Larkin, 2010).

According to researcher Robyn Dawes (1990), the false consensus effect may, in part, be the result of the fact that we tend to spend time with people who are similar to us. People who have a lot in common with us are more likely to engage in the same behaviors and hold similar views, so our perceptions of majority views, argues Dawes, are influenced by exposure to a limited sample. A number of studies have supported this possibility (Krueger & Clement, 1994; Marks & Miller, 1987; Ross, Greene, & House, 1977). For instance, in certain extremist groups, those who belonged to online communities were more likely to overestimate the number of others who shared their views (Wojcieszak, 2008).

Unrealistic Optimism

Optimism, the tendency to see events and situations in a positive light, may also bias us to see *ourselves* in a more positive light. **Unrealistic optimism** is when we tend to imagine that the outcomes of situations will be better for us than for others. For instance, a high school student might imagine he is more likely to get a date to the prom than are his friends. Vera Hoorens and her colleagues (2008) found that college students tend to see themselves as more likely than their fellow students to get good jobs and become financially successful, despite having similar educations, demonstrating that people tend to have unrealistically optimistic predictions about their own futures relative to others in the same circumstances. Unrealistic optimism may also explain why people continue to buy lottery tickets, believing that they will win. Unrealistic optimism also accounts for when we are less likely to think we will encounter negative events than our peers. For example, a few months after September 11, 2001, participants in a study by Lerner and colleagues (2003) were asked to estimate the likelihood that a negative event would befall themselves or another individual. In comparison to themselves, participants were more likely to predict that other people would be directly affected by a violent crime or a terrrorist attack.

While a greater degree of optimism promotes self-efficacy, and while it may lead people to recover more quickly from setbacks and to become

depressed less easily, there are a number of potential hazards to unrealistic optimism as well. One problem with unrealistic optimism is that it can lead us to underprepare for future events. For example, students who are overconfident tend to study less for tests and to receive lower grades than students who have similar abilities but are more pessimistic about those abilities (Norem & Cantor, 1986). The "it won't happen to me" attitude applies to the optimistic bias as well. For instance, college students tend to predict that life-threatening problems and severe illnesses will not affect them. This, in turn, makes students less likely to take precautions against a number of potential hazards to health and life (Weinstein, 1982). Another study found that unrealistic optimism makes people more likely to drive after they have been drinking because they believe they are less likely than others to lose control of their vehicles (Causse et al., 2004). A similar study found that college students who were unrealistically optimistic about their likelihood of experiencing severe problems due to binge drinking were in fact more likely to experience serious alcohol-related problems later on than others (Dillard et al., 2009).

COMPARISON TO OTHERS

When you were in high school, you probably compared your experiences and performance in school with those of your classmates. For example, if you were feeling bad about your performance on a particularly challenging pop quiz, you may have checked with others in the class to see if they also had a hard time. Knowing that your classmates found the quiz as difficult as you did probably made you feel better about your own performance. Regardless of the grade that you actually received, it felt good to know that the quiz was difficult for everyone and that you were not falling behind your peers.

This method of evaluation is described by **social comparison theory**; according to this theory, we compare ourselves to others in different situations because there is no given standard against which to measure our abilities and opinions (Festinger, 1954). However, while other people can serve as a useful frame of reference, we are not always objective in our comparisons. The desire to feel good about ourselves overwhelms the desire to accurately assess our achievements and abilities (Sedikides & Gregg, 2003).

Downward Social Comparison

One clear way to feel better about the self through social comparison is to compare yourself to someone who is less capable or worse off than you are. This process, known as **downward social comparison**, may, for instance, be why television talk shows and reality TV are so popular (Nelson, 2003; Frisby, 1999). Seeing people with broken relationships or dysfunctional families is likely to make you feel better about your own. And seeing people make fools of themselves or treat each other badly is likely to make you feel better about your own behavior. In marriages and dating relationships, couples who engage in downward social comparison with other couples are more likely afterward to feel satisfied about the state of their own relationships (Buunk et al., 2001). And college students who have experienced recent academic setbacks will feel better about themselves when they are exposed to downward comparison information about other students' performances (Aspinwall & Taylor, 1993).

BIRGing

After winning the gold medal in the 1988 Olympic Games, Ben Johnson, a Jamaican-born, Canadian sprinter, was disqualified for steroid use. Psychologist Monika Stelzl and her colleagues noticed that when the Canadian media first reported on Johnson's win, they identified him as

Canadian, but that when they later covered news about his disqualification, they began to label him as Jamaican. Intrigued by these findings, they created a study in which they gave Canadian research participants information about a fictional athlete with a Canadian American identity. They found that in cases where they told participants the fictional athlete had lost, people were more likely to identify him as an American, but that when participants believed he had won, they identified him as a Canadian (Stelzl et al., 2008). What Stelzl and her colleagues observed was an example of what psychologists call **BIRGing**, or "basking in reflected glory," a strategy by which we reinforce our positive self-concepts by identifying ourselves with successful others. You'll probably, for instance, be more likely to wear clothing with the name of your favorite football team on it the day after your team has won a game than on a day after the team has lost. You might even say "We won!" when discussing the victory with other fans. BIRGing also occurs in situations when we can make ethnic, religious, or appearance-based connections to others who have succeeded (Cialdini et al., 1976).

We also engage in the opposite of BIRGing, **CORFing** ("cutting off reflective failure"), when we try to disassociate ourselves from others who have failed or behaved poorly. BIRGing and CORFing are often associated with sports figures and teams, but they can also occur in a number of other situations, such as politics. For instance, after the 2008 presidential election, one study found that people were more likely to keep yard and window signs endorsing Barack Obama on display much longer than those who had signs endorsing John McCain, who lost the election (Miller, 2009).

Self-Handicapping

If you have ever procrastinated on a term paper or decided to go out with your friends on the night before taking an important exam, you *may* have been engaging in **self-handicapping** behavior. Self-handicapping

involves setting up an obstacle before engaging in a task as a way to give ourselves a ready-made excuse in case we don't perform well. We are especially likely to self-handicap when we feel nervous or uncertain about an important performance. For instance, a child feeling nervous about an upcoming piano recital might decide to stop practicing so that if he plays poorly he can tell people that it was due to lack of practice. Similarly, studies have found that students may self-handicap by listening to distracting music while working, by taking drugs or alcohol before engaging in an academic task, or by avoiding studying altogether (McCrea, 2008; Leonardi & Gonida, 2007).

Impression Management: How Do We Represent Ourselves to Others?

> 66 **Be yourself; everyone else is already taken.** —Oscar Wilde 99

How do you want others to perceive you? Which of your characteristics do you value more than others? How does the context affect how you want to be viewed? To some degree, we can control others' impressions of ourselves by emphasizing the information that highlights certain character traits. For instance, if you want people to think you're a hard worker, you might mention the number of hours you spend at your job or the amount of research you've been doing on a paper. If you want people to think you're laid-back, you might make sure they can tell that you're stress free in a stressful situation, or make it clear that you aren't concerned with keeping to a strict schedule. Of course, the way you present yourself will change depending on the situation and the people in it. When you go to a job interview, you will probably choose to emphasize personal qualities like responsibility, organization, and motivation. When you go on a first date, you may play up your charm or sense of humor.

When we want others to think well of us in general, we may use a different form of impression management. Individuals in a work environment may try to increase their influence or likeability with management by complimenting them, agreeing with their opinions, or performing favors for them (Appelbaum & Hughes, 1998). This process, known as **ingratiation**, is a way of controlling others' impressions of us through flattery. Another study, conducted via research in the field, revealed that waiters who complimented couples on their dinner selections received significantly higher tips than those who did not (Seiter, 2007).

Of course, because we want to maintain our self-esteem, we want to believe the complimentary things people say about us, which is why ingratiation can be so effective. Generally in these situations, when

<<< Is America's love of reality TV and TV talk shows inspired **by the self-esteem boost we get from favorably comparing ourselves with others?**

SPOTLIGHT EFFECT the belief that our behavior, our appearance, and even our internal states are obvious to others

SELF-VERIFICATION THEORY a theory wherein we want others to see us as we see ourselves—even when our self-concepts are negative

SELF-MONITORING the process through which people regulate their behavior to be perceived well by others; low self-monitors act consistently across situations, acting according to their personal views, while high self-monitors are constantly monitoring their behavior and adjusting their reactions to fit the situation they are in

there is an additional person present, the person receiving the compliment is much more likely to form a favorable impression of the compliment giver than is the person who is not receiving the compliment (Vonk, 2002). However, there is a catch to ingratiation. If people believe we are not sincere in our attempts to win their approval, the tactic may backfire (Vonk, 2002).

Although we tend to devote a good deal of time and mental energy to the way we present ourselves to others, it may help to know that other people aren't often paying as much attention to us as we think they are. For instance, when giving a presentation, you might start to feel more nervous because you're worried that other people can tell that you're nervous. But chances are your audience probably doesn't notice that your palms are sweaty or that your hands are shaking a little. The belief that our behavior, our appearance, and even our internal states are obvious to others is known as the **spotlight effect**.

How do you feel when you aren't comfortable in your clothes? Chances are, you feel less confident and more exposed—under a proverbial spotlight. Gilovich, Medvec, and Savitsky (2000) demonstrated the spotlight effect by asking college students to walk into a room filled with other people while wearing an embarrassing Barry Manilow T-shirt. Consumed with their own embarrassment and self-consciousness, participants significantly overestimated the number of other people who actually noticed the shirt.

What about self-presentation when it comes to interacting online? If you have a Facebook or MySpace page, you probably realize that it is much easier to control what people think of us when we build an online profile because people only see the

> >>> Is text messaging **a form of impression management?**

information we want them to see. A recent study (Madel & Muncer, 2007) supports the idea that many people prefer text messages and online interaction (like e-mail and instant messenger) to face-to-face interactions or phone calls. This is because in situations where the interaction is less immediate, it is easier for us to control other people's perceptions of us. Later on in this section, you will read about self-presentation in the context of online dating.

SELF-VERIFICATION

If you consider yourself to be an honest person and someone you know has the false impression that you are dishonest, you will probably try to get her to see you as an honest person. But what if you think you are lazy? If someone you know sees you as a hard worker, will you try to change his favorable perception to a less favorable one? Some studies suggest that yes, you will (North & Swann, 2009; Evans & Stukas, 2007). According to **self-verification theory**, we want others to see us as we see ourselves; even when our self-concepts are negative, we still prefer that others perceive our self-concepts as accurate (Swann, Stein-Seroussi, & Gieslder, 1992). Self-verification, even of negative traits, gives us the illusion of having control or ensuring some level of predictability, which is reassuring. In long-term relationships with significant others, we need to self-verify in order to feel secure and develop intimacy (Kraus & Chen, 2009). Because self-verification reduces anxiety and leads to greater harmony in interactions, we are likely to be involved with groups and social organizations that reinforce our perceptions of ourselves (Seyle & Swann, 2007).

SELF-MONITORING

While self-presentation is a general human concern, some people are more likely than others to adapt their self-presentation depending on the situation and social group. Some people try to match the types of people they are with the situations in which they are (Snyder, Berscheid, & Glick, 1985). These individuals, known as high **self-monitors**, are more likely to change their opinions or behaviors to fit the context. Mark Snyder's (1974) self-monitoring scale measures this in people with true/false statements like, "At parties and social gatherings, I do not attempt to do or say things that others will like," and "I laugh more when I watch a comedy with others than when alone."

Assuming that high self-monitors would be more concerned than others with having an attractive dating partner, Snyder, Berscheid, and Glick (1985) performed a study in which they asked male college students to choose one of two women to take on a date. The first woman was highly unattractive—rated 1.87 out of 7 on an attractiveness scale—but participants were told that she was open and outgoing, listened well to others, and valued her sense of humor. The other woman was quite attractive—5.75 out of 7— but was described as being shy, self-centered, and moody. As expected, the participants identified as low self-monitors were more likely to choose the first woman, demonstrating that physical appearance was not of primary concern in their choice of dating partners. The high self-monitors, on the other hand, mostly chose the woman who was more attractive.

Self-monitoring may also play a role in online dating scenarios. As discussed earlier, we can be more selective about how we present ourselves when creating an online profile. It should come as no great surprise that people tend to lie about things like age, salary, and weight— components of our level of attractiveness to potential mates—when creating profiles for a dating Web site. Is there a pattern to the way people lie on dating sites? Hancock, Toma, and Ellison guessed that members of dating Web sites would engage in self-monitoring practices when creating their personal profiles. Noting that men tend to look for physical attractiveness and youth in a dating partner, whereas women are more concerned with social status (education and career), the researchers proposed that women would be more likely to lie about factors like age and weight, whereas men would be more likely to lie about height—a characteristic often associated with status and power. Their findings confirmed that such self-monitoring does occur; women consistently under-reported their weight, while men consistently over-reported their height, though the magnitude of deception was small (Hancock, Toma, & Ellison, 2007).

"Who are you?" may seem like a simple question, but it is clear that our identities are complex and multilayered. Often, they are strongly influenced by external factors and situations, and an inherent need to feel good about ourselves can sometimes make self-understanding challenging and unclear. What has this chapter taught you about yourself? In the next chapter, we'll turn the tables on other individuals and look at how we perceive people in our social environment.

∧
∧ Who is telling the truth? Research shows that almost nine out of
∧ 10 people lie about themselves on their online dating profiles (Hancock et al., 2007).

CHAPTER 04 · Review

Summary

WHAT IS SELF-CONCEPT, AND WHERE DOES IT COME FROM? p. 58

• Our self-concepts are made up of all the various beliefs we hold about ourselves. They develop as we mature, and they are apt to change depending on circumstances and context.

• According to social identity theory, we develop our identity from our group memberships. Culture may impact the influence of the social groups we belong to.

• Our self-concepts are influenced by our behavior (self-perception theory) and our awareness of how close our ideal selves are to our actual selves. Our self-concepts are tied to our motivation too; if we believe we are doing something for its own sake (intrinsic motivation), we are more likely to enjoy it.

IN WHAT WAYS DOES A NEED FOR SELF-ESTEEM MOTIVATE OUR ACTIONS? p. 65

• To maintain a high self-esteem, people often engage in biased thinking when assigning responsibility for the causes of events or outcomes. High self-esteem can lead to more happiness and success, but it can also cause stress and anxiety in attempts to attain it. We also engage in biased, self-serving thinking in the ways we compare ourselves to others.

HOW DO WE REPRESENT OURSELVES TO OTHERS? p. 69

• Because the self occupies an important place in our thoughts, we often believe that we occupy an important place in other people's thoughts, and, as a result, we go to great lengths to control the way others perceive us.

• We may modify our behavior so that our opinions and attitudes seem to match those of the people we are around, or we may use flattery to get others to like us. We feel most comfortable when we are around people who see us as we see ourselves.

Key Terms

affective forecasting the process of predicting the impact future events will have on our overall emotional states 62

attribution deciding who or what is responsible for the outcome of a situation; another way we cope with failure and respond to success in order to maintain self-esteem 67

BIRGing "basking in reflected glory," a strategy by which we reinforce our positive self-concepts by identifying ourselves with successful others 69

collectivism a cultural focus on the self as interdependent and defined by the connectedness of people to one another, in particular, the people closest to them 60

CORFing "cutting off reflective failure," a strategy by which we try to disassociate ourselves from others who have failed or behaved poorly 69

downward social comparison the process of comparing yourself to someone who is less capable or worse off than you are 68

extrinsic motivation the drive to perform an action in response to an external pressure or obligation, to avoid punishment, or to achieve some outside benefit 64

facial feedback hypothesis a hypothesis that states that a change in our facial expressions can lead to a subsequent emotional change 64

individualism at the cultural level, focus on the self as independent from others and defining individual goals over the collective 60

ingratiation a way of controlling others' impressions of us through flattery 69

intrinsic motivation the drive to perform an action because we enjoy it and are likely to engage in it more fully and with greater curiosity and pleasure 64

introspection the process of thinking about your own thoughts 61

self-awareness when attention is brought about on the self; for example, looking in a mirror, standing in front of a crowd, and listening to a recording of your voice 62

self-concept your mental representation or overall sense of "you" 58

self-discrepancy theory a theory in which our concepts of self are influenced by how close our actual selves are to the selves we would like to be 62

self-efficacy a person's belief in his or her ability to achieve certain goals 58

self-esteem a person's evaluation of his or her self-worth 65

self-handicapping a process that involves setting up an obstacle before engaging in a task as a way to give ourselves a ready-made excuse in case we don't perform well 69

self-monitoring the process through which people regulate their behavior to be perceived well by others; low self-monitors act consistently across situations, acting according to their personal views, while high self-monitors are constantly monitoring

their behavior and adjusting their reactions to fit the situation they are in 70

self-perception theory a theory in which, if we are unsure of the attitudes we hold, we look to our behavior and use that to make inferences about our attitudes, much like an outside observer 64

self-schema beliefs about aspects of your identity that organize the processing of information related to the self 58

self-serving attribution a self-protection strategy in which we are likely to believe that external factors are responsible for situations in which we perform poorly 67

self-verification theory a theory wherein we want others to see us as we see ourselves—even when our self-concepts are negative 70

social comparison theory a theory wherein we compare ourselves to others in different situations because there is no given standard against which to measure our abilities and opinions 68

social identity theory a theory in which we develop our identity from our group memberships 60

spotlight effect the belief that our behavior, our appearance, and even our internal states are obvious to others 70

Twenty Statements Test (TST) a measure of self-concept that asks individuals to self-report "who am I?" 60

unrealistic optimism when we tend to imagine that the outcomes of situations will be better for us than for other people 68

Test Your Understanding

MULTIPLE CHOICE

1. Why does research show that you are more likely to be happy with the outcome of a decision when you "go with your gut"?
   a. because if we hesitate, we may lose an opportunity
   b. because we are not always in touch with our true feelings and motivations
   c. because we often make decisions to please others
   d. because most decisions don't really matter anyway

2. Because Clive Wearing's memory was severely impaired:
   a. He had a low self-esteem.
   b. He was unable to remember how to play music.
   c. He had no frame of reference on which to construct his self-concept.
   d. He was highly self-aware.

3. According to self-discrepancy theory:
   a. When others have a poor opinion of us, we are likely to confirm that opinion.
   b. We are more motivated to do things that challenge the way other people see us.
   c. We present different selves in different situations.
   d. If you perceive a large gap between your actual and ideal selves, then you will generally have a more negative self-image.

4. In which situation(s) might you engage in BIRGing?
   a. when your school's football team wins a game
   b. when a family member loses a job
   c. when a friend gets his name in the paper for an accomplishment
   d. when you win a race

5. Which is a hazard of unrealistic optimism?
   a. It may lead you to underprepare for an event.
   b. You may disappoint someone who was counting on you.
   c. It may lead you to perceive others in a more positive light.
   d. You might make others feel insecure about their own abilities.

6. As opposed to Western cultures, Asian cultures tend to:
   a. emphasize the connectedness of people to one another.
   b. emphasize the individual's achievements.
   c. emphasize one's identity as distinct from one's social group.
   d. make choices that will set them apart from others in a group.

7. In which situation(s) might you engage in the false consensus bias?
   a. when you hold a prejudiced view about someone
   b. when you binge after trying to keep yourself to a strict diet
   c. when you think that you are better than everyone else
   d. when your friend tells you that he stole something from a convenience store

8. People with a high self-efficacy:
   a. are more likely to achieve their goals.
   b. are more likely to change their behavior in response to a situation.
   c. have an overall positive feeling about themselves.
   d. are engaging in biased behavior.

9. Dweck and Mueller found that when children were praised for their high intelligence after completing a task that they initially found fun:
   a. they developed strong self-concepts.
   b. they were less likely to take risks that could result in failure on future tasks.
   c. they were likely to tell their friends.
   d. they were likely to help others after they had finished future tasks.

10. If you believe your motivation for performing a certain action is extrinsic, what are you likely to do?
   a. work harder to achieve your goals
   b. spend more time at the task
   c. find other, similar tasks to undertake
   d. lose interest in the task

ESSAY RESPONSE

1. Use your own experience to define and explain social identity theory. In which situations do you find yourself more likely to identify with a group? When are you most likely to see yourself as an individual? In what ways might this be culturally influenced?

2. Based on what you've learned about motivation, make a case for a hypothetical community service program you could implement at your university. What would you do to ensure that students were highly motivated to engage in the work, both now and in their futures?

3. Develop a hypothetical experiment in which you could test the false consensus bias as it applies to cheating on college exams. How would you develop and implement the study?

4. Describe three situations in which social comparison could be a useful tactic, contributing to a healthy self-concept.

5. A number of studies have shown that self-verification reduces anxiety levels. Based on what you now know about self-verification theory and self-concept in general, why might this be the case?

APPLY IT!

Browse a number of online profiles for a social networking site to which you belong (Facebook, MySpace, LinkedIn, Match.com, etc.). Do you notice any self-serving biases in the way people present themselves? Which self-schemata seem to be the most important for people? If you know the people personally, how closely do their profiles match what you know about them? Explain your observations in terms of the concepts you've learned in this chapter.

ANSWERS: 1. b; 2. c; 3. d; 4. a; 5. a; 6. a; 7. a; 8. a; 9. b; 10. d

Remember to check www.thinkspot.com for additional information, downloadable flashcards, and other helpful resources.

SOCIAL PERCEPTION: HOW DO WE PERCEIVE OTHERS?

TO WHAT DO WE ATTRIBUTE PEOPLE'S BEHAVIORS?
HOW DO WE DECIDE WHAT OTHER PEOPLE ARE LIKE?
NONVERBAL COMMUNICATION: HOW DO WE COMMUNICATE WITHOUT WORDS?

Toward

the end of 2009, Americans were stunned to find out that seemingly wholesome golf superstar Tiger Woods was unfaithful to his wife. And not only was he unfaithful, reports stated that he took it to extreme lengths. Suddenly numerous women were coming out of the woodwork to publicly discuss the lewd details of the affairs that went on with Tiger without the knowledge of his model wife, Elin.

Shortly after, TV personality and motorcycle manufacturer Jesse James was exposed for having multiple extramarital affairs that took place behind the back of his wife, actress Sandra Bullock. Mistresses of the two men continued to come forward, and illicit stories about them covered newsstands, airwaves, and television shows throughout much of 2010. After the initial stories broke, each man publicly checked himself into rehabilitation for sexual addiction.

Rumors about why each man acted the way he did became watercooler fodder for months. What did you think at the time? Did Tiger and Jesse cheat on their wives so egregiously because something was so internally wrong that they literally couldn't control themselves? Could it be considered an illness? Or did you think they did it because at their cores, they are simply selfish people who care more about their own needs than those of their loved ones? Did you consider the possibility of situational factors? Maybe the relationships were already on the rocks when Tiger and Jesse chose infidelity. Maybe the pressures of the celebrity spotlight caused these men to act in ways they wouldn't have otherwise.

What causes people to act as they do, and how do we decide to *believe* why people behave the way they do? Why is it that one of your friends thinks Tiger Woods is an inherently horrible person while another feels bad for him? This chapter will take a look at the many ways we perceive others and the psychological theories behind them.

CHAPTER **05**

DISPOSITIONAL ATTRIBUTION inferring that a person's traits, something internal, caused his or her behavior

SITUATIONAL ATTRIBUTION inferring that the situation in which a person is in, something external to the person, caused his or her behavior

CORRESPONDENT INFERENCE THEORY the theory that people base their inferences regarding the source of others' behaviors on whether or not the behavior was freely chosen, if the consequences are distinctive, and if the behavior was socially desirable

COVARIATION THEORY the theory that people base their inferences regarding the source of others' behaviors on whether or not there is a consensus regarding the way one ought to respond, the distinctiveness of the response, and the consistency of the person's response across situations

To What Do We Attribute People's Behaviors?

Two of your friends have vastly different opinions on why Tiger Woods and Jesse James chose to behave the way they did. On one hand, Evan thinks the two men are simply bad people. Why? He says they are selfish and insincere. That sort of explanation is a **dispositional attribution**. Evan thinks their hurtful decisions are the results of inherent parts of their personalities. However, your other friend Natasha gives them the benefit of the doubt. She thinks the men were motivated by already failing relationships. She made a **situational attribution**. This distinction can also be seen as an internal versus external attribution for behavior; a person engages in some act because of something intrinsic to him or her or because of something extrinsic.

CORRESPONDENT INFERENCE THEORY

Why do people make one type of inference over another? Several theories have been developed to explain it. One such theory is **correspondent inference theory** (Jones & Davis, 1965). This theory suggests that people are more likely to attribute behavior to others' personalities based on three factors. The first is whether or not the behavior was freely chosen. If someone

is forced into an action, people will generally not make an attribution to the person's traits. However, if the person chose to act in that way, and could have acted in any other way instead if he or she so desired, a dispositional attribution will be made. For example, if a bank teller smiles at a customer because the bank has imposed a rule that tellers must smile, that behavior does not say anything about the teller's personality because she had to do it. However, if there was no such rule, the teller might be judged as being a friendly person.

The second factor is whether or not the behavior is what would be expected given the situation. For example, if someone acts nicely and respectfully to an old person, one might infer that it is not that the actor is a particularly nice person, but instead that acting in such a way is what one is supposed to do. By contrast, if that same person yells at the old person, completely unprovoked, one would instead consider the actor to be mean.

The third factor is what the consequences of a given action are. If there are multiple positive consequences of an action, it is difficult to isolate which of them may have caused the action. By contrast, if there is only one positive consequence of an action, it can generally be assumed to be the cause. For example, if a microwavable meal tastes terrible but is low in calories, it can be assumed that the consumer may be dieting and bought it because of its low calories. After all, why else would one choose a food that tastes bad? However, if it is also delicious, it is unclear what prompted the purchase, and nothing can be inferred about the buyer.

COVARIATION THEORY

Another theory designed to explain the attributions people make is covariation theory. **Covariation theory** (Kelley, 1972; Kelley & Michela, 1980) focuses on the factors that are present when some behavior occurs and those that are not present when it does not occur—that is, what covaries with the behavior. Like correspondent inference theory, it has three considerations. The first is the consensus regarding a behavior. That is, if most people would behave in a certain way in a given situation, the behavior does not reflect anything unique about the actor. For example, as in the example at the beginning of the chapter, if most people in our society are unfaithful to their spouses, then nothing is notable about the behaviors of Tiger Woods and Jesse James. However, since cheating isn't widely accepted, the behavior reflects something personal.

The second consideration is distinctiveness. This refers to the distinctiveness of the individual's behavior in the given situation as compared with all other situations. If Tiger only cheated once with one woman, then it is likely the situation evoked that isolated behavior from him. However, if he regularly cheated when given the opportunity, it is probably indicative of his personality.

The third and final consideration is consistency. Consistency refers to the reaction of the individual to a particular stimulus over repeated experiences with the stimulus in different situations. If the person always responds in the same way to the stimulus across all contexts, then that behavior can be given a dispositional attribution. If the person does not, then that variation in behavior can be attributed to the context. For example, if every time Jesse encounters a potential mistress he cheats, he may have a disloyal personality. By contrast, if he only cheated after a fight with Sandra, then regardless of whether he is right or wrong, the situation had an influence on his choice.

<<< **"No fat? No sodium? No flavor? I'll buy it!"** It seems there is only one positive outcome for buying this item, **so it's easy to isolate the cause of the action in this case.**

HOW DO BIASES COME INTO PLAY?

These two theories both assume that people are logical and rational in their tendency to attribute causes to behavior. However, as with any social psychological phenomenon, there is a rational as well as a biased side to human behavior and cognition. When deciding whether a behavior is due to an individual's disposition or to the situation, people are biased first and foremost by their own perspectives. When we perform an action, we aren't looking at ourselves; we're looking out at our world, our environment. Therefore, the situation we are in is most salient. By contrast, when we are observing another person's actions, that person is what is most salient to us. We may not even be aware of the entire situation in which that person is. As such, when we are the actor, we tend to make situational attributions for our behavior, and when we are the observer, we tend to make dispositional attributions for the behavior. This is referred to as the **correspondence bias**, or

more commonly as the **fundamental attribution error** (Ross, 1977), so called because it is so basic and frequent in human judgment, at least in individualistic cultures.

This bias can be to the benefit or detriment of the people being judged. For example, when we watch the news, newscasters usually appear to be quite intelligent and informed, and as such, we consider them intelligent people, making a dispositional attribution. However, we neglect to

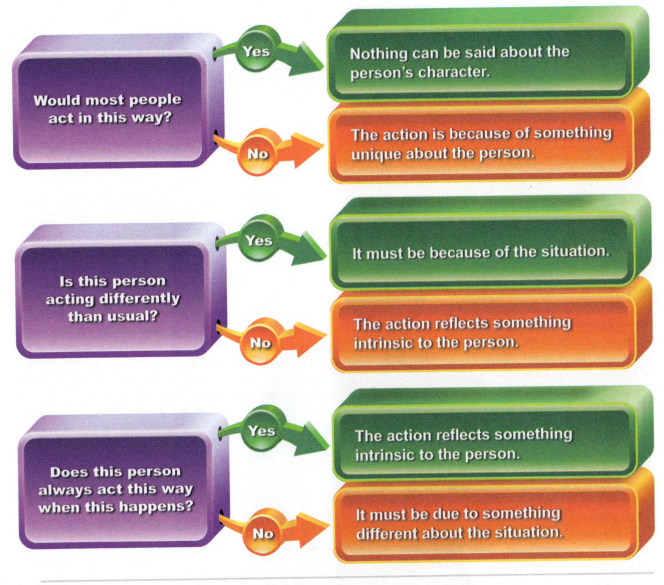

Would most people act in this way?

- Yes → **Nothing can be said about the person's character.**
- No → **The action is because of something unique about the person.**

Is this person acting differently than usual?

- Yes → **It must be because of the situation.**
- No → **The action reflects something intrinsic to the person.**

Does this person always act this way when this happens?

- Yes → **The action reflects something intrinsic to the person.**
- No → **It must be due to something different about the situation.**

Decision Making in Covariation Theory. Consensus, distinctiveness, and consistency all factor into deciding on the source of a behavior.

SPONTANEOUS TRAIT INFERENCE the process of automatically inferring traits from another person's behavior

THREE-STAGE MODEL OF ATTRIBUTION a model in which an observer automatically characterizes a behavior, automatically makes a dispositional inference, and then uses conscious effort to correct for situational constraints if the observer has the cognitive capacity to do so

remember that these people are in prescribed roles and are reading off of cue cards. Although they may, in fact, be intelligent, they are simply performing their roles. Newscasters, just as with any other group of people, vary considerably in intelligence despite appearances. In one longitudinal study lasting 20 years, both CNN and Fox News commentators were not particularly accurate in predicting major events such as presidential elections or the future of the economy (Tetlock, 2005).

The fundamental attribution error was first revealed in work by Jones and Harris (1967). In this study, volunteers were asked to read an essay about Fidel Castro's Cuba and indicate their impressions of the essayist's attitudes toward Cuba. The essay was either pro- or anti-Castro, and, importantly, the essay was either written freely, the opinion advocated chosen by the student, or under constraint, the opinion advocated assigned by an instructor. Not surprisingly, when the essay was one of the ones written freely, subjects reported that the writers' attitudes matched what they wrote in their essays. However, when the essay was written under instruction, subjects *still* reported that they believed the students held the opinion they advocated in the essay. Despite knowing that the essayists had been assigned their positions, subjects made dispositional attributions for those essays.

Subsequent research by Lee Ross and colleagues (Ross, Amabile, & Steinmetz, 1977) demonstrated this effect in a different context. Participants were randomly assigned to either write general knowledge questions that would then be asked of another person or to answer those questions. Questioners wrote a series of questions, derived from their own stores of knowledge. Answerers generally had a low rate of accuracy. Afterward, participants were asked to indicate the general knowledge of both parties. Participants, regardless of condition, consistently rated the questioners as having more general knowledge than the answerers. The answerers were rated as slightly less intelligent than the average student, while the questioners were rated as much more intelligent. Neither party was able to account for the fact that the questioner only knew all the answers because he or she wrote the questions. In fact, subsequent testing showed that the students were equally knowledgeable in general knowledge questions.

This process of attributing traits to others and ignoring the situation occurs quite automatically. Even if we are not asked to form an impression of others and have no particular motivation to do so, we will infer traits about even briefly encountered others (Uleman, 1989; Uleman, Newman, & Moskowitz, 1996). This phenomenon is called **spontaneous trait inferences**. Uleman, Saribay, & Gonzales (2008) asked students to remem-

ber information about target persons—statements reflecting specific behaviors the people exhibited. An example of such a sentence might be, "He pushed the woman out of the way to get onto the train." These students immediately and unintentionally inferred traits about these people—for example, "selfish." Indeed, when provided with single words to act as memory triggers, the ones that were the most helpful were those that reflected the trait rather than other information contained in the sentence. "Selfish" or "mean" would be more helpful than "commuter" or "subway."

Can an individual's culture affect the type of attributions that are made? In individualistic cultures (first discussed in Chapter 1), such as those in the United States and England, people tend to focus on the needs and desires of the individual, emphasizing competition between individuals for success, and reliance on the self for that success and happiness. By contrast, collectivistic cultures, such as those in Japan and India, focus on the needs and desires of the group, prioritizing group goals over personal goals. These collectivistic cultures are less likely than individualistic cultures to use individual personality traits to define people (Miller, 1984; Morris & Peng, 1994). Instead, they are more likely to ascribe situational explanations to behavior than dispositional ones; this is in direct contrast to those in individualistic cultures who engage in the fundamental attribution error.

Notably, these cultural differences become more evident with age, suggesting that increased exposure to the culture and its norms creates these differences in how behavior is explained (Miller, 1984). Additional research (Duff & Newman, 1997; Newman, 1993) has shown that those with a collectivistic orientation will automatically infer situational causes for behavior and will *not* make spontaneous trait inferences, as those who are more individualistic do (Duff & Newman, 1997). Thus these cultural differences exist, even when the individual is not asked to directly make a judgment.

Cognitive Capacity

Does it follow, then, that if you were raised in an individualistic culture, it would be automatic and natural for you to make snap dispositional judgments? If this is the case, then why do Evan and Natasha disagree over Tiger Woods and Jesse James despite having grown up in the same neighborhood?

In the **three-stage model of attribution**, Gilbert, Pelham, and Krull (1988) account for cognition. In the model, an observer automatically characterizes a behavior, automatically makes a dispositional inference, and then uses conscious effort to correct for situational constraints if the observer has the cognitive capacity to do so. If the observer has the time, energy, and motivation, he or she will later adjust the weight she gives to the factors to account further for the situation (Gilbert & Malone, 1995).

For example, you may read a news story about a teenager who was arrested for holding up a local convenience store. A paragraph in, you're thinking about how selfish and violent the teen is. Stealing is always wrong, isn't it? And if he needs money, maybe he

<<< We assume that people in roles in which they are required to appear intelligent **are actually more informed than others**—which is not always true.

should get a job waiting tables like you did in high school. Maybe you toss the paper in the trash. After all, you've automatically characterized the teen's behavior, and you've made your dispositional inference.

But what if you keep reading? You gain new knowledge, and it gives you the cognitive capacity to adjust your evaluation of the situation. You find out that the teen does have a job, but in addition to being a full-time student, he only has pocket money. And that's not enough, since his father is too sick to work and his mother was just laid off. With two other siblings to support, the teen made a misguided decision in order to help his parents make ends meet. Now what do you think? This is how the third stage of the three-stage model of attribution comes into play.

> "Does it follow, then, that if you were raised in an individualistic culture, it would be automatic and natural for you to make snap dispositional judgments?"

Bias and the Need for Cognition

One might argue that "errors" such as the correspondence bias might be due to people's lack of effort in understanding the real reasons behind others' behavior. Some people have what is known as the **need for cognition**, a drive to solve problems; they enjoy thinking, like to analyze everything carefully, and seek to understand their world accurately (Cacioppo et al., 1996). Might these people be less susceptible to the correspondence bias?

Participants in a study examining this question were asked to read a speech either favoring or opposing legal abortion. In all cases, participants were told that the speechwriter was assigned to the position and as such had no choice. Those low in need for cognition exhibited the traditional correspondence bias, believing that the speech's position was indeed the author's true attitude. By contrast, those high in need for cognition took the writer's lack of free choice into account and did not infer that the writer held the opinion espoused in the paper (D'Agostino & Fincher-Kiefer, 1992). Supplementing the original findings by Jones and Harris (1967), this newer research showed that the correspondence bias can be overcome if one is sufficiently motivated to critically examine ideas and uncover the truth.

NEED FOR COGNITION the need that some individuals have to think, solve problems, and understand their world accurately

ACTOR-OBSERVER EFFECT the tendency people have to make dispositional inferences for others' behavior but situational attributions for their own

It is not only effort and motivation to be accurate that can impact one's attributions. Our values and ideology can also alter the types of attributions we make when trying to explain social issues. While both were initially inclined to make dispositional inferences, when those inferences diverged from their ideological beliefs, liberals and conservatives would engage in motivational correction of their beliefs, adjusting to a more situational attribution if doing so would be in line with their beliefs about the world (Skitka et al., 2002; Morgan, Mullen, & Skitka, 2010). For instance, when thinking about AIDS patients, conservatives were more likely to make dispositional attributions for the patients' predicaments, while liberals would initially make dispositional attributions but then adjust to situational attributions, or make no attributions at all (Skitka et al., 2002). Likewise, while liberals tend to make more situational attributions for social problems, conservatives make more situational attributions for military and police misconduct (Morgan, Mullen, & Skitka, 2010).

The Actor-Observer Effect

There is, even in individualistic cultures, among people who are low in need for cognition, one major exception to the correspondence bias—this is when people make causal attributions for our own behavior, and it's called the **actor-observer effect** (Jones & Nisbett, 1971). When we are the actor, we are privy to knowledge about everything that impacted the decision, including the environment in which we were. But when we are the observer, we are focused on the other person himself or herself and not only have less access to, but also pay less attention to, the environmental factors that may be influencing the other person. As such, we pin the responsibility on the person himself or herself—his or her traits.

Further, if the actor is a member of our ingroup, we are more likely to make a situational attribution. But if he or she is in the outgroup, we'll probably make a dispositional attribution. Using former football star O.J. Simpson's trial to illustrate this, Graham, Weiner, and Zucker (1997) showed that black participants were more likely than white participants to blame his murder charges on his ex-wife's behavior instead of his own jealousy. A member of their ingroup, Simpson received a situational explanation from the African Americans involved in the study.

>>> You might be procrastinating on your schoolwork because you've had a rough week and you're tired, but your classmate might conclude that it's because you're lazy. **The actor-observer effect is the fact that we attribute others' behavior to dispositions but our own to the situations.**

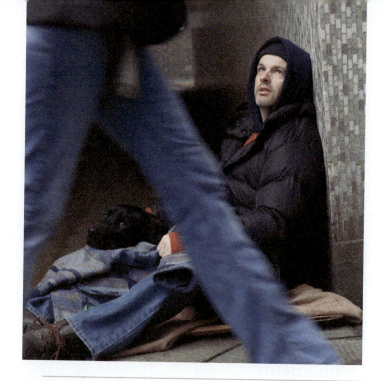

> **BELIEF IN A JUST WORLD** people have to believe the world is fair and adjust their other beliefs to maintain that stance by concluding that bad things happen to bad people and good things happen to good people

Belief in a Just World

It is to our psychological benefit to believe that others are to blame for their own misfortunes; after all, if it was a situation they could not control, those misfortunes could befall us as well. As such, we are motivated to believe that things happen for a just reason—good things happen to good people, and bad things happen to bad people. That is, we have **belief in a just world** (Lerner, 1980). Therefore, since we are evidently good people (in our own opinions), only good things will happen to us, and, thus, we are safe from harm and need not continually fear the future.

Having read that last statement, you are likely to have realized that the extent to which people believe in a just world varies from person to person. Some people, notably those with anxiety or depressive disorders, do fear the future (though belief in a just world is one way of coping with anxiety about the future). However, most people do, to some degree, believe that the world is fair as a self-protective mechanism. The more strongly one holds this belief, the more one will think that people who have fallen on hard times are responsible for their plights.

> " **It is** to our psychological benefit to believe that others are to blame for their own misfortunes; **after all, if it was a situation they could not control, those misfortunes could befall us as well.** "

Whether we attribute the source of people's behavior to disposition or situation is not only important because of what it leads us to believe about others; it also has very serious practical implications. If we blame others for their problems, we are less likely to offer them help, with our hands, wallets, or votes. By contrast, if we blame the situation, we do provide help. If a person has lung cancer and we believe that it is because she smokes, we will not feel bad for her or offer assistance. If we believe that the cancer is due to chance, genetics, or secondhand smoke exposure, we will feel worse for the person and offer whatever help we can provide. This, as mentioned earlier, can to some extent be predicted by political ideology—liberals are more likely to attribute the source of social problems such as poverty to the situation, and thus are more likely to support aid programs such as welfare, whereas conservatives are more likely to attribute it to the person, and thus are against forms of welfare (Skitka et al., 2002; Morgan, Mullen, & Skitka, 2010).

How Do We Decide What Other People Are Like?

Impressions are not formed only deliberately, nor are they formed only after being exposed to a person's behaviors. Rather, they are formed nearly

> ∧ ∧ ∧ Belief in a just world causes us to infer that those who have had bad things happen to them must be bad themselves—**and that we, being good people, will never suffer such a fate.**

instantaneously (see Uleman, Newman, & Moskowitz, 1996 for a review). Social psychological research suggests that it takes only a 10th of a second to form an impression of a person (Willis & Todorov, 2006). Ambady and Rosenthal (1993) illustrated the importance and relevance of these instant first impressions by asking participants to make judgments of teachers based on extremely short, silent video clips of the teachers. The researchers found that these snap judgments were indeed strongly in accordance with end-of-the-semester student evaluations, as well as the principal's ratings, giving viability to first impressions.

To see for yourself how rapidly an entire personality is inferred for another person based on very little information, try this exercise. Think for a minute how you would picture a person described as being intelligent, skillful, industrious, warm, determined, practical, and cautious. Write down for yourself some immediate thoughts about this person—how you're picturing him. Would you want to work with him?

Now consider a different person. This person is described as being intelligent, skillful, industrious, cold, determined, practical, and cautious. Again, quickly write down some thoughts about the person and how you picture him. Would you want to work with him?

Your overall image of these two people is probably quite different. And yet the only difference between the two was that the first was described as being "warm," while the second was described as being "cold." The reason for the influence of these two traits above the others was their centrality to personality; the other traits provided were specific ones that describe particular features of a person, whereas warmth is considered to be a more global trait that can encapsulate an entire personality in one word. Thus, even a one-adjective difference in information provided about another person can create profound differences in the

Dispositional or Situational?

Consider the attribution biases discussed in the chapter—that is, our tendency to attribute others' actions to their dispositions but our own actions to the relevant situations. Focus on the fundamental attribution error—the idea that, at least in individualistic cultures, we are more likely to focus on dispositional explanations for behavior and not take into account the situational constraints. Take one 24-hour period to note all the times you make judgments about another person's behavior. Record the individual's behavior and your initial reaction to it (i.e., did you focus on a dispositional or situational explanation). Take time to consider alternative explanations for why the individuals behaved the way they did and record these as well.

In a separate 24-hour period, record all the occurrences during which you believe others are making judgments about your behavior. Do you think they are making dispositional or situational judgments about your behavior? Think about how your and others' judgments have been affected by attributional biases. Consider what steps you could identify to reduce your own biased impressions in the future. Share your findings with your classmates. What will you learn from this action learning project?

1. You will see how often we all engage in these biases.
2. Research (Lilienfeld, Ammirati, & Landfield, 2009; Gergen, 1973) suggests that by becoming aware of when you engage in these biases, you may be more motivated to avoid them in future interactions.
3. You will gain some insight into why others may react to your behaviors as they do.

Target exhibits a behavior, like eating fast food.

Individualistic culture

Collectivistic culture

Infer a dispositional cause for behavior: "He must eat fast food every day and live an unhealthy lifestyle!"

Infer a situational cause for behavior: "Maybe he was in a rush when he decided to get fast food for lunch."

<<< **Cultural Differences in Attribution.** While we all automatically infer causes for behavior, the types of causes inferred vary dramatically by culture.

overall image formed of that person. This is exactly what Solomon Asch (1946) found in his classic study on impression formation. By altering the adjectives provided about a person to include *cold* instead of *warm*, he dramatically changed the description participants provided about that person (Asch, 1946).

In addition, even within the first few minutes of coming to know a new person, the very first features of the person hold extreme importance. In one of Asch's early studies, some participants were asked to rate a person described as envious, stubborn, critical, impulsive, industrious, and intelligent. Other participants were asked to rate a person described as intelligent, industrious, impulsive, critical, stubborn, and envious. Note that the lists contain the exact same information, only in opposite order. The second group, which learned about the person's positive qualities first, rated the person more highly than the first group, which learned about the person's negative qualities first (Asch, 1946).

Moreover, when he examined the relative impact of each individual word, Asch discovered that the first word on the list was of utmost

PRIMACY EFFECT the phenomenon whereby the first pieces of information to which we are exposed have the most impact on our judgments

RECENCY EFFECT the phenomenon whereby the last pieces of information to which we are exposed have heightened impact on our judgments, relative to information received in the middle

> It can also be extremely difficult to monitor the impression others develop of us **because it is not simply contingent upon our own behavior.**

importance in the impressions formed about the person; this is termed the **primacy effect** (Asch, 1946). This effect states that the first piece of information in a list will have the most impact on impressions formed. The second and third items showed some impact on impressions, though this impact was diminished compared to that of the first item. This suggests that first impressions can be amended to some extent with other information presented prior.

Notably, there is another phenomenon termed the **recency effect**, which states that the information presented last will also dominate in memory and have an effect on impressions (Thorndike, 1935). This may lead one to believe that the primacy effect can be undone, but this is not so. The effect of recent information dominates in our impressions immediately after the information is presented. It does not, however, have the long-term impact on impressions that the primacy effect does. Recently provided information can affect how others see you right now, but the first impression will affect how they see you later.

These impressions are crucial when trying to navigate one's social world; being aware of the initial impression one conveys to others can have a profound impact. It can also be extremely difficult to monitor the impression others develop of us, because it is not simply contingent upon our own behavior. Roles, for example, play a large part in identifying what traits are considered positive for a given person. This is not always a bad thing. We want our mothers to be warm and caring, whereas it is less important for our electricians to act that way; we may simply want them to be professional.

However, these expectations for others can result in discrimi-nation. One such example is when men and women are applying for a new job or a promotion. Men's gender-typed roles dictate that they should be intelligent, assertive, and dominant—the same features one is likely to want in a manager of a company, for example. By contrast, women's gender-typed roles dictate that they should be gentle, nurturing, and submissive—features that differ starkly from managerial features. Women who do not conform to their gender-typed roles are evaluated more negatively by their peers, both male and female, and, despite having characteristics matching those desired in a manager, are promoted or hired much less often (see review by Heilman, 2001). So what does a woman applying for a managerial position do? Due to such role expectations, women are often required to try to strike a difficult balance between the two roles—acting professional and intelligent to convey suitability as a manager, but also being nurturing and prosocial toward co-workers to match what is expected of women. Therefore, it is not at all a simple manner to try to manage others' impressions, and the content of those impressions becomes of high importance.

Such rapid impressions are thus important in many day-to-day encounters. Consider in your own life, how often this is and will be relevant. In a very short time, employers must decide if they will hire you—and you must decide if you want to work for that employer. Do you think that boy or girl across the room is someone you want to approach? And after the first date, do you want to continue to a second? At these times, we know very little about the people we are evaluating, and they know very little about us—but nonetheless, we and they must make character judgments based on this miniscule amount of information.

First impressions are so powerful, in fact, that we need not even be present for them to have an impact (e.g., Widmeyer & Loy, 1988). In an early study by Kelley (1950), students were informed that a lecturer to whom they would subsequently be exposed was either a rather warm person or a rather cold person. The students then listened to the same neutral lecture by that lecturer, regardless of the description they had received, and participated in a group discussion with him. The students who had been told that the lecturer was warm perceived him as a much more effective lecturer and rated him as more positive on several attributes. Moreover, those who were told that the lecturer was warm were much more likely to participate in the discussion (56 percent participated) than those who were told that he was cold (32 percent participated) (Kelley, 1950).

<<< Beautiful faces **have a powerful effect on behavior.**

First impressions of physicality also matter and have profound effects on the way we treat other people. How attractive a person is creates a powerful bias in our behavior, in what is termed the **what is beautiful is good effect** (Dion, Berscheid, & Walster, 1972). While most people do not intend to infer that beautiful equates to good and ugly equates to bad, these associations are, to some extent, automatic in our brains. When people are exposed to pictures of beautiful faces, they are subsequently quicker at categorizing positive words as being positive than if they were exposed to unattractive faces (Olson & Marshuetz, 2005). This is because seeing the beautiful faces makes positive things more accessible, or ready to come to mind, and as such, they are identified more quickly. By contrast, this effect did not occur when people were exposed to pictures of beautiful homes instead of faces, suggesting that there is something particularly powerful, important, and positive about faces. We will revisit the idea of the what is beautiful is good effect in Chapter 12 on attraction, and we will explore additional research about how sometimes being *too* attractive can be detrimental in Chapter 14.

The effect of beauty does not stop with the activation of positive things in our minds. It goes as far as impacting the life expectancies we have for others (Dion, Berscheid, & Walster, 1972). Attractive people are expected to attain more prestigious occupations. In general, they are expected to be happier and more successful. People will even go so far as to change their self-presentation in ways derogatory to the self in the face of beauty. Women exposed to photos of attractive men who they might meet presented themselves as less intelligent when the man was purported to have traditional, conservative values (Zanna & Pack, 1975). The implications of beauty are quite potent.

While the effect of beauty on impressions may be particularly profound, other seemingly irrelevant aspects trigger impressions. Our opinions regarding the music on a person's iPod (Rentfrow & Gosling, 2006) or name (Young et al., 1993) can have an impact on our judgment of that person. For example, people with names associated with older generations (for example, Edith) were viewed as less popular and less intelligent than people with names popular among younger people (Young et al., 1993). People's belongings, Facebook page profiles, and dorm rooms are used to form sweeping impressions of them (Gosling, 2008). Even the pitch of a person's voice is used to infer the masculinity or femininity of the person (Ko, Judd, & Blair, 2006).

The effects of our facial features do not stop with beauty. The size and shape of particular facial features impact whether people are perceived to be kindhearted or mean-spirited. We tend to perceive

>>> What assumptions are you making **about the person who lives here?**

someone as more kindhearted if he has a full, round face; curly hair; long eyelashes; large eyes; a short nose; full lips; and an upturned mouth (Hassin & Trope, 2000). In addition, the more "baby faced" a person is, the more likely people are to give that person the benefit of the doubt, but also to judge the person as weak, naïve, and submissive (Berry & Zebrowitz-McArthur, 1988). In summary, people readily make snap judgments about others based on a variety and wealth of potentially irrelevant factors.

HALO EFFECT

Once we form these sweeping impressions of others, we use them to guide our interpretation of subsequent behaviors. If we form an overall positive impression of another person, then we have what is termed a positive implicit personality theory, a theory centered on the idea of the **halo effect**, about that person. The theory is then applied to whatever the person does thereafter. If we have witnessed behavior that we think implies one positive trait in a person, we are more likely to infer that the person possesses myriad other positive traits as well.

People will fail to distinguish among various behaviors exhibited by a person and assume that they are all positive—for instance, if that person has been judged to be a good worker, her projects and assignments will be uniformly evaluated more positively, even if one slips through the cracks. That worker will be seen as positive on many dimensions of work,

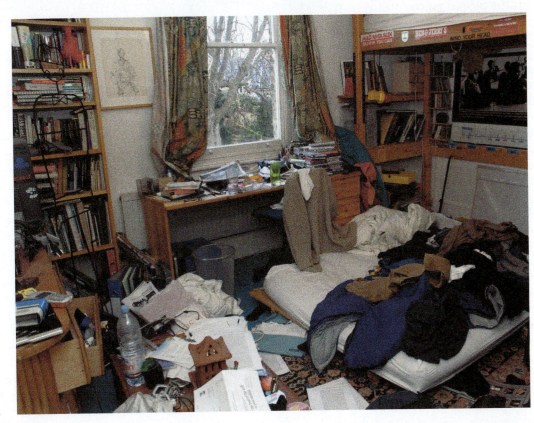

such as initiative, creativity, and diligence, even if she is not necessarily as creative as she is diligent.

In one study demonstrating this effect, students who watched a lecturer who was clearly established as being warm imbued him with other positive features such as attractiveness, likeability, and even a more pleasant accent (Nisbett & Wilson, 1977). And they did this far more than if he had been established as cold. Importantly, these students were completely unaware of why they made these judgments of the lecturer, and instead cited other causes that had not, in fact, differed between condition (exposure to warm versus cold lecturer) and thus could not have accounted for the effect.

CONFIRMATION BIAS

Imagine that you are a staunch supporter of the death penalty. You believe that it deters crime and is a just punishment for severe transgressions. Imagine now that you have read a research article that shows, quite powerfully, that the death penalty does not deter crime, and that over 70 percent of people killed under the death penalty were later exonerated. Would you change your opinion and decide that the death penalty should be abolished? Or would you decide that the research must be flawed?

If you said that you would decide that the research is flawed, most likely, this is what would happen. People defend their existing beliefs even against overwhelming evidence to the contrary. How? By selectively attending to information that supports their opinions and discounting information that does not. This is called the confirmation bias, as we saw in Chapter 1 (Darley & Gross, 1983).

One study that examined the confirmation bias asked participants to watch a video of a nine-year-old girl named Hannah answering academic questions (Darley & Gross, 1983). They were told, prior to watching the video, that Hannah was either from an upper-class, white-collar family and neighborhood (provoking high expectations for her performance) or a lower-class, blue-collar family and neighborhood (provoking low expectations for her performance). Participants who did not watch the video showed slight differences in their evaluation of Hannah's intelligence, congruent with their expectations. Those who did watch the video all saw Hannah answer some difficult questions correctly, but also answer some easy questions incorrectly. After watching the video, despite the mixed evidence provided, the difference in evaluation between conditions became more extreme; those who had expected Hannah to do well rated her as more intelligent, while those who expected her to do poorly rated her as less intelligent. Thus, participants zeroed in on the part of Hannah's performance that supported their existing expectations for her and discounted the rest, thereby providing support, in their own minds, for what they already believed.

This biased examination of the evidence is termed confirmatory hypothesis testing (Snyder & Swann, 1978). For example, in Snyder and Swann's 1978 study, participants were told that they were going to inter-

> " People defend their existing beliefs even against overwhelming evidence to the contrary. "

view someone they had never met in order to get to know that person. They were led to believe that the person was either an introvert or an extrovert. They were then asked to select questions they would ask the other person from an existing list. Participants tended to select questions that would confirm but not disconfirm their beliefs. For instance, those who expected the person to be an extrovert would select questions such as "How do you liven up a party?"—a leading question that virtually demands an answer that sounds extroverted (Snyder & Swann, 1978). In this way, we both passively and actively engage in **belief perseverance**, maintaining our original beliefs in the face of countervailing evidence (Ross, Lepper, & Hubbard, 1975).

SELF-FULFILLING PROPHECY

Once these impressions are formed, confirmation bias suggests that our expectations will influence the way others' behavior is perceived and understood. This has effects not only on our impressions of others but also on how we act toward those others. Importantly, by acting in ways based upon our expectations of the other person, we may unintentionally elicit exactly the behavior we expected, whether or not the person would have acted that way otherwise.

For example, if you are paired with a classmate who you expect to be lazy, you may treat her contributions as less valuable and take more of the work on yourself. And whether or not the classmate is actually lazy, she might see that you're taking most of the responsibility, and she'll take a backseat. This is the premise behind the self-fulfilling prophecy, which says that if we expect that something will happen, we will act in ways that elicit exactly what we expected. We have cognitive constructs that guide our understanding of the world, termed schemas. Schemas, discussed previously in Chapter 3, organize information about something and imbue it with meaning and structure. For instance, rather than thinking of an object as bright, made of glass, and small, we can just think of a light bulb, and all of those features come to mind in one package. We form schemas for what things are "like," such as what a good student is "like," and we use these to infer information about others. These schemas are part of what causes the self-fulfilling prophecy to occur.

In one study, schoolchildren were given a test of their potential for intellectual growth in the next year—or at least, that is what the teachers were made to believe the test assessed (Rosenthal & Jacobson, 1968). In actuality, it assessed the students' IQs. The teachers were provided with false feedback—that is, the students who were identified as having high potential for improvement were selected randomly. At the end of the school year, those who had been identified as having potential for improvement actually showed the most improvement in IQ. The teachers acted in such a way over the course of the school year as to make their own expectations for the children a reality—paying them more attention, giving them more challenging tasks and better feedback, and providing them with more opportunities to engage in class.

Notably, however, this effect was only shown in the lower grades (i.e., younger children). It was not shown among older children (Rosenthal & Jacobson, 1968). It is possible that the effect did not emerge among these children because teachers do not expect as dramatic a change to be possible among older children. It may also have been that these older

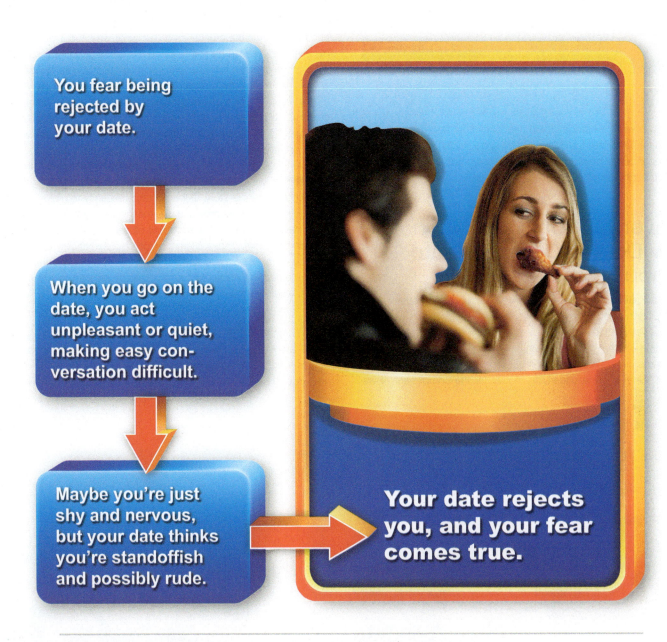

∧
∧ **The Self-Fulfilling Prophecy: How It Happens.** We cause our own expec-
∧ tations to come true by acting in ways that elicit expected behavior from others.

students had established reputations of which the teachers were already aware, and the supposed test results were not enough to undo these preexisting expectations. Even though teachers' expectations can be self-fulfilling, for the most part, the expectations they have are accurate, and a teacher's expectation alone will not cause a student to fail. Nor will the expectation cause a student to rise to the top of the class (Jussim & Harber, 2005). Whatever the reason, this finding suggests that the self-fulfilling prophecy may not be written in stone in all circumstances.

HOW WE CAN BE ACCURATE

This chapter attempted to illuminate many of the ways in which people are imperfect in the way they perceive others. On some level, it may lead you to believe that perceiving another person accurately is hopeless, but that is not the case. For example, we are generally more accurate in per-

ceiving people with whom we are familiar (Kenny, 2000). Indeed, bias and accuracy coexist in our perceptions of others every day, and often one will cause the other. Notably, the assumption that another person is similar to you will increase accuracy in understanding that person (Kenny & Acitelli, 2001).

In addition, when people are motivated to be accurate, they will form more accurate impressions (Kruglanski & Webster, 1996). The theory of social hypothesis testing claims that a high motivation for accuracy will lead people to engage in extensive diagnostic testing, to generate alternative hypotheses, and to take those hypotheses into account as they make decisions (Trope & Liberman, 1996). As such, they are more likely to consider multiple possible sources for others' behaviors before arriving at a decision. Further, research on empathic accuracy, or the ability to discern the thoughts and feelings of others, has shown that many factors increase empathic accuracy, including motivation (Ickes & Simpson, 2004), feedback from targets about their true thoughts and feelings (Marangoni, Garcia, Ickes, & Teng, 1995), and a dependence on the target for one's own positive outcomes to occur (Simpson, Oriña, & Ickes, 2003).

Nonverbal Communication: How Do We Communicate Without Words?

Part of navigating our social environments is deciphering others' true thoughts, feelings, and intentions. This is crucial precisely because they have a powerful impact on us. If a person makes us a promise, we must decide whether or not we trust that person to keep it. If someone compliments us, we must decide if we believe that she is being genuine or if there is some underlying motive for the compliment. If we need a favor, we are most likely to get what we need if we can determine who is the best person to ask. Who is in a good mood and more likely to help? Who has the skill set most appropriate for assisting? These decisions are difficult to make because the inner lives of others are invisible to us—but that does not stop us from inferring the content of those inner lives. We regularly infer the thoughts and feelings of others to try to come to understand them. On what do we base these inferences?

Given that people often do not disclose their true motives, thoughts, and feelings, we must use **nonverbal cues** to try to decipher them. But this is not the whole story. Our automatic tendency to make inferences about others and categorize and give meaning to our world persists even when we are not trying to learn about others or even actively attending to their behaviors. These inferences occur automatically and nonconsciously. In both of these cases, nonverbal cues are paramount. The basic methods of nonverbal communication will lead to inferences by others, whether conscious or not.

EMOTIONAL EXPRESSION

There are many sorts of nonverbal behaviors that people tend to use—including facial expressions, eye movements, and bodily gestures. Facial expressions, for one, are so fundamental to

∧
∧
∧ "Just go. It's fine." **People's nonverbal behaviors can communicate a wealth of information** that may be contradictory to their words.

Λ
Λ **Emotions Across Cultures.** These faces are recognized as reflecting the same emotions
Λ across different cultures.

communication that six basic emotions are conveyed with the same expressions across cultures—happiness, fear, sadness, anger, surprise, and disgust (Ekman, 1994). For example, people in both Western and Eastern cultures will identify a furrowed brow and pursed lips as anger.

Some argue that this constancy reflects the fact that these are the core emotions upon which all other emotions are built; for example,

frustration could be seen as a combination of anger and disgust. In addition, however, the tendency of people across the globe to use the same expressions to reflect these basic emotions suggests the primacy of facial expression in nonverbal communication, no matter the language spoken. The varied muscles in the face all play a role—a crooked smile can convey mischief, while a raised eyebrow can convey doubt or surprise. These expressions can be automatically

SELF-VERIFICATION the motivation of an individual for others to know him or her accurately, including his or her negative features

evoked. For example, when reminded of a positive, loved person in your life, you will likely automatically exhibit positive facial expressions, even when being exposed to *negative* aspects of that person (Andersen & Berk, 1998). While these expressions are very brief and can quickly be covered up with self-regulation, they cannot be altogether prevented. Thus, facial expressions can reflect one's underlying feelings and emotions, whether or not one intends to display them.

One especially notable aspect of facial expression is eye gaze and movement. Without the eyes, interpreting the emotions of others can be a frustrating endeavor. If a person makes eye contact, her intentions seem more genuine, and she seems more confident. In fact, continued eye contact is usually a sign of positive regard and attention. Despite that, an unwavering stare can even be intimidating. Darting eyes may suggest anxiety, while a lowered gaze may suggest shame or guilt. Simply changing one's gaze direction or intensity can powerfully impact what is communicated to others.

The rest of the body, too, conveys information to others about intentions and feelings. Research has shown that gesturing works together with speech to create meaning (McNeill, Cassell, & McCullough, 1994), and as such, gestures are inherently linked to meaning. One fairly straightforward form of body language involves the speed of one's motions. If someone is fidgeting, rubbing his or her arms rapidly, or some other repeated, quick motion, it is easy to infer that the person is aroused, whether in a positive or negative way. Gestures can range from small movements, like a roll of the eyes, to large movements, such as an entire body posture. Importantly, what is communicated by one part of the body may not map onto what is communicated by another part—this is likely due to some part being monitored and regulated by the actor to appear a certain way, while other parts reflect underlying feelings.

It is important to note that differences in the situation can result in the exact same nonverbal behavior being interpreted in very different ways. Imagine that your friend is sitting next to you reading a book. You ask her what she wants to order for dinner, and she shrugs. How would you interpret that behavior? Probably as ambivalent but calm. Now imagine that she is instead your girlfriend, and you asked her if she minded if you went out with your friends instead of staying with her, and she shrugged. How would you interpret that behavior? It would probably be taken as more hostile than in the former example. The gestures were identical, but the interpretation of them hinged on the context. The actions and their subsequent interpretations can also depend on who uses them. For example, if a child cries, people will usually infer that he is sad. If a man cries, many people will (unfortunately!) consider that he is weak or overly sensitive. Much of social psychology rests on this

> "These decisions are difficult to make because the inner lives of others are invisible to us—**but that does not stop us from inferring the content of those inner lives.**"

notion—that our understanding of the world is an intricate interaction of person and situation factors.

DETECTING DECEPTION

Imagine that it's summer and you're living with your parents again until the fall semester begins. You got used to going where you wanted to, when you wanted to, but now your parents want to know everything you do. You really want to go to a concert but you don't have anyone to go with, and your parents would never let you go alone. The night of the concert comes and your parents ask you with whom you're going. What do you do? How will you convince them that your friend really *is* coming with you?

Given all the methods of communication that occur without awareness, one might expect that we would be fairly good at detecting lies in others. However, this is not the case (Ekman, 2001). We are only slightly better than 50 percent accurate at detecting lies—that is, only slightly above chance, or as accurate as we'd be if we flipped a coin. This is in part because we tend to assume that people are generally honest, and as such don't attend to possible clues that they might be being dishonest.

This faulty belief is especially incredible considering that we tend to lie—and often. People tell at least one lie every day (DePaulo & Kashy, 1998), though we don't lie equally to everyone; we mostly lie to strangers, and lie much less often to family and friends. Why might that be? We lie for many reasons. One such reason is self-presentation—we lie so that others will see us how we want to be seen. However, once we know someone well, that person knows us well, too, and it is thus harder to tell a convincing lie.

Moreover, **self-verification** needs may take over (Swann & Read, 1981)—we want others to see us as we see ourselves—and as such, we are less likely to be intentionally dishonest (we were first introduced to this concept in Chapter 4). In addition, we may be somewhat more likely to feel guilty about manipulating a loved one with lies. However, that does not suggest that we do not still lie to loved ones, but that we may do so to spare their feelings or to avoid the repercussions of some misbehavior, for example.

How to Detect Deception

There are several nonverbal behaviors that have been identified as being indicative of deception. For one, the briefly exhibited facial expressions mentioned earlier may be indicative of deception if they differ from the subsequently expressed, intentional facial posturing. Another possibility is that the emotion exhibited by one body part or gesture may vary from another part or gesture. If a person smiles broadly at you but shifts uncomfortably on her feet, she is likely to not be as calm as it may have initially appeared.

What we say is also an indicator of whether or not we are lying. Work by Vrij, Evans, Akehurst, and Mann (2004) shows that people will use

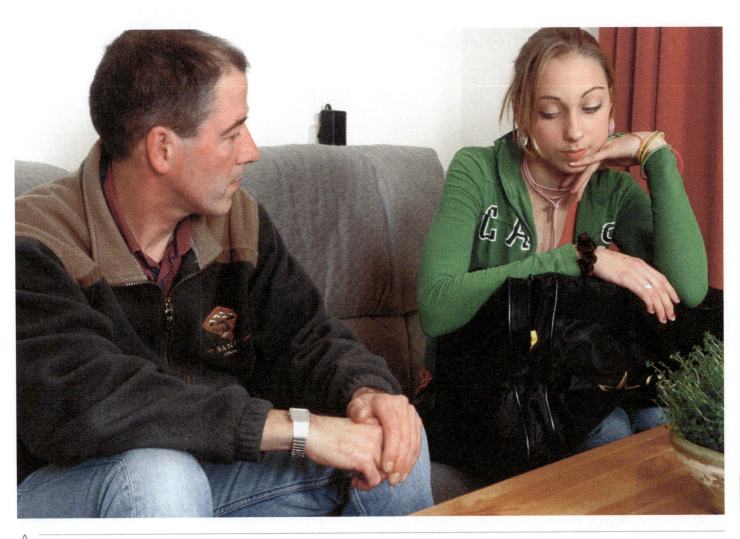

^^^ How do we know **when someone is lying?**

different words when they are lying, and they will use far fewer details in describing the incident than will truth tellers, failing to recount conversation content or describe visual images. Indeed, while verbal cues were indicators of lies (i.e., it accounted for 67 percent of the variance in whether or not people were lying), nonverbal cues were not predictors. As such, while nonverbal cues do exist and can indicate lying, they are not as good as predicting lies in real-life interactions.

Moreover, the nonverbal cues that are typically thought to indicate lying do not always indicate deception. Research by Mann, Vrij, & Bull (2004) showed that police officers who were considered experts at lie detection and had experience in it were only accurate 65 percent of the time, far above typical accuracy rates, in detecting lies. Notably, their use of nonverbal behaviors such as gaze aversion or fidgeting, which are often thought to be indicative of deception, was negatively correlated with accuracy; it *decreased* their rate of accuracy. By contrast, confidence in lie detection ability positively correlated with accuracy, so more confidence actually increased their rate of accuracy. Those who were good at detecting lies were also more likely to report using cues from the story itself, such as the number of details provided to describe it.

Detecting deception remains equally important in online environments, in which many people spend most of their days. However, it

is increasingly difficult. Despite the importance of the words we use, the absence of nonverbal cues creates a deficit in the ability to detect deceit. Liars in an Internet setting used more words, fewer first-person pronouns (e.g., "I"), more third-person pronouns (e.g., "she"), and more terms that referenced the senses (e.g., "saw") (Hancock, Curry, Goorha, & Woodworth, 2008). The increase in words may seem to contrast with liars' tendency to provide less detail, but it may be that liars will embellish under normal conditions, but hesitate to do so when a suspect in a crime for fear of saying something that would reveal the lie. Despite this, the recipient of the lies communicated online, in most cases, was unable to use these cues to detect the lie.

Accuracy in social perception is thus its own area of research, with an abundance of findings examining what facilitates accuracy in understanding others. And in terms of overcoming bias, while it cannot be fully overcome—and in some cases, leads to accuracy—what you have learned in this chapter may enable you to be more aware of these processes occurring in yourself and thereby allow you to correct for them, improving your social perception skills. Teaching people about the biases they have in social perception may enable them to make changes in their ways of perceiving others (Lilienfeld, Ammirati, & Landfield, 2009; Nisbett, Fong, Lehman, & Cheng, 1987).

05

Review

Summary

TO WHAT DO WE ATTRIBUTE PEOPLE'S BEHAVIORS?   p. 76

● Behaviors can be attributed to a person's disposition (traits) or situation. There are both rational processes that go into making these decisions and biased ones. Rational processes include whether or not the action was freely chosen and how distinctive the action is compared to what would be expected in the situation. Biased processes include one's perspective—the fundamental attribution error is when we attribute others' behaviors to their dispositions, but our own to the situation.

● People in individualistic cultures tend to make dispositional attributions quite automatically—termed spontaneous trait inferences. By contrast, those in collectivist cultures will make attributions equally as automatically and unintentionally, but the inferences they make will be situational. Thus, in all cultures, people have the tendency to immediately determine the cause of a given behavior—perhaps reflecting an innate need to understand our world.

HOW DO WE DECIDE WHAT OTHER PEOPLE ARE LIKE?   p. 80

● The content of information we are provided about a person is not the only thing that impacts our impressions; the centrality of the trait to personality as well as its order of presentation impact the extent to which it influences your impressions. Notably, first impressions are key. The primacy effect suggests that the very first thing to which we are exposed has a lot of weight in our evaluations of a person.

● The role that we are in can also influence how our behaviors are understood, as can having beauty or a baby-faced quality. Once we form an opinion of someone else, we are loath to change it—so much so that we seek out information that confirms our original beliefs. Moreover, with our own behavior, we elicit behavior from others that is consistent with our beliefs.

NONVERBAL COMMUNICATION: HOW DO WE COMMUNICATE WITHOUT WORDS?   p. 86

● Communication occurs via many parts of the body, from one's gaze to one's posture. Facial expressions are such a primary method of communication that six basic emotions are identifiable by the exact same expressions across cultures. These expressions can be evoked either consciously or automatically.

● These communications can give an indication of when someone is lying—for example, if one body part suggests one thing is true, but another body part suggests another. Despite the belief that most people are generally honest, people tend to lie at least once per day, though are more likely to do so to strangers than to close friends or family.

● Lacking nonverbal cues can impede people's abilities to detect deception. That said, verbal cues tend to be effective indicators in real-world situations, though there is contradictory evidence regarding whether more or less detail in the telling of a story indicates lying.

Key Terms

actor-observer effect the tendency people have to make dispositional inferences for others' behavior but situational attributions for their own 79

belief in a just world people have to believe the world is fair and adjust their other beliefs to maintain that stance by concluding that bad things happen to bad people and good things happen to good people 80

belief perseverance holding on to one's beliefs, even in the face of contradictory evidence 84

correspondence bias the tendency of people to make dispositional attributions for others' behaviors 77

correspondent inference theory the theory that people base their inferences regarding the source of others' behaviors on whether or not the behavior was freely chosen, if the consequences are distinctive, and if the behavior was socially desirable 76

covariation theory the theory that people base their inferences regarding the source of others' behaviors on whether or not there is a consensus regarding the way one ought to respond, the distinctiveness of the response, and the consistency of the person's response across situations 76

dispositional attribution inferring that a person's traits, something internal, caused his or her behavior 76

fundamental attribution error a more commonly known name for the correspondence bias. The scientific community now leans toward using "correspondence bias" so as not to suggest that these inferences are inherently in "error" 77

halo effect when one positive thing is known or believed about a target person, we tend to infer that the individual is positive overall and thus has other positive features 83

need for cognition the need that some individuals have to think, solve problems, and understand their world accurately 79

nonverbal cues behaviors, gestures, and expressions that convey thought or emotion without words 86

primacy effect the phenomenon whereby the first pieces of information to which we are exposed have the most impact on our judgments 82

recency effect the phenomenon whereby the last pieces of information to which we are exposed have heightened impact on our judgments, relative to information received in the middle 82

self-verification the motivation of an individual for others to know him or her accurately, including his or her negative features 88 situational attribution inferring that the situation in which a person is in, something external to the person, caused his or her behavior 76

spontaneous trait inference the process of automatically inferring traits from another person's behavior 78

three-stage model of attribution a model in which an observer automatically characterizes a behavior, automatically makes a dispositional inference, and then uses conscious effort to correct for situational constraints if the observer has the cognitive capacity to do so 78

what is beautiful is good effect the phenomenon wherein beautiful things are imbued with positivity and activate positive things in the mind 83

Test Your Understanding

MULTIPLE CHOICE

1. Which of these emotions is not one of the core six, recognizable by the same facial expressions across cultures?
   a. fear
   b. anger
   c. sympathy
   d. disgust

2. Why are we bad at detecting deception?
   a. We assume people are honest.
   b. We don't attend to cues that would reveal deception.
   c. We aren't lied to very often so don't have much experience with it.
   d. We endorse stereotypes about what nonverbal behaviors mean.

3. When are we more likely to make a dispositional attribution?
   a. if we are from a collectivistic culture
   b. when we are judging our own behavior
   c. when we have a high need for cognition
   d. when we are judging others' behavior

4. Which of these influences impressions the least?
   a. primacy
   b. concentration
   c. recency
   d. centrality of the trait to personality

5. Belief in a just world does not arise from:
   a. a desire to believe that things happen for a reason.
   b. a belief that we are good, so good things should happen to us.
   c. efforts to ameliorate anxiety about our futures.
   d. depressive disorders.

6. How long does it take to form an impression of someone?
   a. as soon as we learn one fact about that person
   b. 0.1 second after exposure
   c. as soon as we learn one central feature of that person
   d. one second after exposure

7. Why did changing a person's description from including "warm" to including "cold" have such a profound effect on impressions of that person in Asch's (1946) study?
   a. because it was presented last
   b. because it was central to personality
   c. because people were asked to form impressions based on all the words
   d. because people focus on visceral words

8. Exposure to a beautiful face can do all of these except:
   a. activate other positive things in memory.
   b. make you more helpful toward that person.
   c. make you more helpful in general.
   d. make women portray themselves as less intelligent.

9. You meet an employee in your company who is described as "diligent." You later remember him or her as being hardworking. This is an example of:
   a. the halo effect.
   b. confirmation bias.
   c. correspondence bias.
   d. the primacy effect.

10. In the study by Snyder & Swann (1978), if a participant believed that a target person was an introvert, what kind of questions would the participant ask the target?
    a. questions about introverted activities
    b. questions about extroverted activities
    c. questions about his or her hobbies
    d. none; since the person was not socially oriented, there was no point

ESSAY RESPONSE

1. What sorts of cues can we use to detect deception? Discuss the strengths and weaknesses of each.

2. Explain the possible consequences of motivated correction of the correspondence bias for political ideology.

3. Discuss the part social roles play in how behaviors are interpreted by perceivers. Use a concrete example, such as behavior in the workplace, newscasting, or behavior in any position where a person's role impacts what others infer about him or her.

4. Think about the difficulties inherent in finding middle ground on any contentious issue due to the confirmation bias. Discuss what the confirmation bias is and how it can serve to divide people with opposing opinions.

5. Explain what the self-fulfilling prophecy is and the negative impact it can have on social perception. Use the example of teacher expectations for students in your answer.

APPLY IT!

Think about a celebrity you admire. Why do you admire him or her? To what extent has his or her position/role contributed to your positive thoughts about him or her? Would you still admire him or her if he or she were not famous and instead lived next door to you?

ANSWERS: 1. c; 2. a; 3. d; 4. b; 5. d; 6. b; 7. b; 8. c; 9. a; 10. a

Remember to check www.thinkspot.com for additional information, downloadable flashcards, and other helpful resources.

APPLYING SOCIAL PSYCHOLOGY
Business

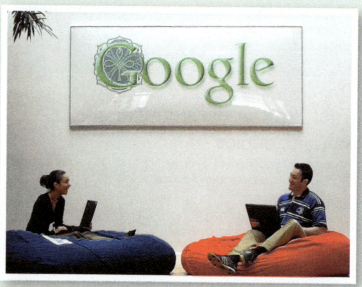

Imagine working for a company that provides free gourmet meals during your lunch break; offers you custom-made milkshakes when you are in the mood for a sugar fix; features an on-site gym, laundry room, hairdresser, and games room; and even provides you with inexpensive massages should you find your working environment too stressful. Throw in a comprehensive health care plan, generous salary and benefits, and the opportunity to bring your pet to work with you every day, and you are probably wondering about the inevitable catch. For once, it seems there isn't one. Google has consistently been named one of *Fortune Magazine*'s top employers because of the numerous perks it offers its employees. In exchange, the company is inundated with more than 3,000 job applications every day, has its pick of the world's brightest and most talented prospective employees, and is able to cultivate a loyal, hardworking workforce. As Google cofounder Larry Page puts it, "It's common sense: Happy people are more productive" (Lashinsky, 2008).

Page's philosophy incorporates some of the principles of industrial-organizational (IO) psychology, a branch of psychology that focuses on workplace productivity and related issues, such as the physical and mental well-being of employees. Both social psychologists and psychologists from other disciplines may specialize in the IO field, performing research to answer questions such as the following: How are applicants selected for jobs? What makes an effective leader? What factors motivate people to work hard, and what influences levels of job satisfaction?

One common issue that falls under the realm of IO psychology is whether or not men are perceived to be more effective leaders than women. As you will learn in the Chapter 9 discussion of leadership, research indicates that people have less favorable attitudes toward female leaders, making it less likely that they will be viewed as effective (Biernat, Crandall, Young, Kobrynowicz, & Halpin, 1998). One study found that female leaders tended to be evaluated negatively when they used stereotypically male leadership styles (for example, demonstrating decisiveness or resilience as opposed to strong interpersonal skills), or when they

Google is consistently considered a top-notch employer thanks to embracing many of the principles of industrial-organizational psychology.

worked in traditionally male-dominated fields, such as college athletics, business, or manufacturing (Eagly, Makhijani, & Klonsky, 1992). These negative evaluations were more pronounced when the evaluators were men than when they were women.

> "On the whole, however, the broad range of research collected on the topic of leadership and gender indicates that male and female managers do not differ any more in effectiveness than managers of the same gender."

Despite these negative attitudes, studies suggest that female managers are comparable to male managers in their effectiveness and differ only in their leadership styles. Whereas women generally adopt a more democratic or participatory style of leadership, men lean toward a more assertive, controlling approach (Eagly & Johnson, 1990). Some researchers report that this gender distinction creates a slight difference in effectiveness based on position requirements—task-oriented positions favor male leaders, whereas female managers perform better in interpersonally oriented roles (Eagly, Karau, & Makhijani, 1995). On the whole, however, the broad range of research collected on the topic of leadership and gender indicates that male and female managers do not differ any more in effectiveness than managers of the same gender.

Personnel selection and evaluation are also areas that lend themselves to the studies of IO psychology. Imagine that you are taking part in a job interview with the managing director of a company. During a particularly enthusiastic response, you sweep a cup of coffee across the table and it lands in the managing director's lap. Is it possible to redeem yourself, or will you (assuming that you are still in the running for the position) be forever remembered as a clumsy, ham-fisted oaf who should never be entrusted with wining and dining prospective clients? Unfortunately, as you learned in Chapter 5, it appears that we never get a second chance to create a first impression; when meeting new people, we make relatively accurate and persistent evaluations about them based on less than 30 seconds of observation (Ambady & Rosenthal, 1993). A recent study identified the neural processes responsible for these snap judgments. During a social encounter, two key regions in the brain sort information based on its personal and subjective significance, essentially formulating a first impression (Schiller et al., 2009). These impressions are often based on nonverbal clues or physical appearance. When observers viewed full-body photographs of 123 strangers in a naturally expressed pose (for example, a smiling expression or an energetic stance), they were able to accurately assess nine out of 10 personality traits, ranging from agreeableness and emotional stability to religiosity and political orientation (Naumann, Vazire, Rentfrow, & Gosling, 2009).

> **Once a first impression has been made, it is difficult to shake off because we have a natural tendency to pay attention to information that supports preconceived stereotypes and ignore information that contradicts them.**

However, first impressions are not always accurate, and supervisors and evaluators often fall prey to the social perception biases discussed in Chapter 5. In the workplace, such social and cognitive bias may work in an employee's favor or may hinder his career progress. For example, research shows that appraisers are more likely to rate an employee favorably if they took part in the initial appraisal or hiring process, even when provided with negative information about that employee (Bazerman, Beekun, & Schoorman, 1982). Appraisers are also likely to fall victim to the halo effect—a failure to differentiate between different aspects of an employee's performance (Cooper, 1981). As a result of the halo effect, employers are prone to assuming that a worker who is friendly and warm is also likely to be efficient and a strong team player, whereas an employee who is antisocial often rates lower on unrelated measures of performance (see Chapter 12 for more information about the halo effect). Researchers have found that the halo effect is particularly prevalent when evaluators rate someone they don't know well, or when a time delay has affected their recollection of an employee's performance (Kozlowski, Kirsch, & Chao, 1986; Murphy & Balzer, 1986).

Once a first impression has been made, it is difficult to shake off because we have a natural tendency to pay attention to information that supports preconceived stereotypes and ignore information that contradicts them, a phenomenon known as confirmation bias (see Chapter 10 for further discussion of the confirmation bias). Thus, once an employer has pigeonholed an employee as lazy, bright, intelligent, useful, or inept, the employer will only be conscious of the employee's actions if those actions support the employer's previous opinion. By making employers and employees aware of these tendencies and the other factors discussed above, social psychology can help increase our knowledge of how to be productive, effective, and happy in the work force.

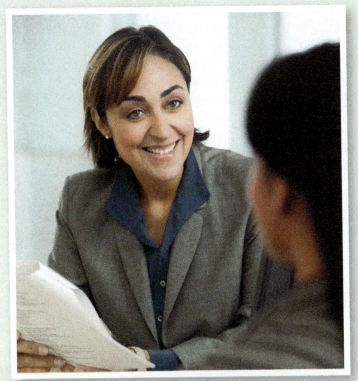

Studies indicate that whether you are in a business environment or a social setting, first impressions last a long time.

ATTITUDES: MAKING EVALUATIONS ABOUT THE WORLD

<<< *What makes us care about*
some issues while remaining
apathetic toward others?

Q

In 2010,

the world witnessed a major oil leak in the Gulf of Mexico. Indeed, calling it a "leak" is quite an understatement—it was very likely the worst environmental disaster in U.S. history. Eleven people died when the British Petroleum (BP) *Deepwater Horizon* oil rig exploded on April 20, 2010. The explosion caused a long pipe that carried oil from the ocean floor into the oil rig to break off. When the rig exploded and sank, it dragged the pipe with it, bending and twisting it across the ocean floor. The pipe ruptured in several places, sending 2.5 million gallons of highly pressurized oil gushing into the Gulf of Mexico every day for over three months. What made matters worse was that the disaster took place 5,000 feet below the surface of the Gulf, making repairs extremely difficult. Scientists say that the long-term damage to the environment caused by the gushing oil is still incalculable. In addition, the economic toll on locals who relied on the Gulf's waters for their livelihood was devastating.

Many Americans were outraged by this unprecedented environmental disaster, immediately calling for bans on offshore drilling and boycotts of BP. Many Americans and others around the globe believed that this disaster would have lasting, if not permanent, ill effects on the ecosystem of the Gulf of Mexico and on the human beings who are a part of that ecosystem. Some people called the company evil, saying it didn't do enough to stop the disaster, and executives instead spent their energy pointing fingers. For other people, though, the BP disaster was just another story on the news. Flipping past the story on TV, or skimming headlines on news Web sites, they thought "Oh, that's a bummer," or didn't even register the disaster at all.

In many cases, this disaster prompted a change in attitude. People who had neutral feelings toward offshore drilling started feeling negative toward it. Does that mean they joined the letter writers and cleanup crews? Not necessarily. As you've likely seen many times in your life, how you feel about something doesn't always correspond to the way you act. In this chapter, we will look at the factors that affect the development of attitudes, what factors predict attitudes, how attitudes change, and if attitudes predict subsequent behavior.

CHAPTER 06

How Do Attitudes Develop?

Social psychologists define **attitudes** in many different ways, and their definitions have changed much over the years (Schwarz & Bohner, 2001). For the purposes of our discussion, however, we will stick with one definition—having an evaluative component toward a stimulus that is made-up of affective, behavioral, and cognitive in formation (Zanna & Rempel, 1988). As you saw in Chapter 5, it takes only a split second to form an attitude about someone or something. In fact, you may not even realize that you've formed an attitude because your mind is constantly and unconsciously judging and analyzing the environment. As you likely know from personal experience, attitudes can vary greatly in strength. Maybe you have a strong aversion to olives and can't even stand the smell of them. There might be a political issue that gets your blood boiling. At the other end of a spectrum, there might be a particular actor you don't really like, but you're not going to refuse to see one of his movies if your friends want to go.

Attitudes might also be ambivalent. The word might be unfamiliar, but it's a safe bet you know *exactly* what this feels like. Let's say you were accepted to a school several hundred miles away from your hometown. You think it could be an exciting new adventure to live so far away from home. At the same time, maybe many of your friends are planning to go to schools in your home state. You're torn—you want new experiences, but you don't want to leave your friends. An **ambivalent** attitude is defined as simultaneously experiencing strong contradictory emotions or motivations.

Think again about the BP disaster in the Gulf. While most people felt badly for the suffering animals and local residents, some were uncertain of where to place blame. How did you feel? Did you blame BP for having a faulty rig, or for not addressing the leak quickly enough? Did you blame the government for not getting more effectively involved? Did you blame politicians for allowing offshore drilling? Maybe you blamed oil consumers for creating such a demand for offshore drilling. Maybe your attitude was ambivalent,

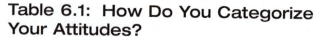

Table 6.1: How Do You Categorize Your Attitudes?

Attitude	Positive Reaction	Negative Reaction	Example
Positive	High	Low	"I love guacamole! It's my favorite dip."
Negative	Low	High	I despise guacamole! I'll never eat a bite."
Indifferent	Low	Low	"I've never tried guacamole so I really have no opinion."
Ambivalent	High	High	"I love guacamole, but I'm allergic to avocados!"

Source: Adopted from: Cacioppo, J. T., Gardner, W. L., & Berntson, G. G. (1997). Beyond bipolar conceptualizations and measures: The case of attitudes and evaluative space. *Personality and Social Psychology Review, 1*, 3–25.

and you experienced conflicting feelings on where the blame should be placed.

As the story developed, you may have cycled through several different attitudes toward the incident. Some people, overwhelmed by media coverage, may have even decided not to care at all about the issue and turned their attention away from it. This, too, is a kind of attitude. Weak or strong, positive, indifferent, negative, or ambivalent—we all have attitudes on everything that comes across our "radars," as Table 6.1 illustrates.

ATTITUDE FORMATION

Many times, attitudes are automatically formed and activated without our even being aware of them—these are called **implicit attitudes** (Fazio & Olson, 2003). Such attitudes are outside of our conscious control. Think about the attitudes you had as a child, and how they have changed. For example, let's say as a child, Tasha was afraid of dogs, despite never having had a negative experience with one. She simply felt afraid when she saw a dog. As she grew up, though, she was able to override that attitude. Tasha told herself that her fear was irrational and sought out interactions with dogs in an effort to overcome her fear. Now, Tasha loves dogs. This is an example of an **explicit attitude**—an attitude that one recognizes and can control (Gawronski & Bodenhausen, 2006; Nosek, 2007).

Psychologist Laurie A. Rudman (2004) pointed out four factors that differentiate between implicit and explicit attitudes. She defined them as early experiences, affective experiences, cultural biases, and cognitive consistency principles. Many social psychologists argue that implicit attitudes stem from early, even forgotten, experiences, while explicit attitudes are formed in reaction to more recent experiences. Affective experiences may also have more effect on implicit attitudes because they have to do with automatic reactions, while explicit attitudes come from a more cognitively controlled mindset. For the same reason, cultural biases have more influence over implicit

∧
∧ We don't often have to think too hard to know **what our**
∧ **attitude about something is.**

rather than explicit attitudes. Finally, cognitive consistency principles affect attitudes through a formula that can be expressed as "I like X, and Y is X, so I must like Y." For example, if you like comedies and you've been invited on a date to see a comedy, you'll probably have a positive attitude about those plans.

Although attitudes are primarily evaluative (Eagly & Chaiken, 1993), both implicit and explicit attitudes comprise three separate components: *affect*, *behavior*, and *cognition*. An *affective* response is based on your emotions, such as feeling badly for victims of the Gulf oil spill. You may also find yourself donating money to a rescue society, which is a *behavior* that demonstrates your attitude toward the spill. Finally, your negative thoughts about BP for not responding quickly to the spill reflected the *cognition* underlying your attitude, as you weighed what they *could* have done against what they *did* do.

When you are evaluating a person, object, event, or idea, your mind weighs both positive and negative information in its analysis; however, research indicates that negative information makes much more of an impact on your attitudes. Put another way, you remember the bad things more than you do the good things when you are forming an attitude about something. This is called the negativity bias (Kunda, 1999; Fiske, 1980; for a review of the negativity bias, see Rozin & Royzman, 2001). It has been suggested that this arose in our manner of processing information because attending to negative information is more crucial for our survival than positive information, so as to avoid any dangers we may encounter.

To determine whether this tendency is truly hardwired, researchers measured the electrical activity in people's brains when they viewed positive photos (e.g., a Ferrari, a pizza), neutral photos, and negative photos (e.g., a mutilated face, a dead cat). The measurements reflected the responsiveness of the brain to the valence of the stimulus—that is, its response the moment the brain recognizes a stimulus as being positive, negative, or neutral. The results showed that there were larger brain waves, reflecting a dramatic increase in brain activity, when participants viewed the negative photos as opposed to when they viewed the positive or neutral photos (Ito et al., 1998). Thus, the brain reacts much more strongly to negative information than to positive or neutral information as soon as the brain recognizes the valence of what its owner is seeing.

We may in fact be hardwired to avoid danger in order to survive, and, as our brains evolved, we developed systems to remember hazardous situations or objects in order to avoid them in the future. The negativity bias might be why politicians these days rely on "negative advertising," making accusations that an opponent will take your money and won't look out for you. Those weaknesses will stick in viewers' brains and possibly draw attention away from the opposing candidate's positive features. We all know from experience that it can go too far and that nobody likes a bully. Particularly vicious attacks on another person may backfire and cast a negative light on the attacker, and that too will be remembered. These examples illustrate how attitudes are based on evaluation, but let's take a closer look at how it happens.

Your Attitude:

The oil spill was a negative occurrence.

Affect:
You felt bad for the victims.

Behavior:
You donated money to charities working to clean up the spill.

Cognition:
You thought BP should have responded more quickly.

The ABCs of the BP Oil Spill. Our attitudes are expressed by and composed of the affect, behavior, and cognition that reflect them.

CLASSICAL CONDITIONING a type of learning by which a neutral stimulus gets paired with a stimulus (UCS) that elicits a response (UCR). Through repeated pairings, the neutral stimulus (CS) by itself elicits the response (CR) of the second stimulus

UNCONDITIONED STIMULUS (UCS) a stimulus that elicits a response automatically, without learning taking place

UNCONDITIONED RESPONSE (UCR) a response that occurs automatically in reaction to some stimulus, without learning taking place

CONDITIONED STIMULUS (CS) a stimulus that, only by repeated association with a particular unconditioned stimulus, comes to evoke the response associated with the unconditioned stimulus

CONDITIONED RESPONSE (CR) a learned response to the conditioned stimulus that was previously a neutral stimulus

MERE EXPOSURE EFFECT the phenomenon whereby objects become better-liked with exposure—we like things more with which we are familiar

NAME-LETTER EFFECT the tendency to show a preference for letters in our own name and prefer stimuli that contain those letters

Classical Conditioning

One example of how attitudes, both negative and positive, develop is in the case of **classical conditioning** (for a review of this concept, see Jones, Olson, & Fazio, 2010). Classical conditioning is a type of learning in which a neutral stimulus gets paired with a stimulus that elicits a response. Once conditioning has occurred through repeated pairings, the neutral stimulus by itself already elicits the response of the second stimulus.

Ivan Pavlov (1927) uncovered this type of conditioning in his famous experiment with dogs. Each time the dogs were given meat, they would salivate. The meat is the **unconditioned stimulus (UCS)** and the salivation is the **unconditioned response (UCR)**, because it occurs automatically without learning. Pavlov added a second stimulus—each time the dogs were given meat, he would ring a bell. Sure enough, after repeated trials, the dogs began to salivate when they heard the bell—even if there was no meat to be found! By association with the unconditioned stimulus, the bell became

the **conditioned stimulus (CS)** and the salivation at the sound of the bell (without presentation of the food) became the **conditioned response (CR)**.

Similarly, our attitudes can be formed by associations. For example, you might associate the smell of baking bread with your loving grandmother, so whenever you smell bread baking you become filled with warm and fuzzy thoughts and feelings. This reaction happens because, over the years, you have smelled the baking bread repeatedly while simultaneously receiving your grandmother's undivided positive attention. You do not have to put any conscious effort into evoking this sort of reaction—it happens quite automatically.

So how can classical conditioning impact attitudes? In the previous example, the positive associations with your grandmother are likely to make you feel positively about bread, too. Notably, these associations need not be purposeful—they can involve two things that occur together completely incidentally. In a recent experiment, participants were shown positive images (e.g., flowers, a mother and child) paired with either Coke or Pepsi (Gibson, 2008). The drink not paired with the positive images was instead paired with negative images (e.g., a graveyard, the word "terrifying"). The participants were then given a completely different task of memorizing an eight-digit number, in order to clear participants' working memory of which soda was associated with which images, as well as to distract them from the purpose of the study. After this distraction, when asked to choose one or the other soda, participants who initially did not favor either brand of soda chose the positively associated soft drink over the negatively associated one, even if they could not remember which soda had been presented with which images. Of course, these sorts of things happen in everyday life, too. For example, if Jack is eating sushi when he learns that his mother has been in a car accident, he may develop a negative attitude toward sushi. Even if he's not entirely aware of it, for him, eating sushi may now be linked with fearful and negative feelings. Associations can come to impact our attitudes toward even the soda we drink and food we eat.

Associations need not be between two objects—there is an inherent association between things with which we are familiar and positive affect, as well as the unfamiliar and negative affect. This, too, may have arisen due to a need to protect ourselves from the unknown. This is called the **mere exposure effect**, which states that simply having been exposed to something increases our liking for it (Zajonc, 1968). Things and people that originally invoke a neutral response grow on us the more we are exposed to them (Mita, Dermer, & Knight, 1977). The mere exposure effect can certainly backfire—have you ever seen the same commercial so many times that it begins to grate on your nerves and you don't even want to think about the product it features, let alone purchase it? Additionally, it doesn't work with stimuli to which you have an initial negative response. If you hate a song the first time you hear it, no amount of continued exposure will make you like it. You will learn more about the mere exposure effect in Chapter 12.

One recent finding that powerfully demonstrates that exposure increases positive regard is called the **name-letter effect** (Nelson & Simmons, 2007; Nuttin, 1987). Research has uncovered that we have a preference for our own names and initials; in fact, we have a tendency to prefer our own initials over any other letters in the alphabet. This finding is used as a measure of implicit self-esteem—if we think well of ourselves, we

<<< If something is paired with food often enough, it might just make you salivate on its own—such as the feeling of increased hunger and salivation after placing a delivery order.

∧
∧ Rewards for good behavior **make people**
∧ **want to practice those good behaviors more often.**

will prefer our initials over other letters and seek them out unconsciously. This can have both a positive and negative impact, however. If your initial matches a positive performance label, you are more likely to perform better. For instance, researchers found that individuals with names like Chris or Derek tended to have lower grades than students with names like Allison or Bob (Nelson & Simmons, 2007). In addition, your first initial may also determine the products that you buy and places you live (Jones et al., 2004; Brendl, Chattopadhyay, Pelham, & Carvall, 2005). Tanya is more likely to live in Tampa and drive a Toyota than Sarah, but Sarah may select Sarasota and a Subaru. It is important to keep in mind, however, that even though this research shows that initials are linked to some outcomes, these studies are correlational only. Remember from Chapter 2, that we learned that we cannot infer that our name *causes* these consequences, as this type of study design only permits conclusions about *relationships* among variables. Of course, classical conditioning is just one theory of how attitudes are developed. Let's examine another theory.

Operant Conditioning

If each time you earned an A on a paper or exam, you received an expensive gift like an iPad or a $100 Target gift card, you might be inclined to try to rack up as many As as possible, right? However, if each time you received a C or lower you were punished by having your cell phone taken away, you would also likely try hard to keep your grades high. This is an example of **operant conditioning**, a method of learning that occurs through rewarding desirable behavior and punishing undesirable behavior. It is a method that

OPERANT CONDITIONING a type of learning in which the frequency of a behavior is determined by reinforcement and punishment

OBSERVATIONAL LEARNING acquiring an attitude or behavior due to the observation of others exhibiting that attitude or behavior

was first discovered by Edward Thorndike and elaborated on by the psychologist B.F. Skinner (1938).

Operant conditioning occurs through the mechanisms of reinforcement and punishment, of which there are two types, positive and negative. *Positive reinforcement* refers to the addition of a desirable item in order to reinforce or increase the likelihood or repetition of a behavior. For example, your parents might offer you money for every A on your report card. *Negative reinforcement*, by contrast, refers to the removal of something unpleasant in order to increase the likelihood of repetition of a behavior—if you improve your grades, you don't have to go to boring tutoring sessions. *Positive punishment* refers to the addition of an undesirable stimulus in order to reduce a behavior. Spanking is an example of this. *Negative punishment* refers to the removal of something pleasurable in order to decrease the frequency of a behavior (for example, if your parents take away your car because your semester grades were too low).

Operant conditioning can influence attitudes as well. If a behavior is reinforced, our attitudes toward it are likely to become more positive, and if it is punished, our attitudes are likely to become more negative. This can even extend to the way we feel about other people. For example, couples who provide each other with reinforcements such as favors, running errands, giving gifts, and so forth, are more likely to be together four months down the line than those who do not provide many rewards (Berg & McQuinn, 1986). Notably, an imbalance in rewards also predicted lesser likelihood of remaining together, in part, due to one partner not receiving sufficient reinforcement, but inevitably also due to issues of inequity in the relationship.

Observational Learning

Observational learning (Bandura, 1977), or modeling, is yet another way by which attitudes can be formed. People develop attitudes about things or other people based on how they see others act. In doing so, they take on the same views of those they observe. For instance, if a girl grows up watching her father act distrustful of a particular racial or ethnic group, she may very likely adopt those same views. Attitudes developed in this way can, however, be reversed, as evidenced in an experiment many of us would probably like to see for ourselves. Each day for four days, children who were initially afraid of dogs witnessed a little boy playing with a dog in a playpen for 20 minutes. After the four days, 67 percent of the dog-phobic children were comfortable enough to climb inside the playpen and play with the dog, even when all others left the room (Bandura, Grusec,

<<< We learn how to act by observing others' behaviors. In this way, children sometimes pick up undesirable behaviors from their parents that can impact the way they approach situations and other people for the rest of their lives.

& Menlove, 1966). Just seeing another child playing with the dog helped the children learn not to fear dogs.

Another more recent study demonstrated the potent effect of observational learning. Ninth graders were exposed to scenes in movies where people were either smoking or not (i.e., the smoking was edited out) (Pechmann & Shih, 1999). Those who watched smokers tended to look favorably upon the smokers' social stature, had an increased sense of positive arousal, and had more intention to smoke compared to those who did not watch smokers. While this is a powerful statement in support of observational learning, these deleterious effects were overcome if the students were shown an anti-smoking advertisement before watching the movie. Therefore, while observational learning can directly impact attitudes toward objects and behaviors, it can be countered with educational techniques that create healthy attitudes before the unhealthy stimulus is encountered.

ASSESSING ATTITUDES

You can usually tell what your friends and acquaintances think about certain people or social objects. You know Dave dislikes Tim's girlfriend because he rolls his eyes almost every time she speaks. It's obvious that

Megan really likes Sean, because she gives him a warm hug as soon as he walks into a room. These indicators let you know what Dave's and Megan's explicit attitudes are. Explicit attitudes are, again, attitudes of which we are aware and that are often obvious to an outsider. For instance, in the beginning of this chapter we talked about attitudes toward the 2010 BP oil disaster. People's actions and words let us know their attitudes about the event. You could tell people felt strongly when they attended a protest, volunteered to clean up a beach, or wrote letters to the President. Explicit attitudes can be assessed by *self-report measures* (discussed in Chapter 2)—questionnaires where participants are asked what they think or how they feel. This method relies on participants willingly and honestly revealing the way they feel about someone or something.

On the flipside, it is impossible to perceive all the attitudes people have about the world around them; in fact, they may not even know what some of their own attitudes are! These implicit attitudes require a more precise method of assessment. If you don't even know how you feel about something, how would a researcher be able to find out? The answer is that researchers have to go undercover, so to speak, and use covert measures to ascertain what your underlying attitudes are about something. One possibility is *unobtrusive observation*.

Implicit Attitudes. If you have implicit knowledge of the stereotypes that Asian Americans are good at math and African Americans are good at sports, **this setup will be more difficult for you, and you will take longer to identify this face.**

Observation (also discussed in Chapter 2) can provide insight into both explicit and implicit attitudes. For example, if Mark is at a party and splits the last piece of pizza with his friend, an observer might think Mark values sharing. Does Mark really value sharing, though, or does he just want people to *think* he does? That is, is Mark's selflessness an implicit, automatically activated reaction toward seeing his friend's desire for that last piece of pizza, or must he activate it with conscious effort to impress others? However, if the same thing happened while Mark and his friend were dining one-on-one, it would suggest that sharing is more likely to be an implicit attitude. One could argue though, that any behavior is, in part, an effort to convince *ourselves* that we are who we want to believe we are.

Of course, measuring such things is incredibly difficult. One measure that does not suffer from these obstacles, and as such is one of the primary covert measures used, is a self-report test called the **Implicit Association Test**, or the **IAT**. (To review additional measures of implicit attitudes, see Fazio & Olson, 2003.) You may be wondering how self-reported data on attitudes can be useful—after all, won't people just lie to make themselves look better? To control for this and increase accuracy of self-report data, researchers use the "bogus pipeline." Basically, participants in a study are led to believe that a nonfunctioning (of course, they don't know it's non-functioning) machine can predict their responses. The researchers conduct a sample trial to show the participant how it works. In studies using this method, individuals are less likely to answer in a socially desirable fashion and instead are more truthful (Jones & Sigall, 1971).

The IAT measures how easily we associate categories with positive or negative descriptions. For instance, a person may associate Indian Americans with intelligence and high achievement, African Americans with dancing ability, or French people with snobbishness. These attitudes may not even be conscious to the person who holds them, and the IAT is one tool that allows us to gain insight into these implicit attitudes. If you're brave enough and interested in self-discovery, you can take the test online and find out not only what your implicit attitudes may be toward different ethnic and racial groups, but also other attitudes such as those you have toward recent presidents of the United States. The test can be found at https://implicit.harvard.edu/implicit/.

The test asks you to quickly categorize words and faces presented on the screen. For instance, in one trial, you may be asked to click the A key if a word is positive or a face is white and click the L key if a word is negative or a face is black. This pairing, if you possess the implicit attitude that black people are associated with negative things and white people are associated with positive things, should be easy and you would press the correct keys more quickly. However, if you held the same attitude and the pairing was negative and white and positive and black, you would have a more difficult time and respond more slowly. It's important to note that the reaction times are measured in terms of milliseconds; these are reactions that occur quickly without conscious control.

Remember, these implicit attitudes reflect associations between concepts—that when the category is encountered, the associated concepts are activated in unconscious memory (see *accessibility*). That does not mean that those associations are endorsed by the person, but simply

>>> **Whether or not our attitudes influence our behavior can depend on a number of factors,** just as all those who want to stop smoking do not necessarily do so, even if they hold the attitude that smoking is bad.

IMPLICIT ASSOCIATION TEST (IAT) test that measures how easily we associate categories with positive or negative attitudes, including measures in categories ranging from racial and religious attitudes to attitudes about presidents

that they have been created by repeated exposure. So if you have been exposed to others' stereotypes that African Americans are lazy, you are likely to have that association in memory even if you do not endorse it.

As such, the IAT is not without controversy. Opponents of the test claim that since it simply measures a person's subconscious association of adjectives with specific social groups, but does not necessarily reflect what the person actually believes, it isn't meaningful. Even if you're Asian American and know very well that every Asian American is not a budding genius, you may have the adjective "smart" associated with Asian American in your mind, and so it will seem as if this is your implicit attitude. A hiring manager may not explicitly endorse stereotypes such as this, and might not actively recruit only Asian Americans, but she may be more likely to hire an Asian American for a position that calls for intelligence. As described in Chapter 5, the person will not know that his or her stereotypes are guiding the decision making because they are not actively endorsed, but they have a deleterious effect nonetheless. In this and many other ways, associations between groups of people and constructs in memory matter, even if they are not believed to be true.

Do Attitudes Influence Behavior?

We have a plethora of attitudes about almost everything, and it seems as though, if we believed in something, we would necessarily act in accordance. But do we? Let's say your best friend is having a birthday bash on Saturday night, but you have a paper due on Monday, and you

haven't even started writing. It is going to require a lot of research and time. Even though education is one of your top priorities, do you stay home on Saturday night and skip the party? The likely answer is no. Despite your positive attitude about your education, that attitude does not come into play in every decision you make. In this case, it's likely because of the competing, stronger positive attitude toward your friend. Likewise, someone might be strongly opposed to offshore drilling and want to help prevent another BP-type disaster. However, this doesn't necessarily mean that she will hop on a plane to the Gulf of Mexico and help with the cleanup, or that she will even pick up the phone and make a 60-second phone call to her congressperson to express her dismay.

WHEN ATTITUDES DO NOT PREDICT BEHAVIOR

The disconnect between attitude and behavior was demonstrated by a classic study conducted by a researcher named LaPiere in 1934. LaPiere was struck by racial prejudice against the Chinese in the United States and wanted to investigate this attitude further. He happened to be traveling with a young Chinese student and his wife when he realized that they were able to find rooms in hotels with no trouble, even in hotels in very prejudiced areas. He traveled all over the United States with the young Chinese couple and remained hidden while the couple went into a variety of restaurants and hotels. LaPiere found that the couple was denied entry to only one establishment out of 66 hotels and 184 restaurants.

Six months later, LaPiere sent questionnaires to those same hotels and restaurants asking if they would be willing to accommodate a Chinese couple. The vast majority of the businesses that responded (92 percent of restaurants and 91 percent of hotels) answered "no," despite having accommodated the Chinese couple earlier. LaPiere noted that the couple had smiled often and hypothesized that their smiles were disarming to the people they encountered, thereby rendering the Americans' racist attitudes less influential on their behavior. So maybe "kill 'em with kindness" actually works! He also speculated that the Chinese couple's unaccented English reduced the employees' tendencies to discriminate. Ultimately, the attitudes of the restaurant and hotel operators did not necessarily predict their behaviors. However, one of the flaws of LaPiere's research is that we don't know if the employees who completed the survey were the same as the ones who had displayed the nondiscriminatory behavior.

In another classic study demonstrating this disconnect, a researcher named Corey (1937) tested 67 university students in an educational psychology class. He first administered a questionnaire to the students to ascertain their attitudes toward cheating. Many of them disapproved of cheating; their attitudes on average suggested a moderate distaste for cheating. Next, every week for five weeks the students were given a five-question true-or-false test. The students gave the test to the researcher, who secretly graded the exams so he or she would know the students' true scores and then returned the exams to the students so that they could grade the exams themselves. Such a scenario allowed the students to cheat by covertly changing their answers to improve their scores while grading.

Corey found that in 76 percent of the cases, students cheated, regardless of their previously stated attitudes toward cheating. Their attitudes toward cheating were completely unrelated to whether or not they actually did so; in fact, the best predictor of cheating was the difficulty of the exam. It seems that these students could talk the talk, but most of them could not walk the walk when it came to being consistent with their attitudes against cheating.

> "Their attitudes toward cheating were completely unrelated to whether or not they actually did so; in fact, the best predictor of cheating was the difficulty of the exam."

HOW ATTITUDES DO INFLUENCE BEHAVIOR

It is not always the case that attitudes do not impact behavior; certainly, it is easy to think of examples from our lives of when they have. More notably, there have been studies showing the dramatic effects our attitudes can have on our lives. Optimism has been shown to improve immune system functioning. One study found that law school students who were more optimistic about their performance had better functioning immune systems than those who were not (Segerstrom & Sephton, 2010). Their immune systems fought more powerfully against a foreign body inserted into their skin, mimicking the response to a foreign body such as a virus or bacterium.

In addition, recent research has found that lung cancer patients with optimistic attitudes tend to live longer than cancer patients with pessimistic attitudes (Novotny et al., 2010). This optimistic attitude was not present only during the onset of disease, but 18 years prior, and the extension of life was present independent of the stage of cancer or whether or not the patient smoked. In addition, the five-year survival rate

^ Sometimes, we truly do base our **actions on reasoned, thoughtful decisions.**

of optimists was 32.9 percent as compared to pessimists who had a survival rate of 21.2 percent. The researchers suggested that the source of this difference may be that pessimistic patients tend to make poorer choices with regard to their cancer treatment. So, sometimes, your attitudes can impact behavior.

Have you ever made a decision after a long period of thoughtful deliberation? Let's take the example of a young woman mired in an emotionally abusive relationship with a boyfriend. She is seriously contemplating leaving him. Perhaps she writes a list of pros and cons about leaving him, and her list of pros—reasons why she should leave him—is much longer than the cons—reasons why she should stay with him. She then develops a positive attitude about the prospect of leaving him. She imagines what those who care about her would think if she left him. Surely her mother would be pleased. And her best friend would be happy as well because she wouldn't have to listen to them fighting all the time. This makes the young woman certain that she can leave her boyfriend, so she sets the intention to do so. The very next day she breaks off the relationship. The young woman breathes a sigh of relief. The deed is done.

The underlying structure of this rational process is what social psychologists refer to as the **theory of planned behavior** (Ajzen & Fishbein, 1977, 1980). This theory suggests that attitudes, social norms, and the perceived control of the individual lead to behavior. Behavioral options are considered, the consequences of each are weighed, and a decision on how to act is made. The theory of planned behavior, in addition, postulates that people will also consider the feasibility of performing the action before committing to it.

So, an intention to form a behavior will arise from this sort of reasoned thinking and will, according to the theory, involve three considerations—one's own attitudes toward the behavior, the attitudes of others toward that behavior (subjective norms), and the perceived feasibility of the behavior (the perceived behavioral control). The decision at which the young woman in the above example arrived was based on those three considerations—her own favorable attitude toward breaking up, the favorable attitudes of people she cares about regarding breaking up, and her belief that she could actually perform the behavior. In combination, these three factors tended to promote the occurrence of the behavior.

Why Attitudes Matter

Attitudes provide us with scaffolding with which to organize our world. For example, if you hold a particularly strong attitude about legalizing marijuana, and are presented with information that supports this attitude, you would tend to consider that information as more reliable than information that argues against your attitude (Munro & Ditto, 1997). Recall the discussion of the confirmation bias in Chapter 1—we tend to seek out and notice information that is consistent with the attitudes or beliefs that we hold. Attitudes also impact our concept of self (that you first learned about in Chapter 4). Attitudes that are important to us help make up our self-concept. Expression of these attitudes is a form of expressing our identity that can impact our self-esteem. For example, if an individual has a strong attitude about not eating animal products, being vegetarian or vegan is an important part of his or her self-concept, and behaviors such as wearing a t-shirt in support of vegetarianism reinforce that attitude.

The attitudes that we hold and that we publicly express impact our social interactions and how others form impressions of us. Attitudes, therefore, can be context-dependent, meaning that how strongly we appear to hold an attitude or whether or not we express an attitude may depend on the social environment that we are in (Schwarz & Bohner, 2001). For example, if you were being interviewed in a room with several individuals who had a very favorable attitude toward a political candidate, and you had a negative attitude toward that same candidate, you might not express your attitude.

FACTORS TO CONSIDER WHEN EVALUATING BEHAVIORS

We've discussed the ways in which attitudes contribute to planned behaviors, and why attitude is important in considering behaviors. There are several other factors we need to consider when evaluating whether our attitudes will correspond to our actual behaviors—strength of attitude, specificity, and accessibility.

Strength of Attitude

You have many different attitudes, and they inevitably vary with regard to how important they are to you. For instance, if you have a particularly strong attitude about the environment, you are more likely to act on that attitude as opposed to a weaker one. Why might this be? There are two reasons—the importance of the attitude to you personally and the extent to which these attitudes are formed based on direct experience.

Most people agree that children learn more in better schools. However, people are much more likely to support paying higher taxes for

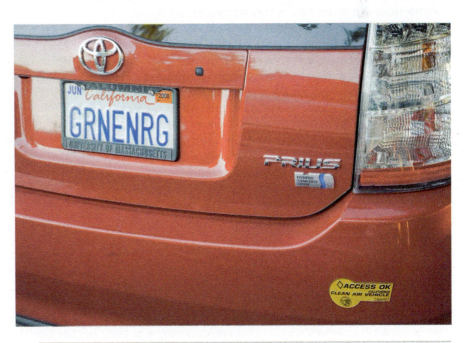

∧
∧ **People don't tend to act on a belief** if they only hold it
∧ halfheartedly.

ACCESSIBILITY the degree to which a concept is active in our consciousness

CHRONIC ACCESSIBILITY accessibility arising from frequent and recent exposure to a construct that has permanence—i.e., it is accessible all of the time

better schools if they have children in the public school system. This is because the issue of better schools is more personally relevant to people with children in the school system. This implies that if something is more important to you, it is going to have more of an impact on your behavior (Crano, 1997; Visser, Krosnick, & Simmons, 2003).

Additionally, if you have been inside a poorly funded school and have seen the quality of education and supplies the children receive, you are more likely to act in support of bettering these schools; for example, you might lobby for higher school taxes. This is because direct experience with an issue makes it more palpable—it can no longer be ignored. For instance, think about the spokespeople for various disease-related charities that you see. What do most have in common? Either they or a loved one have dealt with that disease. In this latter example, the issue is now both personal and one with which they have direct experience, and as such, these spokespeople are some of the most passionate, active supporters of their causes you will find.

> Direct experience with an issue makes it more palpable—**it can no longer be ignored.**

Specificity

Another factor that affects how strongly our attitudes predict behavior is how specific the attitude is. We've already learned that attitudes do not necessarily predict behavior; however, if the attitude is a specific one, tailored to you and a specific situation, it is more likely to predict your behavior. If you are asked, "How important is college to you?" you might give a stock answer that would please your parents. Instead, if you are asked, "How important is it to receive good grades this semester?" your answer may be quite different. College may be important to you, broadly speaking, but whether or not you are motivated to translate that into good grades right now is a very different issue. Similarly, asking participants about their attitudes toward donating money to a homeless shelter is a better indicator of the attitude-behavior link than asking how an individual feels about homeless people in general (Schwarz & Bohner, 2001).

In demonstration of this effect, a recent study asked college students, "How do you feel about using condoms?" Their responses were overwhelmingly positive, whereas their behavior in most cases did not correlate with their responses. However, when the question was posed more specifically, that is, "How do you feel about using condoms every time you have sex in the next month when you are with a new partner?", the participants' responses were much more consistent with their behaviors (Sheeran, Abraham, & Orbell, 1999). As such, when forced to think about specific behaviors at particular moments in time, people are much more likely to report attitudes that are consistent with their eventual behaviors.

Accessibility

Another factor that influences the tendency of our attitudes to impact our behavior is **accessibility** (Fazio, Chen, McDonel, & Sherman, 1982). Accessibility refers to the degree with which a concept is active in our consciousness (Higgins, Rholes, & Jones, 1977). Constructs are made accessible by frequent and/or recent exposure (Higgins & King, 1981). Fazio, Ledbetter, and Towles-Schwen (2000) (see Fazio, 1995 for a review of this concept) suggest that some attitudes we hold may be more accessible than others. For instance, if we are at a political rally, our attitudes about politics may be more accessible than our attitudes about particular types of television programming. A study of voter behavior during the 1984 presidential election showed that attitude accessibility affected the way people voted. People with relatively accessible attitudes (as a result of viewing a televised debate between the candidates) had greater attitude-behavior consistency than people with less accessible attitudes (Fazio & Williams, 1986).

Let's say you've been caring for a friend's pet snake while he's away on vacation for a week. After seeing the snake every day for a week and a half, you might be more likely to think you saw a snake on the ground if you encounter a strangely shaped stick. Not only will something that is accessible come to mind more often, but it will also come to mind more quickly. This is due to the concept of "snake" being **chronically accessible** in your mind. Frequent and recent exposure to a concept means the concept comes to mind more easily. As a student, you might often categorize individuals in terms of their intelligence, because you are in an environment in which you are constantly exposed to the concept of intelligence and measures of intelligence. When a concept is chronically accessible, we are more likely to describe others in terms of that concept (Higgins & King, 1981).

Accessibility of an attitude can directly impact its strength. Recent research demonstrated that when an attitude is made transiently accessible by repeated expression of it, people will report more commitment to the attitude (Holland, Verplanken, & van Knippenberg, 2003). By increasing the strength of the attitude, as mentioned earlier, it will be more likely to translate to behavior. More directly, the previously mentioned research by Fazio & Williams (1986) showed that accessibility can increase behavior toward the object of the attitude. During the 1984 presidential election, townspeople were polled on their attitudes toward the candidates, Ronald Reagan and Walter Mondale. Accessibility of these attitudes was assessed by determining the time it took people to answer questions about these attitudes—faster responses indicated higher accessibility. Subsequently, these people's perceptions of the candidates' performance in debates were assessed, and it was found that greater accessibility predicted a better perceived performance of the preferred candidate. Moreover, those whose attitudes toward their favored candidate were more accessible were more likely to actually vote when the election arrived. As such, accessibility helps attitudes to manifest in actual behavior.

When Does Behavior Influence Attitudes?

Attitudes are complex, and sometimes we may be unaware of them. We may even disagree with our own attitudes. But that doesn't necessarily mean that they're so deeply ingrained that we can't change them. In this section, we will discuss changes in attitudes due to self-persuasion. In Chapter 7, we'll explore the influence of other persuasion—when other individuals bring about a change in our attitudes or behaviors.

Read the following statements and rate how much you agree or disagree with them. **1** = strongly disagree, **2** = disagree, **3** = no opinion, **4** = agree, **5** = strongly agree

1. People talking on cell phones while driving can cause accidents.

2. Children are our future.

3. It is important to save our planet.

4. It is important to study hard.

Answer the following questions:

1. Do you drive while talking on your cell phone?

2. Do you personally spend time mentoring or working with children?

3. Do you engage in environmentally friendly behavior, like recycling?

4. Do you study hard for all of your classes, all of the time?

Are your attitudes consistent with your behavior? How does it make you feel? When you consider your actual behavior, does it make you reconsider how you feel about these issues?

Source: Carkenord, D.M., & Bullington, J. (1993). Bringing cognitive dissonance to the classroom. *Teaching of Psychology, 20,* 41-43.

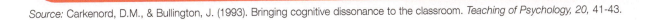

Awareness of Behavior and Attitude Change. Being aware of one's own behavior will often cause a person to modify his or her attitudes to accommodate that behavior as permissible (Carkenoid & Bullington, 1993). What will you do?

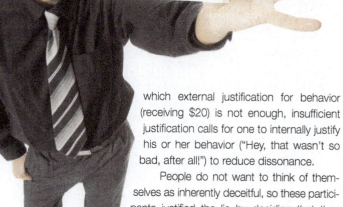

<<< **We look for explanations for our behavior—**and why would we do something for only a dollar?

COGNITIVE DISSONANCE

Did you ever think that if you were paid a lot of money for a task, you might actually like it less than somebody who is paid less money for the same task? It sounds backward, but turns out to be true. Researchers asked college student participants to complete a very boring task that was supposed to be so boring as to verge on unpleasant. Then they paid the participants either $20 or $1 to tell a lie to the next participant awaiting her turn at the study— that the task was actually enjoyable. Afterward, in a confidential interview, the participants who were paid $20 admitted that the task was actually boring. But, interestingly enough, the participants who were paid $1 claimed that the task was somewhat enjoyable (Festinger & Carlsmith, 1959).

Can you surmise why the participants who were paid $20 to lie admitted to being bored while the ones who were paid $1 to lie said that they enjoyed the task? The answer has to do with a concept called **cognitive dissonance**. Cognitive dissonance theory states that people want their behavior to be consistent with their beliefs, and feel uncomfortable with any inconsistency between the two. After all, if you believe something to be true, it would feel strange for you to act in a manner inconsistent with that truth. If people's behaviors are inconsistent (or dissonant), they feel the need to justify or rationalize their behavior. The people who were paid the $20 to lie had the payment as justification for lying. On the contrary, those who were paid $1 did not have a high amount of payment as justification for the lie. The people paid $1 had insufficient justification for telling the lie, so they experienced more discomfort (dissonance) and were more likely to adjust their attitudes to match their behaviors. In situations in which external justification for behavior (receiving $20) is not enough, insufficient justification calls for one to internally justify his or her behavior ("Hey, that wasn't so bad, after all!") to reduce dissonance.

People do not want to think of themselves as inherently deceitful, so these participants justified the lie by deciding that they *actually enjoyed the task*. It is worth noting that no participant cited what is perhaps the truest justification for the lie—that he or she was in the role of "subject" and felt compelled to do what the experimenter asked. Thus, people can be ignorant of the true reasons for their behavior, and in the absence of such information will fill in the blanks with what they *need* to believe is true.

These findings on cognitive dissonance have been used to attempt to promote healthy behaviors in young people by making them aware of the inconsistency between their attitudes and behaviors. In one study, researchers asked sexually active college students to volunteer to develop a speech advocating condom use to other sexually active college students (Stone, Aronson, Crain, Winslow, & Fried, 1994). Students either gave the speech in front of a video camera that they were led to believe would be used to advocate condom use to others, or created the speech but were not led to believe that it would be used for advocacy. In addition, some students were made to read a list of reasons why some young people do not use condoms, to make them mindful of the reasons for condom use failure, while others did not read this list. Students were then asked to indicate how often they used condoms in the past and how often they intended to use them in the future. Finally, students were given the opportunity to discreetly purchase condoms.

Those who were made mindful of the reasons why students do not use condoms, evoking some of the reasons that they themselves have not— and also gave the speech advocating for condom use—were the most likely to purchase condoms at the end of the study and bought the most condoms of any group. In fact, 94 percent of participants in this group made some effort toward condom use, either buying condoms or taking home informational pamphlets. In this way, those who were aware that their own

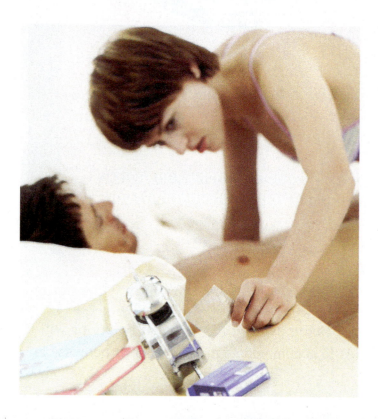

<<< Cognitive dissonance can actually help people **act more in line with their attitudes, such as the importance of safe sex.**

past behavior violated their beliefs about condoms took action to bring their behaviors in line with their beliefs, thereby reducing cognitive dissonance.

In another study that attempted to improve behavior by inducing feelings of hypocrisy—that you say one thing and do another—researchers asked people who were environmentally conscious about their water usage in the shower (Dickerson, Thibodeau, Aronson, & Miller, 1992). Those who were reminded of their own excessive water usage and asked to make a public commitment to take shorter showers, and thus made to feel hypocritical if they took long showers, later took significantly shorter showers than those either not reminded of their usage or not asked to make a commitment. The participants who took shorter showers wanted to rid themselves of the cognitive dissonance they felt between their own environmentally conscious beliefs and the fact that they took long showers.

Sometimes all it takes is effort to make something seem worthwhile. When we spend a lot of time and energy making something happen, we more often than not see value in that accomplishment—even if we shouldn't. Why? Because working hard to achieve something and then finding it wasn't worth the effort is a sure source of cognitive dissonance. To combat this, we justify effort that was spent. This is referred to as effort justification.

An illustration of this concept comes in the form of a study concerning people who were trying to lose weight. Participants were asked to complete high- or low-effort cognitive tasks, none of which were actually proven to help with weight loss. People who completed the high-effort tasks lost an average of over eight pounds, while those who spent less time on low-effort tasks didn't lose weight (Axsom & Cooper, 1985).

In addition to altering our behaviors, dissonance plays a role in affecting our attitudes toward the choices we have already made, as described earlier. Imagine you have been asked to make a choice between two posters to decorate your dorm room. You like both posters equally, but you only have enough space for one. After you've made your decision, you may find that you now like your selected poster better and have a lower opinion of the rejected one. **Post-decision dissonance** results from having to reject one appealing choice in favor of another. To combat this, we enhance our opinions of what we've chosen to justify our choice cognitively.

In a recent study, researchers had participants rate a series of photographs, then choose between pairs of them, and then rate them again. Those who were chosen experienced an increase in rating from the first rating to the second, and those who were not chosen experienced a decrease in rating. Notably, this effect occurred even in amnesiacs who could not remember which items they chose and which they did not. As such, the change in evaluation that occurs when we make a choice occurs relatively unconsciously (Lieberman, Ochsner, Gilbert, & Schacter, 2001).

Interestingly, though, dissonance effects are limited in collectivist cultures. Indeed, Japanese participants were found to only engage in dissonance-reducing attitude changes after being asked to consider the preferences of a self-relevant other person (Kitayama, Snibbe, Markus, & Suzuki, 2004)—that is, they engaged in dissonance-reducing techniques to please others and therefore justify their collectivist ideals. In this way, people from such cultures can believe that what they want is truly what the group wants.

Since the inception of the theory of cognitive dissonance, some modifications to the theory have been provided. One notable modification postulated a four-step model by which attitude change occurs (Cooper & Fazio, 1984):

1. The individual must realize that the attitude-discrepant action has negative consequences.
2. The individual must take personal responsibility for the action.
3. The individual must experience physiological arousal.
4. The individual must attribute the arousal to the action.

POST-DECISION DISSONANCE cognitive dissonance that results from having to reject one appealing choice in favor of another

All four of these factors must be in place for attitude change to occur. Yet, this theory does not take into account the ability of cognitive dissonance to change behavior instead of attitudes. One possible factor may be the extent to which the behavior can be changed—have you made an unalterable choice or taken an unalterable action, or might you change your behaviors in the future? Future research, perhaps, can more precisely delineate when each one will change and when each one will not.

The photo here shows an image of one of Aesop's famous fables. If you are not familiar with it, the story is about a fox who looks longingly at a bunch of grapes and tries repeatedly to reach them. After several attempts he gives up and says, "They must have been sour anyway."

LE RENARD ET LES RAISINS. Fable LIII.

 When something is unattainable, **we tend to devalue it.**

Cognitive dissonance operates in this way—making us believe that we wanted all along what we have and did not want what we do not have.

If you are interested in reading more about cognitive dissonance, you may be interested in the 2007 book *Mistakes Were Made (But Not By Me)*, by Carol Tavris and Elliot Aronson. It describes real-world examples of cognitive dissonance in politics. Cognitive dissonance enables our attitudes to shift so that we are more content with our lot in life than we might otherwise be. In addition, it can compel behavioral change that makes people act more in line with how they wish to behave.

> "Cognitive dissonance enables our attitudes to shift so **that we are more content with our lot in life than we might otherwise be.**"

In the "new look" at cognitive dissonance mentioned earlier, social psychologists Joel Cooper and Russell Fazio (1984) describe four steps involved in the arousal and reduction of cognitive dissonance. First, a behavior that doesn't match an attitude must cause *negative consequences*. Remember those study participants who were offered money to lie about the experiment being interesting? Then, there must be a feeling of *personal responsibility* for the negative outcome of the behavior. For this to happen, the person must feel that he or she had a choice in the matter and that the consequences were to some degree foreseeable. The people who were given $1 to lie about the experiment felt guilty about lying—they were given the choice to lie and knew there would be negative consequences.

The third step in the new model is physiological *arousal*. Cognitive dissonance causes physical discomfort and tension—of course you want to reduce it. Finally, there must be an *attribution* of the arousal to the behavior. The people who got $1 for lying to the next participant knew they felt bad because of what they had done.

Alternative Methods of Self-Persuasion

Cognitive dissonance is just one theory of attitude change. Other researchers have proposed theories to address how behavior may lead to attitude change. Self-perception theory (to which you were first exposed in Chapter 4) suggests that we infer our own attitudes by observing our own behaviors (Bem, 1967, 1972). For instance, if we see ourselves opening the cover of a book we've already read, we may then infer that we really like that book. This theory originated from the idea that

we can infer the true thoughts of others in many cases simply by observing their behavior, without access to their internal states; therefore we should not need access to our own either. Also, emotions often follow rather than precede behaviors, arising as a result of interpreting our behaviors. For example, if people are made to smile while watching something, they will report liking it more than if they are made to frown (e.g., Laird, 2007). Thus, under self-perception theory, attitudes can be adjusted by altering one's behavior.

Stuart Valins demonstrated this theory in an experiment involving male college students. The students were invited to view a series of "centerfolds" while hooked up to electrodes assumed to be measuring their heartbeats. In reality, the experimenter was in control of varying the "heartbeats." While a man looked at a randomly selected photo in the series, the experimenter would speed up the pace of the heartbeat reading, leading the men to believe their heart rates were speeding up in response to viewing one particular photo. When they were invited to take one of the photos home, which do you think they chose? Of course, the vast majority of the men chose the photo they thought got their heart rates revved up, believing this was the photo they liked the most (Valins, 1966).

Once we establish a sense of self, we are motivated to maintain it and reaffirm it. **Self-affirmation theory** (Steele, 1988) states that, in the face of threat, people will try to restore their self-worth by reaffirming their values. But how does this relate to shifting attitudes? Under normal circumstances, people are motivated to maintain existing beliefs as a way of affirming their understanding of themselves. However, if people are allowed to affirm their sense of self in some other way—for instance, by the acquisition of a symbol reflecting a value such as a degree if they place value on their intelligence, or even by thinking or talking about an important part of their identity—they are more open to others' ideas and will process those ideas in less biased ways, opening themselves up to attitude change (Correll, Spencer, & Zanna, 2004).

We are not only concerned with understanding ourselves, but also with how others perceive us. People must create and maintain impressions of themselves that match how they want others to understand them, as described by the theory of **impression management** (e.g., Piwinger & Ebert, 2001). Impression management states that people either consciously or unconsciously attempt to monitor how they appear to others by regulating the information conveyed about themselves in a social interaction. Research suggests that attitudinal shift as a result of cognitive dissonance is much more likely to occur when the counterattitudinal behavior is conducted publicly (Gaes, Kalle, & Tedeschi, 1978). As a result, we are more concerned with appearing consistent with our attitudes to others than we are with actually being consistent, and that concern can drive attitude change.

In many ways, our attitudes define who we are. Attitudes, behavior, and cognition have a reciprocal relationship with one another—it's safe to say you can't study one without studying the others. Research on attitudes helps us to understand our behaviors and interactions with one another. In fact, you might see attitudes as the root of social interactions. Everything we say and do starts with an attitude, whether negative, positive, or somewhere in between. Research allows us to not only understand how attitudes, behaviors, and cognition interact with each other, it also allows an opportunity for change. The more we know about our attitudes and how they are linked (or not linked) to our behaviors, the more resources we will have for ensuring that our attitudes and subsequent behaviors reflect ourselves.

Cognitive Dissonance

Cognitive dissonance is a theory of self-persuasion. When your attitude is inconsistent with your behavior, you are likely to experience an unpleasant feeling (dissonance) and will try to bring your attitude more in line with your behavior. Consider a current behavior that you have that you would like to change (because it is inconsistent with your attitude). For example, maybe your attitude is that you would like to be healthier, but you eat a lot of fast food meals or you don't exercise. Or maybe your attitude is that you care about the environment, but you currently do not recycle. You could just change

your attitude, but for this project we want to bring about a behavioral change. For one week, change your behavior. Plan a healthy diet, exercise daily, or recycle all your plastics. This may be difficult to do, so pick a simple behavior and stick to it. Make a public commitment by writing down the steps you will take to change your behavior. When you feel tempted to return to old behaviors, think about times in the past you've engaged in those behaviors and how you felt when you realized that they were inconsistent with your attitude.

At the end of the week, note your attitude toward the behavior. Now that you have

modified your behavior, how do you feel? Did the attitude grow stronger, or stay the same strength? Did you make cognitive dissonance work for you?

What you will learn from this action learning project:

1. How to bring about a change in your behavior
2. How powerful self-persuasion can be
3. How being aware of discrepancies between actions and attitudes can help you to act more in line with your attitudes

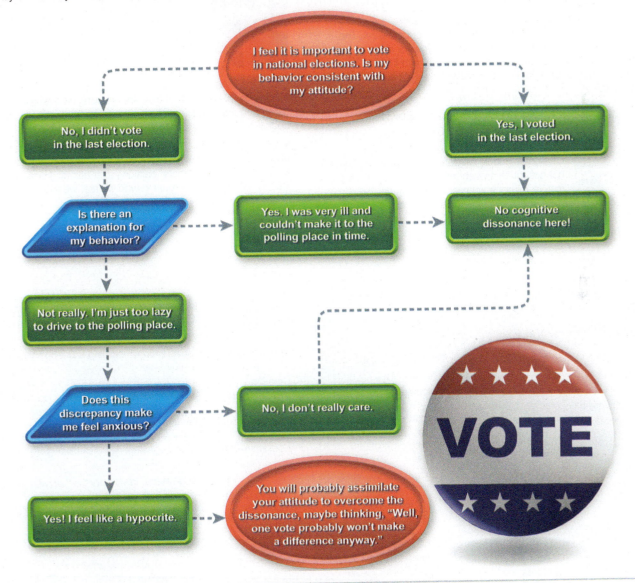

Rock the Vote. Cognitive dissonance operates by arousing anxiety due to an inconsistency between behavior and attitude that we are motivated to eliminate.

06

Review

Summary

HOW DO ATTITUDES DEVELOP?   p. 96

• One way that attitudes can arise is due to conditioning—either classical or operant. Classical conditioning creates an association between two mutually occurring events, while operant conditioning increases or decreases the frequency of a behavior with reinforcements and punishments.

• Attitudes can also arise due to observational learning, wherein we internalize the attitudes of others. In this way, attitudes can be passed on from one person to another.

• Attitudes can be held explicitly (those that are consciously known) or implicitly (associations of which people may not be aware). The methods necessary to assess these different types of attitudes vary considerably. Explicit attitudes can be assessed with simple self-report measures, while implicit attitudes require a subtle method such as the IAT.

DO ATTITUDES INFLUENCE BEHAVIOR?   p. 101

• Attitudes do not inherently imply behavior. Oftentimes people will believe in a cause or principle but not act on it when the opportunity arises. Many factors influence whether or not attitudes will come to impact behavior. The core factors are the strength of the attitude, the specificity of the attitude to the behavior in question, the accessibility of the attitude, and the result of rational decision making.

• The stronger an attitude is, the more likely it is to translate into behavior. Likewise, the more specific the attitude is to the circumscribed behavior, the more it will be relevant for that behavior. The easier an attitude is to bring to mind, whether because of repeated exposure to it or recent exposure to it (both of which increase accessibility), the more it will influence behavior. Finally, if rational thought leads to the decision that a behavior should be done based upon a held attitude, and it is decided that the behavior can be done, it is more likely that the behavior will arise.

WHEN DOES BEHAVIOR INFLUENCE ATTITUDES?   p. 104

• One way in which attitude change occurs is via cognitive dissonance. If people find that they are behaving in a way that is inconsistent with their attitudes, they will shift their attitudes to better match the behavior. This can be used to impact behavior as well, by making people aware that they are behaving inconsistently with a cared-about attitude. In addition, the tendency to be affected by cognitive dissonance is affected by culture.

• Our attitudes can also shift based on observations of our own behavior, our motivation to appear in a particular way to others, or by being more open to others' opinions after affirming core parts of our identity. When we are secure in who we are, we feel freer to consider others' ideas.

Key Terms

accessibility the degree to which a concept is active in our consciousness   104

ambivalence simultaneously experiencing strong contradictory emotions or motivations   96

attitudes having an evaluative component toward a stimulus that is made up of affective, behavioral, and cognitive information   96

chronic accessibility accessibility arising from frequent and recent exposure to a construct that has permanence—that is, it is accessible all of the time   104

classical conditioning a type of learning by which a neutral stimulus (UCS) gets paired with a stimulus that elicits a response (UCR). Through repeated pairings, the neutral stimulus (CS) by itself elicits the response (CR) of the second stimulus   98

cognitive dissonance the anxiety that arises from acting in a way discordant with your attitudes. This anxiety is resolved by adjusting one's attitudes to be in line with the behavior.   106

conditioned response (CR) a learned response to the conditioned stimulus that was previously a neutral stimulus   98

conditioned stimulus (CS) a stimulus that, only by repeated association with a particular unconditioned stimulus, comes to evoke the response associated with the unconditioned stimulus   98

explicit attitudes attitudes of which one is aware, and that one can control   96

Implicit Association Test (IAT) test that measures how easily we associate categories with positive or negative attitudes, including measures in categories ranging from racial and religious attitudes to attitudes about presidents. https://implicit.harvard.edu/implicit/demo/   101

implicit attitudes attitudes that are automatically formed and activated without our even being aware of it   96

impression management the process by which people either consciously or unconsciously attempt to monitor how they appear to others by regulating the information conveyed about themselves in a social interaction, and thus attitude change is more likely when counterattitudinal behavior occurs in public   108

mere exposure effect the phenomenon whereby objects become better-liked with exposure—we like things more with which we are familiar   98

name-letter effect the tendency to show a preference for letters in our own name and prefer stimuli that contain those letters   98

observational learning acquiring an attitude or behavior due to the observation of others exhibiting that attitude or behavior   99

operant conditioning a type of learning in which the frequency of a behavior is determined by reinforcement and punishment   99

post-decision dissonance cognitive dissonance that results from having to reject one appealing choice in favor of another   107

self-affirmation theory the theory that we are more open to attitudinal change when we have recently been given an opportunity to affirm our core values and identity   108

theory of planned behavior the theory that attitudes, social norms, and the perceived control of the individual lead to behavior   103

unconditioned response (UCR) a response that occurs automatically in reaction to some stimulus, without learning taking place   98

unconditioned stimulus (UCS) a stimulus that elicits a response automatically, without learning taking place   98

Test Your Understanding

MULTIPLE CHOICE

1. Which of these methods is best at measuring implicit attitudes?
   a. observation
   b. self-report
   c. introspection
   d. the IAT

2. Which of these events are we most likely to remember?
   a. the A we got in social psychology
   b. the F we got in social psychology
   c. the sound of a clock ticking
   d. the hue of the color magenta

3. You are afraid of thunder. I decide that every time there is a thunderstorm, I will make you hold a rabbit. Now you also fear rabbits. The rabbit is the:
   a. unconditioned stimulus
   b. unconditioned response
   c. conditioned stimulus
   d. conditioned response

4. You made me a delicious dinner. Since I want more dinners made for me, I bring you wine and smile a lot when you cook for me. What am I doing?
   a. positive reinforcement
   b. negative reinforcement
   c. positive punishment
   d. negative punishment

5. Cognitive dissonance causes people to strive to diminish which personality trait?
   a. guilt
   b. hypocrisy
   c. fear
   d. prejudice

6. Why do implicit attitudes influence behavior?
   a. because associations in memory are activated outside of awareness
   b. because we endorse implicit attitudes
   c. because we mimic these attitudes in others
   d. implicit attitudes do not influence behavior

7. Hotel owners did not keep the Chinese couple from staying at their hotels in the research by LaPiere (1934). Which is least likely to be the reason?
   a. the couple exhibited kindness
   b. the couple spoke proper English
   c. the generality of the stereotype versus the specificity of the couple
   d. the owners really didn't mean it when they said they wouldn't admit a Chinese couple

8. Which influences the impact of attitudes on behavior the least?
   a. strength of the attitude
   b. specificity of the attitude
   c. superordinance of the attitude
   d. accessibility of the attitude

9. When you act in a way that is different from how you believe you should, you:
   a. change your behavior
   b. change your attitude
   c. a or b, depending on whether or not the behavior can be changed and the strength of the attitude
   d. neither a nor b

10. What is the best way to get others to listen to your opinions, based on attitude research?
    a. talk louder
    b. allow them to do something affirming their own beliefs
    c. try to provide proof for your opinions
    d. show them that most people share your opinion

ESSAY RESPONSE

1. If some attitudes are acquired through conditioning, consider how we might overcome or undo attitudes that have negative impacts on our lives, such as prejudice.

2. Discuss how observational learning can overcome phobias.

3. When might attitudes influence behavior versus not?

4. Think about how cognitive dissonance operates in the workplace. What from this chapter explains why paying employees more for better work is effective? How might employers increase workplace enjoyment, given that paying employees for work may reduce enjoyment of the tasks themselves?

5. Consider how impression management can impact your attitudes. What does it mean for the self and social relations to say that we change attitudes more when we behave counter-attitudinally in public?

APPLY IT!

Think about your attitude toward school. Regardless of how positive or negative it is, what factors contributed to your acquisition of this attitude? Might conditioning or observational learning have played a role? Might cognitive dissonance be responsible for any decrements in your attitude toward school, perhaps after attending a few parties instead of studying? Or might impression management have kept any positive aspects of your attitude intact?

ANSWERS: 1. d; 2. b; 3. c; 4. a; 5. b; 6. a; 7. d; 8. c; 9. c; 10. b

Remember to check www.thinkspot.com for additional information, downloadable flashcards, and other helpful resources.

APPLYING SOCIAL PSYCHOLOGY
Health

When diagnosing a patient, health psychologists take psychosocial factors, such as stress, into consideration.

When your parents or grandparents visited the doctor, they were probably asked about their medical histories, diets, and any genetic disorders. Today, medical doctors are increasingly incorporating a holistic view of health based on the biopsychosocial model—a concept that views health as the product of a combination of factors, including biological characteristics (for example, genetic predispositions), behavioral issues (for example, stress and relationships), and social conditions (for example, family support or cultural influences). As such, a visit to a doctor today might include questions about one's lifestyle and any recent stressful events. The biopsychosocial model is the underlying concept behind the emerging discipline of health psychology.

In a fast-paced world, we increasingly encounter stress—an unpleasant physical response to events that make us feel threatened or upset our balance in some way. Losing a job, dealing with a troubled family member, coping with financial difficulties, going through a divorce, or grieving the death of a close friend are all common causes of stress. According to a 2008 survey by the American Psychological Association, money and the economy are the top two causes of stress in the United States (Wilbert, 2008). Stress triggers can be divided into three main categories: crises or catastrophes (a natural disaster, motor vehicle accident, or terrorist attack), major life events (the death of a spouse, a divorce, or job loss), and daily stressors (car problems, work issues, waiting in lines, or environmental factors such as noise, heat, and cold). Why do some people seem to bounce back from major catastrophes while others fall apart over minor, daily stresses? Social psychology can help us understand these differences, aiding in the treatment of physical symptoms that manifest as a result of stress. It can also be applied to the health industry in an effort to prevent health problems, as in the following example.

> " Why do some people seem to bounce back from major catastrophes while others fall apart over minor, daily stresses? "

Social psychologists often investigate the effectiveness of various methods of prevention with regard to health and well-being. For instance, most people would agree that reducing teen pregnancy rates is a desirable goal, but what is the best way to go about it? Some schools advocate abstinence-only programs, which focus on encouraging students to refrain from sexual activity until marriage and avoid discussing the use of contraceptives. However, research suggests that abstinence-only education may not be the most effective method of preventing teen pregnancy. Those who receive abstinence-only education are no more likely than those in a control group to abstain from sexual activity or delay the start of sexual activity (Trenholm, Devaney, Fortson, Quay, Wheeler, & Clark, 2007). Instead, studies suggest that comprehensive sexual education classes, which not only promote abstinence but also teach about contraception, sexually transmitted diseases, and relationships, are more effective at reducing teen pregnancy rates (Kohler, Manhart, & Lafferty, 2008).

In addition to researching the effectiveness of various methods of prevention, social psychologists are also involved with changing people's attitudes toward serious health problems and minimizing risk-taking behavior. A key area of research is the prevention of HIV—a virus transmitted through blood, semen, breast milk, and vaginal secretions that may lie dormant for many years but ultimately ravages the body's immune system in the form of AIDS. Over the past 30 years, the number of reported cases of AIDS in the United States has increased from 189 people in 1981 to 470,902 people at the end of 2007 (Avert, 2010). Worldwide, the number of new infections continues to climb in parts of Latin America, North Africa, the Middle East, Eastern Europe, and parts of Asia. Social psychologists have found that the most effective way to prevent the spread of HIV and AIDS is to alter people's beliefs, motivations, and risk-taking behaviors regarding the disease (Gerrard, Gibbons, & Bushman, 1996). Jeffrey Fisher and his

> **The students who publicly advocated the use of condoms and were reminded of their past failures to use them were more likely to buy condoms than those who were not made aware of their hypocritical behavior.**

colleagues (2002) demonstrated this theory by setting up HIV prevention programs in four urban high schools. The programs provided students with accurate information about the disease, motivated students to engage in HIV-preventative behavior, and provided them with the behavioral skills necessary to follow through (i.e., how to use condoms). Fisher found that for an estimated cost of $2.22 per student, condom use increased up to a year later.

Researchers have also found cognitive dissonance—the theory of self-persuasion you learned about in Chapter 6 that states it is uncomfortable to hold two conflicting ideas simultaneously—to be an effective method of influencing people's health-related behavior. Jeff Stone and his colleagues (1994) asked 72 sexually active college students to write a persuasive speech about the importance of safe sex as a method of preventing the transmission of HIV. Half of the participants were filmed giving their speech and told that it would be shown to high school students. They were then asked to make a list of the times that they had failed to use condoms in the past, as a way of making them feel hypocritical about their previous behavior. Later, they were given the opportunity to buy condoms. Stone noted that the students who publicly advocated the use of condoms and were reminded of their past failures to use them were more likely to buy condoms than those who were not made aware of their hypocritical behavior. Similar experiments with cognitive dissonance have been used to help prevent eating disorders (Stice, Trost, & Chase, 2003). Developing techniques to encourage prevention of risky behaviors is just one example of the many useful ways social psychology can be put to practical use in the health industry.

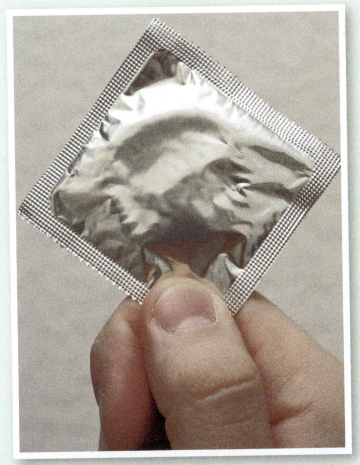

The social psychological theory of cognitive dissonance can be useful in promoting prevention of risky behaviors among college students.

THE POWER OF
PERSUASION

<<< ***Why are flowers the Mother's Day gift of choice?***

WHAT ARE PERSUASIVE MESSAGES, AND WHICH ARE THE MOST EFFECTIVE?
WHAT DOES RESEARCH TELL US ABOUT RESISTING PERSUASION TACTICS?
WHEN SHOULDN'T WE RESIST PERSUASION?

How did

you celebrate last Mother's Day? Did you buy flowers, cards, and trinkets for your mother, grandmother, or any other special women in your life? Did you treat one of these ladies to one of the many well-advertised Mother's Day brunches at a local restaurant?

Overall, U.S. citizens spent nearly $14 billion on Mother's Day gifts in 2009 (Kristof, 2010). According to Nicholas D. Kristof, an op-ed columnist for the *New York Times*, this money could pay for the primary education of 60 million girls around the world currently not attending school—effectively ending female illiteracy. Billions of dollars go toward chocolate, roses, and greeting cards, and to what end? Do these material items contribute to the well-being of the world's mothers and future mothers?

In addition to noting the impact this money could have on illiteracy, Kristof notes that there are other worthy causes that are more deserving of this money than a card that may well find its way into the recycling bin. He suggests that the money spent on one Mother's Day could instead go toward medical procedures that could improve the lives of mothers globally as well as save them from maternal complications. And, says Kristof, wouldn't this be a better way to honor the mothers of the world?

When put so simply, it seems obvious what the answer *should* be. So why do we find ourselves pouring money into Hallmark instead of global efforts to reduce maternal mortality? The answer is in persuasion. Card stores, gift shops, and florists remind us: "Don't forget Mother's Day!"—and they let us know just how to go about making sure we do not do so.

CHAPTER 07

PERSUASION the way people communicate in order to influence other people's attitudes and behaviors

CENTRAL ROUTE a type of processing that occurs when an individual has the ability and motivation to thoroughly listen to and evaluate a persuasive message

PERIPHERAL ROUTE a type of processing that occurs when an individual lacks the ability and motivation to thoroughly listen to and evaluate a persuasive message and is, therefore, influenced by external cues like attractiveness of the speaker

What Are Persuasive Messages?

What are you wearing? Why did you purchase these items? Did you do it because you really like the way your shoes and shirt look and fit? Or did you see a similar style in a magazine and decide it was a good look?

Now scroll through your iPod. Why did you download these songs? Did you find them on your own? Or did a friend recommend that you listen to them? Maybe you heard a song played on a television show, like "Bad Things" by Jace Everett, which spiked in popularity after becoming the theme song for the HBO show "True Blood." Most of us would like to believe that we are independent thinkers, but persuasive forces are all around us. They're in our homes, governments, schools, and the media.

The study of **persuasion**, or the way people communicate in order to influence other people's attitudes and behaviors, started as a central focus of social psychology after World War II prompted an interest in the power of persuasive propaganda. Interest in persuasion has continued to grow since then, particularly in the past few years as the economic crisis that peaked in 2008 has prompted Americans to question how and why we spend our money.

It's no surprise that we do not always spend our money in the most practical of manners. Persuasive forces can provoke irrational spending. What do you think of Kristof's ideas? Has he persuaded you to swap the standard dozen roses and Mother's Day card for an honorary donation to a worldwide educational fund? Probably not, given the amount of time you have spent convinced of the worth of flowers and cards as well as your mother's probable expectations of what constitutes a proper gift. However, if you (and she) haven't yet been persuaded by Kristof's message, it doesn't mean that you will never be convinced. As you will learn in this chapter, it's not always what is said, but how it's said, when it's said, and who says it that carries the power of persuasion.

ROUTES TO PERSUASION

We all want to have what are the "right" attitudes and opinions, but the potential number of issues on which we can have an opinion is infinite. It is nearly impossible to carefully scrutinize every message or evaluate all of the evidence when trying to arrive at a well thought-out opinion, so in our search for what is "right," we must compromise by paying more attention to some information than we do to other information. Early research by Carl Hovland and colleagues (1949, 1953) resulted in the Yale Communication

>>> Do you choose the clothes you wear or **do clothing companies choose for you?**

∧
∧ Sex is a popular method of persuasion
∧ **because it doesn't just sell consumers a product;** it sells them a desired lifestyle.

Model, suggesting that a message will be accepted based on three factors—the communicator of the message, the content of the message, and the audience receiving the message. This research was only the start. But before beginning to understand when people accept persuasive messages, it is important to understand what cognitive faculties enable or disable persuasion. Dual process models of persuasion propose that it occurs through one of two routes—central or peripheral (e.g., Eagly & Chaiken, 1993, 1998; Petty & Cacioppo, 1981).

The **central route** is a type of processing that occurs when an individual has the ability and motivation to thoroughly listen to and evaluate a persuasive message. When booking a hotel for an upcoming vacation, a person using the central route might research the best rates, read several Trip Advisor reviews, and evaluate the amenities available at each option. This is the more analytical approach. Richard Petty and colleagues (2004) argue that attitudes that are developed as a result of using the central route to persuasion "will be more persistent over time, will remain more resistant to persuasion, and will exert a greater impact on cognition and behavior" (p. 75) in comparison to attitudes that are affected by using the peripheral route. For example, if you carefully consider the benefits of donating your Mother's Day gift money to a women's charity, weighing them against the cons, and decide to donate, you are more likely to continue to donate for years to come.

The **peripheral route** is the opposite of the central route. It is a type of processing that occurs when an individual lacks the ability and motivation to thoroughly listen to and evaluate a persuasive message and is therefore influenced only by external cues. Using the previous example, a person using this route might book a hotel based on the flashy photos on the hotel's Web site, a fun-sounding name, or other external factors. This approach involves using more superficial information to make decisions. For example, if you see a beautiful bouquet of flowers and a sign that says, "Give your mom the gift of flowers," you might be more likely to buy these for your mother than you are to donate to a charity in her name.

As a result of peripheral-route processing, several counterintuitive effects can emerge. If we are presented with a poor argument that is presented in an attractive manner, such as an effort to make us buy a flashy car with low gas mileage, we may be persuaded if we process with the peripheral route. In addition, a non-credible source may persuade us if the argument is strong and we process it via the central route; for example, a random college student might make a compelling argument for a political position that, after much deliberation, we decide is correct.

As stated, opinions adopted due to central-route processing are more resistant to change. The reason for this is that when people have the available cognitive resources with which to consider an issue, they rely on the message as well as their own reflections. The more deeply an individual thinks about an issue, the more that attitude will resist change since the issue was considered more carefully. Keep in mind, however, that the link between attitudes and actual behavior can be influenced by other factors, as we saw in Chapter 6. If we must make a snap judgment, even messages adopted via the peripheral route can bring about a change in behavior. For example, if you had to choose a professor but did not have time to thoroughly research each one, how would you select among them? You may decide on an instructor simply because one of your friends said he was a "fun" professor. Of course, as we saw in Chapter 4, first impressions may not always be accurate, so peripheral-route processing is not always best.

> **ELABORATION LIKELIHOOD MODEL (ELM)** a model of persuasion that proposes that there are two different routes, central and peripheral, that an individual may take when processing a message. The route is impacted by cognitive capacity and individual differences of the perceiver

So when do we use one route versus the other? This can be explained by the **Elaboration Likelihood Model (ELM)**, the most prevalent of which is Petty and Cacioppo's 1981 model. The ELM provides a general framework for organizing and understanding the basic processes underlying the effectiveness of persuasive communication by emphasizing how people react to persuasive communication (Petty & Cacioppo, 1986). According to the model, people react to persuasive communication by reflecting on different aspects of a persuasive message as a function of their involvement in the message content and their ability to process the message.

WHAT INFLUENCES WHICH ROUTE WE TAKE?

There are several factors that influence whether we process information via the central or peripheral route.

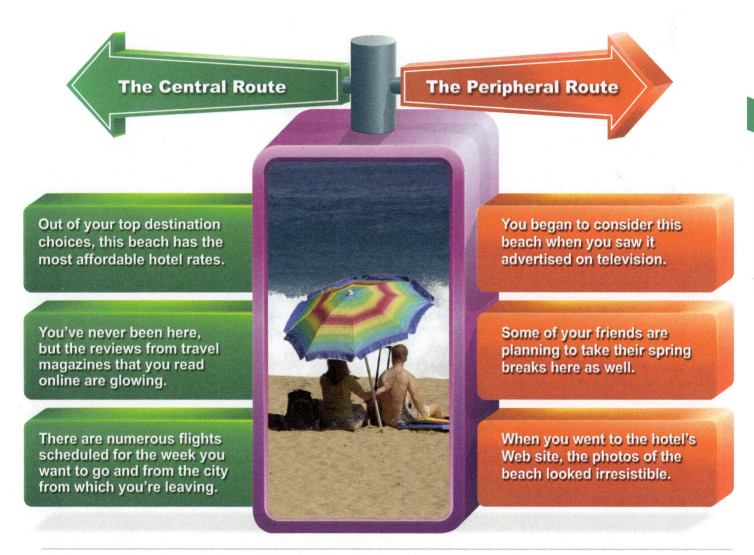

The Central Route

Out of your top destination choices, this beach has the most affordable hotel rates.

You've never been here, but the reviews from travel magazines that you read online are glowing.

There are numerous flights scheduled for the week you want to go and from the city from which you're leaving.

The Peripheral Route

You began to consider this beach when you saw it advertised on television.

Some of your friends are planning to take their spring breaks here as well.

When you went to the hotel's Web site, the photos of the beach looked irresistible.

∧∧∧ **Which Way to Spring Break?** When choosing your last spring break destination, **what types of information influenced you more?**

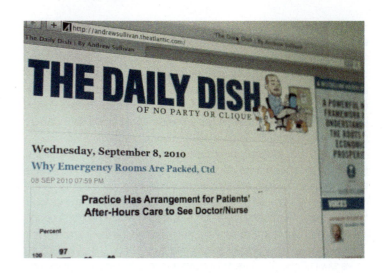

The Source

When it comes to persuasive messages, who the message comes from can be just as important as what is said. The person or organization who delivers the message is called the **source**. The source may be an actor in a commercial, a celebrity spokesperson, or a major media outlet. Much like the packaging on a product, the attractiveness of the source can enhance the power of a persuasive message. This factor is the reason why young, attractive models are used in print ads and television commercials. Apple did not hire Gisele Bündchen for their "Get a Mac" campaign because of her knowledge of computers; they hired her because her physical attractiveness has the power to persuade consumers. Research supports this idea; in a study that asked participants to collect signatures for a petition, researchers found that the success rate was 41 percent for attractive participants and only 32 percent for unattractive participants (Eagly & Chaiken, 1993). We will further explore the impact of attractiveness on social perception in Chapter 12, including if attractiveness can, at times, be a liability.

> "*Apple did not hire Gisele Bündchen for their 'Get a Mac' campaign because of her knowledge of computers;* they hired her because her physical attractiveness has the power to persuade consumers."

The limitations of attractiveness are revealed when an individual has a reason to value the credibility of the source. For example, you would likely take advice from David Beckham on which soccer ball is best for your intramural team, but you might not take his advice on how to rewire a light switch. If you read that a celebrity couple was breaking up, you'd be more likely to believe the rumor if it was written in *The New York Times* than if it was posted on a random celebrity gossip message board. Similarly, you would be more likely to follow skin care advice from a board-certified dermatologist than a cosmetic company representative at a department store. The credibility of a source is an important variable in persuasion. In most cases, the source's credibility is a boon to message persuasiveness (see Pornpitakpan, 2004 for a review), and credibility can be increased by factors such as whether or not the source is perceived as having authority (e.g., Kelman & Hovland, 1953), discussed more in depth later in this chapter. A decrease in credibility can have a tremendous impact. For instance, from 2002 to 2006, the war on terror prompted a marked decrease in perceived credibility of information coming from the White House, both among American citizens and foreigners, and this may have had a negative impact on foreign relations (Corman, Hess, & Justus, 2006).

However, credibility's impact can wane. Research has shown that credibility has a **sleeper effect** (Hovland & Weiss, 1951). In other words, if you learn after receiving a message that the source is of low credibility,

 Do you consider blogs a credible source for late-breaking news?

at the time you will discount the message, but over time you will tend to increasingly support it. The sleeper effect is less likely to occur if a person is informed of the source beforehand than if they receive the message and then find out the source. For example, Justin Long is known for being an actor, not a computer expert. But the more we see his Mac versus PC television commercials, the easier it becomes for us to accept his word on the subject of which computer to purchase. Counterintuitively, a low-credibility source can suppress initial attitude change but increase it over time.

Not all sources need to be as attractive as Megan Fox or as credible as Brian Williams to be persuasive; simply being similar to the message recipient can be effective. Research has shown that sources that are similar to the recipient are more persuasive than those that are different. Consider this: Would you be more persuaded to see a movie that was suggested by your grandfather or your best friend? You and your friend likely have a similar idea of what is funny, scary, or compelling, so you would probably take your friend's suggestion over your grandfather's.

Similarity can apply to a person's background, values, associations, appearance, or any of a number of factors. In one study that investigated the effects of similarity, student participants were asked to read a persuasive essay on an environmental issue written by either a fellow schoolmate or a student from another university (Mackie, Worth, & Asuncion, 1990). Researchers found that participants were more likely to consider the arguments of their classmates than those of students from a different university.

Message recipients can come to perceive similarities through various routes. The source might directly express attitudes that are similar to those of the recipient or a third party might imply the presence of a similarity. It might even be the case that the person simply shares our birthday (Burger, Messian, Patel, del Prado, & Anderson, 2004), and yet this incidental similarity increases persuasiveness as well. Similarity is used to sell a variety of everyday items such as laundry detergent, toothpaste, and cereal. Advertisers establish a target audience (e.g., mothers of young children, seniors, middle-class men) and choose a spokesperson or actor who appears to be a member of that target audience to promote their products. Skin care manufacturer Neutrogena primarily sells to teenage girls suffering from acne, so the company hired teen actresses

Hayden Panettiere and Vanessa Hudgens to persuade young girls to purchase its products.

Another factor influencing source effectiveness is the likeability of the source. Attractiveness and similarity are two factors that may increase liking, but no matter the form of liking, it has an impact. For example, persuasive messages from our own groups' members, who are generally more liked than members of other groups, are more effective (Mackie, Worth, & Asuncion, 1990). In addition, those who are more attractive are more well-liked, increasing communicator persuasiveness (Chaiken, 1979).

It is important to note that most of these factors are *heuristics*—shortcuts that are used to form opinions. They involve use of the peripheral route to persuasion, rather than one that involves systematic processing.

The Message

The actual message is obviously a critical factor in the effectiveness of persuasion. Whether it is verbal or visual, the message has the ultimate duty to get the job done. The message has two main characteristics: message content and message construction. Message content refers to the tactics that may be used to communicate a concept to an audience—the actual words or images used in the message. Message construction refers to how the message is put together (how information should be placed in a message, how long the message should be, and how often the message should be repeated).

<<< Which one of these people is likely to convince you that the iPad will revolutionize the way you study?

VALENCE the degree of attraction or aversion that a person feels toward a specific object, event, or idea

FEAR-BASED APPEAL an attempt to provoke fear in the audience in order to persuade them not to do something

When developing the message content, a source must consider the valence of the message. In psychology, **valence** refers to the degree of attraction or aversion that a person feels toward a specific object, event, or idea. This means that a source must decide if it wants its message to be positive or negative—does it want to attract or repel the audience? Negative messages are typically delivered with **fear-based appeals**. Fear-based appeals attempt to provoke fear in the audience by depicting a personally relevant threat in order to persuade people to modify their behaviors. The effectiveness of fear-based appeals varies and can be affected by individual differences and whether the final message is one of fear or of how to take action to overcome the feared situation. Fear-based appeals seem to be most effective when they attempt to prevent a negative outcome, such as an anti-smoking commercial focusing on avoiding cancer, rather than attempting to promote a positive outcome such as being healthy overall (Lee & Aaker, 2004).

That said, the amount of fear induced can negatively impact persuasion if it is enough to be overwhelming. In one study, researchers gave participants one of three messages about the dangers of not practicing proper oral hygiene habits. Each message varied in the level of intended fear. The study found that the negative message that stimulated mild fear resulted in the most improvement in oral hygiene habits, while the message that stimulated the most fear resulted in the least improvement (Janis & Feshbach, 1953). It may be that people were so afraid that they only wanted to turn away from the message, feeling hopeless rather than empowered enough to act. Other fear-based approaches are unsuccessful because they put the audience on the defensive and prompt members of the audience to argue against the message or dismiss it completely because they believe "that won't happen to me" (Liberman & Chaiken, 2009).

Fear-based approaches are often used to guide audiences away from behaviors that pose health risks. For example, the classic "This is your brain. This is your brain on drugs" campaign aimed to prevent teens from using drugs by inflicting the fear that their brains would fry like an egg if they did. These messages, however, are not always effective.

Recent research shows that how vulnerable a person is can affect his or her likelihood of being persuaded by a fear-based appeal. Men who had sex with men who were at risk for Hepatitis-B were more likely to adopt the perspective that they were at risk if they read a personal account of someone who exhibited normative sexual behaviors (i.e., sexually active but not hypersexual) and became infected than if they were given statistical probabilities of infection. Notably, those who perceived themselves as at-risk were more likely to report an intention to get vaccinated (de Wit, Das, & Vet, 2008). In this way, making people aware that

<<< **Some public service announcements (PSAs) use fear-based approaches** in an attempt to persuade the public to avoid certain unhealthy behaviors.

they were at risk of getting a disease made them more likely to seek out vaccination. Also, if a fear-based appeal shows how to avoid the fear-inducing event, and an implementable solution is provided, then a fear-based message may be successful—for example, getting vaccinated for tetanus (Leventhal, Singer, & Jones, 1965).

Messages with a positive valence can also bring about a change in attitude. Studies suggest that health messages would actually be more effective if the content had a positive valence (Broemer, 2004). For example, an ad that shows a group of friends smiling and laughing while getting a ride home in a taxi would be more effective at convincing audiences not to drink and drive than showing a mangled car and an autopsy report on a drunk driver. But as we discussed earlier, sources must always take their audiences into account. Studies have shown that while Americans are more likely to respond well to positive information, Japanese individuals are more likely to focus on the negative (Noguchi, 2006). So a fear-based approach may be more effective in Japan or other non-Western cultures.

It's not always what is said but how it is said that is important, so when delivering a persuasive message, positive or negative, construction can be just as important as content. Something as simple as the length of a message can influence its effectiveness. The length of the message might serve as a peripheral cue that leads to an unfounded assumption, such as thinking that a longer message must have more support for its position (Petty & Cacioppo, 1984; Wood, 1985). When audiences make this assumption, longer messages will be more persuasive than shorter ones. Imagine that you are reading a newspaper article on the benefits of eating raw food. If the article is a section feature rather than a short vignette, you may develop a more favorable opinion about the subject even if the quality of the information is identical to what would have been presented in the vignette. However, if you process the information via the central route, the length will not matter, only the strength of the argument itself.

The strength of the message, indeed, contributes to its persuasiveness; for example, those who provide compelling reasons for a request are more likely to get others to comply with the request (e.g., Langer, Blank, & Chanowitz, 1978). Furthermore, while it may seem that, to be persuasive, you should focus on your side of the issue and present only the points that support your case, presenting both sides of the argument and refuting the points of the opposing opinion is the most effective method of persuasion. This

form of persuasion relies in part on the central route of processing, since it requires a well thought-out argument and rebuttal of others' arguments. It may be that presenting multiple sides of an issue and refuting counterattitudinal arguments increases the strength of one's own argument.

The way in which people adopt opinions also shifts based on the issue at hand. When people care about an issue, they will expend the effort to deeply and carefully process the arguments in support of and against a given perspective—in other words, they will use the central route. In this case, the argument's strength determines the effectiveness of the persuasive message. However, for individuals not involved in or concerned with an issue, the characteristics of the source of the message will predominate in persuasion. In this case, the person will use the peripheral route (Petty, Cacioppo, & Goldman, 1981).

Given that issues about which we care deeply are those whose messages we process centrally and systematically, these same issues, once we form an opinion on them, are resistant to further persuasion (Zuwerink & Devine, 1996). For example, when an attitude, such as supporting gays serving openly in the military, is important to us, we will be more resistant to strong counterattitudinal messages (i.e., those that differ from what we believe) than individuals for whom this issue is not as relevant or important.

Investment in the issue at hand is just one kind of motivation, and motivation to understand the message being delivered can increase the likelihood of central-route processing (Chaiken, 1980). Motivation is increased not only by the importance of the issue but also its proximity to us, both in time and in space, and so central route processing is increased by proximity as well. The central route is more time-consuming and difficult,

 Short messages lend themselves to billboards.

so a person with less motivation is more likely to engage in peripheral processing, which is easier and requires less analysis (Petty & Cacioppo, 1984; Gass & Seiter, 2003).

Creating circumstances in which such "outcome-relevant involvement" is either high or low can generate motivation. **Outcome-relevant involvement** is the degree to which the economic or social outcome promoted in the message is important to the receiver (Slater, 1997). For example, a message about debt consolidation would have high outcome-relevant involvement to a person who is drowning in credit card debt and student loans. When outcome relevance is high, people are likely to engage in central-route processing. When outcome relevance is low, people are likely to engage in peripheral-route processing.

The Audience

The intended audience of a persuasive message has a tremendous effect on how the message is crafted, as different audiences are influenced in different ways. Audiences are often identified by demographic factors such as age, gender, and education. Each of these demographics reacts to persuasive messages in its own unique way. Research has shown that teens and young adults are the most easily influenced by persuasive messages, making them appealing to advertisers. When compared to adults aged 23 and older, college students aged 18 to 22 have more flexible attitudes and a stronger tendency to submit to authority; therefore, they are more easily influenced by persuasive messages (Krosnick & Alwin, 1989). That said, both younger and older adults are more susceptible to attitude change than middle-aged adults (Visser & Krosnick, 1998). Older adults (aged 55–85) are, in particular, more likely to be persuaded by emotionally meaningful messages, that is, those related to love and caring, than are younger adults (Fung & Carstensen, 2003). This holds true for people across several different races. Once again, the content and type of persuasive message matters.

Similarly, while both men and women are equally persuadable when they are not familiar with a topic (Eagly, 1978), the type of persuasion strategy may be chosen according to apparent gender differences. This discrepancy is due to social roles. In our culture, men tend to assert their independence from others, while women tend to concentrate on promoting cooperation with others. Since men and women react to persuasive messages differently, the type of persuasion strategy used on each gender is different. Women are often more influenced by face-to-face persuasion—which occurs in point-of-sale situations such as purchasing a car—than by impersonal strategies such as direct mail or e-mail advertising. On the other hand, men often have the same reaction to both personal and impersonal messages (Guadagno & Cialdini, 2002).

While sources might use different techniques to persuade their audiences based on gender, there is no formula for persuading any one demographic. The expression, "There's a sucker born every minute," emphasizes the assumption that some people are more easily influenced by persuasive messages than others. Susceptibility to persuasion, however, is a little more complex than simply having gullible genes. Several personality variables play a part in the persuasion process.

One of these personality factors is a need for cognition. *Need for cognition* refers to an individual's tendency to engage in and enjoy effortful cognitive activity. Individuals who have a high need for cognition enjoy thinking abstractly, while those who have a low need for cognition do not seek out and may, in fact, try to avoid situations in which deep thought is needed (Cacioppo & Petty, 1982). Those with a high need for cognition prefer deliberate analysis, having an inherent desire to understand phenomena and a liking of critical thinking and, therefore, are likely to default to the central route rather than the peripheral.

Research suggests that need for cognition also influences a person's need for elaboration. This means that individuals with a high need for cognition are more likely to ask questions and request more details about an issue than individuals with a low need for cognition (Cacioppo, Petty et al., 1996). These high-need individuals are likely to be persuaded by messages that can withstand scrutiny; therefore, the quality of the message is an important aspect of persuading this audience. Individuals who have a low need for cognition are likely to be persuaded by secondary signals such as the attractiveness or popularity of the source (Cacioppo & Petty, 1982).

In a study that tested the individual differences in the need for cognition, researchers divided student participants into two groups and showed each group a different 20-minute clip of the movie *Die Hard* (Gibson & Maurer, 2000). One group viewed a clip in which the lead character John McClain, played by actor Bruce Willis, smokes. The other group viewed a clip in which he doesn't smoke. Nonsmoker participants who had a low need for cognition and who saw McClain smoking reported more favorable attitudes about smoking than the high-need participants who viewed the same clip. Additionally, they reported more willingness to become friends with a smoker than participants who had a high need for cognition.

Susceptibility to persuasion is also influenced by a person's ability to self-monitor her actions. In Chapter 4, we learned that self-monitoring is the tendency to focus on situational or internal cues when deciding how to present the self in a particular situation (Snyder, 1979). In general, most people are concerned with self-presentation (the way they present themselves to others), but that does not mean they are concerned with self-monitoring (the extent to which they adjust their behaviors in response to different situations). Individuals who are high self-monitors promptly change

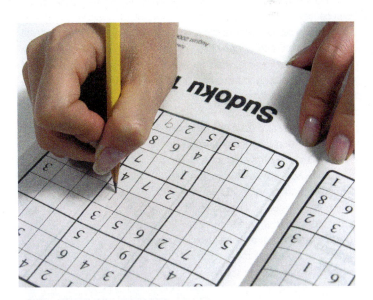

∧
∧ **People with a high need for cognition may enjoy**
∧ **thought-provoking activities** such as solving Sudoku puzzles.

their behaviors in response to the demands of a particular situation. Individuals with low self-monitoring have little concern for changing their behaviors and tend to uphold the same attitudes and opinions regardless of the demands of the situation. For example, a person may frequently curse when around good friends, but may clean up his language when around his parents. However, if he is a low self-monitor, he is likely to keep the same behavior regardless of the context. He would keep cursing regardless of whether he was around his parents or his priest.

> Individuals who are high self-monitors promptly change their behaviors in **response to the demands of a particular situation.**

People who are high self-monitors, then, are more susceptible to shifts in attitude or behavior if such shifts would make them more agreeable to others. When selecting a romantic partner, high and low self-monitors have very different preferences. In a study that examined the difference between these two personality types, researchers asked male college students to pick between two potential romantic partners with very different strengths and weaknesses. One woman was considered attractive (study administrators rated her 5.75 on a seven-point scale of attractiveness), but she was also described as being shy around strangers, self-centered, and moody at times. The other woman was considered unattractive (she only rated 1.88 on the scale of attractiveness), but had several positive personality traits such as a sociable, outgoing nature, emotional stability, thoughtfulness, and a good sense of humor. High self-monitors were more likely to choose the attractive woman with the negative personality. Low self-monitors were more likely to choose the unattractive woman with the positive personality (Snyder, Berscheid, & Glick, 1985). Similarly, a person with high self-monitoring might be persuaded to purchase an attractive, but impractical, sports car if that is valued by her social group, or to vote for a popular, but inexperienced, political candidate.

Even if a person is motivated to process a message due to personal relevance, self-monitoring, or a high need for cognition, if he lacks the ability to focus on the message, then he is still likely to engage in peripheral processing. The inability to focus on a message can be due to a lack of time or the presence of distractions. For instance, television advertisements are often less than a minute long, leaving you to rely on the peripheral aspects of the message—the models, the music, the visual effects—to process the information. Additionally, if you are distracted, it is difficult or impossible to concentrate on the message and process information on a central level. Distractions, thus, force a person to rely on peripheral cues to process messages (Petty, Wells, & Brock, 1976). When processing a message while distracted, people tend to immediately accept the information they receive and then revisit the information later.

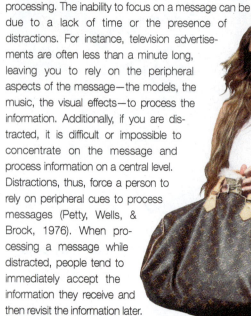

∧
∧ A distracted individual might have a **limited**
∧ **ability to focus on the surrounding messages.**

While it might seem reasonable that sources would want people to focus on their messages, distractions can be beneficial. A persuasive message can be enhanced by distracting the receiver long enough to prevent him or her from developing counterarguments. A political candidate might use vivid images and quick, catchy buzz words to distract the public's attention so that viewers do not examine the candidate's message, experience, or records too closely. If you have ever purposely waited until your parent was watching TV, reading a book, or otherwise occupied to ask for a favor, then you may have experienced the benefits of distraction firsthand.

> A political candidate might use vivid images and quick, catchy buzz words to distract the public's attention **so that viewers do not examine the candidate's message, experience, or records too closely.**

As you might expect, the mood of an audience can influence its susceptibility to persuasion. Have you ever wanted to ask a person for a favor but then held off because you wanted to wait until he or she was in a better mood before you made your plea? You do this because you know that people who are in good moods are more easily persuaded than those who are not. This is true because people who are in good

<<< A woman who is a high self-monitor might buy an expensive purse if she is going to be in a crowd that values popular accessories.

moods typically wish to stay in those good moods, so they are less likely to disrupt their euphoria in order to process information carefully. This leads them to rely on peripheral cues rather than central cues when evaluating a message (Ruder & Bless, 2003). Sources will attempt to put their audience in a good mood by delivering positive emotional messages through words or images. For example, a laundry detergent company might use images of a sunny sky, crystal clear water, and sandy beaches to get a consumer in the mood to say "yes" to a product that has nothing to do with a tropical paradise.

Physical mood cues can affect a person's willingness to accept persuasive arguments as well. In one study, researchers asked participants to either nod their heads in agreement or shake their heads in disagreement while listening to a persuasive message (Briñol & Petty, 2003). Their findings indicated that the head movements had a significant effect on the participants' thoughts about the message; nodding enhanced participants' confidence in their thoughts about the message, while shaking undermined it.

Not all audiences have the same physical cues of happiness or agreement, which is why sources need to be knowledgeable about their audiences, especially if communication is occurring across cultures. For example, in Western culture, the thumbs-up gesture indicates a positive emotion, as if to say, "Hey, all right," but in some Middle Eastern

I'm trying to lose weight. This message is **personally relevant** and I'm **motivated** to take a central route to approaching it.

I only have 20 minutes to go grocery shopping—not enough time to read about fish. **Time** limits my **ability** to process the information any way other than peripherally.

I'm allergic to fish. This message is **not personally relevant** and I will likely only peripherally process the information.

Fish is good for you! Here's why...

I already eat fish but I'm interested in finding out why it's good for me. Tell me more! I have a high **need for cognition,** so I'm more **motivated** to take a central route.

What?! You want me to eat fish? But there's a steak right over there! I'm **distracted** by the steak and therefore less **able** to analyze the benefits of fish.

How Will You Process this Message? How likely are you to respond to an advertisement that lauds the benefits of eating fish?

<<< **Wal-Mart uses greeters to improve the mood of customers** as they walk in the door.

countries, it is considered an obscene gesture and can be the equivalent of giving the middle finger. So giving a movie "two thumbs up" in a country such as Iraq would not be a good way to persuade a person to rush to the theater. Language can also be an issue. When Chevrolet introduced the Nova to Spanish-speaking countries, it created more laughter than sales because in Spanish "no va" translates to "it doesn't go."

> "When Chevrolet introduced the Nova to Spanish-speaking countries, it created **more laughter than sales because in Spanish 'no va' translates to 'it doesn't go.'**"

These cultural differences may be easy to identify, and a source might alter its behavior accordingly, but differences on intimate issues such as how people identify with themselves can be a bit more of a challenge. When cosmetic companies use slogans like "Maybe she's born with it. Maybe it's Maybelline" they are relying on a desire for a type of personal self-enhancement that may only apply to some Western cultures (Morling & Lamoreaux, 2008). The need to alter one's appearance in order to appear more attractive may seem universal in North America and Western Europe, but this kind of sense of self is different from that of much of the rest of the world, particularly in Eastern cultures (Heine & Lehman, 1997).

Westerners have a tendency to think of individuals as having their own attitudes and beliefs. Some cultures have a broader sense of self and individuals within them think of themselves as members of a group with collective attitudes and beliefs. Persuasion in these types of cultures can be difficult

because a source must aim to change the attitude of an entire group, not just the individual. This is not to say that individuals from these cultures would never form attitudes or participate in behaviors that go against the group, but the motivation to do so is much lower. These concepts are directly related to the ideas of individualism and collectivism discussed in Chapter 4.

In the United States, audiences have motivation to stray from the collective culture because we value individuality. That is why, for instance, companies such as Nike allow customers to customize their own shoes. The NIKEiD offers customers their choice of hundreds of different color combinations and even lets buyers embroider their own names or messages on the shoe. This type of customized footwear might be coveted in the United States, but in a collectivist culture like that of Korea, this uniqueness might make a person feel uncomfortable. In Korea, things that are normal, regular, and traditional are the most desirable (Kim & Markus, 1999). When delivering persuasive messages to this audience, sources such as advertisers tend to promote concepts that represent cultural values.

CIALDINI'S SIX WEAPONS OF INFLUENCE

In his book, *Influence* (1984), psychologist Robert Cialdini identified six persuasion techniques, or "weapons," that are useful in specific situations. "The Six Weapons of Influence" include reciprocation, commitment and consistency, social proof, liking, authority, and scarcity.

Reciprocation

The use of reciprocity capitalizes on our desire not to appear as moochers or freeloaders. Most of us do not want to feel indebted to another person or organization, so we often try to repay favors or acts of kindness. It's a classic case of the old give and take: If your friend helps you move a couch, you may return the favor by dog-sitting for a night. In some cases, this persuasion tactic can create an unequal exchange.

Regan (1971) demonstrated the strength of reciprocation in an experiment in which attendees at an art show were offered a complimentary soft drink at the beginning of the show and then asked to buy a 25-cent raffle ticket by the same individuals. The majority of attendees purchased a raffle ticket even if they did not accept the free soft drink. Participants who were not offered a soda were significantly less likely to buy tickets.

You've most likely used reciprocation as a persuasion tactic many times in your life. Have you ever helped out a classmate with a question or problem with the expectation that if *you* ever had a question or problem, that person would help you as a way to return the favor? You may even have saved "favor banks" with several people, passively keeping track of things you have done for others, records you can recall when you need a favor done. Charities such as the March of Dimes use the reciprocation technique when they send prospective donors personalized address labels as "free" gifts and then ask for donations. They hope to persuade people to make a donation by making them feel indebted to the organization because they accepted the gift, even though it was not solicited. Reciprocity has been found to occur even when the individual believes that the person who provided the original favor will not know that the favor was returned (Burger, Sanchez, Imberi, & Grande, 2009), suggesting that this norm does not operate out of a selfish desire for recognition of our acts but rather a desire to restore balance.

∧∧∧ Customization has become a **mainstay of American culture.**

Commitment and Consistency

In Chapter 6, we learned that people like to make sure that their attitudes are in line with their behaviors—if they are not, people experience an unpleasant tension called dissonance. Our attitudes include things we believe about ourselves—for instance, if we are reminded that we believe ourselves to be generous people, we will be more likely to donate to charities requesting money. Likewise, if we value being a good son or daughter, a florist is more likely to be persuasive at selling us flowers if she emphasizes in advertisements that good sons and daughters buy flowers, with images of tearful, grateful mothers hugging their children.

Similarly, when a person makes a commitment, particularly a verbal one, to something, he typically feels internal and external pressures to meet that commitment. The person doesn't want to seem unreliable or weak-willed. As such, he will be sure to act in a way that is consistent with that commitment. For example, if you wanted to collect volunteers for a community outreach program, you might post fliers around campus or send out a mass e-mail to friends, asking people to show up for the program. While simply presenting the information to people may generate some volunteers, you would most likely have more success if you approached or called your friends and classmates personally and asked them to make a verbal commitment to volunteer.

Commitment and consistency is an effective persuasion weapon. In one study, when one group of individuals was approached about putting up a large written sign about safe driving, only 17 percent agreed. However, a second group of individuals was first approached to put up a small three-inch sign. When the second group was approached about putting up the larger, more cumbersome sign, 76 percent agreed to do so (Freedman & Fraser, 1966). This is referred to as the "foot in the door" technique—if we agree to a small favor, it leads us to infer things about ourselves such as, in this

>>> Asking a person to RSVP to an event is a **way of using commitment and consistency as a persuasive technique.**

example, that safe driving is important to us. Once we hold this belief about ourselves, we will act in accordance with it—even if it requires more of a burden. We will explore these ideas and techniques further in Chapter 8.

Social Proof

Social proof, the notion that others' actions suggest to us what is correct, has the power to change what we believe is true in our world. Imagine that you are driving a car and trying to make a left-turn exit out of a crowded mall parking lot. After several minutes of waiting, you finally reach the intersection, but there is a sign that says "No Left Turns." You notice that two cars in front of you turn left. What do you do? Many people would make the turn because the other cars did. In advertising, this principle is referred to as the *bandwagon effect*. Microsoft has used this weapon in its advertising campaign for its search engine Bing with the slogan, "I Bing, U Bing," and the perceived normalcy of buying flowers or chocolates for Mother's Day heavily contributes to the consumer tendency to buy these items instead of making a donation to a women's charity. Indeed, when individuals who were initially going to vote for George Bush in the 1992 Presidential election were told that nominee Bill Clinton was ahead in the polls, they changed their voting behavior (Morwitz & Pluzinski, 1996). This premise also holds a lot of sway in helping behavior, which will be explored in Chapter 13.

Liking

The notion of being persuaded more readily by people we like is a simple concept—we enjoy saying "yes" to requests from people we like and do not enjoy saying "yes" to people we don't like. So the more a person likes you, the more likely it is that you will be able to persuade him or her. For example, imagine you need to purchase a new laptop, so you go to a local electronics store to check out a few different models. The salesperson who helps you is very friendly and even compliments you on your knowledge of computers. You were thinking about purchasing the laptop from an online retailer who offers a free case with each purchase, but you decide to buy the laptop from the store because the salesperson was so

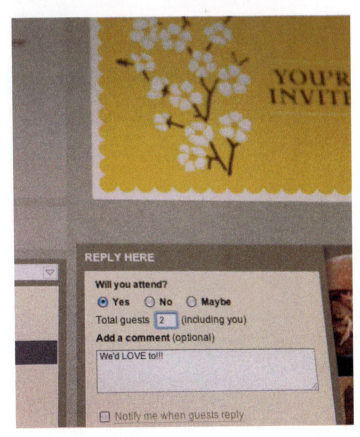

nice and helpful, and also because she complimented you; praise tends to increase liking (e.g., Drachman, DeCarufel, & Insko, 1978).

In addition, you're more likely to buy those flowers for your mother for Mother's Day if the florist is extremely helpful and kind and compliments your quality as a son or daughter for getting flowers. Salespeople know likeability plays a huge role in their pursuits to persuade you to purchase items. Corporations know this as well, which is why companies such as Best Buy spend 5 percent of their payroll on training sales staff to, among other things, make a positive impression on the customer (Kump, 2010).

Authority

In most societies, people are taught to respect authority, both implied and real, especially individuals such as police officers, firefighters, and members of the military. If a police officer asked you to show a form of identification, you probably would not hesitate to take out your driver's license.

But authority figures are not just uniformed public servants; they can come in many different forms. A parent, teacher, pastor, doctor, hotel manager, grocery store supervisor, or any person with a badge or nametag can be seen as an authority figure. Let's say you are eating lunch at a table in a park. A person in plain clothes walks up to you and tells you that you have to move because the table is reserved for a private party. You might be hesitant to move because she does not seem to have any authority over the space. But if she pulls out a badge and states that she is a grounds supervisor for the parks department, wouldn't you be more likely to move? Your motivation in such a case may be less a belief that what the supervisor is doing is correct, and more of a fear of being penalized for inaction, but nonetheless you would act. Research has shown that even in the absence of an obvious punishment for inaction, people will obey authority figures—even to the point of administering lethal shocks to another person—and this will be discussed further in Chapter 8.

Scarcity

People want what they can't have. Diamonds are more valuable than quartz, not because they are necessarily more beautiful, but because they are more scarce. Emphasizing scarcity is a popular way of selling products. Things such as limited-edition shoes or watches make consumers feel as if they have something special that has a value above the purchase price. Scarcity applies to more than just consumer products. Limited-time offers can occur

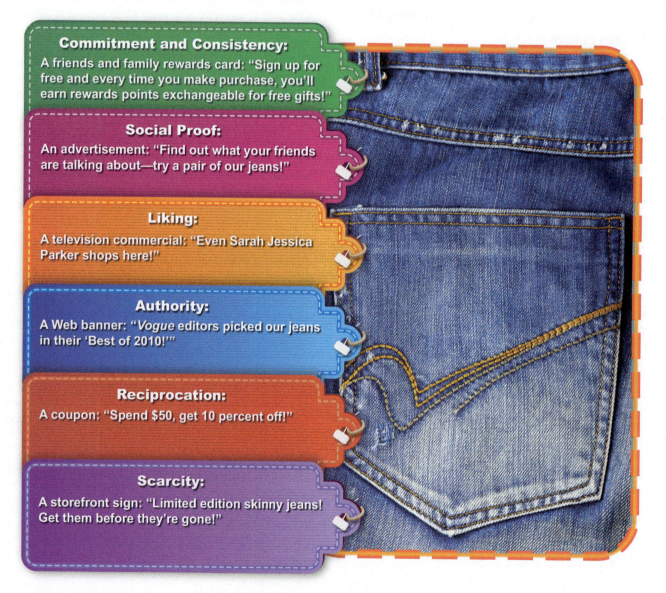

Commitment and Consistency:
A friends and family rewards card: "Sign up for free and every time you make purchase, you'll earn rewards points exchangeable for free gifts!"

Social Proof:
An advertisement: "Find out what your friends are talking about—try a pair of our jeans!"

Liking:
A television commercial: "Even Sarah Jessica Parker shops here!"

Authority:
A Web banner: "*Vogue* editors picked our jeans in their 'Best of 2010!'"

Reciprocation:
A coupon: "Spend $50, get 10 percent off!"

Scarcity:
A storefront sign: "Limited edition skinny jeans! Get them before they're gone!"

How Does the New Store at the Mall Get You in Its Pocket? A single message can be delivered using each of "The Six Weapons of Influence."

in personal relationships. In order to get a person to go out on a date with you, you may project yourself as something special and highlight your unique qualities that cannot be found in anyone else. In other words, you're not a dime a dozen, and you may not be on the market for long.

> "In order to get a person to go out on a date with you, you may project yourself **as something special and highlight your unique qualities that cannot be found in anyone else.**"

The scarcity effect can even occur with something as simple as cookies. People rated cookies in a jar more highly when there were only two cookies in the jar as compared with 10, even though the cookies were all identical. In addition, when the very same cookie jar was emptied but for a few cookies, those remaining cookies received higher ratings than they had when the jar was fuller (Worchel, Lee, & Adewole, 1975).

Now, after retiring from Arizona State University in 2009, Cialdini is using his weapons of persuasion to fight the energy crisis by studying consumer energy efficiency behavior. The U.S. government enlisted Cialdini's expertise when trying to create an initiative that would persuade people to reduce their energy use. In the past, the government had tried incentives, subsidies, educational campaigns, and other methods, but now it hoped to find a cheaper and more effective way to get citizens to flip the switch.

To determine the effectiveness of his "weapons" in this campaign, Cialdini conducted a study in the suburbs of San Diego. Going door-to-door, his team hung signs about energy conservation on doorknobs. Four signs were used, and every week for a month, each home received one at random. The first sign encouraged homeowners to conserve energy for the sake of the environment. The second asked people to do it for the welfare of future generations. The third promoted the financial advantages of

FOREWARNING the process of being informed ahead of time that a favored attitude will be challenged

energy conservation, and the fourth simply stated, "The majority of your neighbors are undertaking energy-saving actions every day."

This fourth sign demonstrated Cialdini's weapon of social proof. At the end of the month, the team checked the energy meters and found that the only homes that showed a significant reduction in energy usage were those that received the fourth sign. Thus, certain methods of persuasion can be more effective in particular situations than in others. Inducing feelings of guilt and responsibility (illustrated by the first two signs) and conveying personal benefits of action (displayed in the third sign) can be effective methods in other situations. But in this context, the tendency of people to do what others were doing was what persuaded them to reduce their energy consumption (Rahim, 2010). After all, they did not want to be the only ones not reducing consumption and look bad. Further, clearly if their neighbors were doing it, it was the right thing to do. We will further discuss the implications of Cialdini's weapons in Chapter 8.

What Does Research Tell Us About Resisting Persuasion Tactics?

So now that you know all of the tactics that different sources use to persuade people, you must be wondering if it is inevitable that we will fall prey to these messages. But we are not defenseless against the power of persuasive messages. Our ability to resist persuasion is influenced by three factors: forewarning, reactance, and inoculation.

FOREWARNING

If a friend yells "heads up" before tossing you an object, you are more likely to catch that object than if he just hurled it at you with no warning. This concept also applies to the processing of persuasive messages. When people are given **forewarning** about a persuasive message, they are being informed ahead of time that an attitude will be challenged. Forewarning allows a person to build up a defense or prepare to resist a persuasive message. For example, if you know ahead of time that a car rental company likes to try to convince customers to buy more optional features with "last-minute offers," then you will be better prepared to say "no, thanks" when the rental representative offers you a deal on an unnecessary upgrade. In a study to examine the effects of forewarning, researchers measured the persuasiveness of a lecture given to teenagers arguing that teenagers should not be allowed to drive. The sample of teenagers was divided into two groups. One group was informed of the topic 10 minutes before the lecture started. The other group was not forewarned of the topic. The group that was forewarned was less convinced by the argument. This is because the delay between a warning and the delivery of a message gives people more time to generate arguments against the message (Petty & Cacioppo, 1977).

REACTANCE

Sometimes we build up such a resistance to a persuasive message that it can have a boomerang effect, making us believe the exact opposite of what the source intends. This occurs frequently in relationships between

<<< What would persuade you to try to **become more energy efficient?**

parents and their children. Have your parents ever expressed disapproval of the person you were dating? How did you respond? Chances are, you ignored your parents' objections, or even liked the person all the more because of the disapproval. This boomerang effect is known as **reactance**. The reactance theory, established by psychologist Jack Brehm in 1966, states that when individuals feel that their freedom is threatened, they instinctively want to restore their freedom by acting in opposition to the freedom-threatening source.

Reactance explains why anti-drug campaigns sometimes backfire. Researchers from Texas State University in San Marcos concluded that anti-drug ads might increase rather than decrease drug usage among college students. After presenting government-funded anti-drug ads to a sample group of 53 college students, researchers found that three out of four students said that they had a *more* favorable impression of drugs after viewing the ads than they had previously. The researchers explained that students saw the ads as exaggerated and nonfactual, which created distrust of the source and its message (Meagher, 2004). So instead of convincing students that drugs are bad, the ads led students to believe that drugs aren't *that* bad. Reactance also explains why warning labels on violent movies or television shows increase viewership by inappropriate audiences. In a study to examine the effects of rating systems on young children, researchers found that ratings that indicated violent, sexual, and other graphic content had a deterrent effect on children younger than age eight but had an enticement effect on children older than 11, especially boys (Bushman & Cantor, 2003).

INOCULATION

Just as we use vaccines to inoculate ourselves and build up resistance to diseases, we sometimes want to inoculate ourselves and build up resistance to persuasive messages. After the Korean War, there were reports of brainwashing among captured troops and civilians. They believed things that were contrary to their native country's ideals and, indeed, the ideals they had possessed when the war began. It was especially perplexing that these people had come to adopt the beliefs of their enemies! Such persuasion is termed the Stockholm syndrome, in which captives come to identify with and even love their captors, adopting their beliefs and acting on their behalf. Psychologists, upon seeing these brainwashed people, were motivated to figure out how to build up resistance to unwanted persuasion so as to help future soldiers and civilians prevent such persuasion in the future.

In 1961, William McGuire and his colleagues developed a technique appropriately called **inoculation** (McGuire & Papageorgis, 1961). To inoculate a person against persuasion, McGuire proposed that the person be exposed to weak attacks on a favored position. The attacks must be weak so that they do not alter the person's opinion on the subject. By defending against the weak attack, a person will be better prepared to face future, possibly stronger, attacks (McGuire, 1964). In the original work, to inoculate participants against arguments against brushing their teeth, participants were provided with some arguments against regular toothbrushing that were then refuted, rendering them weak. These refutations resulted in more support for regular tooth brushing after exposure to stronger anti-brushing messages (McGuire & Papageorgis, 1961). In their studies, the researchers were able to demonstrate that inoculation approaches were more powerful than telling a person that they currently have the correct opinion and should ignore any persuasive tactics (McGuire, 1964). Defense attorneys might use inoculation in their opening statements. They may tell the jury, "The prosecution will try to convince you that one 130-pound man is capable of carrying a 300-pound steel safe 200 yards on his own, in the middle of the day, undetected." The prosecution may have several strong arguments, but the defense wants to point out the weakest parts so that jurors build up a resistance to the prosecution's argument before stronger evidence is exposed in cross-examination.

However, these techniques to resist persuasion do not work equally well for all. The APA developed a Task Force on advertising and children, and found that young children are not capable of employing these resistance techniques and lack the cognitive ability to critically think about advertising. For instance, cereal manufacturers often include the disclaimer that cereal is part of a balanced breakfast. However, research argues that children do not understand this claim and, therefore, will equate the cereal with being a good breakfast in and of itself (Palmer & McDowell, 1981). As a result, in some countries, advertisements to children are restricted. One example of this is the European Union, whose committee on Audiovisual Media Services outlines the restrictions.

When Shouldn't We Resist Persuasion?

Persuasion is not always something to be resisted; in some cases, it is to our benefit to carefully consider new opinions and maybe even shift our own to align with them. For example, in a study in which researchers first validated people's complaints about recycling (e.g., that it was inconvenient) but then delivered a persuasive message about recycling, researchers found success in getting people to partake in this beneficial behavior (Werner, Stoll, Birch, & White, 2002). By "succumbing" to persuasion, people can adopt behaviors that benefit them and their environments.

In addition, there are behaviors that are not only beneficial to adopt but may be a matter of life and death. One of those behaviors is getting tested for HIV, and one factor that can influence this behavior is framing the goal to get tested. Goals can be viewed using a *gain frame* (thinking about what you will gain by approaching them) or a *loss frame* (thinking about what you will lose by avoiding them) (for a review, see O'Keefe & Jensen, 2007). In the case of HIV testing, when people were certain they would test negative, gain-framing (reminding subjects of the peace of mind they would attain once tested) produced more persuasion. However, when people were uncertain, there was a slight increase in the rate of getting tested under loss framing (reminding subjects of the potential problems they would face if they didn't get tested) (Apanovitch, McCarthy, & Salovey, 2003). Similarly, risky behaviors benefit from loss framing, while low-risk behaviors become more likely with gain framing. In one study, this translated to greater condom-related health behavior, such as carrying condoms, when there was a gain frame but greater condom-related relational behavior, such as talking to one's partner about using them, when there was a loss frame (Kiene et al., 2005). Goal framing can also have an impact on such behaviors as smoking cessation (Tasso et al., 2005) and frequency of breast self-examination (Meyerowitz & Chaiken, 1987).

Persuasion can be powerful, for better or worse. Whether it leads you to quit smoking, improve your health, or buy your mother flowers for Mother's Day, it affects your attitudes and behavior all the time. In Chapter 8, we will explore other social influence tactics—including shifts in attitude and behavior as a result of demands made by a perceived authority figure or another individual. We will examine in-depth the effects on one's own attitudes and behaviors that may emerge as a result of desires and compulsions to conform to group norms. As you read Chapter 8, keep in mind all we have learned so far, and how these persuasion techniques might apply to conformity in group situations as well.

Getting Fit and Persuasive

As you have learned from this chapter, persuasion is an art and a science. Creating an effective persuasive message requires creativity as well as a keen understanding of the target audience.

Imagine that your student council is starting a campus-wide campaign to increase student use of the school's new fitness center,

the key to a new push toward health and well-being. The president of the student council has asked you to act as the psychology expert to design the message behind the campaign.

How would you create the persuasive message? Would you try to get students to follow the central or peripheral route? Consider the source, the message, and your audience prior to designing the campaign. Should you design two different advertisements? What measures would you take in minimizing resistance to your

message? To design an effective campaign, you must take into consideration the factors that affect persuasion.

What you will learn from this action learning project:

1. How to bring about a change on campus
2. How to create a persuasive message
3. How to deliver a message through multiple routes

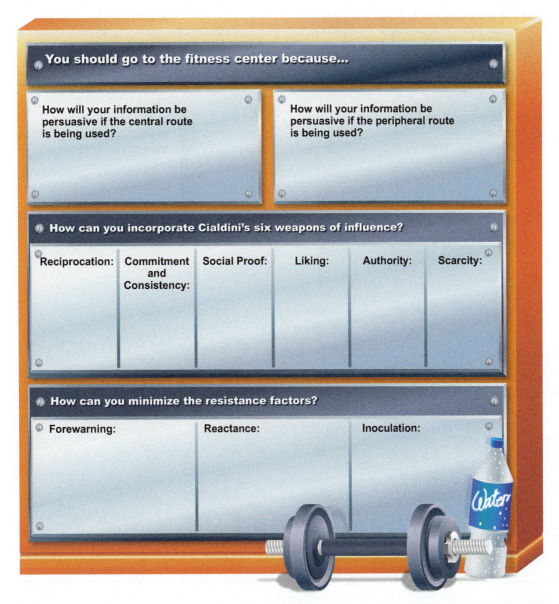

How will you **get your classmates in shape?**

07

• Review

Summary

WHAT ARE PERSUASIVE MESSAGES, AND WHICH ARE THE MOST EFFECTIVE? p. 116

• Persuasion is the strategy of communicating with other people in order to get them to behave in a certain way or change particular attitudes. A number of factors determine how the message recipient will process this information, and the recipient will do so via either the central route or the peripheral route.

• Not all persuasive messages are successful. If they were, recipients would have a harder time making decisions. The person trying to persuade the recipient must consider three factors: the source, or the entity delivering the message; the audience, or the demographics of who is to receive the message; and the message itself, and what tactics might be most suitable to delivering it.

• Psychologist Robert Cialdini has identified "six weapons of influence" that people can use when developing persuasive messages. These are reciprocation, commitment and consistency, social proof, liking, authority, and scarcity. No one way is better than the other; the effectiveness of each depends on the context of the situation.

WHAT DOES RESEARCH TELL US ABOUT RESISTING PERSUASION TACTICS? p. 127

• People are not always susceptible to even the best persuasive messages. This is due to three strategies for resisting persuasion: forewarning, reactance, and inoculation.

• When people are informed ahead of time—or forewarned—that they will be the recipient of a persuasive message, they are afforded the opportunity to think critically about the message they are to receive and to build up a defense against it. Sometimes, a persuasive message can have the boomerang effect, making us believe the exact opposite of what is intended. This is termed reactance. And finally, to inoculate yourself against persuasion, you can expose yourself to weaker attacks relating to the message and responses to them supporting your opinion. In doing so, you will be better prepared for possible stronger attacks in the future.

WHEN SHOULDN'T WE RESIST PERSUASION? p. 128

• Sometimes it is not beneficial to resist persuasion. For example, sometimes persuasion can convince us to engage in actions of benefit to ourselves, such as getting tested for HIV, doing self-breast examinations, or getting vaccinated for tetanus or Hepatitis B.

Key Terms

central route a type of processing that occurs when an individual has the ability and motivation to thoroughly listen to and evaluate a persuasive message 116

Elaboration Likelihood Model (ELM) a model of persuasion that proposes that there are two different routes, central and peripheral, that an individual may take when processing a message. The route is impacted by cognitive capacity and individual differences of the perceiver 117

fear-based appeal an attempt to provoke fear in the audience in order to persuade them not to do something 119

forewarning the process of being informed ahead of time that a favored attitude will be challenged 127

inoculation the process of building up resistance to unwanted persuasion 128

outcome-relevant involvement the degree to which the economic or social outcome promoted in the message is important to the receiver 121

peripheral route a type of processing that occurs when an individual lacks the ability and motivation to thoroughly listen to and evaluate a persuasive message, and is therefore influenced by external cues like attractiveness of the speaker 116

persuasion the way people communicate in order to influence other people's attitudes and behaviors 116

reactance when individuals feel that their freedom is threatened, they instinctively want to restore their freedom 128

sleeper effect the effect whereby the persuasive impact of a non-credible source increases over time; we remember the message but forget the criticisms of it 118

source the person or persons who delivers the message 118

valence the degree of attraction or aversion that a person feels toward a specific object, event, or idea 119

Test Your Understanding

MULTIPLE CHOICE

1. Which is an example of a message that would be persuasive if an individual was taking the central route?
   a. a print ad that says "Your girlfriend will love these shoes"
   b. a commercial that features an attractive model
   c. a speech that uses colorful vocabulary
   d. a food label that highlights nutritional benefits

2. If you do not have the motivation to listen to a central message, you are less likely to rely on cues such as
   a. the length of the message
   b. the message source
   c. the facts in the message
   d. the sound of the message

3. Which of the following audiences is most likely to have high outcome-relevant involvement with a message about the closing of a community senior center?
   a. the director of a community youth center
   b. a real estate developer
   c. a person who attends the senior center
   d. a newspaper journalist

4. Which of Cialdini's weapons is being used if a source uses a police officer to deliver its message?
   a. social proof
   b. liking
   c. reciprocation
   d. authority

5. Which of the following factors is not a major influence on the source of a message?
   a. attractiveness
   b. scarcity
   c. credibility
   d. similarity

6. Which of the following is a person with a low need for cognition likely to enjoy?
   a. doing crossword puzzles
   b. examining food labels
   c. reading owner's manuals
   d. skimming the newspaper

7. The tendency to focus on situational or internal cues when deciding how to present the self in a particular situation is called
   a. self-realization
   b. self-monitoring
   c. self-sufficiency
   d. self-control

8. When a person is in a good mood, she is likely to rely on
   a. peripheral cues
   b. central cues
   c. motivation focus
   d. central focus

9. Which of the following might initiate reactance?
   a. a person being told the subject of a speech
   b. a person being told that they can't do something
   c. a person being told a weak message
   d. a person being told multiple messages

10. What are the benefits of inoculation?
    a. It gives a person time to build up a resistance to a message.
    b. It lets a person know the source ahead of time.
    c. It prevents a person from hearing strong arguments for a message.
    d. It allows counter-arguments to be repeated.

ESSAY RESPONSE

1. Think about the last time you made a decision. Did you come to this decision through the central route or the peripheral route? Explain why.

2. In what way can distraction enhance the persuasiveness of a message?

3. Imagine that you want to persuade a potential employer that you would be a great employee. Which one of Cialdini's "Six Weapons of Influence" would you use in your persuasive message?

4. How does self-monitoring prevent individuals from being persuaded?

5. What do you think causes some individuals to be persuaded by dangerous ideologies? What can be done to prevent this from happening?

APPLY IT!

Find an advertisement for something you recently purchased. How much influence did this advertisement have on you? Is it using the central or peripheral route to appeal to consumers? Which of Cialdini's six techniques do you see at work?

Answers: 1. d; 2. c; 3. c; 4. d; 5. b; 6. d; 7. b; 8. a; 9. b; 10. a

Indecent Influence: The Positive Effects of Obscenity on Persuasion

By CORY R. SCHERER and BRAD J. SAGARIN
Northern Illinois University, DeKalb, IL, USA

This experiment examined the effects of judicious swearing on persuasion in a pro-attitudinal speech. Participants listened to one of three versions of a speech about lowering tuition that manipulated where the word "damn" appeared (beginning, end, or nowhere). The results showed that obscenity at the beginning or end of the speech significantly increased the persuasiveness of the speech and the perceived intensity of the speaker. Obscenity had no effect on speaker credibility.

In 1939, David Selznick, producer of *Gone With the Wind*, was fined $5,000 by the Hollywood Production Code Commission for the profane word that ended Rhett Butler's famous line, "Frankly my dear, I don't give a damn" (Vertres, 1997). Sixty-five years later, US Vice President Dick Cheney used a substantially stronger word when he told Vermont Democratic Senator Patrick Leahy to, in the words of *The Washington Times*, "perform an anatomical sexual impossibility" (Simms, 2004, p. 98). The statement garnered no fine, and Cheney offered no apology. Indeed, in an interview with Neil Cavuto of Fox News, Cheney expressed no regrets, explaining instead that he "felt better afterwards" (FOXNews.com, 2004, ¶101).

Clearly, society's stance against swearing has become more relaxed in recent years. The increasing acceptability of swearing raises the possibility that obscenity could have a positive effect on the percep-

tions of the speaker. In fact, Cheney's use of obscenity actually endeared him to some. As blogger Ravenwood explained, "The more I hear about Vice President Dick Cheney telling Senator Patrick Leahy to go fuck himself, the better I like Cheney" (Ravenwood's Universe, 2004, ¶1). Along these lines, a poster to the bulletin board on Promote Liberty.org argued that Cheney's comment "shows a remarkable degree of restraint on the part of the Vice President yet a willingness to stand up for his personal honor and convictions" (FMeekins, 2004, ¶4).

The present experiment was designed to examine the effects of obscenity on the perceptions of a speaker and the persuasiveness of a speech. However, as the reactions to Cheney's statement suggest, obscenity may have its most positive effect when targeted at a congenial audience. Given this, the present experiment examined the persuasive impact of a single swear word incorporated into a pro-attitudinal speech. The present experiment also examined the effects of obscenity on the perceived intensity and credibility of the speaker.

Swearing and Persuasion

What are the effects of swearing on the influence process? Past research suggests two possibilities: (a) increasing the perceived intensity of the communicator and (b) decreasing credibility.

Intensity

Hamilton, Hunter, and Burgoon (1990) defined intensity as a stylistic feature of language that is expressed through emotionality and specificity. Emotional intensity is the degree of affect in the source's language. Obscene language can be seen as a form of intense language (Bradac, Bowers, & Courtright, 1979).

A study examining motivation for why people swear had female and male college students complete a survey to determine their beliefs about the common motives for their use of obscenity and why others use obscenity (Fine & Johnson, 1984). The study examined 10 possible motives: to express anger, to emphasize feelings, out of habit, peer pressure, to relieve tensions and frustrations, because the word is taboo, to act cool, to get attention, because the word is acceptable, and lack of another word. Across gender, the motives of expressing anger and emphasizing feelings were found to be of greatest importance.[1]

Fine and Johnson's (1984) results demonstrate that the emphasis of feelings is an important motive for swearing. Furthermore, people recognize that other people swear, in part, to emphasize feeling. In this regard, Mulac (1976) found that a speaker can demonstrate strong emphasis about a topic by using obscene language, but the obscene language detracts from other aspects of how the speaker is perceived. Nonetheless, in regards to persuasion, Fine and Johnson's results suggest that if an audience

[1] Although people swear to express anger, they also swear to express other emotions such as happiness. At the 2003 Grammy awards, for example, Bono of the rock group U2 used an obscenity to express how happy he was with the fact that his band had just won an award.

Sidebar notes:

When you read Chapter 11 about aggression, revisit this idea. How can language be used as a tool for aggression? Do you swear?

Would obscene language in a speech be a characteristic of a message using the central route to persuasion or the peripheral route to persuasion?

hears a speaker swear when giving a speech on a particular topic, then the audience might infer that the speaker is emphasizing feelings. Acknowledgement of such a point might motivate the audience to take particular note of the argument and, quite possibly, to be especially influenced by the communication.

In fact, research supports the idea that speakers can increase persuasion by increasing the intensity of their language. According to a causal model by Bradac, Bowers, and Courtright (1980) based on reinforcement expectancy theory, language intensity influences attitude change through two steps: language intensity affects source evaluation and source evaluation affects attitude change. If swear words act as strong or intense language, then obscenity may increase persuasion in the same way as other forms of intense language. However, unlike some other forms of intense language, swearing may negatively impact source evaluation by reducing credibility.

Credibility

In *Cursing in America*, Jay (1992) claims that cursing at an inappropriate time will reduce a speaker's credibility, persuasiveness, and perceived professionalism. Therefore, Jay cautions that swearing for persuasive reasons should be used only when the speaker has nothing to lose.

Past research on obscenity and persuasion supports Jay's (1992) concern. For example, Bostrom, Baseheart, and Rossiter (1973) examined reactions to people who swear. This experiment looked at the persuasive effects of three types of profane language: religious (e.g., damn), excretory (e.g., shit), and sexual (e.g., fuck) obscenity. The participants listened to a tape-recorded interview about a topic and evaluated the topic before and after listening to the tape. Overall, Bostrom et al. (1973) did not find support for the prediction that

obscenity would increase persuasion. Another study conducted by Hamilton (1989) found that obscenity increased audience disgust with the message and negative perceptions of the source.

However, the lack of persuasion effects in these studies may have stemmed from the choice of topics, which were counter-attitudinal for most participants. For counter-attitudinal topics, listeners may use swearing as an excuse to reject the message. On the other hand, swearing may increase persuasion for pro-attitudinal topics. Nevertheless, given Jay's (1992) caution, the present experiment examined the possible detrimental effects of obscenity on the credibility of the speaker.

The Current Experiment

The current experiment examined the effects of swearing on the persuasive impact of a speech and the intensity and credibility of the speaker. Because of the dearth of evidence for the persuasive power of obscenity, the present experiment used swearing in a manner optimized for its effectiveness: one relatively mild swear word ("damn") was placed at the beginning or end of a pro-attitudinal speech.

Method

Participants. A total of 88 introductory psychology students from a large Midwestern university participated in partial fulfillment of a course requirement.

Design and procedure. The participants were randomly assigned to one of three conditions (no swear word, swear word at the beginning of the speech, swear word at the end). After giving informed consent, participants were seated in front of a computer and instructed to follow the instructions on the computer.

The computer played a 5-minute videotaped speech about

the topic of lowering tuition at a different university, a pro-attitudinal topic of low relevance to the participants. When the participants finished watching the speech, they completed scales that measured their attitudes on the topic and their perceptions of the speaker. After the participants finished, they were probed for suspicion and debriefed.

Materials. There were three speeches of similar length. The speeches discussed the topic of lowering tuition at a different university. The speeches had a mixture of strong and weak arguments. Strong arguments included how students have to take into account how much school will cost when deciding where to go and how the school will be saving the students money. Weak arguments included how the school could use lowering tuition as a selling point and how the community will be more attractive to businesses because the students would have more money to spend in the town. Judicious swearing was operationalized as a single instance of the relatively inoffensive word "damn." The swear word appeared either at the beginning ("... that lowering of tuition is not only a great idea, but damn it, also the most reasonable one for all parties involved.") or end ("Damn it, I think lowering tuition is a great idea.") of the speech. The control speech was the same speech without the swear word.[2]

The speeches were delivered in a video format on a computer screen using Medialab experimental software (Jarvis, 2002). The male speaker could be seen from midchest up in front of a neutral background. The speaker attempted to maintain the same tone for every speech.

There were two surveys that assessed the participants' attitudes about the speaker and the speech. The first survey was a nine-item scale that asked questions about the participants' attitudes toward the speaker. The questions of most interest were the three questions about

[2]The experiment contained an additional condition with swearing in the middle of the speech. Unfortunately, this condition inadvertently confounded the placement of the swear word with its use ("... then the alumni may feel that the damn school already has taken enough money from them."). This condition did not differ from the control condition on persuasion, speaker intensity, or speaker credibility, but given the confound, it is unclear whether the lack of an effect was due to the placement of the swear word or its use.

Why is this important to the validity of the experiment? What would happen to the results if all of the arguments were either strong or weak?

Can you think of intense language that would be an alternative to swearing? How might the impact of swearing change depending on the source, the message, or the audience?

The researchers are utilizing replication, which you first learned about in Chapter 2, to build on previous findings about obscenity and persuasion. What are some other ways to replicate this idea?

the intensity of the speaker (how passionately, strongly, and enthusiastically did the speaker feel) and three questions about the credibility of the speaker (how credible, trustworthy, and knowledgeable the audience found the speaker). There were an additional three questions about how similar the speaker was to the participant (was the speaker like them, similar to them, and akin to them) that were used for further study. The second survey was a four-item scale that asked about the participants' attitudes about lowering tuition (how much did they like the idea of lowering tuition, how much did they think it was a good idea at the school that was implementing the plan, would they implement such a plan at their school, and did the speech make them feel more positive or negative towards the idea). All questions used similar seven-point response options with all points labeled (e.g., not at all credible, not credible, somewhat not credible, neutral, somewhat credible, credible, very credible).

Results

The purpose of the present experiment was to examine the effects of swearing on the perceptions of the speaker and the persuasiveness of the speech. These were tested using a series of univariate ANOVAs comparing the three conditions on each dependent variable (speaker intensity, speaker credibility, and attitude about topic; see Table 1). Each dependent variable displayed good internal consistency (intensity: $\alpha = .87$, credibility: $\alpha = .83$, and attitude about topic: $\alpha = .82$). Speaker intensity was correlated with speaker credibility ($r = .28$, $p = .009$) and with attitude about the topic ($r = .35$, $p, .001$). Speaker credibility did not correlate with attitude about the topic ($r = .12$, $p = .267$).

Swearing had a significant effect on participants' attitudes about lowering tuition, $F(2, 85) = 3.751$, $p = .027$. Follow-up contrasts showed that the speeches with

the swear word at the beginning or end were significantly more persuasive than the control speech (see Table 1). The speeches with the swear word in the beginning and end did not significantly differ from each other. Swearing also had a significant effect on participants' perceptions of the intensity of the speaker, $F(2, 85) = 3.473$, $p = .035$. Follow-up contrasts revealed the same pattern as for attitudes about lowering tuition: swearing at the beginning or end of speech led to significantly higher perceptions of speaker intensity than no swearing. Swearing did not significantly impact perceptions of speaker credibility, $F(2, 85) = 0.052$, $p = .945$.[3]

Mediational analysis. To test whether the effects of swearing on persuasion were fully or partially mediated by increased intensity, three regression analyses were conducted (Baron & Kenny, 1986). In each of these regressions, the three conditions were represented by two contrast vectors. Contrast vector 1 (CV1) compared the beginning and end conditions against the control condition. Contrast vector 2 (CV2) compared the beginning condition against the end condition. CV1 represented the comparison of interest. CV2 was included to fully represent the three conditions in the regression equations.

In the first regression, intensity was regressed on the contrast vectors. Consistent with the ANOVA results above, CV1 was a significant predictor of intensity, $B = -.395$, $SE_B = .152$, $\beta = -.270$, $t = -2.599$, $p = .011$. In the second regression, attitude toward lowering tuition was regressed on the contrast vectors. Also consistent with the ANOVA results, CV1 was a significant predictor of attitude toward lowering tuition, $B = -.938$, $SE_B = .352$, $\beta = -.276$, $t = -2.661$, $p = .009$. In the third regression, attitude toward lowering tuition was regressed on the contrast vectors and intensity. CV1 remained a significant predictor, $B = -.067$,

$SE_B = .031$, $\beta = -.228$, $t = -2.131$, $p = .036$, although the beta was reduced somewhat, suggesting partial mediation. Speaker intensity approached significance, $B = .075$, $SE_B = .046$, $\beta = .174$, $t = 1.628$, $p = .107$. It should be noted, however, that although the experimental manipulation allows a causal interpretation of the effect of swearing on intensity and persuasion, the relationship between intensity and persuasion is correlational, and the data are consistent with other possible causal relationships.

Discussion

The purpose of this experiment was to examine the effects of judicious swearing on persuasion in a pro-attitudinal speech. Results demonstrated that swearing at the beginning and at the end of the speech led to more positive attitudes about the topic and greater perceptions of speaker intensity. These results provide the first demonstration of the persuasive power of obscenity, and they suggest that judiciously used obscenity can increase persuasion, at least within the context of a pro-attitudinal speech.

Mediational analyses suggested that speaker intensity partially mediated the effects of swearing on persuasion, although the effect of intensity on persuasion in the final regression equation was not statistically significant. This may be due to a lack of statistical power. Additional research should be conducted to further test the mediational effect. These findings are congruent with the idea that language intensity can lead to higher levels of attitude change and they suggest that swear words can be used in a similar way to other forms of intense language.

In the present experiment, swearing had no impact on speaker credibility. In regards to credibility, it is possible that swearing may be affecting credibility both positively and negatively, leading to an

Think about the primacy and recency effects you learned about in Chapter 5. What can you conclude about these effects from the results of this experiment?

Do you think the results of this experiment would be the same had the use of obscenity been abundant?

[3] When looking at the expertise and trustworthiness components of credibility separately, the results were similarly nonsignificant—expertise: $F(2, 85) = 0.184$, $p = .832$, trustworthiness: $F(2, 85) = 0.224$, $p = .800$.

Table 1 Effects of One Swear Word on Persuasiveness of a Speech and Perceptions of the Speaker

	No obscenity (control)	Obscenity at the beginning	Obscenity at the end
Attitude about lowering tuition	4.14 $SD = 0.40$	4.42[a] $SD = 0.45$	4.34[a] $SD = 0.41$
Speaker intensity	4.40 $SD = 1.03$	4.89[a] $SD = 0.81$	5.02[a] $SD = 0.98$
Speaker credibility	4.91[a] $SD = 0.73$	4.91[a] $SD = 0.75$	4.98[a] $SD = 0.76$

Scales range from 1–7 with higher values indicating more persuasion, greater intensity, and greater credibility. Means within a row that share a superscript are not significantly different.

overall null effect. ==Obscenity could impact credibility positively because the use of obscenity could make a credible speaker appear more human.== Consistent with this, Aune and Kikuchi (1993) found that language intensity increased source credibility in a pro-attitudinal message. However, obscenity could also impact credibility negatively because the use of obscenity could be seen as inappropriate for a credible speaker. Future work is needed to tease apart the relationship between swearing and the different aspects of credibility: expertise and trustworthiness. It is also possible that credibility would have greater importance in a counter-attitudinal speech in which the audience might be motivated to reject the speech by derogating the qualities of the speaker.

Limitations and future directions. As described above, the present experiment was designed to examine the persuasive power of obscenity in an optimal setting: a pro-attitudinal speech containing a single, relatively mild swear word. Future studies could examine whether obscenity's persuasive effect is limited to this domain. Are there situations in which obscenity can increase persuasion even in a counter-attitudinal speech? Would obscenity be more or less useful if the message arguments are all strong or weak? What would be the effects of using stronger (and potentially more offensive) swear words? Would an increase in the number of swear words increase their persuasive impact? It might be the case that the effects of swearing on persuasion are curvilinear; additional

swear words may increase a message's persuasive impact only to the extent that they are perceived as appropriate. Once the swearing becomes excessive, however, it may backfire.

Manuscript received 11 April 2005

Manuscript accepted 11 April 2006

References

Aune, R. K., & Kikuchi, T. (1993). Effects of language intensity similarity on perceptions of credibility, relational attributions, and persuasion. *Journal of Language and Social Psychology, 12,* 224–238.

Baron, R. M., & Kenny, D. A. (1986). The moderator–mediator variable distinction in social psychological research: Conceptual, strategic, and statistical considerations. *Journal of Personality and Social Psychology, 51,* 1173–1182.

Bostrom, B. N., Baseheart, J. R., & Rossiter, C. M. (1973). The effects of three types of profane language in persuasive messages. *The Journal of Communication, 23,* 461–475.

Bradac, J., Bowers, J., & Courtright, J. (1980). Lexical variations in intensity, immediacy and diversity: An axiomatic theory and causal model. In R. N. St. Clair & H. Giles (Eds.), *The social and psychological contexts of language* (pp. 294–317). Newbury Park, CA: Sage.

Bradac, J., Bowers, J. A., & Courtright, J. (1979). Three language variables in communication research: Intensity, immediacy and diversity. *Human Communication Research, 5,* 257–269.

Fine, M. G., & Johnson, F. L. (1984). Female and male motives for using obscenity. *Journal of Language and Social Psychology, 3,* 59–74.

FMeekins (2004, July 3). Hillary high horse. Message posted to http://www.promoteliberty.org/phpbb2/viewtopic.php?t = 65

FOXNews.com (2004). *Transcript: Interview with Dick Cheney,* Retrieved September 20, 2004, from http://www.foxnews.com/printer_friendly_story/0,3566,123 792,00.html

Hamilton, M., Hunter, J., & Burgoon, M. (1990). An empirical investigation of an axiomatic model of the effect of language intensity on attitude change. *Journal of Language and Social Psychology, 9,* 235–255.

Hamilton, M. A. (1989). Reactions to obscene language. *Communication Research Reports, 6,* 67–69.

Jarvis, B. (2002). *MediaLab2001 (Version 2002.1.4) [Computer software].* New York: Empirisoft Corporation.

Jay, T. (1992). *Cursing in America.* Philadelphia: John Benjamins Publishing Company.

Mulac, A. (1976). Effects of obscene language upon three dimensions of listener attitude. *Communication Monographs, 43,* 300–307.

Ravenwood's Universe (2004). *Cheney said what needed to be said,* Retrieved September 20, 2004, from http://www.ravnwood.com/archives/003261.shtml

Simms, P. (2004, July 26). New details surface. *The New Yorker,* Retrieved September 20, 2004, from http://www.newyorker.com/shouts/content/?040726sh_shouts

Vertes, A. D. (1997). *Selznick's vision: Gone with the Wind and Hollywood filmmaking.* Austin, TX: University of Texas Press.

Which of Cialdini's six weapons of influenced discussed in Chapter 7 does this idea apply to?

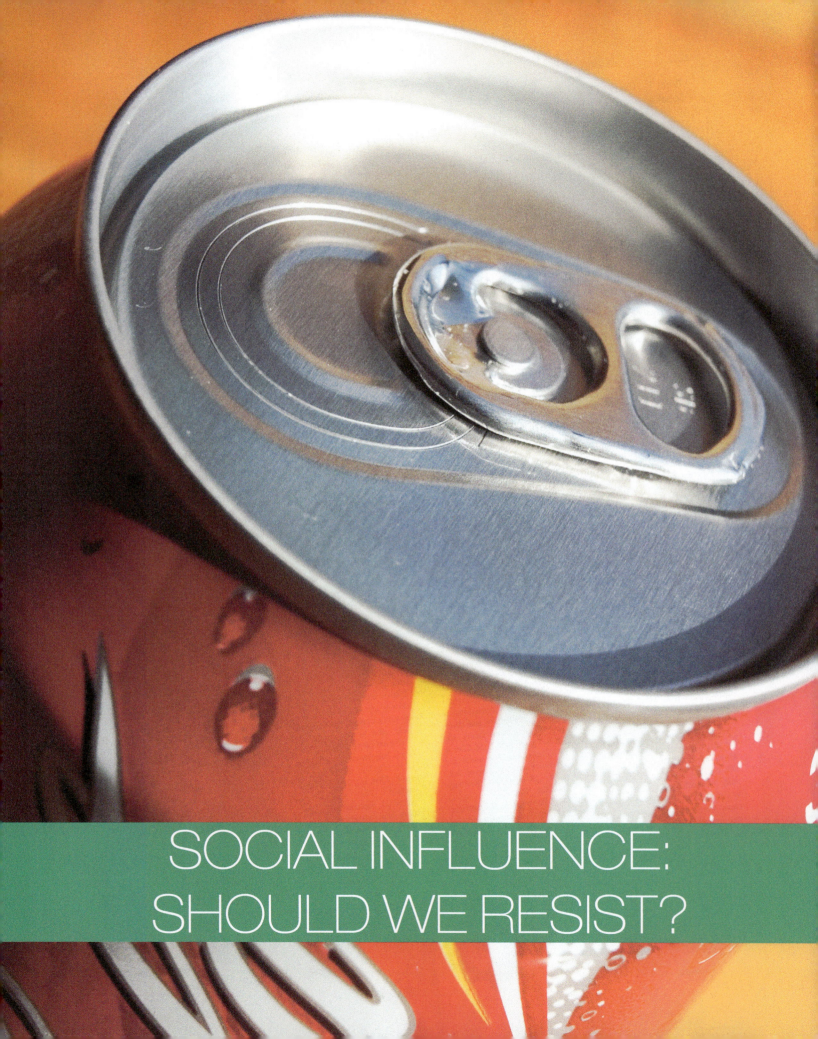

SOCIAL INFLUENCE: SHOULD WE RESIST?

<<< What do our names for these drinks tell us about social influence?

HOW DO SOCIAL ROLES AND SOCIAL NORMS DEFINE THE WAYS IN WHICH WE BEHAVE?
WHAT FACTORS AFFECT AND PROMOTE CONFORMITY?
WHAT METHODS DO PEOPLE USE TO GET OTHERS TO COMPLY WITH REQUESTS?
HOW DO AUTHORITY FIGURES GET US TO OBEY THEM?

It's spring

break, and you've decided to join your friend Jake for a visit to his hometown in a state you've never visited before. You're at the movie theater one night, ordering snacks before you head in to see the movie. You have your candy and your popcorn, and are just about to order a beverage. You open your mouth, ask for what you want to drink—and the woman behind the concessions counter looks at you like you have two heads.

Confused, you turn to Jake, who immediately starts to laugh. Why? What's so funny about asking for something to drink? To you, what you've ordered makes perfect sense, but Jake and the woman behind the counter have grown up calling those carbonated beverages something else entirely. In fact, these beverages have many different names, depending on where you are in the world—"pop" in the midwestern United States, "soda" in the Northeast, "co-coler" in Georgia and Alabama, "bubbler" in New England, "cold drink" in Louisiana, "scoosh" in Scotland, "fizzy drink" in the United Kingdom, "cooldrink" in South Africa . . . wherever you go, they're calling it something else (von Schneidemesser, 1996)!

These differences are, perhaps surprisingly, the topic of much debate and research. People can get quite heated about which is the "right" name—in fact, bring the question up in the dining hall at school and see what happens. If you have friends from different regions or parts of the world, chances are you'll find yourself in the middle of an argument!

The fact that people in different regions conform to certain names for beverages is an illustration of social influence, a concept that will be discussed in great detail in this chapter. As you read, think about how you might behave the next time you go to the movies with Jake— would you continue to order using the word you're accustomed to using, or would you bend to the expectations of the people around you in this unfamiliar city?

CHAPTER **08**

How Do Social Roles and Norms Define the Ways in Which We Behave?

You're at a party with friends. It's a great place to observe the ways in which people interact, so you decide to sit back and watch what's going on around you. In the corner, you see your friend Mark talking to Jane, who you know he likes. You notice she has a habit of rubbing her arm as she speaks with Mark. As you watch them, you notice that Mark has started rubbing his arm when he talks, too.

Now, if you weren't studying social psychology, you probably wouldn't have been observing their behaviors closely enough to pick up on this. It leaves you wondering, though. Is Mark intentionally mimicking Jane's behavior, and for what benefit?

It's highly unlikely that Mark is *intentionally* rubbing his arm. In fact, it's highly unlikely that he is even fully conscious of the fact that he is doing so—or that Jane is rubbing hers. Instead, Mark is probably exhibiting what is known as the **chameleon effect**. Coined by Tanya Chartrand and John Bargh (1999), this term refers to "the non-conscious mimicry of the postures, mannerisms, facial expressions, and other behaviors of one's inter-action partner, such that one's behavior passively and unintentionally changes to match that of others in one's current social environment."

Chartrand and Bargh (1999) demonstrated this effect in a study in which students had a 10-minute interaction with a confederate under the guise of discussing photographs for use in another experiment. The students each interacted with two different confederates in two separate sessions. During the interactions, the confederates varied their mannerisms, smiling, shaking their feet, or rubbing their faces; the second confederate would exhibit mannerisms that the first hadn't. The researchers observed that students smiled more times per minute when partnered with a smiling confederate rather than a neutral one, and shook their feet or rubbed their faces more often when that behavior was exhibited by the confederate.

If you're thinking the students might have been mimicking the confederates on purpose, Chartrand and Bargh (1999) thought of that, too. At the end of each session, they asked the students if anything had stood out about the other participant. Not one student pointed out the target mannerisms, demonstrating that the chameleon effect is not conscious.

So what is the mechanism behind this chameleon effect, which calls to mind the lizard's ability to match its surroundings? Chartrand and Bargh point to a perception-behavior link through which perceiving an action being done by another person makes someone more likely to do that same action. The chameleon effect may serve an important social function, according to Chartrand and Bargh. Being "in sync" with someone else's behaviors and mannerisms allows for easier interactions between people. In a second experiment, they had confederates match the behaviors of some study participants but not others. The participants who had been mimicked responded more favorably to the confederate than those who had not been (1999). It may be that we mimic others when we want to be liked or are feeling a bit out of place. It certainly explains why Mark was rubbing his arm, doesn't it?

Have you ever wondered why, when you see someone else yawning, you usually end up yawning, too? Psychologist Robert Provine (2005) explored this question through an experiment in which he exposed people to a five-minute video of a man yawning repeatedly. As he expected, 55 percent of viewers yawned. Only 21 percent of people watching a video of a man smiling yawned. He determined that seeing a yawning face stimulates "mirror neurons" in the brain (Rizolatti, & Craighero, 2004). These neurons are responsible for our mimicking witnessed actions. The "yawn effect" can be seen as another example of the chameleon effect.

The chameleon effect is just one way in which we describe the social influence exerted upon us in our daily lives. Social influence, which occurs when our attitudes, cognitions, or behaviors are affected by another person or group, can be seen in persuasion (which you learned about in Chapter 7), conformity, compliance, and obedience. We'll discuss those last three later in the chapter. First, we must address the concepts in which much of social influence takes root—social roles and social norms.

∧∧∧ The term *chameleon effect* describes the tendency to nonconsciously mimic the behaviors of someone with whom one is interacting.

SOCIAL ROLES

Monique is a 21-year-old woman. She's a student, majoring in psychology, who also works part-time at Target and volunteers once a week at the local animal shelter. She's the sister of 7-year-old twin boys, lives with her parents, and spends most Saturdays with her girlfriends at the beach. While all of this adds up to make one individual person, do you think Monique's behaviors and mannerisms

At School:
- Polite
- Attentive
- Dresses modestly
- Completes work and asks questions

<<< **Monique's Social Roles.** As we move through the day, we change our behaviors to meet the expectations of various social roles.

At Work:
- Helpful
- Cheerful
- Dresses in uniform
- Helps customers and keeps store tidy

At Play:
- Active
- Loud
- Dresses casually
- Listens to music and laughs with friends

the odd feeling that sometimes comes with seeing someone "out of context."

Fulfilling the expectations of social roles can have serious consequences, as evidenced in a study known as the Stanford Prison Experiment (Zimbardo, 1971; Haney & Zimbardo, 1998). College students volunteered to spend time in a simulated prison in Stanford's psychology department. Half of the students took on the role of guards, while the other half became prisoners. The "guards" were given billy clubs and permission to enforce rules. Very quickly, the students settled into their roles—and the expectations that came along with those roles. The guards devised humiliating punishments for the prisoners, some of whom rebelled and some of whom became apathetic to the situation. The students fell so fully into their roles that the researcher had to call off the two-week experiment after only six days. How do you think the lessons of this study can be applied to social roles outside of the laboratory?

remain exactly the same as she moves through all of these spheres of her life?

Of course not. At the beach, you'll find Monique wearing a bathing suit and laughing loudly as she goofs around with her friends. When she babysits her brothers, she can't show the same behaviors—she must be a responsible older sister. At work, she wears clothing you'd never see her wearing in class, and the way she interacts with customers is very different from the way she does with her friends at the beach. Though she is still Monique in all of these settings, she must play different roles throughout her life, and these roles dictate which behavior is called for. Through the course of your day, your **social role**, or the expectations for the ways in which you should behave in a given situation, may change many times. Think about all of the different circles in which you move as a student, a member of your family, an employee, and so on. How do you behave differently in your social roles?

The social influence exerted by the expectations of social roles is pretty well ingrained. We expect people within certain roles to act a certain way. How would you react if you saw one of your professors dancing at a local club? It might throw you off, because you expect him to behave within the confines of his social role of "professor." Remember, though, that he, like you, has many other social roles—you just don't normally see him in those roles. This explains

SOCIAL NORMS

Imagine you are visiting your friend Olivie in Paris. When she introduces you to her family, each member greets you warmly, giving you a quick kiss on each cheek. You find this is repeated when you meet some of Olivie's friends for lunch. You're not used to making such close contact with unfamiliar people, but you know this kind of greeting is common in France, so you relax and accept the warm gesture.

You expect lunch to be rather quick, maybe an hour if you get caught up in conversation, but three hours pass without anyone making a move to leave the table. You're feeling a little antsy, since you're not used to lingering so long, but it seems normal to everyone else, so you just go along with it.

Hand-in-hand with social roles go **social norms**. These are the patterns of behavior that are accepted as normal, and to which an individual is expected to conform in a particular group or culture. You might think of them as rules indicating how you're expected to behave. These

DESCRIPTIVE NORMS how people typically behave in a given group or situation

INJUNCTIVE NORMS behaviors of which people typically *approve* or *disapprove* of in a given group or situation

rules can be explicit (a sign saying "No Shirt, No Shoes, No Service" posted on the door of a convenience store) or implicit (you just *know* you're not supposed to stand close to someone using an ATM).

In many ways, social norms are internalized. Because we feel uncomfortable about violating social norms, we often conform to the group norm so we don't stick out. In fact, in new situations such as those you might experience when visiting Olivie in Paris, people are likely to pick up norms quickly by looking to those around them to model expected behavior. Of course, this isn't limited to vacations in foreign cities—think about the last time you started at a new job or school. How did you learn what was expected of you? We want to be accepted, so we accept the influence of social norms. But how do these norms develop in the first place? In the first half of the 20th century, one of the founders of social psychology, Muzafer Sherif (1937), set out to answer this question. He wanted to know how norms develop and how strong their influence can be.

In his approach to answering these questions, Sherif made use of a setup in which people are placed in a dark room and exposed to a stationary point of light. In this situation, most people perceive that the light is moving because there are no points of reference for location or distance in a completely dark room. This perception of movement is called the autokinetic phenomenon.

What does this have to do with social norms? Sherif knew that people perceive the stationary light as moving different distances. By placing several people in the room at once, he found that those people influenced one another when asked what the light was doing. There

was no discussion or debate between participants, but after several trials they would start to conform to a group norm. Then, when people were exposed to the light individually, they continued to describe the movement in ways that were consistent with the group norm. Sherif had demonstrated that norms can change what people actually believe.

Descriptive and Injunctive Norms

Social norms describe behavior that is considered to be "normal," but does this single definition fit every situation? Consider drinking among college students. Is there a difference between how much a "normal" student *should* drink and how much a "normal" student *does* drink? A 2007 study examined how social norms determine drinking behaviors in college students (Lee et al., 2007). The researchers found that students tend to overestimate how much their peers drink, and that this overestimation is positively correlated with drinking behavior (meaning there was an increase in drinking). They also found that college students tend to perceive that their peers are more approving of alcohol consumption than they actually are, and that this estimation is also associated with heavier drinking (Lee et al., 2007). This study demonstrates the influence of two different kinds of social norms: descriptive norms and injunctive norms.

Descriptive norms describe how people typically behave in a given group or situation. These are generally pretty easy to follow. There isn't anything to analyze, as they're based on raw behavior. You might think of descriptive norms as birds in a flock or fish in a school, following the behavior of those around them. **Injunctive norms**, on the other hand, involve perceptions of which behaviors are acceptable or unacceptable. Injunctive norms are behaviors of which people typically *approve* or *disapprove* of in a given group or situation. Subscribing to these norms is based on understanding the moral rules of a society. Both kinds of norms motivate human action. Every day, you see examples of people doing what is socially approved and of people simply doing what is popular!

> Social norms dictate many areas of our lives—even the ways in which we greet one another—and can vary greatly from one culture to another.

A perfect example of this is littering, for which the injunctive norm has become that one should *not* litter. In 1994, Robert Cialdini described his work researching the effect of descriptive norms on littering. Several years earlier, he and his team set up an experiment in which they hoped to manipulate norms that would lead people to litter. They gave people an opportunity to litter after finding flyers on their car windshields.

The environment varied—it was either clean or fully littered—and the researchers added another variable by having a confederate either model littering or throwing the flyer in a trashcan. By introducing these variables, they were manipulating the perceived descriptive norm. They found that people were more likely to litter when they watched a confederate model littering, particularly in areas that were already fully littered. Cialdini and his fellow researchers (2004) also found that people were least likely to litter when they watched a confederate litter in a clean environment. They speculated that this was because the confederate's action drew attention to the anti-littering descriptive norm represented by the clean environment (Cialdini, 2004).

Descriptive norms are often called upon in public service announcements. Cialdini criticized this method, arguing that more effective PSAs focus on injunctive norms. To illustrate this, he conducted an experiment at Arizona's Petrified Forest National Park (Cialdini, 1994). In an effort to curb the rampant theft from the park, there were prominently placed signs calling out the problem, announcing that 14 tons of petrified wood are taken from the park each year by visitors removing small pieces at a time. Cialdini showed that by pointing out the harmful prevalence of the problem, these signs are describing the norm for the park.

He suggested instead that the park focus on using the injunctive norm (that people do not steal from the Petrified Forest National Park) to combat the problem. A new sign was created. It included the words, "Please don't remove the petrified wood from the park, in order to preserve the national state of the Petrified Forest," and featured a picture of a lone visitor stealing wood, with a red circle-and-bar symbol over the offender's hand. This calls out an individual's action that goes against the norm. In the end, the second campaign was successful. There was about five times as much theft with the original descriptive norm-based signs as there was with the new signs (Cialdini, 1994).

Pluralistic Ignorance

As was stated before, people tend to accept social norms out of the desire to be accepted. What happens, though, when our drive to be accepted is so strong that we go along with social norms despite privately rejecting them? What happens when each individual in a group engages in this outward acceptance and private rejection, believing that everyone else accepts the norm?

You've probably seen this phenomenon demonstrated in one or more of your classes along the way. Let's say you're in a difficult math class, and you're just not getting it. Your professor asks if anyone has any questions. "Yes! About a hundred!" you think, but before raising your hand, you look around the room. All of your classmates are staring straight ahead, and no other hands are raised. You don't want to look stupid—after all, it seems like everyone else is getting it—so you keep your hand down. Only a week later,

<<< They might all be confused, but pluralistic ignorance leads them to stay silent for fear of looking stupid in front of their classmates.

PLURALISTIC IGNORANCE a type of norm misperception that occurs when each individual in a group privately rejects the norms of the group, but believes that others accept them

CONFORMITY a type of social influence in which an individual changes his or her behaviors to stay in line with social norms

PUBLIC CONFORMITY a type of conformity that occurs when we feel pressured to conform to group norms. When publicly conforming, people pretend to agree with the group, but privately think the group is wrong

PRIVATE CONFORMITY a type of conformity that occurs when people truly believe the group is right; occurs even in the absence of group members

INFORMATIONAL SOCIAL INFLUENCE a type of influence that occurs when one turns to members of one's group to obtain accurate information

NORMATIVE SOCIAL INFLUENCE a type of influence that occurs when one goes along with a group because one wants to be accepted

when the professor ditches a lesson plan in favor of reviewing the material based on the class's dismal performance on a quiz, do you figure out that everyone else felt just like you did. Of course, most of the time, we don't ever get any hints that pluralistic ignorance has been at work.

Pluralistic ignorance is a type of norm misperception that occurs when each individual in a group privately rejects the norms of the group, but believes that others accept them. It also often plays out in the development (or nondevelopment!) of romantic relationships. Out of fear of rejection, you might not pursue someone in whom you are interested, fearing the person isn't into you. Of course, the other person is feeling the exact same way and doesn't call you, which only serves as evidence for your suspicion that he is not interested. Your failure to call serves as the same evidence for him, and you both end up missing out on a potential relationship.

Descriptive norms, injunctive norms, pluralistic ignorance—what keeps us following these rules of social influence?

What Factors Affect and Promote Conformity?

Let's say you're in line at the grocery store, and you're in a real hurry. Ahead of you are three people, each with 15–20 items in their baskets. The second person in line has reached into her purse only to pull out, of all things, a checkbook. You feel like you're going to be in line forever. So why don't you just step in front of the woman with the checkbook and get on with your day? It sounds crazy to even suggest it, doesn't it? People just don't do things like that. But why?

Conformity is the driving force that keeps you following social norms like patiently waiting your turn in the grocery store. It's a type of social influence in which we change our behaviors to stay in line with those norms. This concept was explored in a classic study by Solomon Asch in the early 1950s. Asch wanted to explore the forces of social influence, particularly those that come into play when our own judgments or actions don't match up with those reached or demonstrated by others.

Asch asked study participants to respond to a series of problems in which they were asked to select which of three comparison lines was the same length as a standard line. Each participant was joined by several other participants who were, unbeknownst to the original participant, really confederates, meaning they were part of the research team. For many of the problems, the assistants stated incorrect answers out loud, before the participant gave an answer. All of the confederates gave the same incorrect answer.

Keep in mind, these judgments were quite simple, so it must have seemed odd to the participants that these other people were agreeing on an answer that was clearly incorrect. What was the participant to do? Should he be the "odd man out" and give the correct answer, or go along with the group, despite knowing that the answer they gave was most likely wrong?

Asch (1951, 1955) found that most people chose the latter. Although he reported that many subjects experienced observable conflict with publicly conforming, 37 percent of all answers were conforming. Some people even reported "I am wrong; they are right" when questioned. It is important to note that although 75 percent of subjects conformed at least once across the 12 trials, participants could also sometimes resist conformity. Of the subjects, 95 percent did provide at least one correct answer going against the group at least once.

Many of the participants in Asch's experiment were probably exhibiting public conformity, which occurs when we feel pressured to conform to group norms. When publicly conforming, people pretend to agree with the group, but privately think the group is wrong. Private conformity, on the other hand, occurs when people truly believe the group is right. This type of conformity occurs even in the absence of group members.

There are actually two different kinds of influence that lead to conformity. When you turn to members of your group to obtain accurate information, you are demonstrating informational social influence. There are various situations in which this might occur, such as when a situation is ambiguous and you're not sure what to do, or when immediate action is necessary during a crisis. In such cases, we depend upon others for what to do, or to ease our fears. Informational social influence most often leads to private conformity to the group's views. This kind of influence was demonstrated in Sherif's moving light experiment—remember that participants continued to give the group's agreed-upon answer, even when they later encountered the situation alone.

On the other hand, normative social influence occurs when you go along with a group because you want to be accepted. This kind of influence and the resulting public conformity were demonstrated in Asch's line experiment. Despite their feelings that the group was wrong,

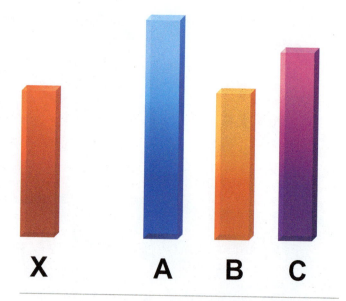

X   A   B   C

∧ For Asch's study, participants were asked
∧ to identify which of the three comparison lines
on the right matched the length of the standard line
on the left.

<table>
<tr>
<td>

Informational Social Influence:

- **Ambiguous situations**
- **Need information right away**
- **When immediate action is necessary**
- **When we are afraid and need to ease our fears**
- **Leads to private conformity**

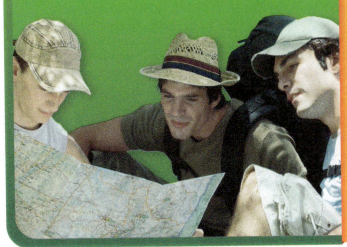

</td>
<td>

Normative Social Influence:

- **When meeting new people**
- **At a party**
- **When we want to be accepted**
- **When we are seeking approval**
- **Leads to public conformity**

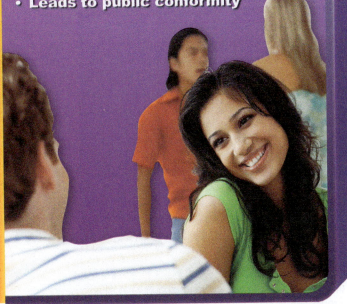

</td>
</tr>
</table>

∧
∧ **Social Influence: Informational or Normative?** Seeking information or striving to be
∧ accepted?

---

participants were still highly likely to give the group's answers as their own. Sometimes, we would rather be wrong than risk social disapproval.

FACTORS AFFECTING CONFORMITY

Recent research has shown how conformity manifests in the brain (Klucharev, Hytonen, Rijpkema, Smidts, & Fernandez, 2009). Using functional magnetic resonance imaging, scientists demonstrated that conformity is based on mechanisms within the brain that are associated with reinforcement learning. They found that conflict with group opinion triggers a "prediction error" signal that flares when there is a difference between the expected and actual outcomes of a situation. This response is centered on the *rostral cingulated zone*, which plays a role in monitoring behavioral outcomes, and the *nucleus accumbens*, which is involved in the anticipation and processing of rewards. Action in this reward-processing part of the brain explains our automatic adjustment to go with the majority (in this particular study, the majority's judgment of facial attractiveness). Our brains, it seems, are wired to put out an alert when we make the mistake, as one of the researchers described it, "of being too different from others."

Characteristics of the Group

You've just settled in to study for tomorrow's huge exam. Your grade in the class is on the edge, and if you do well tomorrow morning, you might just make an A. You've promised yourself you won't be distracted, that you'll keep your mind focused on the goal. Suddenly, your roommate bursts through the door, exclaiming, "25 cent wing night! Come on, we'll go for like an hour, and then you'll still have plenty of time to study."

It's easy to turn him down, with a promise to go next week and an explanation that your grade is riding on this exam. He leaves you alone, and you open your text, a little disappointed that you can't join him, but proud of yourself for sticking to your guns.

Let's rewind. Now, instead of your roommate bursting through the door, it's your roommate *and* four of your friends. Suddenly it's a lot harder to say "no," isn't it? As the size of a group increases, so does the impact of conformity. Asch's experiment demonstrated this. When participants faced their tasks with only one confederate present, almost every participant went with his or her original answer without being swayed by the confederate. When two confederates were present, 14 percent of the participants conformed to the influence of the group,

SOCIAL IMPACT THEORY a theory that suggests that social influence depends on the strength, immediacy, and number of source persons relative to the target person(s)

giving the wrong answer on at least one trial. Adding another confederate led to 32 percent of all answers conforming to the group norm (Asch, 1951, 1955). However, there is a limit to the number of individuals that can continue to increase the level of conformity. In Asch's work, adding three individuals led to an increase in conformity, but after that, the addition of another person did not significantly affect levels of conformity (Asch, 1956; Gerard, Wilhelmy, & Conolley, 1968). Thinking about the example from the beginning of this chapter, the next time you go to the movies in that city, you might be more likely to conform to the local name for that Sprite if you're surrounded by people in line than if it were just you and the server behind the counter.

This effect can be explained by **social impact theory** (Latane, 1981), which suggests that social influence depends on the strength, immediacy, and number of source persons relative to the target person(s). The strength of a source comes from status, ability, or relationship to a target person. You're more likely to comply to influence from someone you see as competent or of higher status than yours. Immediacy has to do with how close a source person is to a target person. You're more likely to comply with using the local name for that carbonated beverage at the concessions counter than the one you use back home, miles and miles away. Finally, as the number of source people increases, so does their influence. Again, think about that line of people behind you. If there were just one person behind you, you wouldn't be nearly as likely to conform to giving that local name.

Demographic Variables

The degrees to which people conform, and in what situations, are not one-size-fits-all. Likelihood of conformity is dependent upon factors such as age, gender, and culture. You probably already know from your own experience that conformity to norms set by one's parents decreases with age, as conformity to norms set by one's peers increases. One classic study of students in the 3rd, 6th, 9th, 11th, and 12th grades confirmed this (Berndt, 1979). Students responded to hypothetical situations in which peers encouraged them to behave in antisocial, prosocial, or neutral ways. For all types of behavior, peer conformity peaked in sixth or ninth grade. In a second study by the same researchers, children in those same grades responded to situations testing conformity to peers or parents. As you might have already guessed from your own experience, conformity to parents decreased steadily with age and was negatively correlated with conformity to peers. Recall what you learned about correlations in Chapter 2. In this example, as one variable increased, the other decreased, so as conformity to parents decreased, conformity to peers increased.

Let's say you are talking with a group of friends about plans for Friday night. Three of the people in the group want to go to a party a friend is having, but one isn't interested. She would much rather go into the city to hear a classmate's band play. Ten minutes of arguing later, the dissenter has started to cave, saying, "OK, maybe the party would be more fun, but I'm not sure." After another five minutes, she's in complete agreement that everyone will go to the party. Do you think this conformity would have been more or less likely if the dissenter had been a man? It seems like an odd question, but gender plays a role in how likely a person is to conform.

Traditionally, women tend to be more concerned with interpersonal relationships than men are. As such, are women more readily influenced to conform? Researchers Alice Eagly and Carole Chrvala (1986) explored this question by assigning subjects to groups containing two males and two females in addition to the subject. Subjects were given those group members' opinions, which were represented as being different from opinions that subjects themselves had given earlier in the study.

After seeing the group members' opinions, subjects were asked to give their opinions again, with their fellow group members either having or not having surveillance over the newly given opinions. While the tendency of men to conform was not affected by surveillance, women conformed more with the group opinion with surveillance than without it. Age was also a factor—in subjects under 19 years old, surveillance had no effect on conformity (Eagly & Chrvala, 1986).

So it would seem that gender is a factor in conformity in group pressure situations, but not in private situations. If there is no one around to observe any change that may take place, women don't conform any more or less than men do. Why, if a woman would not conform privately, would she be so much more likely to bend to group pressure? Some researchers believe it is due in part to the expectations of women in many societies. Women are often expected to foster interpersonal relationships and encourage harmony within a group. Often, this is accomplished through giving in to the group (Wood & Stagner, 1994).

These gender differences do, however, depend on familiarity with material, which determines how comfortable people are with a given task. In one study, male and female participants were asked to answer questions on stereotypically feminine, masculine, or gender neutral topics. They were also given the percentage of people who agreed or disagreed with each question. Female participants conformed to the majority more on the masculine items, while men conformed more with the feminine items (Sistrunk & McDavid, 1971). Faced with unfamiliar material, people are more likely to go with the group. In another study, men resisted influence to conform to incorrect answers about stereotypically masculine topics, while women held their ground on stereotypically feminine topics, showing that comfort with a topic leads to less conformity (Cacioppo & Petty, 1980).

> "Why, if a woman would not conform privately, would she be so much more likely to bend to group pressure?

Cultural differences also play a major role in an individual's likelihood to conform. In a meta-analysis of conformity studies using a task similar to that in Asch's classic work, researchers found that countries with collectivist cultures tend to show higher levels of conformity than those with more individualistic cultures (Bond & Smith, 1996). Why? In collectivist countries, conformity is often seen as the "glue" that holds society together, whereas in individualistic cultures, conformity is usually seen as something to be avoided.

Of course, these are not hard and fast rules. Women and individuals from collectivist cultures may be more likely to conform in general, but it depends on the situation and task.

RESISTING THE PULL OF CONFORMITY

In July 2010, the prime minister of Iceland, Johanna Sigurdardottir, made history—for the second time. In 2009, she became the world's first openly gay head of state, and in 2010, she and her partner of seven years took advantage of the full marriage equality in Iceland and were married. Though Iceland is one of the few nations around the world that allows marriage equality for gay and lesbian citizens, there is still some bias present (Melloy, 2010).

Iceland lacks the fervent campaigns that mark the U.S. campaigns against marriage equality, but same sex marriage is still not fully accepted. Imagine the pressure to conform that people in positions of power must feel. All eyes are on them, and the public will judge. Sigurdardottir may very well have decided to conform to the prescribed image for a head of state, but instead she chose to live her life according to what is right for her and for her family. The drive toward conformity is a strong one, but it is one that can, and sometimes should, be resisted.

Finding an Ally

Let's say you don't agree with a policy at your school. Would you make your voice heard? It can be pretty scary to resist conformity on your own, can't it? This is where the power of having an ally comes in. In Asch's line study, he found that the introduction of a confederate who agreed with the study participant reduced conformity by about 80 percent (Asch, 1951).

Two experiments from the research team of Vernon Allen and John Levine (1969) demonstrate the strength of having an ally. In the first, they found that people conformed to the group less often when a confederate didn't go along with the majority. In the second, they found that even a seemingly incompetent ally decreased conformity (1971). Simply having another person who is willing to stand up to the majority can have a powerful effect.

Motivation

The issue of conformity is a complicated one, particularly in an individualistic society such as the United States, in which individual freedoms are highly valued, yet people for the most part are expected to conform to social norms. To some people, the very word calls to mind weak-minded individuals who blindly go along with society. Of course, it's not that simple or that dire. Indeed, we all conform to some degree, and conformity can be positive. Can you imagine what would happen if we all refused to conform to the social norms associated with waiting in line at the grocery store or obeying traffic signals?

Resistance to conformity is driven by a high need for individuality, particularly in situations in which people feel they're just one of the crowd. This motivates behaviors that are aimed at reestablishing a sense of being different. Individuals who demonstrate a high need for uniqueness are less swayed by the pressure to conform and agree less with the majority (Imhoff, 2009).

Despite the image of the "nonconformist" in popular culture as a sullen teen who rejects anything "normal," resistance to conformity can have a profound impact. In many cases throughout history, we have nonconformists to thank for social progress, particularly since the punishment for resisting conformity can sometimes be great. Without the willingness of key individuals to resist conformity, would the civil rights movement have started? Would the feminist movement have gotten off the ground? Would Sigurdardottir be able to live her life openly? Often, the motivation to resist conformity comes from a deep belief that large-scale societal change is necessary.

Minority Influence

Most of the time, the social influence of conformity is carried out by a majority. Sometimes, though, we find cases of **minority influence**, a process in which a small number of people within a group guide a change in the group's attitude or behavior. How does this work? When the minority is very firm in their beliefs, unwilling to give in to pressure from the majority, others start to believe that those in the minority may actually be right.

Research has shown that, while people publicly shy away from aligning themselves with a deviant point of view, minority influence can be profound, leading to the private conformity that comes with an actual change

<<< Icelandic prime minister Johanna Sigurdardottir broke conformity when **she became the first openly gay head of state, and did so again when she married her longtime partner in July 2010.**

in viewpoint (Wood, Lundgren, Ouelette, Busceme, & Blackstone, 1994). This can, in fact, lead to an improvement in thinking, as an exposure to a strong opposing viewpoint forces cognitive effort and leads to more original thinking (Erb, Bohner, Schmilzle, & Rank, 1998).

Of course, conformity can be a positive force. As we discussed earlier, conformity to the injunctive norm of not littering and to another, more recently developed injunctive norm—recycling—has led to greater stewardship of the environment. Conformity can help us take care of ourselves and those around us. Think about the norms at your school. The expectation to conform to campus values such as the rejection of cheating and plagiarism serves to protect students. It might be rejected by "nonconformists," but these individuals often are not thinking about how the full picture of conformity can benefit society.

> "Conformity can help us take care of ourselves and those around us."

What Methods Do People Use to Get Others to Comply with Requests?

Your sister has just come home from the mall. As soon as she gets in the door, she throws a shopping bag from Gap into your lap. "I can't believe I just bought that," she groans. You pull a dress from the bag. It's not ugly, really, but it's definitely not *her*. You ask her why she bought it. She answers, "I tried it on and didn't really like it, but the saleswoman said it looked really good. Before I knew it, I was at the register with that dress in my hand. I'm returning it tomorrow!"

How often have you agreed to do something simply because somebody asked you to do it? Favors for friends, letting people cut ahead of you in line at the store, buying something you don't really want because a salesperson nudges you toward purchasing it—these are all examples of **compliance**. Compliance is a form of social influence involving direct requests from one person to another.

The effect of simply requesting a certain behavior of an individual has been studied in various situations, including a study involving a copy machine at a library. Three different requests for cutting in line were used (Langer, Blank, & Chanowitz, 1978). For the first, participants were asked, "Excuse me. I have five pages. May I use the Xerox machine?" In the second version, the words "because I'm in a rush" were added to the request. In the third, participants were asked, "Excuse me. I have five pages. May I use the Xerox machine because I have to make some copies?"

Both the second and third versions include the word "because," which would signal a *reason* for having to cut in line. Look again at the third, though, and you'll find that there isn't any real reason given. This didn't seem to matter, though. While more study participants complied when the

request was justified (94 percent complied with the second request, compared to the 60 percent who did with the first request), the *appearance* of a reason was all that was needed. Given the third request, in which no justification was actually given, 93 percent of participants still complied. Remember the concept of automatic processing from Chapter 3? Sure sounds like it's at work here, doesn't it?

Words aren't even always necessary for compliance. Briñol and Petty (2003) conducted a study that showed that, sometimes, all it takes is getting someone to nod his or her head in agreement. In a series of experiments, participants were prompted to either nod or shake their heads while listening to a persuasive message, and then were asked to what degree they were influenced by the messages. When the messages were strong, nodding produced more persuasion than shaking. When the messages were weak, the reverse was the case. Something as simple as head movements can have profound impacts on a person's thoughts about a message.

THE SIX PRINCIPLES OF COMPLIANCE

In the mid-1990s, social psychologist Robert Cialdini set out to study compliance. He determined that the best way to do so was to study individuals who depended upon their abilities to persuade others. He called these individuals *compliance professionals*—individuals such as salespeople, people who work in advertising, fund-raisers, politicians—anyone whose livelihood is directly tied to his or her powers of persuasion.

To study these individuals and their methods of prompting compliance, Cialdini went undercover, working in fund-raising, sales, and other fields that depend upon compliance. He found that while people may use many different methods of gaining compliance, all of these methods are based on six principles. They are *friendship or liking*, *commitment or consistency*, *scarcity*, *reciprocity*, *social validation*, and *authority* (Cialdini, 1994). We first discussed these as "weapons of influence" in Chapter 7, and now we will explore each of these in more detail.

Friendship or Liking

Let's say your friend has asked you to save him a seat at the movies. No problem, right? Now let's say the same request has been made by a stranger or by someone you don't like. Suddenly, the likelihood of your compliance is pretty low, right? It seems fairly obvious—we are more likely to comply with requests from people we like than with those from people we don't like or don't know.

Persuasive techniques that take advantage of this principle are called **ingratiation techniques**—techniques in which we get others to like us so they are more likely to comply with a request. Flattery is a great example of this—remember your sister and the dress she didn't like but bought anyway?

Even just a *sense* of familiarity can affect degrees of compliance. Researchers have found that participants were more likely to agree to a request for a donation to charity from a stranger who had the same first name or birthday than when there were no such similarities between the participant and the stranger (Burger, Messian, Patel, del Prado, & Anderson, 2004). As small as the connection might be, it still enhanced the drive to comply.

Commitment or Consistency

You're heading into class when a classmate approaches, asking you to sign a petition to stop animal testing in the campus labs. If you already agree with his or her position, you're far more likely to sign than if you disagree. This is an illustration of the commitment or consistency principle of compliance. Once you're already committed to a position, you are more willing to comply with requests that reflect that position.

One persuasive technique that depends upon this principle is the **foot-in-the-door technique**, which begins with a small request. Once that request is granted, the requester makes a larger target request. You've seen this in play if you've ever been to a large "warehouse" store like Costco or BJ's. It's so easy to take that free sample, isn't it? The requester knows that once that sample is in your hands, it will be easier to persuade you to comply with the target request: buying the full-sized product. Research suggests that this technique does indeed lead to increased compliance (Freedman & Fraser, 1966).

Another technique based on the commitment or consistency principle is the **lowball technique**. In this technique, once an individual agrees with an offer, the requester adds on additional costs, making the offer less attractive. Why, after an offer has been made less attractive, doesn't the target of the offer just walk away? This is where the idea of commitment comes in. Once the initial commitment has been made, it's harder to say "no," even when the offer has changed. For example, your friend asks you to drive him or her to the airport so he or she can fly home to visit his or her parents. Only after you've already agreed does he or she mention that his or her flight is at 7 a.m., and that you'll need to pick him or her up at 5 a.m. Had your friend mentioned the time before you complied with the request, you might not have agreed to the arrangement. As unattractive as the prospect of getting up at 4 a.m. to drive to the airport may be, you probably won't back out now, because you have already made the commitment.

> " Why, after an offer has been made less attractive, **doesn't the target of the offer just walk away?** "

Scarcity

If something is hard to get or if supplies are running out, you're more likely to comply with a request. Items that seem to be in short supply suddenly seem more desirable, and we don't want to feel left out. Think about what happens around the holiday season at the end of each year. There's usually some hot new toy or gadget that's the "must have" gift of the year. How many news stories have you heard about parents getting into fistfights over these toys? It's the principle of scarcity at work.

One classic study confirmed the effectiveness of perceived scarcity. Worchel, Lee, and Adewole (1975) asked participants to rate the attractiveness of and the cost they'd be willing to pay for cookies. They found that ratings were significantly higher when there were only two cookies in the jar as opposed to when there were 10 cookies available.

Reciprocity

When you do a favor for someone, you expect he or she will be willing to do one for you next time you ask, right? The principle of reciprocity works because you are usually more willing to comply with a request from someone who has previously complied with a request from you.

The principle of reciprocity is central to a method known as the **door-in-the-face technique**. Here, the requester makes an initial offer that is much larger than the target offer, in the hope that the final offer will have the appearance of the requester doing a favor for the target person. This technique comes into play in a classic study carried out by Cialdini and his colleagues (Cialdini, Vincent, Lewis, Catalan, Wheeler, & Darby, 1975). They asked college students if they would be willing to commit to unpaid

positions as counselors for juvenile delinquents for two hours a day for the next two years. Not one person agreed. However, when the request was modified to ask the students to serve as chaperones on a two-hour trip to the zoo with the juvenile delinquents, half of the students agreed. When the zoo request was made without the initial proposition of a counseling position, only 17 percent of the students complied (Cialdini, Vincent, Lewis, Catalan, Wheeler, & Darby, 1975). In the end, it appeared that the researchers were making an offer of reciprocity—that they were willing to help the students out by making the offer more manageable.

Another technique that depends upon the principle of reciprocity is the **that's-not-all technique**. Using this technique, an initial request is followed by adding something that makes the offer more attractive. Infomercials are notorious for using this technique—in fact, the very words "That's not all!" are often used in those television advertisements.

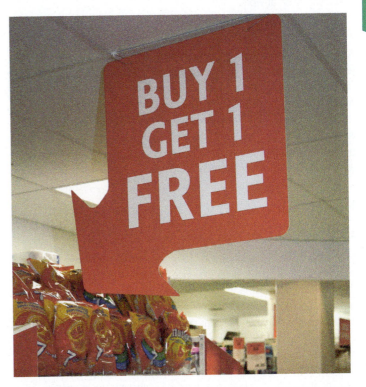

∧ ∧ ∧ **Two for the price of one?** The that's-not-all technique relies on the principle of reciprocity, **throwing in something extra to make you feel like you're getting something free.**

This technique works in part because it seems like a negotiation, even though it's used when the target of the request hasn't yet had a chance to respond to the offer. As a salesperson adds additional products or incentives, the customer feels an obligation to purchase the product because it seems that the salesperson is making concessions—again, tapping into that principle of reciprocity. The effectiveness of this technique was illustrated in an experiment with a bake sale (Burger, 1986). Cupcakes were either sold with two cookies together for 75 cents, or the cupcakes alone were priced at 75 cents, with the two cookies being thrown in "for free." The success rate of the first offer was 40 percent, while the "that's not all!" offer made for successful sales 73 percent of the time.

Social Validation

The principle of social validation depends upon our willingness to comply with a request that is in line with what we believe is the norm for people like ourselves. We want to fit in (again, the power of social norms at work!), so we go along with requests that seem to match up with what others are doing.

In fact, the principle of social validation was the one Cialdini most often encountered during his studies of compliance (2001). Think about all of the ads you've seen or heard in which a company claims its product is the best-selling or most popular on the market—it's the principle of social validation at work.

Authority

After an appointment with a doctor, you're most likely going to follow her advice or pick up the medication she prescribed. When you see a police car flashing its lights behind you, you're most likely going to pull over. We are generally more likely to comply with requests from people who appear to have authority. This influence often comes from the perception that authority figures are experts. In the next section, you will read about just how far this compliance can go, and the dangers that are associated with an excessive drive toward complying with authority figures.

How Do Authority Figures Get Us to Obey Them?

In Chapter 2, you were introduced to Stanley Milgram's infamous studies on **obedience**, a form of social influence in which an authority figure is able to simply order someone to do something. His experiments, in which he led study participants to believe they were administering electric shocks to an unseen person whenever that person gave an incorrect answer to a question (Milgram, 1963), rocked the world of social psychology and brought ethical concerns to the forefront of discussions of (and subsequent changes to) acceptable research methods because participants believed they were administering potentially lethal shocks to another individual. Despite Milgram's assertion that he debriefed all participants and a

survey showing that 84 percent of participants were either "glad" or "very glad" to have participated in the experiment, ethical concerns prevent research like his from being conducted today.

The principle of authority that plays a part in driving compliance is the central factor in obedience. Milgram's research depended upon perception of authority. Carried out in a lab at Yale University, run by a research scientist, the study resulted in 70 percent of participants continuing to administer shocks to the generator's limit. When Milgram ran his studies out of a ramshackle lab with no associations with Yale, the rate of obedience with administering the shocks dropped to 48 percent. When the experimenter was not perceived to be a scientist, but instead another participant, compliance dropped to 20 percent.

We'd probably like to think that an experiment like Milgram's wouldn't get the same results today. But nearly 50 years later, despite ethical constraints, researchers have recently been able to replicate Milgram's experiment (Burger, 2009). Jerry Burger, a professor at Santa Clara University, is one of those researchers. Burger had observed that many people think the results would be different today, that the lessons of the Holocaust and an awareness of the dangers of blind obedience would lead people to resist the pressure of the authority figure.

To comply with ethics guidelines, Burger put several safeguards in place. He lowered the top range of the generator to 150 volts, the level

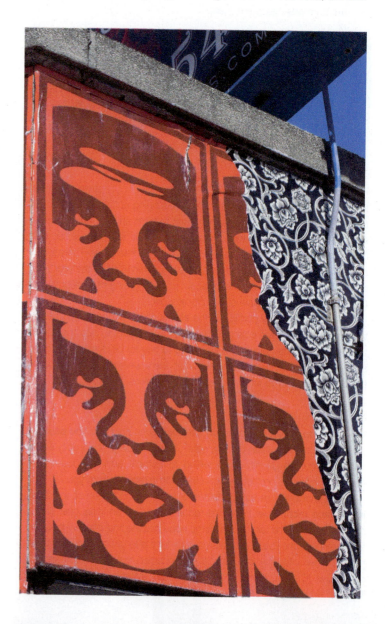

>>> **Shepard Fairey's** street art is recognizable and **carries a powerful message.**

ACTION LEARNING

Using Compliance Techniques

Is there a particular cause about which you care deeply, one for which you feel you could do something major, if only you had some assistance from your peers or the community? Now that you have learned about a variety of compliance techniques based on Cialdini's six principles, why not apply them and finally drum up some of that support you've been hoping for?

Turn on the television, and you'll see compliance principles and techniques used in an effort to get you to do your part as a consumer. Research has demonstrated that compliance techniques are useful in more noble pursuits as well. In a study by Brownstein & Katzev (1985), 89 people were asked to contribute a dollar to a museum after having been exposed to one of three different techniques. Using the foot-in-the-door technique, researchers first asked patrons to sign a petition in support of the museum. Researchers used the door-in-the-face technique by initially asking for a $5 contribution and then reducing the request. Finally, patrons were exposed to the lowball procedure—they were asked to

contribute 75 cents, and were then asked to add an additional 25 cents in support of the museum's children's program.

Generally, it was found that the lowball procedure was the most effective of the three techniques, and that the foot-in-the-door technique was the least effective (Brownstein & Katzev, 1985). Why do you think the compliance techniques varied in their effectiveness in this scenario? Which of the various compliance techniques do you think might be most effective in asking for support for your selected cause?

For this project, select a cause for which you wish to garner support from your community. In order to test compliance techniques, remember that there should be some request you will make of your potential supporters. Here are some ideas for a possible cause:

1. An organization for which you would like to raise money through an event such as a bake sale or through directly asking for donations (e.g., your psychology club, a local children's school, or a homeless shelter)
2. An elected position, such as on your school's student government, to bring about change
3. A research fund or drive to which you would like to contribute money
4. Another cause that is important to you

Select three compliance techniques and/or principles (e.g., foot-in-the-door, door-in-the-face, and scarcity) and write out in your own words how they work. Apply the three techniques to your chosen cause by developing three different requests that can be used to ask for support. Approach people in your community and ask for support using one of the requests you developed, using the three requests on different people. Evaluate which of the techniques is most successful—do they all work equally well, or is one more successful than the others? Are there any additional factors that may have affected rates of compliance?

What will you learn from this action project?

1. Explain how three compliance techniques work.
2. Use compliance techniques to request support for a selected cause, and help contribute to that cause.
3. Evaluate which compliance technique is most successful for use in supporting a selected cause.

Using Compliance Techniques for a Good Cause

What Cause Is Important to You?	
Technique 1:	Results:
Technique 2:	Results:
Technique 3:	Results:
Which compliance technique is most successful for your cause?	

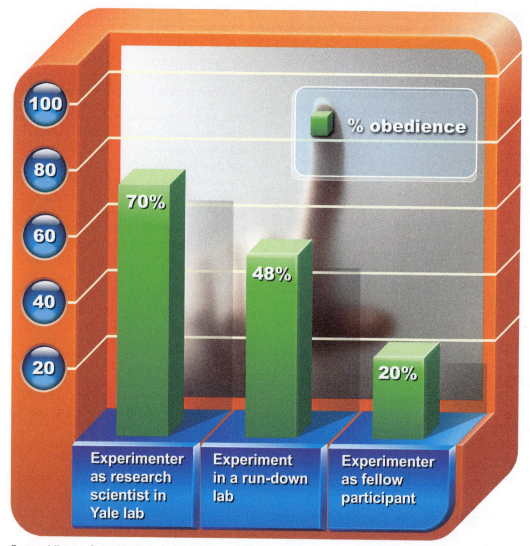

% obedience

100
80
70%
60
48%
40
20
20%

Experimenter as research scientist in Yale lab

Experiment in a run-down lab

Experimenter as fellow participant

Source: Milgram, S. (1963). Behavioral study of obedience. *Journal of Abnormal and Social Psychology, 67*(4).

Degrees of Disobedience. Whether or not we obey depends upon the perceived level of authority, as demonstrated in Milgram's controversial study on obedience.

in Milgram's study at which nearly every participant paused and expressed reluctance to continue. Participants in Burger's study were told at least three times they could withdraw and still receive the $50 payment. They were also given a lower sample shock (to show the generator was real) than that given in Milgram's study.

His study may not have directly mimicked Milgram's, but it is nonetheless useful. What he found may be a bit disheartening though. Despite our supposed awareness of the dangers of blind obedience, and the historical examples of the horrors that can result, Burger's experiment resulted in only slightly lower levels of obedience than those found in Milgram's original work (Burger, 2009).

OBEDIENCE OUTSIDE THE LAB

Would you eat a big jar of worms right now? How about let yourself be locked in a glass box full of snakes and cockroaches? Of course not, right? The very idea of doing either of these things seems just plain crazy.

Now, what if you could win a trip to Las Vegas or a new car by doing one of these things? *What if you were on television*?

Reality shows like *Fear Factor*, which feature stunts like the ones above (and those would be considered tame by the show's standards!), depend upon contestants' willingness to do things they would never normally do. For prizes, yes, but many believe the real motivation comes from being on television. Of course, we don't only see the potential dangers of obedience carried out in reality television. There are plenty of real-world examples that serve as warnings against blind obedience.

Think about the prisoner abuses carried out by soldiers who were "just following orders" at Abu Ghraib. When the trial began in 2004, the question on everyone's mind was: What makes good people do bad things? Zimbardo, who carried out the Stanford Prison Experiment we discussed earlier, served as an expert witness for several of the soldiers on trial. He argued that social modeling and group conformity, paired with stress and a lack of accountability, played roles in the obedience that led soldiers to act in appalling ways (Dittman, 2004).

On a smaller scale, but no less horrifying, is the story of a nightmarish interrogation that took place at a McDonald's in Mt. Washington, Kentucky. Following instructions given by a "police officer" on the phone, the store manager subjected a terrified employee to an "examination" and sexual abuse carried out by the manager's fiancée. The man on the phone was, of course, not a police officer. Rather, this was the latest in a long line of hoax calls carried out by a voyeuristic prison guard (ABC News, 2005). The perceived authority of the caller coupled with the presentation of an unfamiliar situation led the store manager to blindly trust and obey the voice on the phone.

Bringing Milgram to Prime Time

The motivation of the promise of TV time was illustrated, to disturbing effect, on French television in March 2010. Eighty contestants on a game show signed contracts in which they agreed to inflict electric shocks on other contestants. They were told that there would be no prizes, as it was a new show and this was a test episode, but were offered a small fee for their participation.

The setup was much like that in Milgram's experiment. Contestants were instructed to administer an electric shock, up to 460 volts, to another contestant whenever he answered a question incorrectly. The overwhelming majority obeyed, despite his screams of protest. When the final shock of 460 volts was administered, the man fell silent—presumably he had passed out or even died. Only 16 of the 80 contestants stopped before that last shock. What could drive people to follow orders until they potentially killed a man?

> **When the final shock of 460 volts was administered, the man fell silent—presumably he had passed out or even died.**

As it turned out, this was no game show. The contestant being shocked was an actor, who screamed and writhed as the "shocks" were administered. It was all for a documentary called *Game of Death*, which cast a critical eye on the trend of reality television, in which contestants are asked to carry out harmful or humiliating tasks. Many of the "contestants" in the show later said they wanted to stop, but that they were convinced by the presenter to keep going. One admitted with regret that she kept going despite the fact that her grandparents were Jewish Holocaust victims.

Has television become the ultimate authority? *Game of Death* producer Christophe Nick argued that on television, under the guise of a game, you can get people to do anything. Even if your partner screams, you are still in a game. In a game, he said in an interview about the documentary, the rules are skewed. A psychologist involved with the show said the results serve as a lesson that rules must be explained to children, rather than simply imposed upon them, and that people must be taught to disobey when a situation calls for it (Chazan, 2010).

Cults and Obedience

In the mid-1970s, the Peoples Temple, a cult-like organization that started in the mid-1950s in Indianapolis, Indiana, moved its headquarters to San Francisco. As the group became more politically active, they started to face opposition in San Francisco, prompting another move—this time to a remote settlement, dubbed Jonestown, in Guyana.

There the group lived until 1978, when Congressman Leo Ryan of California, in response to concern from relatives of some of the members of the Peoples Temple, traveled to Guyana to investigate. His party received a polite reception, but things quickly spun out of control as some members of the cult expressed desire to defect and return to the United States with Ryan. As his party attempted to leave, three were shot and killed. Fearing imprisonment and the dissolution of the cult, Jones ordered his followers to commit mass suicide. Large vats of Kool-Aid were laced with cyanide, and though a few people escaped, the vast majority of his group obeyed. Some helped their children drink the Kool-Aid before drinking it themselves, their final act of obedience to their leader.

>>> **Jim Jones and the members of the Peoples Temple** serve as a haunting example of just how far obedience can go.

STRATEGIES FOR RESISTING OBEDIENCE

Despite the power exerted by authority figures, there are ways in which obedience can be resisted. This can be done by changing authority or changing proximity (Milgram, 1963).

Changing Authority

One way in which obedience can be resisted is by taking away the perceived authority level from the authority figure. Remember that Milgram (1963) did not get nearly as many people to comply when the person urging them to push the button was perceived to be another participant, rather than a researcher. We often believe authority figures are willing to take responsibility for actions they have ordered. If it is perceived that the person does not have a high enough level of authority, people are less willing to follow her orders.

Changing Proximity

It's a classic suspense-movie scenario. You can stop one of three events, and you must make a choice between them. One will result in the death of your best friend, the second will result in the deaths of 20 people in your town, and the third will result in the deaths of 200 people in a foreign country. If your instinct is to save your friend, you are not alone. Proximity is a powerful factor. Because you are more proximal to your best friend, you are naturally more inclined to want to save him.

In Milgram's study, he found that obedience levels were significantly reduced the closer the participant was to the person being shocked, with the lowest levels occurring when participants were required to touch their partners. Proximity of the authority figure was also a factor, with lower levels of obedience when the experimenter gave instructions over the phone or via a tape recorder, rather than in person (Milgram, 1963).

Often, as Milgram discovered, we behave in ways that cognitively, we don't necessarily want to. Social roles and norms play a large part in defining how we think we should behave and how we do. This sometimes results in obeying and conforming, but it also helps us persuade others to conform in ways we wish them to. These social influence techniques can be used to both harm and help. So next time you change your attitudes or behaviors, consider the influence that others have on your decision.

Review

Summary

HOW DO SOCIAL ROLES AND SOCIAL NORMS DEFINE THE WAYS IN WHICH WE BEHAVE?   p. 138

• Social influence occurs when our attitudes or behaviors are affected by another person or group. This influence is rooted in social roles and social norms.

• We expect people within certain social roles to act according to our expectations for those roles. Social norms might vary from culture to culture and group to group, and provide guidance for how we are expected to behave in a particular place or group. Descriptive norms describe how people typically behave, while injunctive norms define what is acceptable behavior.

WHAT FACTORS AFFECT AND PROMOTE CONFORMITY?   p. 142

• Through changing our behaviors to stay in line with social roles and social norms, we engage in conformity. Conformity can be public, which occurs when one feels pressure to follow a group, or private, which occurs when one comes to truly believe that the group is right.

• There are many reasons for conforming, including when we need to decide what to do in an ambiguous situation, or when we want to be accepted by the group. Conformity is affected by group size as well as demographic variables.

WHAT METHODS DO PEOPLE USE TO GET OTHERS TO COMPLY WITH REQUESTS?   p. 146

• Compliance is based on six basic principles, upon which different compliance techniques are built. These techniques are used to influence someone through a direct request. Often, all that is needed for compliance is the appearance of a reason.

HOW DO AUTHORITY FIGURES GET US TO OBEY THEM?   p. 148

• The findings of Stanley Milgram's infamous 1963 study still hold true today—people seem to be willing to follow the orders of an authority figure, even if it means hurting someone else. The effect has been made even greater with the invention of various reality television shows.

• While there are certainly positive aspects to authority and obedience, there are many dangers associated with the kind of blind obedience seen in Milgram's study. Levels of obedience can be changed by changing the authority level of the person giving orders or by changing proximity.

Key Terms

chameleon effect the nonconscious mimicry of the postures, mannerisms, facial expressions, and other behaviors of one's interaction partner, such that one's behavior passively and unintentionally changes to match that of others in one's current social environment   138

compliance a form of social influence involving direct requests from one person to another   146

conformity a type of social influence in which an individual changes his or her behaviors to stay in line with social norms   142

descriptive norms how people typically behave in a given group or situation   140

door-in-the-face technique a persuasive compliance in which the requester makes an initial offer that is much larger than the target offer, in the hope that the final offer will have the appearance of the requester doing a favor for the target person   147

foot-in-the-door technique a compliance technique that begins with a small request that, when granted, leads to a larger request   147

informational social influence a type of influence that occurs when one turns to

members of one's group to obtain accurate information   142

ingratiation techniques techniques in which we get others to like us so they are more likely to comply with a request   146

injunctive norms behaviors of which people typically *approve* or *disapprove* in a given group or situation   140

lowball technique a compliance technique in which a target accepts a "low-cost" offer, only then to be told that there are additional hidden costs   147

minority influence a process in which a small number of people within a group guide a change in the group's attitude or behavior   145

normative social influence a type of influence that occurs when one goes along with a group because one wants to be accepted   142

obedience a form of social influence in which an individual orders another person to do something   148

pluralistic ignorance a type of norm misperception that occurs when each individual in a group privately rejects the norms of the group,

but believes that others accept them   142

private conformity a type of conformity that occurs when people truly believe the group is right; occurs even in the absence of group members   142

public conformity a type of conformity that occurs when we feel pressured to conform to group norms. When publicly conforming, people pretend to agree with the group, but privately think the group is wrong   142

social impact theory a theory that suggests that social influence depends on the strength, immediacy, and number of source persons relative to the target person(s)   144

social norms patterns of behavior that are accepted as normal, and to which an individual is expected to conform, in a particular group or culture   139

social role expectations for the ways in which an individual should behave in a given situation   139

that's-not-all technique a compliance technique in which an initial request is followed by adding something that makes the offer more attractive   147

Test Your Understanding

MULTIPLE CHOICE

1. People most likely engage in the chameleon effect to:
   a. allow for easier interaction through shared mannerisms.
   b. make fun of someone.
   c. subtly influence another person's behavior.
   d. exert power over one another.

2. Muzafer Sherif studied social norms using:
   a. the chameleon effect.
   b. the autokinetic phenomenon.
   c. brain imaging.
   d. surveys.

3. _____ norms involve perceptions of what we should do in a typical setting.
   a. social
   b. injunctive
   c. descriptive
   d. confederate

4. Which is an example of pluralistic ignorance?
   a. Ten people at a party drink five beers each, believing that the rest of the group finds this normal and acceptable. Privately, all of them believe it to be excessive, but don't want to look stupid.
   b. In Asch's line trials, the participants gave the wrong answers because those were the answers given by a group of confederates.
   c. A student raises his hand in class to ask about a lecture because he thinks everyone else might have been confused by it.
   d. All of these are incorrect.

5. _____ is a type of social influence in which we change our behaviors to stay in line with norms.
   a. compliance
   b. obedience
   c. conformity
   d. norm adjustment

6. Some studies have shown that women are more likely than men to:
   a. conform to group opinions.
   b. resist conformity.
   c. conform to group opinions only in private situations.
   d. conform to group opinions only in public situations.

7. _____ is a form of social influence involving direct requests.
   a. conformity
   b. compliance
   c. pluralistic ignorance
   d. a social role

8. Which of the following is an example of the door-in-the-face technique?
   a. getting a free sample at the food court in the mall, then being asked if you want to buy a sandwich
   b. being offered a coupon for milk in exchange for buying cookies, only to be told after you've agreed to buy the cookies that they are out of milk
   c. being told that there are only five left of the shirt you are on the fence about ordering
   d. being asked to make a $100 donation, and then to make a $25 donation when the first request is refused

9. Which of the following is an example of the lowball technique?
   a. getting a free sample at the food court in the mall, then being asked if you want to buy a sandwich
   b. agreeing to a flight and hotel vacation package through a travel agent, and when the agent adds on extra service fees, you still purchase it
   c. being told that there are only five left of the shirt you are on the fence about ordering
   d. being asked to make a $100 donation, and then to make a $25 donation when the first request is refused

10. Burger's 2009 study found that:
    a. Milgram's 1963 findings have not changed much over time.
    b. people are less likely to obey authority figures than they were in the 1960s.
    c. compliance techniques are based on six principles.
    d. people are willing to do just about anything on television.

ESSAY RESPONSE

1. Provide examples of three social roles that you fill. How does your behavior change between these roles? Why?

2. You have been asked to plan a public service campaign for a social issue. Explain how you would use what you have learned about descriptive and injunctive norms to shape the campaign.

3. Choose a situation such as a trip to the grocery store or driving to work. Name one descriptive norm for people in that situation, and one injunctive norm. What is the difference?

4. Describe examples of when informational social influence and normative social influence might occur. What is the difference between the two?

5. How might you design an ethically acceptable experiment to test the boundaries of obedience? Why would this experiment be effective?

APPLY IT!

Think of a social norm you can safely (and legally!) break. Do so. What happens? Observe the reactions of your breaking that norm.

ANSWERS: 1. a; 2. b; 3. b; 4. a; 5. c; 6. a; 7. b; 8. d; 9. b; 10. a

Remember to check www.thinkspot.com for additional information, downloadable flashcards, and other helpful resources.

THE POWER
OF THE GROUP

On

January 28, 1986, the world was shocked when the *Challenger* space shuttle exploded only seconds after launching. While the explosion itself was an incredible tragedy, what is perhaps more upsetting is that it could have possibly been prevented. Reports indicate that engineers and other workers found problems with equipment on the shuttle, but no one went through the process of properly addressing these issues. Though individuals had identified problems, the groups of people working on the shuttle launch refused to acknowledge the problems, or to delay the launch until the problems were resolved. This sad example of what we call "groupthink" indicates how groups can alter an individual's behavior. Though some found errors, the collective response was simply to drive forward and complete the ultimately fatal launch. The *Challenger* launch is an example of how a group can negatively impact a person's behavior. But fortunately, group interaction doesn't always have to have a negative result.

People join groups for all kinds of reasons. Some people happen to end up in a group simply because they are in the same place at the same time, although these people are not united. Some individuals look actively for groups to join because they want to make new friends, while others want to work collaboratively to accomplish a common goal. Some people may live alone and crave the social interaction that groups provide, while others like the diversion from the stress of everyday life.

Most people become part of at least one group in one way or another, and every group serves a different purpose. A group can consist of two or three people, such as a study group, or it can be larger and include hundreds or thousands of members, like a political party. Sometimes our membership in a group is temporary—such as participation in an intramural sports team—while other times it may be lifelong, such as membership within a church. The accepted behaviors of a group become norms for us as individuals and determine how we act when surrounded by other members. Whether we are functioning as part of a family or as members of a social committee, the influence of the group leads us down paths we would not normally walk alone.

This chapter will help you to understand what defines a group, how groups influence individual behavior, and the factors that determine how decisions are made within groups. We will also take a look at conflicts, their causes, and methods for solving them.

CHAPTER **09**

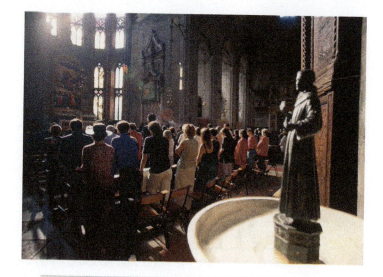

What Defines a Group?

A **group** is defined as two or more people who are seen as a unit and interact with one another (Shaw, 1981). Some groups—such as sports teams or work groups—have members who know each other personally and work together in order to achieve a common goal. The members of these groups recognize themselves as being part of a group. Other groups contain people who do not know each other and are grouped together only by similar interests or characteristics. Your sex, culture and race place you within groups, but you don't necessarily know every other person in those groups. For example, you probably connect more strongly with other people who speak your language than with those who do not, whether or not you have personal interactions or relationships with them. You are grouped in with these people simply because you share some type of commonality.

We all join groups; sometimes our memberships are short-lived, like when you're part of a group waiting in line at Subway. Other times, we belong to groups for life, like our families or religious groups. Regardless of how long you are in a group or how insignificant it might seem, each group you are part of serves a different purpose.

COHESION

Groups have different degrees of **cohesion**, or the extent to which they are connected. They may be comprised of a random selection of people who have little in common with one another, except that they find themselves in the same place at the same time. If you're waiting in line for a sandwich at Subway, for example, there is no reason to assume you share any of the same characteristics or goals as the people in front of

∧
∧ *Religious groups have a high level of*
∧ *cohesion because their members share a*
belief that the group has great importance.
What else creates cohesion in a religious group?

you or behind you. But you *are* all there for a reason—you're hungry! This is the only factor making you cohesive as a group.

On the other hand, groups can be made up of people who are united in terms of a shared intimacy, history, or background, as in the case of religious groups or families. People in these groups tend to have high levels of communication with each other, as well as common goals and a shared belief that the group is of great importance. They also have a high level of cohesion and are usually more subject to stereotypes because their behaviors are consistent over time. Furthermore, they are often stereotyped because their particular characteristics make them more distinguishable from other groups (Yzerbyt, Corneille, & Estrada, 2001).

Most established groups possess common motives and goals, as well as defined roles and statuses; this, in turn, results in the formation of a social rank or hierarchy of dominance among group members. Groups are also characterized by their accepted norms and values, as well as a clear system of rewards and penalties when those norms are upheld or violated (Sherif & Sherif, 1956).

People serve different roles in order to fulfill various goals in a group. In some cases, roles are assigned or voted upon,

<<< *Groups come in all shapes and sizes.* **Most have common goals that determine the actions of each individual.** *How many groups do you belong to?*

> ∧ ∧ ∧ **Experienced athletes typically feel more driven to succeed** when they are being watched.

like that of a class president, whereas in other cases, people acquire roles due to their personal characteristics. Think about the group of friends with whom you spend the most time. Often one friend is better at making decisions for the group, while another helps keep peace when conflict arises. Think about the Stanford Prison Experiment (Zimbardo, 1969) we discussed in Chapter 2. The students chosen to be prisoners quickly fell into their roles and demonstrated varied behavior ranging from rebellion to emotional distress. The guards in the prison adopted different approaches to their newfound power in relation to one another: Some were harsher with prisoners, while others attempted to compensate or help prisoners through lenience. Though the students were initially all just volunteers, they quickly embraced their designated roles. Regardless of the social network to which we may belong, the group often influences our individual behavior. We are not always simply *in* a group; we become *part* of it. Our own actions are often a result of the presence of other people. This includes experiences within our families or workplaces and extends to our relationships with friends.

In fact, recent research indicates that your friends can affect your health just as much as your family can. In a long-term study of 12,067 people, researchers found that a person's social network can influence alcohol intake. Think about it. If your friends spend Friday and Saturday nights drinking, you probably do too. Specifically, the study showed that an individual who spends a lot of time with a heavy drinker is 50 percent more likely to drink to excess as well. A person could even be up to 36 percent more likely to drink heavily if a friend of a friend does. When attempting to treat a person for alcoholism, his or her social networks should be taken into account as a possible hindrance to the attainment of sobriety (Rosenquist, Murabito, Fowler, & Christakis, 2010). This is just one example of the many impacts a group like one's social network can have on one's life.

How Does a Group Influence Individual Behavior?

Being around others can influence a person to act in certain ways, whether negatively or positively. Have you ever shown up to a class to which your professor was 10 or 15 minutes late? There were probably students who thought it was a good idea to leave before waiting a sufficient amount of time for the teacher to arrive. The original idea to leave may have been the suggestion of just a couple of people; however, after some of the other students who had planned to wait discussed the idea with their classmates, the suggestion to leave became more appealing and acceptable to them. The group influence moved these individuals to make a decision that they might not have made alone.

Groups can and do move us to action. If you've ever been at a sporting event or a rock concert, you are probably aware of your inclination to ramp up your behavior as the crowd grows. Conversely, groups also influence us to choose *not* to act on occasion. Have you ever not voiced your opinion because you thought the rest of the group would not agree with you? Worrying what other people might think is a part of human nature that has both benefits and drawbacks, which you will see shortly. Three examples in which the presence of others affects individual behavior include social facilitation, social loafing, and deindividuation.

SOCIAL FACILITATION

You probably possess a talent or a set of skills that others may not. If you are a gifted and confident singer, you are likely to show even more proficiency in front of an audience. To many skilled performers, the feeling of being "on stage" propels them to perform with even more accuracy and passion than if they were alone. This trend toward stronger performance in the presence of others is called social facilitation.

In one of the seminal studies in social psychology, Norman Triplett (1898) showed that the mere presence of others affects behavior and generally heightens performance. To support his finding that cyclists' racing times were faster when they competed against each other than when they competed against a clock, Triplett tested his idea by having multiple teens compete to wind a fishing reel as fast as possible. What he found was that the subjects wound the reel faster when one or more other people were also winding a fishing reel (Triplett, 1898).

Zajonc (1965) later developed this idea into the theory of social facilitation. However, while having others present can facilitate performance, some studies have shown that the presence of others can at times hinder performance (Zajonc, 1965). Think of a time when you had to make an oral presentation to your class. If public speaking does not come naturally to you, or if it frightens you, then you may not have performed as well as you wanted. Hindered performance in the company of others tends to occur with activities that individuals find somewhat difficult.

> " Groups can and do move us to action. If you've ever been at a sporting event or a rock concert, you are probably aware of your inclination to ramp up your behavior as the crowd grows. "

Zajonc noted that when we have an audience, we become stimulated to succeed at the task at hand; the physiological arousal we experience because of the audience amplifies our dominant response (1965). Consequently, if the task is a familiar one, our dominant response will most likely result in improved performance. If the task is less familiar, however, decreased performance can often occur because our dominant tendency isn't established like it is in a more familiar task. Depending on our dominant response to a given task, the presence of an audience may have a positive or negative impact on our success. However, we end up responding, we can see that being in front of an audience strongly influences us.

What Leads to Arousal?

We evidently experience increased arousal when we are in the presence of an audience. Why is this? Research indicates there are three factors that may lead to increased arousal: mere presence, evaluation apprehension, and distraction.

Mere presence is the idea that the presence of other people is enough to cause us physical arousal, whether negative or positive (Zajonc, 1965). In a study using cockroaches, Zajonc, Heingartner, and Herman (1969) found that being self-conscious is not necessarily the only reason people perform poorly in front of a group. Zajonc and his team placed cockroaches in mazes made out of clear tubes and recorded the time it took each cockroach to reach the end of the maze using two different scenarios—in the presence of other cockroaches and by themselves. When cockroaches were tested in the more complex maze in the presence of other cockroaches,

the bugs took more time to reach the end than they did when they were by themselves. This study showed that cockroaches, which do not have the same self-awareness as humans, also experienced weakened performance with a difficult task in the presence of other cockroaches.

Evaluation apprehension is the idea that one's performance will be hindered or heightened due to approval or disapproval from others. When we feel that we will be judged by the people watching us, we become self-conscious and thus apprehensive about our abilities, and these feelings can negatively affect our performance.

A classic example of evaluation apprehension can be seen in sports teams "choking" during the most important game of the season. During the 2004 American League Championship Series, the New York Yankees won the first three games of a seven-game series with the Boston Red Sox. At the end of Game 4, the Yankees were ahead by one run, but ended up losing the game to Boston. Boston went on to win the next three games and the series. This was a historic choke, with the Yankees becoming the only major league team in history to lose a seven-game series after starting off the series 3–0 (Krupa, 2009).

In many different sports, studies have shown that some teams have greater tendencies to lose critical games—such as championship playoffs—on their home turfs (Baumeister & Steinhilber, 1984). A rationale for this tendency is that performing in front of a supportive audience when the pressure is on increases self-awareness and leads to thinking too much about what is at stake. Being self-conscious can produce harmful results for the team and lead to devastating losses (Wallace, Baumeister, & Vohs, 2005).

Social facilitation may also be explained by what is known as **distraction conflict theory**, which is the idea that a person performing a task in front of others experiences a conflict of attention between the audience and the task at hand (Baron, 1986). When the individual is tackling simple tasks, this can increase his or her motivation to succeed because of the awareness that he or she is being watched. But if the task is difficult, studies show that the time it takes to complete it increases with the presence of an audience, making it harder for us to focus (Baron, Moore, & Sanders, 1978; Groff,

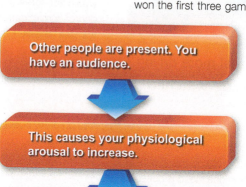

Other people are present. You have an audience.

This causes your physiological arousal to increase.

Your dominant response is enhanced.

This is a new task for you. The presence of an audience compounds your nervousness and your performance suffers.

You've done this task many times, you're confident, and you enjoy it. The presence of an audience boosts your performance.

Social Facilitation: When the Going Gets Tough.

The presence of an audience can propel us to excel at the task at hand if it is something we are comfortable doing. But research has shown that the less capable we are at a task, the more poorly we will perform in front of an audience.

Baron, & Moore, 1983). For instance, do you ever find yourself struggling to parallel park with a passenger in the car more so than you do when you're driving alone?

SOCIAL LOAFING

Around the same time that Norman Triplett was conducting his work with cyclists, Max Ringelmann was also conducting work on the influence of groups. In contrast with Triplett's findings, however, Ringelmann found that the presence of others actually decreased performance in certain group tasks where individual contributions were not identified (Ringelmann, 1913). This occurrence, known as social loafing, is the tendency among individuals performing a group task to exert less effort than if they were performing the task alone.

The reasoning for this phenomenon is that people feel less pressure to perform to the best of their abilities when they know others will pick up the slack. People working in a group feel less responsible to give it their all because the burden is not solely theirs; therefore, they are less concerned about the opinions of others. Social loafing also occurs because group members feel their contribution is not that important. To expand upon this theory of social loafing, Latane, Williams, and Harkins (1979) conducted a study that showed that individuals who were asked to clap and shout as part of a group did so significantly softer and less forcefully than when they were asked to clap and shout alone. The researchers measured the noise level of an individual's claps and shouts as compared to the noise of the group. While the level did increase, it didn't increase proportionally to the number of people in the group. In the end, it was clear that the individuals of the group were not clapping or shouting as loudly as they had when they performed the tasks alone.

Social loafing is a trait exhibited by adults and children alike. In fact, it has even been shown to occur in children as young as five (Smith, Kerr, Markus, & Stasson, 2001). In families with several children, the youngest of the bunch will sometimes learn to walk and talk later in life than did the older siblings. This is due to the tendency of the older children to perform tasks for the baby, such as getting a toy that she wants or asking a parent for something.

Social loafing is a trait that can be found across the globe; however, it is more prevalent in certain groups compared to others. Individualist cultures, like those of the United States and most Western nations, are more prone to social loafing than collectivist cultures. People in collectivistic cultures, such as those found in East Asia, are generally more interconnected, so they tend to understand the necessity of each person contributing to the group effort. These cultures are more aware of what social loafing can do to the group. Because of this awareness, social loafing is less prevalent (Karau & Williams, 1993).

Within individualistic cultures, prevalence of social loafing can be further determined by gender. In general, men tend to be more individualistic than women, causing men to be more prone to social loafing (Karau & Williams, 1993).

It should be noted that there are differences that affect the level of social loafing among individuals, for instance, the need for cognition. If you need to understand and acquire the skills or knowledge stemming from a group project, you are less inclined to loaf because the contributions you make are more valuable to you and your future goals (Smith, Kerr, Markus, & Stasson, 2001).

In your academic career, you have probably been involved in numerous group assignments. Depending on your experiences and your own work habits, you may have differing opinions on a particular group dynamic. Do you prefer to work alone or with a group? If you do not like working in groups, what are some of your reasons? You are probably well aware of the inclination of some students to perform less work within a group, leaving the bulk of the productivity to fall upon the more motivated students. Usually, if individual performance is not assessed, or if all students are given the same grade, social loafing may occur (Aggarwal & O'Brien, 2009; North, Linley, & Hargreaves, 2000; Comer, 1995).

It may seem unavoidable that certain people will exert less commitment to a group project; however, social loafing is less likely to occur when one of three things happens. The first is when group members believe that their individual work will be acknowledged by the assessor. When a member knows that his or her personal contributions will be validated, he or she tends to exert more effort because there is more at stake for him or her personally. Williams, Nida, Baca, and Latane (1989) demonstrated this idea through their research. Specifically, they found that relay swimmers achieved faster results when their individual times were recognized than when their times were lumped in with the group.

Another factor that reduces social loafing is an increase in each group member's level of commitment (Karau & Williams, 1993). This is more likely to happen when it is established that each person's contributions are necessary for a successful outcome. The belief that one's personal

∧
∧
∧ **A study led by Alan Ingham and his team (1974) showed that when blindfolded students were led to believe that others were pulling behind them in a game of tug of war,** *they exerted less effort than when they knew they were pulling alone.*

work will have a positive bearing on the entire group's performance causes an individual to work harder and more steadily toward the common goal.

A third factor in the reduction of social loafing is task importance. When there is more at stake for team members personally, they are more motivated to put forth greater effort in their personal contributions. For example, people in an office collaborating on a group project that has the potential to yield them promotions will view the task as having greater importance. With the possible outcome of a pay raise, individuals are more motivated to work harder, despite other members' less fervent efforts.

A study by Brickner, Harkins, & Ostrom (1986) showed that students who were assigned to evaluate a plan that would require exams to be comprehensive were more inclined to loaf when the proposal would not affect their own academics, but rather those of future students or students at other schools. Students who learned that the proposed change would immediately affect their lives next year worked harder at the group evaluation of the proposal. Increasing the personal importance of the task to the students caused the students to be more motivated to put forth effort and not loaf.

ACTION LEARNING

Practice Reducing Social Loafing

How many times have you found yourself frustrated because you felt that you were taking on more than your fair share of a group project? How many times do you find yourself on the other side of the line, kicking back and letting others take on more responsibility for the work? What influenced your choices in these cases?

Next time you are assigned to work on a group project with other students, apply this action learning project. Consider the potential impact social loafing may have on your group. Explain to your classmates what social loafing is. Chances are they already know people slack off in groups but what they don't know is that it's something social psychologists study. Let the other students know that there are some solutions to social loafing—making each group member's contributions identifiable, increasing the level of individual commitment, and increasing the importance of the task.

Brainstorm with your group members how you can apply these three solutions to social loafing to your project in order to ensure that your work as a group is productive and meaningful. Once the project is complete, write up a summary of the techniques you used and evaluate their effectiveness. Share your results with the rest of your classmates.

What will you learn from this action project?

1. Use social psychological principles to increase the productivity and success of a working group.
2. Educate others about resolving the problems associated with group work to enhance each individual's experience.
3. Practice strategies to help you become an effective leader in future group projects.

Eliminating the Loafing. How will you eliminate social loafing on your next group project?

DEINDIVIDUATION

Can a group lead us to lose our senses of self and engage in behaviors that we normally wouldn't perform if we were by ourselves? This occurrence, known as **deindividuation**, is when a person lets go of self-consciousness and control and does what the group is doing—usually with negative goals or outcomes.

Deindividuation happens when individuals feel anonymous within a group and because of that anonymity, also feel empowered to act upon a situation. Mobs, especially sports mobs, are an excellent example of deindividuation. In 1992, after the Chicago Bulls defeated the Portland Trail Blazers and earned their second consecutive NBA championship title, Bulls fans in Chicago partied themselves into a riot. Over 1,000 people were arrested for looting, mob action, and several other charges (Abramowitz, 1992). In the midst of the celebration of their team's championship win, their behavior unraveled into chaos. What would cause people to act like this?

Zimbardo (1969) identified three antecedent conditions associated with deindividuation: arousal, anonymity, and reduced feelings of responsibility. Following the Bulls-Trail Blazers championship game, Bulls fans were excited, or aroused, by the win. In addition, the large number of fans in the crowd gave individuals the feeling of anonymity. Because people were feeling excited and anonymous, they felt less individual responsibility for their actions. This explains why groups of people in certain cults or in mobs experience a loss of self-restraint and subsequently commit acts that they normally would not if they were alone.

The theory of deindividuation was tested in an experiment involving two groups of female students from New York University (Zimbardo, 1970). One group wore hoods that obscured all of their faces except their eyes, while the other group of women remained uncovered. They were then directed to decide how much electric shock would be administered to the subjects of the study. The researchers found that, when given a choice, the hooded students would have administered twice as much electric shock to the subjects as the women who were not hidden behind the hoods. It should be noted that no actual electric shock was administered; the researchers were simply trying to determine what effect the women's anonymity would have on their actions. A study conducted by Diener, Fraser, and Kelem (1976) found that children who wore costumes (facilitating anonymity) and were a part of a group chose to steal candy and money more often than those who were identified by name, or those who were presented with the choice to steal by themselves. The highest

instance of stealing candy and money was in the groups of children in costumes who were not asked to identify themselves; clearly, what provoked the transgression in the study was the combination of both anonymity and group behavior.

> " **The researchers found that, when given a choice, the hooded students would have administered twice as much electric shock to the subjects as the women who were not hidden behind the hoods.** "

This understanding of human behavior can explain why people in certain cult-type organizations become moved to commit acts of violence—the deindividuation propels them toward more active participation in the group experience. As we see in these two studies, the women and the children who experienced the most deindividuation were most likely to choose the more violent or less acceptable choice. For these members, if everyone around them was doing something, and if they couldn't be identified, it felt acceptable to go along with the group mentality.

In one of the more famous examples of group members experiencing deindividuation, the Heaven's Gate cult committed a group suicide in March 1997. The leader of the cult, Marshall Applewhite, convinced the group that suicide was the only way to take their souls to the next spiritual level. Though their ages ranged from mid-20s to early 70s, all of the members of the cult participated in the suicide. Their identification with the group and the resulting behavior illustrates classic deindividuation. Another more common example of this is manifested in the way soldiers are processed into boot camp. The soldiers are

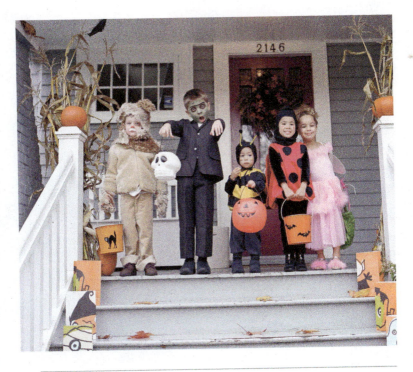

∧∧∧ Children in costumes that created a sense of anonymity chose to steal candy more often when they were in a group **than when they were alone or had been identified by name.**

RISKY SHIFT

Risky shift (Stoner, 1961) is the tendency for people in groups to take greater risks than individual members would. The belief is that the shared risk makes each person's individual risk seem less hazardous.

Risky shift is somewhat related to social loafing, in that it involves less accountability on the part of an individual. Wallach, Kogan, and Bem (1962) found that in a group setting, people are more willing to take greater risks because responsibility is spread out among members, and the support of others lessens anxiety over a risky choice. Another reason for risky shift is that highly confident risk takers in the group tend to persuade less confident group members to take greater chances (Collins & Guetzkow, 1964).

Further, group members' social standings are often determined by the extent to which they will take risks, causing people to take more chances in order to maintain a high status within the group (Brown, 1965). Bateson (1966) offered an additional suggestion that this shift occurs when members increasingly focus on a risky action until they become so used to the notion that the perceived risk lessens.

While initially it seemed that people tended to make riskier decisions in group contexts, other research has discovered that the group setting can actually cause a more conservative decision to be made. This occurrence can be a result of a phenomenon known as *group polarization*.

GROUP POLARIZATION

Group polarization (Moscovici & Zavalloni, 1969) is the tendency for an attitude or belief to become magnified for individual group members after

stripped of everything that differentiates them from each other, including their hair. They are required to dress in uniforms and behave according to standards set by the Army. This causes a loss of self, and ultimately a stronger identification with the group orchestrating that loss.

As we learned in Chapter 4, the way a person identifies himself or herself is linked to his or her behavior. Think back to Chapter 4's discussion of self-awareness at length—how might that connect to the concept of deindividuation? As Mullen, Migdall, and Rozell (2003) discovered in their study on self-awareness, when a person feels anonymous they experience a decreased self-awareness and decreased social identity. The researchers asked participants to fill out a survey on identity in four different scenarios: in front of a mirror, wearing a hood, after filling out a family tree, and in a controlled environment with no additional variables. The results showed the link between self-awareness and social identity; those participants who wore the hood felt less self-aware and less able to identify themselves socially. The hood created a loss of identity, and so deindividuation occurred.

Recent research has proposed a SIDE model of deindividuation—*social identity deindividuation* (Postmes, Spears, & Lea, 1999). This model argues that deindividuation occurs not because there is a loss of identity, but because there is a shift from identification with oneself to identification with the group. Once the person has made this shift, this leads them to conform to the group's norms. Whether a person loses his self-awareness and conforms to the group or actually adopts the group's identity, deindividuation results in a person acting like other members of a group instead of the way he would alone.

How Does a Group Make Decisions?

Think about a group to which you belong. Have any recent decisions been made that affected the entire group? Maybe at your restaurant job, management made the decision to pool tips to be divided among the staff instead of letting each person keep the tips he or she earned individually. Or maybe your class voted to change a due date for an assignment so that it was better suited to people's schedules. If a decision was made recently, did you agree with it? Do you think it was fairly made? The sections that follow present three factors that affect group decision making: risky shift, group polarization, and groupthink.

When the Group Takes a Gamble: Which Seems Riskier? It's easier for an individual to make a riskier move in a group, because the responsibility of a poor result is then diffused.

discussing an issue with the group as a whole (for a review, see Isenberg, 1986). The dominant attitude among group members becomes stronger when people discuss their feelings—whether favorable or oppositional—about a certain topic (Brauer, Judd, & Jacquelin, 2001). In their 2001 study on social stereotypes, Brauer, Judd, and Jacquelin found that when students in a low-prejudice group talked about racial issues, their attitudes became even more accepting of different races. However, when students in a high-prejudice group discussed the same issues, they became even more prejudiced.

Let's say you had a problem with a recent rash of burglaries in your neighborhood and you talked to neighbors who shared your thoughts and feelings about the events. As a group, you would become more inclined to feel threatened and want to take measures to protect yourselves. Because of the group's supporting beliefs, all members might experience a heightened conviction in their opinion. A common tendency is for group members to feed on the emotions of others and become even more passionate—in this case incensed—about an issue.

A study by McCauley and Segal (1987) found that group polarization is present in terrorist organizations all over the word. The study showed that people are not born terrorists, nor do people wake up one day and begin committing homicidal and suicidal terrorist acts. Rather, the terrorist mentality is the product of growing extremist beliefs among like-minded members of a group. Consider the fact that most, if not all, suicide bombers are a part of a larger organization. The group may initially form to discuss their grievances. However, as they share ideas and feelings, their perspectives become more and more extreme due to their isolation from moderate influences.

Group polarization frequently occurs in juries during deliberation. In one study, jurors watched a reenactment of a murder trial, and the results of the deliberation demonstrated group polarization. Before meeting to deliberate, most jurors leaned toward a guilty verdict, but after deliberation, they felt that not only should the verdict be guilty, but that the punishment should be more extreme than they had indicated prior to discussion with other jurors (Hastie, Penrod, & Pennington, 1983). Bray and Noble (1978) conducted a study that also showed group polarization at work. When students at the University of Kentucky, after listening to a recorded murder trial, decided on the (assumed guilty) murderer's sentence, students who were leaning toward harsher sentences generally increased the years in prison after deliberation. Those students who were leaning toward fewer years in prison tended to decrease the years required after deliberating with other jurors. One exception to group polarization occurs in juries when the initial verdict is not-guilty, and also when the evidence is not incriminating (MacCoun & Kerr, 1988). This usually results in significantly more lenient sentences after deliberation. If even a minority of the jury leans toward acquittal, if there is a not-guilty verdict or less incriminating evidence, the jurors will move toward a more lenient sentence (instead of always tending toward harsher sentences even if there is a dissenting voice of leniency in the group).

You can get a glimpse at group polarization any day by surfing the Internet. The Web is an abundant source of group forums, message boards, and chat and game rooms that allow millions of users to share their thoughts and feelings, participate in hobbies, and empathize or commiserate with one other. For example, Web sites devoted to self-help groups, such as Alcoholics Anonymous or those for military wives, offer virtual meeting places for people with similar interests and concerns to encourage one another and give and receive support in their struggles. Cass Sunstein (2001) discusses the phenomenon of people choosing to interact with only those people who share their prejudices and ideas. This choice to filter out opposing viewpoints can certainly be harmful to open

dialogue and exposure to new ideas. One study found that extremist Web sites feed off of connectivity to other extremist sites, and often the links between these sites escalate the hate and prejudice already present on a site (Gertsenfeld, Grant, & Chang, 2003).

Most Web sites aren't used to espouse racism or spread hateful messages, as we know. The social networking site Facebook is teeming with groups and fan pages, which users can "like" in an effort to back any given cause, and many virtual groups provide millions of people the opportunity to find solace or comfort in the company of people who believe what they believe.

Think about the sites you visit on the Internet. Do any of these offer group membership, whether formally or informally? What are some of the groups you belong to within those social networks? What are the shared beliefs? Do you see an inclination within yourself to feel more passionately about your views after communicating with the people in the groups to which you belong?

There are essentially two explanations for group polarization. The first cause is *social comparison*, which occurs when someone is conscious of how others perceive them, and adjusts accordingly in order to retain a favorable position within a group (Isenberg, 1986). In this instance a person is constantly evaluating the norms of the group as they perceive them, and then repositioning themselves to suit that group dynamic. The other cause is *persuasion* or persuasive arguments, as we discussed in Chapter 7. In both cases the result of the influence is group polarization.

GROUPTHINK

Groupthink is a manner of thinking that happens when group members, faced with an important decision, become so focused on the decision being passed smoothly that they overlook other, possibly more fruitful,

∧
∧
∧ Due to a grassroots Facebook campaign, Betty White hosted *Saturday Night Live*, boosting the show's ratings.

options (Janis, 1982). The mentality of the group can actually produce negative results because their desire for harmony supersedes a practical evaluation of other solutions. Being caught up in the group's goals can skew decision making and produce unanticipated consequences, as we learned from the chapter opener.

Janis (1982) coined the term *groupthink* after examining the Bay of Pigs invasion of 1961. The Bay of Pigs invasion is historically considered a complete and perfect failure. President John F. Kennedy and his advisors, who attended some of the country's best universities, approved an invasion of Cuba using Cuban exiles as invaders. One of the biggest mistakes of the United States was counting on situations that never came to fruition, nor seemed likely to happen in the first place, such as assuming exiles would use guerilla warfare in nearby mountains. However, the closest mountain range was 80 miles away and required the exiles to pass through a huge swamp. Fidel Castro's soldiers easily captured the exiles, and the mission was subsequently linked to the U.S. government. What seemed like a sound plan quickly turned disastrous and left Kennedy's

∧
∧ **Engineers opposed the launch of the *Challenger***
∧ **in 1985 because of potential dangers caused by**
freezing temperatures. Group pressures to
launch, however, took precedence over the
engineers' warnings and resulted in the
destruction of the shuttle and the lives of all
seven on board.

advisors wondering what went wrong. Janis determined that Kennedy's cabinet was so overconfident and enthusiastic in their mission that they did not entertain any possible problems with the plan. The group stifled any dissenters in order to preserve the self-assurance in which the newly elected administration reveled.

Groupthink usually occurs when two factors are present: a strong unity among group members, and emergent group norms. **Group norms** are rules or expectations regarding desirable behaviors that group members strive to follow. Group norms determine the behavior of members in an attempt to maintain harmony within the group. Individuals not wanting to cause a ruckus or be judged by the group are swayed by the motivation to preserve and act accordingly with group norms.

Solutions to Groupthink

Janis (1982) believed that groupthink is preventable and can be avoided by following a few simple practices: being open to criticism; working with diverse people, including members outside of the group; and training members in group decision making.

One study found that groups whose norms include being open to constructive criticism tend to make better decisions (Postmes, Spears, & Cihangir, 2001). Willingness to listen to outside opinions helps prevent the groupthink mentality. Another method of preventing groupthink is to ensure a diverse group of people is involved in decision making. A study that included racially diverse people with various backgrounds discovered that the groups with more diversity resulted in more varied opinions and essentially less groupthink (Antonio et al., 2004). Another key to eradicating groupthink is to educate the group making the decisions about the dangers of bias and of groupthink itself (Stewart & Stasser, 1995). Finally, researchers have found that information sharing in decision-making sessions can lead to better decisions (Larson, Foster-Fishman, & Keys, 1994).

After the disastrous Bay of Pigs invasion, Kennedy rethought his decision-making process during the Cuban missile crisis a year later. At the time, tensions between the United States and the Soviet Union were extremely tense. When Kennedy learned that the Soviets were housing nuclear missiles in Cuba, he took steps to avoid groupthink by listening to advice and courses of action from leaders and experts in different fields and having committees debate the ultimate solution. The United States decided to quarantine Cuba in an effort to prevent additional missiles from being housed on the island. Ultimately, the Soviet Union removed its missiles from Cuba without conflict.

LEADERSHIP STYLE

Another factor that affects the process of group decision making is the type of leader the group has. While good leaders possess similar traits, they are separated into two categories: **transformational** and **transactional**. Transactional leaders are those who reward good behavior, but ultimately only take action when something goes wrong. Transformational leaders work on building relationships and group goals throughout their time in leadership. Both types are effective, but transformational leaders tend to produce better performance among the group because they nurture trust among members and build identification with, and excitement for, lofty group goals. Transformational leaders welcome new approaches for problem solving and create internal motivation among group members (Charbonneau, Barling, & Kelloway, 2001).

Charismatic, transformational leaders often believe that when people are inspired by a passionate and visionary leader, they will follow more easily due to genuine admiration. Furthermore, they believe that the best way to motivate followers is to envelop them in enthusiasm and energy for the tasks at hand. Transformational leaders strive to transform not only the

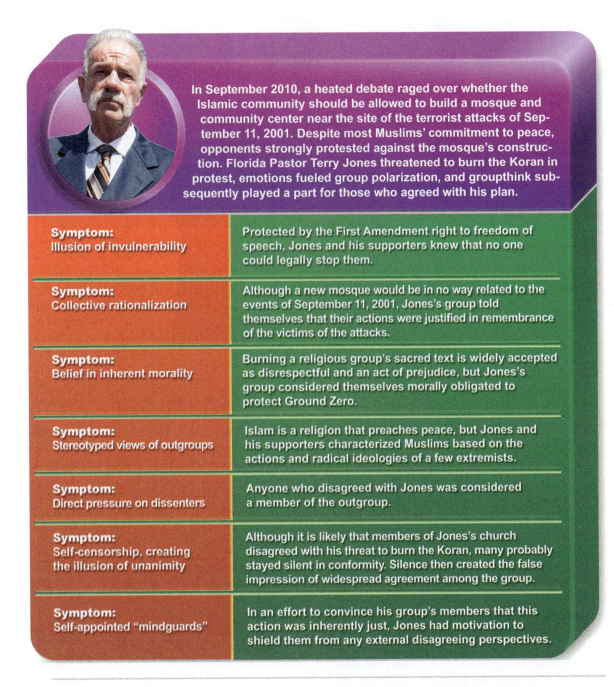

In September 2010, a heated debate raged over whether the Islamic community should be allowed to build a mosque and community center near the site of the terrorist attacks of September 11, 2001. Despite most Muslims' commitment to peace, opponents strongly protested against the mosque's construction. Florida Pastor Terry Jones threatened to burn the Koran in protest, emotions fueled group polarization, and groupthink subsequently played a part for those who agreed with his plan.

Symptom: Illusion of invulnerability	Protected by the First Amendment right to freedom of speech, Jones and his supporters knew that no one could legally stop them.
Symptom: Collective rationalization	Although a new mosque would be in no way related to the events of September 11, 2001, Jones's group told themselves that their actions were justified in remembrance of the victims of the attacks.
Symptom: Belief in inherent morality	Burning a religious group's sacred text is widely accepted as disrespectful and an act of prejudice, but Jones's group considered themselves morally obligated to protect Ground Zero.
Symptom: Stereotyped views of outgroups	Islam is a religion that preaches peace, but Jones and his supporters characterized Muslims based on the actions and radical ideologies of a few extremists.
Symptom: Direct pressure on dissenters	Anyone who disagreed with Jones was considered a member of the outgroup.
Symptom: Self-censorship, creating the illusion of unanimity	Although it is likely that members of Jones's church disagreed with his threat to burn the Koran, many probably stayed silent in conformity. Silence then created the false impression of widespread agreement among the group.
Symptom: Self-appointed "mindguards"	In an effort to convince his group's members that this action was inherently just, Jones had motivation to shield them from any external disagreeing perspectives.

Group Polarization and the Seven Symptoms of Groupthink.
These seven symptoms of groupthink are a collective form of reducing any dissonance (for more on cognitive dissonance, see Chapter 4) that group members may feel when threatened.

group as a whole but also the members within the network, believing that members will transform themselves through their contributions to the group. These leaders view their followers as products of the transformation; however, when the group and its members are happy with the way things are and do not want to be transformed, transformational leaders are likely to become frustrated. Some names of transformational leaders you might recognize are Richard Branson of Virgin, and Steve Jobs of Apple, Inc.

One of the disadvantages of transformational leadership is that followers can mistake their leader's passion and confidence for what is actually taking place. Just because a leader is excited and determined to succeed does not necessarily mean that the group will prevail. While passionate leaders have indeed accomplished great things, a successful outcome is not always the case.

Transformational leaders can also become burdens to their followers by way of their relentless energy for accomplishing a goal. While a leader's energy is a necessary ingredient in getting people motivated, it can often backfire and cause people to give up. A final drawback to the style of transformational leaders is their inclination to not see the details but rather focus on the end product. If no one takes care of the details for them, these leaders often end up failing.

Transactional leaders, while also successful, tend to see less fruitful results than transformational leaders. Although there has been much debate about its limitations, transactional leadership continues to be a popular approach with many directors. These leaders believe in a clear ladder of authority and consider people on lower rungs to be subordinates and therefore required to follow the instructions set forth by their manager.

Transactional leaders reward good work and work efficiently to solve problems (Burns, 1978). They assume that individuals work harder when they are aware of potential rewards for producing results, as well as penalties for not working effectively. While the consequences of poor work are not always explicit, transactional leaders ensure that those under their direction understand that there will be punishments for not keeping pace.

Have you ever been a leader in a group? Perhaps you were a summer camp counselor or the head of a youth group in your hometown. Or maybe you plan to become a leader in your career, such as a teacher or principal. Based on the descriptions of the two types of leadership styles, what kind of leader do you want to be, or what kind of leader have you been in the past?

Certain traits have been associated with great leaders, and both men and women can be effective leaders. However, many people do not consider women to be as effective leaders as men, an assessment that often places an undue burden on women, who can and do make skilled, successful leaders.

A 1990 study found that women in leadership roles received more negative criticism when they gave specific comments and offered arguments on a given topic than men in the same scenario who said the same things as the women (Butler & Geis, 1990). What's more, people tend to negatively judge and devalue the authority of female leaders who express anger, whereas men are viewed as more powerful and better leaders when they become angry (Brescoll & Uhlmann, 2008). People also tend to look down upon women who take on more traditionally "male" leadership styles, such as autocratic or directive styles, or when they occupy historically male-dominated positions (Eagly, Makhijani & Klonsky, 1992).

Whether male or female, strong leaders often possess the same traits. They are consistently intelligent, dominant, and extroverted, and they can initiate, plan, and delegate responsibilities. They also tend to be decisive, use shrewd judgment, and are strong communicators (Zaccaro, 2007). Think of one of your favorite teachers. He or she likely possesses most of these traits. Men and women both have the ability to lead, and each can do so transactionally or transformationally.

<<< Do you consider President Barack Obama **a transformational or transactional leader?**

How Are Conflicts Among Groups Resolved?

Leadership isn't the only element that contributes to the success or failure of a group. We experience conflicts every day, whether within ourselves, or with other people, times, or events. Not a day goes by in which we are not faced with some sort of problem that requires a solution. If you were to reflect upon this day, in particular, you could probably come up with a handful of conflicts you have already resolved or plan to resolve. **Conflict** can be defined as the perceived incompatibility of actions, goals or ideas. Conflicts are usually most intense when they involve groups of people.

With one look at a news channel, you are bombarded with stories of conflicts between groups. Pro-life protestors regularly quarrel with pro-choice abortion clinic employees and patients; Republicans frequently clash with Democrats; celebrities who want more privacy consistently fight with paparazzi; and recently, the press has refused British Petroleum's request to keep photographers away from the scene of the oil clean-up in the Gulf of Mexico. Conflict is an inevitable part of life. In this section, we will look at the usual causes of conflicts, as well as common attempts to solve them.

CAUSES OF CONFLICT

There are numerous reasons people enter into conflicts. The causes are similar on all scales—from the smallest dispute, such as a quarrel with a spouse or loved one, to a racial clash among citizens of the same country, to an international conflict among warring nations. No matter how big or small the conflicts, the reasons we enter into them are very similar. The most prevalent factors that lead to conflict are realistic group competition, attribution bias, communication errors, and biased perceptions.

Realistic Group Conflict Theory

When groups of people compete for resources, they enter into **realistic group conflict** (Coser, 1956; Sherif, 1966). In a classic study investigating the effect of competition on producing conflict, Muzafer Sherif divided two groups of boys at summer camp. These two groups functioned independently of each other until, after a time, they were brought together. The two groups had already formed bonds, and once they were confronted with each other, their identification as separate groups in competition with one another increased. This type of conflict stems from the threat of not having any access to already limited resources, such as money, land, or power.

<<< **Regardless of their professional performances,** politicians like Hillary Clinton and Sarah Palin endure a certain type of scrutiny **that their male counterparts do not.**

Even if the people in these groups come from the same backgrounds and lead similar lives, much like the boys at the camp, a desperate need for resources can quickly catapult them into competition and conflict.

For example, Southern Nigeria is plagued by fighting over its oil resources. Instead of being used to eliminate poverty and stave off pollution, the resources are a cause of conflict as different groups attempt to acquire more oil and exert power over one another (Harsch, 2007). Another instance is that of Sierra Leone's "blood diamonds," the small diamonds that are smuggled and sold to finance violent battles over control of the diamond fields (Harsch, 2007).

Attributional Bias

When we judge people's personalities based on incomplete evidence, such as an isolated act or behavior, fundamental attribution error (first discussed in Chapter 5) occurs. If you have ever witnessed a stranger yelling at her children in a supermarket, you probably assumed that the woman was a bad mother who had no patience for her children. Your judgment was based on what you saw in an isolated timeframe.

What you probably did not take into account was that the woman may have been having a bad day and that her children may have been behaving in a way she had already warned them about several times. She could have been a very loving mother who doted on her children. Under similar circumstances as the mother at the grocery store, we, or people we know well, might have acted in the same way. When we form these opinions without knowing the relevant context, we are demonstrating attributional bias.

As you learned in Chapter 6, in one study about this bias (Jones & Harris, 1967), subjects listened to people reading pro- and anti-Fidel Castro essays. Though the audiences were warned that the essays were randomly assigned, the observers tended to believe that the readers who read the essays in favor of Castro were actually supporters of the Cuban dictator. Even though they knew better, the situational information the audience had caused an attribution bias against the readers. How can attribution bias contribute to creating conflict?

Another manifestation of this type of bias is termed **hostile attribution bias** (Dodge, Price, Bachorowski, & Newman, 1990). This type of bias occurs when people assume that the intentions of another person are hostile and intended to inflict harm or stress on their own lives. Baron and Richardson (1994) determined that hostile attribution bias causes people to assume an antagonistic intent on the part of others, even when there is none. This generally shows up when the wronged party feels disrespected or threatened in some manner and may, as a result, react to the behavior in an aggressive way (Halligan, Cooper, Healy, & Murray, 2008).

In everyday life, this bias could occur anywhere, such as at a club. If you walked up to the bar to order a drink and there was a group of people looking in your direction and laughing, you might assume they were laughing at you. You would also probably feel that they were being hostile toward you and that they were mean people. This, in turn, would cause you to feel hostility toward them for laughing (and maybe even become violent or antagonistic with the group). What you would not have realized is that they were laughing at a funny commercial on the TV behind you.

In order to avoid this bias and the reactions it causes within us, it is wise to have a general awareness of the tendency. By noticing our

incomplete understanding of other people's intentions, we can begin to release the negative bias when a situation arises and avoid making incorrect attributions.

Blaming other people when we do not achieve our own goals is also a feature of attribution bias. As humans, when we feel that our goals have been obstructed, we generally try to pinpoint the reasons for the negative outcome. Assuming that another party has interfered with our goals can lead to an intense conflict, even if other people actually had no involvement in the situation. Being biased in attributing blame for an unrealized goal plays an important role in conflict and can often cause disputes that did not need to take place.

Has there been a time in your life when you mistakenly thought that another person was responsible for thwarting your goals? Attribution bias shows up in our lives when we feel suspicious of other people's intentions.

Communication Errors

Another reason for conflict stems from communication errors. The way we communicate with each other often leads to conflict, since all of us have different ways of expressing ourselves. We each bring to the table different behaviors, perspectives, and backgrounds that are not always compatible or comprehensible with those of the people with whom we interact.

If you grew up in a family in which members communicated by yelling, you might enter into a conflict later on with someone who grew up in a family where yelling did not occur. If you attended schools where teachers constantly praised your efforts—whether or not they produced excellent results—you might enter into conflict with a college professor who criticizes your work, even though you have put forth great effort.

Have you ever known a person who was very blunt in the way he criticized you? Instead of phrasing his criticism in a helpful or polite way, it seemed as if he came right out and judged you in a manner that hurt your feelings or made you angry. Studies have revealed that this type of disapproval can result in vengeful feelings on the part of the wronged person and can lead to a series of conflicts that

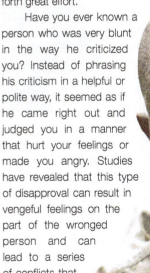

>>> In conflict over the scarce mineral resource of diamonds, **factions in Sierra Leone often come to bloody battles for control of the lucrative diamond fields.**

do not necessarily involve people with opposing views (Baron, 1990; Cropanzano, 1993). This explains why there might be a person at your job toward whom you feel animosity because of a bad first impression.

Biased Perception

A third cause for conflict stems from a **biased perception** of the intentions of others. This occurs when we think we are justified in our own thoughts and actions but believe that others are biased in *their* beliefs and behaviors.

Perceiving other people in this manner often amplifies differences in opinions and unduly stresses conflicts of interest among groups or individuals. Studies have shown that a biased perception occurs most often for groups or individuals in powerful or controlling positions (Keltner & Robinson, 1997). A biased perception among powerful groups often leads to an inaccurate opinion of other groups with opposing viewpoints. Powerful groups that experience perception bias tend to believe that their stance is more rational or neutral than it actually is (Keltner & Robinson, 1997).

One method researchers use to examine the effects of social conflict is called the "Prisoner's Dilemma" (Rapoport, 1960). Let's say Alex and Jack are caught vandalizing a freshman dormitory in a fraternity hazing prank. Campus security knows Alex and Jack committed the prank together, but the guard only has adequate evidence for a lesser punishment. The security guard decides to offer an incentive to each one as he interrogates them separately.

The guard tells each student that if one of them confesses and the other doesn't, the confessor will get immunity while the student who does not confess will get kicked out of his frat—a punishment to the fullest extent. If both Alex and Jack confess, they will each be punished by having to clean the men's bathrooms for a semester. But if neither confesses, each will receive only a mark on his record—a mere slap on the wrist. If you were Alex and had no way of talking to Jack, what would you do? The choice you make will almost surely cause a conflict based on how you and Jack perceive each other's actions.

Another manifestation of biased perception is in *hostile media phenomenon*. This occurs when a person views supposedly unbiased media coverage as biased against whatever perspective they hold. In a study on hostile media phenomenon, researchers discovered that participants assumed the media held a bias against whatever position they held, no matter which side of the argument they were on (Vallone, Ross, & Lepper, 1985). Here we see bias perception occurring between individuals and the media.

RESOLVING CONFLICT

It has been said that every problem has a solution—or that there *are* no problems, only solutions. Resolving conflict is such a necessary action that entire law firms are dedicated to solving disagreements between groups. People who possess strong negotiating skills can make healthy

livings from the conflicts of others. Negotiation occurs everywhere, every day, in businesses and non-profit organizations, as well as in the government, during legal proceedings, and among nations. It also happens in personal situations such as marriage, divorce, and parenting.

The two most common forms of resolving group conflict are bargaining and a process known as GRIT. These techniques can be used in personal relationships and also in international relations.

Bargaining

When you first got your driver's license, you probably tried to convince your hesitant parents to let you borrow the car on a Friday night. Maybe they did not want you to take it out and they told you their reasons for their reluctance. You probably countered with your own reasons as to why it would be a good idea. Ultimately, if they allowed you to borrow the car for the night, you probably had to make some concessions, such as agreeing to be home by a certain hour or allowing only one other person to ride with you. In order to persuade your parents to come to a decision that would make everyone happy, you went through the process of bargaining.

Bargaining, also known as negotiation, is the most common means for resolving a conflict. It occurs when two disputing parties come together, either in person or through representatives, to discuss ideas for resolving their disagreements. Bargaining typically involves each party making offers, counteroffers, and concessions in order to reach a resolution.

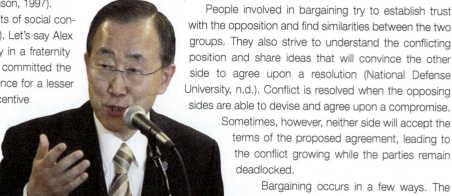

People involved in bargaining try to establish trust with the opposition and find similarities between the two groups. They also strive to understand the conflicting position and share ideas that will convince the other side to agree upon a resolution (National Defense University, n.d.). Conflict is resolved when the opposing sides are able to devise and agree upon a compromise. Sometimes, however, neither side will accept the terms of the proposed agreement, leading to the conflict growing while the parties remain deadlocked.

Bargaining occurs in a few ways. The people involved in the process use specific tactics in order to convince the opposing side to concede to their desires by diminishing their goals so that they will instead settle for something less desirable. Negotiators do this, first by offering an extreme proposal that favors the side that wants it. Then, they try to convince the opponent to make more concessions than they normally would. Third, they express that their party will cease negotiations if they do not get what they want and will instead find someone else who either will offer better

∧
∧ **Conflicts often require the help of a third, neutral party like the United**
∧ **Nations** in order to be resolved.

results or agree to their terms as is (Thompson, 1998).

Negotiators view the bargaining process as having two potential outcomes: one in which there is a winner and a loser, and one in which everyone wins. The latter result is generally more preferable since it provides gains for the individuals on both sides of the conflict. In order to achieve this "win-win" outcome from the bargaining process, each side must exhibit not only the willingness to listen to what the other side wants, but also possess a genuine concern for what is important to the opponent.

A historic example of when bargaining produced a mutually favorable outcome is that of the Louisiana Purchase in 1803. On behalf of President Thomas Jefferson, politicians James Monroe and Robert Livingston traveled to France with the intention of buying the port of New Orleans and the state of Florida for the sum of $2 million from Emperor Napoleon I. The French, however, countered with the offer of selling them the entire state of Louisiana, but not Florida, for $15 million.

In return, the United States received many benefits, including a tariff agreement on French and Spanish goods entering the country through Louisiana. By negotiating with the French government, Monroe and Livingston ended up doubling the size of the United States in the matter of a day (The Negotiator Magazine, 2005).

Think of a time when you bargained personally with someone else like a parent or your significant other, resulting in either a win-win or a win-lose deal. What concessions did either you or the other person make? What techniques did you each use to get what you wanted? What factors went into making the ultimate decision? If you won the conflict, how did you feel for yourself and for the other person? If you lost, what impression did you take away from the other person?

> "Negotiation occurs everywhere, every day, in businesses and non-profit organizations, as well as in the government, during legal proceedings, and among nations."

GRIT

Diffusing a conflict can seem almost impossible when both parties are set on having their own way. Even if a person or group on one side of the dispute wants to take actions that might end or change the conflict, doing so imposes great risks for the entire group. Individuals within a group who take measures to find a way to agree with the opposition might be viewed as traitors by their own groups. People on opposite sides of the disagreement are likely to be angry or mistrustful of each other and might reject any peacemaking attempts. They might misunderstand measures to resolve the conflict and view the negotiators as devious or deceitful.

A way to try to avoid these pitfalls is to use what is known as "graduated and reciprocated initiatives in tension reduction," or **GRIT**, which is a step-by-step formula for de-escalating a conflict (Osgood, 1962). The term GRIT was later shortened to stand for "gradual reduction in tension" because that is precisely what it helps people do—work gradually through a problem with the use of compromise to reduce tension between opposing groups.

Using the GRIT method, one party involved in the dispute begins to weaken the conflict by making a small concession to the opposing side and then asking them to concede something as well. If the adversary accepts the concession and makes an equal compromise, then the first party makes a second concession, setting in place a chain of peacemaking measures (Conflict Research Consortium, 1998). These concessions include taking responsibility for previous errors, or simply expressing the willingness to begin compromising (Kriesberg, 2003).

GRIT stands for "graduated and reciprocated initiatives in tension reduction"; a step-by-step formula for de-escalating a conflict that involves unilateral concessions and quick reciprocation by the opposition

The goal of GRIT is to establish trust and cooperation between disputing groups, leading to quick reciprocation in the form of concessions made by either side. The idea behind it is that it increases one party's credibility and persuades the other party to act in a similar manner of concession-making.

When disputing parties use the GRIT method, conflicts become more manageable and thus more easily resolved. The GRIT formula results in a higher probability of both parties feeling satisfied with the ultimate agreement, as well as the transformation of their opinions of the opposing side. In a study of this method, researchers found that 90 percent of the conflicts that used GRIT were resolved with a mutually beneficial agreement, whereas only 65 percent of the disputes treated with a non-GRIT approach resulted in mutually beneficial outcomes (Lindskold & Han, 1988).

Historically, GRIT has led to favorable outcomes for both sides involved in a conflict. One example involved the tensions resulting from Egypt's declaration in 1948 that it would not officially recognize Israel nor accept communications from Israeli contacts. In 1978, however, the Egyptian president changed his stance when he said that he would visit Israel to communicate with its leader if he was invited to do so. In turn, Israel soon invited the president of Egypt and crowds welcomed him with enthusiasm. Both sides then began to work on resolving their conflict. When a stalemate was reached, U.S. President Jimmy Carter stepped in and helped to organize a peace treaty that both parties signed, thus ending the conflict that had lasted for 30 years (Kriesberg, 2003). Without concessions being made by both Egypt and Israel, a peaceable outcome might never have been reached.

An understanding of the influence groups can have on our personal behavior, as well as the reasons we enter into conflicts and the means for resolving them, can assist you in the way you relate to other people. Specifically, being aware of social facilitation, social loafing, and evaluation apprehension can help you understand why you behave in certain ways in front of others. Now that you're aware of deindividuation, group polarization, and groupthink, you'll be conscious of how a group dynamic changes your opinion or causes you to make choices you might not otherwise make. With an understanding of leadership styles, factors that cause conflict, and ways to diffuse conflict, you can operate in groups of varied dynamics and help solve problems. And a greater awareness of human behavior in groups can allow you to move beyond asking why people act the way they do and begin asking how you can take measures to improve group interactions and resolve conflicts effectively.

>>> **What differences do you think we'd see in the world** if leaders like Iran's Mahmoud Ahmadinejad made an effort to implement GRIT?

• Review

Summary

WHAT DEFINES A GROUP? p. 156

● A group is defined as two or more people who appear to be united to some extent. Most groups are formed intentionally and have members who know each other personally and work together in order to achieve a common goal. Some groups, however, are formed solely as a result of common characteristics, such as race or gender.

● Most groups possess common motives and goals, as well as established roles and clear statuses, meaning that there is a social rank or hierarchy of dominance among group members. Groups are also characterized by their accepted norms and values, as well as a clear system of rewards and penalties when those norms are adhered to or violated.

HOW DOES A GROUP INFLUENCE INDIVIDUAL BEHAVIOR? p. 157

● Social facilitation affects individual behavior in that the presence of other people can drive a person to perform better than when alone. The effects of social loafing on individual behavior can be seen when a group task causes some members to put forth less effort when they know others will carry the weight of the project.

● Deindividuation affects an individual when a person lets go of self-consciousness and control and does what the group is doing, usually with negative goals or outcomes. This occurs when a person is moved by the group experience and does things that, without the group for support, she would not normally do.

HOW DOES A GROUP MAKE DECISIONS? p. 162

● Many groups are moved to make decisions after group polarization has occurred. Group polarization is the tendency for an attitude or belief to become magnified for group members after discussing an issue with the group. The dominant attitude among group members becomes stronger when people discuss their feelings—whether favorable or oppositional—about a certain topic.

● Groups often make decisions when influenced by groupthink. This manner of thinking happens when group members, faced with an important choice, become so focused on making a smooth, quick decision that they overlook other, possibly more fruitful, options. The mentality of the group can actually produce negative results because their desire for harmony supersedes a practical evaluation of other solutions. Being caught up in the group's goals can skew decision making and produce unanticipated consequences.

HOW ARE CONFLICTS AMONG GROUPS RESOLVED? p. 166

● Groups typically use the process of bargaining in order to resolve conflict. This involves the two disputing parties coming together to discuss ideas for resolving their disagreements. Bargaining typically includes each party making offers, counteroffers, and concessions in order to reach a resolution.

● GRIT is a method that allows parties to work gradually through a problem with the use of compromises. One party begins to weaken the conflict by making a small concession to the opposing side and by asking them to concede something as well. If the adversary accepts the concession and makes an equal compromise, then the first party makes a second concession, setting in place a chain of peacemaking measures.

Key Terms

bargaining a means of resolving conflict that involves each side of the dispute making offers, counteroffers, and concessions *168*

biased perception the belief that we are justified in our own thoughts and actions but that others are biased in their beliefs and behaviors *168*

cohesion the degree to which a group is connected *156*

conflict the perceived incompatibility of actions, goals, or ideas *166*

deindividuation the tendency for an individual within a group to let go of self-awareness and restraint and do what the group is doing *161*

distraction conflict theory the idea that a person performing a task in front of others experiences a conflict of attention between the audience and the task at hand, thus increasing the motivation to succeed when completing simple tasks *158*

evaluation apprehension the idea that one's performance will be hindered or heightened due to approval or disapproval from others *158*

GRIT stands for "graduated and reciprocated initiatives in tension reduction"; a step-by-step formula for de-escalating a conflict that involves unilateral concessions and quick reciprocation by the opposition *169*

group two or more people who are seen as a unit and interact with one another *156*

group norms rules or expectations regarding desirable behaviors that group members strive to follow *164*

group polarization the tendency for an attitude or belief to become magnified within a group after members discuss an issue amongst themselves *162*

groupthink a manner of thinking that happens when the desire for harmony in a decision-making group overrides a realistic evaluation of other solutions *163*

hostile attribution bias occurs when people assume that the intentions of another person are hostile *167*

realistic group conflict the theory that conflict stems from competition for limited resources such as money, land, power or other resources *166*

risky shift the tendency for people in groups to take greater risks than if the actions were to be taken by individual members alone   *162*

transactional leader a leader who believes in a ladder of authority and considers people on

lower rungs to be subordinates and therefore required to follow the instructions set forth by their manager; this type of leader rewards good work and works efficiently to solve problems   *164*

transformational leader a leader who believes in inspiring his followers with energy and devotion, thereby transforming the group and its members   *164*

Test Your Understanding

MULTIPLE CHOICE

1. Which of the following is not a trait of a typical group?
   a. similar beliefs
   b. anger over perceived injustices
   c. cohesion
   d. the presence of leaders and followers

2. Which psychological researcher is credited with being the first to study the theory of social facilitation?
   a. Baron
   b. Ringelmann
   c. Zajonc
   d. Triplett

3. Which of the following is not a reason that social loafing occurs?
   a. the feeling of less accountability
   b. less pressure to perform when others will pick up the slack
   c. the fear of performing when there is an audience
   d. the feeling that an individual's contribution is not important

4. Which term describes the tendency for a person in a group to lose self-awareness and go along with the group?
   a. deindividuation
   b. social loafing
   c. bargaining
   d. social facilitation

5. Which term best describes the tendency for group members to develop a more extreme position when in a group setting?
   a. groupthink
   b. deindividuation
   c. group polarization
   d. social loafing

6. Which of the following is not true of transformational leaders?
   a. They nurture trust among group members.
   b. They are passionate and energetic.
   c. They create intrinsic motivation within their followers.
   d. They believe in punishment for poor work.

7. What is an example of attribution bias?
   a. You see a stranger kick a soda machine and assume that he is an angry person.
   b. You believe you are justified in your own thoughts and actions but think that other people are biased in their beliefs and behaviors.
   c. Your professor harshly criticizes your work and you develop a dislike for her.
   d. You give a fantastic oral presentation because you enjoy public speaking.

8. Which is not involved in the bargaining process?
   a. One side makes an initial offer.
   b. The other side makes a counter offer.
   c. One side makes a concession with no expectation that the opposition will also make a concession.
   d. Both sides try to find similarities with each other.

9. Which event is not an example of the successful use of bargaining to resolve a conflict?
   a. the Louisiana Purchase
   b. the Cuban missile crisis
   c. hostage situations
   d. the Iraq war

10. Which is a step-by-step method for resolving a conflict?
    a. hostile attribution bias
    b. realistic group conflict
    c. GRIT
    d. none of the above

ESSAY RESPONSE

1. Explain how deindividuation involves aspects of both social facilitation and social loafing.

2. How can a group member strive to decrease social loafing among other members?

3. Describe how and where group polarization occurs on the Internet. Find an example and explain how group polarization came about and what the implications could be.

4. Discuss the differences between a transactional and a transformational leader. What are the drawbacks of each, and which style do you think is better?

5. Give an example of an imaginary conflict that could use GRIT as a solution. Devise potential elements of the conflict, as well as potential concessions made by both sides, and then determine the ultimate outcome.

APPLY IT!

Write a journal entry about a time when you exhibited attribution bias. What happened to cause you to make a judgment? Do you think you were fair in your criticism? Now that you understand what fundamental attribution error is, how could that knowledge have affected your understanding of the other person? How will you use this understanding in future, similar scenarios?

ANSWERS: 1. b; 2. d; 3. c; 4. a; 5. c; 6. d; 7. a; 8. c; 9. d; 10. c

Remember to check www.thinkspot.com for additional information, downloadable flashcards, and other helpful resources.

Law

As you've learned in Chapter 9, groups can wield quite a bit of influence over individuals. One field in which this is prominently illustrated is law. In a court trial, once a jury has been presented with all the available evidence in a case, several factors may influence the decision-making process. Social psychologists have conducted research in two key areas: the processes involved in group decision making and the influence of demographic factors such as the defendant's physical appearance and ethnicity.

Most juries are not in agreement when they first enter the jury room; however, nearly all manage to reach a consensus following deliberations, indicating that some form of group influence has occurred. In the classic film *Twelve Angry Men*, Henry Fonda stars as a juror who is firmly convinced that the defendant is not guilty, ultimately transforming an 11–1 jury in favor of conviction into a 12–0 jury in favor of acquittal. Research suggests that this situation would be extremely unlikely in a real trial; majority opinion usually prevails. One study found that nine out of 10 juries reach the verdict favored by the majority on the first ballot (Kalven & Zeisel, 1966); however, minority influence occasionally sways a jury's verdict, particularly if those in the minority are confident, persistent, and consistent in their opinions (Gordijn, De Vries, & de Dreu, 2002).

The influence of a group may also magnify individuals' initial viewpoints. Group polarization suggests that group discussions may magnify individuals' initial viewpoints, making them more extreme. This tendency can lead to the group making a riskier decision when working together than when acting as individuals, known as the risky shift phenomenon. For example, when students listened to a 30-minute tape of a murder trial in which the defendant was found guilty, those who believed in strong punitive measures increased the recommended prison sentence from 56 years to 68 years

Social psychologists work with experts to examine multiple areas of a trial, including jury selection, evaluating eye witness accounts, and jury deliberation.

> ❝ **Does the concept of "innocent until proven guilty" automatically make juries inclined to favor the defendant?** ❞

following deliberations, while students who were initially more lenient decreased their recommended sentence from 38 years to 29 years (Bray & Noble, 1978). In a study of 69 juries in Massachusetts (compiled from citizens on jury duty), Hastie, Penrod, and Pennington (1983) found that when given an unlimited amount of time to debate a reenactment of an actual murder case, most jurors' initial leanings intensified following deliberations. Prior to discussion, four out of five jurors believed that the accused was guilty, but they favored a manslaughter verdict. Following deliberations, nearly all the jurors believed in the guilt of the accused, and most opted for the stronger verdict of second-degree murder.

Does the concept of "innocent until proven guilty" automatically make juries inclined to favor the defendant? Research suggests that most jurors become more lenient during deliberations, particularly if the evidence is not highly incriminating (MacCoun & Kerr, 1988). Additionally, juries that are initially leaning toward acquittal will rarely return a conviction (Stasser, Kerr, & Bray, 1981). This tendency to favor the accused is known as the leniency bias, a phenomenon that likely occurs because jurors in favor of acquittal need only produce a reasonable doubt in their fellow jurors, whereas those in favor of conviction must eliminate any doubt at all.

Demographic factors also come into play when applying social psychology to law. In 2010, troubled actress Lindsay Lohan was released from jail, having served less than two weeks of her 90-day sentence; socialite Paris Hilton served just five days of her 45-day sentence in 2007. Authorities attributed the early releases to prison overcrowding, but might the celebrities' appearances have played a role in their preferential treatment? Research suggests that the attractiveness of a defendant may play a part in decisions made within the legal system, including the likelihood of a guilty verdict and the length of sentence given (Lieberman, 2002; Downs & Lyons, 1991). When Downs and Lyons examined the fines and bail set for over 2,000 people in Texas accused of a misdemeanor or felony offense, they discovered that more attractive criminals (as rated by outside observers) were given lighter penalties. Those rated extremely unattractive received an average fine of $1,384.18, compared with an average fine of $503.74 for people who were rated extremely attractive. Why might this be the case? Researchers suggest that a less attractive defendant may

" Those rated extremely unattractive received an average fine of $1,384.18, compared with an average fine of $503.74 for people who were rated extremely attractive. "

look more like the "type of person" to commit a crime, that people perceive crimes committed by more attractive defendants to be less serious, and that society holds a general belief that attractive people are unlikely to participate in criminal actions (Nauert, 2010).

Other demographic factors unrelated to the offense may also help or hinder a defendant in court. Research shows that when race is not a prevalent factor during a trial, jurors tend to favor defendants of their own race or ethnic background (Sommers & Ellsworth, 2000). In a series of mock trials, Sam Sommers and Phoebe Ellsworth found that white mock jurors rendered more punitive judgments and formed more negative impressions when a criminal defendant was black as opposed to white, while black mock jurors demonstrated the opposite pattern.

In a real-life example, when former football star O.J. Simpson was on trial for the murder of his ex-wife Nicole Brown and her friend Ronald Goldman, jury consultants for the defense team predicted that race would play an important part in the trial and that black women would prove to be Simpson's strongest defenders. A consultant for the prosecution came up with similar findings; however, prosecutor Marcia Clark rejected the advice, believing that black women would turn on Simpson when they heard about his history of domestic violence. The results of the 1995 trial supported the consultants' findings—Simpson was acquitted after just four hours of jury deliberation (Toobin, 1996).

An awareness of the types of biases that occur in and out of the courtroom can help to reduce prejudicial behaviors in the legal system. For example, witnesses have been known to report false memories of crime scenes after being asked unintentionally leading questions. But when police detectives are trained to interact objectively with eyewitnesses, the likelihood of corrupting the witnesses' memories is greatly reduced (Köhnken, Milne, Memon, & Bull, 1999). Social psychological research is used to educate juries and law enforcement officials about the possibility of bias and plays an important role in bias reduction.

Are juries biased in favor of more attractive defendants? Research shows that attractive people receive lighter sentences than their average-looking peers.

STEREOTYPES, PREJUDICE, AND DISCRIMINATION:

CAUSES AND CONSEQUENCES

By the

second week of camp, tensions between the two groups had reached fever pitch. The Eagles had written off their fellow campers, the Rattlers, as a rough bunch that swore too much, while the Rattlers made equally negative snap judgments about the Eagles. When the Rattlers won a crucial tug-of-war competition, the Eagles responded by stealing their rivals' flag and burning it. Goaded into action, the Rattlers raided the Eagles' camp, stealing the group leader's jeans and painting them orange. They carried the jeans as a flag the next day, emblazoned with the taunt "The Last of the Eagles." Incensed, the Eagles launched a retaliatory raid on the Rattlers' camp, flinging dirt around the cabin and overturning camp beds.

The rivalry between the Eagles and the Rattlers might sound like a synopsis of a recent episode of *Survivor* or a similar reality show, but you might be surprised to learn that it was actually part of a social psychology experiment that took place more than half a century ago. Researcher Muzafer Sherif and his colleagues wanted to see whether it was possible to instill prejudice between two similar groups by developing group norms and values and then placing the two groups in competition with each other

(Sherif, Harvey, White, Hood, & Sherif, 1954). They took two groups of 11- to 12-year-old boys (all of similar religious, educational, socioeconomic, and geographical backgrounds) to a two-week summer camp in the western United States. With the researchers acting as camp counselors, the groups—who were initially unaware of one another's presence—participated in teambuilding activities such as camping and cooking. During this first stage, each group established a cohesive group identity, with hierarchies and social norms.

As you may have guessed from the opening paragraph, once the two groups were made aware of each other, intergroup rivalry broke out, creating a strong sense of "us" and "them." Derogatory names were used, and the two groups refused to eat meals together. However, during the final stage of the experiment, the researchers managed to reduce intergroup friction by replacing competitive goals with goals that could be achieved only if the two teams worked together. The Robbers Cave Experiment, as it came to be known, showed how quickly stereotypes and prejudices develop but also demonstrated how they can be abated through the development of interdependent goals.

CHAPTER **10**

PREJUDICE a negative learned attitude toward particular groups of people

DISCRIMINATION a behavior directed toward a group of people based solely on their membership in that group

What Are Stereotypes, Prejudice, and Discrimination?

When terrorists flew commercial passenger jet airliners into the World Trade Center towers and the Pentagon on September 11, 2001, most people blamed the suicide bombers for the devastating events and their aftermath. Some individuals, however, held a different viewpoint. Following the horrific attacks, Baptist pastor Jerry Falwell broadcasted a statement on the Christian television program *The 700 Club* indicating that feminists, gays, and lesbians were partly to blame for the terrorists' actions. During a heated rant, he stated that civil rights groups such as the ACLU and other organizations that had helped to "secularize" America had invoked God's anger, leaving the country vulnerable to attack. Falwell ended his speech with an undeniable accusation: "I point the finger in their face and say 'you helped this happen'" (CNN, 2001).

Although Falwell later retracted his allegations and issued an apology, his comments revealed an explicit **prejudice** against particular groups of people; his statement indicated that he held negative feelings about feminists, gays, and lesbians based on the fact that they belong to a certain group. Prejudice often leads to **discrimination**—behavior directed against people solely because they are members of a particular group. During the Robbers Cave Experiment mentioned at the beginning of the chapter, the members of the Eagles camp discriminated against members of the Rattlers camp, purely on the basis that they belonged to a different campsite and stole or intentionally damaged their property.

Prejudice and discrimination have to do with attitudes and behaviors—prejudice is the affective or attitudinal component of the equation, and discrimination is where our behavior comes in. They have their roots in a cognitive component that starts with automatic processing—that "shortcut" thinking that leads us to make sweeping generalizations called stereotypes.

Most of us would probably strongly reject the idea that we hold similar prejudices to Falwell or that we actively discriminate against people on the basis of their race, gender, or sexual orientation. However, whether we admit it to ourselves or not, we are all guilty of forming stereotypes—general beliefs about groups of people. Stereotypes can contain negative or positive information—think about the stereotype that all Asians are smart, or the one that says all African Americans are good at sports. Still, it's important to remember that even if a stereotype seems to say something good about someone, it's still an overgeneralization that can lead to prejudice.

Have you ever been cut off in traffic by an elderly driver and instantly thought to yourself that people over the age of 75 shouldn't be allowed on the road? Or have you seen a group of young men wearing hooded sweatshirts and nervously crossed to the other side of the street? Do you buy into the assessment that all Italians are good lovers or that "white men can't jump"? Our brains save us time and energy by classifying people and objects into categories, and stereotyping provides us with useful basic information about the world around us; however, this can often lead us to draw false conclusions about people, resulting in prejudice and discrimination. Encountering that group of young men wearing hoodies is an example of a stereotype that has led to discrimination—the choice to cross the street because you don't want to go anywhere near them. Once a stereotype has been formed, it is difficult to dispel, because we have a tendency to reject new information that does not support our stereotype and accept only information that encourages our preconceived viewpoint (Munro & Ditto, 1997). Alternatively, we may subtype a stereotyped target who doesn't end up fitting the stereotype, deciding that she isn't really part of that group, or is somehow an exception to the rule (Weber & Crocker, 1983).

While stereotypes are difficult to dispel, they are not static. Stereotypes change as a group's role changes over time. Often, stereotypes are used to rationalize a group's role, as demonstrated in a 1990 study of gender stereotypes. Researchers found that people attributed role-based stereotypical descriptions in response to a division of labor between sexes—"city workers" versus "child raisers." They determined that people rationalize the division by attributing gender-based personality differences (women are more nurturing, so they must be the child raisers, for example) (Hoffman & Hurst, 1990). Stereotypes of groups also change as group status changes (e.g., Ross & Nisbett, 1991).

> "Prejudice and discrimination have to do with attitudes and behaviors—prejudice is the affective or attitudinal component of the equation, and discrimination is where our behavior comes in.

<<< **Following the 2001 terrorist attacks,** comments made by evangelical Christians Jerry Falwell and Pat Robertson **displayed explicitly prejudiced attitudes.**

You might think of prejudice and discrimination as being personal issues, but in fact some types of prejudice are institutionalized. **Racism** and **sexism** are examples of institutional practices that result in discrimination against individuals on the basis of their race or gender. Another type of institutionalized prejudice is heterosexism. The "Don't Ask, Don't Tell" policy prevents gay and lesbian individuals from serving openly in the military. Here, heterosexism is the backbone of a governmental policy, making this discriminatory practice accepted and "normal."

Prejudice is more rampant than you might imagine. A 2009 report by the Southern Poverty Law Center counted 932 active hate groups in the United States. Each of these groups has beliefs or practices that attack or malign a specific group of people, typically because of their race or ethnicity. Although many of these groups restrict their activities to posting hateful messages on Web sites, some actively promote acts of violence against immigrants or ethnic minorities, creating a climate of fear among vulnerable communities (SPLC, 2009). Prejudice can lead to devastating consequences, as evidenced by the Holocaust of the 1930s and 1940s to the hate crimes we continue to see today.

RACISM an institutional practice that discriminates against individuals on the basis of their race

SEXISM an institutional practice that discriminates against individuals on the basis of their gender

RACIAL PREJUDICE the tendency to hold a hostile attitude toward an individual because of his or her racial background

RACISM

Imagine being denied a table in a restaurant purely on the basis of the color of your skin. Under the Jim Crow laws in the United States, racial segregation was a reality until well into the 1950s, denying blacks equal access to schools, public facilities, and public transportation. Although racial segregation is no longer in existence, **racial prejudice**—the tendency to hold a hostile attitude toward an individual because of his or her racial background—remains a cause for concern.

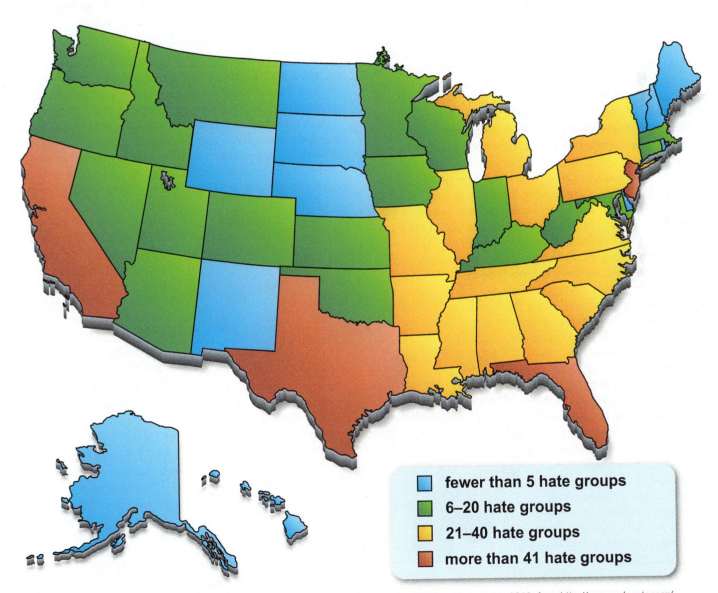

(light blue)	fewer than 5 hate groups
(green)	6–20 hate groups
(yellow)	21–40 hate groups
(orange)	more than 41 hate groups

Source: Based on SPLC. (2009). Active U.S. hate groups. *Southern Poverty Law Center.* Retrieved August 17, 2010, from http://www.splcenter.org/get-informed/hate-map.

 Hate Groups in America. There are 932 hate groups currently operating in the United States.

GENDER PREJUDICE the tendency to hold a hostile attitude toward an individual because of his or her gender

GENDER STEREOTYPES people's ideas about how men and women behave based on socially and culturally defined beliefs

In the famous Supreme Court case *Brown v. Board of Education of Topeka, Kansas,* Thurgood Marshall and his team referred to the studies of social psychologists Kenneth and Mamie Clark as evidence for the destructive effects of racial segregation. The Clarks produced drawings and dolls of black and white children and asked a number of black preschool and elementary school children to indicate their preferences. They also asked the children to color line drawings using the crayon that was closest to their skin color. Results showed that black children often preferred the white doll and drawing and often colored the line drawing a shade lighter than their skin tones. Some of the children's responses indicated that they perceived white as "good" and "pretty," and thought of black as "bad" and "ugly," leading the researchers to conclude that at the tender age of six or seven, black children had already accepted their inferior status in society (Clark & Clark, 1947). By illustrating how the "separate but equal" system reinforced negative stereotypes and a sense of inferiority among black children, the "doll test" assisted in ending racial segregation in the United States. These studies were used in a brief arguing that children would benefit from integrated schools in a case that went before the Supreme Court in the early 1950s. *Brown vs. Board of Education* was resolved on May 17, 1954, when the Supreme Court unanimously decided that school segregation violated the Fourteenth Amendment.

Although racial segregation ended more than half a century ago, overt racial prejudice in the United States persists through hate groups and individual attitudes. Interestingly, many Americans view other people as being racially prejudiced but are unable to identify themselves as such. In a 1997 Gallup poll, white Americans estimated 44 percent of their peers to be high in prejudice (5 or higher on a 10-point scale); however, just 14 percent of those surveyed gave themselves a similarly high score (Whitman, 1998). Prejudice and bias occur within racial groups, as well. Research has shown that we have a tendency to be able to recognize faces of familiar others, including those in our own racial groups, more readily than those of different racial groups (see Meissner & Brigham, 2001, for a review of this concept). The tendency has even been demonstrated in infants as young as three months old (Bar-Haim, Ziv, Lamy, & Hodes, 2006). This is reflected in the brain; different areas of the brain become more active when recognizing someone of the same race versus someone of a different race (Golby, Gabrieli, Chiao, & Eberhardt, 2001). When white students viewed people with darker skin (either black faces or white faces with darker skin tone), the brain showed higher activity in the amygdala (Ronquillo et al., 2007).

Research shows that attitudes that drive racist jokes and workplace discrimination can lead to a collective mentality that allows people to carry out horrific actions against whole groups. Genocide carried out in Europe during the Holocaust, in Rwanda against the Tutsis,

> ∧∧ **Until the 1950s,** the United States maintained a policy of racial segregation **in schools and public places.**

and against other groups throughout history is rooted in institutionalized prejudice. Images and rhetoric are spread until a population has internalized prejudices, allowing them to participate in such inhuman plots.

Like stereotypes, prejudices toward groups also change over time, depending on the concerns and ideologies of a given group, as well as current events. In recent years, prejudice against immigrants has risen, with Germans harboring more prejudices toward Turks, the British toward West Indians and Pakistanis, and Americans toward Latin Americans (Pettigrew & Tropp, 2006). In recent years, groups of American citizens, part of the Minutemen movement, have taken it upon themselves to patrol the Mexico-United States border, looking for people crossing into the United States illegally. Hundreds of volunteers, taken in by the rhetoric of the movement, have participated in these patrols—sometimes with deadly results, as in the case of the shooting of a 10-year-old girl and her father (McKinley, 2009).

SEXISM

When Dr. Sagan Tuli joined Harvard Medical School as a qualified neurosurgeon, she expected to be treated like any other member of the staff. Instead, Tuli, who is Harvard's only female spinal neurosurgeon, was subjected to months of harassment, ridicule, and intimidation from her male peers. During a 2007 surgery, the chairman of the neurosurgery department commented, "You are just a girl. Are you sure you can do that?" Tuli was eventually awarded $1.6 million after winning a sex discrimination lawsuit (Kowalczyk, 2009).

Unfortunately, cases such as this are not that uncommon. Both men and women may be subject

> ∧∧ Studies suggest that children learn traditional gender roles **from a young age.**

to gender discrimination or **gender prejudice** in the workplace, in which they are treated unequally due to attitudes based on their sex. Such prejudice arises from **gender stereotypes**—people's ideas about how men and women behave based on socially and culturally defined beliefs. Gender stereotypes differ from other stereotypes because they are prescriptive rather than merely descriptive—in other words, they indicate what many people in a particular culture believe that men and women should be. These stereotypes are reinforced by common phrases such as "Big boys don't cry" and "Girls don't play with trucks." As gender roles have evolved in society, gender stereotypes have also changed (Eagly, 1987).

Studies show that gender stereotypes are formed very early in life. For example, researchers showed 24-month-olds paired pictures of men and women performing identical activities that were traditionally masculine (hammering, taking out the garbage), traditionally feminine (putting on makeup, feeding a baby), or neutral (reading, turning on a light). The results indicated that the children paid a lot more attention to pictures that were gender-inconsistent when the activities were traditionally feminine (for example, a man putting on makeup) than when the activities were traditionally masculine (for example, a woman taking out the garbage). This aligned with the role division

within the subjects' homes—the women were far more likely to perform typically masculine activities such as taking out the garbage than the men were to perform typically feminine activities such as putting on makeup. The infants were, therefore, more surprised when they saw men performing female activities than the other way around (Serbin, Poulin-Dubois, & Eichstedt, 2002).

As with attitudes toward racial prejudice, attitudes toward women and gender roles have changed over the past few decades. In 1967, 56 percent of first-year college students agreed that married women should confine their activities to the home and family; by 2002, the number of students in agreement had dropped to 22 percent (Sax et al., 2002). The widespread support for Hillary Clinton as the Democratic presidential nominee in the 2008 election is another clear reflection of changing attitudes toward the role of women in positions of power. A 2007 Gallup poll found that 88 percent of Americans would be willing to vote for a qualified female candidate—up from 57 percent in 1967 and just 33 percent in 1937 (Jones, 2007).

Despite changing attitudes, gender prejudice remains a prevalent issue, both in the United States and in other parts of the world. In many parts of Asia, sons are more highly prized than daughters, contributing to a rise in

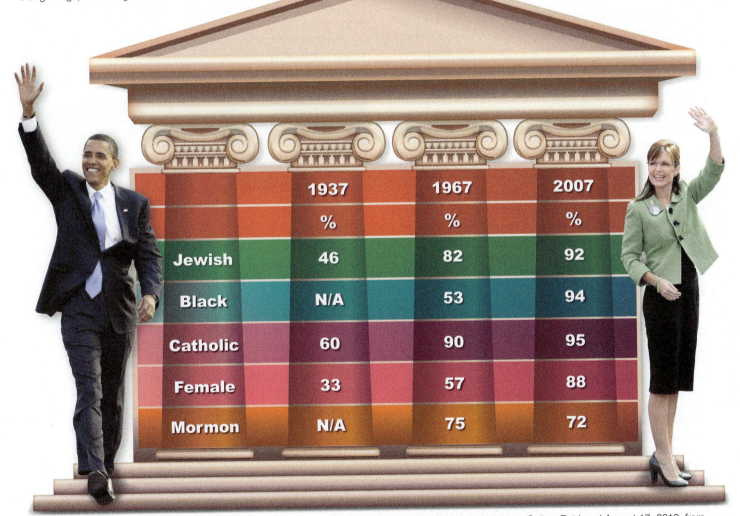

	1937 %	1967 %	2007 %
Jewish	46	82	92
Black	N/A	53	94
Catholic	60	90	95
Female	33	57	88
Mormon	N/A	75	72

Source: Jones, J.M. (2007). Some Americans reluctant to vote for Mormon, 72-year-old presidential candidates. *Gallup.* Retrieved August 17, 2010, from http://www.gallup.com/poll/26611/some-americans-reluctant-vote-mormon72-year-oldpresidential-candidates.aspx.

∧
∧ **Americans' Willingness to Accept a Nontraditional President.** American attitudes
∧ regarding women and racial minorities in positions of power **have changed drastically over the past century.**

AMBIVALENT SEXISM the contradictory attitudes of hostile sexism and benevolent sexism

OLD-FASHIONED RACISM overt, oppressive acts and feelings toward a group of people based on their race

MODERN RACISM negative feelings toward a group of people based on their race, manifested in more subtle forms of racism

OLD-FASHIONED SEXISM overt sexism, characterized by the endorsement of traditional gender roles, differential treatment of men and women, and stereotypes about lesser female competence

MODERN SEXISM internalized negative feelings toward a group of people based on their gender, characterized by a denial of continued discrimination, antagonism toward women's demands, and lack of support for policies designed to help women in work and education

the number of sex-selective abortions. The natural sex ratio is roughly 1.05 to 1, meaning that about 105 male babies are born for every 100 female babies. But in China, for example, the ratio is about 120 boys for every 100 girls, and in areas such as Guangdong and Hainan, the imbalance has reached 135 to 100 (Jacoby, 2008). And as a result, millions of young men in Asia are unable to find mates, fueling a devastating kidnapping trade in which young girls fetch a high price as child brides for lonely single men (Sheridan, 2009). In other countries, discrimination against women extends to domestic and sexual violence and so-called honor killings. Globally, up to six out of 10 women experience sexual or physical violence in their lifetimes (United Nations, 2010).

In the United States, psychologists have found that gender attitudes are often contradictory. Peter Glick and Susan Fiske (2001) describe this phenomenon as **ambivalent sexism**. On the one hand, men experience *hostile sexism*, in which they feel resentful about women's abilities and make derogatory remarks about the female sex. On the other hand, men also experience *benevolent sexism*, feeling paternalistic toward women and wanting to demonstrate chivalrous behavior (a more acceptable form of sexism, but a contributor to negative female stereotypes nonetheless). In a study of 19 nations across six continents, Glick and others (2000) found evidence of ambivalent sexism all over the world, noting that it is most prevalent in people from countries with the greatest degree of economic and political inequality between the sexes.

How Do We Measure Stereotypes, Prejudice, and Discrimination?

What does it mean to be prejudiced? Is prejudice a conscious decision that we make or an automatic response? A study by Patricia Devine (1989) indicates that stereotypes may bias our perceptions and responses, even if we don't personally agree with them. The mere fact that we are aware of a particular stereotype through images in the media or through stories told by family members or friends is enough to automatically activate the stereotype when we encounter members of the group involved. Devine illustrated this distinction between automatic and controlled processes by exposing white participants (who varied in their self-reported level of prejudice) to subliminal presentations on a computer monitor. One group of participants was exposed to a high level of prime words related to stereotypes about black people (for example, *welfare, ghetto, lazy,* and *oppressed*), while a second group was exposed to a lower level of stereotype-related words. The prime words were presented subliminally, appear-

ing on the screen so fast that the participants were unaware they had been exposed to them. Devine noted that those who had been exposed to a high number of stereotype-related words were more likely to activate the African American stereotype, interpreting ambiguous behavior by an African American in a more negative, hostile light. This was the case even among participants who did not consciously endorse the stereotype in question, suggesting that stereotype activation is automatic for individuals, whatever their true beliefs and values.

So if stereotyping is a function of automatic processing, does that mean that stereotyping is inevitable? Can stereotyping be prevented? The answer is complex—stereotyping is not something that can be flipped on and off like a switch. Yes, stereotypes are triggered automatically, as evidenced in Devine's study. However, there are factors that make activation more or less likely to happen.

Some stereotypes come to mind more quickly and easily for some people than for others. This depends upon one's environment. Activation of a stereotype for someone who is Mexican is going to happen more easily for someone living near the Mexican-American border in Texas than it is for someone living in Maine. Additionally, while stereotypes can be activated even in people who don't express much prejudice, triggers are usually much stronger in people who already feel prejudice toward a certain group.

Because stereotypes are a function of automatic processing, it takes more carefully controlled processing to overcome them. You will read more about that in the later section on combating stereotypes.

> *If stereotyping is a function of automatic processing,* **does that mean that stereotyping is inevitable?**

In the case of African Americans, researchers have noted a difference between **old-fashioned racism**—overt oppressive acts and feelings—and **modern racism**—more internalized feelings that blacks are "pushing too hard, too fast, and into places they are not wanted" (McConahay, 1986, pp. 92–93) and a general attitude that discrimination no longer exists; therefore, policies such as affirmative action are unnecessary. McConahay used an Old-Fashioned Racism Scale and a Modern Racism Scale to test people's attitudes. Both scales included questions on the topic of racism in a Likert format, enabling participants to choose *strongly agree, agree, neutral, disagree,* or *strongly disagree* in response to statements such as "Over the past few years, Blacks have received more economically than they deserve." As McConahay predicted, people scored higher on the Modern Racism Scale than on the Old-Fashioned Racism Scale.

Janet Swim and her co-researchers (1995) found a similar distinction between **old-fashioned sexism** and modern beliefs about women, noting that although overt sexism is less common in today's society, **modern sexism**—characterized by the denial of continued discrimination, antagonism toward women's demands, and a lack of support for policies designed to help women in work and education—is alive and well. Swim and her colleagues conducted a study comparing an Old-Fashioned Sexism Scale and a Modern Sexism Scale along the same lines as McConahay's tests and found that men scored higher on the Modern Sexism Scale than the Old-Fashioned Sexism Scale. They also scored higher than women on both tests.

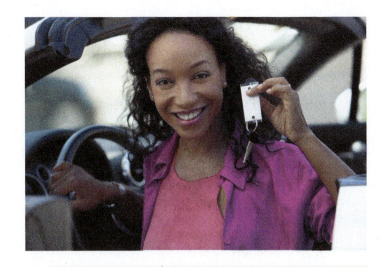

∧
∧ **Will the dealer charge this woman more**
∧ **because of her race and gender?** According to
researchers, black women pay up to 8 percent
more for a new vehicle than white males.

But do these attitudes translate into real-world behaviors? Some studies would suggest they do. When a research team visited 90 Chicago-area car dealers and used a uniform strategy to try to negotiate the lowest price on a new car, they discovered that the dealers altered their "best price" according to the buyer's race and gender. On a car costing the dealer around $11,000, white males were offered a final price averaging $11,362, white females were given an average price of $11,504, black males were offered $11,783, and black females were charged $12,237—almost 8 percent more than the rate given to white males (Ayres, 1991). Other studies have noted discrepancies between the treatment of whites, blacks, and Hispanics at traffic stops. While black, white, and Hispanic drivers are equally likely to be pulled over by police, blacks and Hispanics are more likely to be searched or arrested than white drivers, and police officers are more likely to threaten or use force with non-white civilians than with their white counterparts (Associated Press, 2007).

COVERT MEASURES

Efforts to measure unconscious prejudicial reactions to racial and gender differences, among others, seem to support Devine's theory that bias is often unconscious and unintended, but present nonetheless. In a series of experiments by Anthony Greenwald and his colleagues (1998, 2000), the researchers proved that many white students more quickly associate positive adjectives with pictures of white faces and negative adjectives with pictures of black faces, indicating an implicit racial bias.

>>> **In tests that use virtual reality simulation,** participants are more likely to mistakenly shoot at an image of a black person than at an image of a white person.

During the Implicit Association Test (IAT), subjects were measured on the time it takes to associate faces with positive or negative words (for example, pairing a white face with the word *good* or a black face with the word *bad*). The IAT indicated that most people hold implicit negative stereotypes about people of a different race from themselves. Researchers Kurt Hugenberg and Galen Bodenhausen (2003) took these IAT results and used them to show that people with stronger implicit prejudices are more likely to perceive anger in ambiguous black faces than in ambiguous white faces. Neurological studies indicate that people have a natural tendency to classify others as part of a racial "ingroup" or "outgroup." By tracking event-related brain potentials (ERPs), which reflect brain electrical activity in response to discrete stimuli, researchers are able to examine the range of processes that occur when people perceive racial ingroup and outgroup members. Studies have shown that stereotype-based processing is evident within 100 milliseconds of encountering a stigmatized group member (Ito, Thompson, & Cacioppo, 2004).

Such bias can have serious consequences in certain scenarios. For example, Joshua Correll and his colleagues (2002) as well as Anthony Greenwald and others (2003) conducted an experiment using a virtual reality simulation, in which they invited student participants to "shoot" or "not shoot" images of men who suddenly appeared onscreen holding either a gun or a harmless object such as a flashlight or a bottle. Given less than a second to respond to each figure, the students (who were predominantly white or Asian) wrongly shot at black targets 35 percent of the time, compared with a 26 percent error rate for white targets. Similar studies by Keith Payne (2001) and Charles Judd and colleagues (2004) concluded that when primed with black faces, people were more likely to mistake a harmless object for a gun than when confronted with white faces. Studies such as these may help to explain why unarmed black men such as Steven Eugene Washington, who was shot by police in Koreatown, Los Angeles in March 2010, lose their lives simply for reaching into a pocket or touching a waistband while being confronted by law enforcement officials.

IS PREJUDICE ON THE DECLINE?

At the beginning of the 19th century, the idea that women in the United States should be allowed to vote seemed preposterous to many; today it seems equally implausible that women in some parts of the world (for example, in Saudi Arabia) are currently not allowed to vote. Other prejudicial attitudes have changed even faster. In 1942, most Americans

AVERSIVE RACISM the attitudes of whites who openly endorse egalitarian views but discriminate in ways they're able to rationalize

agreed that there should be separate sections for black people and white people on streetcars and buses (Hyman & Sheatsley, 1956). By the 1960s, overtly hostile attitudes of whites toward blacks were on the decline, and by the 1990s they had reached historic lows (Schuman, Steeh, Bobo, & Kyrsan, 1997). Issues that once caused deep social divisions—whether whites and blacks should be allowed to drink from the same water fountains, stay in the same hotel rooms, or go to the same schools—seem fairly ridiculous now that we have elected a black president to run the country.

Although there is little doubt that attitudes have changed overall, prejudice still exists in various forms. Recent research shows that 20 percent of gay, lesbian, and bisexual persons have experienced a crime based on their sexual orientation (Herek, 2009). Religious groups are also an ongoing target—eight years after September 11, 58 percent of Americans felt that there remained "a lot of discrimination against" Muslims (Pew, 2009). In 2008, law enforcement agencies in the United States reported a total of 7,780 hate crimes, 51 percent of which were racially motivated and 20 percent of which were motivated by religious bias (FBI, 2009). And even though Barack Obama won the 2008 presidential election, one study of racial and political attitudes in voters concluded that had there been no white racial prejudice, Obama would have received 6 percent greater support (Fournier & Tompson, 2008).

Some psychologists believe that prejudice has not been dispelled but has merely transitioned into a more subtle form, with people unwilling to admit, either to themselves or others, how they truly feel. Many white people, some argue, have learned to say the right thing but have not truly internalized the ideals that would classify them as nonracist (Jackman & Jackman, 1983). Psychologists Samuel Dovidio and John Gaertner (2000) coined the term **aversive racism** to describe the attitudes of whites who openly endorse egalitarian views but discriminate in subtle ways they're able to rationalize. They investigated changes in aversive racism over a 10-year period and found that self-reported prejudice was lower in 1998 to 1999 than it was in 1988 to 1989, but that white participants showed discrimination against black job candidates when differences between the strengths of black and white candidates were ambiguous (Dovidio & Gaertner, 2000).

This argument, that prejudice and discrimination is not gone but is simply more subtly expressed, is supported by behavioral bias identified in various social experiments. In one case, M.I.T. researchers sent 5,000 resumes out in response to 1,300 employment advertisements. Applicants who were randomly assigned typically "white" names, such as Emily or Greg, received one callback for every 10 resumes sent. Applicants who were randomly assigned typically "black" names, such as Lakisha or Jamal, received one callback for every 15 resumes sent—a far lower success rate than their white-sounding counterparts (Bertrand & Mullainathan, 2004).

> "Many white students showed mild approval toward the photos on their friends' social networking sites, **but privately found them offensive.**"

What Are the Sources of Stereotyping and Prejudice?

When students at the University of California, San Diego, held an off-campus "Compton Cookout" to mock Black History Month in February 2010, reactions were mixed. Some viewed the event—which invited guests to wear gold teeth in the style of rappers from the Los Angeles suburb of Compton, eat watermelon, and dress in baggy athletic wear—as a form of harmless entertainment, while others were outraged and staged a protest in the chancellor's office.

But what determines people's responses to events such as the "Compton Cookout?" A study by Brendesha Tynes and her colleague Suzanne Markoe (2010) reveals that reactions to racially themed parties depend on people's races and their attitudes toward diversity. Showing 217 ethnically diverse college students images from racially themed parties (for example, photos of people dressed in blackface makeup to attend a "gangsta" party), Tynes and Markoe prompted them to respond as if they were writing on a friend's profile on a social networking site. They found that 58 percent of black students and 21 percent of white students were bothered by the pictures, while those who held the "color-blind" racial attitude of the post-Civil Rights era were more likely to be ambivalent to them. However, Tynes and Markoe also noted that this "color-blind" ideal commonly valued by white students, in which race and racism purportedly no longer exist and, therefore, should not be addressed, was detrimental to race relations on college campuses. Many white students showed mild approval toward the photos on their friends' social networking sites, but privately found them offensive. Stereotypes and prejudice originate from several different sources: how we were brought up, the way that our brains classify individuals as part of an ingroup or an outgroup, and motivating factors such as group competition and individual emotional status.

SOCIAL LEARNING

Imagine growing up in a household in which the use of derogatory terms such as *fag* and *dyke* was actively encouraged. Your attitude toward the homosexual community would likely be very different than if you grew up in a same-sex household or a household in which the use of such terms resulted in being deprived of television for a week. Children often form their attitudes about people in different groups by watching and listening to their parents. For example, if a child hears a parent express a negative opinion about someone who holds different religious beliefs, or sees a parent avoid interacting with people who hold these beliefs, the child is more likely to form negative beliefs about people in this group (Towles-Schwen & Fazio, 2001). Similarly, children who are raised by obese mothers tend to exhibit more positive attitudes toward individuals who are obese, whereas children who are raised by slender mothers show an implicit preference for slimmer individuals (Rudman, Phelan, & Heppen, 2007).

Parents are not the only people who are capable of influencing our attitudes and behaviors—peers, too, serve as yardsticks by which we measure our social responses. When a friend or classmate expresses a prejudicial attitude, laughs at a joke that invokes a stereotype, or takes part in a discriminatory act, he contributes to the formation and perpetuation of stereotypes (Crandall, Eshleman, & O'Brien, 2002). For example, studies have shown that when white students heard someone express a racist viewpoint, they were later less likely to take a strong antiracist standpoint than people who had not been exposed to racially prejudiced comments. On the flip side, students who heard someone condemn racism were more likely to express antiracist opinions when later asked how their school should address issues related to racism (Blanchard, Crandall, Brigham, & Vaughn, 1994).

Another source related to social learning is the concept of the **authoritarian personality**, a personality type that favors obedience to authority and intolerance of people lower in status, first theorized by Theodor Adorno and his colleagues (1950). In an attempt to get at the psychological roots that allowed Nazi Germany to lead the killing of millions of people, they found that individuals who showed hostility toward Jews also showed hostility to other minorities. These people also shared the traits of submission to authority and intolerance for weakness. Generally, such people face harsh discipline as children, and project their fears and hostility onto others.

COGNITIVE SOURCES

Many of us like to think that we are immune from stereotyping, but numerous everyday experiences tell us otherwise. Imagine that you are driving to visit a friend and another car cuts in front of you at an intersection. You glare out of your window at the other driver and notice that he or she is of the opposite gender. What do you say? Most people have a tendency to use a flurry of expletives, followed by a comment about what bad drivers men or women are. Why is this type of interaction such a common phenomenon? In part, it happens because our brains classify people and objects into categories (e.g., Bar-Haim et al., 2006; Sherman et al., 2009).

Just as biologists classify animals into categories, so too do people divide each other into groups according to their race, gender, and other common attributes. This process of **social categorization** helps us to form impressions quickly and enables us to use previous experiences to shape new interactions. For example, if you have had problems communicating with an older person because she is hard of hearing, you might develop a tendency to speak slower and louder around people over a certain age when you first meet them. Studies have shown that the practice of placing people into categories begins at a very early

AUTHORITARIAN PERSONALITY a personality type that favors obedience to authority and intolerance of people lower in status

SOCIAL CATEGORIZATION the process of dividing people into categories according to their race, gender, and other common attributes

OUTGROUP HOMOGENEITY EFFECT the tendency to see outgroup members as similar to one another but ingroup members as diverse individuals

INGROUP FAVORITISM the natural tendency to favor an ingroup versus an outgroup

age. Young babies are able to differentiate between people in various racial groups, showing a preference for faces that belong to their own race. In a study of 36 infants from three groups—white babies who had primarily experienced an all-white environment, black babies who had primarily experienced an all-black environment, and black babies who had experienced a mixed-race environment—researcher Yair Bar-Haim and colleagues (2006) found that when shown pairs of photos of black and white faces, the babies who had been raised in an all-white or all-black environment spent significantly more time looking at faces from their own race. Conversely, babies who had been raised in a mixed-race environment showed no preference for either black faces or white faces, indicating that early exposure to people of other races may block the development of own-race preference.

Categorizing individuals into ingroups and outgroups might save our brains time and energy, but it is not without consequences. Researchers have found that people tend to learn features about majority groups earlier than features about minority groups. When we learn about minority groups, we focus on features that differentiate them from the majority, magnifying perceived differences between groups (Sherman et al., 2009). Because we have a tendency to exaggerate the differences between our own ingroups and other outgroups, minimizing perceived similarities and maximizing perceived differences, stereotypes are formed and reinforced. This cognitive habit is explained by two phenomena—the **outgroup homogeneity effect** and **ingroup favoritism**.

Outgroup Homogeneity

Think back to a sports match you have played in the past. You may be a valuable member of a team: the top goal scorer, the fastest runner, or the strongest defender. Other members of your team probably have their own unique capabilities on the field and you may socialize with them after training, familiarizing yourself with their likes and dislikes, their family backgrounds, and their goals and aspirations. Now picture one of the teams against which you have played. Do you see the players as similar individuals with unique qualities, or as a single entity that must be defeated? In all likelihood, you took the latter view, perceiving the rival team as a homogenous group with few individual characteristics.

The outgroup homogeneity effect refers to our tendency to see outgroup members as similar to one another,

<<< We all like to think that we don't stereotype, but negative interactions between drivers of the opposite sex frequently prove otherwise.

but ingroup members as diverse individuals. This effect is evident in numerous situations around the world. You have probably heard liberals refer to conservatives as a group of "gun-toting religious nuts" and listened to conservatives dismiss liberals as "bleeding-heart socialists." Teenagers are often categorized as rude, thoughtless, and uncivilized, while the elderly are frequently thought of as stubborn, helpless, or old-fashioned. To ingroup members, people in an outgroup may even seem to look alike. For example, people are less accurate when it comes to distinguishing and recognizing faces of racial outgroups, especially if they are unfamiliar with these other groups (Chiroro, Tredoux, Radaelli, & Meissner, 2008). The difficulty with cross-race identification has proven to be tragic in some cases—Cuban American Orlando Boquete served 23 years in prison for a crime he did not commit because a white woman mistakenly identified him as the man who had sexually assaulted her in her Florida home. Boquete was eventually released in 2006 when DNA test results proved him innocent (Dwyer, 2007).

Studies indicate that this same-race bias occurs early on in life—babies as young as nine months of age are better able to discriminate between faces within their own ethnic group than those from other ethnic groups (Kelly, Quinn, Slater, Lee, Ge, & Pascalis, 2007). This phenomenon likely results from familiarity with one's own race and may be reversed if we become intimately familiar with another race. In a study of Korean children who were adopted by white families when they were between the ages of three and nine, researchers found that the children were better able to recognize white faces than Asian ones (Sangrigoli, Pallier, Argenti, Ventureyra, & de Schonen, 2005). Conversely, Korean children who grow up in Korea are better able to recognize Asian faces than white ones.

Why do we tend to perceive outgroups as homogenous? One reason is a lack of familiarity. If we have little personal contact with a particular group of people, we are unlikely to notice subtle differences between them and more inclined to lump them all together as a group. We may perceive our own ingroup to be homogenous when we first join but change our opinion over time as we become more familiar with individual group

members (Ryan & Bogart, 1997). For example, during the Robbers Cave Experiment, none of the boys in either camp initially knew one another, yet by the end of the first week, each group had established a coherent identity with leaders, social norms, and hierarchies. A lack of familiarity with the other group—the outgroup—resulted in stereotyping and name-calling, with each group making sweeping generalizations about the other.

Ingroup Favoritism

As soon as groups are formed, people have a natural tendency to favor an ingroup over an outgroup. This preference is so strong that we even categorize ingroup words such as *we* or *us* more favorably than outgroup words such as *they* or *them* (Otten & Wentura, 1999). Ingroup favoritism often results in discriminatory behavior. For example, jurors often give shorter sentences to those accused of a crime when the accused is within their same ethnic group (Sommers & Ellsworth, 2000). Why might this occur? One reason for ingroup favoritism is self-interest; we are more likely to favor those in our ingroup because they are more likely to favor us in return (Vivian & Berkowitz, 1992). During the Robbers Cave Experiment, the Eagles were more likely to support members of their own camp, who could provide them with food, prizes, and help with chores, than members of the Rattlers' camp who were of no practical use to them. As illustrated by the strong group bonds within the two camps, ingroup favoritism is more likely when people identify heavily with their group and when group norms are a prominent part of group mentality (Gagnon & Bourhis, 1996).

Sometimes, people see their own groups as naturally superior to other groups. This is referred to as having a **social dominance orientation** (Pratto et al., 1994; Sidanius & Pratto, 1999). They believe social groups should be ordered according to worth, and that superior groups should have more wealth and power. People with such an orientation usually hold negative stereotypes and prejudices against other groups, often out of a fear that the "superior" group's status is being somehow threatened.

Attributional Biases

In Chapter 5, we discussed attribution errors that we make for others' behaviors. The fundamental attribution error is the tendency to focus on dispositional explanations for an individual's behavior, without taking the situation into consideration. Likewise, attribution errors may be applied to an entire group. When we begin to favor an ingroup over an outgroup, we risk committing an **ultimate attribution error**—the tendency to explain the behavior of groups in terms of internal dispositional factors, without taking the situational constraints into consideration (Pettigrew, 1979). Thus, negative outgroup behavior is attributed to dispositional attributes of the entire group (for example, you read a newspaper report about a black man shooting someone and conclude that it happened because all black men are violent), whereas positive outgroup behavior is attributed to an exceptional case or an example of good fortune (for example, you read a newspaper report about a woman taking over a company and conclude that she must be related to the owner). Several studies support Pettigrew's analysis. For

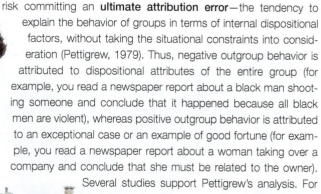

<<< Children are more likely to recognize faces from within their own racial group, **or the racial group with which they are most familiar.**

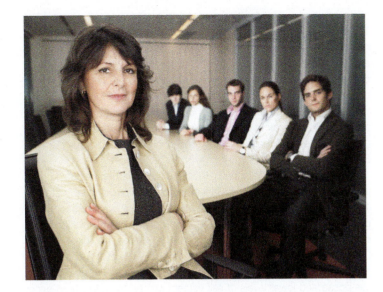

∧
∧ **Was this woman simply in the right place at the**
∧ **right time, or did her capable personality and**
hard work propel her to the top? Studies show
that female successes are more likely to be
attributed to luck than to ability.

example, researchers found that white students were more likely to think
a shove was violent (due to dispositional factors) when it came from a
black person than when it came from a white person (Duncan, 1976).
Gender prejudice is also evident with regard to ultimate attribution errors.
Upon reviewing 58 separate experiments, researchers found that male
successes in traditionally masculine tasks were more likely to be considered a result of ability than were female successes. Meanwhile, male failures were more likely attributed to poor luck or low effort than were female
failures. (Swim & Sanna, 1996).

Another attributional bias is the **just-world hypothesis**, in which
people believe that victims of misfortune deserve what happens to
them. According to the hypothesis, we have a strong desire or need to
believe that the world is a predictable, dependable place, where people
get what they deserve. To live happy, fulfilling lives, we have to assume
that our actions will have predictable consequences. As a result, when

we encounter evidence that suggests the world is not a reliable, fair
place to live, we attempt to restore the balance by convincing ourselves
that no injustice has occurred. For example, a recent survey of 1,000
Londoners found that one in 10 respondents believed that most rape
claims are "probably false," and more than half of the female respondents thought that there were situations in which the rape victim was to
blame for the attack. Almost 20 percent of people agreed that a rape
victim was partly to blame for being attacked if she went to the
attacker's home (Bindel, 2010). By deciding that a woman has done
something "wrong" by having a drink with a defendant or wearing
provocative clothing, female jurors at a rape trial are able to reassure
themselves that rape won't happen to them as long as they don't do
anything similar. We invoke the just-world hypothesis every time we tell
ourselves that a homeless person is simply lazy and needs to get a job,
that an AIDS patient must be promiscuous or a drug addict, or that a
person imprisoned for a crime he or she didn't commit must have done
something wrong to arouse suspicion in the first place.

MOTIVATIONAL FACTORS

Imagine that you are going camping for the weekend with friends or
family. When you get to the campsite, you find that there is a limited
supply of hot water in the showers and very little firewood with which
to start a campfire. Another group arrives late in the afternoon and
pitches their tent next to yours. Are you more likely to welcome the
new arrivals or suddenly become possessive over the firewood and
the hot water? According to the **realistic group conflict theory**,
when different groups are in competition for resources, they tend to
close ranks and favor ingroup members while discriminating against
outgroup members (Esses, Jackson, & Armstrong, 1998). Animosity
between different racial groups and different genders is therefore a
result of individuals' self-interest in terms of competition for land,
wealth, or even jobs when the economy is in decline. During the
Robbers Cave Experiment, the Rattlers and the Eagles became possessive over *their* campground and *their* baseball diamond as soon
as an element of competition was introduced to the summer camp
experience.

In the current economic climate, you may have noticed an increase
in grumblings about the number of immigrants coming to the United
States and "taking our jobs," as well as a stronger push for tighter border controls. One study found that when Americans assessed the similarities between their ingroup and Mexican immigrants on work-related
traits, they felt more threatened than when differences were highlighted.

<<< **According to the realistic group conflict**
theory, competition between groups
increases when resources are scarce.

RELATIVE DEPRIVATION discontent caused by the belief that we might fare badly in comparison with people in other groups

In other words, the notion that Mexican-American immigrants might be as equally skilled and hardworking as American workers made the Americans perceive the immigrants as more able to compete effectively in the job market and, thus, a greater threat. This threat resulted in higher levels of prejudice against Mexican immigrants (Zárate, Garcia, Garza, & Hitlan, 2004). Discontent caused by the belief that we might fare badly in comparison with people in other groups is known as **relative deprivation**. For example, if you are told that you, as an American, are unlikely to get accepted to the university of your choice because the school is prioritizing applications from foreign students, you are more likely to hold prejudicial attitudes toward foreign students and support policies that limit the number of non-American students at your university.

Relative deprivation describes the feeling of being threatened by another group; by the same token, we want to be part of a successful group. According to social identity theory, part of our self-esteem is derived from the groups to which we belong—when we affiliate with successful groups, our feelings of self-worth increase (Tajfel & Turner, 1986). For example, when President Obama was elected in 2008, you may have heard someone say (or commented yourself) that it was a proud moment for African Americans. The 2008 elections also inspired feelings of pride among women from both ends of the political spectrum, who celebrated the groundbreaking achievements of Democratic Senator Hillary Clinton and Republican Governor Sarah Palin. Sporting events often arouse positive feelings of self-worth; you may have cheered when American swimming champion Michael Phelps won eight gold medals during the 2008 Olympic Games, or witnessed the recent demonstration of national pride in Spain following the final of the 2010 soccer World Cup.

Sometimes, it doesn't take much to identify as part of a group. This is shown through the *minimal ingroup paradigm*. Even members of randomly determined groups in which members are unfamiliar with each other feel connected and will show preference for one another. In one study, students were randomly assigned to groups but told the assignment was based on preference for a Klee or Kandinsky painting. When the students were tasked with assigning points to their classmates, they awarded more points to individuals who shared the same group label, even without knowing those individuals personally (Tajfel & Billig, 1974).

The flipside of social identity theory is that although belonging to a particular group may help to build feelings of self-worth and self-esteem, it often occurs at the expense of outgroups. Derogating outgroup members leads to increases in self-esteem, especially when our ingroup is important to us (Branscombe & Wann, 1991; Hodson, Dovidio, & Esses, 2003). For example, one study of black and white high school gang members in Orlando, Florida, found that gang members of both ethnicities possessed lower levels of self-esteem compared to their non-gang peers and had fewer role models (Wang, 1994). Other researchers found that threatening individuals' self-esteem by giving them false task-failure feedback automatically caused an increase in their tendency to stereotype others. When white students received negative feedback from an experimenter, they became more likely to make word completions related to black stereotypes than participants who received positive or no feedback (for example, they would be more likely to complete the stem –ITOR as *JANitor* rather than *MONitor*). It seems that, unfortunately, negative evaluations of those who belong to stereotyped groups can serve to restore our damaged self-esteem (Spencer, Fein, Wolfe, Fong, & Dunn, 1998; Fein & Spencer, 1997).

Logically, one might conclude that people with high self-esteem need not participate in ingroup favoritism; however, it appears that the opposite is true. Research suggests that people with high self-esteem favor their own groups to a greater extent than those who have low self-esteem (Aberson, Healy, & Romero, 2000).

Members of small minority groups tend to feel greater loyalty than individuals in majority groups **because members of the minority group feel unique.**

What factors affect our tendency to put down other groups and strongly favor our own? The practices of ingroup favoritism and outgroup derogation are more likely to occur under three specific conditions: being part of a small ingroup, having marginal status within a group, and feeling inferior as a group.

Being part of a small minority ingroup inspires greater group loyalty than being part of a majority group because members feel unique (Brewer & Pickett, 1999). Have you ever heard of a White Studies Club? How about the Heterosexual Historical Society? Chances are these groups do not exist because people in majority groups are unable to distinguish themselves from the masses through their skin color or sexuality. However, you have probably noticed an Asian Students Union, a Lesbian, Gay, Bisexual, and Transgender Community Center, or a Muslim Community Association in your local area.

A person's status within a group can also influence how likely she is to put down members of outgroups. Those with marginal status are more likely to derogate others, particularly in front of ingroup members. A study by Noel, Wann, and Branscombe (1995) found that peripheral members of fraternities and sororities were more likely to put down outgroups in public than in private, presumably because they wanted to demonstrate their group-oriented behavior to core fraternity or sorority members in order to gain acceptance. In a separate study of women in sororities, Jennifer Crocker and her colleagues (1987) also noted that sorority women with high self-esteem who considered themselves to be in a low-status sorority strongly derogated other sororities, whereas women with high self-esteem in prestigious sororities showed little bias against other sorority women.

Finally, when ingroups as a whole feel threatened with inferiority, they are more likely to take pleasure in another group's failure—a concept known as intergroup schadenfreude. For example, during a study of Dutch soccer fans, researchers found that participants took greater pleasure in the defeat of Germany in the 1998 soccer World Cup quarterfinals when they were reminded that the Dutch team had lost to Brazil in the same competition (Leach, Spears, Branscombe, & Doosje, 2003).

Moods and Emotions

Most of us would be horrified to think that being in a good mood might bring out subconscious prejudices within us; however, research suggests that both positive and negative emotions may affect our ability to think clearly, resulting in a tendency to resort to preconceived stereotypes. For example, when we are in a good mood, we are less likely to think things through carefully. Whereas negative emotions such as sadness indicate that we need to pay close attention to people around us, positive emotions such as happiness imply that systematic processing is unnecessary (Schwarz, 1990).

Recall what you learned in Chapter 7. This is just like persuasion—when we're happy, we don't want to think too much. Researchers (Bodenhausen, Kramer, & Süsser, 1994) tested this theory by inducing mood states in a group of participants. Some were asked to write about happy past experiences (inducing a positive mood condition), while others were asked to write about neutral experiences (inducing a neutral mood condition). The participants were then presented with a

<<< **Could your happy mood inadvertently cause you to rely on stereotypes?**

description of a student allegedly involved in misconduct (such as assaulting someone or cheating on a test). When asked to rate the student's guilt, participants in happy moods were more likely than those in neutral moods to rate "Juan Garcia" guilty compared with the identical "John Garner." Another study found that students who had been put in positive moods by being given favorable feedback about a previous task were more likely to shoot Muslim targets in a computer game than students in neutral moods (Unkelbach, Forgas, & Denson, 2007).

Negative moods can also affect our tendencies to resort to stereotypes. Emotions that arouse us (for example, anger or fear) reduce the amount of cognitive resources available to us and limit our ability to think clearly and logically, thus increasing the likelihood of stereotyping. A study by Wilder (1993) showed that people who are anxious are less likely to differentiate among members of a group and will assimilate a deviant member into the group as a whole rather than acknowledging the individual as a contradiction of the stereotype. Under these conditions, when a member of the outgroup behaves in a positive way that contradicts expectations, members of the ingroup recall the entire outgroup, including that member, as behaving in a manner consistent with the stereotype. For example, if a teenager politely holds open a door for an anxious elderly lady while a group of the teenagers' friends rudely barge past, the elderly lady is unlikely to remember anything other than a group of teenagers rudely pushing past her. Other emotional states may also affect our judgment—as noted earlier, when we are feeling low about ourselves, we are more likely to derogate others.

What Are the Consequences of Stereotyping?

Are there any real dangers to stereotyping? Most psychologists would argue "yes;" the practice of pigeonholing others into specific categories influences our perception of other people and affects our behaviors, as well as the behaviors of the stereotyped groups. To illustrate the first point, researchers Darley and Gross (1983) asked subjects to rate the academic ability of a young girl named Hannah, who was shown on video taking an achievement test. The subjects were led to believe that Hannah came from either a high or a low socioeconomic background. Those who believed that Hannah came from a higher socioeconomic background rated her as having significantly higher motivation and cognitive skills than those who believed she came from a lower socioeconomic background. Even though the material shown on the video was ambiguous (Hannah answered some questions correctly and some incorrectly), the subjects cited specific elements of her behavior during the test as "evidence" of her ability level.

Our tendency to search for information that supports our initial viewpoint is known as confirmation bias. For example, in the "Little Hannah" study described previously, participants already believed that children from higher socioeconomic groups were more capable than children from lower socioeconomic groups and looked for information in

Sources of Stereotyping and Prejudice. Stereotyping and prejudice originate from several different sources.

the video to support their beliefs. We are guilty of using confirmation bias every time we get stuck behind a particularly slow mother and child at a supermarket checkout and conclude that all mothers with young children will delay us in a line. In reality, the situation may have occurred only a handful of times, but our natural instinct is to remember stereotype-consistent information and forget or ignore stereotype-inconsistent facts, such as the times that we encounter a highly efficient family at a checkout, a polite teenager, or a capable elderly driver (Lyons & Kashima, 2003).

Stereotyping not only influences our perception of other people; it can ultimately lead us to interact with people in ways that influence their behavior. When this occurs, it is known as a self-fulfilling prophecy—a belief that causes itself to be true. For example, in one study, researchers Robert Rosenthal and Lenore Jacobson (1968) gave elementary school children a test and told teachers that some of their students had an unusually high level of intelligence. In reality, the students had been picked at random and were no more gifted than the rest of the students in the class. Nonetheless, when the students who had been singled out were retested at the end of the school year, Rosenthal discovered that their IQ scores had risen by 10 to 20 points.

Although in this instance, the self-fulfilling prophecy brought about a positive impact, in many cases, it can limit people as a result of others' negative expectations. For example, research demonstrated that nonverbal cues from interviewers elicited poor performance of job applicants (Word, Zanna, & Cooper, 1979). Studies have also shown that men in high-power positions give subordinate women fewer assignments than their male counterparts and generally have lower expectations of them in the workplace (Vescio, Gervais, Snyder, & Hoover, 2005). As a result, women in subordinate positions feel less confident and their performances suffer, fulfilling their bosses' expectations that they are not as competent as their male peers. Every time we talk down to someone of a different race, treat an elderly person as frail and incompetent, or patronize someone with a physical disability, we are helping to create a self-fulfilling prophecy.

STEREOTYPE THREAT

A further consequence of stereotyping is **stereotype threat**, or being at risk of confirming the negative stereotype about a group one belongs to. For example, although he might not believe it, a person from a low socioeconomic group may be aware that societal expectations with regard to his career

^
^ We have a tendency to remember
^ information that supports preconceived
stereotypes, **but are they always correct?**

prospects are extremely low—people would not generally expect someone who grew up in a ghetto to become the CEO of a high-ranking company. As a result, that person may feel additional pressure when he attends a job interview, negatively impacting his performance during the interview. A study by Claude Steele and Joshua Aronson (1995) gave black and white college students at Stanford University a difficult test using items from the GRE verbal exam. One group of students was told that their performance on the exam would prove to be a good indicator of their underlying intellectual abilities, while a second group was told that the test was simply a problem-solving exercise and was not diagnostic of ability. The results showed that black students performed equally well as white students when the test was non-diagnostic but much worse when they believed the test was indicative of their intelligence levels. Steele and Aronson concluded that the black students, while just as intelligent as their white counterparts, performed worse when their racial identity was made salient.

Similar results have been found with other stereotyped groups. When researchers showed male and female undergraduates (all of whom were good at math) a set of six television commercials before asking them to complete a difficult math test, the female undergraduates' performance on the test differed according to the content of the commercials they had seen. Those who were shown commercials containing female stereotypes (for example, an advertisement depicting a woman so excited about an acne product that she bounced on her bed) scored lower than their male peers on the test, whereas those who were shown counter-stereotypical commercials (for example, an advertisement showing a woman exhibiting detailed knowledge of auto engineering) scored equally high. The males' test scores were consistent across both groups (Davies, Spencer, Quinn, & Gerhardstein, 2002).

How Can We Combat Stereotyping and Prejudice?

Is anyone immune to stereotyping? Recent research indicates that one particular group of people might be able to avoid forming racial stereotypes. A study (Santos, Meyer-Lindenberg, & Deruelle, 2010) of 20 children

with the neurological disorder Williams syndrome (WS) found that the youngsters did not engage in racial bias about other ethnic groups. Twenty children with the disorder and 20 children who did not have WS were asked to associate pictures of light-skinned and dark-skinned people with characters in stories. Children without WS tended to associate positive characteristics with pictures of light-skinned children and negative characteristics with pictures of dark-skinned children, whereas children with the disorder showed no signs of racial bias. Since the youngsters with WS retained the same patterns of gender stereotyping shown in other children, the researchers speculated that racial bias stems from a different brain process. People with WS show abnormal activity in the amygdala—the part of the brain involved in responding to social threats and triggering unconscious negative emotional reactions to people of a different race. Racial stereotypes, therefore, are likely linked to social fear.

Although the results of the Williams syndrome study may provide us with valuable information about the causes of stereotypes and prejudice (and possible solutions to help combat them), the research is preliminary and will need to be replicated in larger samples and among different age groups before reliable conclusions can be drawn (see Chapter 2 for more information about research methods). In the meantime, we can attempt to combat stereotypes and prejudice using four different techniques: increased equal contact with people in minority groups, increased interdependence between groups, better education, and improved personal motivation. As noted earlier in the chapter, most efforts to combat stereotyping and prejudice must rely on controlled processing, as it takes much effort to overcome the brain's desire to categorize and identify things effortlessly.

^
^ **Anxiety caused by the belief that we might**
^ **inadvertently conform to a** negative cultural
stereotype may affect our performance at
school and in the workplace.

CONTACT HYPOTHESIS the belief that increased communication and contact between different racial groups reduces levels of prejudice and discrimination

JIGSAW CLASSROOM TECHNIQUE teaching method that focuses on small-group activities and fosters a cooperative rather than competitive environment

CONTACT HYPOTHESIS

As Kenneth and Mamie Clark proved with the "doll test" in the 1940s (referred to earlier in this chapter), racial segregation reinforces discrimination and causes black children to develop a sense of inferiority and self-hatred. Conversely, the **contact hypothesis** argues that increased communication and equal contact between different racial groups reduces levels of prejudice and discrimination. For example, in a study of two public housing projects in New York City that were desegregated in the late 1940s, researchers found that randomly selected white housewives held their black neighbors in higher esteem and were considerably more in favor of interracial housing (75 percent to 25 percent) than housewives who lived in segregated developments (Deutsch & Collins, 1951). However, other studies showed little decrease in prejudice following desegregation, with some even noting an increase. In 1998, Thomas Pettigrew reviewed all the existing work on the contact hypothesis and came to the conclusion that contact situations that fostered the development of friendship are the most likely to reduce prejudice because friendship tends to generate positive orientations, such as empathy, and reduce negative emotions, such as anxiety (Pettigrew, 1998).

> "Contact situations that fostered the development of friendship are the most likely to reduce prejudice **because friendship tends to generate positive orientations, such as empathy, and reduce negative emotions, such as anxiety.**"

GROUP INTERDEPENDENCE

In 1954, Gordon Allport theorized that increased contact between minority groups was not sufficient to reduce prejudice, but decreased prejudice may occur in four conditions: when both groups have equal status within a situation, when they have institutional support (for example, the support of laws, authorities, or customs), when there is intergroup cooperation, and when both groups have common goals (Allport, 1954). The Robbers Cave Experiment provides a useful example of the last two conditions; when the camp's water supply was shut down and both the Eagles and the Rattlers had to work together in order to fix an outlet faucet, the two teams celebrated their joint success without name calling or bickering about which group should get a drink first.

This method of intergroup cooperation is used within today's classrooms to reduce racial conflict and promote better learning. The **jigsaw classroom technique**, developed in Texas by Elliot Aronson and colleagues (1978), uses a cooperative jigsaw structure, in which each student's role is essential for the successful completion of a project.

EDUCATION

Stereotyping can be reduced through training and education. Following the assassination of Dr. Martin Luther King, Jr., in 1968, elementary schoolteacher Jane Elliott decided to give her all-white class a lesson in discrimination, as you first read about in Chapter 1. After telling students that people with blue eyes were clever, quick, and likely to succeed, whereas people with brown eyes were untrustworthy, lazy, and stupid, she divided the class into blue-eyed and brown-eyed children and laid out a set of rules in which the superior group had extra privileges. Elliott discovered that the children's attitudes quickly changed — blue-eyed students became arrogant and behaved aggressively toward brown-eyed children on the playground, while brown-eyed children became timid and subdued. When Elliott told the class a few days later that she had made a mistake and swapped the color superiorities around, the same situation happened in reverse (Tozer, Violas, & Senese, 1993).

Research shows that participating in demonstrations of discrimination such as the one described previously is an effective technique for reducing prejudice; however, it is important for people to actually participate in an exercise. Merely watching a lecture or a video does not seem to change prejudicial attitudes (Byrnes & Kiger, 1990). Other types of education include training in statistical reasoning to learn about how we often mistakenly pair two things together. On a computer simulation task, police officers are initially more likely to shoot unarmed black suspects than unarmed white suspects, but following repeated computer training that shows a lack of connection between a suspect's race and the likelihood that he or she is carrying a weapon, officers are able to eliminate racial bias (Plant, Peruche, & Butz, 2005). Another study demonstrated that diversity training can reduce implicit racial prejudice. Researchers found evidence that participants' cognitive processes actually changed as stereotyping was reduced (Rudman, Ashmore, & Gary, 2001).

MOTIVATION

Can we become less prejudiced simply by choosing to do so? Although stereotyping is (to an extent) an automatic response, being motivated to reduce our reliance on stereotypes is a key factor in eliminating prejudice. For example, a study was conducted in which participants were asked to decide whether an object presented along with a black face or a white face was related to sports. The researchers found that, although participants tended to misidentify neutral objects as sports-related when depicted with black faces, this bias could be eliminated with training. The researchers also noted that participants who were highly motivated to respond without prejudice were especially effective at eliminating the bias (Peruche & Plant, 2006).

Sometimes, when people are made aware of their stereotypical attitudes, they will make a conscious effort to change their beliefs and behaviors. Monteith's (1993) research suggests that low-prejudiced individuals who are made aware of their prejudiced responses feel a strong sense of guilt and self-dissatisfaction and subsequently make an effort to inhibit responses to racist or homosexual jokes. Even high-prejudiced individuals who are confronted about their prejudicial comments are less likely to espouse their views in the future. However, their motivation usually stems from a desire to avoid being perceived by others as prejudiced, rather than a desire to eliminate prejudice itself (Plant & Devine, 1998). In general, though, an awareness of the language we use and the comments we make can reduce the use of stereotypes, especially if we have a personal desire to do so.

At the beginning of this chapter, you read about the Robbers Cave experiment, in which psychologists were able to create tension and prejudice between two groups of campers. Importantly, the experiment also showed one way of breaking down such prejudices—through creating goals for the campers that forced them to work together. The "real world" is more complicated than the camp scenario, but it does offer an important lesson—as strong a hold as stereotypes, prejudices, and discrimination can have, they can be overcome. The brain's preference for the automatic processing that leads to snap judgments and preferences for ingroups is strong, and it can lead to biases that we aren't even fully aware are there. Several techniques, however, can help combat the stereotypes that lead to discrimination and prejudice against others. Most of the techniques rely on harnessing the more effortful controlled processing that forces us to look objectively at the world around us rather than making an easy, quick assessment.

ACTION LEARNING

The Jigsaw Classroom

Following the desegregation of schools in Austin, Texas, in the early 1970s, Aronson and his colleagues noted that the fear and distrust felt by various racial groups toward each other was being fueled by a competitive element within the classroom. They shifted the emphasis from competition to cooperation by developing a learning technique in which classes were divided into small groups that were diversified in terms of race, ethnicity, and gender. Each student within the group was responsible for one specific part of a project, and, just as in a jigsaw puzzle, each student's part was essential for the successful completion of the project. Once the students had completed their research, they had to report back to the rest of their group, encouraging each member to listen to one another in order to learn the necessary material. The researchers noted that this new method encouraged children who were typically unwilling to speak up in class to participate, increasing their self-confidence. It also encouraged children who would usually ridicule others to help them out for the sake of the group, fostering better group relations. Aronson's jigsaw technique has since been used in many other settings, including businesses, in order to facilitate social learning, increase self-confidence, and reduce stereotyping and prejudice.

Select a group that you would like to work with—maybe a campus club, members of your dormitory, or children in a local school. Choose a skill or an idea that would be worthwhile to learn and divide participants into small groups. Assign individuals within each group a task, making sure that the number of tasks is equivalent to the actual number of individuals. Once the tasks are complete, have the groups reunite to share their new knowledge with one another, and then have the entire group come back together to share what they have learned. How did this technique work out? Did you find that individuals and groups cooperated well together? What are the advantages of using this method?

What will you learn from this action project?

1. Learn how to implement a technique to foster cooperation among individuals.
2. Learn how to reduce competitive instincts within a large-group setting.
3. Get firsthand experience with a social psychologically tested concept to reduce stereotyping.

If you would like to learn more about the jigsaw classroom, visit http://www.jigsaw.org/.

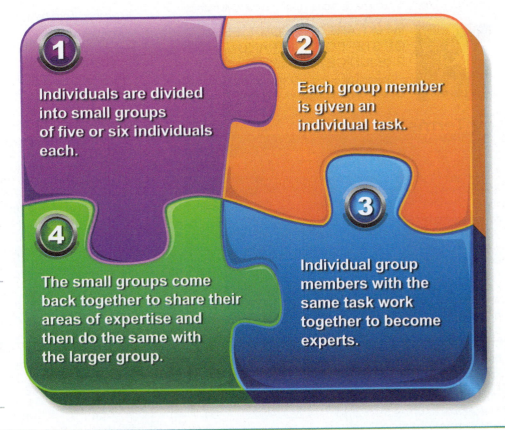

>>> **The Jigsaw Classroom.** The jigsaw classroom technique fosters cooperation and reduces stereotyping and prejudice.

1. Individuals are divided into small groups of five or six individuals each.

2. Each group member is given an individual task.

3. Individual group members with the same task work together to become experts.

4. The small groups come back together to share their areas of expertise and then do the same with the larger group.

• Review

Summary

WHAT ARE STEREOTYPES, PREJUDICE, AND DISCRIMINATION? p. 176

• Prejudice is a negative learned attitude toward particular groups of people. Prejudice often leads to discrimination, or negative behavior directed toward members of a particular group. Common types of prejudice are racial prejudice and gender prejudice.

• Stereotypes may bias our perceptions and responses even if we do not personally agree with them. Neurological studies indicate that people have a natural tendency to classify others as part of a racial "ingroup" or "outgroup." This often translates into real-world behaviors, such as racial profiling.

HOW DO WE MEASURE STEREOTYPES, PREJUDICE, AND DISCRIMINATION? p. 180

• The discussion of stereotypes goes back to the difference between automatic and controlled processing, as stereotyping is a function of the quicker automatic processing. Researchers have found different measures of stereotyping and racism in the distinction between old-fashioned and modern racism.

• Covert measures of prejudice work to uncover bias that is unconscious, and often unintended. While some people say prejudice is a thing of the past, tests such as the Implicit Association Test help to uncover such phenomena as hidden bias and aversive racism.

WHAT ARE THE SOURCES OF STEREOTYPING AND PREJUDICE? p. 182

• Stereotyping and prejudice originate from several different sources: how we were brought up, the

way that our brains classify individuals as part of an ingroup or an outgroup, and motivating factors such as group competition and individual emotional status.

• Groups are motivated to compete for resources, such as jobs, land, or wealth. When resources are scarce, groups tend to close ranks, favoring ingroup members and discriminating against outgroup members.

WHAT ARE THE CONSEQUENCES OF STEREOTYPING? p. 187

• Stereotyping influences our perception of people and their behavior. Our natural instinct is to remember stereotype-consistent information but to ignore information that contradicts the stereotype. When we interact with people based on a preconceived stereotype, we influence their behavior, creating a self-fulfilling prophecy.

• A further consequence of stereotyping is stereotype threat, or the fear held by people in minority groups that they might conform to a negative cultural stereotype. Anxiety caused by stereotype threat affects people's performances at school and in the workplace.

HOW CAN WE COMBAT STEREOTYPING AND PREJUDICE? p. 189

• We can attempt to combat stereotypes and prejudice using four different techniques: increased contact with people in minority groups, increased interdependence between groups, better education, and improved personal motivation.

• The jigsaw classroom is one example of increasing interdependence between groups. Students work in a cooperative rather than competitive environment, gaining self-confidence and learning how to work with people from different racial and ethnic groups.

Key Terms

ambivalent sexism the contradictory attitudes of hostile sexism and benevolent sexism *180*

authoritarian personality a personality type that favors obedience to authority and intolerance of people lower in status *183*

aversive racism the attitudes of whites who openly endorse egalitarian views but discriminate in ways they're able to rationalize *182*

contact hypothesis the belief that increased communication and contact between different racial groups reduces levels of prejudice and discrimination *190*

discrimination a behavior directed toward a group of people based solely on their membership in that group *176*

gender prejudice the tendency to hold a hostile attitude toward an individual because of his or her gender *179*

gender stereotypes people's ideas about how men and women behave based on socially and culturally defined beliefs *179*

ingroup favoritism the natural tendency to favor an ingroup versus an outgroup *183*

jigsaw classroom technique teaching method that focuses on small-group activities and fosters a cooperative rather than competitive environment *190*

just-world hypothesis the tendency for people to believe that the world is fair and just; therefore, victims of misfortune deserve what happens to them *185*

modern racism negative feelings toward a group of people based on their race, manifested in more subtle forms of racism *180*

modern sexism internalized negative feelings toward a group of people based on their gender, characterized by a denial of continued discrimination, antagonism toward women's demands, and lack of support for policies designed to help women in work and education *180*

old-fashioned racism overt, oppressive acts and feelings toward a group of people based on their race *180*

old-fashioned sexism overt sexism, characterized by the endorsement of traditional gender roles, differential treatment of men and women, and stereotypes about lesser female competence *180*

outgroup homogeneity effect the tendency to see outgroup members as similar to one another but ingroup members as diverse individuals *183*

prejudice a negative learned attitude toward particular groups of people *176*

racial prejudice the tendency to hold a hostile attitude toward an individual because of his or her racial background *177*

racism an institutional practice that discriminates against individuals on the basis of their race *177*

realistic group conflict theory the idea that when different groups are in competition for resources, they tend to close ranks, favoring ingroup members and discriminating against outgroup members *185*

relative deprivation discontent caused by the belief that we might fare badly in comparison with people in other groups *186*

sexism an institutional practice that discriminates against individuals on the basis of their gender *177*

social categorization the process of dividing people into categories according to their race, gender, and other common attributes *183*

social dominance orientation seeing one's own group as naturally superior to other groups *184*

stereotype threat fear or anxiety held by people in minority groups that they might conform to a negative cultural stereotype *189*

ultimate attribution error the tendency to explain the behavior of groups in terms of internal dispositional factors, without taking the situational constraints into consideration *184*

Test Your Understanding

MULTIPLE CHOICE

1. Which of the following is an example of modern racism?
   a. dismissing the idea that racism exists in today's culture
   b. supporting the segregation of white people and black people
   c. refusing to hire a person of an ethnic minority because of the color of his or her skin
   d. banning people of a particular race from a restaurant or other business

2. Ambivalent sexism is most likely to occur
   a. in first-world countries.
   b. in third-world countries.
   c. in countries where men and women have equal rights and equal opportunities.
   d. in countries where there is a high degree of economic and political inequality between the sexes.

3. Which of these statements about stereotyping is NOT true?
   a. We form stereotypes very early on in life.
   b. Stereotyping is avoidable if children are taught early in life.
   c. Awareness of a stereotype in the media is enough to activate it in real life.
   d. Stereotyping is an automatic process that helps us classify people and objects.

4. What does the Implicit Association Test (IAT) primarily measure?
   a. gender bias
   b. racial bias
   c. political bias
   d. age bias

5. Stereotyping and prejudice can originate from all of the following, except
   a. social learning.
   b. cognitive bias.
   c. geographical origin.
   d. motivational factors.

6. The inability to accurately distinguish people of other races results from
   a. ingroup favoritism.
   b. ultimate attribution error.
   c. the just-world hypothesis.
   d. the outgroup homogeneity effect.

7. Terry's classmates have been hiking all morning and decide to stop for lunch at the same time as another group. When Terry's teacher enters the shop, she notices that there are not enough sandwiches for both groups. Because there are only enough sandwiches for one group, Terry's group starts to make comments about the competitiveness of the second group. At the same time, the other group starts calling Terry's group names because they are buying up all the sandwiches. This demonstrates
   a. the realistic group conflict theory.
   b. intergroup schadenfreude.
   c. social identity theory.
   d. the contact hypothesis.

8. If we are in a good mood, we are
   a. less likely to stereotype others.
   b. more likely to stereotype others.
   c. unable to stereotype others.
   d. equally likely to stereotype others.

9. Which of these techniques does not help to combat stereotyping and prejudice?
   a. increased contact with people in minority groups
   b. increased interdependence between groups
   c. increased personal motivation
   d. increased competition between groups

10. Hannah walks past a homeless man on the street and tells herself that he is probably a drug addict who is entirely responsible for his own situation. Hannah is using
    a. the just-world hypothesis.
    b. confirmation bias.
    c. the contact hypothesis.
    d. a stereotype threat.

ESSAY RESPONSE

1. What are the differences between old-fashioned prejudice (for example, old-fashioned racism and old-fashioned sexism) and modern prejudice? Provide an example of each.

2. Describe the main principles of the jigsaw classroom technique and explain how it utilizes one of the four methods used to combat prejudice.

3. Explain how social categorization contributes to the formation and reinforcement of stereotypes.

4. Describe the advantages and disadvantages of belonging to an ingroup. Include examples of the outgroup homogeneity effect and ingroup favoritism in your answer.

5. Explain how our perceptions of other people may result in a self-fulfilling prophecy. Include an example of a self-fulfilling prophecy in your answer.

APPLY IT!

Find a newspaper or magazine article that discusses the consequences of gender prejudice around the world (for example, sex-selective abortion in India or China). What are the long-term implications of such prejudice? What measures are being taken to prevent it?

ANSWERS: 1. a; 2. d; 3. b; 4. b; 5. c; 6. d; 7. a; 8. b; 9. d; 10. a

Remember to check www.thinkspot.com for additional information, downloadable flashcards, and other helpful resources.

NEWSWEEK

See Baby Discriminate

By PO BRONSON AND ASHLEY MERRYMAN
Published: September 5, 2009

> Based on your reading of the research presented in Chapter 10, what are other potential variables that could impact this relationship?

> Were you raised in an environment where people openly discussed race? What role do you think cognitive dissonance (see Chapter 6) played in the discomfort these parents felt?

Kids as young as 6 months judge others based on skin color. What's a parent to do?

At the Children's Research Lab at the University of Texas, a database is kept on thousands of families in the Austin area who have volunteered to be available for scholarly research. In 2006 Birgitte Vittrup recruited from the database about a hundred families, all of whom were Caucasian with a child 5 to 7 years old.

The goal of Vittrup's study was to learn if typical children's videos with multicultural storylines have any beneficial effect on children's racial attitudes. Her first step was to give the children a Racial Attitude Measure, which asked such questions as:

How many White people are nice?
(Almost all) (A lot) (Some) (Not many) (None)
How many Black people are nice?
(Almost all) (A lot) (Some) (Not many) (None)

During the test, the descriptive adjective "nice" was replaced with more than 20 other adjectives, like "dishonest," "pretty," "curious," and "snobby."

Vittrup sent a third of the families home with multiculturally themed videos for a week, such as an episode of *Sesame Street* in which characters visit an African-American family's home, and an episode of *Little Bill*, where the entire neighborhood comes together to clean the local park.

In truth, Vittrup didn't expect that children's racial attitudes would change very much just from watching these videos. Prior research had shown that multicultural curricula in schools have far less impact than we intend them to—largely because the implicit message "We're all friends" is too vague for young children to understand that it refers to skin color.

Yet Vittrup figured explicit conversations with parents could change that. So a second group of families got the videos, and Vittrup told these parents to use them as the jumping-off point for a discussion about interracial friendship. She provided a checklist of points to make, echoing the shows' themes. "I really believed it was going to work," Vittrup recalls.

The last third were also given the checklist of topics, but no videos. These parents were to discuss racial equality on their own, every night for five nights.

At this point, something interesting happened. Five families in the last group abruptly quit the study. Two directly told Vittrup, "We don't want to have these conversations with our child. We don't want to point out skin color."

Vittrup was taken aback—these families volunteered knowing full well it was a study of children's racial attitudes. Yet once they were aware that the study required talking openly about race, they started dropping out.

It was no surprise that in a liberal city like Austin, every parent was a welcoming multiculturalist, embracing diversity. But according to Vittrup's entry surveys, hardly any of these white parents had ever talked to their children directly about race. They might have asserted vague principles—like "Everybody's equal" or "God made all of us" or "Under the skin, we're all the same"—but they'd almost never called attention to racial differences.

They wanted their children to grow up colorblind. But Vittrup's first test of the kids revealed they weren't colorblind at all. Asked how many white people are mean, these children commonly answered, "Almost none." Asked how many blacks are mean, many answered, "Some," or "A lot." Even kids who attended diverse schools answered the questions this way.

More disturbing, Vittrup also asked all the kids a very

blunt question: "Do your parents like black people?" Fourteen percent said outright, "No, my parents don't like black people"; 38 percent of the kids answered, "I don't know." ==In this supposed race-free vacuum being created by parents, kids were left to improvise their own conclusions—many of which would be abhorrent to their parents.==

Vittrup hoped the families she'd instructed to talk about race would follow through. After watching the videos, the families returned to the Children's Research Lab for retesting. To Vittrup's complete surprise, the three groups of children were statistically the same—none, as a group, had budged very much in their racial attitudes. At first glance, the study was a failure.

Combing through the parents' study diaries, Vittrup realized why. Diary after diary revealed that the parents barely mentioned the checklist items. Many just couldn't talk about race, and they quickly reverted to the vague "Everybody's equal" phrasing.

Of all those Vittrup told to talk openly about interracial friendship, only six families managed to actually do so. And, for all six, their children dramatically improved their racial attitudes in a single week. Talking about race was clearly key. Reflecting later about the study, Vittrup said, "A lot of parents came to me afterwards and admitted they just didn't know what to say to their kids, and they didn't want the wrong thing coming out of the mouth of their kids."

We all want our children to be unintimidated by differences and have the social skills necessary for a diverse world. The question is, do we make it worse, or do we make it better, by calling attention to race?

The election of President Barack Obama marked the beginning of a new era in race relations in the United States—but it didn't resolve the question as to what we should tell children about race. Many parents have explicitly pointed out Obama's brown skin to their young children, to reinforce the message that anyone can rise to become a leader, and anyone—regardless of skin color—can be a friend, be loved, and be admired.

==Others think it's better to say nothing at all about the president's race or ethnicity—because saying something about it unavoidably teaches a child a racial construct.== They worry that even a positive statement ("It's wonderful that a black person can be president") still encourages a child to see divisions within society. For the early formative years, at least, they believe we should let children know a time when skin color does not matter.

What parents say depends heavily on their own race: a 2007 study in the *Journal of Marriage and Family* found that out of 17,000 families with kindergartners, nonwhite parents are about three times more likely to discuss race than white parents; 75 percent of the latter never, or almost never, talk about race.

In our new book, *NurtureShock,* we argue that many modern strategies for nurturing children are backfiring—because key twists in the science have been overlooked. Small corrections in our thinking today could alter the character of society long term, one future citizen at a time. The way white families introduce the concept of race to their children is a prime example.

For decades, it was assumed that children see race only when society points it out to them. However, child-development researchers have increasingly begun to question that presumption. They argue that children see racial differences as much as they see the difference between pink and blue—but we tell kids that "pink" means for girls and "blue" is for boys. "White" and "black" are mysteries we leave them to figure out on their own.

It takes remarkably little for children to develop in-group preferences. Vittrup's mentor at the University of Texas, Rebecca Bigler, ran an experiment in three preschool classrooms, where 4- and 5-year-olds were lined up and given T-shirts. Half the kids were randomly given blue T-shirts, half red. The children wore the shirts for three weeks. During that time, the teachers never mentioned their colors and never grouped the kids by shirt color.

The kids didn't segregate in their behavior. They played with each other freely at recess. But when asked which color team was better to belong to, or which team might win a race, they chose their own color. They believed they were smarter than the other color. "The Reds never showed hatred for Blues," Bigler observed. "It was more like, 'Blues are fine, but not as good as us.'" When Reds were asked how many Reds were nice, they'd answer, "All of us." Asked how many Blues were nice, they'd answer, "Some." Some of the Blues were mean, and some were dumb—but not the Reds. ==Bigler's experiment seems to show how children will use whatever you give them to create divisions—seeming to confirm that race becomes an issue only if we make it an issue.== So why does Bigler think it's important to talk to children about race as early as the age of 3?

If these children did not learn to stereotype and hold negative opinions about other races, then this suggests that racism isn't fully the result of social learning. If it's not, then why do you think these children came to such conclusions?

What is your opinion? What is the most ideal way to handle this topic with children? After learning about stereotype threat in Chapter 10, how do you think discussing President Barack Obama's race would affect both black and white children?

How does this experiment compare to Jane Elliott's blue eyes/brown eyes demonstration?

What does this tell us about the nature or nurture debate first discussed in Chapter 1? Do you think the results of this experiment give us any definitive evidence for one side or the other?

Think about how Bronson and Merryman's Diverse Environment Theory is similar to the contact hypothesis you learned about in Chapter 10.

Her reasoning is that kids are developmentally prone to in-group favoritism; they're going to form these preferences on their own. Children naturally try to categorize everything, and the attribute they rely on is that which is the most clearly visible.

We might imagine we're creating color-blind environments for children, but differences in skin color or hair or weight are like differences in gender—they're plainly visible. Even if no teacher or parent mentions race, kids will use skin color on their own, the same way they use T-shirt colors. Bigler contends that children extend their shared appearances much further—believing that those who look similar to them enjoy the same things they do. Anything a child doesn't like thus belongs to those who look the least similar to him. The spontaneous tendency to assume your group shares characteristics—such as niceness, or smarts—is called essentialism.

Within the past decade or so, developmental psychologists have begun a handful of longitudinal studies to determine exactly when children develop bias. Phyllis Katz, then a professor at the University of Colorado, led one such study—following 100 black children and 100 white children for their first six years. She tested these children and their parents nine times during those six years, with the first test at 6 months old.

How do researchers test a 6-month-old? They show babies photographs of faces. Katz found that babies will stare significantly longer at photographs of faces that are a different race from their parents, indicating they find the face out of the ordinary. Race itself has no ethnic meaning per se—but

children's brains are noticing skin-color differences and trying to understand their meaning.

When the kids turned 3, Katz showed them photographs of other children and asked them to choose whom they'd like to have as friends. Of the white children, 86 percent picked children of their own race. When the kids were 5 and 6, Katz gave these children a small deck of cards, with drawings of people on them. Katz told the children to sort the cards into two piles any way they wanted. Only 16 percent of the kids used gender to split the piles. But 68 percent of the kids used race to split the cards, without any prompting. In reporting her findings, Katz concluded: "I think it is fair to say that at no point in the study did the children exhibit the Rousseau type of color-blindness that many adults expect."

The point Katz emphasizes is that this period of our children's lives, when we imagine it's most important to not talk about race, is the very developmental period when children's minds are forming their first conclusions about race.

Several studies point to the possibility of developmental windows—stages when children's attitudes might be most amenable to change. In one experiment, children were put in cross-race study groups, and then were observed on the playground to see if the interracial classroom time led to interracial play at recess. The researchers found mixed study groups worked wonders with the first-grade children, but it made no difference with third graders. It's possible that by third grade, when parents usually recognize it's safe to start talking a little about race, the developmental window has already closed.

The other deeply held assumption modern parents have is what Ashley and I have come to call the Diverse Environment Theory. If you raise a child with a fair amount of exposure to people of other races and cultures, the environment becomes the message. Because both of us attended integrated schools in the 1970s—Ashley in San Diego and, in my case, Seattle—we had always accepted this theory's tenets: diversity breeds tolerance, and talking about race was, in and of itself, a diffuse kind of racism.

But my wife and I saw this differently in the years after our son, Luke, was born. When he was 4 months old, Luke began attending a preschool located in San Francisco's Fillmore/Western Addition neighborhood. One of the many benefits of the school was its great racial diversity. For years our son never once mentioned the color of anyone's skin. We never once mentioned skin color, either. We thought it was working perfectly.

Then came Martin Luther King Jr. Day at school, two months before his fifth birthday. Luke walked out of preschool that Friday before the weekend and started pointing at everyone, proudly announcing, "That guy comes from Africa. And she comes from Africa, too!" It was embarrassing how loudly he did this. "People with brown skin are from Africa," he'd repeat. He had not been taught the names for races—he had not heard the term "black" and he called us "people with pinkish-whitish skin." He named every kid in his schoolroom with brown skin, which was about half his class.

My son's eagerness was revealing. It was obvious this was something he'd been wondering about for a while. He was relieved to have been finally given the key. Skin color was a sign of ancestral roots.

Over the next year, we started to overhear one of his white friends talking about the color of their skin. They still didn't know what to call their skin, so they used the phrase "skin like ours." And this notion of ours versus theirs started to take on a meaning of its own. As these kids searched for their identities, skin color had become salient.

Soon, I overheard this particular white boy telling my son, "Parents don't like us to talk about our skin, so don't let them hear you."

As a parent, I dealt with these moments explicitly, telling my son it was wrong to choose anyone as his friend, or his "favorite," on the basis of skin color. We pointed out how certain friends wouldn't be in our lives if we picked friends for their color. Over time he not only accepted but embraced this lesson. Now he talks openly about equality and the wrongfulness of discrimination.

Not knowing then what I do now, I had a hard time understanding my son's initial impulses. Katz's work helped me to realize that Luke was never actually colorblind. He didn't talk about race in his first five years because our silence had unwittingly communicated that race was something he could not ask about.

The Diverse Environment Theory is the core principle behind school desegregation today. Like most people, I assumed that after 30 years of desegregation, it would have a long track record of scientific research proving that the Diverse Environment Theory works. Then Ashley and I

began talking to the scholars who've compiled that very research.

In the summer of 2007, led by the Civil Rights Project, a dozen scholars wrote an amicus brief to the U.S. Supreme Court supporting school desegregation in Louisville, Ky., and Seattle. By the time the brief reached the court, 553 scientists had signed on in support. However, as much as the scientists all supported active desegregation, the brief is surprisingly circumspect in its advocacy: the benefits of desegregation are qualified with words like "may lead" and "can improve." "Mere school integration is not a panacea," the brief warns.

UT's Bigler was one of the scholars heavily involved in the process of its creation. Bigler is an adamant proponent of desegregation in schools on moral grounds. "It's an enormous step backward to increase social segregation," she says. However, she also admitted that "in the end, I was disappointed with the amount of evidence social psychology could muster [to support it]. Going to integrated schools gives you just as many chances to learn stereotypes as to unlearn them."

The unfortunate twist of diverse schools is that they don't necessarily lead to more cross-race relationships. Often it's the opposite. Duke University's James Moody—an expert on how adolescents form and maintain social networks—analyzed data on more than 90,000 teenagers at 112 different schools from every region of the country. The students had been asked to name their five best male friends and their five best female friends. Moody matched the ethnicity of the student with the race of each named friend, then compared

the number of each student's cross-racial friendships with the school's overall diversity.

Moody found that the more diverse the school, the more the kids self-segregate by race and ethnicity within the school, and thus the likelihood that any two kids of different races have a friendship goes down.

Moody included statistical controls for activities, sports, academic tracking, and other school-structural conditions that tend to desegregate (or segregate) students within the school. The rule still holds true: more diversity translates into more division among students. Those increased opportunities to interact are also, effectively, increased opportunities to reject each other. And that is what's happening.

As a result, junior-high and high-school children in diverse schools experience two completely contrasting social cues on a daily basis. The first cue is inspiring—that many students have a friend of another race. The second cue is tragic—that far more kids just like to hang with their own. It's this second dynamic that becomes more and more visible as overall school diversity goes up. As a child circulates through school, she sees more groups that her race disqualifies her from, more lunchroom tables she can't sit at, and more implicit lines that are taboo to cross. This is unmissable even if she, personally, has friends of other races. "Even in multiracial schools, once young people leave the classroom, very little interracial discussion takes place because a desire to associate with one's own ethnic group often discourages interaction between groups," wrote Brendesha Tynes of the University

Think about your own school and the schools you've attended in the past. Have you witnessed the same phenomenon? Why do you think this is the case? What implications might it suggest?

What do you think is the reason for children's need for ingroups and outgroups? What are the potential consequences?

In Chapter 10, you learned about old-fashioned and modern racism and sexism. How might the two different types of racism and sexism play a role in Katz's observation?

of Illinois at Urbana-Champaign.

All told, the odds of a white high-schooler in America having a best friend of another race is only 8 percent. Those odds barely improve for the second-best friend, or the third-best, or the fifth. For blacks, the odds aren't much better: 85 percent of black kids' best friends are also black. Cross-race friends also tend to share a single activity, rather than multiple activities; as a result, these friendships are more likely to be lost over time, as children transition from middle school to high school.

I can't help but wonder—would the track record of desegregation be so mixed if parents reinforced it, rather than remaining silent? It is tempting to believe that because their generation is so diverse, today's children grow up knowing how to get along with people of every race. But numerous studies suggest that this is more of a fantasy than a fact.

Is it really so difficult to talk with children about race when they're very young? What jumped out at Phyllis Katz, in her study of 200 black and white children, was that parents are very comfortable talking to their children about gender, and they work very hard to counterprogram against boy-girl stereotypes. That ought to be our model for talking about race. The same way we remind our daughters, "Mommies can be doctors just like daddies," we ought to be telling all children that doctors can be any skin color. It's not complicated what to say. It's only a matter of how often we reinforce it.

Shushing children when they make an improper remark is an instinctive reflex, but often the wrong move. Prone to categorization, children's brains can't help but attempt to generalize rules from the examples they see. It's embarrassing when a child blurts out, "Only brown people can have breakfast at school," or "You can't play basketball; you're white, so you have to play baseball." But shushing them only sends the message that this topic is unspeakable, which makes race more loaded, and more intimidating.

To be effective, researchers have found, conversations about race have to be explicit, in unmistakable terms that children understand. A friend of mine repeatedly told her 5-year-old son, "Remember, everybody's equal." She thought she was getting the message across. Finally, after seven months of this, her boy asked, "Mommy, what's 'equal' mean?"

Bigler ran a study in which children read brief biographies of famous African-Americans. For instance, in a biography of Jackie Robinson, they read that he was the first African-American in the major leagues. But only half read about how he'd previously been relegated to the Negro Leagues, and how he suffered taunts from white fans. Those facts—in five brief sentences were omitted in the version given to the other children.

After the two-week history class, the children were surveyed on their racial attitudes. White children who got the full story about historical discrimination had significantly better attitudes toward blacks than those who got the neutered version. Explicitness works. "It also made them feel some guilt," Bigler adds. "It knocked down their glorified view of white people." They couldn't justify in-group superiority.

Minority parents are more likely to help their children develop a racial identity from a young age. April Harris-Britt, a clinical psychologist and professor at the University of North Carolina at Chapel Hill, found that all minority parents at some point tell their children that discrimination is out there, but they shouldn't let it stop them. Is this good for them? Harris-Britt found that some preparation for bias was beneficial, and it was necessary—94 percent of African-American eighth graders reported to Harris-Britt that they'd felt discriminated against in the prior three months.

But if children heard these preparation-for-bias warnings often (rather than just occasionally), they were significantly less likely to connect their successes to effort, and much more likely to blame their failures on their teachers—whom they saw as biased against them.

Harris-Britt warns that frequent predictions of future discrimination ironically become as destructive as experiences of actual discrimination: "If you overfocus on those types of events, you give the children the message that the world is going to be hostile—you're just not valued and that's just the way the world is."

Preparation for bias is not, however, the only way minorities talk to their children about race. The other broad category of conversation, in Harris-Britt's analysis, is ethnic pride. From a very young age, minority children are coached to be proud of their ethnic history. She found that this was exceedingly good for children's self-confidence; in one study, black children who'd heard messages of ethnic pride were more engaged in school and more likely to attribute their success to their effort and ability.

That leads to the question that everyone wonders

but rarely dares to ask. If "black pride" is good for African-American children, where does that leave white children? It's horrifying to imagine kids being "proud to be white." Yet many scholars argue that's exactly what children's brains are already computing. Just as minority children are aware that they belong to an ethnic group with less status and wealth, most white children naturally decipher that they belong to the race that has more power, wealth, and control in society; this provides security, if not confidence. So a pride message would not just be abhorrent—it'd be redundant.

Over the course of our research, we heard many stories of how people—from parents to teachers—were struggling to talk about race with their children. For some, the conversations came up after a child had made an embarrassing comment in public. A number had the issue thrust on them, because of an interracial marriage or an international adoption. Still others were just introducing children into a diverse environment, wondering when and if the timing was right.

But the story that most affected us came from a small town in rural Ohio. Two first-grade teachers, Joy Bowman and Angela Johnson, had agreed to let a professor from Ohio State University, Jeane Copenhaver-Johnson, observe their classrooms for the year. Of the 33 children, about two thirds were white, while the others were black or of mixed-race descent.

It being December, the teachers had decided to read to their classes *'Twas the Night B'fore Christmas,* Melodye Rosales's retelling of the Clement C. Moore classic. As the teachers began reading, the kids were excited by the book's depiction of a family waiting for Santa to

come. A few children, however, quietly fidgeted. They seemed puzzled that this storybook was different: in this one, it was a black family all snug in their beds.

Then there was the famed clatter on the roof. The children leaned in to get their first view of Santa and the sleigh as Johnson turned the page—

And they saw that Santa was black.

"He's black!" gasped a white little girl.

A white boy exclaimed, "I thought he was white!"

Immediately, the children began to chatter about the stunning development. At the ripe old ages of 6 and 7, the children had no doubt that there was a Real Santa. Of that they were absolutely sure. But suddenly there was this huge question mark. Could Santa be black? And if so, what did that mean?

While some of the black children were delighted with the idea that Santa could be black, others were unsure. A couple of the white children rejected this idea out of hand: a black Santa couldn't be real.

But even the little girl the most adamant that the Real Santa must be white came around to accept the possibility that a black Santa could fill in for White Santa if he was hurt. And she still gleefully yelled along with the Black Santa's final "Merry Christmas to All! Y'all Sleep Tight."

Other children offered the idea that perhaps Santa was "mixed with black and white"—something in the middle, like an Indian. One boy went with a two-Santa hypothesis: White Santa and Black Santa must be friends who take turns visiting children. When a teacher made the apparently huge mistake of saying that she'd never seen Santa, the children all quickly corrected her: everyone had seen Santa at the mall. Not that that clarified the situation any.

The debate raged for a week, in anticipation of a school party. The kids all knew Real Santa was the guest of honor.

Then Santa arrived at the party—and he was black. Just like in the picture book.

Some white children said that this black Santa was too thin: that meant that the Real Santa was the fat white one at Kmart. But one of the white girls retorted that she had met the man and was convinced. Santa was brown.

Most of the black children were exultant, since this proved that Santa was black. But one of them, Brent, still doubted—even though he really wanted a black Santa to be true. So he bravely confronted Santa.

"There ain't no black Santas!" Brent insisted.

"Lookit here." Santa pulled up a pant leg.

A thrilled Brent was sold. "This is a black Santa!" he yelled. "He's got black skin and his black boots are like the white Santa's boots."

A black-Santa storybook wasn't enough to crush every stereotype. When Johnson later asked the kids to draw Santa, even the black kids who were excited about a black Santa still depicted him with skin as snowy white as his beard.

But the shock of the Santa storybook was the catalyst for the first graders to have a yearlong dialogue about race issues. The teachers began regularly incorporating books that dealt directly with issues of racism into their reading.

And when the children were reading a book on Martin Luther King Jr. and the civil-rights movement, both a black and a white child noticed that white people were nowhere to be found in the story. Troubled, they decided to find out just where in history both peoples were.

AGGRESSION

<<< Girls are often the surprising culprits behind bullying and cyberbullying.

WHAT IS THE NATURE OF AGGRESSION?
WHAT ARE THE THEORIES OF AGGRESSION?
WHAT INFLUENCES AGGRESSION?
HOW CAN WE REDUCE AGGRESSION?

In the

fall of 2009, 15-year-old Phoebe Prince and her family moved from their native Ireland to the small community of South Hadley, Massachusetts. Phoebe started as a freshman at South Hadley High School and quickly began a romantic relationship with a well-liked senior. Her immediate popularity drew resentment from some of the other girls in school. To intimidate her, the girls and a few of their male friends bumped into Phoebe in the halls, sent her threatening text messages, and called her derogatory names to her face. Despite complaints from Phoebe's mother, school officials did not intervene. The harassment escalated, and on January 14, 2010, Phoebe committed suicide. Although disputed by school officials and defense attorneys, the primary motivation for her suicide was likely the relentless bullying she endured from her classmates. Felony charges were brought against six teens— four girls and two boys—for stalking and civil rights violations. Phoebe's case and a rash of other bullying-related deaths have influenced a number of anti-bullying laws in 41 states (Hampson, 2010). The circumstances surrounding Phoebe's death are still under investigation.

Educational psychologists recognize the kind of situation described previously as a new kind of bullying. Unlike the male, social delinquent stereotype of the past, these new bullies are generally good-looking, athletic, accomplished students, and are comfortable around authority figures (Hampson, 2010). The way teens bully has changed as well. The Internet has taken bullying out of the schoolyard and into cyberspace, and mobile devices facilitate harassment 24 hours a day. Cyberbullying includes the use of texts, instant messaging, Web sites, or e-mails to threaten, intimidate, or humiliate a person. Four in 10 teens have experienced cyberbullying, and girls are twice as likely to be the victims and perpetrators of this kind of harassment (University of Gothenburg, 2010). The instigators of cyberbullying are often motivated by frustration, anger, retaliation, and at times, simple boredom. The majority of teens who have been bullied online do not tell their parents because they worry they'll lose computer access, they fear nothing will change even if they do report the problem, or they worry that their parents won't understand (Mishna, Saini, & Solomon, 2009). Adults often misunderstand the concept of bullying and chalk it up to a simple tiff between teens. What they fail to understand is that bullying is an aggressive behavior that entails an imbalance of strength and power. If administrators and parents would attempt to understand this changing phenomenon better, then tragedies such as the death of Phoebe Prince may be prevented.

CHAPTER 11

201

AGGRESSION behavior, either verbal or physical, that is used to intentionally harm another individual

HOSTILE (AFFECTIVE) AGGRESSION a behavior that occurs when the primary goal of an action is to make the victim suffer

INSTRUMENTAL AGGRESSION a behavior that occurs when the primary goal of an action is not to make the victim suffer, but to attain a non-injurious goal

What Is the Nature of Aggression?

Consider the following situations: (1) A woman walking home from a night out with friends is knocked out with a mallet and sexually assaulted. (2) A man is sitting at a red light. When the light turns green, the person in the car behind him lays on the horn and yells at the man to move. (3) A teenager is texting while driving and rear-ends another vehicle, killing a family of four. (4) A pet owner hits his dog with a rolled-up newspaper after the dog disobeys him.

Which of these instances is considered aggression? Your answer will depend on your definition of aggression. Many people assume that aggression involves inflicting harm on another person, but what if the harm was unintentional, such as in the case of the teenager? And what if no physical harm occurs, such as in the case of the man at the red light? And what if the target is not a person, as in the case of the pet owner? Aggression takes many forms and can have multiple effects, so it can be tricky to specifically define. **Aggression** can be generally defined as a behavior, either verbal or physical, that is used to intentionally harm another individual.

> "Aggression takes many forms and can have multiple effects, **so it can be tricky to specifically define.**"

Acts of aggression seem to be the way many people attempt to release frustration or address conflicts. If you flip on the news or open a newspaper, you will read about acts of rape, murder, and armed assault. These are the types of behaviors you may primarily associate with aggression. What you may not realize is that there are probably acts of aggression in your everyday life that fly under the radar, such as a verbal argument with a coworker, a harsh e-mail from a friend, or a case of the silent treatment from a significant other. These behaviors may not seem overtly aggressive, but when you examine the purpose of the acts—to harm another—then the aggression behind them is revealed. Social psychologists are interested in the causes of aggressive behavior and have sought to achieve a better understanding of its nature through research. They anticipate that the better we understand human nature, the better equipped we are to prevent aggressive acts. Let's examine what social psychologists already know about aggression.

Aggression comes in two forms: hostile and instrumental. **Hostile (or affective) aggression** occurs when anger leads to aggression and the primary goal of an action or behavior is to make the victim suffer. Individuals who participate in emotional aggression, then, are simply seeking to harm or

injure the target of their attack. The 2008 brutal beating of a Florida teen is an example of emotional aggression. A young girl from Polk County, Florida was badly beaten by a group of six girls and two boys who kicked and punched her until she was unconscious. The girls recorded their attack on a cell phone camera so that they could post it on YouTube (CBS/AP, 2008).

In contrast, **instrumental aggression** occurs when the primary goal of the action is not to make the victim suffer, but to attain a non-injurious goal. An individual who participates in instrumental aggression will harm or injure another as a way of obtaining various rewards such as control of a situation or improved self-esteem. Chicago Bears linebacker Brian Urlacher breaking through an offensive line and knocking a quarterback to the ground is an example of instrumental aggression. His motivation behind the action isn't to physically harm the quarterback; it's to establish dominance for his team and to keep his opponent away from the end zone in an ultimate effort to win the game.

Instrumental aggression is often used as a method of coercion to help a person "get his way." Acts of intimidation, such as threatening injury or demanding control, demonstrate behavior intended to improve the aggressor's situation and harm another in the process. An angry diner who yells at a waiter and demands to be compensated for unsatisfactory service is exhibiting instrumental aggression. At times, the primary goal of this type of aggression is hard to detect, such as when the goal involves a person's sense of self. When people participate in instrumental aggression to improve their self-esteem, they

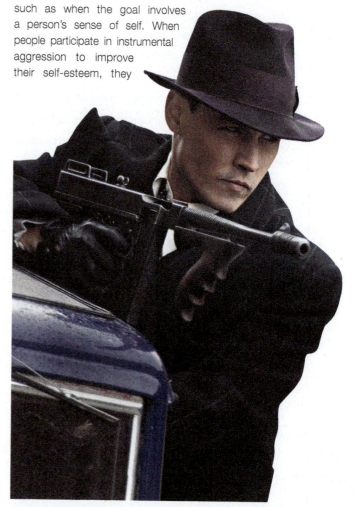

Armed robbery is a form of instrumental aggression, as the primary goal is obtain money, **not to harm another.**

attempt to build themselves up by bringing others down. Phoebe Prince's case is an example of instrumental aggression. Bullies often tease others as a way to make themselves feel better.

GENDER DIFFERENCES

When we think of an act of hostile aggression, we often think of the aggressor as male. This is because of the informal assumption that males are more aggressive than females. This notion is supported by the overwhelming number of reports of male aggression in the news and other forms of media, as well as by research. When asked whether they had ever participated in any aggressive actions, males reported a higher incidence of aggressive behavior than did females (Harris, 1994). Furthermore, males are more likely than females to be targets of aggression (Buss, 2004; Daly & Wilson, 1989).

While these studies support what many of us already believe, further research on gender differences in aggression reveal that the issue is a bit more complex (Hyde, 1984; Bettencourt & Miller, 1996; Lightdale & Prentice, 1994). Meta-analysis and reviews of literature suggest that the gender differences are not that large (Hyde, 1984; Bettencourt & Miller, 1996), and the disparity in aggression between genders is dependent on how aggression is defined. Studies have found that males ultimately tend to be more physically aggressive, while females are more relationally aggressive (Crick & Grotpeter, 1995; Anderson & Huesmann, 2003). In other words, female aggression is more likely to manifest itself through hurting relationships by engaging in gossip, excluding a person from a group or activity, or telling lies (Tapper & Boulton, 2004, 2005; Huesmann et al., 2003; Crick & Rose, 2000).

Provocation, or the lack thereof, considerably affects this disparity. When men are provoked in any way, they are significantly more likely to act aggressively than are females. However, when provocation is not involved, the disparity seems to disappear (Bettencourt & Miller, 1996). Similarly, gender differences in aggression are heightened in situations in which aggression is required or expected, typically by some sort of social role. The term "man up," used in situations in which a man is expected to take an aggressive approach to something, exemplifies this type of social expectation (Baron & Richardson, 1994).

The type of aggression also affects the disparity. Research has shown that males are more likely than females to participate in direct aggression. **Direct aggression** is an action or behavior that is clearly derived from the aggressor and is aimed directly at the target—for example, punching, pushing, yelling, and using insulting language. On the other hand, females are more likely than males to participate in indirect aggression. **Indirect aggression** is an action or behavior that is not clearly derived from the aggressor, where it is not obvious to the target that he or she has been the victim of aggression. Examples of this include spreading rumors

and gossiping, creating social isolation, or framing others for something they did not do. So while a man is more likely to get into a brutal brawl with someone, a woman is more likely to spread a nasty rumor (Eagly & Wood, 1991).

Research suggests that men and women also differ when it comes to their respective attitudes toward aggression. Men tend to report less guilt or anxiety about their aggressive behavior than women, while women report more concern about the possibility that their aggressive behavior could cause a threat to their personal safety, as in the case of retaliation. Research also suggests that men and women are apt to have contrasting views of what aggression represents. Women tend to hold an **expressive view of aggression**, in which aggression is used as a way to express anger and reduce stress. Men, on the other hand, tend to hold

	Physical	Verbal
Direct	Punching	Name calling
Indirect	Refusal to shake hands	Spreading a rumor

Types of Aggression. Aggression can be a combination of direct, indirect, verbal, and physical behavior.

^^ In 2008, Texas teenagers Amina and Sarah Yaser Said were shot to death by their father **because they supposedly dishonored their family by dating non-Muslim boys.**

an instrumental view of aggression, in which the aggression is used to gain social or material rewards (Campbell, Muncer, & Gorman, 1993).

Researchers have worked to account for the gender differences in aggression. One explanation is that the levels of testosterone in people's bodies influence their levels of aggression (Mazur & Booth, 1998; Olweus, Mattson, Schally, & Low, 1988). Men naturally have more testosterone, so they tend to be more aggressive. These correlational studies show that there is a relationship between the amount of testosterone and the level of aggression in young boys (Chance, Brown, Dabbs, & Casey, 2000), adults (Banks & Dabbs, 1996), and in women (Dabbs & Hargrove, 1997).

However, it is important to note that additional research suggests that it is not the level of testosterone alone that accounts for increased aggression. Research comparing individuals of different income levels finds that men with high income levels have low rates of delinquency regardless of their levels of testosterone, yet the rate of delinquency for low-income men varies with level of testosterone (Dabbs & Morris, 1990). Others have looked at socialization and gender roles and found that males and females are taught differently about the costs and benefits of aggression (Eagly & Steffen, 1986). There isn't just one reason for the gender differences in aggression; hormone levels, gender roles, and methods of socialization all contribute to the way men and women exhibit aggression.

CULTURAL DIFFERENCES

While we often think of aggression as triggered by the actions of another person, it can also be triggered by cultural factors. A culture's system of values, beliefs, and norms may suggest that aggression is appropriate or even necessary in certain circumstances. Countries with individualistic cultures like the United States have different ways of thinking and behaving than those with collectivist cultures like China, for example, and these differences, along with general beliefs and values, contribute to the varied ways aggression manifests itself in different cultures.

> " A culture's system of values, beliefs, and norms may suggest that aggression is appropriate **or even necessary in certain circumstances.** "

In cultures where the law is weak and citizens need to protect themselves, the act—or even the threat—of violence is considered to be essential. Under these conditions, any threat to a person or his or her possessions must be met with retaliation or he or she could be viewed as an easy target and have his or her survival put at risk. Social psychologists refer to these types of cultures as **cultures of honor** (Nisbett & Cohen, 1996). In cultures of honor, strong norms suggest that aggression is an appropriate response to an insult or threat to one's honor.

The Southern United States was one of the first focuses of social psychologists' research on cultures of honor. One study by Nisbett and Cohen (1996) found higher instances of violence in that region. In another study, Southerners were more likely than Northerners to respond with aggression

and show physical signs of distress when their honor was challenged by insults (Cohen et al., 1996). You may have also witnessed this type of culture in movies. In an old western, a cattle driver might challenge a crooked sheriff to a duel because the sheriff insulted the man's livelihood. Or in a Japanese period piece, you may see a young warrior set out on a mission to seek revenge on a man who dishonored the young warrior's family. While these situations often seem larger than life on-screen, they remain present in the real world.

Cultures of honor often exist in conditions where law enforcement is weak or lacking, wealth is portable and can be stolen, and financial security is absent (Cohen & Nisbett, 1997). It may seem like this type of culture died with the Wild West, but there are several present-day examples of cultures of honor around the world—including in the inner cities of the United States and other developed countries, as well as those in the remote regions of Europe and Asia. Individuals living in a housing project in Detroit might develop a culture of honor as law enforcement tends to be ineffective in such areas, residents own few possessions, and they have little financial security. Citizens of this culture may feel compelled to present the threat of violence or participate in violent behavior as a means to protect themselves from potential threats. Showing off a gun, aligning oneself with a gang, or making verbal threats might achieve this goal.

Individuals in cultures of honor sometimes perpetrate *honor killings*, which have become a searing human rights issue. Honor killings occur when one family member kills another because the victim has somehow "shamed" the family. Typically, this is perpetrated by a father, brother, or husband on a daughter, sister, or wife. Honor killings are based on the belief that women are considered the property of the family and their bodies are repositories of the family's honor (Amnesty International, 2010). If a woman or girl is accused, or even suspected, of participating in behavior that could damage the reputation of her family, she is likely to endure brutal retaliation from fellow family members. This retaliation can result in serious bodily injury and even death.

In 1997, Marzouk Abdel Rahim, a tile maker from Cairo, brutally murdered his 25-year-old daughter and then dismembered her body because he felt that her relationship with a male friend dishonored their family. Abdel Rahim displayed no regrets for his action, and in a statement to the press declared that, "honor is more precious than my own flesh and blood." He served only two months in jail for his crime (Jehl, 1999). Honor killings are most prevalent in Arab nations, where traditions are tightly adhered to. Leaders of these nations are often close-lipped about the subject, but some governments, such as Jordan's under King Abdullah, have lifted the lid on public discussion of honor killings. They have worked in conjunction with modernizers and traditionalists to respond to this issue with appropriate sensitivity.

Arabs contend that attention to their society's role in the phenomenon of honor killings is a result of the Western world's tendency to see them as backward. In the United States, when a man kills his wife based on the suspicion that she is cheating, it is viewed as a crime of passion. Or when a gang member kills a member of a rival gang because the rival disrespected, or "dissed," one of his boys, it is seen as an unfortunate consequence of urban living. But when crimes with similar motivations happen in the Arab world, they are considered barbarous and incomprehensible (Jehl, 1999). Still, despite these arguments, the fact remains that Western nations punish murderers regardless of the motivation, while many Arab governments traditionally choose to look the other way or merely issue slaps on the wrist when it comes to honor killings.

What Are the Theories of Aggression?

Through formal and informal observation, we know that human beings frequently engage in aggressive behavior, but we don't know exactly *why*. The nature of aggression, the forces from which it originates, and the factors that impact its occurrence are contentious topics among social psychologists (Baron & Richardson, 1994). Theoretical perspectives on aggression typically fall into three general categories: instinct, frustration, and social learning.

INSTINCT AND EVOLUTION

Psychologists who follow the **instinct theory** believe that aggression is an innate and inevitable force. Sigmund Freud and Konrad Lorenz were two of the leading proponents of this theory. Freud believed that aggression stems from a self-destructive impulse and that humans must act out that impulse in order to release negative energy and return to a state of calm—a behavior Freud refers to as a "death drive." Lorenz agreed that aggression is unlearned and universal, but viewed the behavior from an evolutionary perspective. He believed that through evolution, humans developed a fighting instinct similar to that found in animals. Over the course of many years, our ancestors found that aggressive behavior benefited them as a method of gaining resources, eliminating competition, threatening rivals, and defending against assailants. According to instinct theory, the natural need for aggression gets stronger over time.

Instinct theory is not without flaws. It does not take into account the differences in aggressive behavior among various societies. If all humans share the same desire to act aggressively, how can we explain why some societies are historically peaceful while others are violent, or why every human does not overtly express her aggressive desires (Hornstein, 1976)? Instinct theory must concede that the way humans express their aggression is a learned behavior, regardless of whether that expression is physical, verbal, direct, or indirect. For example, you and your friend might both have the innate desire to act aggressively, but you may have learned to express that aggression by verbally venting to others while

your friend may have learned to release aggression through physical force. Another problem with instinct theory is that the logic behind it is circular. When a person asks why people aggress, the answer is that it is due to instinct. When discussion about how we know aggression is instinctual arises, instinct theory falls back on the simple fact that people do aggress.

Another related theory that looks at our origins for explanations of aggression is evolutionary theory. This theory examines the evolutionary drive to survive and posits that our aggression evolved out of necessity in order to simply exist. One study claims that the need to obtain limited resources necessary for survival resulted in adaptive aggressive behavior (Tooby & Cosmides, 1988). It is important to remember that simply because the need arose and aggression became a part of the evolutionary process, this doesn't necessarily mean everyone is aggressive.

GENETICS

Another way of explaining the individual differences in aggressive behavior is by considering biological factors. Our individual biological makeup is believed to be a fundamental factor that influences our behavior.

Instinct theory suggests that humans, **like animals in the wild, have an innate desire to protect their personal safety, their family's safety,** and their possessions through aggressive behavior.

Like blue eyes or detached earlobes, a tendency toward extreme aggression can be genetic. Researchers in the Netherlands discovered a genetic mutation in a Dutch family that appears to cause periodic outbursts of aggression in its maternally linked male possessors. Because the problem only affects the men in the family, it is likely a problem with a recessive gene on the X chromosome, and after years of research, the defect was isolated in one gene area (Morell, 1993). Researchers could not clearly affirm whether this gene creates a problem for individuals outside of that particular family. Over-generalizing the results of genetic research could be dangerous, as people could push for prenatal screening for the aggressive gene. This information is, however, another step closer to answering the central questions about the origins of aggression.

When trying to identify aggressive behavior, research can look directly at the brain. Scientists have used the Single Photon Emission Computerized Tomography (SPECT) system to identify regions of the brain that relate to aggression. SPECT generates a color picture of the blood flow and activity in the brain (Hirono, 2000). Unusual increases and decreases in activity that are vital to causing aggression are typically found in the left temporal lobe. Aggressive men tend to have too much or too little activity in that area, limiting their ability to control their actions. Identifying the areas of abnormality allows doctors to prescribe customized drug treatment for individuals to help balance the activity in their brains.

Biochemical Influences

Conflicting studies have shown that heredity alone cannot determine whether or not a person is going to behave aggressively. An individual's blood chemistry also influences the propensity to aggressive behavior. If you've ever watched an episode of MTV's *The Jersey Shore* and observed cast members getting into drunken bar brawls, then you know that alcohol can unleash aggression when individuals are provoked. Laboratory experiments and legal statistics back up that observation. In 55 percent of in-home assaults and 65 percent of homicides, the assailant and/or the victim had been drinking (American Psychological Association, 2004). Alcohol has a tendency to enhance aggressive behavior by reducing people's self-awareness and their ability to self-monitor while focusing their attention on provocative sources (Bartholow & Heinz, 2006). While aggressive behavior does not occur in every person who throws back a drink, it does have a strong correlation with heavy drinking, especially in the case of those who already expect that their disposition will become more aggressive when alcohol is involved. Results from a 2006 study that included a sample of 212 men and women revealed that alcohol increases aggression among heavy drinkers who expect alcohol to increase their aggression or who are dispositionally aggressive (Barnwell, Borders, & Earleywine, 2006).

Human hormones, and particularly testosterone, can also be a key biological factor that influences aggressive behavior. Researchers from Georgia State University studied the testosterone levels, crime, and prison misbehavior of 692 prison inmates and found that male inmates who had committed personal crimes that were violent or sexual in nature

>>> **Authorities investigated the role of "roid rage"—** caused by an increase in testosterone due to anabolic steroids—**in professional wrestler Chris Benoit's killing of his wife and child and his subsequent suicide.**

> *If you've ever watched an episode of MTV's The Jersey Shore and observed cast members getting into drunken bar brawls, then you know that* **alcohol can unleash aggression when individuals are provoked.**

had higher testosterone levels than inmates who committed property crimes of larceny, drug possession, and burglary. They also found that those inmates with higher levels of testosterone violated more prison rules, especially rules that involved confrontation (Dabbs, Carr, Frady, & Riad, 1995). While testosterone, like aggression, is typically associated with men, it impacts women as well. In one study, women who were given doses of testosterone so that their levels of the hormone became equal to those of men became less aware of aggression-deterring threat signals like facial expressions of anger, fear, and disgust, making them more susceptible to aggression themselves (van Honk & Schutter, 2007). Injecting a person with testosterone, male or female, will not automatically make him or her aggressive, but in general, higher levels of this hormone are associated with aggressive behavior when a person is provoked, just as lower levels are associated with less aggressive behavior.

Researchers can also look directly at brain activity. Low levels of the neurotransmitter serotonin can cause compromised impulse control in the frontal lobes, as serotonin plays a considerable role in the regulation of emotions and social functioning, domains that are closely related to aggression. Research has shown that in humans as well as primates, low serotonin is often found in violence-prone children and adults. As with

genetics, however, it is not accurate to simply state that biochemical makeup can create an individual who is predisposed to aggressive behavior. There has been no evidence to support the idea of a "violent brain" that works independently from a person's surroundings and circumstances, so we must understand that there are environmental factors as well as natural factors that influence aggressive behavior.

Psychopathy, a risk factor for aggression, has been linked to abnormalities in brain regions associated with morality and emotions, as well as with reduced activity in the prefrontal cortex (Blair, 2001, 2007; Glenn & Raine, 2009). Psychopaths operate with their own self-interest in mind, and their aggression is used to that end rather than for emotional reasons. These individuals are also less sensitive to social responses that help deter aggression, similar to the female subjects who were given testosterone and were less responsive to such signals. It is imperative to remember that the studies on aggression are correlational, and so they do not indicate causation. These studies are useful in identifying variables that are related to one another, but there coulds, of course, be other variables that contribute to aggression.

FRUSTRATION AGGRESSION

As a student, you probably understand frustration all too well. You spend hours studying for a test, but end up with a less than impressive grade. You need to get to class, but you cannot find your notebook anywhere and you need it for an open-note test. These types of situations will typically lead to **frustration**, which is a feeling of being upset or annoyed by the inability to reach a goal or perform an activity.

The **frustration aggression theory** (Dollard et al., 1939) suggests that frustration precedes aggression. This theory states that frustration triggers the inclination for aggression because our motivation for aggression increases when our current behavior is interrupted or we are prevented from reaching a goal. What do you do when you can't find that lost notebook or other misplaced item? Do you forcefully toss around nearby objects or mumble obscenities to yourself? A classic study of the frustration aggression theory occurred in 1941 when researchers showed a group of children a room full of attractive toys, but did not allow all of the children to play with the toys right away. Researchers found that the children who had to delay their play, and thus became frustrated, engaged in more aggressive behavior in their play once they were allowed access to the toys (Barker, Dembo, & Lewin, 1941). Later research, however, failed to find more than mild support of this theory, so it cannot be concluded that frustration alone leads to aggression or that aggression is always preceded by frustration (Burstein & Worchel, 1962). In 1989, Leonard Berkowitz revised the frustration aggression theory; he found that frustration produced anger, and anger could then lead to aggression, but did not necessarily always do so.

Relative deprivation (Merton & Kitt, 1950; Crosby, 1976; Bernstein

& Crosby, 1980) is a common cause of frustration that can lead to aggression. We experience relative deprivation when we compare ourselves to others and feel deprived of something, leading to feelings of frustration. Some researchers have suggested that the riots in Los Angeles in 1992 after four policemen accused of beating Rodney King were acquitted were fueled by relative deprivation (Brush, 1996; Miller, 2001). The economic downturn in the area caused tension and frustration to build, particularly because the lower income families in the area bore the brunt of the economic change. When the verdict in the highly publicized case was read, residents of L.A. were already highly agitated and experiencing a feeling of injustice due to their worsening financial situation.

Finally, one more notable theory of aggression is **cognitive-neoassociation theory**. This theory posits that when a person experiences something with a negative result, such as pain or discomfort, aggressive behavior can often occur in the wake of that experience (Berkowitz, 1998). Another aspect of the theory indicates that when a person is simply in the presence of an object related to aggression, that person is more likely to display aggression (Berkowitz & LePage, 1967).

SOCIAL LEARNING

Social learning theory suggests that human aggression is largely learned by observing the aggressive behavior of other people and is reinforced by consequences such as punishments or rewards in the individual's environment. Psychologist Albert Bandura developed social learning theory, also referred to as social cognitive theory, during the 1960s.

>>> Frustration aggression theory suggests that waiting in a long line **might trigger aggressive behavior.**

MODELING a process by which a person mimics another's behavior

REINFORCEMENT an action or process that strengthens a behavior

GENERAL AGGRESSION MODEL (GAM) a theory that builds on the social learning theory and provides a more integrative framework for specific theories of aggression by including situational and personal variables

> "Reinforcement can come from the behavior of parents and peers, as well as from media sources such as television, movies, and video games."

Modeling

Bandura conducted several studies involving observational learning, or modeling. **Modeling** is a process by which a person mimics another's behavior. Bandura believed that children could learn to engage in aggressive behavior by observing that behavior, both in real life and in the media (Bandura, Ross, & Ross, 1963). Bandura's famous Bobo doll study exhibited the power of modeling on aggression in children. In the study, a sample of preschool-aged children watched a video that showed an adult forcefully tossing, kicking, and punching an inflatable toy, which researchers referred to as a Bobo doll (a five-foot-tall doll with a weighted bottom that would pop back up when it was knocked down). The adults in the video displayed very specific physical and verbal signs of aggression, including striking the doll with a mallet, sitting on the doll, punching it in the nose, tossing it in the air, and repeating phrases such as, "sock him," "kick him," "hit him down," "throw him in the air," and "pow." The children were then placed in a mildly frustrating situation in which they were given some of their favorite toys only to have them taken away a few minutes later.

The children were eventually introduced to the Bobo doll along with other toys such as stuffed animals, baby dolls, and crayons. Without the children's knowledge, researchers observed the children for 20 minutes. The observers noted that the children who watched the video of the adults striking the Bobo doll were far more likely to strike their own dolls than a control group who did not watch the video (Bandura, Ross, & Ross, 1961), showing that the children learned to display aggression. The Bobo doll study, along with follow-up studies that involved exposure to prerecorded aggression, was one of the first lines of research to suggest a link between violence on TV and violence in real life. We will discuss this link in more detail later on in this chapter.

Reinforcement

The second component of social learning theory is reinforcement. **Reinforcement** is an action or process that strengthens a behavior, and

is a part of operant conditioning, which we discussed in Chapter 6. Reinforcement can be positive (adding in something that is pleasant or desirable) or negative (the removal of an unpleasant or aversive stimulus).

While one would think that aggressive behavior is typically met with punishment (e.g., a teenager getting suspended from school for fighting), it is frequently met with positive reinforcement that might not be considered. For example, if a man knocks a woman down and steals her purse, the man's aggressive behavior is rewarded with the valuable contents of the woman's purse. Children who learn to associate aggressive behavior with positive reinforcement will be more likely than children who learn to associate the behavior with punishment to participate in aggressive behavior in the future (Bandura, Ross, & Ross, 1961).

In another Bobo doll study, children watched one of three videos of an individual either being punished, rewarded, or receiving no consequences for aggressing against the Bobo doll (Bandura, 1965). The children who had seen the individual rewarded for beating up the Bobo doll showed the same behavior toward doll. An unexpected finding, however, was that children who watched the video that resulted in no consequences also engaged in aggressive behavior toward the doll, perhaps because it appeared that they could engage in violence without being punished.

Reinforcement can come from the behavior of parents and peers, as well as from media sources such as television, movies, and video games. In 2005, researchers from Iowa State University conducted a study in which participants were asked to play one of three versions of a car-racing video game: a version in which all violence was punished (i.e., points were deducted), a version in which all violence was rewarded (i.e., points were added), and a nonviolent version in which aggressive behavior had no impact on the player's score (Carnagey & Anderson, 2005). Results of the study showed that rewarding violent game actions increased hostile emotions, aggressive thinking, and aggressive behavior in participants. Punishing violent behavior increased hostile emotions; however, it did not increase aggressive behavior or aggressive thinking. The results suggest that positive reinforcement of violent actions can increase aggressive behavior, cognitions, and affect (Carnagey & Anderson, 2005).

<<< According to social learning theory, a child who watches his or her parents aggressively argue will be more likely to engage in similar aggressive verbal behavior than a child of calmer parents.

Aggressive Behavior:
A child steals a toy from a classmate.

Positive Reinforcement:
The child is rewarded by getting to play with the toy.

Negative Punishment:
The child loses not only that toy but all of the toys for the rest of the day.

Future Behavior:
The child is more likely to act aggressively during play again.

Future Behavior:
The child is less likely to act aggressively during play again.

The Reinforcement Chain Reaction. When aggressive behavior is met with positive reinforcement, it is more likely to lead to future aggressive behavior than when it is met with negative punishment.

GENERAL AGGRESSION MODEL

The **General Aggression Model (GAM)** builds on the social learning theory and provides a more integrative framework for specific theories of aggression by including different types of input variables (Anderson, Bushman, & Groom, 1997). According to GAM, two major types of input variables can trigger events that may eventually lead to blatant aggression—factors that relate to current situations, or situational factors, and factors that relate to the individuals involved, or personal factors. Situational factors are elements of the present situation that increase aggression: for example, factors such as verbal insults, the presence of a weapon, the presence of an intimidating figure, and overall frustration or discomfort. Personal factors are whatever a person brings to the present situation like attitudes, behavioral tendencies, and beliefs. Biological factors (e.g., hormones and genetics) are included in personal factors (Carnagey & Anderson, 2005).

Input variables must influence several different processes at a variety of levels before they can increase or decrease aggressive behavior. GAM suggests three routes of influence: affective state, cognitive state, and arousal state. The affective state filters information and can initiate aggressive feelings and their outward signs, such as an angry glare or "the evil eye." The cognitive state processes information and can initiate aggressive thoughts or can stir up beliefs and attitudes about

aggression. The arousal state determines what stimulates a person and can increase personal excitement. Depending on an individual's understanding of a present situation and the environmental factors involved, he or she employs either thoughtful action (e.g., restraining his or her anger) or impulsive action (e.g., releasing his or her anger through aggressive acts). This chain of events ultimately determines whether, and in what form, aggression occurs (Bushman & Anderson, 2002).

What Influences Aggression?

Now that you understand the various theories of aggression, let's examine specific factors and conditions that may influence aggression. Based on surveys, correlational and experimental studies, social psychologists have found that aversive experiences, cues in the environment, and the effects of the media can create a powerful cocktail for personal aggression.

AVERSIVE EXPERIENCES

Imagine that you are at a summer music festival. It's one of the hottest days of the year, and it seems like everyone in a 50-mile radius is in attendance. The crowd is so dense that you hardly notice the broken bottle under your feet, and you end up slicing your foot on it as you make your way toward the main stage. The cut is pretty deep and painful,

How do you react when you get a lower grade than you think you deserve?

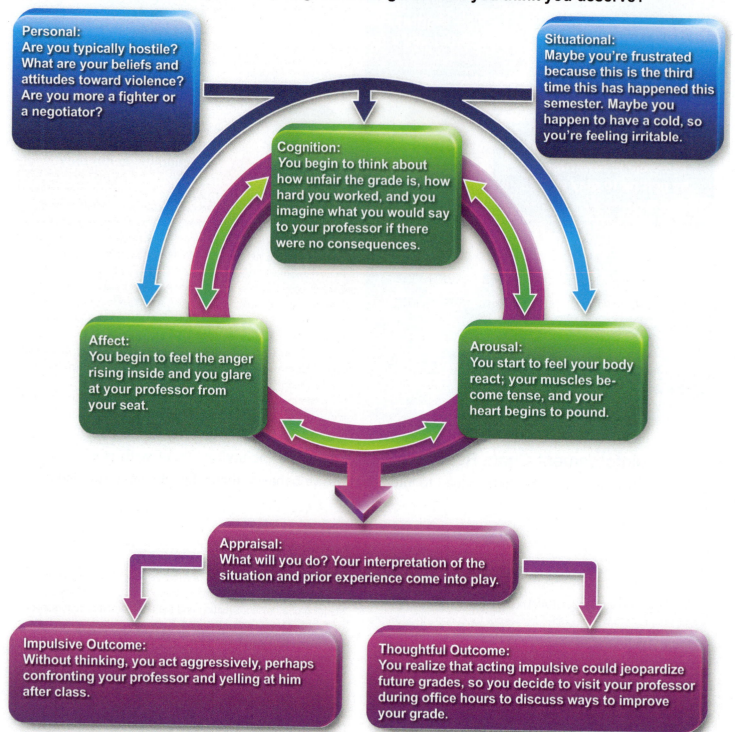

Personal:
Are you typically hostile? What are your beliefs and attitudes toward violence? Are you more a fighter or a negotiator?

Situational:
Maybe you're frustrated because this is the third time this has happened this semester. Maybe you happen to have a cold, so you're feeling irritable.

Cognition:
You begin to think about how unfair the grade is, how hard you worked, and you imagine what you would say to your professor if there were no consequences.

Affect:
You begin to feel the anger rising inside and you glare at your professor from your seat.

Arousal:
You start to feel your body react; your muscles become tense, and your heart begins to pound.

Appraisal:
What will you do? Your interpretation of the situation and prior experience come into play.

Impulsive Outcome:
Without thinking, you act aggressively, perhaps confronting your professor and yelling at him after class.

Thoughtful Outcome:
You realize that acting impulsive could jeopardize future grades, so you decide to visit your professor during office hours to discuss ways to improve your grade.

Source: Based on Bushman, B. J., & Anderson, C. A. (2002). Violent video games and hostile expectations: A test of the General Aggression Model. *Personality and Social Psychology Bulletin, 28,* 1679–1689.

The General Aggression Model. The General Aggression Model (GAM) looks at the person in the given situation. It proposes that aggression is affected by several factors, including current internal state, personal understanding, and decision making.

∧
∧ Between 1967 and 1971, riots broke out in
∧ 79 U.S. cities. **More occurred on hot days than on cooler days, and none of them occurred during the winter.**

so you know that you need to find a first aid tent to get help. Moving back through the crowd is nearly impossible. Your foot is beginning to throb, and the sun is beating down on you. How are you feeling right now? Are you cursing under your breath about the people who carelessly discarded their bottles on the ground? Are you tempted to shove all the people in front of you in order to make your way out of the crowd? Even a typically passive person could be tempted to act aggressively during such an aversive experience.

An **aversive experience** is an undesirable experience that may include pain, discomfort, overcrowding, or attack. Pain can be a powerful force that increases aggression in humans. Psychologist Leonard Berkowitz and his colleagues from the University of Wisconsin conducted a study in which students submerged one hand in either tepid water or bitterly cold water. The students whose hands were in the bitterly cold water described more feelings of irritability and annoyance than those whose hands were in the tepid water. This group was also more willing to inflict an unpleasant noise on another study participant. These results prompted Berkowitz to conclude that aversive experience, rather than frustration, is the primary instigator of aggressive behavior. It may be the culprit for bringing out the worst in us, as those made miserable often make others miserable (Berkowitz 1983, 1989, 1998). Misery loves company, right?

AROUSAL

It is easy to comprehend how certain experiences can spark aggressive behavior, as many of us have been in conditions that make our blood boil (e.g., being stuck in a stuffy plane stranded on the runway). What about the experiences that make our hearts pound? Types of arousal such as those associated with exercise or sexual excitement can have an effect on our aggression. Imagine that you've just had a vigorous workout at the gym; you took a lung-busting cardio class or lifted some serious weights. When you get back to the locker room, you find that the showers are out of order, so you can't clean up before you go to an appointment that you have scheduled. What do you do? Do you forcefully throw down your towel? Do you go to the front desk and give the gym manager a piece of your mind? Since this is merely a hypothetical situation and you have not

actually received the physiological arousal from a workout, you may not think that you would have a very strong reaction to this situation. But what you may not realize is that the arousal you receive from a workout may work up some aggressive feelings.

One study on arousal and behavior conducted by psychologists Stanley Schachter and Jerome Singer (1962) included 184 male college students who were taking an introductory psychology class at University of Minnesota. Participants were placed in private rooms and told that the study was examining the effects of vitamin injections on visual skill. Each participant was asked if he would be willing to receive an injection of "Suproxin," a name that was invented by the study administrators. The students who agreed to the injection received either adrenaline or saline, the latter of which served as a placebo. The individuals who were injected with the adrenaline were divided into three groups: informed (those who were told that the "Suproxin" produced side effects such as hand shaking and heart pounding, and who were therefore prepared for the effects of the adrenaline), misinformed (those who were told to expect effects that would not actually be produced by the drug, such as numb feet), and ignorant (those who were given no instructions of what to expect). Participants were then placed in a waiting room in which a confederate would either create a euphoria situation by entertaining the participant or an anger situation by annoying the participant.

In both the euphoria situation and the anger situation, the informed group showed the least emotion. Researchers concluded that this occurred because participants had an explanation for why they felt aroused (the injection). They believed that it wasn't the confederate's behavior that was making their body react—it was the drug. On the other hand, the misinformed and ignorant groups showed both increased happiness and increased anger in the simulated situations because they could not explain why their feelings were aroused.

These findings support the researchers' concept of a two-factor theory of emotional states that explains how appraisal shapes emotion.

∧
∧ The arousal a football player receives from
∧ vigorous exercise **may cause him to have increased anger when a play does not work and increased happiness when his team scores.**

You're waiting in line at a hot dog stand on the beach on a sweltering day. The line is long, and all you want is some water. As you wait, the experience becomes more and more aversive. What would trigger an aggressive action?

Arousal:
As the sun beats down on you, your heart rate increases, your skin feels like it's burning, and you begin to sweat.

Angry feelings:
You think about how thirsty you feel, and you start to get angry at how long the line is taking. Why would serving hot dogs take *this* much time?

Aggressive thoughts:
It occurs to you that you could just cut in line; after all, these people want hot dogs and you just want water. Or maybe you envision yourself telling the kids behind the stand to hurry it up.

**You can't take it anymore!
Will you take aggressive action?**

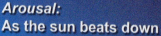

Aversive Experiences. Aggressive behavior can stem from aversive situations, which can create arousal, aggressive feelings, or aggressive thoughts.

The theory says that physiological arousal in different emotions is completely the same; we simply label the arousal according to the information that we have available (Schachter & Singer, 1962). Under this principle, the anger you might feel in response to the situation at the gym could be reduced if you understood that physiological arousal had revved up your emotions. With that said, the evidence for the two-factor theory is mixed (Marshall & Zimbardo, 1979; Maslach, 1979). Something that grew out of the two-factor theory is the excitation-transfer theory (Zillmann, 1983, 1996): a person may experience arousal in one situation, and that may not fully dissipate before another situation occurs. The excitement from the first situation can transfer to another event, and the same kind of arousal (anger, aggression, etc.) will also transfer to that second scenario.

Other research notes that any arousal, even sexual arousal, can increase aggression (Cantor, Zillmann, & Einseidel, 1978). It is important

to note that arousal can be misinterpreted. If a man is reprimanded at work and becomes upset, he may return home and display anger toward his family, even though his anger is actually meant for the workplace. Finally, we should remember that arousal is not a necessary component of emotions (Reisenzein, 1983).

CUES IN THE ENVIRONMENT

What do you think of when you see a gun? Safety, danger, or violence? According to Leonard Berkowitz and other psychologists, the sight of a weapon such as a gun is an environmental cue that can prime aggressive thoughts (Anderson, Benjamin, & Bartholow, 1998; Berkowitz & LePage, 1967; Berkowitz, 1993). In a study conducted by Berkowitz and his colleague LePage, participants were given electric shocks by a study administrator. Later, the participants were given the opportunity to shock the administrator. During the study, some participants were sitting at a table with the shock machine and two badminton rackets; others were at a table with both the machine and a 12-gauge shotgun and a 38-caliber revolver. All objects were supposedly left behind from a previous experiment. The results showed that participants who sat at the table with the guns gave more electric shocks to the administrator than those participants who sat at the table with the racket (Berkowitz & LePage, 1967). Berkowitz conducted a similar study with children. He found that children who had recently played with toy guns were more willing to knock down another child's tower of blocks (Berkowitz, 1968).

These studies suggest that environmental cues such as guns can create hostile thoughts and subsequently instigate aggressive actions. Berkowitz associates the rate of handgun crime with handgun ownership. Though controversial, Berkowitz's claim is supported by statistics showing that gun owners are 2.7 times more likely to be murdered, almost always by a family member or close friend who would have been most likely to have had visual exposure to the gun (Kellerman, 1993).

Interestingly, another study notes that the weapon priming effect is seen when the gun is viewed as a tool of violence, rather than a hunting tool (Bartholow et al., 2005). This was demonstrated when hunters saw a hunting rifle and did not experience an increase of aggressive thoughts, while non-hunters did experience an increase. The awareness of the rifle changed the reaction and resulting presence or lack thereof of aggressive thoughts.

Other factors that can contribute to increased instances of aggression are higher temperatures and consumption of alcohol. Studies have shown a link between increased aggression and higher temperatures due to the increase in physical arousal that accompanies higher temperatures (Anderson, Deuser, & DeNeve, 1995). Research has also found a connection between alcohol use and aggression. In one study, people who had consumed alcohol were more likely to give a higher number of electric shocks to an opponent than those who hadn't had alcohol, even if they were not doing so in response to provocation (Bailey & Taylor, 1991).

MEDIA VIOLENCE

Famed film director Oliver Stone is quoted as saying, "Film is a powerful medium. Film is a drug. Film is a potential hallucinogen. It goes into your eye. It goes into your brain. It stimulates, and it's a dangerous thing. It can be a very subversive thing." (British Broadcasting Corporation, 1995) While Stone's comments may be slightly tongue-in-cheek, many people believe that violence in the media is a very real threat to our society. They feel that exposure to aggressive behavior via television, movies, music, or books can cause children and even adults to act aggressively. This belief has been supported by research (Bushman & Anderson, 2001; Bushman & Huesmann, 2001) and many health organizations, but as you have learned so far in this chapter, aggression is not as simple as "monkey see, monkey do." It is generally agreed upon that media has some influence on behavior, but how and to what extent? There are correlational studies on this subject, from which we can only infer a relationship, and then there are experimental studies, which allow us to isolate possible causal variables (review research methodology in Chapter 2). Let's examine this issue, but

> ∧
> ∧ Does this collection of guns ignite
> ∧ feelings of **aggression in you?**

keep in mind that the results of the research should not be interpreted to mean that all people who watch television will commit acts of violence.

Models Aggression

On April 20, 1999, two male students walked into Columbine High School in Littleton, Colorado, wearing black trench coats and toting semi-automatic handguns, shotguns, and explosives. Within an hour, the boys killed 12 fellow students, one teacher, and themselves. To witnesses, the event was like a scene right out of a movie. Was it? Many different factors were blamed for this tragedy—poor parental supervision, lack of moral initiatives in school, and availability of guns.

But it was exposure to violence in the media that drew the most attention. The boys' attack was nearly identical to a fantasy scene from the 1995 film *The Basketball Diaries* in which the protagonist, played by Leonardo DiCaprio, walks down the halls of his school in a trench coat and randomly shoots classmates with a shotgun. Many people believe that children and adults who are exposed to violent behavior through the media will likely model that behavior in real life, as in Bandura's Bobo doll study, discussed earlier (Freedman, 2002). While the event was eerily similar to the movie, we shouldn't assume this was the reason the act was perpetrated; there were many factors in play here, including the reality that the boys were social outcasts, and they had been bullied.

Television in particular is often pinpointed as the largest provider of violent messages, as it is the most accessible medium to the average American. While it might be common for some children to imitate the kicks they see in a kung fu cartoon or some adults to try to replicate a grappling move they see during a televised mixed martial arts fight, it does not mean that everyone is likely to model violent behavior displayed through the media. If that were the case, millions of people would tote samurai swords and administer violent vengeance on anyone who crossed them, a la Uma Thurman in Quentin Tarantino's graphically violent *Kill Bill* movies.

There are certain things we can look at to get a glimpse into the likelihood of aggression in children. Dodge's social information processing theory is a five-step model that outlines a child's response to a problematic situation (Dodge, 1986; Crick & Dodge, 1994). A child moves through the model successfully, or possibly is hindered by bias and deficient ability to process the situation; the child who fails to navigate the problem is more likely to have aggressive behavior. This study proposes how cognition mediates aggression in children, and may ultimately help mitigate aggression in children if they can learn to respond to problems in different ways. The five steps—encoding social cues, interpreting social cues, searching for a response, evaluating a response, and enacting—can be applied to how children process information coming from the media.

Primes Aggression

The media does not have to be a how-to guide in order to influence aggression; it can simply *prime* thoughts and feelings of aggression, which may eventually lead to aggressive behavior. Violent video games are often accused of priming aggressive thoughts and feelings in children and teens. In a study investigating the effect that violent video games have on aggression, researchers randomly assigned two video games to members of a group of 43 participants. Some played *Mortal Kombat* (a violent video game), and others played *Tiger Woods PGA Tour* (a nonviolent video game). After the participants played their assigned game, they performed a retaliation reaction time task with a study administrator. The participant set the punishment levels (punishment was in the form of noise) for the administrator during the task. Researchers found that the participants who played the violent video game used higher levels of noise when they were in the punisher role. It was concluded that the violent video game primed the aggressive feelings of participants, causing them to act out their aggression on the study administrator (Bartholow & Anderson, 2002).

Music, and particularly music with explicit lyrics, is also a media source that can prime aggressive behavior. In the way that "Let's Get It Started" by the Black Eyed Peas might get you pumped to perform your best in a game, songs with violent lyrics might get you primed for aggression. In a 2006 study, participants were asked to listen to either a song with misogynistic lyrics such as Bloodhound Gang's "A Lapdance is So Much Better When the Stripper's Crying," and Dr. Dre's "Bitches Ain't Shit," or a song with more neutral lyrics such as Miley Cyrus's "The Climb" (Fischer & Greitemeyer, 2006). Participants were told that they were participating in a music survey. After participants listened to their assigned song, they were asked to prepare a sample of hot sauce for another participant, who was secretly one of the study administrators. The participants heard the administrators state that they did not enjoy spicy foods and were told that they could dish out as large of a sample as they wished with the knowledge that the administrator would be required to drink the entire sample.

The results of the survey showed that participants who heard the misogynistic lyrics gave more hot sauce to female administrators than to male administrators. The group who listened to the neutral lyrics did not show a discrepancy in sample sizes. The results of this survey suggest that misogynistic lyrics can prime aggressive feelings against women and cause individuals to model the behavior described in the lyrics.

Repeated Exposure to Violence

As we discovered from social learning theory, aggressive responses are stimulated in individuals either by their personal experiences or by their observation of others. Actors on television or in the movies serve as models for viewers, and with more than half of major actors shown on network television continuously involved in violent interactions, it is likely that television actors are frequent models of aggressive behavior. As we learned from Bandura, viewers are likely to imitate aggressive models if the behavior is rewarded or goes unpunished. Repeated exposure to rewarded or unpunished violence may lead viewers to believe that if others can constantly behave aggressively without being punished, then that behavior is acceptable for them as well. In a recent analysis, more than 5,000 hours of programming on network and cable broadcasts showed violence being rewarded 15 percent of the time and unpunished 73 percent of the

time (Federman, 1997). FX's *The Shield* and Showtime's *Dexter* are shows that frequently exhibit violent behavior being rewarded.

This repeated exposure to violent media, particularly violence that is rewarded, can desensitize a viewer to the violence. When **desensitization** occurs, a viewer's physiological reactions to violence are reduced as a result of repeated exposure. According to an American Psychological Association task force report on television and American society, by the time the average child completes elementary school, he or she will have viewed more than 8,000 murders and more than 100,000 other assorted acts of violence on television. The emergence of online streaming of television shows on computers and personal mobile devices allows even more frequent and extreme acts to be displayed inside and outside of the home.

How Can We Reduce Aggression?

Let's think about what we have learned so far in this chapter. Observations, genetics, biochemical makeup, culture, aversive experiences, arousal, environmental cues, and the media can all potentially lead us to act aggressively. With all of these factors encouraging us to act aggressively, why isn't everyone in the world in constant opposition? Well, aggression is not inevitable. In fact, recent studies show that the United States is not becoming more violent, but that homicides and other crimes are actually decreasing (Anderson & Huesmann, 2003). Aggression can be reduced and even prevented in many cases through several strategies. The source of the aggression might impact, which prevention strategy is most effective in any given situation.

PUNISHMENT

As we learned from Bandura's social learning theory, children are likely to model aggressive behavior if they see that behavior rewarded. Similarly, they are less likely to model aggressive behavior if that behavior is punished. For example, when the children in the Bobo doll study were shown a video that displayed an adult kicking the doll and then getting yelled at for doing so, the children were less likely to model the aggressive form of play.

Unfortunately, punishment alone is not completely effective, because several types of aggression stem from impulsive reactions. A man punches another man who makes a quick and threatening move toward him. A woman yells out a threatening curse word when the person in the car next to her cuts her off. When people act impulsively, they do not have time to think about the consequences of their actions. Let's use the death penalty as an example. This punishment is used as a deterrent for heinous crimes such as murder, but murders are typically committed on impulse and without premeditation. The vast majority of the evidence shows that the death penalty is no more effective as a deterrent for murder than imprisonment. States with the death penalty do not have lower rates of criminal homicide than states without the death penalty. In fact, during the early 1970s, death-penalty states averaged an annual rate of 7.9 criminal homicides per 100,000 people, while states without the death penalty averaged a rate of 5.1 per 100,000 (American Civil Liberties Union, 1990). Also,

∧∧∧ Reports from the Kaiser Foundation state that 81 percent of parents have seen their children **model either positive (e.g., helping) or aggressive (e.g., punching or hitting) behaviors from TV.**

abolishing the death penalty does not raise violence in the community (Archer & Gaertner, 1984). Even for non-physical aggression, individuals may not think about the possible consequences or punishment for their behavior. The assailants in Phoebe Prince's case, discussed in the opening of the chapter, most likely did not consider that spreading rumors and sharing insults could cause a person's death and subsequently send them to jail.

MODELING NON-AGGRESSION

One of the major flaws in the use of punishment as a method to reduce aggression is that it does not show the individual an example of acceptable behavior. It does not draw a distinction between how a situation is handled with aggression and how it can be appropriately handled without aggression. Just as the modeling concept can lower inhibitions and encourage imitation when aggressive behavior is observed, it can also increase self-control and encourage obedience when non-aggressive behavior is observed. A television program that shows a protagonist who typically does the "right thing" (e.g., solves conflicts with peaceful discussion, displays self-control) can serve as a non-aggressive model. Incorporating these types of models in children's lives through positive television programming or organizations such as Big Brother, Big Sister can help children learn how to control their aggression and become less violent adults.

TRAINING

One of the best methods for reducing aggression is to prevent it before it happens. Training individuals to engage in non-aggressive conflict resolution strategies can help to accomplish this. In 2006, psychologists Sandra Jo Wilson and Mark Lipsey collected data from 249 studies of school violence prevention programs and found that these types of programs were effective in reducing violence, particularly in the case of programs that engaged students with behavioral problems. In these programs, students were taught problem-solving skills, conflict resolution techniques, and emotion-control strategies. After completion of a given program, the percentage of students who participated in violent or disruptive behavior was reduced from 20 percent to 13 percent (Wilson & Lipsey, 2006). The kids who were charged in the Phoebe Prince case are prime examples of those who should participate in programs that work to prevent violence in schools—perhaps if people are given non-violent tools to deal with peers with whom they have conflicts, fewer stories like Phoebe's will end so tragically.

<<< How often do you wish that you could immediately take back something you said in a verbal argument? **Many of our aggressive acts are triggered by impulse, so we do not take the time to consider the consequences.**

ACTION LEARNING

Action Learning Project: Reducing Aggression

The tragedy at Columbine that was previously mentioned was unfortunately not the only occurrence of its type. Among other recent school violence incidents, the nation was rocked in 2007 when Seung-Hui Cho went on a murderous rampage at Virginia Tech in which he killed 32 people and then himself. What can be done to protect students from violence from elementary school all the way through college? What have you learned in this chapter that applies?

Consider teaching others to reduce and even prevent violence by introducing the General Aggression Model. Design a violence prevention workshop for children based on the GAM. Use the chart below to organize your ideas, and draw out the model in terms that a young child could understand. Be sure to simplify the terms and concepts. Explain how this type of education could decrease some of the bullying that children and teenagers experience at school. Contact your campus child development center or a local elementary school to

see if you can share your project with them. Ask your instructor if you can present your project in class to show how social psychology can be applied.

What you will learn from this action learning project:

1. How social psychology theories can help reduce or even prevent aggression
2. How to educate others about reducing aggression
3. How children react to non-aggressive modeling

How Will You React? Explaining the General Aggression Model to Children			
Inputs	Personal:		Situation:
Routes	Affect:	Cognition:	Arousal:
Outcomes	Thoughtful Action:		Impulsive Action:

Summary

WHAT IS THE NATURE OF AGGRESSION? p. 202

• Social psychologists are interested in what causes aggressive behavior and have sought for several years to achieve a better understanding of its nature through research. They anticipate that the better we understand human nature, the better equipped we are to prevent aggressive acts.

• Aggression comes in two forms: hostile (affective) and instrumental. Hostile aggression occurs when the primary goal of an action or behavior is to make the victim suffer. Individuals who participate in hostile aggression, then, are simply seeking to harm or injure the target of their attack. Instrumental aggression occurs when the primary goal of the action is not to make the victim suffer, but to attain a non-injurious goal. An individual who participates in instrumental aggression will harm or injure another as a way of obtaining various rewards such as control of a situation or improved self-esteem.

• While we often think of aggression as being triggered by the actions of another person, it can also be triggered by cultural factors. A culture's system of values, beliefs, and norms may suggest that aggression is appropriate, or even necessary, in certain circumstances. In cultures where the law is weak and citizens need to protect themselves, the act or even the threat of violence is considered to be essential.

WHAT ARE THE THEORIES OF AGGRESSION? p. 205

• Freud believed that aggression stems from a self-destructive impulse and that humans must act out that impulse in order to release negative energy and return to a state of calm—a behavior Freud refers to as a "death drive." Lorenz believed that through evolution, humans developed a fighting instinct similar to that found in animals.

• Social learning theory suggests that human aggression is largely learned by observing the aggressive behavior of other people and is affected by consequences such as punishment or reward in the individual's environment. Psychologist Albert Bandura developed social learning theory, also referred to as social cognitive theory, during the 1960s.

• The General Aggression Model (GAM) builds on the social learning theory and provides a more integrative framework for specific theories of aggression by including input variables. According to the GAM, two major types of input variables can trigger events that may eventually lead to blatant aggression—factors that relate to current situations, or situational factors, and factors that relate to the individuals involved, or personal factors.

WHAT INFLUENCES AGGRESSION? p. 209

• There are several factors that influence aggression, including aversive experiences, arousal, and cues in the environment. Aversive experiences can come in the form of pain, discomfort, or personal attacks. Arousal from sources such as exercise and sex can be transformed into aggression. Environmental cues such as guns or other weapons increase the likelihood of aggression.

• Viewing violence either in person or on television can increase aggressive behavior, particularly when individuals are provoked. It can also desensitize viewers to violence, making them less aware of the harmful results of their actions.

HOW CAN WE REDUCE AGGRESSION? p. 214

• Aggression is not inevitable. It can be reduced and even prevented in many cases through several strategies. The source of the aggression might impact which prevention strategy is most effective in a given situation.

• Children are likely to model aggressive behavior if they see that behavior rewarded. Similarly, they are less likely to model aggressive behavior if that behavior is punished.

• Just as the modeling concept can lower inhibitions and encourage imitation when aggressive behavior is observed, it can also increase self-control and encourage obedience when non-aggressive behavior is observed.

Key Terms

aggression behavior, either verbal or physical, that is used to intentionally harm another individual *202*

aversive experience an undesirable experience that may include pain, discomfort, overcrowding, or attack *211*

cognitive-neoassociation theory a theory that suggests that when a person experiences something with a negative result, such as pain or discomfort, aggressive behavior can often occur in the wake of that experience *207*

culture of honor a culture in which strong norms suggest that aggression is an appropriate response to an insult or threat to one's honor *204*

desensitization when physiological reactions to violence are reduced as a result of repeated exposure *214*

direct aggression an action or behavior that is clearly derived from the aggressor and is aimed directly at the target *203*

expressive view of aggression a method of aggression in which aggression is used as a way to express anger and reduce stress *203*

frustration a feeling of being upset or annoyed by the inability to reach a goal or perform an activity *207*

frustration aggression theory a theory stating that frustration precedes aggression because our motivation for aggression increases when our current behavior is interrupted or we are prevented from reaching a goal *207*

General Aggression Model (GAM) a theory that builds on the social learning theory and provides a more integrative framework for specific theories of aggression by including situational and personal variables *209*

hostile (affective) aggression a behavior that occurs when the primary goal of an action is to make the victim suffer *202*

indirect aggression an action or behavior that is not clearly derived from the aggressor, and where it is not obvious to the target that he or she has been the victim of aggression *203*

instinct theory a theory in which aggression is an innate and inevitable force *205*

instrumental aggression a behavior that occurs when the primary goal of an action is not to make the victim suffer, but to attain a non-injurious goal *202*

modeling a process by which a person mimics another's behavior *208*

reinforcement an action or process that strengthens a behavior *208*

social learning theory a theory that suggests that human aggression is largely learned by observing the aggressive behavior of other people and is reinforced by consequences such as punishment or reward in the individual's environment *207*

Test Your Understanding

MULTIPLE CHOICE

1. Which of the following situations is an example of hostile (affective) aggression?
   a. A baseball player rushes the pitcher's mound after being hit by a ball.
   b. A basketball player elbows an opponent in the eye after a rebound.
   c. A football player knocks down a receiver after he catches the ball.
   d. A soccer player steps on the foot of an official while going for the ball.

2. What group would most likely be the target of aggression?
   a. men
   b. teens
   c. the elderly
   d. women

3. Which of the following is an example of indirect aggression?
   a. a verbal insult to a person's face
   b. a punch in the stomach
   c. a rumor that is told in secret
   d. a noticeable snub at a party

4. What is the flaw in the instinct theory?
   a. It only applies to animals and does not apply to human behavior.
   b. It does not take into account the differences in behavior between individuals.
   c. It does not include verbal aggression.
   d. It does not take history into consideration.

5. Which of the following is not a biological force of aggression?
   a. genetics
   b. biochemical makeup
   c. hormones
   d. observations

6. Reinforcements influence aggression by
   a. creating additional frustration
   b. rewarding behavior
   c. regulating stimuli
   d. increasing environmental cues

7. According to GAM, what are elements of a given situation that can increase aggression?
   a. biological variables
   b. situational factors
   c. personal factors
   d. instinct variables

8. Which of the following is not an element of an aversive experience?
   a. discomfort
   b. knowledge
   c. attack
   d. pain

9. Through what method of influence does television induce violence?
   a. modeling
   b. authoritarianism
   c. frustration
   d. reiteration

10. Which of the following is a method to reduce aggression?
    a. increased arousal
    b. genetic engineering
    c. non-aggressive modeling
    d. appraisal

ESSAY RESPONSE

1. Is the fighting a soldier engages in during wartime considered emotional or instrumental aggression? Why? Can it be both?

2. Give an example of a culture of honor in the United States and explain the forces that impact that culture.

3. How do biological factors work with environmental factors to impact aggression?

4. What reinforcements and punishments (positive and negative) might be involved in a physical fight between two men over a woman they both have interest in?

5. How strongly does television influence your behavior? Have you ever modeled the behavior of an actor?

APPLY IT!

Conduct your own study on the effects of violent song lyrics. Ask your friends to bounce a ball against a wall as they listen to a song that includes lyrics about violence and then a song that includes neutral lyrics. Notice the change, if any, in the force your participant uses while listening to each song.

ANSWERS: 1. a; 2. d; 3. c; 4. b; 5. d; 6. b; 7. b; 8. b; 9. a; 10. c

Remember to check www.thinkspot.com for additional information, downloadable flashcards, and other helpful resources.

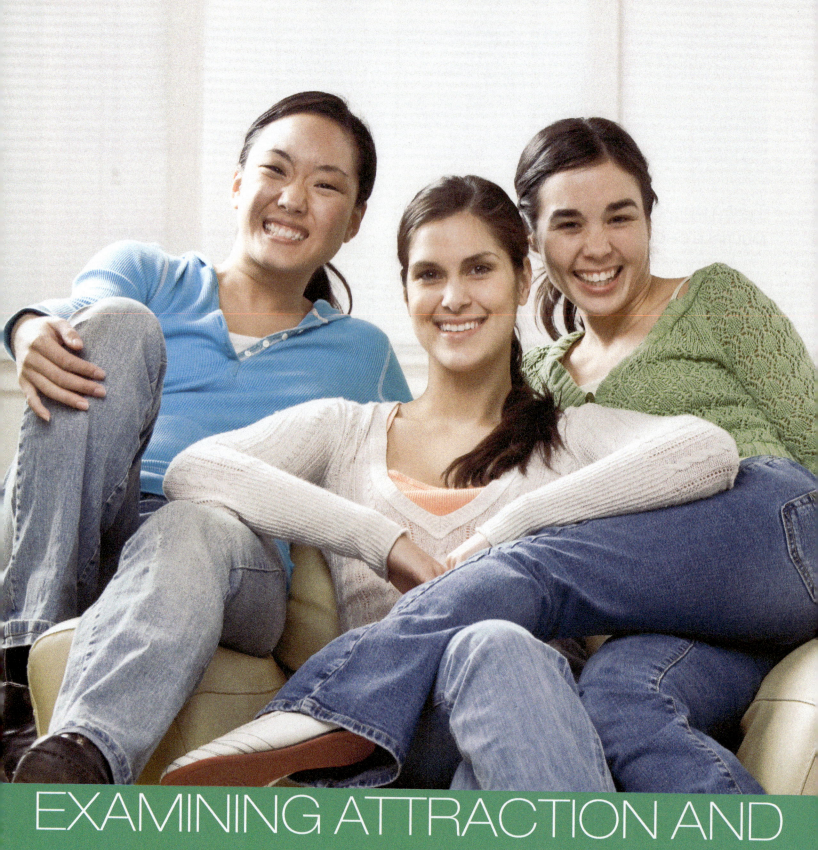

EXAMINING ATTRACTION AND CLOSE RELATIONSHIPS

Jessica

knows what she'll hear before she even picks up the phone.

"Hey, sweetie, what are you having?"

They call it their cocktail hour. It's been the routine for 10 years now, ever since Karen, Jessica's best friend since sixth grade, had to move to Atlanta for work. Every Thursday evening at eight o'clock, without fail, Jessica's phone rings. The two women sit in their living rooms at opposite ends of the East Coast and talk about everything that's happened over the week.

As she waits for this week's call, and the familiar question, Jessica thinks about the 25 years that have been marked by this friendship. *I don't know what I would do without her*, she thinks, recalling Karen's soothing voice on the other end of the line when Jessica's mother was diagnosed with breast cancer, and the joyful tears they shed together when Karen's daughter was born.

They know everything about each other, and have been each other's support through it all: struggling through class with the legendary mean history teacher, the crushes, the disastrous first attempts at learning to drive, the agonizing process of deciding where to go to college, engagements, marriages, an ill parent, a birth, a divorce.

Of course, the two women talk throughout the week—a day doesn't pass without at least a few e-mails between them. Still, there's something about this Thursday evening ritual that provides a foundation for the rest of the week. No matter what the week throws at her, Jessica knows there's someone out there who is pulling for her.

Deep in thought about her relationship with Karen, Jessica is startled when the phone rings. She smiles, settles into the cushions of the sofa, and picks up the phone, eager to hear her best friend's voice on the other end.

"Hey, sweetie, what are you having?"

Reading about Jessica and Karen, were you reminded of a close relationship you have? How does this relationship impact your life? What drew you to this person in the first place? In this chapter, you will explore how attraction leads to relationships (both close friendships and romantic relationships), and how those relationships are developed and defined.

CHAPTER **12**

NEED FOR AFFILIATION the desire to establish and maintain rewarding interpersonal relationships

It might seem like an obvious conclusion, but studies have demonstrated that friendships foster a sense of positive well-being across a person's lifetime. Friends boost our self-esteem and help us to learn social roles and social norms that allow us to succeed within a group (Hartup & Stevens, 1997).

It's not just our social lives that benefit from friendship. Numerous longitudinal studies have shown that both men and women with close friends actually have better health outcomes than people without such friendships. People with solid networks of friends also generally seem to live longer (Giles, Glonek, Luszcz, & Andrews, 2005) and overall are happier than individuals who are not as social (see Argyle, 1987 for a review). A 2010 study shows that a high level of social interaction might improve our survival odds by 50 percent. In fact, the researchers who conducted that study argue that low social interaction compares to smoking 15 cigarettes a day or being an alcoholic, is worse than not exercising, and is twice as harmful as obesity (Holt-Lunstad, Smith, & Layton, 2010).

Even at the neural level, the effects of social interactions or a lack thereof are clearly demonstrated (Eisenberger, Lieberman, & Williams, 2003). Studying the hypothesis that the brain registers social pain in a similar way to physical pain, researchers scanned study participants who were playing a virtual ball-tossing game. The participants were ultimately excluded from the game. It was discovered that the parts of the brain that respond to physical pain were active during exclusion, showing that the distress caused is indeed similar to visceral pain.

So it would seem that friendship is good for us. What, though, draws us to other people in the first place? Our urge to surround ourselves with other people is driven by the **need for affiliation**, or the desire to establish and maintain rewarding interpersonal relationships (Baumeister & Leary, 1995; MacDonald & Leary, 2005; McAdams, 1989). Of course, this motive is different for everyone—you might describe

yourself as a "people person," while someone else might consider herself a "loner"—but the general tendency is toward achieving a balance.

This desire for balance was demonstrated in a study in which researchers asked college students to carry pagers for four days (O'Connor & Rosenblood, 1996). When the pagers went off, as triggered by the researchers, students recorded whether they were alone or with others at that moment, as well as whether they *wanted* to be alone or with others at that time. The response a student gave usually predicted the situation he or she would be in the next time the pager went off (for example, a student who said she wanted to be alone when paged at 1 p.m. would then be found alone when paged at 2 p.m.). This study demonstrates how people choose their own needs to be with others or to seek solitude.

The affiliation motive describes our desire to have rewarding interpersonal relationships. What, though, leads to a rewarding relationship, and how do we define what it means to be rewarding? The specifics are different for everyone, but at the basic level, there are certain characteristics that define attraction and close relationships.

What Leads to Attraction?

"All the girls get prettier at closing time, oh, they all begin to look like movie stars ... If I could rate them on a scale from one to 10, I'm looking for a nine but eight could work right in. Few more drinks and I might slip to five or even four" (Baker-Knight, 1975).

Attraction is a funny thing, isn't it? As tongue-in-cheek as the song "Don't All the Girls Get Prettier at Closing Time" might be, it voices an astute observation of the game of finding love. You might even be surprised to learn that this song's thesis was actually used as a hypothesis for a study on attraction conducted by James Pennebaker and his colleagues (1979). Those "beer goggles" that people joke about have some truth to them—both men and women are perceived as more attractive by members of the opposite sex (the study didn't consider potential same-sex pairings) as a night out at a bar progresses. It might not have anything to do with the beer, either. It could be that, as the clock ticks away, people who want to meet a potential partner readjust the way they see the "options" around them.

What is it, though, that creates a sense of attraction, anyway? Of course, we're not just talking about attraction to potential romantic partners, but potential friends as well. In many ways, attraction boils down to just being around someone.

∧ ∧ ∧ As the night goes on and the prospect of going home alone looms, **do people become more attractive to one another?**

PROXIMITY, MERE EXPOSURE, AND INTERACTION

It's the first day of freshman orientation. Brian has found himself in the dining hall, surrounded by a sea of unfamiliar faces. He gets his lunch and sits down at his assigned table with the rest of his orientation group, feeling so overwhelmed, he barely even glances at the student next to him. The next day, he finds himself sitting next to the same person again, and they introduce themselves. Brian and Keith chat a little about how orientation is going and about what classes they are going to be taking. A few days later, in his first day of English Composition, Brian notices that Keith is in the same class. They decide to sit next to one another—after all, it's nice to see a familiar face, isn't it? By the end of the school year, Brian and Keith are close friends and decide to become roommates for the next school year.

Obviously, attraction has to start with contact. You can't get to know someone and decide if you are a good match for friendship or a romantic relationship without first meeting. This is why attraction starts with your physical surroundings. The people with whom you come into contact are determined by where you work, what classes you take, what dorm you live in, and so on. The repeated contact that results from these arrangements is based on **proximity**, the physical closeness between two individuals (Festinger, Schachter, & Back, 1950). The smaller the physical distance, the more likely the two people will experience repeat contact, and the development of mutual attraction. Numerous studies have shown that proximity is one of the best predictors of friendship (e.g., Festinger, Schachter, & Back, 1950; McPherson, Smith-Lovin, & Cook, 2001; Back, Schmukle, & Egloff, 2008).

In Brian and Keith's example, you can see why proximity is so important. Related to this is the concept of *functional distance*, which describes how often individuals come into contact with one another. Functional distance contributes to relationship development (Newcomb, 1961). People who live or work close to one another are more likely to become acquainted and form friendships. People are also generally more likely to form relationships with—or at least favor—individuals they anticipate meeting, due to an effect called "anticipation of interaction." Studies have found that when female college students were given information about two women and were told they were going to interact with one of them, they consistently preferred the woman they were told they were going to meet (Darley & Berscheid, 1967; Miller & Marks, 1982).

Of course, stereotypes may play a role in how positive this anticipation effect is. For example,

Gurwitz and Markus (1978) found that when female participants were told they were going to interact with a homosexual or heterosexual man, the typical effect of anticipation on liking was found. However, when male participants were told the same thing, they rated the homosexual male target as less favorable than male participants who did not anticipate meeting him.

The effect created by proximity is called **mere exposure**, which hypothesizes that the mere repeated exposure of an individual to a stimulus is enough for an increase in favorable response to that stimulus (Zajonc, 1968). In other words, the more you see a person, the more likely you are to like that person. This might not work, though, when an initial response is negative—in fact, repeated exposure in that case can lead to even stronger dislike!

The effect of mere exposure was demonstrated in a study conducted in a college course (Moreland & Beach, 1992). One assistant attended class 15 times over the course of a semester, a second attended 10 times, a third attended five times, and a fourth did not attend a single class. None

Attraction starts with proximity and mere exposure—the simple fact that two students are in the same class makes it more likely that they will become friends.

of the assistants actually interacted with the students. At the end of the semester, when the students were shown photos of the four assistants and asked how much they liked each one, it was found that the number of times an assistant had been present in class was directly related to how much she was liked.

The mere exposure effect even works with photographs. In one study (Moreland & Zajonc, 1982), subjects viewed photographs of faces and rated them for likeability and similarity. The faces that they saw more often were rated as more likeable and more similar to themselves. Another study (Mita, Derma, & Knight, 1977) illustrating the mere exposure effect assumed that we are more often exposed to our mirror images, and that our friends and lovers are more frequently exposed to our true images. The researchers found that subjects reliably preferred their mirror images over their true images, and the opposite held true for friends and lovers viewing images of the person. More recently, Back, Schmukle, and Egloff (2008) found that when students were randomly assigned seats for a semester, the students sitting together felt friendlier toward one another in comparison to other students sitting farther away from one another.

Of course, the reason that proximity and mere exposure are so important to attraction is that they lead to interaction. It is only through interaction that people learn enough information about each other to find out if they are a good match. Sometimes, though, interaction comes without proximity. Interactions through social networking sites like Facebook don't benefit from geographic proximity, but they can still have positive effects (McKenna, Green, & Gleason, 2002). During a study in which people met online prior to meeting in person, they tended to report more favorable impressions of one another in comparison with pairs who first met in person. New proximity-based smartphone applications take advantage of this by allowing people to digitally start a date with individuals who are in close geographic proximity. Proximity, mere exposure, and interaction make up just one piece of the puzzle, though. Another factor that plays a major role in pulling people together is the perception of physical attractiveness.

THE IMPACT OF PHYSICAL ATTRACTIVENESS

You're waiting at a bus stop when an individual approaches you with a clipboard, asking if you'd like to sign a petition against a Wal-Mart being built in the community. This person flashes you a smile with amazing white teeth. You notice the person has really nice eyes, and a great body. Does this matter? Could the fact that this person is highly attractive have anything at all to do with whether or not you add your name to the petition?

You might like to think the answer is "No," that you'll choose whether or not to sign the petition based on how you feel about the issue.

As much as we might not want to admit it, a person's level of attractiveness does impact interactions with others. Research using this petition scenario found that the more attractive the experimenter was, the more signatures he was able to get (Chaiken, 1979). The findings suggest that attractive individuals wield more persuasive power than their unattractive counterparts. Additional research has revealed advantages such as the tendency for physically attractive men and women to earn more money than their peers (Hamermesh & Biddle, 1994). In fact, Hamermesh and Biddle (1994) discovered a salary "plainness penalty" of about 5 to 10 percent.

After studying the difference in earnings between attractive people and their less attractive counterparts, one of the researchers who conducted that study wanted to find out if attractiveness contributes to the perception of skills and productivity that people believe lead to differences in pay. In 2005, Hamermesh & Parker studied students' ratings of their professors based on six independent measures of beauty, and they found that those who were considered better-looking received higher ratings for their instructional skills. The impact was larger for male instructors than for female instructors, and the difference between those who were considered the least attractive (in the bottom 10th percentile of attractiveness) and those who were considered the most attractive (those in the 90th percentile) was substantial.

Wait a minute, though. What about all of those sayings like "beauty is in the eye of the beholder"? If physical attractiveness is a subjective measure, how can it be studied in this way? It could be that physical attractiveness is actually an objective characteristic that can be measured and studied. People tend to assume that what is considered attractive differs greatly between cultures, but it turns out that's not necessarily true.

Studies that have examined the question of physical attractiveness as an objective characteristic have found that the concept of attraction really doesn't differ across cultures. In one study, Asian and Hispanic students who had recently arrived in the United States, along with white Americans, rated the attractiveness of Asian, Hispanic, black, and white women in photographs (Cunningham, Roberts, Wu, Barbee, & Druen, 1995). There was a high level of correlation between their ratings. The same thing happened when white and black American men rated the attractiveness of black women in photographs. A similar study comparing what Korean and U.S. students find attractive showed a high degree of similarity in their standards of attractiveness (McArthur & Berry, 1987).

Yet another study showed that even as children, people of different cultural backgrounds found the same features, such as big eyes and prominent cheekbones, attractive in photographs of people of different races, genders, and ages (Langlois, Ritter, Roggman, & Vaughn, 1991). This indicates a generalized definition of what is considered attractive. It also demonstrates that preferences for attractiveness are not, as previously thought, gradually learned through socialization but may be somehow "hardwired." For example, the researchers pointed out that previous work has shown that infants look longer at and seem to prefer attractive female faces.

Interestingly, social psychologists have found that people show a preference for faces in which the features aren't very different from the average. Langlois and Roggman (1990) presented college students with actual yearbook photos and computerized photos that "averaged" the features from four to 32 of those photos consistently preferred the faces that had been created. In fact, the more faces that had been averaged, the more the students liked them. The researchers speculated that this preference may be due to the perceived familiarity of those computerized faces—because they incorporate so many faces, they are less distinctive and therefore seem more familiar.

This effect of preference for "averaged" images has been found to extend to nonhuman species and even inanimate objects (Halberstadt & Rhodes, 2003). Although much of the research uses self-reporting of perceptions of attractiveness, other research has used physiological measures (Winkielman, Halberstadt, Fazendeiro, & Catty, 2006) such as facial EMGs

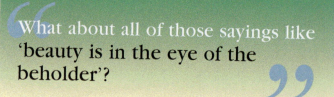

"What about all of those sayings like 'beauty is in the eye of the beholder'?"

"What Is Beautiful Is Good"

In a study on the "what is beautiful is good" stereotype, researchers found that a physical attractiveness stereotype exists in which it is assumed that attractive people have better personalities and lives (Dion, Berscheid, & Walster, 1972). The researchers also concluded that physical attractiveness can have a profound impact on social interactions and influence. They point out that the advantage physically attractive people have in dating may be even greater than previously assumed because of the belief that beautiful people attract wealth and happiness.

They do concede that they don't know how the stereotype determines patterns of social interaction, but that it would be strange if people didn't behave in line with the stereotype, and that social interaction shaped by the stereotype has been reported anecdotally. As an example of this, they point to previous research showing that even social workers used to dealing with many kinds of people often find it difficult to think of a pretty girl as having committed a crime. Beautiful women, it seems, are not often convicted (Dion, Berscheid, & Walster, 1972). Do you agree with these conclusions, or do you believe something else could explain the way the "what is beautiful is good" stereotype is at play?

Think about the influence of attraction on your interactions with others. Has an individual's level of attractiveness influenced whether or not you pursued a relationship with that person? To show the impact that level of attractiveness has on our perceptions of others, replicate research testing the "what is beautiful is good" stereotype. Consider showing people two different images of a male or female target person (make sure that the target individuals share the same basic demographics). Ask 10 other people to rate the level of attractiveness of each of the target individuals. Then ask a series of other questions to determine if attractiveness impacts the impression that was formed. For example, you may want to ask how much money people think the target individuals make on a scale of 1 to 7, with 1 being a very low amount and 7 being a very high amount, or how intelligent people think the target individual might be on the same scale.

You may want to revisit Chapter 2 on research methods to help you successfully plan this research. Develop a hypothesis. When you have completed your research, consider alternative explanations for your findings. Did your demonstration go as planned or were there issues that may have impacted your results? Share your results with your classmates and discuss how the "what is beautiful is good" stereotype may have influenced your perceptions of others.

What will you learn from this action project?

1. Develop a hypothesis concerning how level of attractiveness affects interactions.
2. Prepare a social psychological study to test a question.
3. Analyze the results of a social psychological study.

Examples of the photos you might use for your target individuals. Be sure your selected individuals match across all traits other than their levels of attractiveness.

that are not as susceptible to biased responses. Facial studies on averaging also show a preference for facial images that are symmetrical, in which the left and right side are mirror images of one another (see Rhodes, 2006 for a review). Yet another study further demonstrated our preference for symmetry; participants were more attracted to dancers whose features were physically symmetrical (Brown et al., 2005).

Why Is Attraction Important?

It's pretty clear from the research we've discussed that being attractive is a desirable trait and can impact interpersonal relationships. Physical appearance is the most visible trait in social interactions, and for better or worse, it has a high degree of impact on those interactions. A 1972 experiment sought to find whether or not people assume that physically attractive people also possess desirable personality traits and expect them to lead better lives (for example, to be better husbands or wives) (Dion, Berscheid, & Walster, 1972). The researchers noted that folk psychology has long contained theories that a given person's outward appearance is enough to forecast personality. The results of the experiment uncovered the existence of a "what is beautiful is good" stereotype in which it is assumed that physically attractive people are somehow "better" in other aspects of life, and that their lives are happier. Others (Eagly, Ashmore, Makhijani, & Longo, 1991; Hatfield & Sprecher, 1986; Cash, Gillen, & Burns, 1977; Watkins & Johnson, 2000) have shown that attractive people are perceived as being more successful, happier, more sociable, and better job applicants than unattractive individuals. These studies also serve as further evidence of a somewhat universal standard of attractiveness. If standards varied widely, then this stereotype would not hold much weight in our daily interactions as well as in our friendships and in interpersonal attraction.

> *Physical appearance is the most visible trait in social interactions, and for better or worse, it has a high degree of impact on those interactions.*

SIMILARITY

Opposites attract. It's a fact of life, right? Repeated over and over in popular culture (just how many romantic comedies start out with the couple absolutely hating one another?), it's become one of those hard and fast truths about dating—you just have to be different for it to work. Studies of relationships, however, have largely contradicted the popular belief.

Overall, we tend to like people who are similar to us in terms of demographics, attitudes, or experiences. This can be explained with the **matching hypothesis**, which was proposed by sociologist Erving

Goffman (1952). Goffman hypothesized that people are more likely to form long-standing relationships with others whose social attributes match theirs. This is true of romantic relationships as well as friendships (Cash & Derlega, 1978). Research has shown that pairs based on complementary interests and behaviors have better, longer lasting relationships (e.g., Aube & Koestner, 1995). Others have shown that partners with similar levels of physical attractiveness express more liking for each other (e.g., Walster, Walster, Berscheid, & Dion, 1971). Of course, couples don't *always* match in levels of attractiveness. However, research (Buss & Barnes, 1986; Byrne, 1961; Murstein & Christy, 1976; Feingold, 1988) has documented that matching attitudes, senses of humor, and attachment styles (Klohnen & Luo, 2003) can result in initial attraction. For instance, Donald Trump's looks may not rival those of his former spouses, but personal tastes and common opinions may have drawn them to each other.

In fact, this tendency toward pairing with people with whom we share similar traits can actually be expressed as a proportion! That's right—there is a formula that can predict attraction between two individuals. The **proportion of similarity** divides the number of topics on which two people express similar views by the total number of topics on which they have communicated (Byrne & Nelson, 1965). The proportion that results can then be put into a formula that predicts attraction—the higher the proportion of similarity, the more the pair will like one another.

This idea has a flipside in Rosenbaum's (1986) **repulsion hypothesis**, which states that similarity doesn't actually have any effect on attraction. Instead, Rosenbaum suggests that people are repulsed by dissimilarity. His hypothesis was later shown to be wrong (Smeaton, Byrne, & Murnen, 1989), but there's still value to the research—dissimilarity does in fact have a slightly stronger effect on attraction than does similarity (e.g., Tan & Singh, 1995).

RECIPROCITY

Similarity is just one factor that helps to predict attraction; another is **reciprocity**, which is the exchange of what we receive for what we get, which can include liking those who like us back (Aron, Dutton, Aron, & Iverson, 1989; Kenny, 1994). Many people begin friendships or romantic relationships based on this belief—we are attracted to those who like us. The belief that someone likes you can lead you to reveal more about yourself to the person over time (Collins & Miller, 1994). This helps to build trust in a relationship, which in turn strengthens it. We like people who share personal information with us. In one study (Vittengl & Holt, 2000), college students had short conversations with strangers. Those who revealed more about themselves reported being in a better mood after the conversation than those who did not reveal as much—they also reported liking their conversation partners more than those who were more closed off.

How Do Early Parent-Child Interactions Impact Future Relationships?

The first personal contact most people make is with a parent. From the moment we take our first breaths, we are ready to interact with other people. It's well known that infants are highly sensitive to facial expressions as well as sounds and movements made by people. Think about the times you have seen a baby interact with an adult—the adult probably engaged in baby talk and shot big grins and other exaggerated facial expressions at the baby. As he did, the baby might have cooed or giggled. The baby is being entertained, but there is deeper work going on here. As a parent interacts with an infant, he lays the groundwork for how the infant will experience interpersonal relationships over her lifetime.

Our brains are wired to encourage this interaction. When faced with nonthreatening signals from a stranger, the hormone oxytocin, which facilitates social recognition, is released. This leads to a feeling of trustworthiness (Zak, Kurzban, & Matzner, 2005). This is important in facilitating relationships as we come into contact with new people, and the same principle is at work between parents and children.

Oxytocin has been linked to a clearly defined set of maternal bonding behaviors such as affectionate touch and vocalizations, as well as frequent checking of the infant, leading some researchers to consider it a "bonding hormone" (Feldman, Weller, Zagoory-Sharon, & Levine, 2007). Though many people assume the strongest bond between a parent and child is that involving the mother, a similar biological encouragement for cuddling has been found in fathers. In fact, it seems that men are as "hardwired" to bond with their children as women are (Gordon, Zagoory-Sharon, Leckman, & Feldman, 2010).

Psychology professor Ruth Feldman found that oxytocin levels increase in fathers as well as in mothers after childbirth. The hormone is linked to feeling calm and connected, which encourages the behaviors

that will educate the infant about positive social interactions. Dr. Feldman found that fathers' oxytocin levels were comparable to those found in mothers, and that the levels rose the more the men cuddled their babies. The more they cuddled, the more oxytocin was released, and the better they felt. Of course, it's all for a reason. The loop has to start with positive interaction with the baby (Shellenbarger, 2009).

Developmentally, these first human interactions are critical to our attitudes about ourselves, others, and trust. Long before a child acquires any language skills, he has already started developing a style of interacting with others. This is called an **attachment style** (Ainsworth et al., 1978; Bowlby, 1969, 1973), or the degree of security experienced in interpersonal relationships.

ATTACHMENT STYLES

You might be surprised to learn that much of what we know about attachment begins with taking baby rhesus monkeys away from their mothers. Psychologist Harry Harlow (1958) gave baby monkeys a choice of surrogate "mothers" after the separation—one made of terrycloth and another made of wire. He found that the monkeys clung to their cloth mother for security and comfort, and chose the wire mother only when it provided food. He also found that the monkeys, after being separated from their cloth mothers for a few days and then reunited, clung to the surrogates in lieu of exploring their surroundings. Through these studies, he illustrated the importance of physical connection and that feeding was not, as previously thought, the most important factor in bonding.

Mary Ainsworth and her colleagues (1978) and John Bowlby (1969, 1973) were among the first to bring attachment studies to human subjects. Ainsworth introduced a method in the same vein as Harlow's monkey studies with the Strange Situation paradigm, in which a mother and baby would be introduced to an unfamiliar woman. The baby would briefly be left with the woman, and then would be left alone. It was found that the children were less confident in exploring and playing when their mothers were not present. Ainsworth and Bowlby conducted such important work that it didn't just add to the scientific literature, it also influenced public policy involving children. (For a review of their work and its impact, see Bretherton, 1992.)

Bowlby's research led to the assumption that infants develop two basic attitudes during early interactions with adults. Self-esteem is developed through the emotional reactions of the infant's caregiver. A caregiver who smiles at and cuddles the infant helps to build a sense that the infant is valued and loved, while a caregiver who behaves coldly toward the infant is laying the groundwork for the child to feel unloved and unvalued.

<<< **Our very first interactions** have profound impacts on our later interpersonal relationships.

The second attitude that starts to develop at this time is **interpersonal trust**. Before her first words, the infant develops a perception that the caregiver is trustworthy and reliable (or the opposite). Interpersonal trust, which involves the belief that people are generally trustworthy and dependable as opposed to the opposite, is the attitude that underlies the development of attachment styles. Studies have drawn parallels between attachment styles and adult relationships—as young lovers, people long for physical affection and feel distress when separated, just as babies do in relation to their mothers (Shaver & Hazan, 1993; Fraley, 2002)

> "Self-esteem is developed **through the emotional reactions of the infant's caregiver.**"

Basically, attachment styles can be boiled down to a formula describing the levels of self-esteem and interpersonal trust. A person can be high in both, low in both, or high in one and low in the other. These attachment styles, developed so early in life, have a great impact on our adult lives. Bowlby (1988) argued that there is a link between the type of attachment style an infant has and the type of relationships that he will have later in life, and others have echoed this argument (Feeney & Noller, 1990; Hazan & Shaver, 1987). Rainer Banse (2004) showed that marital status and success may be predicted from knowing both partners' attachment styles. This is the case for both opposite-sex and same-sex relationships (Ridge & Feeney, 1998; Robinson, 1999). There is some disagreement when it comes to the number of styles, but following the above formula gives us four basic attachment styles.

Secure Attachment Style

If a person is high in both self-esteem and interpersonal trust, she has a **secure attachment style**. Seven in 10 infants, and about as many adults, exhibit this type of attachment style (Baldwin et al., 1996; Jones & Cunningham; 1996; Mickelson, Kessler, & Shaver, 1997). This is the most successful of the attachment styles. People with this style tend to form lasting and satisfying relationships over the courses of their lives.

Fearful-Avoidant Attachment Style

At the other end of the spectrum, someone who is low in both self-esteem and interpersonal trust is described as having a **fearful-avoidant attachment style**. People with this style are usually unable to form close relationships, or their relationships are not fulfilling. Several studies have demonstrated that people with this attachment style tend to focus on how they are similar to or different from their friends, which strongly impacts the natures of the relationships (Gabriel et al., 2005).

Preoccupied Attachment Style

People who are low in self-esteem but high in interpersonal trust exhibit the **preoccupied attachment style**. This style is also referred to as "anxious-ambivalent." They find it easy to form relationships, as they crave closeness and the approval of others. The preoccupied attachment style can be seen as a bit self-destructive, as for all of their craving for closeness, people with this style expect to be rejected because they believe they are not worthy of attention or love. Anxious lovers tend to report more emotional ups and downs with their relationships than those with secure or avoidant styles (Davis, Shaver, & Vernon, 2004). It's also been demonstrated that individuals with this style perceive their partners as less supportive (Campbell, Simpson, Boldry, & Kashy, 2005; Collins & Feeney, 2004).

Dismissive Attachment Style

A combination of high self-esteem and low interpersonal trust results in the **dismissive attachment style**. The high self-esteem leads people to believe they are worthy of good relationships, but the low level of interpersonal trust means they expect the worst of others and therefore are fearful of getting close to people.

Can Attachment Styles Change?

Once an attachment style has been established, that doesn't necessarily mean it is set in stone. Many social psychologists do believe it remains constant (e.g., Klohnen & Bera, 1998). However, there is certainly evidence that our relationship experiences, both good and bad, can lead to a change in attachment style (e.g., Brennan & Bosson, 1998; Baldwin & Fehr, 1995; Keelan, Dion, & Dion, 1994; Scharfe & Bartholomew, 1994). People who have relationship experiences that leave them feeling vulnerable (e.g., a traumatic breakup), for example, have been found to change attachment styles (Davila & Cobb, 2003). Of course, this can go both ways; a particularly positive relationship experience can lead to an increase in secure attachment style (Ruvolo, Fabin, & Ruvolo, 2001).

Though our attachment styles took form when we were infants, they continue to shape the way we interact with our friends and romantic partners for the rest of our lives. They play a role in how we approach and define romantic love—but of course, attachment style is not the only factor in those approaches and definitions.

What Factors Influence and Define Romantic Love?

Paul and Maria have been hanging out with the same group of friends since they all started school together last year. They've always liked one another, but lately things have just been *different*. When they're out with their friends, they find themselves sitting right next to each other

Secure Attachment Style:
High in self-esteem
High in interpersonal trust
Most successful style
Forms long-lasting and satisfying relationships

Fearful-Avoidant Attachment Style:
Low in self-esteem
Low in interpersonal trust
Unable to form close relationships
Relationships are not fulfilling

Preoccupied Attachment Style:
Low in self-esteem
High in interpersonal trust
Self-destructive
Craves closeness
Expects to be rejected

Dismissive Attachment Style:
High in self-esteem
Low in interpersonal trust
Expects the worst out of other people
Fearful of getting too close

Sources: Ainsworth, M. D. S., Blehar, M. C., Waters, E., & Wall, S. (1978). Patterns of attachment: A psychological study of the strange situation. Hillsdale, NJ: Lawrence Erlbaum.
Bowlby, J. (1969). Attachment and loss: Vol. I: Attachment. New York: Basic Books.
Bowlby, J. (1973). Attachment and loss: Vol. II: Separation: Anxiety and anger. New York: Basic Books.
Bowlby, J. (1988). A secure base: Parent-child attachment and healthy human development. New York: Basic Books.

Attachment Styles. The relationship between self-esteem and interpersonal trust **defines your attachment style.**

more and more often. To top it off, Maria will sometimes catch Paul looking at her and then turning away, and she could swear she sees him blushing!

Obviously, these two are attracted to one another, but what factors will turn this attraction into a romantic relationship? For the most part, romantic love can be influenced by the same factors that affect other relationships. Paul and Maria are affected by proximity and mere exposure since they're in the same group of friends, and they enjoy the same activities—there you see similarity and the matching hypothesis at play.

THE ROLE OF GENDER

As Paul and Maria move toward a romantic relationship, they are probably seeking different things from the relationship. Much of this has to do with their individual personalities, of course, but some can also be attributed to their genders. For men and women in heterosexual relationships, different aspects of potential mates carry more weight than others. Evolutionary psychologists suggest that whether or not we are interested in becoming parents, our genetic histories and our ancestors' drives to pass on their genes play a major role in our selections of romantic partners. Our preferred mate choices, these psychologists argue, are based on reproductive potential, which is manifested in different ways in males and females (e.g., Geary, Vigil, & Byrd-Craven, 2004). For example, it's suggested that men have developed a more powerful desire for a variety of sex partners, with the explanation that more partners means more opportunities to successfully reproduce (Buss, 2002).

There may be a reason for the emphasis men seem to place on physical attractiveness in potential female partners, according to evolutionary determinants. Beauty may be associated with fertility, and early men may have had more reproductive success with female mates selected according to physical attractiveness, which is indicative of youth and good health—both considered important in the process of reproduction and childbirth. There may also be evolutionary reasons for men's preferences for "beautiful" long hair and symmetrical faces (Jacobi & Cash, 1994; Hughes, Harrison, & Gallup, 2002). While a man may not be looking to start a family with every woman he dates, he still may be predisposed to seek out women who are considered beautiful (Buss, 2002).

Women, of course, are also drawn to potential mates that are physically attractive, as discussed earlier in this chapter. Evolutionary psychologists suggest that women don't care as much about physical attractiveness in men because men's reproductive years aren't as limited as women's are; therefore, youth is not as much of a factor in mate selection. Instead, they argue that women are more highly attracted to men who have access to resources, because those resources translate to an ability to protect and care for a family (Buss, 2002; Kenrick, Neuberg, Zierk, & Krones, 1994).

Now, before you throw this book across the room, grumbling that you can't just make broad generalizations about what men and women are looking for in their romantic partners, you should know that not everyone agrees with this perspective. Research indicates that *both* women and men prefer wealthy and healthy mates (Miller, Putcha-Bhagavatula, & Pederson, 2002). Cultural influences may now be more powerful than

evolutionary ones, and the argument that reproductive potential is the key to romance is not universally accepted.

Additionally, gender differences are not as great when individuals are asked about long-term relationship goals (Kenrick, Sadalla, Groth, & Trost, 1990). Both genders are more selective when it comes to picking a long-term mate (Stewart, Stinnett, & Rosenfeld, 2000). Another criticism of the evolutionary perspective is its lack of explanation for male homosexuality. However, new research (Vasey & Vanderlann, 2010) does argue that male same-sex attraction can be explained by the kin selection hypothesis. According to this hypothesis, homosexual men may perpetuate family genes by acting as "helpers in the nest," helping with the care of nieces and nephews.

PASSIONATE LOVE

As Paul and Maria fall in love with one another, their relationship is new and exciting. They find that their feelings are intense, at some times even overwhelming. They spend all of their free time together and one's heart seems to skip a beat when the other approaches. Paul and Maria are in the throes

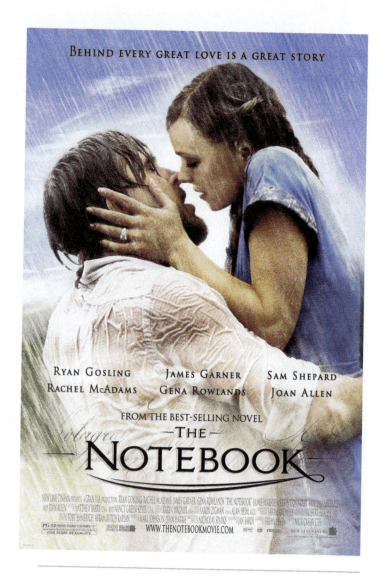

^^ Once mutual attraction has been established, how does it turn into a romantic relationship?

^^^ When two people are in the throes of passionate love, **they feel as if they cannot live without each other.**

Passionate Love:

Characterized by intense longing for one's partner

Thrilling

Roller-coaster of emotions

First experienced in adolescence

Can be triggered by scary or intense experiences

Often present at the beginning of a romantic relationship

Companionate Love:

Calm and stable

Characterized by shared values and life experiences

Marked by a deep sense of trust

Most often present in couples that have been together for a long time

∧
∧ **Passionate and Companionate Love.** Over time, the thrill of new love usually fades,
∧ and a calmer kind of love takes its place.

of **passionate love**, defined by Elaine Hatfield (1988) as a state of intense longing for union with another. Hatfield and her colleague Susan Sprecher actually developed a Passionate Love Scale, rating feelings for another person on a range from "extremely passionate" to "extremely cool," for use in family therapy with adolescents, who aren't quite sure how to deal with the intensity of passionate love, experiencing these feelings for the first time. They contended that the first appearances of passionate love coincide with puberty (Hatfield & Sprecher, 1986; Hatfield, 1988).

Hatfield theorizes passionate love, identified by such behaviors as a couple gazing into one another's eyes and feeling like they're on an emotional "roller coaster," as the steering of a state of arousal into an emotional state. She maintains that heightened arousal is the same no matter what emotion is involved. Think about it. If your heart is pounding and your body is trembling, you might be experiencing fear, anger, or joy, but the physical response is the same. By this theory, any source of arousal should intensify feelings of passion—as long as a possible target of that passion is present. Could a fearful situation, then, lead to feelings of love?

Can Fear Lead to Passionate Love?

It's a classic action movie scene. A beautiful woman is in danger. Maybe she's been kidnapped, or has been locked in a cage with a hungry tiger, or is being dangled off the edge of a skyscraper by a crazed villain. Whatever the circumstances may be, the hero swoops in and saves the day. Then what happens? They fall madly in love, of course!

It's easy to roll our eyes at these romantic pairings between heroes and their damsels in distress, but they could actually reflect a basic truth about passionate love. There's some pretty substantial evidence showing that sexual attraction occurs with increased frequency when people are in strong emotional states. The **excitation transfer** process suggests that arousal from one stimulus, a scary movie or a roller coaster, can be transferred to the second stimulus, a person (Zillmann, 1971). The evidence includes studies such as one conducted by Dutton and Aron (1974) in which male passersby were contacted by an attractive female interviewer either on a fear-arousing suspension bridge or a non-fear-arousing bridge. The men were asked to fill out questionnaires using Thematic Apperception Test pictures, which are assumed to tap into a subject's unconscious to uncover repressed feelings. The sexual content of stories written by subjects was significantly greater for men who had been contacted on the fear-arousing bridge. Participants who were approached on that bridge misattributed their arousal (marked by racing heart rate and heavier breathing) to the woman interviewing them, rather than to the bridge. These men were more likely to call the woman after the experience than those who met her on the non-fear-arousing bridge. The differences were not present for subjects who were contacted by a male interviewer.

> **"** It's easy to roll our eyes at these romantic pairings between heroes and their damsels in distress, **but they could actually reflect a basic truth about passionate love. "**

It's hard to believe, but those action movies could actually contain a few realistic elements!

COMPANIONATE LOVE

Maybe their relationship progresses to the point that Paul and Maria get married. After years together, their state of passionate love shifts into a different kind of love. While passionate love is intense and exciting, **companionate love** is more stable and calm. It's the affection we feel for people with whom our lives are deeply intertwined. Companionate love is characterized by shared attitudes, values, and life experiences, as well as deep feelings of trust in the other person.

Passionate love is thrilling, but eventually all thrills must come to an end. That doesn't mean the relationship ends or the love stops, though. It just changes into the more sustainable and comfortable companionate love.

Sometimes, though, this cooling of passionate love goes through a transitional period. As the excitement and novelty fade, people can become disillusioned, particularly if they believe romance is essential for the continuation of a marriage. Some social psychologists believe rising divorce rates can be attributed in part to the rising importance of intense positive emotional experiences, like the "high" of passionate love. It's hard

to keep that kind of emotional state up, but that doesn't stop some people from clinging to the dream (Simpson, Campbell, & Berscheid, 1986).

More recent research suggests that being in a long-term relationship doesn't necessarily mean one has to give up on passionate love and make a complete shift to companionate love. Romantic love can exist in long-term marriages and is in fact a sign of well-being and high self-esteem in long-married couples (Acevedo & Aron, 2009).

THE TRIANGULAR THEORY OF LOVE

As the relationship between Paul and Maria develops and changes, we call it love, but what does that mean? What components add up to create *love*? Robert Sternberg (1986, 1997) found a way to explain it through his **triangular theory of love**. He suggests that there are three components that make up love: *intimacy* (feelings of closeness and connectedness), *passion* (physical attraction and sexual consummation), and *commitment* (both in the decision that one loves another and to maintain the love). The amount of love felt by an individual depends on the strength of these components, and the kind of love depends on the strength of each component in relation to the others.

We've discussed passionate and companionate love, but Sternberg's triangular model actually results in *eight* different types of love, as people can experience love as all three components, two of the components, just one of them, or even none of them (Sternberg, 1986). Where might companionate love and passionate love (which Sternberg describes as romantic love) fall on the model? Think about what characterizes those types of love, and which of the three components would be strongest.

ROMANTIC LOVE ACROSS CULTURES

If Paul and Maria had grown up in a country such as China or India, would they place as much importance on the connections they are forming with each other now? Would they even see each other as potential partners, or envision marrying one another?

Definitions of romantic love vary across cultures. One study that explored differences in romantic love along the lines of individualist and collectivist cultures found that viewpoints can be quite different (Dion & Dion, 1993, 1996). Romantic love seems to be a more important basis for marriage in individualist cultures than it is in collectivist cultures. Likewise, individualist cultures place more value on psychological intimacy between romantic partners. The research also discussed the impact of individualism on romantic love, particularly the aspects of individualism that make developing psychological intimacy problematic.

Other research has determined that there are some similarities in the way different cultures conceptualize love. For example, Hong Kong Chinese and British respondents in one study both showed at least a moderate belief in the role of predestiny and fate in relationship development (Goodwin & Findlay, 1997). The Chinese respondents, however, scored significantly higher on endorsement of those beliefs than their British counterparts did.

Not all romantic relationships are based on initial passionate love. For example, studies on arranged marriages in India (Gupta & Singh, 1982; Myers, Madathil, & Tingil, 2005) find that even though these unions are not by choice, there is no difference in the long-term satisfaction within the relationships in comparison to marriages of choice.

IS MARRIAGE THE END GOAL OF ROMANTIC LOVE?

In imagining Paul and Maria moving through the stages of a relationship, we've assumed that they get married, but not all romantic

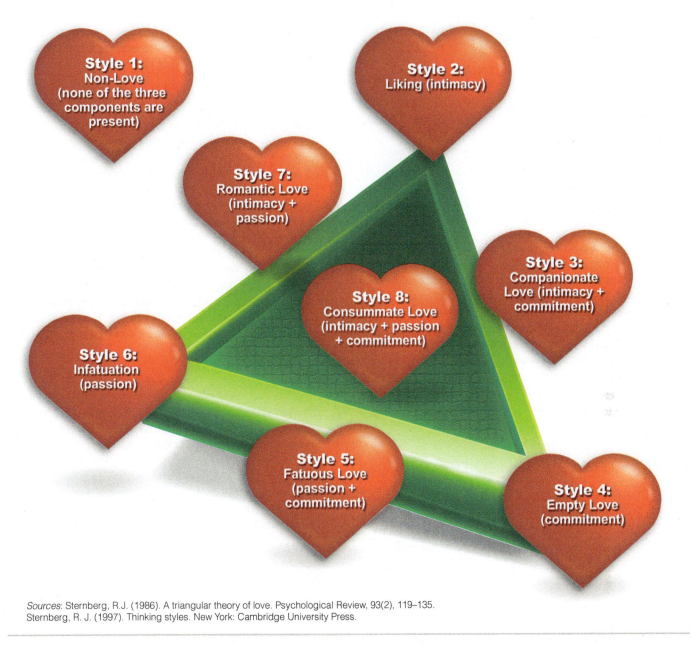

Sources: Sternberg, R.J. (1986). A triangular theory of love. Psychological Review, 93(2), 119–135. Sternberg, R. J. (1997). Thinking styles. New York: Cambridge University Press.

Sternberg's Triangular Theory of Love. Through different arrangements of three basic components of love (intimacy, commitment, and passion), **eight distinct types of love can be experienced.**

relationships end in marriage. Some people see marriage as the "goal" of a romantic relationship, but should it be? Research to determine whether marriage has a positive effect is complicated. Some research shows that marriage benefits individuals' economic well-being, the well-being of their children, and their overall health (e.g., Lerman, 2002; Schoenborn, 2004). Other studies show that it's not marriage alone that predicts better health and well-being—that people must be *satisfied* with their marriages to reap these benefits. These studies suggest that single individuals generally have better health than their unhappily married counterparts (e.g., Holt-Lunstad, Birmingham, & Jones, 2008).

There are also cultural considerations in the question of marital satisfaction. In the United States, many people cannot imagine being paired off for an arranged marriage, but some research shows that people in arranged

marriages actually experience more satisfaction than those who chose their partners (Xiaohe & Whyte, 1990). However, other research shows that there isn't any difference in satisfaction between people in arranged marriages versus those who married for love (Myers, Madathil, & Tingle, 2005).

It must be noted, too, that most of the research on marriage and long-term relationships has been on opposite-sex couples. Part of the reason for this are bans on same-sex marriages. However, we can assume that same-sex couples would also experience the same benefits and challenges of marriage. In fact, a 2010 study for the *American Journal of Public Health* suggests that the ban on gay marriage has had a negative impact on the mental health of gay, lesbian, and bisexual individuals (Mustanski, 2010). The study found an increase in mood disorders, generalized anxiety disorder, and alcohol use disorders among gay, lesbian, and bisexual individuals living in states with gay

SOCIAL EXCHANGE THEORY an economic model of human behavior in which people make decisions based on maximizing benefits and minimizing costs in relationships

EQUITY THEORY theory that relationships are most satisfying when the ratio between benefits and contributions is similar for both partners

INVESTMENT those resources that have been devoted to a relationship that cannot be retrieved

EXCHANGE RELATIONSHIP a relationship in which partners expect strict reciprocity

COMMUNAL RELATIONSHIP a relationship in which partners expect mutual responsiveness to one another's needs

marriage bans. It's argued that, in addition to illustrating the ill effects of keeping people from the benefits of marriage, this study clearly demonstrates the negative effect of institutionalized discrimination. Other recent research looking at same-sex couples who are in civil unions or long-term relationships adds support to the idea that same-sex couples experience the same benefits from long-term relationships as do opposite-sex couples (Balsam, Beauchaine, Rothblum, & Solomon, 2008; Gottman, Levenson, Swanson, Swanson, Tyson, & Yoshimoto, 2003). A longitudinal study by Kurdek (2004) showed that same-sex couples were just as happy as, if not happier than, opposite-sex couples. (See Peplau & Fingerhut, 2007, for a review of research on same-sex couples.)

How Are Relationships Maintained?

So far, we've discussed how friendships and romantic relationships start, but how do people keep them going? There have been several theories proposed to predict how long and how well a relationship is maintained.

SOCIAL EXCHANGE THEORY

The first of these theories is the **social exchange theory** (Thibaut & Kelley, 1952, 1959), an economic theory of behavior that argues that people base behaviors on maximizing benefits and minimizing costs in relationships. Following this theory, relationships that offer more benefits and fewer costs (including the work it takes to maintain the relationship) will naturally last longer and be more fulfilling than those that carry more costs and fewer benefits. The frequency and rate of increase of rewards also matter (Berg & McQuinn, 1986)—couples who experience greater increases in rewards over the course of a relationship tend to stay together longer. The same effect has been found in heterosexual couples as well as homosexual couples (Kurdek, 1991).

Of course, timing is everything. The social exchange theory doesn't usually apply to the early stages of a relationship. People don't tend to worry about costs of relationship in the first throes of passion or during

---

>>> What keeps couples together?

The answer may lie in several theories of relationship maintenance.

the honeymoon (Hays, 1985). In addition to timing, another important consideration is how well rewards actually address each partner's needs—social exchange isn't just about quantity, but quality (Lawrence et al., 2008).

EQUITY THEORY

Have you ever been in a relationship in which you felt you worked much harder than the other person, and that he or she got more out of it without having to lift a finger? Chances are, it didn't last too long. This can be explained through the **equity theory** (Walster, Walster, & Traupmann, 1978), which states that relationships are most satisfying when the ratio between benefits and contributions is similar for both partners. (For a review of this theory, see Sprecher & Schwartz, 1994; Van Yperen & Buunk, 1994.)

This theory isn't without its critics, who argue that the evidence is sometimes contradictory to the theory. However, Van Yperen, and Buunk (1990) argue that there are individual differences in importance of equity. For example, if couples place high importance on exchange, then the perception of equity is important to the satisfaction level of the relationship.

THE INVESTMENT MODEL

Once you've devoted certain things to a relationship—time, self-disclosure, energy—there is no way to get them back. These resources that cannot be retrieved are **investments** (Rusbult, 1983, 1991). The investments you make in a relationship are directly linked to the commitment you feel to that relationship. If you've put a lot into it, it's harder to break it off. Think about someone you've dated for two weeks versus someone you've dated for two years—you're generally more willing to work through problems if you have more invested in a relationship. Research findings tend to support this model across time (Rusbult, 1983).

EXCHANGE AND COMMUNAL RELATIONSHIPS

Yet another way of looking at the maintenance and satisfaction of relationships is through examining the differences between exchange and communal relationships (Clark, 1984). **Exchange relationships** are those in which partners expect strict reciprocity, while **communal relationships** are those in which partners expect mutual responsiveness to one another's needs.

Criticism:

"You never think about how I feel. You just do whatever you want!"

Attacking one's partner or aspects of the relationship

Contempt:

"You're the laziest person I've ever met."

Acting as if one is repulsed by his or her partner

Defensiveness:

"You know how busy I've been. Why didn't you just call the restaurant yourself instead of expecting me to do it?"

Protecting oneself over all else, making excuses

Stonewalling:

"I'm just too busy to talk about this right now."

Emotional withdrawal and refusal to communicate

Source: Gottman, J. (1994). Why marriages succeed or fail...and how you can make yours last. New York: Simon & Schuster.

The Four Horsemen. John Gottman identified four conflict styles that can bring about the end of a relationship.

Exchange relationships are usually limited to strangers and casual acquaintances, or between business partners. Strong communal relationships, on the other hand, exist between close friends, romantic partners, and family members. In these relationships, people seek to take care of one another without expecting anything in return. (For a review of these types of relationships, see Clark & Pataki, 1995.)

What Role Does Conflict Play in Relationships?

"I just don't even want to look at you right now!" she yells and, before you know it, the door has been slammed in your face. What started out as a

perfectly normal evening has now somehow ended in a massive fight, and you're not even sure how you got there.

Fighting with a friend or lover is never fun, but it certainly isn't unusual. Relationships have the potential to improve your mood and overall health, but they aren't without their challenges. All close relationships will involve some conflict—it simply can't be avoided.

While conflict can be part of a healthy relationship, there are certain conflict styles that can be quite destructive. In fact, John Gottman, a leading marriage researcher from the University of Washington, identified four styles, calling them the "Four Horsemen of the Apocalypse" because they can usher in the end of a relationship. They are criticism, contempt, defensiveness, and stonewalling (Gottman, 1994).

NEGATIVE ATTRIBUTIONAL STYLE occurs when a person explains his or her partner's behaviors in negative ways

Criticism is characterized by attacking aspects of one's partner or of the relationship. *Contempt* is marked by one acting as if he is repulsed by his partner. One exhibits *defensiveness* when she will protect the self over all else, often through making excuses, and *stonewalling* involves emotional withdrawal and refusal to communicate. They all sound like they could kill a relationship, don't they? And they can; research has shown that relationships in which these behaviors are shown lead to lower satisfaction over time in women (Huston & Vangelisti, 1991). According to Gottman (1994), there are gender differences in the use of techniques. For instance, men are more likely to use stonewalling. Gottman (1994) also argues that stonewalling and contempt are especially likely to predict divorce.

THE IMPACT OF ATTRIBUTIONS

Sarah is walking out of her morning class when she sees her boyfriend, Will, waiting for her. Without a word, he hands her two tickets to see Muse, one of her favorite bands. She'd had to work when tickets for the show went on sale, and had been disappointed that she was going to miss out on seeing them. Looking at the tickets, and then at Will's smiling face, she thinks, "Best boyfriend ever! He is so sweet!"

In Chapter 5, you learned about Harold Kelley's theory of attributions, that "common sense psychology" we use to explain everyday events. We attribute behaviors to internal or external causes as we try to make sense of what is going on around us. Usually, we make beneficial attributions for things that happen to ourselves and our loved ones. You might make an excuse for your partner's negative behavior, attributing it to an external factor. Positive behavior, like Will buying Sarah those Muse tickets, is attributed to an internal factor—that Will is a thoughtful boyfriend and cares about Sarah.

What if, though, Sarah didn't attribute Will's positive behavior to a positive factor? What if she instead attributed it to something negative? Let's say, upon seeing the tickets, Sarah's first thought was "What did he do this time?"

Here, Sarah is falling into a **negative attributional style**. This occurs when a person explains her partner's behaviors in negative ways. We're all familiar with the classic scenario, often used in comedy, in which a man brings his wife flowers, only to have her assume he's done something wrong—he's cheating on her, or has screwed up at work. These traps lead to lower marital satisfaction, usually because they increase conflict within a relationship.

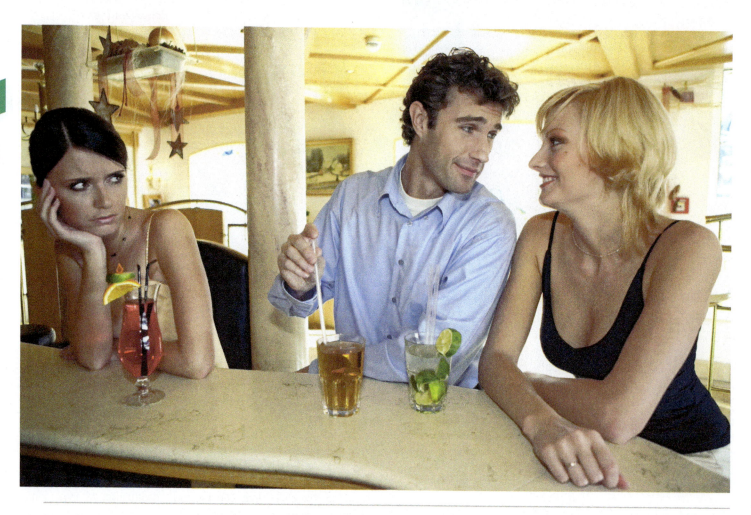

∧
∧ Is seeing your partner talk to an **attractive person** enough to get you feeling jealous? **There**
∧ **could be an evolutionary reason.**

In a study of attribution, researchers asked married couples to rate their trust in their partners and then to discuss a common relationship problem. After the discussion, participants rated their beliefs about their partners during the discussion. Two years later, the participants were shown video of their discussion and were asked once again to rate their beliefs about their partners. People who had made negative attributions in the first part of the study reported less trust in their partners during the two-year follow-up. Likewise, people who reported lower trust in the first part of the study made negative attributions for their partners' behavior in the second part of the study (Miller & Rempel, 2004).

THE GREEN-EYED MONSTER

How do you feel when you see your partner chatting up an attractive person at a party? It's normal to feel a little pang of jealousy over any potential threat to your relationship. Men and women both experience jealousy, but do they experience it in the same ways, and in reaction to the same experiences?

Once again, evolutionary psychologists have a possible answer. Participants in one study were asked to imagine their partners flirting with someone at a party (Dijkstra & Buunk, 1998). Male participants were more jealous when they imagined their partners flirting with someone powerful and successful, while female participants were more likely to report feelings of jealousy when imagining their partners flirting with really physically attractive people.

The potential for jealousy over different behaviors also seems to be divided along gender lines (Buss, Larsen, Westen, & Semmelroth, 1992). When men and women were asked if they would be more upset if their partner had sexual intercourse with or formed a deep emotional attachment to another person, 60 percent of the men said they would be more upset by sexual infidelity. Of the women who were surveyed, 83 percent said they would be more upset by the emotional infidelity.

Evolutionary psychology suggests that men should fear sexual infidelity because it could result in the use of their resources to raise another man's child. A woman, on the other hand, would be more threatened by emotional infidelity because it threatens resources that support her children.

ARE THERE BENEFITS IN THE DISSOLUTION OF A RELATIONSHIP?

Sometimes people just drift apart. Nothing bad happened, it's just that the relationship has run its course. This is common with friendships, but the same is not generally true with romantic relationships or marriages. The dissolution of a marriage can be particularly difficult, as all of the energy a couple has put into building a life together can suddenly seem like a waste of time.

Partners deal with a relationship that is "on the rocks" in either active or passive ways (Rusbult & Zembrodt, 1983). An active response can take the form of making a move to end the relationship or working to improve it. A passive response is, of course, the opposite—a person in a troubled relationship might just wait and hope that it gets better.

Our automatic response tends to be to see breakups as a bad thing. One's trust in others takes a hit, belongings are divided, friends choose sides—it can be hard to see much good coming out of the dissolution of a relationship. Why, then, do so many people say, "It's for the best"?

There's no doubt that the end of a relationship causes feelings of sadness, but there is some positive effect. Think of it this way: Everything you learned about yourself in the formation, duration, and dissolution of a relationship only makes you better prepared for the next one. Evidence of personal growth can be divided into several groupings: person positives, relational positives, and environment positives (Tashiro & Frazier, 2003). Person-positive personal growth is marked by the development of attitudes such as greater confidence in what experiences you can handle. Relational positives involve lessons about yourself in relation to others, such as learning relationship skills or knowing not to let yourself fall so hard so quickly. Finally, environment positives focus on the world around you. You might see a break-up as a way to refocus on the importance of your friends or schoolwork.

<<< "Hey, man, it's all for the best." Is there truth in these commonly used words of comfort?

12 • Review

Summary

WHAT LEADS TO ATTRACTION?   p. 220

● Attraction starts with proximity, which leads to repeat contact between people. This repeated contact, described as mere exposure, increases the likelihood of attraction.

● Physical attraction impacts interaction; we are more likely to react positively to someone who is physically attractive. We are also attracted to people with whom we share similar traits or beliefs.

HOW DO EARLY PARENT-CHILD INTERACTIONS IMPACT FUTURE RELATIONSHIPS?   p. 224

● Our brains are wired to encourage interaction between parents and children. The release of the hormone oxytocin leads to feelings of trust and calm.

● Early interactions with parents and caregivers lead to the development of attachment styles. These styles describe the relationship between self-esteem and interpersonal trust. They affect the way we define and interact within relationships.

WHAT FACTORS INFLUENCE AND DEFINE ROMANTIC LOVE?   p. 226

● Romantic relationships are defined in terms of passionate and companionate love. Passionate love is frequently seen at the beginning of a relationship, when two people feel intense longing toward one another. It usually cools into the more stable and calm companionate love.

● Robert Sternberg's triangular theory of love describes the relationship between three possible components of love. His model results in eight different types of love.

HOW ARE RELATIONSHIPS MAINTAINED?   p. 232

● Social exchange theory argues that relationship satisfaction comes from weighing the benefits of a relationship against the costs. Similar to this is equity theory, in which relationship maintenance can be predicted based on similarity between partner's ratios of benefits to contributions in a relationship.

● The more you've invested in a relationship, the more you're willing to work at maintaining it.

WHAT ROLE DOES CONFLICT PLAY IN RELATIONSHIPS?   p. 233

● Conflict is a normal part of any relationship; however, there are four conflict styles, identified by John Gottman, that usually result in the end of a relationship. The negative attributional style can also cause serious problems within a relationship.

● The dissolution of a relationship is often considered a bad thing, but it can result in personal growth. This growth is measured in three types of positive outcomes.

Key Terms

attachment style the degree of security experienced in interpersonal relationships *225*

communal relationship a relationship in which partners expect mutual responsiveness to one another's needs *232*

companionate love the affection we feel for people with whom our lives are deeply intertwined *230*

dismissive attachment style a conflicted, insecure attachment style characterized by high self-esteem and low interpersonal trust *226*

equity theory theory that relationships are most satisfying when the ratio between benefits and contributions is similar for both partners *232*

exchange relationship a relationship in which partners expect strict reciprocity *232*

excitation transfer the process by which arousal from one stimulus can be transferred to the second stimulus, a person *230*

fearful-avoidant attachment style the most insecure of the attachment styles, characterized by low self-esteem and low interpersonal trust *226*

interpersonal trust involves the belief that people are generally trustworthy and dependable as opposed to the opposite and is the attitude that underlies the development of attachment styles *226*

investment those resources that have been devoted to a relationship that cannot be retrieved *232*

matching hypothesis the hypothesis that people are more likely to form longstanding relationships with others whose social attributes match with theirs and with those who are similar in physical attractiveness *224*

mere exposure the hypothesis that the mere repeated exposure of an individual to a stimulus is enough for an increase in favorable response to that stimulus *221*

need for affiliation the desire to establish and maintain rewarding interpersonal relationships *220*

negative attributional style occurs when a person explains his or her partner's behaviors in negative ways *234*

passionate love a state of intense longing for union with another *229*

preoccupied attachment style a conflicted, insecure attachment style characterized by low self-esteem and high interpersonal trust *226*

proportion of similarity an equation that divides the number of topics on which two people express similar views by the total number of topics on which they have communicated, resulting in a prediction of attraction *224*

proximity physical closeness; the smaller the physical distance, the more likely the two people will experience repeat contact, which could lead to the development of mutual attraction *221*

reciprocity the exchange of what we receive for what we get, which can include liking those who like us back *224*

repulsion hypothesis states that similarity doesn't actually have any effect on attraction *224*

secure attachment style the most successful of the attachment styles, characterized by high self-esteem and high interpersonal trust *226*

social exchange theory an economic model of human behavior in which people make decisions based on maximizing benefits and minimizing costs in relationships *232*

triangular theory of love Robert Sternberg's theory that love is made of three components: intimacy, passion, and commitment *230*

Test Your Understanding

MULTIPLE CHOICE

1. The hypothesis that repeated contact with a stimulus is enough for an increase in favorable response to that stimulus is called _____.
   a. mere exposure
   b. proximity
   c. interaction
   d. attachment

2. Studies of the concept of physical attractiveness across cultures have found that
   a. people from Asian countries tend to favor smaller features.
   b. collectivist cultures place very little emphasis on physical attractiveness.
   c. there is very little difference in what is considered physically attractive by people from different cultures.
   d. people from the United States tend to favor large eyes and prominent cheekbones.

3. According to evolutionary psychologists
   a. men seek out physically attractive mates while women seek out mates with access to resources.
   b. there is really no difference in what men and women want in a potential romantic partner.
   c. women seek out younger mates while age isn't a factor for men.
   d. women seek out mates who are physically attractive, but men value youth above all in a partner.

4. Interaction between parents and their infants is encouraged by the release of
   a. melatonin.
   b. oxytocin.
   c. adrenaline.
   d. estrogen.

5. Which attachment style results from low self-esteem paired with high interpersonal trust?
   a. secure attachment style
   b. fearful-avoidant attachment style
   c. preoccupied attachment style
   d. dismissive attachment style

6. Which attachment style results from high self-esteem paired with low interpersonal trust?
   a. secure attachment style
   b. fearful-avoidant attachment style
   c. preoccupied attachment style
   d. dismissive attachment style

7. The type of love often seen in long-term relationships and characterized by stability and calm is called
   a. passionate love.
   b. comfortable love.
   c. companionate love.
   d. real love.

8. Robert Sternberg's triangular theory of love describes the relationship between
   a. intimacy, loneliness, and passion.
   b. intimacy, passion, and commitment.
   c. commitment, loneliness, and attractiveness.
   d. commitment, passion, and loyalty.

9. One of the "Four Horsemen," *stonewalling* involves
   a. emotional withdrawal.
   b. acting as if you are repulsed by your partner.
   c. ignoring everything your partner says.
   d. complaining about your partner.

10. When one explains his or her partner's behavior in a negative way, he or she is showing evidence of
    a. criticism.
    b. denial.
    c. contempt.
    d. negative attributional style.

ESSAY RESPONSE

1. Explain the process that leads to attraction, using an example.
2. Is physical attractiveness a subjective trait, or can it be measured objectively? Explain your reasoning.
3. Define each of the four attachment styles, and give an example of a representative relationship for each.
4. Compare and contrast passionate and companionate love. How does one lead to the other?
5. How does the negative attributional style lead to distrust and negative feelings in a relationship?

APPLY IT!

Choose five of the eight possible types of love from Robert Sternberg's triangular theory of love. Find examples from television, movies, or books that exemplify each of the types you selected. How do these examples reflect these types of love?

ANSWERS: 1. a; 2. c; 3. a; 4. b; 5. c; 6. d; 7. c; 8. b; 9. a; 10. d

Remember to check www.thinkspot.com for additional information, downloadable flashcards, and other helpful resources.

THINK READINGS

SCIENTIFIC AMERICAN MIND

How Science Can Help You Fall in Love

By ROBERT EPSTEIN

Published: January/February 2010

> Why do you think vulnerability can play such a large part in the success of a relationship? Think about what you learned in Chapters 4 and 5. How might self-disclosure play a role in romance?

> Epstein attributes this effect in large part to an increase in people opening up to one another. But what role do you think proximity, mere exposure, and interaction—factors you learned about in Chapter 12—played in his experiment?

Nothing is more fulfilling than being in a successful love relationship. Yet we leave our love lives entirely to chance. Maybe we don't have to anymore

The best way to get students interested in scientific studies is to give them hands-on experiences that get them excited about the subject matter. In chemistry courses, teachers accomplish that with test tubes and mysterious liquids. In a course I taught recently at the University of California, San Diego, on relationship science, I piqued my students' interest with exercises on, well, *love*.

To begin, I invited eight students who did not know each other to come to the front of the auditorium, where I paired them up randomly. I then asked each individual to rate, on a scale of 1 to 10, how much he or she liked, loved, or felt close to his or her partner. Then I asked the couples to look deeply into each other's eyes in an exercise I call Soul Gazing.

There was some giggling at first and then some very intense gazing. After two minutes, I again asked for the numbers. The result? A modest 7 percent increase in loving (meaning 1 point added for one person in one couple), an 11 percent increase in liking, and a whopping 45 percent increase in closeness. There were gasps and cheers in the audience. When I asked everyone in the class to pair up for two minutes of gazing, 89 percent of the students said the exercise increased feelings of intimacy.

And that was just the beginning....

Eye Contact

About 50 percent of first marriages fail in the U.S., as do two thirds of second marriages and three quarters of third marriages. So much for practice! We fail in large part because we enter into relationships with poor skills for maintaining them and highly unrealistic expectations. We also tend to pick unsuitable partners, mistakenly believing that we are in love simply because we feel physical attraction.

That combination of factors sets us up for failure: eventually—often within a mere 18 months— the fog of passion dissipates, and we begin to see our partner with new clarity. All too often we react by saying, "Who are *you?*" or "You've *changed.*" We might try hard for years after that to keep things going, especially if children are in the picture. But if we start out with the wrong person and lack basic tools for resolving conflicts and communicating, the chances that we will succeed are slim to none.

Over the years, having looked carefully at the fast-growing scientific literature on relationship science and having conducted some new research of my own, I have come to believe that there is a definite fix for our poor performance in romantic relationships. The fix is to extract a practical technology from the research and then to teach people how to use it.

At least 80 scientific studies help to reveal how people learn to love each other. A 1989 study by psychologist James D. Laird of Clark University and his colleagues inspired my Soul Gazing exercise. The researchers showed that mutual eye gazing (but not gazing at hands) produced rapid increases in feelings of both liking and loving in total strangers. Mutual gazing is like staring, but with an important difference: for many mammalian species, staring is both intended and received as a threat. Try it on a New York subway if you have any doubts about its efficacy. In mutual gazing, however, people are giving each other *permission* to stare; that is, they are being *vulnerable* to each other, and that is the key element in emotional bonding. The vulnerability created when people are in war zones can

Fast Facts

Lessons on Love

1 » About half of first marriages fail in the U.S., as do two thirds of second marriages and three quarters of third marriages. We fail in large part because we enter into relationships with poor skills for maintaining them and highly unrealistic expectations.

2 » The fix for our poor performance in romantic relationships: extract a practical technology from scientific research on how people learn to love each other—and then teach individuals how to use it.

3 » A study of arranged marriages in which love has grown over time hints that commitment, communication, accommodation and vulnerability are key components of a successful relationship. Other research indicates that sharing adventures, secrets, personal space and jokes can also build intimacy and love with your partner.

SCIENTIFIC AMERICAN MIND, Vol. 20, Pages 26–33 Copyright 2010 Scientific American

create powerful emotional bonds in seconds, and even hostages sometimes develop strong attachments to their captors, a phenomenon called the Stockholm syndrome.

Signs of vulnerability in an animal or another person bring out tendencies in many people to provide care and protection—to be drawn to that being and to like or even love him or her. And as research in social psychology has shown for decades, when a person is feeling vulnerable and thus agitated or otherwise aroused, he or she often looks around for clues about how to interpret and label those feelings. The body is saying, "I'm aroused, but I'm not sure why," and the environment is suggesting an answer, namely, that you're in love.

A Technology of Affection

Soul Gazing is one of dozens of exercises I have distilled from scientific studies that make people feel vulnerable and increase intimacy. Love Aura, Let Me Inside and Secret Swap are other examples of fun, bond-building activities that any couple can learn and practice [see box on preceding page].

Students could earn extra credit in my course by trying out such techniques with friends, romantic interests or even total strangers. More than 90 percent of the students in the course reported using these methods successfully to improve their relationships, and more than 50 of the 213 students submitted detailed reports about their experiences. Nearly all the reports documented increases in liking, loving, closeness or attraction of between 3 and 30 percent over about a month. In a few cases, ratings tripled. (Students did

not need to enhance their relationships to receive extra credit; all they had to do was document their use of the techniques.)

The few exceptions I saw made sense. One heterosexual male saw no positive effects when he tried the exercises with another male; moreover, the experience made him "uncomfortable." When he tried them with a female, however, his intimacy ratings increased by 25 percent—and *hers* increased by 144 percent!

A student named Olivia attempted the exercises with her brother, mother, a good friend and a relative stranger. Soul Gazing failed with her brother because he could not stop giggling. When she and her mom tried the Secret Swap—an activity that creates vulnerability when people disclose secrets to each other—intimacy ratings increased by 31 percent. Exercises she tried with her friend boosted ratings between 10 and 19 percent, but most impressive was the outcome of gazing with someone she barely knew: a 70 percent increase in intimacy.

One student did the assignment with her husband of five years. The couple, Asa and Gill, tried out eight different exercises, and even though their "before" scores were usually very high (9s and 10s), every exercise they tried increased their scores by at least 3 per-

cent. Overall, Asa wrote, "I noticed a drastic change in our bond for one another. My husband seems more affectionate now than he was, for

Love-Building

Exercises

Here are some fun exercises, all inspired by scientific studies, that you can use to deliberately create emotional intimacy with a partner— even someone you barely know:

1 » **Two as One.** Embracing each other gently, begin to sense your partner's breathing and gradually try to synchronize your breathing with his or hers. After a few minutes, you might feel that the two of you have merged.

2 » **Soul Gazing.** Standing or sitting about two feet away from each other, look deeply into each other's eyes, trying to look into the very core of your beings. Do this for about two minutes and then talk about what you saw.

3 » **Monkey Love.** Standing or sitting fairly near each other, start moving your hands, arms and legs any way you like—but in a fashion that perfectly imitates your partner. This is fun but also challenging. You will both feel as if you are moving voluntarily, but your actions are also linked to those of your partner.

4 » **Falling in Love.** This is a trust exercise, one of many that increase mutual feelings of vulnerability. From a standing position, simply let yourself fall backward into the arms of your partner. Then trade places. Repeat several times and then talk about your feelings. Strangers who do this exercise sometimes feel connected to each other for years.

5 » **Secret Swap.** Write down a deep secret and have your partner do the same. Then trade papers and talk about what you read. You can continue this process until you have run out of secrets. Better yet, save some of your secrets for another day.

6 » **Mind-Reading Game.** Write down a thought that you want to convey to your partner. Then spend a few minutes wordlessly trying to broadcast that thought to him or her, as he or she tries to guess what it is. If he or she cannot guess, reveal what you were thinking. Then switch roles.

7 » **Let Me Inside.** Stand about four feet away from each other and focus on each other. Every 10 seconds or so move a bit closer until, after several shifts, you are well inside each other's personal space (the boundary is about 18 inches). Get as close as you can without touching. (My students tell me this exercise often ends with kissing.)

8 » **Love Aura.** Place the palm of your hand as close as possible to your partner's palm without actually touching. Do this for several minutes, during which you will feel not only heat but also, sometimes, eerie kinds of sparks.

—R.E.

ROBERT EPSTEIN is a contributing editor for *Scientific American Mind* and former editor in chief of *Psychology Today*. He holds a Ph.D. in psychology from Harvard University and is a longtime researcher and professor. He is currently working on a book called *Making Love: How People Learn to Love and How You Can Too* (www.MakingLoveBook.com).

> What do you think of Epstein's exercises? How do you think you would feel if you tried them with a significant other, a family member, or a stranger?

Extra Credit for Love

Jocelyn, aged 21, and Brian, aged 25, are students at the University of California, San Diego, where they tried some of the love-generating techniques they learned in the author's class on relationship science. These graphs show changes in feelings of liking (blue), closeness (pink) and loving (red) over six weeks. Each week the students tried one exercise. At the outset, they liked each other fairly well but experienced little closeness or love. In the first week, the gazing technique had a big effect on closeness, especially for Brian. By the sixth week, Jocelyn's love for Brian had risen from a 1 to a 6 on a 10-point scale, and Brian's love for Jocelyn had climbed from a 2 to a 7. Brian and Jocelyn might have made progress without the exercises, but both felt the activities had helped.

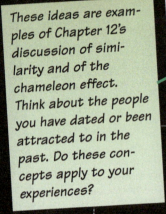

These ideas are examples of Chapter 12's discussion of similarity and of the chameleon effect. Think about the people you have dated or been attracted to in the past. Do these concepts apply to your experiences?

Schemas about what love is and should be differ across cultures, as Epstein describes in this article. In Chapter 3, you learned about the role optimism can play in our lives. How do you think the Western idea of destiny's role in love can make us happy or unhappy?

which I am really grateful." She also reported a bonus: a substantial drop in the frequency with which she and her spouse called attention to their past mistakes. This change probably came about because the couple was now, as a result of my course, broadly interested in enhancing their relationship.

Taking Control

The students in my course were doing something new—taking *control* over their love lives. We grow up on fairy tales and movies in which magical forces help people find their soul mates, with whom they effortlessly live happily ever after. The fairy tales leave us powerless, putting our love lives into the hands of the Fates.

But here is a surprise: most of the world has never heard of those fairy tales. Instead more than half of marriages on our globe are brokered by parents or professional matchmakers, whose main concerns are long-term suitability and family harmony. In India an estimated 95 percent of the marriages are arranged, and although divorce is legal, India has one of the lowest divorce rates in the world.

(This is starting to change, of course, as Western ways encroach on traditional society.)

Young couples in India generally have a choice about whether to proceed, and the combination of choice and sound guidance probably accounts for the fact that studies of arranged marriages in India indicate that they measure up well—in, for example, longevity, satisfaction and love—against Western marriages. Indeed, the love experienced by Indian couples in arranged marriages appears to be even more robust than the love people experience in "love marriages." In a 1982 study psychologists Usha Gupta and Pushpa Singh of the University of Rajasthan in Jaipur, India, used the Rubin Love Scale, which gauges intense, romantic, Western-style love, to determine that love in love marriages in India does exactly what it does in love marriages here: it starts high and declines fairly rapidly. But love in the arranged marriages they examined started out low and gradually *increased*, surpassing the love in the love marriage about five years out. Ten years into the marriage the love was nearly twice as strong.

How do they do it? How do people in some arranged marriages build love deliberately over time— and can we do it, too?

Studies in Intimacy

Dozens of scientific studies illuminate how people fall in love—and hint at techniques for building strong relationships. Here are 10 kinds of investigations that are helping to inspire a new technology of love.

1 ›› Arousal. Studies by researchers such as psychologist Arthur Aron of Stony Brook University show that people tend to bond emotionally when aroused, say, through exercise, adventures or exposure to dangerous situations. Roller coaster, anyone? See the Falling in Love exercise on page 29.

2 ›› Proximity and familiarity. Studies by Stanford University social psychologists Leon Festinger and Robert Zajonc and others conclude that simply being around someone tends to produce positive feelings. When two people consciously and deliberately allow each other to invade their personal space, feelings of intimacy can grow quickly. See the Let Me Inside exercise on page 29.

3 ›› Similarity. Opposites sometimes attract, but research by behavioral economist Dan Ariely of Duke University and the Massachusetts Institute of Technology and others shows that people usually tend to pair off with those who are similar to themselves—in intelligence, background and level of attractiveness. Some research even suggests that merely imitating someone can increase closeness. See the Monkey Love exercise on page 29.

4 ›› Humor. Marriage counselors and researchers Jeanette and Robert Lauer showed in 1986 that in long-term, happy relationships, partners make each other laugh a lot. Other research reveals that women often seek male partners who can make them laugh—possibly because when we are laughing, we feel vulnerable. Know any good jokes?

5 ›› Novelty. Psychologist Greg Strong of Florida State University, Aron and others have shown that people tend to grow closer when they are doing something new. Novelty heightens the senses and also makes people feel vulnerable.

6 ›› Inhibitions. Countless millions of relationships have probably started with a glass of wine. Inhibitions block feelings of vulnerability, so lowering inhibitions can indeed help people bond. Getting drunk, however, is blinding and debilitating. Instead of alcohol, try the Two as One exercise on page 29.

(continue)

Over the past few years I have been interviewing people in arranged marriages in which love has grown over time. One of these couples is Kaiser and Shelly Haque of Minneapolis, who have been happily married for 11 years and have two bright, welladjusted children. Once he had a secure life in the U.S., Kaiser, an immigrant from Bangladesh, returned to his native country to let his family know he was ready for matrimony. The family did the rest. After just one meeting with Shelly—where, Kaiser said, there was "like at first sight"—the arrangements were made. "We've grown to love each other and to get to know each other over time," Kaiser says. "The sparks are getting bigger, and I think we can do even better in the future."

Kaiser and Shelly are not atypical. A study that Mansi Thakar, a student at the University of Southern California, and I presented at the November 2009 meeting of the National Council on Family Relations included 30 individuals from nine countries of origin and five different religions. Their love had grown, on average, from 3.9 to 8.5 on a 10-point scale in marriages lasting an average of 19.4 years.

These individuals identified 11 factors that contributed to the growth of their love, 10 of which dovetailed beautifully with the scientific research I reviewed in my course. The most important factor was commitment, followed by good communication skills. The couples also identified sharing secrets with a spouse, as well as accommodation—that is, the voluntary altering of a partner's behavior to meet the other person's needs. Seeing a spouse in a vulnerable state (caused by injury or illness) was also singled out. There are many possible lessons here for Westerners, among them: do things deliberately that make you vulnerable to each other. Try experiencing danger, or thrilling simulations of it, as a couple.

The results conflicted with those of American studies in only one respect: several of the subjects said their love grew when they had children with their spouse. Studies in the U.S. routinely find parenting to be a threat to feelings of spousal love, but perhaps that tendency results from the strong feelings and unrealistic expectations that launch our relationships. The stress of raising children tends to disrupt those expectations and ultimately our positive feelings for each other.

Creating Love

A careful look at arranged marriage, combined with the knowledge accumulating in relationship science, has the potential to give us real control over our love lives—without practicing arranged marriage. Americans want it all—the freedom to choose a partner and the deep, lasting love of fantasies and fairy tales. We can achieve that kind of love by learning about and practicing techniques that build love over time. And when our love is fading, we can use such techniques to rebuild that love. The alternative— leaving it to chance—makes little sense.

Further Reading

- **An Exploratory Study of Love and Liking and Type of Marriages.** Usha Gupta and Pushpa Singh in *Indian Journal of Applied Psychology,* Vol. 19, pages 92–97; 1982.
- **Love Games.** Mark Robert Waldman. Tarcher/Putnam, 2000.
- **Steps toward the Ripening of Relationship Science.** Harry T. Reis in *Personal Relationships,* Vol. 14, pages 1–23; 2007.
- **Handbook of Relationship Initiation.** Susan Sprecher, Amy Wenzel and John Harvey. Psychology Press, 2008.
- The author's ongoing survey of arranged marriages (including how to participate) is at **http://ArrangedMarriageSurvey.com**
- Test your relationship skills at **http://MyLoveSkills.com**

7 » **Kindness, accommodation and forgiveness.** A variety of studies confirm that we tend to bond to people who are kind, sensitive and thoughtful. Feelings of love can emerge especially quickly when someone deliberately changes his or her behavior—say, by giving up smoking or drinking—to accommodate our needs. Forgiveness often causes mutual bonding, because when one forgives, one shows vulnerability.

8 » **Touch and sexuality.** The simplest touch can produce warm, positive feelings, and a backrub can work wonders. Even getting very near someone without actually touching can have an effect. Studies by social psychologist Susan Sprecher of Illinois State University, among others, also show that sexuality can make people feel closer emotionally, especially for women. There is danger here, however: confusing sexual attraction with feelings of love. You cannot love someone without knowing him or her, and attraction blinds people to important characteristics of their partner.

9 » **Self-disclosure.** Research by Aron, Sprecher and others indicates that people tend to bond when they share secrets with each other. Once again, the key here is allowing oneself to be vulnerable. See the Secret Swap exercise on page 29.

10 » **Commitment.** We are not that good at honoring our relationship commitments in the U.S., but studies by researchers such as psychologist Ximena Arriaga of Purdue University suggest that commitment is an essential element in building love. People whose commitments are shaky interpret their partners' behavior more negatively, for one thing, and that can be deadly over time. Covenant marriage— currently a legal option only in Arizona, Arkansas and Louisiana— is a new kind of marriage (emerging from the evangelical Christian movement) involving a very strong commitment: couples agree to premarital counseling and limited grounds for divorce. Conventional marriage in America can be abandoned easily, even without specific legal cause (the so-called no-fault divorce).

—R.E.

What do you think the answer is? Are any couples in your family the result of an arranged marriage? How would you feel if you knew that your parents would choose your future spouse?

"A careful look at arranged marriage, combined with the knowledge accumulating in relationship science, has the potential to give us real control over our love lives."

How might a person's gender affect the way one person in a couple reacts to the other in a vulnerable state? What did you learn in Chapter 12 about the way men and women differ in expressing their affection for each other?

PROSOCIAL BEHAVIOR:
WHY WE HELP, AND WHY WE DON'T

In 2006,

upon observing a Mercedes Coupe and a homeless man across the street, a 14-year-old girl remarked to her father that if the owner of the Coupe had a less expensive car, the difference in money could feed the homeless man. She continued to press her parents about the issue of inequality, motivated to do something. Her mother asked her, "What do you want to do, sell our house?"

And that's exactly what they did.

The Salwen family sold their house, donated half of the proceeds to charity, and moved into a more modest home. Over time, they donated $800,000 toward ending hunger in Ghana. In *The Power of Half* (2010), father and daughter Kevin and Hannah Salwen chronicle their experience and encourage others to do as they did—not necessarily to sell their houses, but to define their lives, not by how much they own but by what they give to others. Since moving to the smaller house, the Salwens report being happier; not only have they done something good for others, but the move has brought them closer together as a family, both physically and emotionally.

What makes some people give so incredibly generously—selling their home in order to give to others—while others give nothing? Even on a much smaller scale, what will lead someone to help—for instance, offering an elderly person a seat on the subway or bus—when so many people do not?

Psychological research has investigated the factors that contribute to and impede helping behavior. Moreover, there has been extensive debate about what helping *is*. In other words, is helping always a selfish act, or can it be done purely selflessly? Even the Salwens admit that helping others has provided them with enormous gratification and improved their family life. "The Money Song" from the Broadway musical *Avenue Q* contains the line, "When you help others, you can't help helping yourself" (Lopez & Marx, 2003). If that's true, can helping others ever be a truly selfless act? In order to answer this question, it is important to understand the reasons, both emotional and intellectual, for why people are driven to help.

In this chapter, we will examine the many factors that contribute to why people help others. We will also explore the different kinds of helping—selfish and selfless—in order to determine what differentiates them and to what extent it matters. We will investigate the five-step model that determines when people will help and when they will not, and what the obstacles are to providing and receiving help. Finally, we will explore how we might increase helping behavior, both in our own lives and in the lives of others.

243

CHAPTER 13

Why Do We Help?

Helping behavior, in the psychological literature, has been shown to take many forms. Broadly speaking, **prosocial behavior** is behavior intended to benefit others; it is a positive form of social action (Wispé, 1972; Staub, 1978). This form of behavior can be either **egoistic**, meaning that it is done for selfish reasons, or **altruistic**, meaning that it is done for purely selfless reasons. Why might someone decide to help or not to help, and what motivations might underlie that decision? Can you think of a unique time in American history when many individuals engaged in prosocial behavior?

In the wake of the September 11, 2001 terrorist attacks, the rate of blood donation skyrocketed (Glynn, Busch, Schreiber, Murphy, Wright, Tu, & Kleinman, 2003). In fact, immediately after the attacks, donation centers had to turn away eligible donors—they did not have the ability to accommodate so many. At other times, however, there is a nearly constant shortage of blood, and donation centers desperately seek donors. Why were so many people eager to donate during a crisis, but reluctant to donate during ordinary times?

One possible explanation is that when someone's sense of order and moral righteousness is threatened by violent and hateful acts such as those committed on September 11, he responds by "**morally cleansing**," or reaffirming his commitment to his values (Skitka, Saunders, Morgan, & Wisneski, 2009). In this way, individuals were able to reassure themselves that they and others in their ingroup were morally trustworthy, even though the outgroup of the terrorists was not.

In the case of the outpouring of help immediately after September 11, another possibility is that the personal relevance of the attacks made helping others somewhat soothe the trauma. Indeed, recent neurobiological research has shown that making charitable donations activates the same brain regions—the regions of the mesolimbic reward system—that are activated upon the receipt of monetary rewards (Moll, Krueger, Zahn, Pardini, de Oliveira-Souza, & Grafman, 2006). This suggests that giving to those in need makes a person feel just as good as if she had just received a reward. Another possibility is that, after the attacks, people helped out of genuine empathy toward the victims and their families. In truth, there are many possible reasons, all of which are likely to be true to some extent, for some people.

Next, we will consider some of the predominant theories of why people help when they do; keep in mind, though, that it is rare that there is only one reason. In truth, it is far more likely that, at any given time, there are multiple motives behind the decision to help.

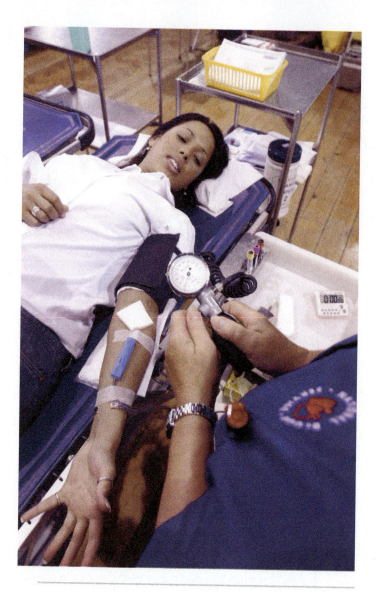

∧
∧ Why do we engage in actions that **will**
∧ **benefit others?**

EGOISTIC MODELS

Several models postulate that selfish motivations are at the core of people's decisions to help others. Specifically, the *negative state relief model* and *cost-benefit analysis* are two models that describe how people consider the outcomes of their helpful behaviors.

Negative State Relief Model

People will provide help to others to feel good about themselves. Prosocial behavior has positive psychological effects on individuals, notably increasing their happiness (Piliavin, 2003). People will also provide help to alleviate their negative state while observing or thinking about another's suffering; this is known as the **negative state relief model** (Cialdini, Kenrick, & Baumann, 1982). Witnessing another's suffering can induce **empathy**—which includes both a cognitive and emotional component and includes the feeling of compassion for others and that of seeing the world through the eyes of another individual (Eisenberg & Miller, 1987). If a friend complains about his tough class for the third day in a row, you feel compassion toward him, and you imagine how he feels to be overwhelmed by coursework. Seeing him in distress motivates you to help him in an effort to alleviate his suffering. So you offer to spend a couple of hours helping him organize his notes, hoping it will give him some relief.

You might also help someone to help yourself, which also fits this model. Selfish motives such as gaining respect from your peers, making yourself feel better, or actually being rewarded can lead to helping (Batson, 1998). Whatever the reason, the negative state relief model of motivation can actually lead to sustained helping (Omoto & Snyder, 1995). When researchers investigated volunteers' motives for helping people with AIDS and tracked how long those volunteers continued to work, they found that people who were there for more selfless reasons were actually less likely to keep volunteering. Somewhat unexpectedly, the people who were volunteering for more selfish reasons, such as wanting to make friends, kept volunteering longer.

Cost-Benefit Analysis

People are more inclined to help others when their own outcomes can be improved by helping. They will weigh the needs of the other person with their own needs to determine if helping will prove too costly to themselves. This decision-making process is termed a **cost-benefit analysis** (Dovidio, Piliavin, Gaertner, Schroeder, & Clark, 1991; Piliavin, Dovidio, Gaertner, & Clark, 1981). It includes weighing any potential threats to the self, including personal harm, emotional harm, and any harm that may befall one's reputation due to association with a member of a stigmatized group (Batson, O'Quin, Fultz, Vanderplas, & Isen, 1983; Midlarsky & Midlarsky, 1973; Edelmann, Childs, Harvey, Kellock, & Strain-Clark, 1984; Piliavin & Piliavin, 1972; Staub, 1974; Snyder, Omoto, & Crain, 1999). People are not only motivated to help when it does not cause them harm; they will also help if it brings them rewards, such as money (Wilson & Kahn, 1975), improved mood (Gueguen & De Gail, 2003), improved skill (Perlow & Weeks, 2002), increased popularity and recognition from others (Fisher & Ackerman, 1998; Reddy, 1980), maintenance of a good reputation (Johnson, Erez, Kiker, & Motowidlo, 2002), personal gratification (Smith, Keating, & Stotland, 1989; Utne & Kidd, 1980), or even a simple "thank you" (McGovern, Ditzian, & Taylor, 1975).

In addition to the motivation people have to improve their frame of mind, their existing mood impacts the perceived costs and benefits of

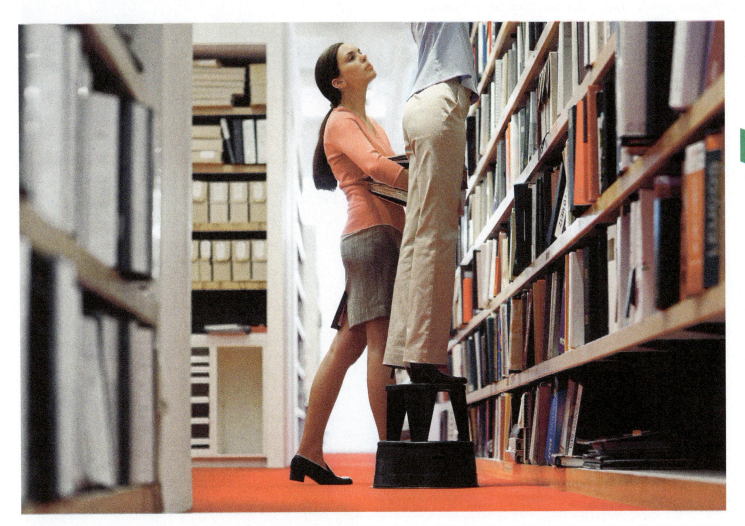

∧
∧ People sometimes help others for their own gain, such as when people do internships. **Doing**
∧ **the work for free benefits the employer but also provides benefits to the student, such as increased skill and experience as well as a reference.**

EMPATHY-ALTRUISM MODEL OF PROSOCIAL BEHAVIOR a model suggesting that true altruism is a product of empathy; this empathy can create nurturing feelings toward a target or a goal to increase the target's welfare

RECIPROCITY NORM the idea that if others help us, we should help them, and that if we help them, they will help us

SOCIAL RESPONSIBILITY NORM the idea that we have social responsibility to help others; the extent to which this extends to outgroup members varies by culture

helping. Those in good moods will be more likely to focus on the rewards of helping rather than the costs, and these rewards will come to mind more easily; even finding a dime or getting a cookie can enhance one's mood and subsequently increase the desire to help others (Isen, 1970; Isen, Clark, & Schwartz, 1976; Isen & Levin, 1972; Isen, Shalker, Clark, & Karp, 1978). Moreover, people will also help others in an effort to try and maintain their own existing positive moods—to avoid it slipping because of the other person's dilemma (Wegener & Petty, 1994). In this way, mood further impacts people's tendency to provide help.

ALTRUISTIC MODEL OF HELPING

On a winter day in 2007, a young man waiting for a train in a New York subway station suddenly began convulsing and collapsed. He managed to get to his feet, but was so disoriented he stumbled to the edge of the platform and fell to the tracks. As the headlights of the approaching train bore down on the dazed man, another man on the platform made an amazing choice. Leaving the side of his two daughters, 50-year-old Wesley Autrey jumped to the tracks, laying on top of the other man, pressing him down as far as he could, between the rails. The train roared over them, five cars passing so closely they smudged Autrey's hat with black grease. Miraculously, both men were okay (Buckley, 2007).

In contrast to the above-mentioned models that propose that helping is driven by egoistic motivations, the **empathy-altruism model of prosocial behavior** (Batson, 1991) suggests that helping can occur for altruistic reasons as well. Specifically, the theory states that someone will be more likely to help another person if that other person's welfare is at stake. This is particularly the case if the helper has nurturing feelings toward the other person. In fact, protecting another's well-being is often enough to encourage helping behavior, even if no egoistic motivations to help exist (Batson & Oleson, 1991)—and, remarkably, even when helping is costly to oneself (Toi & Batson, 1982). This suggests that people truly can help in selfless ways— that altruistic behavior exists and is not an artifact of egoistic motivations.

During the 1980s, researchers (Batson, Duncan, Ackerman, Buckley, & Birch, 1981; Batson, Dyck, Bran, Watson, Powell, McMaster, & Griffitt, 1988) published studies testing the empathy-altruism model. They wanted to show that ego-based motives can't explain the helping that takes place when people feel empathy. Participants were presented with a woman named "Elaine." To elicit empathy, participants were told that Elaine was very much like them in terms of values and interests. After watching Elaine react badly to a pair of electric shocks, participants were told they could take the remaining eight shocks for her. Half were told they could leave if they didn't take the shocks for Elaine, and the other half were told they must stay and watch Elaine take the rest. People who were given the choice to leave did so—except when they felt empathetic concern for

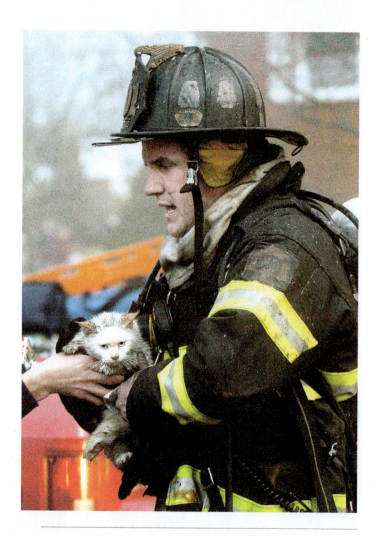

∧
∧ People will help those in need if they feel
∧ nurturing feelings toward them, **even in the
absence of any selfish motivations.**

Elaine. When empathy was introduced, it didn't matter if they were given an escape option—people stayed and helped.

Although taking the perspective of another individual can impact helping, Batson's model is not without criticism (Cialdini, Brown, Lewis, Luce, & Neuberg, 1997; Schaller & Cialdini, 1988). Critics say that conditions leading to empathy also lead to a greater sense of overlap between the self and the other. They argue that this means that the impulse to help isn't just a selfless response to the suffering other, but is also directed toward the self. When this overlap was considered in studies, the impact of empathy was eliminated.

" **When empathy was introduced, it didn't matter** if they were given an escape option—people stayed and helped. "

Batson and colleagues (Batson, 1991; Batson, Duncan, Ackerman, Buckley, & Birch, 1981; Toi & Batson, 1982) proposed that the reason prosocial behavior increases with the presence of nurturing feelings and the desire to increase another's welfare is because these emotions involve empathy. The researchers found that heightened feelings of empathy do indeed predict altruism—helping when no selfish reasons are present. However, there is considerable debate as to whether an altruistic personality really exists. Even if we do not receive tangible awards for helping, there are other intangibles that certainly compensate us—such as feeling good about helping someone.

NORMS

There are two social norms that may affect when people engage in prosocial behavior: reciprocity and social responsibility. These norms can operate without us being aware of them and drive us to certain behaviors without our knowledge. They can also motivate us consciously, whether through a desire to conform to society's standards for their own sake, or through an awareness of how certain behaviors might benefit us and/or others. Of course, there are regional differences in helping within the United States. One aspect of this is actually population density (Levine, Martinez, Brase, & Sorenson, 1994). The denser the population of a city, the less likely people are to help strangers. Of 36 cities examined, Louisville, Kentucky, and Rochester, New York, emerged as two of the most helpful cities, while Los Angeles, California, and New York City ranked close to the bottom.

Reciprocity Norm

One such norm is the **reciprocity norm**, which suggests that people usually help others who have helped them (Wilke & Lanzetta, 1970). Doing a favor for someone increases the likelihood of getting that favor returned. In one classic study (Regan, 1971), participants engaged in a series of interactions with a partner in which they were encouraged to think favorably of him—by witnessing him behave nicely and reasonably—or think poorly of him, after seeing him act unpleasantly. After that, each participant received a soda from the partner, received a soda from the experimenter, or did not receive one at all. Later, the partner asked participants to purchase some raffle tickets and complete a questionnaire assessing their attitudes toward the individual. The results revealed that liking the partner did not impact the likelihood that the participants would buy the tickets. Instead, those who received a soda from the partner bought more tickets than those in the other two groups, and responses to the questionnaire revealed that this was due to feeling compelled to reciprocate.

In fact, this inclination toward reciprocating is even present in children as young as 21 months old. In a study done by Dunfield and Kuhlmeier (2010), babies were introduced to two actresses. One offered each baby a toy, but due to the incline of the table, the toy rolled away and the child was unable to receive it. The other actress showed the baby the toy but did not offer it. In both cases, the child did not gain access to the toy. Then, the two actresses sat next to each other in front of the baby. The experimenter then placed a toy on the table in front of the baby so that it fell off, and both actresses reached for the toy but were unable to get it. The baby could reach the toy, however, and, upon picking it up, was more likely to hand the toy to the actress who had tried to give the baby the toy earlier. In this way, babies remembered an attempt at helpful behavior and returned the favor, thus supporting the idea of the reciprocity norm (Dunfield & Kuhlmeier, 2010).

But what if the baby had been able to get the toy? Would the positive outcome overwhelm the effect of reciprocity? In this same study, some babies were exposed to one actress who, like in the first study, attempted to give the child the toy but could not. Instead of also being exposed to an actress who would not give the baby the toy, however, they were introduced to an actress who successfully gave the baby the toy. In this second stage, babies were no more likely to give the toy to the actress who succeeded than the one who did not. Even infants were able to recognize that the two actresses' intentions were the same—both positively oriented toward the infant—and they responded with reciprocation to both (Dunfield & Kuhlmeier, 2010).

Social Responsibility Norm

Another norm that impacts helping is the **social responsibility norm**. It states that a person will feel more compelled to help others if he feels a sense of responsibility to his society and its members (Berkowitz & Daniels, 1963). One prominent example of this is donations to charity and social activism—people giving time or money to causes in which they believe. In 2008, Americans alone donated $307.65 billion to charity—a staggering amount, considering that 2008 was the first full year of a major recession (Giving USA Foundation, 2009). In 2009, 63.4 million Americans volunteered for one organization or another (Bureau of Labor Statistics, 2010).

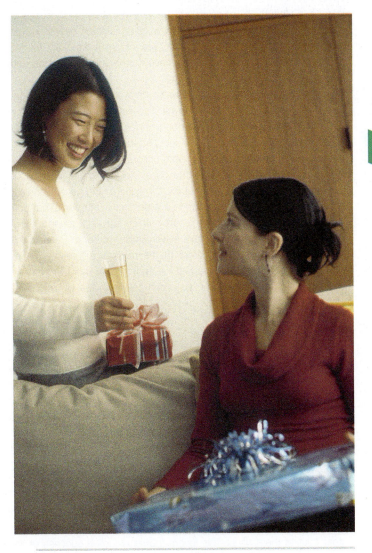

∧
∧ People expect that those for whom they do
∧ a favor will do a favor back when requested,
and indeed that reciprocity tends to occur.

> "People's tendencies to help out in certain ways **can vary based on specific cultural norms.**"

However, this sort of generous giving occurs only when we feel that the victims are not responsible for their situation; if we cast blame on the victim, we will not help. Consider the perception of some individuals toward AIDS patients who become ill due to a transfusion, versus their perception of those who become ill due to unsafe sex or drug use (Chapple, Ziebland, & McPherson, 2004; Marlow, Waller, & Wardle, 2010). Even medically trained staff exhibits less helping toward patients whose injuries they perceive to be avoidable (Mackay & Barrowclough, 2005). The extent to which disease or injury onset is seen as controllable—as evidenced through increased feelings of pity for those who could not control it—predicts helping behavior (Dooley, 1995). As you learned in Chapter 5, however, people vary in the sorts of causes for which they will provide help, and this variation is partly based on their morals and ideologies. For example, liberals are more likely to help people with afflictions perceived to have controllable causes than are conservatives (Skitka, 1999).

Furthermore, people's tendencies to help out in certain ways can vary based on specific cultural norms. For instance, Indians are more likely than Americans to offer their bone marrow for transplant to a wider variety of potential recipients—including strangers on the other side of the world (Baron & Miller, 2000). Both cultural groups are less likely to help outgroup members, but Americans are also more likely to fail sometimes at helping ingroup members living locally. In general, Indians tend to feel more social obligation to a wider variety of people, but both Indians and Americans have criteria by which they limit to whom they would donate—Indians just have fewer limiting criteria. Researchers have also noted that, in addition to the regional differences based on population density we've already noted, help is more likely to be provided in a rural rather than an urban setting in the United States (Levine, 1997; Steblay, 1987).

EVOLUTIONARY REASONS

Some theorists speculate that we help others because it promotes the evolution of our species and the continuation of our genetic line. It has been suggested that genes "selfishly" desire to be passed on to promote species survival and in doing so, create unselfish behavior in the individual organism (Dawkins, 1976). This line of thought is not necessarily opposed to the cultural, emotional, and intellectual lines of reasoning discussed earlier, but it places the most emphasis on genetics as the source of our varied motivations to help. This theory basically argues that genes are only out for themselves.

The theory also includes the concept of **kin selection**, which refers to the tendency of people to help their close relatives, even at great cost to themselves; this favors the reproductive success of the person's relatives over her own survival. This is illustrated by Vasey and VanderLann's 2010 study on Samoan homosexual men. Those men, called *fa'afafine* in Samoa, indirectly contribute to the survival prospects of their family's genes by offering help and support to their nieces and nephews.

Additional studies support the theory of kin selection. Burnstein, Crandal, and Kitayama (1994) found that study participants were more likely to help individuals who were genetically related to them, especially in life-or-death situations. Other research (Korchmaros & Kenny, 2001) has suggested that it is important to not only look at genetic closeness, but also emotional closeness. When participants were asked to decide to which family member they would donate an organ, decisions were based party on kinship and partly on emotional closeness. (For a review of kin selection, see Stewart-Williams, 2007.)

When Do We Help?

Many theories, then, provide possible explanations for why we help when we do. Each of these explanations may hold true in its own relevant circumstances, but knowing *why* people help when they do is only part of the story. It is also important to understand *when* people will help, and one major theory by Bibb Latane and John Darley, from the late 1960s and early 1970s, has made a tremendous contribution toward this understanding.

THE DECISION MODEL OF BYSTANDER INTERVENTION

In 1964, a young woman named Kitty Genovese was brutally murdered outside her home. The original story reported by newspapers said that she had been stabbed repeatedly and cried out for help within earshot of 38 people, but none of these people did anything to help her (Gansberg, 1964). The attacker left the scene and returned to it, continuing his assault, and Kitty kept crying for help, but still no one came. This version of the story has since been shown to be untrue; as it turns out, more than one person did call the police, but Kitty had crawled out of sight and so it was unclear that she continued to need help. In addition, many people thought that it had been a lovers' quarrel rather than a stabbing. One man shouted at the attacker, causing him to flee. While the original version of the story was what prompted the wealth of research done on helping behavior, the true version of the story also reveals many of the core reasons why people choose not to provide help.

Kitty Genovese's murder was not an isolated occurrence. In 1974, 25-year-old Sandra Zahler was beaten to death in an apartment of the building that overlooked the site of the Genovese attack. Neighbors again said they heard screams and "fierce struggles" but did nothing (McFadden, 1974). In 1995, a woman named Deletha Ward was severely beaten by a man before she jumped into a river to escape from the attack, resulting in her death. No one on the bridge where this extended and brutal attack occurred attempted to intervene (Associated Press, 1996). Even in the past few years, there have been several horrifying stories of failure to help others in dire situations. In 2008, Dewayne Taylor was attacked by an unknown assailant with a hammer on the Philadelphia subway. Surveillance video showed at least 10 people who witnessed the attack, but did nothing to intervene (Associated Press,

Egoistic Theory:
Will comforting my upset friend make *me* feel better? Do the benefits outweigh the costs?

Altruistic Theory:
Will comforting my friend satisfy my instinct to be nurturing and my desire to improve her well-being?

Norms-Based Theory:
Will my friend be there for me in the future when the roles are reversed? Is it my social responsibility as a friend to offer a shoulder to cry on?

Evolutionary Theory:
Is this friend also related to me? Would helping her essentially be helping our family?

∧
∧
∧ **Getting by With a Little Help from Your Friends.** Each theory that has been offered to explain helping behavior provides different reasons for such behavior—**and more than one can apply in a given situation.**

2008). In 2009, a 15-year-old girl was gang raped while 10 people watched and did nothing (Huffington Post, 2009).

Even those who put themselves at risk to help others are not always assisted; in 2010, a homeless man named Hugo Tale-Yax rushed to the aid of a woman who was being attacked. During the intervention, he was stabbed. He bled to death on the sidewalk as no less than 20 people walked by and did nothing (Livingston, Doyle, & Mangan, 2010). People's failure to help others in serious situations is not uncommon, and no

number of heinous occurrences seems to prevent it from happening again and again. So what can we do to ensure that help is provided when it is needed?

Darley and Latane (1968) were pioneers in the effort to understand when people will help and when they will not, using both laboratory experiments and field research. They developed the **decision model of bystander intervention**, a series of criteria that must be met before a bystander will provide help in an emergency. In the first step, the

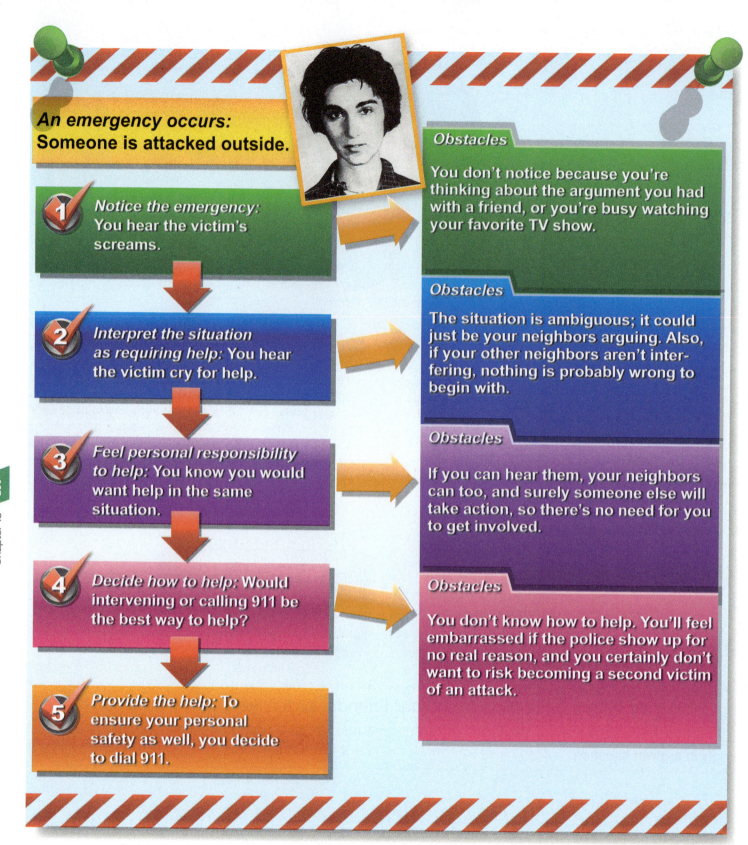

250

**An emergency occurs:
Someone is attacked outside.**

1 **Notice the emergency:** You hear the victim's screams.

Obstacles
You don't notice because you're thinking about the argument you had with a friend, or you're busy watching your favorite TV show.

2 **Interpret the situation as requiring help:** You hear the victim cry for help.

Obstacles
The situation is ambiguous; it could just be your neighbors arguing. Also, if your other neighbors aren't interfering, nothing is probably wrong to begin with.

3 **Feel personal responsibility to help:** You know you would want help in the same situation.

Obstacles
If you can hear them, your neighbors can too, and surely someone else will take action, so there's no need for you to get involved.

4 **Decide how to help:** Would intervening or calling 911 be the best way to help?

Obstacles
You don't know how to help. You'll feel embarrassed if the police show up for no real reason, and you certainly don't want to risk becoming a second victim of an attack.

5 **Provide the help:** To ensure your personal safety as well, you decide to dial 911.

When Will You Help? Darley and Latane (1968) argue that these steps must be followed to permit helping in an emergency to occur; however, there are many obstacles that stand in the way, as illustrated by the deaths of Kitty Genovese and Deletha Ward.

bystander must notice that there is a need for help. The tendency to notice a need is influenced by factors such as being in a hurry (Darley & Batson, 1973). Seminary students sent to an adjacent building for an appointment encountered a man sitting in a doorway, clearly in distress. Of the students who had been sent to the appointment with no sense of urgency, almost two-thirds stopped to help the man. Those who had been sent off in a hurry and told they were late, were far less likely to help; only 10 percent of "late" participants stopped to help the man. Even when these students were headed to give a presentation on the parable of the Good Samaritan (which advocates treating others as you would like them to treat you), they didn't stop to offer help.

Concerns about oneself can therefore affect whether or not a need for help is noticed. Indeed, even being overly concerned with some facet of one's life can reduce the likelihood of noticing someone's need for help; in other words, if you are preoccupied with thoughts about tomorrow's final, you will be self-focused rather than other-focused, and therefore distracted from external cues. One's thoughts, as well as many aspects of one's environment, can act as distractions from the situation.

Proximity to the event and vividness of the event also can contribute to whether or not the need is recognized. In the true Kitty Genovese story, Kitty's cries for help did not make it clear that she had been stabbed, and so neighbors believed it was a lovers' quarrel. Moreover, after her lungs were punctured in the initial attack, it was unlikely that she could have screamed for help at all. Finally, when she crawled away in an effort to escape, she inadvertently placed herself out of sight of her neighbors, and so what was truly happening to her was unclear.

In the second step, the bystander must interpret the situation as requiring help. Ambiguous situations are thus responded to less readily. For example, have you ever seen a visually impaired person crossing the street? You may wonder, "Does that person need help? Will he be offended if I offer to help, or will he appreciate the gesture?" In situations like this, helping is less common.

Another factor that contributes to bystander inaction in a potential emergency is called pluralistic ignorance (Latane & Darley, 1968). This is when a person may privately think there may be an emergency, but seeing others do nothing leads her to infer that there is no need to provide help. In Latane and Darley's 1968 study, participants were placed in a room to answer a questionnaire. As they did, smoke began streaming into the room. When participants were alone, 75 percent reported the smoke. When participants were accompanied by two confederates who ignored the smoke, only 10 percent of them reported the smoke; and when they were accompanied by two other participants, neither of whom were told what was going on and both of whom saw the smoke, only 38 percent reported the smoke.

In Kitty Genovese's case, when the neighbors reported believing the attack to be a lovers' quarrel, their belief was likely validated, in part, by each neighbor seeing the other neighbors do nothing—at least nothing that they could see, such as someone running outside to stop the attacker. In this way, the inaction of others confirmed the belief that nothing was wrong.

Upon recognizing the need for help, people must then feel a personal responsibility to help. As more people are present, each individual is less likely to help, a phenomenon known as the **bystander effect** (Latane & Darley, 1968). That there is danger in numbers can be explained by each individual person feeling less of a personal responsibility for providing help; this is called **diffusion of responsibility**. In fact, even thinking about other people can reduce the likelihood of helping (Garcia, Weaver, Moskowitz, & Darley, 2002). If a person feels responsible for helping, then he is more likely to do so.

BYSTANDER EFFECT a phenomenon in which as more people are present, each individual is less likely to help

DIFFUSION OF RESPONSIBILITY a decreased feeling of responsibility to help in a group; if an emergency arises in a group setting, it is less likely that any one person will help than if someone was witnessing the emergency alone, because being in a group decreases each person's feeling of personal responsibility to help

In Darley and Latane's 1968 study examining the bystander effect, participants were exposed to the sounds of another student having an epileptic seizure. These sounds made very clear what was happening and that help was needed. Participants who were alone were faster to report the emergency than those who believed they were in the company of others—they were not actually able to see these others, but believed they were nearby. The more people participants believed were present, the slower they were to respond.

Moreover, sometimes we do not take responsibility for helping because we are embarrassed; this, too, may have accounted for the failure to help in the seizure study, as people may have felt embarrassed about interfering with its outcome. In another example, in 1993, 38 people witnessed two 10-year-old boys dragging a two-year-old boy for 2.5 miles but did not interfere because the boys said that they were the two-year-old's brothers. The two-year-old, James Bulger, was subsequently brutally murdered by those boys. It is fair to suppose that each person who saw the boy being dragged along and did nothing will regret it for the rest of his or her life. A lesson learned the hard way—if something seems amiss, and you hesitate to act out of embarrassment, it's often worth it to set those feelings aside and act anyway. You might just save a life.

In the next step of the decision model of bystander intervention, people must decide how to assist the person in need. If an obvious solution presents itself, people are more likely to provide effective help; however, if they do not know how to help or do not think that they could execute the helping act, they are less likely to do so. For instance, people with Red Cross training are more likely to provide effective assistance to those in need—not only do they know how to help, but they are confident in their abilities to administer the help, and so they engage in procedures that could save lives (Shotland & Heinold, 1985).

Such competence can actually increase the likelihood of helping. If someone is unsure of how to help, she may hesitate to act or be embarrassed to try to act. For instance, those trained in first aid or CPR are more likely to provide help than those not trained (Cramer, McMaster, Bartell, & Dragna, 1988; Shotland & Heinold, 1985). Thus, having any information regarding how to help would be beneficial in increasing the amount of help given.

There have been some differences found in how men and women help and the situations in which the genders will help. Men tend to be more likely to help in "heroic" ways—assisting with car trouble or rescuing a drowning child, for example (Eagly & Crowley, 1986; Penner, Dertke, & Achenbach, 1973; Piliavin & Unger, 1985). Women tend to help in more long-term, nurturing ways, such as providing emotional support or taking in an elderly parent (Aries & Johnson, 1983; McGuire, 1994). The source of these differences may not be genetic, but instead may be due to the gender norms that men should be heroic and women should be nurturing, or perhaps men's and women's beliefs about their own capabilities (Eagly & Crowley, 1986). A woman may not believe she has the strength to pull the child out of the pounding waves, and a man may not believe

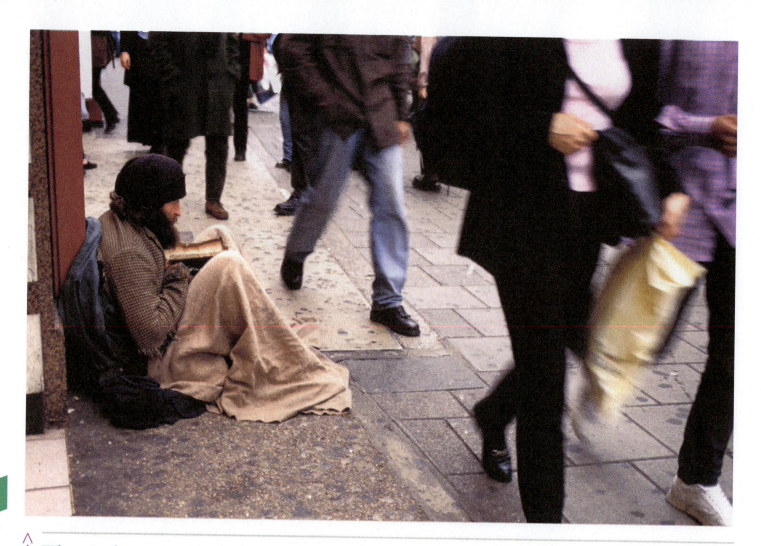

∧∧∧ When in the company of others, **we are less likely to help a person in need than when we are alone.**

that he would know how to tend to the needs of an elderly person. These gender differences in helping have been demonstrated to hold up across cultures (Johnson et al., 1989).

The final step in the decision model is the actual provision of help. In doing this, bystanders must consider a variety of factors, including how to implement their chosen way of helping. One important thing to note is that helpers must consider their own safety as well. If direct intervention is possible, then it ought to be done; however, if the person providing help places her own life at risk, and thus may not be of much assistance to the victim either, it might be better to provide help in a more indirect way, such as by calling 911. In many places, the value of helping others is held in such high regard that laws and rules have been created to protect people who act in good faith to help others. Good Samaritan protections in the United States and Canada focus on protecting people from being prosecuted or sued for injury or wrongful death as a result of helping another person. In Europe, the philosophy behind Good Samaritan laws is quite different—there, the failure to help someone in need when one is able to do so is actually criminalized.

USING THE FIVE STEPS TO HELP

Knowing the circumstances under which people provide each other with help, how can we ensure that we receive help when we need it? One way is to try to reduce the ambiguity of the situation—make it clear that there

is indeed an emergency occurring, and it is something in which others should intervene (Clark & Word, 1972). For instance, if you are being robbed, it might be wise to yell out quite specifically that you are being robbed and that someone should call 911. You might also benefit from stating that you do not know your attacker so that others do not think it is a lovers' quarrel, like in Kitty Genovese's situation (Shotland & Straw, 1976). In addition, to avoid diffusion of responsibility, if it is possible to select a bystander and request help specifically from him, do so, and make eye contact if you can (Moriarty, 1975; Shotland & Johnson, 1978; Shotland & Stebbins, 1980). By isolating one person and pleading with him for help, it becomes clear that he is the only person who can help, and is thus *responsible* for helping. Making such a clear request for assistance from an individual increases your odds of getting the help you need. People often believe that if they request help, others will not offer it (Flynn & Lake, 2008), but this is not the case. People can be quite responsive to direct requests for assistance in clear emergency situations.

What Are Other Influences on Helping?

In addition to the decision model of bystander intervention, there are other factors that contribute to increased or decreased likelihood of someone choosing to help another person in need.

Decision Model of Bystander Intervention

College campuses can often be dangerous places for young women. A 2010 analysis of the eight Ivy League schools as well as MIT, Duke, Stanford, and the University of Chicago found that three-quarters of the schools and the areas around them had sex offense rates 83 percent higher than the United States national rape average (Sullivan, 2010). But just as every student has a right to pursue an education at your school, every student also has the right to feel secure. You and your fellow students can work together as a community to promote a safe environment, but how would you respond if you saw someone being attacked? How would you respond if you were attacked?

Using what you've learned about Latane and Darley's five-step model of helping, design an educational campaign to help students become more knowledgeable about how to act in an emergency—both as the victim and as a potential witness. Imagine your school's Web site administrator has asked you to design a page to help students understand what to do in case of an emergency such as sexual assault. How would you describe and make the five-step model engaging for your classmates? Describe each step thoroughly, and don't forget to include a description of all of the obstacles that can arise when attempting to provide help. Make sure to do research on what's available on your campus. For instance, in discussing Step 4 (deciding how to help), be sure to include all resources available to students at your school—campus crisis hotlines, ways to get in touch with campus security, the closest locations for emergency phones and safe houses, etc. Find out what your school has to offer. Consider resources that don't currently exist but could be implemented at your school.

What will you learn from this action learning project?

1. Understand how to use social psychological research to increase prosocial behavior, and consider how to make your campus environment a safer place.

2. Learn how to teach people to monitor their own behavior in order to avoid falling prey to the obstacles to helping someone.

3. Become more likely to provide help in future situations. Experiments by Beaman and his colleagues (1978) demonstrated that when individuals learn about research on why people do and do not provide help, they are more likely to take responsibility in a situation that looks like someone needs help.

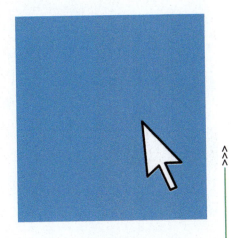

MOOD

Earlier in the chapter, you saw how one model of helping suggests that we help others to alleviate negative emotions. Can a positive mood also impact helping? It's been found that being in a good mood can lead to an increase in helping behavior by bystanders (Isen, Clark, & Schwartz, 1976; Carlson, Charlin, & Miller, 1988; North, Tarrant, & Hargreaves, 2004). In one study also mentioned earlier (Isen & Levin, 1972), participants were more likely to help others after experiencing positive events that presumably put them in a good mood, such as receiving cookies or finding a dime left in a payphone.

Just as you learned in Chapter 10 when you read about stereotypes, when you are in a good mood, you don't want to destroy that mood. Therefore, some researchers argue that we help others in an effort to maintain that good mood (Isen & Levin, 1972; Wegener & Petty, 1994). Another reason people are more helpful when they are in a good mood is that a good mood raises self-awareness. As you learned in Chapter 4, this heightened sense of self-awareness causes us to match our behavior to our actual self. In fact, we are more likely to engage in helping behaviors when in front of a mirror (Batson et al., 1999), a situation in which, as research has shown, we become more self-aware.

ATTRACTION

Another factor is attraction, whether due to appearance, behavior, or other qualities (Dovidio & Gaertner, 1983; Harrell, 1978; Kelley & Byrne, 1976; Kleinke, 1977). For instance, Benson, Karabenick, and Lerner (1976) showed that even when helping is anonymous and there is only a very slim chance of ever meeting the person helped, the attractiveness of the person requiring assistance leads to helping. In their study, people in phone booths discovered a completed graduate school application accompanied by a photograph of the applicant and an envelope addressed to the school. The photograph varied in attractiveness (attractive or unattractive), race (white or black), and gender of the applicant. When the applicant was attractive, people were much more likely to go ahead and mail the application than if the applicant was unattractive. In addition, there was an effect of race; whites were helped more than blacks by the all-white study subjects (for a review of helping and effects of race, see Saucier, Miller, & Doucet, 2005). There were no gender effects, either based on the gender of the helper or person being helped. This study showed that people were more likely to help others whom they perceived as attractive. Notably, these people had no reason to believe that they would ever meet these applicants in real life, so they were not potential candidates for a romantic relationship or even a friendship. Thus, the participants' helpfulness toward these attractive others was not designed to elicit any tangible goals for the helper, and yet the difference in helping still emerged.

> "Can a positive mood also impact helping?"

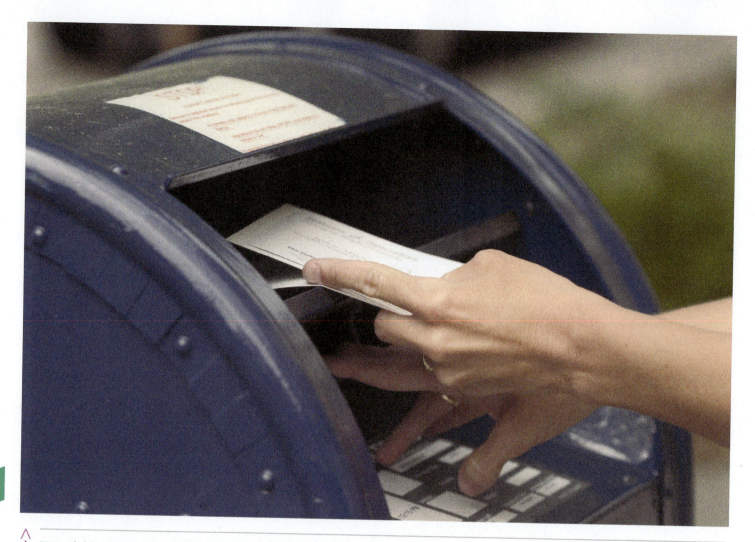

Would **attractiveness** make you more likely to **help someone you may never meet?**

SIMILARITY

Similarity also plays a role in likelihood of being helped. People are more likely to help others who are perceived to be similar to them than those individuals who are not (Dovidio, 1984). This effect will even be present in people who share the same birthday (Burger, Messian, Patel, del Prado, & Anderson, 2004). This may be the case, in part, because similarity leads to attraction (Byrne, 1971). What is similar is familiar, and people prefer what is familiar (Zajonc & Rajecki, 1969). This similarity can consist of being part of the same group, even if the party in distress is a stranger. In one study, students were made to think about their favorite soccer team, thereby activating their identity as a fan of that team. Each participant was then made to walk to another building, purportedly to be shown a video. On the way, he encountered a student who was injured and either wearing a shirt of the participant's favorite team, a shirt of a competitor, or a shirt with no team name. The injured student received more help when wearing a shirt of the participant's favorite team than when wearing either of the other kinds of shirts (Levine, Prosser, Evans, & Reicher, 2005). People who are fans of the same soccer team form an ingroup, and generally speaking, we are more likely to help ingroup rather than outgroup members (Levine et al., 2005).

When it comes to similarity and demographics, things get a little complicated. Reviews show that the impact of race is particularly complex (Crosby, Bromley & Saxe, 1980; Saucier, Miller, & Doucet,

2005). In general, whites and blacks discriminate against the opposite race equally. Some research shows that we are more likely to help same-race victims (Benson, Karabenick, & Lerner, 1976; Gaertner, 1973; Sissons, 1981). Much of this research is done only with black and white participants. However, some studies involving face-to-face interactions find that individuals are more likely to help victims of different races (Dutton, 1971; Katz, Sohn, & Zalk, 1975). Additionally, more recent research looking at volunteerism and race finds that both black and white participants attended the same amount of training sessions, and their contributions were equally evaluated by supervisors (Morrow-Howell, Elliott, & Ozawa, 1990).

Other factors include the sexual orientation of the individual requiring help. For instance, Gore, Tobiasen, and Kayson (1997) found that when a male or female victim made a telephone call to a participant and asked for help with reaching a girlfriend or boyfriend, 80 percent of heterosexuals versus 48 percent of homosexuals received help.

MIMICRY

Another positive influence on helping is mimicry. People tend to mimic one another somewhat automatically and will even mimic strangers in their language and bodily gestures. This mimicry tends to increase prosocial behavior (Chartrand & Bargh, 1999; van Baaren, Horgan, Chartrand, & Dijkmans, 2004). In a study, participants who were

ALTRUISTIC PERSONALITY a proposed personality composite consisting of five traits, each of which correlates positively with helping behavior: empathy, internal locus of control, belief in a just world, a sense of social responsibility, and low egocentrism

mimicked were more helpful and generous toward others than were participants who hadn't been mimicked (van Baaren et al., 2004). This increase in helpfulness wasn't limited to the person doing the mimicking, as you might expect. Rather, it extended to others with whom the participants came into contact.

Other studies have shown the same effect of increased helping behavior toward the mimicker as well as others incidentally encountered (van Baaren, Holland, Kawakami, & van Knippenberg, 2004). Being mimicked seems to increase prosocial orientation; research by Stel, van Baaren, and Vonk (2007) found that mimicry led to more charitable donations. One possible reason for this is that if others act as we do, we infer that they are similar to us. Another possibility is that this mimicry is an effort on our part to develop a common way of interacting—a shared perspective on the world and the way in which "things are done." Research has shown that establishing a shared reality with another person is a crucial way in which people bond and understand their worlds (Hardin & Higgins, 1996), and such a bond and shared understanding could promote helping behavior between people. Mimicry may also lead to feelings of empathy, which, in turn, result in an increase in helping behavior (Stel, van Baaren, & Vonk, 2007; Stel & Vonk, 2010). Stel and Vonk (2010) report that mimickers experienced more empathy in comparison to non-mimickers, leading to more help.

In studying mimicry, neuroscience complements social psychological research. Researchers have identified mirror neurons—brain cells that respond both when an action is performed and when that same action is observed in another—in both monkeys and humans (Iacoboni et al., 1999). Some researchers (Ramachandran, 2006) think that mirror neurons are critical to understanding the function of mimicry. Although this research is still in its infancy, the findings provide an interesting neurological look at empathy.

ALTRUISTIC PERSONALITY

In addition to all of these situational factors, one dispositional one may exist—an **altruistic personality**. Individuals thought to have this personality possess five traits that research has shown seem to correlate with helping behavior: empathy, an internal locus of control (leading those

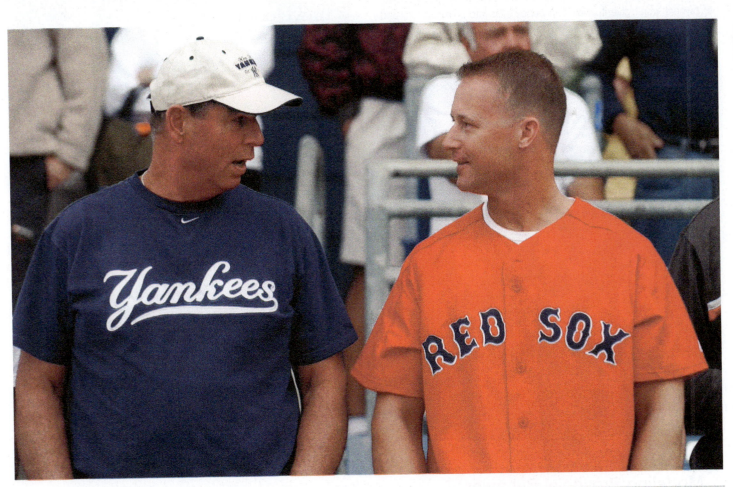

We are less likely to help people in whom we perceive a lack of similarity to ourselves.

people to consider themselves responsible for and able to control the circumstances around them), belief in a just world, a sense of social responsibility, and low egocentrism (Bierhoff, Klein, & Kramp, 1991). A 1991 study found all of these traits in people who had helped victims of traffic accidents (Bierhoff, Klein, & Kramp, 1991). As such, they may be used to predict people's tendencies to engage in helping behaviors.

MODELING

Another factor that increases the likelihood of help being given is the modeling of prosocial behavior (Bryan & Test, 1967). As discussed in previous chapters, people learn how to behave in part by observing how others behave (Bandura, 1962, 1965). The same is true with regard to helping behavior. If people observe others engaging in prosocial behavior—whether in the moment of an emergency or during repeated occasions earlier in their lives—they are more likely to do so themselves (Bryan & Test, 1967). Participants witnessed a driver in need being helped by another person (Bryan & Test, 1967). Sometime later, they encountered another driver in need who was not being helped. Seeing the first driver being helped increased the likelihood of participants helping the second driver (though it's worth noting that these drivers were alone, so the bystander effect is not applicable here). In this way, people use others' actions as cues for what they should do themselves.

Role models need not be physically present—they can be media figures as well (Forge & Phemister, 1987). In one experiment (Sprafkin, Liebert, & Poulos, 1975), children watched one of three video segments. One was a segment from *Lassie* in which Lassie hides her puppy so that her owners won't give it away. The puppy slips into a mine shaft, and Lassie's owner risks his life to save the puppy. Another was a segment from *Lassie* that did not involve any helping behavior. The third was a clip

from *The Brady Bunch* that emphasized family values and interaction. The children were then asked to listen to headphones for the sound of a dog barking—the headphones were supposedly emitting sounds from a kennel. They were told that if they heard a dog barking, they were to push a "help" button. Children who watched the clip where Lassie's owner saved the puppy held the button much longer than those exposed to the other videos; the results implied that the children learned from models in the media.

HOW IT FEELS TO BE HELPED

One final factor that influences helping is the way it feels to be helped. At first, it might seem that those being helped should be grateful—and in some cases, such as emergencies, they are. However, they aren't always grateful. Let's say you just finished working on a paper for your English literature course. You feel like you know a lot about the subject, and you're proud of your work. As it's coming out of the printer, your roommate happens to pick it up and immediately starts pointing out places in which it could be improved. How would that make you feel? Insulted, most likely. Research has shown that help that threatens one's self-esteem is unwelcome (Nadler, Fisher, & Itzhak, 1983; Shrout, Herman, &

> **Research has shown that help that threatens one's self-esteem is unwelcome.**

^ ^ ^ **Modeling Prosocial Behavior.** If we are exposed to role models who exhibit prosocial behavior, **we are more likely to exhibit such behaviors ourselves.**

∧
∧ **Help is only welcome** when it is offered with genuine intentions and **does not insult the target of**
∧ **the help** or threaten his or her self-esteem.

Bolger, 2006), and if the helper appears to exude an air of superiority, the help is seen as unwelcome as well. If we *feel* like we need help, we feel bad (Newsom, 1999). Help provided by enemies (Nadler, Fisher, & Streufert, 1974) or someone with many resources (Nadler & Fisher, 1974) has a negative effect on the person being helped. Overall, help is best received when the person being helped believes the helper is genuinely interested in helping (Ames, Flynn, & Weber, 2004) and is not doing so to humiliate, patronize, or demean.

up and help us when needed. Researchers (Mares & Woodard, 2005) conducted a meta-analysis, reviewing the existing literature on models for children's behavior found on television. Children who watched prosocial content had more positive interactions with others, exhibited more altruistic behavior, held fewer stereotypes, and were less aggressive. In addition, older children (around age six) benefited more than younger children (around age three), perhaps because they had the intellectual capacity to understand the meaning of the modeled behavior. Also, students who viewed a video clip of musicians thanking their mentors—thus showing

How Can We Increase Prosocial Behavior?

Now that we know what leads to prosocial behavior and what precludes it, how can we attempt to increase it in the general population? As we learned in Chapters 7 and 8, whether or not we get what we want often depends on the way we ask.

As we saw earlier, modeling helping behavior increases the likelihood of it occurring (e.g., Bryan & Test, 1967). As such, by modeling helping behavior to other people, we can increase the chances that they will step

> "Children who watched prosocial content had more positive interactions with others, **exhibited more altruistic behavior, held fewer stereotypes, and were less aggressive.**"

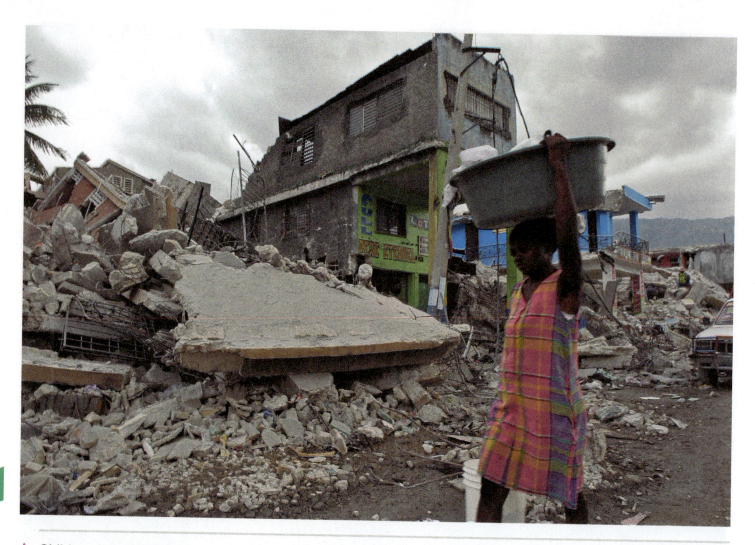

∧
∧   **Children, as well as adults,** are more likely to engage in helpful acts after witnessing others—even
∧   those in the media—do so. **One group's fundraiser for the victims of the Haiti earthquake illustrated this.**

appreciation for their prosocial behaviors toward the musicians—were more likely to volunteer to help the experimenter than those who viewed a neutral or humorous video clip (Schnall, Roper, & Fessler, 2010).

When my four-year-old son's preschool class learned about the 2010 earthquake in Haiti, they worked for two weeks making fresh lemonade and baked goods to sell as a fundraiser. They also decided to have a "race for Haiti," asking people to contribute $1 donations to compete with the kids in a race. Of course, their fundraising efforts were a huge success, and the experience will be something they carry with them as an example of the power of helping for the rest of their lives. Viewing prosocial behavior—and engaging in it—can lead to more of such behavior.

ATTRIBUTIONS

You're eating lunch with a friend when he casually asks if he can borrow your notes for the afternoon class you have together. "I just didn't bother taking any," he says, "and we have that exam on Friday." How would you react? Is it likely that you would comply with his request? Now, what if he'd said, "I try to take organized notes, but I feel like I'm looking at gibberish when I try to study. Would you please help me out?"

Chances are, you'd be more likely to help him in the second scenario, right? A research study (Barnes, Ickes, & Kidd, 1979) tested that very same

scenario, except the request was made by phone. The caller received much more help when he claimed to have tried and failed than when he admitted to not even bothering with taking notes.

When we consider helping others, a certain degree of importance is placed on our feelings about the person's responsibility. Even when the situation is less cut-and-dry, the effect is more or less the same. Pamela Dooley (1995) had study participants read stories about someone who had just been diagnosed with AIDS. Participants felt more pity and expressed more willingness to help when they read that the person contracted the disease through a blood transfusion than when they read it was through

> **When we consider helping others, a certain degree of importance is placed on our feelings about the person's responsibility.**

sexual activity or drug use. It seems we tend to be more willing to help another when we feel a situation is, to some degree, out of her control.

EDUCATION

People are receptive to learning about different behavioral choices and the psychological principles that attempt to explain them. This effect is what Kenneth Gergen (1973) termed the **enlightenment effect**, and it suggests that learning about psychology can bring about changes in behavior. Research has shown that learning about the bystander effect results in an increase in helping in group situations (Beaman et al., 1978). Thus, by reading this chapter and learning about what leads to helping behavior and what blocks or discourages it, you are already modifying your own future behavior. From now on, when you encounter an emergency situation, you

ENLIGHTENMENT EFFECT the effect wherein learning about how humans fall prey to obstacles to helping can aid us in overcoming those obstacles in the future; it extends to benefits from learning about other human biases

will be aware of the bystander effect and may be more conscious of the fact that you are only failing to help because there are others around. And perhaps you will then help, and maybe even save a life.

This awareness not only extends to how you will react in an emergency situation, but also how you will go about your day-to-day life. You may not be able to make a grand gesture, like the Salwens selling their home in the opening vignette, but you'll be surprised at the differences that small prosocial acts can make, both in your life and the lives of others.

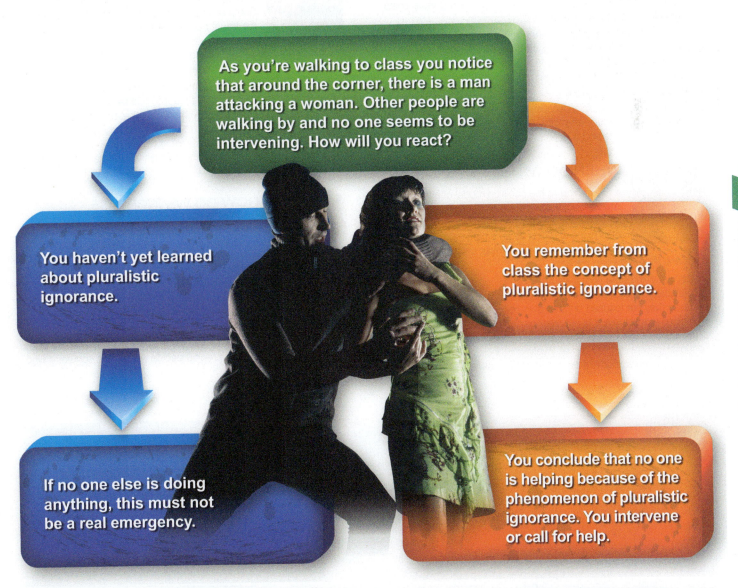

As you're walking to class you notice that around the corner, there is a man attacking a woman. Other people are walking by and no one seems to be intervening. How will you react?

You haven't yet learned about pluralistic ignorance.

You remember from class the concept of pluralistic ignorance.

If no one else is doing anything, this must not be a real emergency.

You conclude that no one is helping because of the phenomenon of pluralistic ignorance. You intervene or call for help.

Enlightened About Pluralistic Ignorance. By learning about psychological theories that help you understand your own thought processes and behaviors, you can avoid falling prey to the obstacles that may prevent you from helping others in need.

Summary

WHY DO WE HELP?   p. 244

• People may provide each other with help, otherwise termed *prosocial behavior*, for a variety of reasons. Some of these reasons may be egoistic (selfishly motivated) or altruistic (selflessly motivated).

• Egoistic models of prosocial behavior include the influences of existing negative mood, the desire to improve one's mood, and the relative costs and benefits of helping. Being in a negative mood, having no desire to improve one's mood, and perceiving more costs than benefits tend to decrease helping.

• Altruistic models of prosocial behavior include the influences of empathy, nurturing feelings toward the target, and a goal to promote the target's welfare on the likelihood of helping behavior. Each of these factors tends to increase helping.

• Models that discuss the influence of norms suggest that the norm of reciprocity increases helping, because we expect that if we help others, they will help us (and they often do). They also suggest that social norms about when helping is appropriate impact our tendency to help.

WHEN DO WE HELP?   p. 248

• According to the decision model of bystander intervention, there are five steps that are required for helping to occur: noticing the emergency, interpreting the situation as an emergency, feeling a personal responsibility to help, deciding how to help, and then providing the help.

• Being aware of the obstacles that arise in completing each step can enable you to overcome them. People do not notice emergencies because they are focused on their own concerns or are otherwise distracted—or the event is not clear or nearby. People do not interpret situations as emergencies when they are ambiguous, when the relationship between the parties involved is unclear, or when pluralistic ignorance occurs; if others do not seem to think there is an

emergency, we decide there must not be one. People do not accept responsibility for helping in groups—all the more when other people are present (diffusion of responsibility). Finally, people will not be able to decide how to help if they do not have the appropriate knowledge set or are insecure in that knowledge.

WHAT ARE OTHER INFLUENCES ON HELPING?   p. 252

• Many other factors can influence helping behavior. Some of these factors include the attractiveness of the target person (whether physical or in terms of personality), the similarity of the helper to the target person, behavioral mimicry of the helper, the helper having the five traits composing an "altruistic personality," and modeling of helping behavior.

• People do not always welcome help. Sometimes it is embarrassing to need help; people sometimes want to feel self-sufficient. People often do not like to be helped with matters that are tied to their self-esteem; in particular, they want to be able to accomplish things on their own in areas important to them. If the helper exudes superiority while helping, it will also make the help less welcome and less appreciated. Indeed, such assistance may hurt more than it helps.

HOW DO WE INCREASE PROSOCIAL BEHAVIOR?   p. 257

• People's tendency to help can be increased by others modeling prosocial behavior to them. Models can be real-life people or people in the media. Older children tend to benefit more from this sort of modeling, and it is prosocial behavior that must be modeled for helping to increase—not just positive behavior in general.

• By being educated about psychological principles related to prosocial behavior, you can apply them to your real-life situations and possibly catch yourself before you decide not to help someone who is truly in need.

Key Terms

altruistic having a selfless motivation for helping   244

altruistic personality a proposed personality composite consisting of five traits, each of which correlates positively with helping behavior: empathy, internal locus of control, belief in a just world, a sense of social responsibility, and low egocentrism   255

bystander effect a phenomenon in which as more people are present, each individual is less likely to help   251

cost-benefit analysis the act of weighing the relative costs and benefits of helping to decide whether or not to provide the help   245

decision model of bystander intervention the model derived by Bibb Latane and John Darley that explains the five steps required to provide help to someone in need and what can interfere

with successful completion of each of these steps   249

diffusion of responsibility a decreased feeling of responsibility to help in a group; if an emergency arises in a group setting, it is less likely that any one person will help than if someone was witnessing the emergency alone, because being in a group decreases each person's feeling of personal responsibility to help   251

egoistic having a selfish motivation for helping   244

empathy having compassion for others and a feeling of seeing the world through the eyes of another individual   244

empathy-altruism model of prosocial behavior a model suggesting that true altruism is a product of empathy; this empathy can create

nurturing feelings toward a target or a goal to increase the target's welfare   246

enlightenment effect the effect wherein learning about how humans fall prey to obstacles to helping can aid us in overcoming those obstacles in the future; it extends to benefits from learning about other human biases as well   259

kin selection the tendency of people to help their biological relatives over nonfamily members, even at great cost to themselves, thus favoring the reproductive success of one's relatives over his or her own survival   248

morally cleansing engaging in actions that restore, in one's own mind, the proper moral order   244

negative state relief model a model positing that the reason people help others is to improve their own negative mood 244

prosocial behavior behavior designed to help another person 244

reciprocity norm the idea that if others help us, we should help them, and that if we help them, they will help us 247

social responsibility norm the idea that we have social responsibility to help others; the extent to

which this extends to outgroup members varies by culture 247

Test Your Understanding

MULTIPLE CHOICE

1. Charitable donations activate the same brain region that is activated when
   a. we smile.
   b. we receive a monetary reward.
   c. we eat something we like.
   d. we are praised by a classmate.

2. Which of these does not factor into a cost-benefit analysis?
   a. emotional harm to oneself
   b. someone saying "thank you"
   c. increased popularity from helping
   d. emotional harm to the target

3. Why does positive mood influence helping?
   a. Rewards are more accessible.
   b. Penalties are more accessible.
   c. You like the target better.
   d. none of these

4. In the empathy-altruism model of prosocial behavior, what promotes helping?
   a. similarity
   b. nurturing feelings
   c. reciprocity norm
   d. attraction

5. According to research, if you give someone a soda and then ask him to buy your raffle tickets, he will
   a. buy more tickets.
   b. want to buy more tickets but not do it.
   c. offer to tell friends about the raffle.
   d. offer you a soda.

6. According to the decision model of bystander intervention, why might we not notice a need for help?
   a. distractions
   b. being self-focused
   c. distance from event
   d. all of the above

7. If others do not act as though there is an emergency happening, you will interpret the event as a nonemergency. This is called
   a. diffusion of responsibility.
   b. egoism.
   c. reciprocity effect.
   d. pluralistic ignorance.

8. People who have decided to help must figure out how to do so. What is not something that would stop them at this stage?
   a. feeling embarrassed
   b. limited time to help
   c. having no training in how to help
   d. lack of confidence in how to help

9. Which of these is a trait not necessarily possessed by someone with an altruistic personality?
   a. empathy
   b. social responsibility
   c. extroversion
   d. belief in a just world

10. Sometimes we don't want to be helped. Which of these is not a reason why?
    a. The person has fewer resources than we do.
    b. Doing it on our own is important to our self-esteem.
    c. The helper exudes superiority.
    d. The person has more resources than we do.

ESSAY RESPONSE

1. Consider the negative state relief model. Can we ever say for sure that this is not the cause of a given helpful behavior? What might we have to do to discount the possibility that the improvement of negative mood is the cause?

2. What does it take to help when doing so is costly to oneself? Consider the research in this chapter in your explanation.

3. The reciprocity norm was shown by infant research to be somewhat innate. What are the possible reasons for this? Consider evolutionary possibilities as well as perspectives regarding the individual's and culture's interests.

4. Consider why attraction might lead us to help someone whom we are likely never to meet. Discuss any egoistic, altruistic, normative, and alternative reasons that may exist.

5. Modeling has profound effects on long- and short-term behavior. Discuss some ways in which parents can inadvertently influence their children and we can inadvertently influence our peers.

APPLY IT!

Think about any time you've been out with your friends and seen a scuffle of some sort. Maybe you saw a couple fighting outside a restaurant. Maybe you saw two men shouting about something on the street. Maybe you saw a woman striking a child, or a man dragging an animal down the street. How could you have fairly assessed whether or not there was an emergency? How could you have responded in a way that would have provided needed help to a potential victim while still ensuring your own safety?

ANSWERS: 1. b; 2. d; 3. a; 4. b; 5. a; 6. d; 7. d; 8. b; 9. c; 10. a

Remember to check www.thinkspot.com for additional information, downloadable flashcards, and other helpful resources.

TH!NK READINGS

PSYCHOLOGICAL SCIENCE

The Smell of Virtue: Clean Scents Promote Reciprocity and Charity

By KATIE LILJENQUIST, CHEN-BO ZHONG and ADAM D. GALINSKY

Published: February 4, 2010

> "*The smell and taste of things remain poised a long time. . .and bear unfaltering, in the tiny and almost impalpable drop of their essence, the vast structure of recollection."*
> (Proust, 1928, p. 65)

As Proust's words so eloquently express, a familiar smell can transport us to an exact time and place in our past. Indeed, psychologists have found that scents can dutifully retrieve images and feelings from the deepest recesses of the mind (Chu & Downes, 2000; Doop, Mohr, Folley, Brewer, & Park, 2006). Not only do smells activate memories, they can also influence judgment (Schnall, Haidt, Clore, & Jordan, 2008) and even regulate behavior. For example, Holland, Hendriks, and Aarts (2005) found that exposure to citrus cleaning scents enhanced the mental accessibility of cleaning-related constructs and led participants to maintain a cleaner environment while eating. Based on the symbolic association between physical and moral purity, we introduce a provocative possibility: clean smells might not only regulate physical cleanliness, but may also motivate virtuous behavior. Indeed, moral transgressions can engender literal feelings of dirtiness (Zhong & Liljenquist, 2006). Just as many symbolic associations are reciprocally related

(Lakoff, 1987), such as coldness and loneliness (Zhong & Leonardelli, 2008) or darkness and depravity (Frank & Gilovich, 1988), morality and cleanliness may also be reciprocally linked. In the current research, we investigate whether clean scents can transcend the domain of physical cleanliness and promote virtuous behavior.

Experiment 1: Promoting Reciprocity

Experiment 1 tested the impact of clean scents on reciprocating trust. We chose this behavior because Aristotle advocated justice in exchange as a primary "moral virtue" (Aristotle, c330BC/1999) and because studies have identified traits like fairness and generosity as central to moral identity (Aquino & Reed, 2002).

Twenty-eight participants (12 female) were individually assigned to either a *clean-scented* room or a *baseline* room. The only difference between the two rooms was a spray of citrus-scented Windex in the clean-scented room.

In both conditions, participants engaged in a one-shot anonymous trust game (Berg, Dickaut, & McCabe, 1995) involving two parties: a sender and receiver. In a typical trust game,

the sender is given money that he can choose to keep or "invest" with an anonymous receiver. Any money sent is tripled, and the receiver then decides how to split the tripled money. For example, if the sender passes all of the money and the receiver reciprocates this trust by returning half of the tripled amount, both would be better off. However, sending money can be risky if the receiver chooses to exploit the sender and keep all the invested money (Camerer, 2003).

All the participants in the current experiment were told they had been randomly assigned to play the role of the *receiver* and that their ostensible counterpart had decided to send them the full amount ($4) which was now tripled to $12. They had to decide how much money to keep or return to the sender. Participants could exploit their counterpart by keeping all the money or they could honor the trust by returning some portion to the other party.

As predicted, participants in the clean-scented rooms returned significantly more money than those in the baseline condition, $t(26) = 2.64$, $p = .01$, $d = 1.03$ (see Table 1). The clean-scented room led participants to resist exploitation and reciprocate the trusting behavior of the sender.

Table 1 Reciprocation of trusting behavior in Experiment 1. Volunteerism and donation rate in Experiment 2. Standard deviations are in parentheses.

	Experiment 1 Money Returned	Experiment 2 Volunteering Interest	Willingness to Donate
Clean Scent	$5.33 (2.01)	4.21 (1.86)	22%
Baseline (No Scent)	$2.81 (2.81)	3.29 (2.04)	6%

Margin notes:

Based on what you learned in Chapter 13, which influences on prosocial behavior might this symbolic association be most closely linked to?

This result demonstrates the reciprocity norm discussed in Chapter 13. But how might an egoistic model of prosocial behavior explain the outcome? How would an altruistic model of helping explain it?

Experiment 2: Promoting Charity

Experiment 2 was designed to replicate the conceptual pattern of Experiment 1 by exploring whether clean scents would motivate another aspect of moral virtue: charity (Aristotle, c330BC/1999; Machan, 1998). Ninety-nine undergraduate students (50 female) were individually assigned to either a *clean-scented* room (sprayed with Windex) or a *baseline no-scent* room and asked to work on a packet of unrelated tasks. Included in the packet was a flier requesting volunteers for a charity, Habitat for Humanity. Participants indicated their interest level in volunteering for future Habitat efforts (1–7 scale), specified the activities they would like to assist with, and selected whether they wanted to donate funds to the cause (yes/no). To rule out mood as a driver of the effects of clean scents, participants completed a shortened version of the PANAS (Watson, Clark & Tellegen, 1988).

As predicted, participants in the clean-scented environment expressed greater interest in volunteering than control participants, $t(97) = 2.33$, $p = .02$, $d = .47$. Additionally, a greater proportion of participants in the clean-scented rooms indicated a willingness to donate money, $\chi^2(1, N = 99) = 4.78$, $p = .03$ (see Table 1). Room scent had no impact on positive nor negative affect (p's > .20), and when controlling for affect, room scent continued to have a significant effect on volunteerism and donation rate (p's < .05). Because our charity measures captured intentions, future research should measure behavior directly.

Discussion

Two experiments demonstrated that clean scents not only motivate clean behavior, but also promote virtuous behavior by increasing the tendency to reciprocate trust and to offer charitable help. Capitalizing on the fact that abstract concepts are often symbolically derived from the concrete environment (Emerson, 1836), our results suggest that olfactory cues can trigger virtuous behaviors that are related to cleanliness at only a symbolic level. The link from cleanliness to virtuous behavior appears to be a nonconscious one: in neither experiment did participants recognize an influence of scent on their behavior, and in Experiment 2, perceived cleanliness did not differ by condition nor correlate with the effects.

These findings carry important implications for environmental regulation of behavior. Evidence abounds of how people lose their moral footing, how saints become sinners. However, there is much less understanding of what can lead sinners toward the path of virtue. By demonstrating that the association between morality and cleanliness is bidirectional, the current research identifies an unobtrusive way—a clean scent—to curb exploitation and promote altruism.

Beyond olfactory cues, there is the possibility that visual cleanliness can also influence morality (Liljenquist, Zhong, & Galinsky, 2008), which is consistent with the "broken windows" theory of crime that argues damage and disrepair in the environment promote lawless behavior. The current findings suggest there is some truth to the claim that cleanliness is next to godliness; clean scents summon virtue, helping reciprocity prevail over greed, and charity over apathy.

References

Aquino, K., & Reed, A. II. (2002). The self-importance of moral identity. *Journal of Personality and Social Psychology, 83,* 1423–1440.

Aristotle. (1999). *Aristotle: Nicomachean ethics.* (T. H. Irwin, Trans.). Indianapolis, IN: Hackett Publishing Company. (Original work published c330BC).

Berg, J., Dickaut, J., & McCabe, K. (1995). Trust, reciprocity and social history. *Games and Economic Behavior, 10,* 122–42.

Camerer, C. (2003). *Behavioral game theory: Experiments in strategic interaction.* Princeton, New Jersey: Princeton University Press.

Doop, M., Mohr, C., Folley, B., Brewer, W., & Park, S. (2006). Olfaction and memory. In W. Brewer, D. Castle, & C. Pantelis (Eds.), *Olfaction and the brain.* (pp. 65–82) Cambridge: Cambridge University Press.

Emerson, R. W. (1836). Nature. In A.R. Fersonson & J.F. Carr (Eds.), *The essays of Ralph Waldo Emerson* (pp. 315–332). Cambridge, MA: Belknap Press.

Frank, M. G., & Gilovich, T. (1988). The dark side of self-and social perception: Black uniforms and aggression in professional sports. *Journal of Personality and Social Psychology, 54(1),* 74–85.

Holland, R.W., Hendriks, M., & Aarts, H. (2005). Smells like clean spirit: Nonconscious effects of scent on cognition and behavior. *Psychological Science, 16(9),* 689–693.

Lakoff, G. (1987). *Women, fire, and dangerous things.* Chicago, IL: University of Chicago Press.

Liljenquist, K. A., Zhong, C., & Galinsky, A. D. (2008, August). Environmental cleanliness and the regulation of ethical behavior. In F. Gino (Chair), *Environmental and outcome-based influences on unethical behavior.* Paper presented at Academy of Management, Anaheim, CA.

Machan, T. R. (1998). *Generosity: Virtue in the civil society.* Washington D.C.: Cato Institute.

Proust, M. (1928), *Swann's way* (C. K. Scott-Moncrieff, Trans.). New York: The Modern Library.

Schnall, S., Haidt, J., Clore, G. L., & Jordan, A. H. (2008). Disgust as embodied moral judgment. *Personality and Social Psychology Bulletin, 34,* 1096–1109.

Watson, D., Clark, L. A., & Tellegen, A. (1988). Development and validation of brief measures of positive and negative affect: The PANAS scale. *Journal of Personality and Social Psychology, 54,* 1063–1070.

Wilson, J. Q., & Kelling, G. L. (1982). Broken windows: The police and neighborhood safety. *Atlantic Monthly, 249,* 29–38.

Zhong, C. B., & Leonardelli, G. J. (2008). Cold and lonely: Does social exclusion literally feel cold? *Psychological Science, 19(9),* 838–842.

Zhong, C., & Liljenquist, K. A. (2006). Washing away your sins: Threatened morality and physical cleansing. *Science, 313,* 1451–1452.

If cleanliness was able to motivate people to return a favor, how did it motivate people to behave prosocially of their own accord? Why might the negative state relief model factor into this?

How might this finding factor into whether or not a person chooses to give money to a homeless person? How does it tie into the idea that attraction and similarity influence helping behavior?

Now that you have a well-rounded idea of the different ways research methods are implemented in social psychology, how would you use replication to strengthen the findings of this experiment?

GLOSSARY

accessibility   the degree to which a concept is active in our consciousness (p. 104)

actor-observer effect   the tendency people have to make dispositional inferences for others' behavior but situational attributions for their own (p. 79)

affective forecasting   the process of predicting the impact future events will have on our overall emotional states (p. 62)

aggression   behavior, either verbal or physical, that is used to intentionally harm another individual (p. 202)

altruistic   having a selfless motivation for helping (p. 244)

altruistic personality   a proposed personality composite consisting of five traits, each of which correlates positively with helping behavior: empathy, internal locus of control, belief in a just world, a sense of social responsibility, and low egocentrism (p. 255)

ambivalence   simultaneously experiencing strong contradictory emotions or motivations (p. 96)

ambivalent sexism   the contradictory attitudes of hostile sexism and benevolent sexism (p. 180)

amygdala   a small structure found in the medial temporal lobe of the brain's limbic system that is involved in automatic processing and emotion (p. 43)

anchoring and adjustment heuristic   a heuristic in which we use a number as a starting point on which to anchor our judgment (p. 48)

applied research in social psychology   the use of the ideas of social psychology to address issues in other fields (p. 9)

archival studies   research that entails culling information from existing records ranging from magazine articles to Web site analytics (p. 27)

attachment style   the degree of security experienced in interpersonal relationships (p. 225)

attitudes   having an evaluative component toward a stimulus that is made up of affective, behavioral, and cognitive information (p. 96)

attribution   deciding who or what is responsible for the outcome of a situation; another way we cope with failure and respond to success in order to maintain self-esteem (p. 67)

authoritarian personality   a personality type that favors obedience to authority and intolerance of people lower in status (p. 183)

automatic processing   the processing of information "on the fly," using schemas as shortcuts (p. 42)

availability heuristic   a rule used to estimate the likelihood of a given occurrence based on how easily one can recall an example of that occurrence (p. 44)

aversive experience   an undesirable experience that may include pain, discomfort, overcrowding, or attack (p. 211)

aversive racism   the attitudes of whites who openly endorse egalitarian views but discriminate in ways they're able to rationalize (p. 182)

bargaining   a means of resolving conflict that involves each side of the dispute making offers, counteroffers, and concessions (p. 168)

base rate fallacy   an erroneous conclusion reached when the representative heuristic is used to draw a conclusion without considering the base rate (p. 46)

basic research in social psychology   the fundamental ideas behind behavior and cognitive processes (p. 9)

belief in a just world   people have to believe the world is fair and adjust their other beliefs to maintain that stance by concluding that bad things happen to bad people and good things happen to good people (p. 80)

belief perseverance   holding on to one's beliefs, even in the face of contradictory evidence (p. 84)

biased perception   the belief that we are justified in our own thoughts and actions but that others are biased in their beliefs and behaviors (p. 168)

BIRGing   "basking in reflected glory," a strategy by which we reinforce our positive self-concepts by identifying ourselves with successful others (p. 69)

bystander effect   a phenomenon in which as more people are present, each individual is less likely to help (p. 251)

central route   a type of processing that occurs when an individual has the ability and motivation to thoroughly listen to and evaluate a persuasive message (p. 116)

chameleon effect   the nonconscious mimicry of postures, mannerisms, facial expressions, and other behaviors of one's interaction partner, such that one's behavior passively and unintentionally changes to match that of others in one's current social environment (p. 138)

chronic accessibility   accessibility arising from frequent and recent exposure to a construct that has permanence—i.e., it is accessible all of the time (p. 104)

classical conditioning   a type of learning by which a neutral stimulus gets paired with a stimulus (UCS) that elicits a response (UCR). Through repeated pairings, the neutral stimulus (CS) by itself elicits the response (CR) of the second stimulus. (p. 98)

cognitive dissonance   the anxiety that arises from acting in a way discordant with your attitudes. This anxiety is resolved by adjusting one's attitudes to be in line with the behavior (p. 106)

cognitive-neoassociation theory   a theory that suggests that when a person experiences something with a negative result, such as pain or discomfort, aggressive behavior can often occur in the wake of that experience (p. 207)

cohesion   the degree to which a group is connected (p. 156)

collectivism   a cultural focus on the self as interdependent and defined by the connectedness of people to one another, in particular, the people closest to them (p. 60)

communal relationship   a relationship in which partners expect mutual responsiveness to one another's needs (p. 232)

companionate love   the affection we feel for people with whom our lives are deeply intertwined (p. 230)

compliance   a form of social influence involving direct requests from one person to another (p. 146)

conditioned response (CR)   a learned response to the conditioned stimulus that was previously a neutral stimulus (p. 98)

conditioned stimulus (CS) a stimulus that, only by repeated association with a particular unconditioned stimulus, comes to evoke the response associated with the unconditioned stimulus (p. 98)

confederate an individual who is part of the research team and is placed in the experiment to play a particular role (p. 12)

confirmation bias the tendency to notice information that confirms one's beliefs and to ignore information that disconfirms one's beliefs (p. 13, 84)

conflict the perceived incompatibility of actions, goals, or ideas (p. 166)

conformity a type of social influence in which an individual changes his or her behaviors to stay in line with social norms (p. 142)

confound any difference other than the levels of the independent variable between the experimental group and the control group (p. 31)

contact hypothesis the belief that increased communication and contact between different racial groups reduces levels of prejudice and discrimination (p. 190)

control group the group that does not get the main treatment in an experiment, but is used as a baseline to compare results with the experimental group (p. 29)

controlled processing a type of mental processing that takes purposeful thought and effort as decisions or courses of action are weighed carefully (p. 42)

CORFing "cutting off reflective failure," a strategy by which we try to disassociate ourselves from others who have failed or behaved poorly (p. 69)

correlational research research in which researchers do not manipulate variables but observe whether there is a relationship between two variables (p. 27)

correspondence bias the tendency of people to make dispositional attributions for others' behaviors (p. 77)

correspondent inference theory the theory that people base their inferences regarding the source of others' behaviors on whether or not the behavior was freely chosen, if the consequences are distinctive, and if the behavior was socially desirable (p. 76)

cost-benefit analysis the act of weighing the relative costs and benefits of helping to decide whether or not to provide the help (p. 245)

counterfactual thinking the tendency to imagine alternative outcomes for an event (p. 50)

covariation theory the theory that people base their inferences regarding the source of others' behaviors on whether or not there is a consensus regarding the way one ought to respond, the distinctiveness of the response, and the consistency of the person's response across situations (p. 76)

culture of honor a culture in which strong norms suggest that aggression is an appropriate response to an insult or threat to one's honor (p. 204)

debriefing procedure of giving participants a full explanation of the hypothesis being tested, procedures used to deceive participants, and the reasons for deception (p. 33)

deception providing participants with false or incomplete information (p. 33)

decision model of bystander intervention the model derived by Bibb Latane and John Darley that explains the five steps required to provide help to someone in need and what can interfere with successful completion of each of these steps (p. 249)

deindividuation the tendency for an individual within a group to let go of self-awareness and restraint and do what the group is doing (p. 161)

dependent variable the variable the experimenter does not control that is used to measure whether the change in the independent variable has an effect (p. 29)

descriptive norms how people typically behave in a given group or situation (p. 140)

descriptive research research used to obtain information regarding the current status of a population or phenomena to describe the who, what, when, where, and how questions with respect to variables or conditions in a situation (p. 25)

desensitization when physiological reactions to violence are reduced as a result of repeated exposure (p. 214)

differential construal the act of judging circumstances differently (p. 13)

diffusion of responsibility a decreased feeling of responsibility to help in a group; if an emergency arises in a group setting, it is less likely that any one person will help than if someone was witnessing the emergency alone, because being in a group decreases each person's feeling of personal responsibility to help (p. 251)

direct aggression an action or behavior that is clearly derived from the aggressor and is aimed directly at the target (p. 203)

discrimination a behavior directed toward a group of people based solely on their membership in that group (p. 176)

dismissive attachment style a conflicted, insecure attachment style characterized by high self-esteem and low interpersonal trust (p. 226)

distraction conflict theory the idea that a person performing a task in front of others experiences a conflict of attention between the audience and the task at hand, thus increasing the motivation to succeed when completing simple tasks (p. 158)

dispositional attribution inferring that a person's traits, something internal, caused his or her behavior (p. 76)

door-in-the-face technique a compliance technique in which the requester makes an initial offer that is much larger than the target offer, in the hope that the final offer will have the appearance of the requester doing a favor of the target person (p. 147)

double-blind study study in which neither the experimenter nor the participant knows which group is experimental and which is control (p. 32)

downward social comparison the process of comparing yourself to someone who is less capable or worse off than you are (p. 68)

egoistic having a selfish motivation for helping (p. 244)

Elaboration Likelihood Model (ELM) a model of persuasion that proposes that there are two different routes, central and peripheral, that an individual may take when processing a message. The route is impacted by cognitive capacity and individual differences of the perceiver. (p. 117)

empathy having compassion for others and a feeling of seeing the world through the eyes of another individual (p. 244)

empathy-altruism model of prosocial behavior a model suggesting that true altruism is the product of empathy;

this empathy can create nurturing feelings toward a target or a goal to increase the target's welfare (p. 246)

enlightenment effect the effect wherein learning about how humans fall prey to obstacles to helping can aid us in overcoming those obstacles in the future; it extends to benefits from learning about other human biases as well (p. 259)

equity theory theory that relationships are most satisfying when the ratio between benefits and contributions is similar for both partners (p. 232)

evaluation apprehension the idea that one's performance will be hindered or heightened due to approval or disapproval from others (p. 158)

evolutionary perspective a perspective that focuses on the physical and biological predispositions that result in human survival (p. 10)

exchange relationship a relationship in which partners expect strict reciprocity (p. 232)

excitation transfer the process by which arousal from one stimulus can be transferred to the second stimulus, a person (p. 230)

experimental group in an experiment, the group that gets the main treatment or manipulation (p. 29)

experimental research research that attempts to control all the factors (like a potential third variable) that may affect the results of an experiment (p. 28)

experimenter bias bias exhibited by the experiment administrator in inadvertently but subtly changing his or her behavior toward participants because of knowledge of which group is control and which group experimental; this also occurs when the researcher subconsciously shows bias in his or her evaluation of results in an effort to reach the desired conclusion (p. 32)

explicit attitudes attitudes of which one is aware and that one can control (p. 96)

expressive view of aggression a method of aggression in which aggression is used as a way to express anger and reduce stress (p. 203)

external validity the extent to which results apply to a general population (p. 28)

extrinsic motivation the drive to perform an action in response to external pressure or obligation, to avoid punishment, or to achieve some outside benefit (p. 64)

facial feedback hypothesis a hypothesis that states that a change in our facial expressions can lead to a subsequent emotional change (p. 64)

false consensus effect a phenomenon that causes individuals to assume that everyone shares the same opinion they do (p. 13)

fear-based appeal an attempt to provoke fear in an audience in order to persuade them not to do something (p. 119)

fearful-avoidant attachment style the most insecure of the attachment styles, characterized by low self-esteem and low interpersonal trust (p. 226)

foot-in-the-door technique a compliance technique that begins with a small request that, when granted, leads to a larger request (p. 147)

forewarning the process of being informed ahead of time that a favored attitude will be challenged (p. 127)

framing heuristic a rule that guides decision making based on the framework in which a situation or item is presented (p. 49)

frustration a feeling of being upset or annoyed by the inability to reach a goal or perform an activity (p. 207)

frustration aggression theory a theory stating that frustration precedes aggression because our motivation for aggression increases when our current behavior is interrupted or we are prevented from reaching a goal (p. 207)

fundamental attribution error a more commonly known name for the correspondence bias. The scientific community now leans toward using "correspondence bias" so as not to suggest that these inferences are inherently in "error" (p. 77)

gender prejudice the tendency to hold a hostile attitude toward an individual because of his or her gender (p. 179)

gender stereotypes people's ideas about how men and women behave based on socially and culturally defined beliefs (p. 179)

General Aggression Model (GAM) a theory that builds on the social learning theory and provides a more integrative framework for specific theories of aggression by including situational and personal variables (p. 209)

GRIT stands for "graduated and reciprocated initiatives in tension reduction"; a step-by-step formula for de-escalating a conflict that involves unilateral concessions and quick reciprocation by the opposition (p. 169)

group two or more people who are seen as a unit and interact with one another (p. 156)

group norms rules or expectations regarding desirable behaviors that group members strive to follow (p. 164)

group polarization the tendency for an attitude or belief to become magnified within a group after members discuss an issue amongst themselves (p. 162)

groupthink a manner of thinking that happens when the desire for harmony in a decision-making group overrides a realistic evaluation of other solutions (p. 163)

halo effect when one positive thing is known or believed about a target person, we tend to infer that the individual is positive overall and thus has other positive features. (p. 83)

heuristics simple rules that reduce mental effort and allow us to make decisions or judgments quickly (p. 44)

hindsight bias the tendency to think that one knew that something would occur all along (p. 12)

hostile (affective) aggression a behavior that occurs when the primary goal of an action is to make the victim suffer (p. 202)

hostile attribution bias occurs when people assume that the intentions of another person are hostile (p. 167)

hypothesis a proposed explanation that can be either supported or disproven with statistics or observations (p. 22)

illusion of control the perception of uncontrollable events as being controllable (p. 49)

Implicit Association Test (IAT) test that measures how easily we associate categories with positive or negative attitudes, including measures in categories ranging from racial and religious attitudes to attitudes about presidents (http://implicit.harvard.edu/implicit/demo/) (p. 101)

implicit attitudes attitudes that are automatically formed and activated without our even being aware of it (p. 96)

impression management the process by which people either consciously or unconsciously attempt to monitor how they appear to others by regulating the information conveyed about themselves in a social interaction, and thus attitude change is more likely when counterattitudinal behavior occurs in public (p. 108)

independent variable the variable the experimenter has control over and can alter (p. 29)

indirect aggression an action or behavior that is not clearly derived from the aggressor, and where it is not obvious to the target that he or she has been the victim of aggression (p. 203)

individualism at the cultural level, focus on the self as independent from others and defining individual goals over the collective (p. 60)

informational social influence a type of influence that occurs when one turns to members of one's group to obtain accurate information (p. 142)

informed consent when subjects are told at the beginning of a study as much information as possible about the participation in the study to determine if they would like to be involved (p. 33)

ingratiation a way of controlling others' impressions of us through flattery (p. 69)

ingratiation techniques techniques in which we get others to like us so they are more likely to comply with a request (p. 146)

ingroup favoritism the natural tendency to favor an ingroup versus an outgroup (p. 183)

injunctive norms behaviors of which people typically approve or disapprove of in a given group or situation (p. 140)

inoculation the process of building up resistance to unwanted persuasion (p. 128)

instinct theory a theory in which aggression is an innate and inevitable force (p. 205)

institutional review board (IRB) a committee that has been established to approve and oversee research that involves human and non-human subjects (p. 33)

instrumental aggression a behavior that occurs when the primary goal of an action is not to make the victim suffer, but to attain a non-injurious goal (p. 202)

internal validity the ability to infer cause and effect; that the variable was manipulated was the only factor to change across conditions and so was what led to the observed effect (p. 28)

interpersonal trust involves the believe that people are generally trustworthy and dependable as opposed to the opposite and is the attitude that underlies the development of attachment styles (p. 226)

intrinsic motivation the drive to perform an action because we enjoy it and are likely to engage in it more fully and with greater curiosity and pleasure (p. 64)

introspection the process of thinking about your own thoughts (p. 61)

investment those resources that have been devoted to a relationship that cannot be retrieved (p. 232)

jigsaw classroom technique teaching method that focuses on small-group activities and fosters a cooperative rather than competitive environment (p. 190)

just-world hypothesis the tendency for people to believe that the world is fair and just; therefore, victims of misfortune deserve what happens to them (p. 185)

kin selection the tendency for people to help their biological relatives over non-family members, even at great cost to themselves, thus favoring the reproductive success of one's relatives over his or her own survival (p. 248)

limbic system the area of the brain thought to be crucial to emotional processing and memory (p. 43)

lowball technique a compliance technique in which a target accepts a "low-cost" offer, only then to be told that there are additional hidden costs (p. 147)

matched samples design research design in which two or more groups of individuals are identical, or matching, in terms of the third variable (p. 27)

matching hypothesis the hypothesis that people are more likely to form long-standing relationships with others whose social attributes match theirs and with those who are similar in physical attractiveness (p. 224)

mere exposure the hypothesis that the mere repeated exposure of an individual to a stimulus is enough for an increase in favorable response to that stimulus (p. 221)

mere exposure effect the phenomenon whereby objects become better-liked with exposure—we like things more with which we are familiar (p. 98)

minority influence a process in which a small number of people within a group guide a change in the group's attitude or behavior (p. 145)

modeling a process by which a person mimics another's behavior (p. 208)

modern racism negative feelings toward a group of people based on their race, manifested in more subtle forms of racism (p. 180)

modern sexism internalized negative feelings toward a group of people based on their gender, characterized by a denial of continued discrimination, antagonism toward women's demands, and lack of support for policies designed to help women in work and education (p. 180)

mood congruence effect the fact that we are more likely to remember positive information when in a positive mood, and negative information when in a negative mood (p. 51)

mood dependent memory the fact that the mood we are in when we learn information may serve as a retrieval clue when we try to remember that information (p. 51)

morally cleansing engaging in actions that restore, in one's own mind, the proper moral order (p. 244)

name-letter effect the tendency to show a preference for letters in our own names and prefer stimuli that contain those letters (p. 98)

natural selection the process whereby individuals with certain characteristics are more frequently represented in subsequent generations are the result of being better adapted for their environments (p. 11)

naturalistic observation research that involves watching behavior in a real-world setting (p. 25)

need for affiliation the desire to establish and maintain rewarding interpersonal relationships (p. 220)

need for cognition the need that some individuals have to think, solve problems, and understand their world accurately (p. 79)

negative attributional style occurs when a person explains his or her partner's behaviors in negative ways (p. 234)

negative state relief model a model positing that the reason people help others is to improve their own negative mood (p. 244)

negativity bias the tendency for people to be more sensitive to and more likely to notice and remember negative information, which then influences the evaluation of people and situations (p. 49)

nonverbal cues behaviors, gestures, and expressions that convey thought or emotion without words (p. 86)

normative social influence a type of influence that occurs when one goes along with a group because one wants to be accepted (p. 142)

obedience a form of social influence in which an individual orders another person to do something (p. 148)

observational learning acquiring an attitude or behavior due to the observation of others exhibiting that attitude or behavior (p. 99)

old-fashioned racism overt, oppressive acts and feelings toward a group of people based on their race (p. 180)

old-fashioned sexism overt sexism, characterized by the endorsement of traditional gender roles, differential treatment of men and women, and stereotypes about lesser female competence (p. 180)

operant conditioning a type of learning in which the frequency of a behavior is determined by reinforcement and punishment (p. 99)

operational definition a definition that assigns one or more specific operational conditions to an event and then identifies how those conditions should be measured (p. 22)

optimistic bias the belief that bad things will happen to other people and that an individual is more likely to experience good things in life (p. 50)

outcome-relevant involvement the degree to which the economic or social outcome promoted in the message is important to the receiver (p. 121)

outgroup homogeneity effect the tendency to see out-group members as similar to one another but ingroup members as diverse individuals (p. 183)

overconfidence barrier a state of having more confidence in one's judgment or control over a situation that is really justified (p. 50)

participant bias bias that occurs when a participant's suspicions, expectations, or assumptions about the study influence the result (p. 31)

passionate love a state of intense longing for union with another (p. 229)

peer review a process by which experts in the field review and comment on each other's work (p. 22)

peripheral route a type of processing that occurs when an individual lacks the ability and motivation to thoroughly listen to and evaluate a persuasive message, and is therefore influenced by external cues like attractiveness of the speaker (p. 116)

perseverance effect the tendency for a schema to remain intact, even when it comes up against discrediting information (p. 41)

persuasion the way people communicate in order to influence other people's attitudes and behaviors (p. 116)

placebo effect a measurable or observable improvement in health or behavior that is not attributed to medication or any other treatment given (p. 32)

pluralistic ignorance when a person may privately think there may be an emergency, but seeing others do nothing leads him or her to infer that there is no need to provide help (p. 142)

post-decision dissonance cognitive dissonance that results from having to reject one appealing choice in favor of another (p. 107)

prefrontal cortex the part of the brain that plays a role in higher-order thinking, including judgment, decision making, and evaluation (p. 43)

prejudice a negative learned attitude toward particular groups of people (p. 176)

preoccupied attachment style a conflicted, insecure attachment style characterized by low self-esteem and high interpersonal trust (p. 226)

primacy effect the phenomenon whereby the first pieces of information to which we are exposed have the most impact on our judgments (p. 82)

prime to activate a schema through a stimulus (p. 40)

private conformity a type of conformity that occurs when people truly believe the group is right; occurs even in the absence of group members (p. 142)

proportion of similarity an equation that divides the number of topics on which two people express similar views by the total number of topics on which they have communicated, resulting in a prediction of attraction (p. 224)

prosocial behavior behavior designed to help another person (p. 244)

proximity physical closeness; the smaller the physical distance, the more likely two people will experience repeat contact, which could lead to the development of mutual attraction (p. 221)

public conformity a type of conformity that occurs when we feel pressured to conform to group norms. When publicly conforming, people pretend to agree with the group, but privately think the group is wrong (p. 142)

racial prejudice the tendency to hold a hostile attitude toward an individual because of his or her racial background (p. 177)

racism an institutional practice that discriminates against individuals on the basis of their race (p. 177)

random assignment a required technique in an experiment to be able to infer cause and effect; every participant has an equal chance of being assigned to any group in the experiment (p. 29)

reactance when individuals feel that their freedom is threatened, they instinctively want to restore their freedom (p. 128)

realistic group conflict the theory that conflict stems from competition for limited resources such as money, land, power, or other resources (p. 167)

realistic group conflict theory the idea that when different groups are in competition for resources, they tend to close ranks, favoring ingroup members and discriminating against outgroup members (p. 185)

recency effect   the phenomenon whereby the last pieces of information to which we are exposed have heightened impact on our judgments, relative to information received in the middle (p. 82)

reciprocity   the exchange of what we receive for what we get, which can include liking those who like us back (p. 224)

reciprocity norm   the idea that if others help us, we should help them, and that if we help them, they will help us (p. 247)

reinforcement   an action or process that strengthens a behavior (p. 208)

relative deprivation   discontent caused by the belief that we might fare badly in comparison with people in other groups (p. 186)

reliable   consistent measurements (p. 22)

replication   repeating a study to verify effects, usually with a different sample of participants (p. 23)

representativeness heuristic   a rule used to estimate the likelihood of an event based on how well it fits with your expectations of a model for that event (p. 46)

repulsion hypothesis   states that similarity doesn't actually have any effect on attraction (p. 224)

research question   the query that is the first step in the research process (p. 21)

risky shift   the tendency for people in groups to take greater risks than if the actions were to be taken by individual members alone (p. 162)

sample   selection of who or what will be tested in the research process (p. 22)

schema   an automatically created cognitive framework that helps guide the way we think about and understand the society around us (p. 40)

scientific method   an approach to thinking that involves using systematic observations, measurements, and experiments to assess information (p. 13)

secure attachment style   the most successful of the attachment styles, characterized by high self-esteem and high interpersonal trust (p. 226)

selective filtering   paying more attention to sensory information that fits a given schema, at the same time filtering out information that is inconsistent (p. 42)

self-affirmation theory   the theory that we are more open to attitudinal change when we have recently been given an opportunity to affirm our core values and identity (p. 108)

self-awareness   when attention is brought about on the self; for example, looking in a mirror, standing in front of a crowd, and listening to a recording of your voice (p. 62)

self-concept   your mental representation or overall sense of "you" (p. 58)

self-discrepancy theory   a theory in which our concepts of self are influenced by how close our actual selves are to the selves we would like to be (p. 62)

self-efficacy   a person's belief in his or her ability to achieve certain goals (p. 58)

self-esteem   a person's evaluation of his or her self-worth (p. 65)

self-fulfilling prophecy   a prediction that causes itself to come true (p. 42)

self-handicapping   a process that involves setting up an obstacle before engaging in a task as a way to give ourselves a ready-made excuse in case we don't perform well (p. 69)

self-report/survey method   a form of data collection in which participants are asked to rate or describe their own behavior or mental state (p. 27)

self-monitoring   the process through which people regulate their behavior to be perceived well by others; low self-monitors act consistently across situations, acting according to their personal views, while high self-monitors are constantly monitoring their behavior and adjusting their reactions to fit the situation they are in (p. 70)

self-perception theory   a theory in which, if we are unsure of the attitudes we hold, we look to our behavior and use that to make inferences about our attitudes, much like an outside observer (p. 64)

self-schema   beliefs about aspects of your identity that organize the processing of information related to the self (p. 58)

self-serving attribution   a self-protection strategy in which we are likely to believe that external factors are responsible for situations in which we perform poorly (p. 67)

self-verification   the motivation of an individual for others to know him or her accurately, including his or her negative features (p. 88)

self-verification theory   a theory wherein we want others to see us as we see ourselves—even when our self concepts are negative (p. 70)

sexism   an institutional practice that discriminates against individuals on the basis of their gender (p. 177)

single-blind study   study in which two groups of participants are not told whether they are given the real treatment or the placebo and therefore do not know in which group they are (p. 32)

situational attribution   inferring that the situation in which a person is in, something external to the person, caused his or her behavior (p. 76)

sleeper effect   the effect whereby the persuasive impact of a non-credible source increases over time; we remember the message but forget the criticisms of it (p. 118)

social categorization   the process of dividing people into categories according to their race, gender, and other common attributes (p. 183)

social cognitive perspective   a perspective that builds on behavioral theories and demonstrates that an individual's cognitive process influences and is influenced by behavior associations (p. 11)

social comparison theory   a theory wherein we compare ourselves to others in different situations because there is no given standard against which to measure our abilities and opinions (p. 68)

social dominance orientation   seeing one's own group as naturally superior to other groups (p. 184)

social exchange theory   an economic model of human behavior in which people make decisions based on maximizing benefits and minimizing costs in relationships (p. 232)

social facilitation   the enhancement of a well-learned performance when another person is present (p. 6)

social identity theory   a theory in which we develop our identity from our group memberships (p. 60)

social impact theory   a theory that suggests that social influence depends on the strength, immediacy, and number of persons relative to the target person(s) (p. 144)

social influence   the process through which other people affect an individual's thoughts or actions (p. 4)

social learning perspective   a perspective that stresses the particular power of learning through social reinforcements and punishments (p. 11)

social learning theory   a theory that suggests that human aggression is largely learned by observing the aggressive behavior of other people and is reinforced by consequences such as punishment or reward in the individual's environment (p. 207)

social loafing   a phenomenon that occurs when individuals make less of an effort when attempting to achieve a particular goal as a group than they would if they were attempting to achieve the goal on their own (p. 6)

social norms   patterns of behavior that are accepted as normal, and to which an individual is expected to conform, in a particular group or culture (p. 139)

social perception   the process through which individuals form impressions of others and interpret information about them (p. 4)

social responsibility norm   the idea that we have social responsibility to help others; the extent to which this extends to outgroup members varies by culture (p. 247)

social role   expectations for the ways in which an individual should behave in a given situation (p. 139)

sociocultural perspective   a perspective that focuses on the relationship between social behavior and culture (p. 10)

source   the person or persons who delivers the message (p. 118)

spontaneous trait inference   the process of automatically inferring traits from another person's behavior (p. 78)

spotlight effect   the belief that our behavior, our appearance, and even our internal states are obvious to others (p. 70)

stereotype   a type of schema in which we apply generalized information to an individual based on the group to which he or she belongs (p. 41)

stereotype threat   being at risk of confirming the negative stereotype about a group one belongs to (p. 189)

that's-not-all technique   a compliance technique in which an initial request is followed by adding something that makes the offer more attractive (p. 147)

theory   a general framework for understanding a concept that allows us to describe, explain, and predict behavior (p. 21)

theory of planned behavior   the theory that attitudes, social norms, and the perceived control of the individual lead to behavior (p. 103)

third variable   any other factor that could be responsible for the observed effect (p. 27)

three-state model of attribution   a model in which an observer automatically characterizes a behavior, automatically makes a dispositional inference, and then uses conscious effort to correct for situational constraints if the observer has the cognitive capacity to do so (p. 78)

transactional leader   a leader who believes in a ladder of authority and considers people on lower rungs to be subordinates and therefore required to follow the instructions set forth by their manager; this type of leader rewards good work and works efficiently to solve problems (p. 164)

transformational leader   a leader who believes in inspiring his followers with energy and devotion, thereby transforming the group and its members (p. 164)

triangular theory of love   Robert Sternberg's theory that love is made of three components: intimacy, passion, and commitment (p. 230)

Twenty Statements Test (TST)   a measure of self-concept that asks individuals to self-report "Who am I?" (p. 60)

ultimate attribution error   the tendency to explain the behavior of groups in terms of internal dispositional factors, without taking situational constraints into consideration (p. 184)

unconditioned response (UCR)   a response that occurs automatically in reaction to some stimulus, without learning taking place (p. 98)

unconditioned stimulus (UCS)   a stimulus that elicits a response automatically, without learning taking place (p. 98)

unrealistic optimism   when we tend to imagine that the outcomes of situations will be better for us than for other people (p. 68)

valence   the degree of attraction or aversion that a person feels toward a specific object, event, or idea (p. 119)

valid   when a variable measures what it is supposed to measure (p. 22)

variables   stimuli or characteristics that can take on different values, such as level of attraction or age (p. 22)

what is beautiful is good effect   the phenomenon wherein beautiful things are imbued with positivity and activate positive things in the mind (p. 83)

ABC News (2005, November 10). Restaurant shift turns into nightmare. *ABC News Primetime*. Retrieved November 30, 2010, from http://abcnews.go.com/Primetime/story?id=1297922&page=1.

Aberson, C. L., Healy, M. R., & Romero, V. L. (2000). Ingroup bias and self-esteem: A meta-analysis. *Personality and Social Psychology Review, 4*, 157–173.

Abramowitz, M. (1992, June 16). Bulls' NBA victory sparks Chicago riots. *The Washington Post*. Retrieved November 30, 2010, from http://www.washingtonpost.com/wpsrv/sports/nba/longterm/jordan/articles/riot92.htm.

Acevedo, B. P., & Aron, A. (2009). Does a long-term relationship kill romantic love? *Review of General Psychology, 13*(1), 59–65.

Adorno, T. W., Frenkel-Brunswik, E., Levinson, D. J., & Sanford, R. N. (1950). *The authoritarian personality*. New York: Harper and Row.

Aggarwal, P. & O'Brien, C. (2009). Social loafing on group projects: Structural antecedents and effect on student satisfaction. *Journal of Marketing Education, 31*, 76–85.

Ainsworth, M. D. S., Blehar, M. C., Waters, E., & Wall, S. (1978). *Patterns of attachment: A psychological study of the strange situation*. Hillsdale, NJ: Lawrence Erlbaum.

Ajzen, I., & Fishbein, M. (1977). Attitude-behavior relations: A theoretical analysis and review of empirical research. *Psychological Bulletin, 84*, 888–918.

Ajzen, I., & Fishbein, M. (Eds.). (1980). *Understanding attitudes and predicting social behaviour*. New Jersey: Prentice-Hall.

Alexander, B. (2006, February 14). The science of love. *MSNBC.com*. Retrieved May 4, 2010, from http://www.msnbc.msn.com/id/11102123/.

Allen, T. J., Sherman, J. W., Conrey, F. R., & Stroessner, S. J. (2009). Stereotype strength and attentional bias: Preference for confirming versus disconfirming information depends on processing capacity. *Journal of Experimental Social Psychology, 45*(5), 1081–1087.

Allen, V., & Levine, J. (1969). Consensus and conformity. *Journal of Experimental Social Psychology, 5*(Fall), 389–399.

Allen, V., & Levine, J. (1971). Social support and conformity: The role of independent assessment of reality. *Journal of Experimental Social Psychology, 7*, 48–58.

Allport, G. W. (1954). *The nature of prejudice*. Reading, MA: Addison-Wesley.

Amabile, T. M., Hennessey, B. A., & Grossman, B. S. (1986). Social influences on creativity: The effects of contracted-for reward. *Journal of Personality and Social Psychology, 50*, 14–23.

Ambady, N., & Rosenthal, R. (1993). Half a minute: Predicting teacher evaluations from thin slices of nonverbal behavior and physical attractiveness. *Journal of Personality and Social Psychology, 64*(3), 431–441.

American Civil Liberties Union (1990). Uniform crime reports. *ACLU*. Retrieved August 8, 2010, from http://www.aclu.org/capital-punishment/case-against-death-penalty#5.

American Psychological Association (2004). Violence in the media: Psychologists help protect children from harmful effects. *American Psychological Association*. Retrieved August 18, 2010, from http://www.apa.org/research/action/protect.aspx.

Ames, D., Flynn, F. J., & Weber, E. (2004). It's the thought that counts: On perceiving how helpers decide to lend a hand. *Personality and Social Psychology Bulletin, 30*(4), 461–474.

Amnesty USA (2010). *Amnesty USA*. Retrieved August 7, 2010, from http://amnestyusa.org.

Andersen, S. M., & Berk, M. S. (1998). The social-cognitive model of transference: Experiencing past relationships in the present. *Current Directions in Psychological Science, 7*(4), 109–115.

Andersen, S. M., & Chen, S. (2002). The relational self: An interpersonal social-cognitive theory. *Psychological Review, 109*(4), 619–645.

Anderson, C. A. (1997). Effects of violent movies and trait hostility on hostile feelings and aggressive thoughts. *Aggressive Behavior, 23*, 161–178.

Anderson, C. A., Benjamin, A. J. Jr., & Bartholow, B. D. (1998). Does the gun pull the trigger? Automatic priming effects of weapon pictures and weapon names. *Psychological Science, 9*, 308–314.

Anderson, C. A., Bushman, B. J., & Groom, R. W. (1997). Hot years and serious and deadly assault: Empirical test of the heat hypothesis. *Journal of Personality and Social Psychology, 73*, 1213–1223.

Anderson, C. A., Deuser, W. E., & DeNeve, K. (1995). Hot temperatures, hostile affect, hostile cognition, and arousal: Tests of a general model of affective aggression. *Personality and Social Psychology Bulletin, 21*, 434–448.

Anderson, C. A., & Huesmann, L. R. (2003). Human aggression: A social-cognitive view (pp. 296–323). In M. A. Hogg & J. Cooper (Eds.) *The Handbook of Social Psychology, Revised Edition*. London: Sage Publications. (2007). Reprinted in M. A. Hogg & J. Cooper (Eds.) (pp. 259–287). The Sage Handbook of Social Psychology, London: Sage Publications.

Antonio, A. L., Chang, M. J., Hakuta, K., Kenny, D. A., Levin, S., & Milem, J. F. (2004). Effects of racial diversity on complex thinking in college students. *Psychological Science, 15*, 507–510.

Apanovitch, A. M., McCarthy, D. & Salovey, P. (2003). Using message framing to motivate HIV testing among low-income ethnic minority women. *Health Psychology, 22*, 60–67.

Appelbaum, S. H., & Hughes, B. (1998). Ingratiation as a political tactic: Effects within the organization. *Management Decision, 36*(2), 85–95.

Archer, D., & Gaertner, R. (1984). *Violence and crime in cross national perspective*. New Haven, CT: Yale University Press.

Argyle, M. (1987). *The psychology of happiness*. London: Methuen.

Aries, E., & Johnson, F. (1983). Close friendship in adulthood: Conversational content between same-sex friends. *Sex Roles, 9*(11), 83–96.

Armor, D. A., & Taylor, S. E. (2002). When predictions fail: The dilemma of unrealistic optimism. In T. Gilovich, D. Griffin, & D. Kahneman (Eds.), *Heuristics and Biases: The Psychology of Intuitive Judgment*. Cambridge, UK: Cambridge University Press.

Aron, A., Dutton, D. G., Aron, E. N., & Iverson, A. (1989). Experiences of falling in love. *Journal of Social and Personal Relationships, 6*, 243–257.

Aronson, E., Blaney, N., Stephan, C., Sikes, J., & Snapp, M. (1978). *The jigsaw classroom*. Beverly Hills, CA: Sage.

Asch, S. E. (1946). Forming impressions of personality. *Journal of Abnormal and Social Psychology, 41*, 258–290.

Asch, S. E. (1951). Effects of group pressure upon the modification and distortion of judgments. In H. Guetzkow (Ed.), *Groups, leadership, and men*. Pittsburgh, PA: Carnegie Press.

Asch, S. E. (1955). Opinions and social pressure. *Scientific American, 193*, 31–35.

Asch, S. E. (1956). Studies of independence and conformity: A minority of one against a unanimous majority. *Psychological Monographs, 70*.

Ash, M. G. (1992). *Kurt Lewin: Person, werk, umfeld*. Frankfurt: Peter Lang.

Aspinwall, L. G., & Taylor, S. E. (1993). Effects of social comparison direction, threat, and self-esteem on affect, self-evaluation, and expected success. *Journal of Personality and Social Psychology, 64*(5), 708–722.

Associated Press (1996). Jury convicts man of murder in death at Belle Isle bridge. *The Blade*: Toledo, Ohio.

Associated Press (2007, April 29). Black, Latino drivers fare worse in traffic stops. Retrieved August 2, 2010, from http://www.msnbc.msn.com/id/18383182/.

Associated Press (2008, September 10). Police arrest man in Pa. subway hammer attack. *MSNBC*. Retrieved November 30, 2010, from http://www.msnbc.msn.com/id/26638199/.

Astin, A. W. (1998). The changing American college student: Thirty-year trends, 1966–96. *Review of Higher Education, 21*(2), 115–135.

Aube, J., & Koestner, R. (1995). Gender characteristics and relationship adjustment: Another look at similarity-complementary hypothesis. *Journal of Personality, 63*(4), 879–903.

Avert (2010). AIDS statistics. *Avert*. Retrieved October 11, 2010, from http://www.avert.org/usa-statistics.htm.

Axsom, D., & Cooper, J. (1985). Cognitive dissonance and psychotherapy: The role of effort justification in inducing weight loss. *Journal of Experimental Social Psychology, 21*, 149–160.

Ayres, I. (1991). Fair driving: Gender and race discrimination in retail car negotiations. *Harvard Law Review, 104*, 817–872.

Back, M. D., Schmukle, S. C., & Egloff, B. (2008). Becoming friends by chance. *Psychological Science: A Journal of the American Psychological Society, 19*(5), 439–440.

Bailey, D. S., & Taylor, S. P. (1991). Effects of alcohol and aggressive disposition on human physical aggression. *Journal of Research in Personality, 25,* 334–342.

Bailey, R. (2006, August 11). Don't be terrorized: You're more likely to die of a car accident, drowning, fire, or murder. *Reason.com.* Retrieved November 30, 2010, from http://reason.com/archives/2006/08/11/dont-be-terrorized.

Baker-Knight, T. (1975). Don't all the girls get prettier at closing time. [Recorded by Mickey Gilley]. On *The Best of Mickey Gilley, Vol. 2.* BMI.

Baldwin, M. W., & Fehr, B. (1995). On the instability of attachment style ratings. *Personal Relationships, 2,* 247–261

Baldwin, M. W., Keelan, J. P. R., Fehr, B., Enns, V., & Koh-Rangarajoo, E. (1996). Social cognitive conceptualization of attachment styles: Availability and accessibility effects. *Journal of Personality and Social Psychology, 71,* 94–109.

Balsam, K. F., Beauchaine, T. P., Rothblum, E. D., & Solomon, S. E. (2008). Three-year follow-up of same-sex couples who had civil unions in Vermont, same-sex couples not in civil unions, and heterosexual married couples. *Developmental Psychology, 44*(1), 102–116.

Bandura, A. (1962). Social learning through imitation. In M. R. Jones (Ed.), *Nebraska Symposium on Motivation.* Lincoln, NE: University of Nebraska Press.

Bandura, A. (1965). Behavioral modification through modeling procedures. In L. Krasner & L. P. Ullman (Eds.), *Research in Behavior Modification.* New York: Holt, Rinehart and Winston.

Bandura, A. (1965). Influence of models' reinforcement contingencies on the acquisition of imitative responses. *Journal of Personality and Social Psychology, 1,* 589–595.

Bandura, A. (1977). Self-efficacy: Toward a unifying theory of behavioral change. *Psychological Review, 84*(2), 119–215.

Bandura, A. (1977). *Social learning theory.* New York: General Learning Press.

Bandura, A., Grusec, J. E., & Menlove, F. L. (1966). Observational learning as a function of symbolization and incentive set. *Child Development, 37,* 499–506.

Bandura, A., Ross, D., & Ross, S. (1961). Transmission of aggression through imitation of aggressive models. *Journal of Abnormal and Social Psychology, 63,* 575–582.

Bandura, A., Ross, D., & Ross, S. A. (1963). Imitation of film-mediated aggressive models. *Journal of Abnormal Social Psychology, 66,* 3–11.

Banks, T. & Dabbs, J. M. Jr. (1996). Salivary testosterone and cortisol in a delinquent and violent urban subculture. *The Journal of Social Psychology, 136*(1), 49–56.

Banse, R. (2004). Adult attachment and marital satisfaction: Evidence for dyadic configuration effects. *Journal of Social and Personal Relationships, 21,* 273–282.

Bar-Haim, Y., Ziv, T., Lamy, D., & Hodes, R. M. (2006). Nature and nurture in own-race face processing. *Psychological Science, 17,* 159–163.

Bargh, J. A., Chen, M., & Burrows, L. (1996). Automaticity of social behavior: Direct effects of trait construct and stereotype activation on action. *Journal of Personality and Social Psychology, 71,* 230–244.

Barker, R., Dembo, T., & Lewin, K. (1941). Frustration and aggression: An experiment with young children. *University of Iowa Studies in Child Welfare, 18,* 1–314.

Barnes, R. D., Ickes, W., & Kidd, R. F. (1979). Effects of the perceived intentionality and stability of another's dependency on helping behavior. *Personality and Social Psychology Bulletin, 5,* 367–372.

Barnwell, S., Borders, A., & Earleywine, M. (2006). Alcohol-aggression expectancies and dispositional aggression moderate the relationship between alcohol consumption and alcohol-related violence. *Aggressive Behavior, 32*(6), 517–525

Baron, J., & Miller, J. G. (2000). Limiting the scope of moral obligations to help: A cross-cultural investigation. *Journal of Cross-Cultural Psychology, 31*(6), 703–725.

Baron, R. A. (1986). Distraction-conflict theory: Progress and problems. In L. Berkowitz (Ed.), *Advances in Experimental Social Psychology* (Vol. 19). Orlando, FL: Academic Press.

Baron, R. A. (1990). Countering the effects of destructive criticism: The relative efficacy of four interventions. *Journal of Applied Psychology, 75,* 235–245.

Baron, R. A., & Richardson, D. R. (1994). *Human Aggression* (2nd ed.). New York: Plenum.

Baron, R. S., Moore, D., & Sanders, G. S. (1978). Distraction as a source of drive in social facilitation research. *Journal of Personality and Social Psychology, 36,* 816–824.

Bartholow, B. D., & Anderson, C. A. (2002). Effects of violent video games on aggressive behavior: Potential sex differences. *Journal of Experimental Social Psychology, 38,* 283–290.

Bartholow, B. D., Anderson, C. A., Carnagey, N. L., & Benjamin, A. J. Jr. (2005). Interactive effects of life experience and situational cues on aggression: The weapons priming effect in hunters and non-hunters. *Journal of Experimental Social Psychology, 41,* 48–60.

Bartholow, B. D., & Heinz, A. (2006). Alcohol and aggression without consumption: Alcohol cues, aggressive thoughts, and hostile perception bias. *Psychological Science, 17,* 30–37.

Bateson, M., Nettle, D., & Roberts, G. (2006). Cues of being watched enhance cooperation in a real-world setting. *Biology Letters, 3,* 412–414.

Bateson, N. (1966, April). Familiarization, group discussion, and risk taking. *Journal of Experimental Social Psychology, 2*(2), 119–129.

Batson, C. D. (1991). *The altruism question: Toward a social-psychological answer.* Hillsdale, NJ: Lawrence Erlbaum Associates.

Batson, C. D. (1998). Altruism and prosocial behavior. In D. Gilbert, S. Fiske, & G. Lindzey (Eds.), *The handbook of social psychology,* 4th edition (Vol. 2, pp. 282–316). New York: McGraw-Hill.

Batson, C. D., Duncan, B. D., Ackerman, P., Buckley, T., & Birch, K. (1981). Is empathic emotion a source of altruistic motivation? *Journal of Personality and Social Psychology, 40*(2), 290–302.

Batson, C. D., Dyck, I. L., Bran, J. R., Watson, J. G., Powell, A. L., McMaster, M. R., & Griffitt, C. (1988). Five studies testing two new egoistic alternatives to the empathy-altruism hypothesis. *Journal of Personality and Social Psychology, 55,* 52–77.

Batson, C. D., & Oleson, K. C. (1991). Current status of the empathy-altruism hypothesis. In M. S. Clark (Ed.), *Review of personality and social psychology: Vol. 12. Prosocial behavior* (pp. 62–85). Newbury Park, CA: Sage.

Batson, C. D., O'Quin, K., Fultz, J., Vanderplas, M., & Isen, A. M. (1983). Influence of self-reported distress and empathy on egoistic versus altruistic motivation to help. *Journal of Personality and Social Psychology, 45,* 706–718.

Batson, C. D., Thompson, E. R., Seuferling, G., Whitney, H., & Strongman, J. A. (1999). Moral hypocrisy: Appearing moral to oneself without being so. *Journal of Personality and Social Psychology, 77,* 525–537.

Baumeister, R. F. (1991). *Escaping the self.* New York: Basic Books.

Baumeister, R. F., Campbell, J. D., Krueger, J. I., & Vohs, K. D. (2003). Does high self-esteem cause better performance, interpersonal success, happiness, or healthier lifestyles? *Psychological Science in the Public Interest, 4*(1), 1–44.

Baumeister, R. F., & Leary, M. R. (1995). The need to belong: Desire for interpersonal attachments as a fundamental human motivation. *Psychological Bulletin, 117,* 497–529.

Baumeister, R. F., & Steinhilber, A. (1984). Paradoxical effects of supportive audiences on performance under pressure: The home field disadvantage in sports championships. *Journal of Personality and Social Psychology, 47,* 85–93.

Bazerman, M. H., Beekun, R. I., & Schoorman, F. D. (1982). Performance evaluation in a dynamic context: A laboratory study of the impact of a prior commitment to the ratee. *Journal of Applied Psychology, 67*(6), 873–876.

Beaman, A. L., Barnes, P. J., Klentz, B., & McQuirk, B. (1978). Increasing helping rates through information dissemination: Teaching pays. *Personality and Social Psychology Bulletin, 4,* 406–411.

Beaman, A. L., Diener, E., & Klentz, B. (1979). Self-awareness and transgression in children: Two field studies. *Journal of Personality and Social Psychology, 37,* 1835–1846.

Bem, D. J. (1965). An experimental analysis of self-persuasion. *Journal of Experimental Social Psychology, 1*(3), 199–218.

Bem, D. J. (1967). Self-perception: An alternative interpretation of cognitive dissonance phenomena. *Psychological Review, 74*(3), 183–200.

Bem, D. J. (1972) Self-perception theory. In L. Berkowitz (Ed.), *Advances in experimental social psychology* (Vol. 6, pp. 1–62). New York: Academic Press.

Benson, P. L., Karabenick, S. A., & Lerner, R. M. (1976). Pretty pleases: The effects of physical attractiveness, race, and sex on receiving help. *Journal of Experimental Social Psychology, 12,* 409–415.

Berg, J. H., & McQuinn, R. D. (1986). Attraction and exchange in continuing and noncontinuing dating relationships. *Journal of Personality and Social Psychology, 50*(5), 942–952.

Berkowitz, L. (1968). The concept of aggressive drive: Some additional considerations. In L. Berkowitz (Ed.) *Advances in Experimental Social Psychology.* New York: Academic Press.

Berkowitz, L. (1983). Aversively stimulated aggression: Some parallels and differences in research with animals and humans. *American Psychologist, 38*, 1135-1144.

Berkowitz, L. (1989). Frustration-aggression hypothesis: Examination and reformulation. *Psychological Bulletin, 106*, 59-73.

Berkowitz, L. (1993). Pain and aggression: Some findings and implications. *Motivation and Emotion, 17*, 277.

Berkowitz, L. (1998). Affective aggression: The role of stress, pain, and negative affect. *Human Aggression: Theories, Research, and Implications for Social Policy*. San Diego, CA: Academic Press.

Berkowitz, L., & Daniels, L. (1963). Responsibility and dependency. *Journal of Abnormal Social Psychology, 66*, 429-436.

Berkowitz, L., & LePage, A. (1967). Weapons as aggression-eliciting stimuli. *Journal of Personality and Social Psychology, 7*, 202-207.

Berndt, T. J. (1979). Developmental changes in conformity to peers and parents. *Developmental Psychology, 15*(6), 608-616.

Bernstein, M., & Crosby, F. (1980). An empirical examination of relative deprivation theory. *Journal of Experimental Social Psychology, 16*, 442-456.

Berry, D. S., & Zebrowitz-McArthur, L. (1988). What's in a face? Facial maturity and the attribution of legal responsibility. *Personality and Social Psychology Bulletin, 14*(1), 23-33.

Bertrand, M., & Mullainathan, S. (2004). Are Emily and Greg more employable than Lakisha and Jamal? A field experiment on labor market discrimination. *The American Economic Review, 94*(4), 991-1013.

Bettencourt, A. B., & Miller, N. (1996). Gender differences in aggression as a function of provocation: A meta-analysis. *Psychological Bulletin, 199*, 422-447.

Bierhoff, H. W., Klein, R., & Kramp, P. (1991). Evidence for the altruistic personality from data on accident research. *Journal of Personality, 59*(2), 263-280.

Biernat, M., Crandall, C. S., Young, L. V., Kobrynowicz, D., & Halpin, S. M. (1998). All that you can be: Stereotyping of self and others in a military context. *Journal of Personality and Social Psychology, 75*, 301-317.

Bindel, J. (2010, February 19). Blame the rapist, not the victim. *The Guardian.* Retrieved August 3, 2010, from http://www.guardian.co.uk/lifeandstyle/2010/feb/19/blame-the-rapist.

Blair, R. J. R. (2001). Neuro-cognitive models of aggression, the antisocial personality disorders and psychopathy. *Journal of Neurology, Neurosurgery, and Psychiatry, 71*, 727-731.

Blair, R. J. (2007). Dysfunctions of medial and lateral orbitofrontal cortex in psychopathy. *Annals of the New York Academy of Sciences, 1121*, 461-479.

Blanchard, F. A., Crandall, C. S., Brigham, J. C., & Vaughn L. A. (1994). Condemning and condoning racism: A social context approach to interracial settings. *Journal of Applied Psychology, 79*, 993-997.

Bodenhausen, G. V., Kramer, G. P., & Süsser, K. (1994). Happiness and stereotypic thinking in social judgment. *Journal of Personality and Social Psychology, 66*, 621-632.

Bond, M. H., & Cheung, T. S. (1983). College students' spontaneous self-concept: The effect of culture among respondents in Hong Kong, Japan, and the United States. *Journal of Cross-Cultural Psychology, 14*(2), 153-171.

Bond, R. A., & Smith, P. B. (1996). Culture and conformity: A meta-analysis of studies using Asch's (1952, 1956) line judgment task. *Psychological Bulletin, 119*, 111-137.

Bordel, S., et al. (2007). Naïve explanations of road accidents: Self-serving bias and defensive attribution. *Psihologia Resurselor Umane Revista Asociatiei de Psihologie Industriala si Organizationala. 5*(2), 36-47.

Bower, G. H. (1987). Commentary on mood and memory. *Behaviour Research and Therapy, 25*, 443-456.

Bowlby, J. (1969). *Attachment and loss: Vol. I: Attachment*. New York: Basic Books.

Bowlby, J. (1973). *Attachment and loss: Vol. II: Separation: Anxiety and anger*. New York: Basic Books.

Bowlby, J. (1988). *A secure base: Parent-child attachment and healthy human development.* New York: Basic Books.

Boyd, R., & Richerson, P. J. (1985). *Culture and the evolutionary process*. Chicago, IL: University of Chicago Press.

Boysen, S. T., & Himes, G. T. (1999). Current issues and emergent theories in animal cognition. *Annual Reviews in Psychology, 50*, 683-705.

Branscombe, N. R., & Wann, D. L. (1991). The positive social and self-concept consequences of sport team identification. *Journal of Sport and Social Issues, 15*, 115-127.

Brauer, M., Judd, C. M., & Jacquelin, V. (2001). The communication of social stereotypes: The effects of group discussion and information distribution on stereotypic appraisals. *Journal of Personality and Social Psychology, 81*, 463-475.

Bray, R. M., & Noble, A. M. (1978). Authoritarianism and decisions of mock juries: Evidence of jury bias and group polarization. *Journal of Personality and Social Psychology, 36*, 1424-1430.

Brehm, J. W. (1966). *A Theory of Psychological Reactance*. New York: Academic Press.

Brendl, C. M., Chattopadhyay, A., Pelham, B. W., & Carvall, M. (2005). Name-letter branding: Valence transfers when product-specific needs are active. *Journal of Consumer Research, 32*, 405-415.

Brennan, K. A., & Bosson, J. K. (1998). Attachment-style differences in attitudes toward and reactions to feedback from romantic partners: An exploration of the relational bases of self-esteem. *Personality & Social Psychology Bulletin, 24*, 699-714.

Brescoll, V. L., & Uhlmann, E. L. (2008). Can an angry woman get ahead? Status conferral, gender, and expression of emotion in the workplace. *Psychological Science, 19*, 268-275.

Bretherton, I. (1992). The origins of attachment theory: John Bowlby and Mary Ainsworth. *Developmental Psychology, 28*, 759-775.

Brewer, M. B., & Chen, Y. R. (2007). Where (who) are collectives in collectivism? Toward conceptual clarification of individualism and collectivism. *Psychological Review, 114*(1), 133-151.

Brewer, M. B., & Pickett, C. L. (1999). Distinctiveness motives as a source of the social self. In T. Tyler, R. Kramer, & O. John (Eds.), *The psychology of the social self* (pp. 71-87). Hillsdale, NJ: Erlbaum.

Brickner, M. A., Harkins, S. G., & Ostrom, T. M. (1986). Effects of personal involvement: Thought provoking implications for social loafing. *Journal of Personality and Social Psychology, 51*, 763-769.

Briñol, P., & Petty, R. E. (2003). Overt head movements and persuasion: A self-validation analysis. *Journal of Personality and Social Psychology, 84*, 1123-1139.

British Broadcasting Corporation (1995). The killing screens. *Panorama Programme*.

Broemer, P. (2004). Ease of imagination moderates reactions to differently framed health messages. *European Journal of Social Psychology, 34*, 103-119.

Brown, R. (1965). *Social psychology*. New York: Free Press.

Brown, W. M., Cronk, L., Grochow, K., Jacobson, A., Liu, C. K., Popovic, Z., & Trivers, R. (2005). Dance reveals symmetry especially in young men. *Nature, 438*, 22-29.

Brownstein, R. J., & Katzev, R. D. (1985). The relative effectiveness of three compliance techniques in eliciting donations to a cultural organization. *Journal of Applied Social Psychology, 15*(6), 564-574.

Brush, S. G. (1996). Dynamics of theory change in the social sciences: Relative deprivation and collective violence. *Journal of Conflict Resolution, 40*(4), 523-545.

Bryan, J. H., & Test, M. A. (1967). Models and helping: Naturalistic studies in aiding behavior. *Journal of Personality and Social Psychology, 6*, 400-407.

Buckley, C. (2007, January 3). Man is rescued by stranger on subway tracks. *The New York Times*. Retrieved November 30, 2010, from http://www.nytimes.com/2007/01/03/nyregion/03life.html.

Bureau of Labor Statistics (2010). *Volunteering in the United States, 2009*. Retrieved November 30, 2010, from http://www.bls.gov/news.release/volun.nr0.htm.

Burger, J. M. (1986). Increasing compliance by improving the deal: The that's-not-all technique. *Journal of Personality and Social Psychology, 51*, 277-283.

Burger, J. M. (2009). Replicating Milgram: Would people still obey today? *American Psychologist, 64*(1), 1-11.

Burger, J. M., Messian, N., Patel, S., del Prado, A., & Anderson, C. (2004). What a coincidence! The effects of incidental similarity on compliance. *Personality and Social Psychology Bulletin, 30*, 35-43.

Burger, J. M., Sanchez, J., Imberi, J. E., & Grande, L. R. (2009). The norm of reciprocity as an internalized social norm: Returning favors even when no one finds out. *Social Influence, 4*, 11-17.

Burns, R. B. (1978). The relative effectiveness of various incentives and deterrents as judged by pupils and teachers. *Educational Studies, 4*, 229-243.

Burnstein, E., Crandall, C., & Kitayama, S. (1994) Some neo-Darwinian decision rules for altruism: Weighing cues for inclusive fitness as a function of the biological importance of the decision. *Journal of Personality and Social Psychology, 67*, 779.

Burstein, E., & Worchel, P. (1962). Arbitrariness of frustration and its consequences for aggression in a social situation. *Journal of Personality, 30*, 528-541.

Bushman, B. J., & Anderson, C. A. (2001). Media violence and the American public: Scientific facts versus media misinformation. *American Psychologist, 56*, 477-489.

Bushman, B. J., & Anderson, C. A. (2002). Violent video games and hostile expectations: A test of the General Aggression Model. *Personality and Social Psychology Bulletin, 28*, 1679-1689.

Bushman, B. J., & Cantor, J. (2003). Media ratings for violence and sex: Implications for policymakers and parents. *American Psychologist, 58*(2), 130-141.

Bushman, B. J., & Huesmann, L. R. (2001). Effects of televised violence on aggression (pp. 223-254). In D. Singer & J. Singer (Eds.), *Handbook of Children and the Media*, Thousand Oaks, CA: Sage Publications.

Buss, D. M. (2002). Human Mating Strategies. *Samfundsokonomen, 4*, 47-58.

Buss, D. M. (2004). *The Evolution of Desire* (rev. ed.). New York: Basic Books.

Buss, D. M., & Barnes, M. (1986). Preferences in human mate selection. *Journal of Personality and Social Psychology, 50*(3), 559-570.

Buss, D. M., Larsen, R. J., Westen, D., & Semmelroth, J. (1992). Sex differences in jealousy: Evolution, physiology, and psychology. *Psychological Science, 3*, 251-255.

Butler, D., & Geis, F. L. (1990). Nonverbal affect responses to male and female leaders: Implications for leadership evaluations. *Journal of Personality and Social Psychology, 58*, 48-59.

Buunk, B. P., Oldsersma, F. L., & deDreu, C. K. W. (2001). Enhancing satisfaction through downward comparison: The role of relational discontent and individual differences in social comparison orientation. *Journal of Experimental Social Psychology, 37*(6), 452-467.

Byrne, D. (1961). Interpersonal attraction and attitude similarity. *Journal of Abnormal and Social Psychology, 62*(3), 713-715.

Byrne, D. (1971). *The attraction paradigm.* New York: Academic Press.

Byrne, D., & Nelson, D. (1965). Attraction as a linear function of proportion of positive reinforcements. *Journal of Personality and Social Psychology, 1*, 659-663.

Byrnes, D. A., & Kiger, G. (1990). The effect of a prejudice-reduction simulation on attitude change. *Journal of Applied Social Psychology, 20*, 341-356.

Cacioppo, J. T., Amaral, D. G., Blanchara, J. J., Cameron, J. L., Carter, C. S., Crews, D. . . . Quinn, K. J. (2007). Social neuroscience: Progress and implications for mental health. *Perspectives on Psychological Science, 2*, 99-123.

Cacioppo, J. T., Gardner, W. L., & Berntson, G. G. (1997). Beyond bipolar conceptualizations and measures: The case of attitudes and evaluative space. *Personality and Social Psychology Review, 1*, 3-25.

Cacioppo, J. T., & Petty, R. E. (1980). Sex differences in influenceability: Toward specifying the underlying processes. *Personality and Social Psychology Bulletin, 6*, 651-656.

Cacioppo, J. T., & Petty, R. E. (1982). The need for cognition. *Journal of Personality and Social Psychology, 42*, 116-131.

Cacioppo, J. T., Petty, R. E., Feinstein, J. A., Jarvis, W., & Blair, G. (1996). Dispositional differences in cognitive motivation: The life and times of individuals varying in need for cognition. *Psychological Bulletin, 119*(2), 197-253.

Caldwell, T. (n.d.). Media sensationalism about crime defies statistical trends toward lower crime rates. *Helium.* Retrieved July 13, 2010, from http://www.helium.com/items/175618-media-sensationalism-about-crime-defies-statistical-trends-toward-lower-crime.

Campbell, A., Muncer, S., & Gorman, B. (1993). Sex and social representations of aggression: A communal-agentic analysis. *Aggressive Behavior, 19*, 125-135.

Campbell, L., Simpson, J. A., Boldry, J. G., & Kashy, D. A. (2005). Perceptions of conflict and support in romantic relationships: The role of attachment anxiety. *Journal of Personality and Social Psychology, 88*, 510-531.

Campbell, W. K., & Sedikides, C. (1999). Self-threat magnifies the self-serving bias: A metanalytic integration. *Review of General Psychology, 3*(1), 23-43.

Cantor, J. R., Zillmann, D., & Einseidel, E. F. (1978). Female responses to provocation after exposure to aggressive and erotic films. *Communication Research, 5*, 395-412.

Carkenord, D. M., & Bullington, J. (1993). Bringing cognitive dissonance to the classroom. *Teaching of Psychology, 20*, 41-43.

Carlson, M., Charlin, V., & Miller, N. (1988). Positive mood and helping behavior: A test of six hypotheses. *Journal of Personality and Social Psychology, 55*, 211-229.

Carnagey, N. L., & Anderson, C. A. (2005). The effects of reward and punishment in violent video games on aggressive affect, cognition, and behavior. *Psychological Science, 16*, 882-889.

Cartwright, D. (1979). Contemporary social psychology in historical perspective. *Social Psychology Quarterly, 42*, 82-93.

Cash, T. F., & Derlega, V. J. (1978). The matching hypothesis: Physical attractiveness among same-sex friends. *Personality and Social Psychology Bulletin, 4*, 240-243.

Cash, T. F., Gillen, B., & Burns, D. S. (1977). Sexism and beautyism in personnel consultant decision making. *Journal of Applied Psychology, 62*, 301-310.

Causse, P. et al. (2004). Alcohol-related accident-risk perception by young drivers: Some determinants of comparative optimism. *Le Travail Humain: A Bilingual and Multidisciplinary Journal in Human Factors, 67*(3), 235-256.

CBS/AP (2008). Teens arrested over filmed beating. *CBS News.* Retrieved August 17, 2010, from http://www.cbsnews.com/stories/2008/04/08/national/main4000740.shtml.

Centers for Disease Control and Prevention (2010). *2009 H1N1 flu ("swine flu") and you.* Retrieved May 14, 2010, from http://www.cdc.gov/h1n1flu/qa.htm.

Chaiken, S. (1979). Communicator physical attractiveness and persuasion, *Journal of Personality and Social Psychology, 37*(8), 1387-1397.

Chaiken, S. (1980). Heuristic versus systematic information processing and the use of source versus message cues in persuasion. *Journal of Personality and Social Psychology, 39*, 752-756.

Chance, S. E., Brown, R. T., Dabbs, J. M. J., & Casey, R. (2000). Testosterone, intelligence, and behavior disorders in young boys. *Personality and Individual Differences, 28*, 437-445.

Chapple, A., Ziebland, S., & McPherson, A. (2004). Stigma, shame and blame: A qualitative study of people with lung cancer. *British Medical Journal, 328*, 1470.

Charbonneau, D., Barling, J., & Kelloway, E. K. (2001). Transformational leadership and sports performance: The mediating role of intrinsic motivation. *Journal of Applied Social Psychology, 31*, 1521-1534.

Chartrand, T. L., & Bargh, J. A. (1999). The chameleon effect: The perception-behavior link and social interaction. *Journal of Personality and Social Psychology, 76*, 893-910.

Chazan, D. (2010, March 18). Row over "torture" on French TV. *BBC News.* Retrieved November 30, 2010, from http://news.bbc.co.uk/2/hi/8573755.stm.

Chen, S. (2009, October 30). Gang rape raises question about bystanders' role. *CNN.com.* Retrieved June 3, 2010, from http://www.cnn.com/2009/CRIME/10/28/california.gang.rape.bystander/index.html.

Chen, S., Boucher, H. C., & Tapias, M. P. (2006). The relational self revealed: Integrative conceptualization and implications for interpersonal life. *Psychological Bulletin, 132*, 151-179.

Childs, D. (2008, June 25). 'Trust drug' oxytocin unbelievable for now. *ABC News.* Retrieved June 3, 2010, from http://abcnews.go.com/Health/MindMoodNews/story?id=5242531&page=1.

Chiroro, P. M., Tredoux C. G., Radaelli, S., & Meissner, C. A. (2008). Recognizing faces across continents: The effect of within-race variations in the own-race bias in face recognition. *Psychonomic Bulletin & Review, 15*, 1089-1092.

Cialdini, R. (1984). *Influence: Science and Practice* (5th Edition). Needham Heights, MA: Allyn & Bacon.

Cialdini, R. B. (1994). *Influence: The psychology of persuasion.* New York: Quill.

Cialdini, R. B. (2001). The science of persuasion. *Scientific American, 284*, 76-81.

Cialdini, R. B. (2003). Crafting normative messages to protect the environment. *Current Directions in Psychological Science, 12*, 105-109.

Cialdini, R. B. (2004). Crafting normative messages to protect the environment. *Current Directions in Psychological Science, 12*(4), 105-109.

Cialdini, R. B., Borden, R. J., Thorne, R. J., Walker, M. R., Freeman, S., & Sloan, L. R. (1976). Basking in reflected glory: Three (football) field studies. *Journal of Personality and Social Psychology, 34*(3), 366-375.

Cialdini, R. B., Brown, S. L., Lewis, B. P., Luce, C., & Neuberg, S. L. (1997). Reinterpreting the empathy-altruism relationship: When one into one equals oneness. *Journal of Personality and Social Psychology, 73*(3), 481-494.

Cialdini, R. B., Kenrick, D. T., & Baumann, D. J. (1982). Mood as a determinant of prosocial behavior in children and adults. In N. Eisenberg (Ed.), *The development of prosocial behavior* (pp. 339-359). New York: Academic Press.

Cialdini, R. B., Reno, R. R., & Kallgren, C. A. (1990). A focus theory of normative conduct: Recycling the concept of norms to reduce littering in public places. *Journal of Personality and Social Psychology, 58*(6), 1015-1026.

Cialdini, R. B., Vincent, J. E., Lewis, S. K., Catalan, J., Wheeler, D., & Darby, B. L. (1975). A reciprocal concessions procedure for inducing compliance: The door-in-the-face technique. *Journal of Personality and Social Psychology, 31,* 206-215.

Claremont Graduate University (2010). Oxytocin: Trust, touch, and the economy. *Media Services.* Retrieved June 3, 2010, from http://www.cgu.edu/pages/4627.asp.

Clark, K. B., & Clark, M. P. (1947). Racial identification and preference in Negro children. Retrieved July 2, 2010, from http://i2.cdn.turner.com/cnn/2010/images/05/13/doll.study.1947.pdf.

Clark, M. S. (1984). Record keeping in two types of relationships. *Journal of Personality and Social Psychology, 47*(3), 549-557.

Clark, M., & Pataki, S. (1995). Interpersonal processes influencing attraction and relationships. In A. Tesser (Ed.), *Advanced Social Psychology* (pp. 283-331). St. Louis: McGraw-Hill.

Clark, R. D. III, & Word, L. E. (1972). Why don't bystanders help? Because of ambiguity? *Journal of Personality and Social Psychology, 24,* 392-400.

CNN (2001, September 1). *Falwell apologizes to gays, feminists, lesbians.* Retrieved July 27, 2010, from http://archives.cnn.com/2001/US/09/14/Falwell.apology/.

Cohen, D., Nisbett, R. E., Bowdle, B. F., & Schwartz, N. (1996). Insult, aggression, and the Southern culture of honor: An "experimental ethnography." *Journal of Personality and Social Psychology, 70,* 945-960.

Cohen, D., & Nisbett, R. (1997). Field experiments examination the culture of honor: The role of institutions in perpetuating norms about violence. *Personality & Social Psychology Bulletin, 23,* 1188.

Cohen, J. D. (2005). The Vulcanization of the human brain: A neural perspective on interactions between cognition and emotion. *Journal of Economic Perspectives, 19*(4), 3-24.

Collins, B. E., & Guetzkow, H. (1964). *A social psychology of group processes for decision-making.* New York: Wiley.

Collins, N. C., & Feeney, B. C. (2004). Working models of attachment shape perceptions of social support: Evidence from experimental and observational studies. *Journal of Personality and Social Psychology, 87,* 363-383.

Collins, N. L., & Miller, L. C. (1994). Self-disclosure and liking: A meta-analytic review. *Psychological Bulletin, 116*(3), 457-475.

Comer, D. (1995). A model of social loafing in real work groups. *Human Relations, 48,* 647-667.

Conflict Research Consortium (1998). Step-by-step de-escalation (GRIT). Retrieved November 30, 2010, from http://www.colorado.edu/conflict/peace/treatment/grit.htm.

Cooley, C. H. (1902). *Human nature and the social order.* New York: Schocken Books.

Cooper, J., & Fazio, R. H. (1984). A new look at dissonance theory. *Advances in Experimental Social Psychology, 17,* 229-265.

Cooper, W. H. (1981). Ubiquitous halo. *Psychological Bulletin, 90,* 218-244.

Corey, S. M. (1937). Professed attitudes and actual behavior. *Journal of Educational Psychology, 28*(4), 271-280.

Corman, S. R., Hess, A., & Justus, Z. S. (2006). Credibility in the global war on terrorism: Strategic principles and research agenda. Consortium for Strategic Communication, Arizona State University.

Correll, J., Park, B., Judd, C. M., & Wittenbrink, B. (2002). The police officer's dilemma: Using ethnicity to disambiguate potentially threatening individuals. *Journal of Personality & Social Psychology, 83,* 1314-1329.

Correll, J., Spencer, S. J., & Zanna, M. P. (2004). An affirmed self and an open mind: Self-affirmation and sensitivity to argument strength. *Journal of Experimental Social Psychology, 40,* 350-356.

Coser, L. A. (1956). *The functions of social conflict.* Glencoe, IL: Free Press.

Craik, F. I. M., Moroz, T. M., Moscovitch, M., Stuss, D. T., Winocur, G., Tulving, E., & Kapur, S. (1999). In search of the self: A positron emission tomography study. *Psychological Science, 10,* 26-34.

Cramer, R. E., McMaster, M. R., Bartell, P. A., & Dragna, M. (1988). Subject competence and minimization of the bystander effect. *Journal of Applied Social Psychology, 18,* 1133-1148.

Crandall, C. S., Eshleman, A., & O'Brien, L. T. (2002). Social norms and the expression and suppression of prejudice: The struggle for internalization. *Journal of Personality and Social Psychology, 82,* 359-378.

Crano, W. D. (1997). Vested interest, symbolic politics, and attitude-behavior consistency. *Journal of Personality and Social Psychology, 72*(3), 485-491.

Crick, N. R., & Dodge, K. A. (1994). A review and reformulation of social information processing mechanisms in children's social adjustment. *Psychological Bulletin, 115,* 74-101.

Crick, N., & Grotpeter, J. (1995). Relational aggression, gender, and social-psychological adjustment. Child Development, 66(3), 710-722.

Crick, N., & Rose, A. (2000). Toward a gender-balanced approach to the study of social-emotional development. *Toward a Feminist Developmental Psychology.* Routledge: New York, NY, 153-168.

Crocker, J. (2002). The costs of seeking self-esteem. *Journal of Social Issues, 58,* 597-615.

Crocker, J., & Luhtanen, R. K. (2003). Level of self-esteem and contingencies of self-worth: Unique effects on academic, social, and financial problems in college freshmen. *Personality and Social Psychology Bulletin, 29,* 701-712.

Crocker, J., & Park, L. E. (2004). The costly pursuit of self-esteem. *Psychological Bulletin, 130,* 392-414.

Crocker, J., Thompson, L., McGraw, K., & Ingerman, C. (1987). Downward comparison, prejudice, and evaluation of others: Effects of self-esteem and threat. *Journal of Personality and Social Psychology, 52,* 907-916.

Cropanzano, R. (Ed.) (1993). *Justice in the workplace.* Hillsdale, NJ: Erlbaum.

Crosby, F. J. (1976). A model of egoistical relative deprivation. *Psychological Review, 83,* 85-113.

Crosby, F., Bromley, S. & Saxe, L. (1980). Recent unobtrusive studies of black and white discrimination and prejudice: A literature review. *Psychological Bulletin, 87,* 546-563.

Cunningham, J. A., & Selby, P. L. (2007). Implications of the normative fallacy in young adult smokers aged 19-24 years. *American Journal of Public Health, 97*(8), 1399-1400.

Cunningham, M. R., Roberts, A. R., Barbee, A. P., Druen, P. B., & Wu, C. H. (1995). "Their ideas of beauty are, on the whole, the same as ours": Consistency and variability in the cross-cultural perception of female physical attractiveness. *Journal of Personality and Social Psychology, 68,* 261-279.

Cunningham, W. A., Johnson, M. K., Gatenby, J. C., Gore, J. C., & Banaji, M. R. (2003). Neural components of social evaluation. *Journal of Personality and Social Psychology, 85*(4), 639-649.

Dabbs, J. M. Jr., Carr, T. S., Frady, R. L., & Riad, J. K. (1995). Testosterone, crime, and misbehavior among 692 male prison inmates. *Personality and Individual Differences, 18,* 627-633.

Dabbs, J. M. Jr., & Hargrove, M. F. (1997). Age, testosterone, and behavior among female prison inmates. *Psychosomatic Medicine, 59,* 477-480.

Dabbs, J. M. Jr., & Morris, R. (1990). Testosterone, social class, and antisocial behavior in a sample of 4,462 men. *Psychological Science, 1,* 209-211.

D'Agostino, P. R., & Fincher-Kiefer, R. (1992). Need for cognition and the correspondence bias. *Social Cognition, 10*(2), 151-163.

Daly, M., & Wilson, M. (1989). Homicide and cultural evolution. *Ethology and Sociobiology, 10,* 99-110.

Darley, J. M., & Batson, C. D. (1973). "From Jerusalem to Jericho": A study of situational and dispositional variables in helping behavior. *Journal of Personality and Social Psychology, 27,* 100-108.

Darley, J. M., & Berscheid, E. (1967). Increased liking as a result of the anticipation of personal contact. *Human Relations, 20,* 29-39.

Darley, J. M., & Gross, P. H. (1983). A hypothesis-confirming bias in labeling effects. *Journal of Personality and Social Psychology, 44*(1), 20-33.

Darley, J. M., & Latane, B. (1968). Bystander intervention in emergencies: Diffusion of responsibility. *Journal of Personality and Social Psychology, 8*(4), 377-383.

Davies, P. G., Spencer, S. J., Quinn, D. M., & Gerhardstein, R. (2002). All consuming images: How demeaning commercials that elicit stereotype threat can restrain women academically and professionally. *Personality and Social Psychology Bulletin, 28,* 1615-1628.

Davila, J., & Cobb, R. J. (2003). Predicting change in self-reported and interviewer-assessed attachment security: Tests of the individual and life-stress model. *Personality and Social Psychology Bulletin, 29,* 859-870.

Davis, D., Shaver, P. R., & Vernon, M. L. (2004). Attachment style and subjective motivations for sex. *Personality and Social Psychology Bulletin, 30*(8), 1076–1090. Previously presented at Annual Meeting of the Western Psychological Association, Portland, OR, 2000.

Dawes, R. M. (1990). The potential nonfalsity of the false consensus effect. In R. M. Hogarth (Ed.), *Insights in decision making: A tribute to Hillel J. Einhorn* (pp. 179–199). Chicago: University of Chicago Press.

Dawkins, R. (1976). *The selfish gene.* Oxford: Oxford University Press.

de Vries, L. (2005). Opposites attract, but marry? *CBS News.* Retrieved July 5, 2010, from http://www.cbsnews.com/stories/2005/02/14/health/webmd/main674003.shtml.

de Wit, J. B. F., Das, E., & Vet, R. (2008). What works best: Objective statistics or a personal testimonial? An assessment of the persuasive effects of different types of message evidence on risk perception. *Health Psychology, 27*(1), 110–115.

DePaulo, B. M., & Kashy, D. A. (1998). Everyday lies in close and casual relationships. *Journal of Personality and Social Psychology, 74*(1), 63–79.

Destin, M., & Oyserman, D. (2010). Incentivizing education: Seeing schoolwork as an investment, not a chore. *Journal of Experimental Social Psychology, 43,* 505–512.

Deutsch, M., & Collins, M. E. (1951). *Interracial housing: A psychological evaluation of a social experiment.* Minneapolis, MN: University of Minnesota.

Devine, P. (1989). Stereotypes and prejudice: Their automatic and controlled components. *Journal of Personality and Social Psychology, 56,* 5–18.

Dickerson, C., Thibodeau, R., Aronson, E., & Miller, D. (1992). Using cognitive dissonance to encourage water conservation. *Journal of Applied Social Psychology, 22,* 841–854.

Diener, E., Fraser, S. C., Beaman, A. L., & Kelem, R. T. (1976). Effects of deindividuation variables on stealing among Halloween trick-or-treaters. *Journal of Personality and Social Psychology, 33*(2), 178–183.

Dijkstra, P., & Buunk, B. P. (1998). Jealousy as a function of rival characteristics: An evolutionary perspective. *Personality and Social Psychology Bulletin, 24,* 1158–1166.

Dillard, A. J., Midboe, A. M., & Klein, W. M. P. (2009). The dark side of optimism: Unrealistic optimism about problems with alcohol predicts subsequent negative event experiences. *Personality and Social Psychology Bulletin, 35*(11), 1540–1550.

Dion, K. K., Berscheid, E., & Walster, E. (1972). What is beautiful is good. *Journal of Personality and Social Psychology, 24,* 285–290.

Dion, K. K., & Dion, K. L. (1996). Cultural perspective on romantic love. *Personal Relationships, 3,* 5–17.

Dion, K. L., & Dion, K. K. (1993). Individualistic and collectivistic perspectives on gender and the cultural concept of love and intimacy. *Journal of Social Issues, 49,* 53–69.

Dittman, M. (2004). What makes good people do bad things? *Monitor on Psychology, 35*(9), 68.

Dodge, K. A. (1986). A social information processing model of social competence in children. In M. Perlmutter (Ed.), *Minnesota Symposium on Child Psychology* (Vol. 18, pp. 77–125). Hillsdale, NJ: Erlbaum.

Dodge, K. A., Price, J. M., Bachorowski, J., & Newman, J. P. (1990). Hostile attributional tendencies in severely aggressive adolescents. *Journal of Abnormal Psychology, 99,* 385–392.

Dollard, J., Doob, L. W., Miller, N. E., Mowrer, O. H., & Sears, R. R. (1939). *Frustration and aggression.* New Haven, CT: Yale University.

Dooley, P. A. (1995). Perceptions of the onset controllability of AIDS and helping judgments: An attributional analysis. *Journal of Applied Social Psychology, 25*(10), 858–869.

Dovidio, J. F. (1984). Helping behavior and altruism: An empirical and conceptual overview. In L. Berkowitz (Ed.), *Advances in experimental social psychology* (Vol. 17, pp. 361–427). New York: Academic Press.

Dovidio, J. F., & Gaertner, S. L. (1983). Race, normative structure, and help-seeking. In B. M. DePaulo, A. Nadler, & J. D. Fisher (Eds.), *New directions in helping* (Vol. 2, pp. 285–302). New York: Academic Press.

Dovidio, J. F., & Gaertner, S. L. (2000). Aversive racism and selection decisions: 1989 and 1999. *Psychological Science, 11*(4), 315–319.

Dovidio, J. F., Piliavin, J. A., Gaertner, S. L., Schroeder, D. A., & Clark, R. D. III. (1991). The arousal: Cost-reward model and the process of intervention: A review of the evidence. In M. S. Clark (Ed.), *Review of personality and social psychology: Vol. 12. Prosocial behavior* (pp. 86–118). Newbury Park, CA: Sage.

Downs, C., & Lyons, P. (1991). Natural observations of the links between attractiveness and initial legal judgments. *Personality and Social Psychology Bulletin, 17,* 541–547.

Drachman, D., DeCarufel, A., & Insko, C. (1978). The extra credit effect in interpersonal attraction. *Journal of Experimental Social Psychology, 14,* 458–459.

Duff, K., & Newman, L. S. (1997). Individual differences in the spontaneous construal of behavior: Idiocentrism and the automatization of the trait inference process. *Social Cognition, 15*(3), 217–241.

Duncan, B. L. (1976). Differential social perception and attribution of intergroup violence: Testing the lower limits of stereotyping of blacks. *Journal of Personality and Social Psychology, 34,* 590–598.

Dunfield, K. A., & Kuhlmeier, V. A. (2010). Intention-mediated selective helping in human infants. *Psychological Science, 21,* 523–527.

Dutton, D. G. (1971). Reactions of restaurateurs to blacks and whites violating restaurant dress regulations. *Canadian Journal of Behavioural Science, 3,* 298–302.

Dutton, D. G., & Aron, A. P. (1974). Some evidence for heightened sexual attraction under conditions of high anxiety. *Journal of Personality and Social Psychology, 30*(4), 510–517.

Dweck, C. S. (1999). *Self-theories: Their role in motivation, personality and development.* Philadelphia, PA: The Psychology Press.

Dwyer, J. (2007, February 11). Fugitive. *The New York Times.* Retrieved August 2, 2010, from http://www.nytimes.com/2007/02/11/magazine/11Boquete.t.html.

Eagly, A. H. (1978). Sex differences in influenceability. *Psychological Bulletin, 85*(1), 86–116.

Eagly, A. (1987) *Sex differences in social behavior: A social-role interpretation.* Hillsdale, NJ: Erlbaum.

Eagly, A. H., Ashmore, R. D., Makhijani, M. G., & Longo, L. C. (1991). What is beautiful is good, but . . . : A meta-analytic review of research on the physical attractiveness stereotype. *Psychological Bulletin, 110,* 109–128.

Eagly, A. H., & Chaiken, S. (1993). *The Psychology of Attitudes,* Fort Worth, TX: Harcourt Brace Jovanovich.

Eagly, A. H., & Chaiken, S. (1998). Attitude structure and function. In D. T. Gilbert, S. T. Fiske, & G. Lindzey (Eds.), *The Handbook of Social Psychology* (4th ed., Vol. 1, pp. 269–322). New York: McGraw-Hill.

Eagly, A. H., & Chrvala, C. (1986). Sex differences in conformity: Status and gender role interpretations. *Psychology of Women Quarterly, 10*(3), 203–220.

Eagly, A. H., & Crowley, M. (1986). Gender and helping behavior: A meta-analytic review of the social psychological literature. *Psychological Bulletin, 100,* 283–308.

Eagly, A. H., & Johnson, B. T. (1990). Gender and leadership style: A meta-analysis. *Psychological Bulletin, 108,* 233–256.

Eagly, A. H., Karau, S. J., & Makhijani, M. G. (1995). Gender and the effectiveness of leaders: A meta-analysis. *Psychological Bulletin, 117,* 125–145.

Eagly, A. H., Makhijani, M. G., & Klonsky, B. G. (1992). Gender and the evaluation of leaders: A meta-analysis. *Psychological Bulletin, 111,* 3–22.

Eagly, A., & Steffen, V. J. (1986). Gender and aggressive behavior: A meta-analytic review of the social psychological literature. *Psychological Bulletin, 100,* 309–330.

Eagly, A. H., & Wood, W. (1991). Explaining sex differences in social behavior: A meta-analytic perspective. *Personality and Social Psychology Bulletin, 17,* 306–315.

Edelmann, R. J., Childs, J., Harvey, S., Kellock, I., & Strain-Clark, C. (1984). The effect of embarrassment on helping. *Journal of Social Psychology, 124,* 253–254.

Eich, E., Macauley, D., & Ryan, L. (1994). Mood dependent memory for events of the person al past. *Journal of Experimental Psychology: General, 123,* 201–215.

Eisenberg, N., & Miller, P. (1987). The relation of empathy to pro-social and related behaviors. *Psychological Bulletin, 101,* 91–119.

Eisenberger, N. I., Lieberman, M. D., & Williams, K. D. (2003). Does rejection hurt? An fMRI study of social exclusion. *Science, 302,* 290–292.

Ekman, P. (1994). Strong evidence for universals in facial expressions: A reply to Russell's mistaken critique. *Psychological Bulletin, 115*(2), 268–287.

Ekman, P. (2001). *Telling lies: Clues to deceit in the marketplace, politics, and marriage.* New York: W. W. Norton & Co.

Epley, N., & Gilovich, T. (2006). The anchoring and adjustment heuristic: Why the adjustments are insufficient. *Psychological Science, 17,* 311–318.

Erb, H., Bohner, G., Schmälzle, K., & Rank, S. (1998). Beyond conflict and discrepancy: Cognitive bias in minority and majority influence. *Personality and Social Psychology Bulletin, 24*(6), 620–633.

Erskine, J. A. K. (2008). Resistance can be futile: Investigating behavioural rebound. *Appetite, 50,* 415-421.

Esses, V. M., Jackson, L. M., & Armstrong, T. L. (1998). Intergroup competition and attitudes toward immigrants and immigration: An instrumental model of group conflict. *Journal of Social Issues, 54*(4), 699-724.

Evans, A. N., & Rooney, B. J. (2008). *Methods in pyschological research.* Thousand Oaks, Calif.: Sage Publishing.

Evans, L., & Stukas, A. A. (2007). Self-verification by women and responses of their partners around issues of appearance and weight: "Do I look fat in this?" *Journal of Social and Clinical Psychology. 26*(10), 1163-1188.

Farr, R. M. (1996). *The roots of modern social psychology.* Cambridge, MA: Blackwell Publishing.

Fast, N. J., & Tiedens, L. Z. (2010). Blame contagion: The automatic transmission of self-serving attributions. *Journal of Experimental Social Psychology, 46*(1), 97-106.

Fazio, R. H. (1995). Attitudes as object-evaluation associations: Determinants, consequences, and correlates of attitude accessibility. In R. E. Petty, & J. A. Krosnick (Eds.), *Attitude Strength: Antecedents and Consequences* (pp. 247-282). Hillsdale, NJ: Erlbaum.

Fazio, R. H., Chen, J., McDonel, E. C., & Sherman, S. J. (1982). Attitude accessibility, attitude-behavior consistency, and the strength of the object-evaluation association. *Journal of Experimental Social Psychology, 18,* 339-357.

Fazio, R. H., Ledbetter, J. E., & Towles-Schwen, T. (2000). On the costs of accessible attitudes: Detecting that the attitude object has changed. *Journal of Personality and Social Psychology, 78,* 197-210.

Fazio, R. H., & Olson, M. A. (2003). Attitudes: Foundations, functions, and consequences. In M. A. Hogg & J. Cooper (Eds.), *The Handbook of Social Psychology.* London: Sage, 139-160.

Fazio, R. H., & Olson, M. A. (2003). Implicit measures in social cognition research: Their meaning and use. *Annual Review of Psychology, 54,* 297-327.

Fazio, R. H., & Williams, C. J. (1986). Attitude accessibility as a moderator of the attitude-perception and attitude-behavior relations: An investigation of the 1984 presidential election. *Journal of Personality and Social Psychology, 51*(3), 505-514.

FBI (2009). *2008 hate crime statistics.* Retrieved July 27, 2010, from http://www.fbi.gov/ucr/hc2008/incidents.html.

Federman, J. (Ed.) (1997). *National television violence study.* Santa Barbara: University of California, Center for Communication and Social Policy.

Feeney, J. A., & Noller, P. (1990). Attachment styles as a predictor of adult romantic relationships. *Journal of Personality and Social Psychology, 58,* 281-291.

Fein, S., & Spencer, S. J. (1997). Prejudice as self-image maintenance: Affirming the self through derogating others. *Journal of Personality and Social Psychology, 73,* 31-44.

Feingold, A. (1988). Matching for attractiveness in romantic partners and same-sex friends: A meta analysis and theoretical critique. *Psychological Bulletin, 104,* 226-235.

Feldman, R., Weller, A., Zagoory-Sharon, O., & Levine, A. (2007). Evidence for a neuroendocrinological foundation of human affiliation: Plasma oxytocin levels across pregnancy and the postpartum period predict mother-infant bonding. *Psychological Science, 18*(11), 965-970.

Festinger, L. (1954). A theory of social comparison processes. *Human Relations, 7,* 117-140.

Festinger, L. (1957). *A theory of cognitive dissonance.* Stanford, CA: Stanford University Press.

Festinger, L., & Carlsmith, J. M. (1959). Cognitive consequences of forced compliance. *Journal of Abnormal and Social Psychology, 58*(2), 203-210.

Festinger, L., Schachter, S., & Back, K. (1950). *Social pressures in informal groups: A study of human factors in housing.* New York: Harper.

Fischer, P. & Greitemeyer, T. (2006). Music and aggression: The impact of sexual-aggressive song lyrics on aggression-related thoughts, emotions, and behavior towards the same and the opposite sex. *Personality and Social Psychology Bulletin, 32,* 1165-1176.

Fischhoff, B. (2007). An early history of hindsight research. *Social Cognition, 25*(1), 10-13.

Fisher, J. D., Fisher, W. A., Bryan, A. D., & Misovich, S. J. (2002). Information-motivation-behavioral skills model-based HIV risk behavior change intervention for inner-city high school youth. *Health Psychology, 21*(2), 177-186.

Fisher, R. J., & Ackerman, D. (1998). The effects of recognition and group need on volunteerism: A social norm perspective. *Journal of Consumer Research, 25,* 262-275.

Fiske, S. T. (1980). Attention and weight in person perception: The impact of negative and extreme information. *Journal of Personality and Social Psychology, 38,* 889-906.

Flynn, F. J., & Lake, V. K. B. (2008). If you need help, just ask: Underestimating compliance with direct requests for help. *Journal of Personality and Social Psychology, 95,* 128-143.

Forgas, J. P., Bower, G. H., & Krantz, S. (1984). The influence of mood on perceptions of social interactions. *Journal of Experimental Social Psychology, 20,* 497-513.

Forge, K. L., & Phemister, S. (1987). The effect of prosocial cartoons on preschool children. *Child Study Journal, 17*(2), 83-86.

Fournier, R., & Tompson, T. (2008, September 21). Poll: Racial misgivings of Dems an Obama issue. *Associated Press.* Retrieved August 15, 2010, from http://www.ap.org/elections2008/fournier/fournier_092108.pdf.

Fox, K. (1997). Mirror, mirror: A summary of research findings on body image. *Social Issues Research Centre.* Retrieved June 3, 2010, from http://www.sirc.org/publik/mirror.html.

Frager, R. (1970). Conformity and anti-conformity in Japan. *Journal of Personality and Social Psychology, 15,* 203-210.

Fraley, R. C. (2002). Introduction to the special issue: The psychodynamics of adult attachments–bridging the gap between disparate research traditions. *Attachment and Human Development, 4,* 131-132.

Freedman, J. (2002). *Media violence and its effect on aggression: Assessing the scientific evidence.* Toronto, ON: University of Toronto Press.

Freedman, J. L., & Fraser, S. C. (1966). Compliance without pressure: The foot-in-the-door technique. *Journal of Personality and Social Psychology, 4,* 196-202.

Frisby, C. M. (1999, August). When bad things happen to bad people: Using social comparison theory to explain affective consequences of viewing TV talk shows. A paper presented to the Mass Communication and Society Division at the Association of Education in Journalism and Mass Communication Convention, New Orleans, LA.

Frost, K., Frank, E., & Maibach, E. (1997). Relative risk in the news media: A qualification of misrepresentation. *American Journal of Public Health, 87*(5), 842-845.

Fung, H. H., & Carstensen, L. L. (2003). Sending memorable messages to the old: Age differences in preferences and memory for emotionally meaningful advertisements. *Journal of Personality and Social Psychology, 85,* 163-178.

Gabriel, S., Carvallo, M., Dean, K., Tippin, B., & Renaud, J. (2005). How I see me depends on how I see we: The role of attachment style in social comparison. *Personality and Social Psychology Bulletin, 31,* 1561-1572.

Gaertner, S. L. (1973). Helping behavior and racial discrimination among liberals and conservatives. *Journal of Personality and Social Psychology, 25,* 335-341.

Gaes, G. G., Kalle, R. J., & Tedeschi, J. T. (1978). Impression management in the forced compliance situation: Two studies using the bogus pipeline. *Journal of Experimental Social Psychology, 14*(5), 493-510.

Gagnon, A., & Bourhis, R. Y. (1996). Discrimination in the minimal group paradigm: Social identity or self-interest? *Personality and Social Psychology Bulletin, 22,* 1289-1301.

Gallup, G. G. (1977). Chimpanzees: Self recognition. *Science, 167*(914), 86-87.

Gansberg, M. (1964). Thirty-eight who saw murder didn't call police. *The New York Times.*

Garcia, S. M., Weaver, K., Moskowitz, G. B., & Darley, J. M. (2002). Crowded minds: The implicit bystander effect. *Journal of Personality and Social Psychology, 83,* 843-853.

Gass, R. H., & Seiter, J. S. (2003). *Persuasion, Social Influence, and Compliance Gaining* (2nd ed.). Boston, MA: Allyn & Bacon.

Gawronski, B. (2003). Implicational schemata and the correspondence bias: On the diagnostic value of situationally constructed behavior. *Journal of Personality and Social Psychology, 84*(6), 1154-1171.

Gawronski, B., & Bodenhausen, G. V. (2006). Associative and propositional processes in evaluation: An integrative implicit and explicit attitude change. *Psychological Bulletin, 132,* 692-731.

Geary, D. C., Vigil, J., & Byrd-Craven, J. (2004). Evolution of human mate choice. *The Journal of Sex Research, 41*(1), 27-42.

Gerard, H. B., Wilhelmy, R. A., & Conolley, E. S. (1968). Conformity and group size. *Journal of Personality and Social Psychology, 8,* 79-82.

Gergen, K. J. (1973). Social psychology as history. *Journal of Personality and Social Psychology, 26*(2), 309–320.

Gerrard, M., Gibbons, F. X., & Bushman, B. J. (1996). The relation between perceived vulnerability to HIV and precautionary sexual behavior. *Psychological Bulletin, 119,* 390–409.

Gerstenfeld, P. B., Grant, D. R., & Chang, C. P. (2003). Hate online: A content analysis of extremist websites. *Analyses of Social Issues and Public Policy, 3*(1), 29–44.

Gibson, B. (2008). Can evaluative conditioning change attitudes toward mature brands: New evidence from the Implicit Association Test. *Journal of Consumer Research, 35*(1), 178–188.

Gibson, B., & Maurer, J. (2000). Cigarette smoking in the movies: the influence of product placement on attitudes toward smoking and smokers. *Journal of Applied Social Psychology, 30*(7), 1457–1473.

Gigerenzer, G. (2004a). Dread risk, September 11, and fatal traffic accidents. *Psychological Science, 15*(4), 286–287.

Gigerenzer, G. (2004b). Fast and frugal heuristics: The tools of bounded rationality. In D. Koehler & N. Harvey (Eds.), *Blackwell handbook of judgment and decision making* (pp. 62–88). Oxford, UK: Blackwell.

Gilbert, D. (2006). *Stumbling on Happiness.* New York: Random House.

Gilbert, D. T., & Ebert, J. E. J. (2002). Decisions and revisions: The affective forecasting of escapable outcomes. Unpublished manuscript, Harvard University.

Gilbert, D., & Malone, P. (1995). The correspondence bias. *Psychological Bulletin, 117,* 21–38.

Gilbert, D., Pelham, B., & Krull, D. (1988). On cognitive busyness: When person perceivers meet persons perceived. *Journal of Personality and Social Psychology, 54,* 733–740.

Gilbert, D. T., Pinel, E. C., Wilson, T. D., Blumberg, S. J., & Wheatley, T. (1998). Immune neglect: A source of durability bias in affective forecasting. *Journal of Personality and Social Psychology, 75,* 617–638.

Giles, L. C., Glonek, G. F., Luszcz, M. A., & Andrews, G. R. (2005). Effect of social networks on 10-year survival in very old Australians: The Australian longitudinal study of aging. *Journal of Epidemiology and Community Health, 59,* 574–579.

Gilovich, T. (1990). Differential construal and the false consensus effect. *Journal of Personality and Social Psychology, 59*(4), 623.

Gilovich, T., Medvec, V. H., & Savistsky, K. (2000). The spotlight effect in social judgment: An egocentric bias in estimates of the salience of one's own actions and appearance. *Journal of Personality and Social Psychology, 78,* 211–222.

Gilovich, T., Vallone, R., & Tversky, A. (1985). The hot hand in basketball: On the misperception of random sequences. *Cognitive Psychology, 17,* 295–314.

Giving USA Foundation (2009). *U.S. charitable giving estimated to be $307.65 billion in 2008.* Retrieved August 25, 2010, from http://www.givingusa.org/press_releases/gusa/GivingReaches300billion.pdf.

Glenn, A. L. & Raine, A. (2009). Psychopathy and instrumental aggression: Evolutionary, neurobiological, and legal perspectives. *International Journal of Law & Psychiatry, 32,* 253–258.

Glick, P., & Fiske, S. T. (2001). An ambivalent alliance: Hostile and benevolent sexism as complementary justifications of gender inequality. *American Psychologist, 56,* 109–118.

Glick, P., Fiske, S. T., Mladinic, A., Saiz, J. L., Abrams, D., Masser, B., Adetoun, B., & López, L. W. (2000). Beyond prejudice as simple antipathy: Hostile and benevolent sexism across cultures. *Journal of Personality and Social Psychology, 79,* 763–775.

Glynn, S. A., Busch, M. P., Schreiber, G. B., Murphy, E. L., Wright, D. J., Tu, Y., & Kleinman, S. H. (2003). Effect of a national disaster on blood supply and safety: The September 11 experience. *Journal of the American Medical Association, 289*(17), 2246–2253.

Goffman, E. (1952). On cooking the mark out: Some aspects of adaptation to failure. *Psychiatry, 15,* 451–463.

Golby, A. J., Gabrieli, J. D. E., Chiao, J. Y., & Eberhardt, J. L. (2001). Differential responses in the fusiform region to same-race and other-race faces. *Nature Neuroscience, 4,* 845–850.

Goodwin, R., & Findlay, C. (1997). "We were just fated together" ... Chinese love and the concept of yuan in England and Hong Kong. *Personal Relationships, 4,* 85–92.

Gopnik, A., Meltzoff, A. N., & Kuhl, P. K. (1999). *The scientist in the crib: What early learning tells us about the mind.* New York: HarperCollins.

Gordijn, E. H., De Vries, N. K., & de Dreu, C. K. W. (2002). Minority influence on focal and related attitudes: Change in size, attribution, and information processing. *Personality and Social Psychology Bulletin, 28,* 1315–1326.

Gordon, I., Zagoory-Sharon, O., Leckman, J., & Feldman, R. (2010) Oxytocin and the development of parenting in humans. *Biological Psychiatry, 68*(4), 377–382.

Gore, K., Tobiasen, M., & Kayson, W. (1997). Effects of sex of caller, implied sexual orientation of caller, and urgency on altruistic response using the wrong number technique. *Psychological Reports, 80,* 927–930.

Gosling, S. (2008). *Snoop: What your stuff says about you.* New York: Basic Books.

Gottman, J. (1994). *Why marriages succeed or fail ... and how you can make yours last.* New York: Simon & Schuster.

Gottman, J. M., Levenson, R. W., Swanson, C., Swanson, K., Tyson, R., & Yoshimoto, D. (2003). Observing gay, lesbian and heterosexual couples' relationships: mathematical modeling of conflict interaction. *Journal of Homosexuality, 45*(1), 65–91.

Graham, S. (2001, August 10). Parkinson's patents feel the placebo effect. *Scientific American.* Retrieved June 3, 2010, from http://www.scientificamerican.com/article.cfm?id=parkinsons-patients-feel.

Graham, S., Weiner, B., & Zucker, G. (1997). An attributional analysis of punishment goals and public reactions to O. J. Simpson. *Personality and Social Psychology Bulletin, 23,* 331–346.

Greenwald, A. G., Banaji, M. R., Rudman, L. A., Farnham, S. D., Nosek, B. A., & Rosier, M. (2000). Prologue to a unified theory of attitudes, stereotypes, and self-concept. In J. Forgas (Ed.), *The role of affect in social cognition* (pp. 308–330). Cambridge, UK: Cambridge University Press.

Greenwald, A. G., McGhee, D. E., & Schwartz, J. L. K. (1998). Measuring individual differences in implicit cognition: The Implicit Association Test. *Journal of Personality and Social Psychology, 74,* 1464–1480.

Greenwald, A. G., Oakes, M. A., & Hoffman, H. (2003). Targets of discrimination: Effects of race on responses to weapons holders. *Journal of Experimental Social Psychology, 39,* 399–405.

Groff, B. D., Baron, R. S., & Moore, D. L. (1983). Distraction, attentional conflict, and drivelike behavior. *Journal of Experimental Social Psychology, 19,* 359–380.

Guadagno, R.E., & Cialdini, R.B. (2002). Online persuasion: An examination of gender differences in computer-mediated interpersonal influence. *Group Dynamics: Theory Research and Practice, 6,* 38–51.

Gueguen, N., & De Gail, M. (2003). The effect of smiling on helping behavior: Smiling and Good Samaritan behavior. *Communication Reports, 16,* 133–140.

Gupta, U., & Singh, P. (1982). Exploratory study of love and liking and type of marriages. *Indian Journal of Applied Psychology, 19,* 92–97.

Gurwitz, S., & Marcus, M. (1978). Effects of anticipated interaction, sex and homosexual stereotypes on first impressions. *Journal of Applied Social Psychology, 8*(1), 47–56.

Gusnard, D. A., Akbudak, E., Shulman, G. L., & Raichle, M. E. (2001). Medial prefrontal cortex and referential mental activity: Relation to a default mode of brain function. *Proceedings of the National Academy of Sciences, 98,* 4259–4264.

Halberstadt, J., & Rhodes, G. (2003). It's not just average faces that are attractive: Computer-manipulated averageness makes birds, fish, and automobiles attractive. *Psychonomic Bulletin and Review, 10,* 149–156.

Halligan, S., Cooper, P., Healy, S., & Murray, L. (2008). The attribution of hostile intent in mothers, fathers, and their children. *Journal of Abnormal Child Psychology, 35*(4), 594–604.

Hamermesh, D. S & Biddle, J. E, (1994). Beauty and the labor market. *American Economic Review, 84*(5), 1174–1194.

Hamermesh, D. S. & Parker, A. (2005). Beauty in the classroom: instructors' pulchritude and putative pedagogical productivity. *Economics of Education Review, 24*(4), 369–376.

Hampson, R. (2010). "A 'watershed' case in school bullying?" *USA Today.* Retrieved July 31, 2010, from http://www.usatoday.com/news/nation/2010-04-04-bullying_N.htm.

Hancock, J.T., Curry, L., Goorha, S., & Woodworth, M.T. (2008). On lying and being lied to: A linguistic analysis of deception. *Discourse Processes, 45,* 1–23.

Hancock, J.T., Toma, C., & Ellison, N. (2007). The truth about lying in online dating profiles. *Proceedings of the ACM Conference on Human Factors in Computing Systems* (CHI 2007), 449–452.

Haney, C., & Zimbardo, P. G. (1998). The past and future of U.S. prison policy: Twenty-five years after the Stanford Prison Experiment. *American Psychologist, 53,* 709–727.

Hardin, C. D., & Higgins, E. T. (1996). Shared reality: How social verification makes the subjective objective. In R. M. Sorrentino, E. T. Higgins (Eds.), *Handbook of motivation and cognition: The interpersonal context* (Vol. 3, pp. 28-84). New York: Guilford Press.

Harlow, H. (1958). The nature of love. *American Psychologist, 13*, 673-685.

Harrell, W. A. (1978). Physical attractiveness, self-disclosure, and helping behavior. *Journal of Social Psychology, 104*, 15-17.

Harris, M. B. (1994). Gender of subject and target as mediators of aggression. *Journal of Applied Social Psychology, 24*, 453-471.

Harsch, E. (2007). Conflict resources: From 'curse' to blessing. *Africa Renewal, 20*(4), 17.

Hartup, W. W., & Stevens, N. (1997). Friendships and adaptation in the life course. *Psychological Bulletin, 121*, 355-370.

Hassin, R., & Trope, Y. (2000). Facing faces: Studies on the cognitive aspects of physiognomy. *Journal of Personality and Social Psychology, 78*(5), 837-852.

Hastie, R., Penrod, S. D., & Pennington, N. (1983). *Inside the jury*. Cambridge, MA: Harvard University Press.

Hastie, R., Penrod, S., & Pennington, N. (1983). What goes on in a jury deliberation. *American Bar Association Journal, 69*, 1848-1853.

Hatfield, E. (1988). The passionate love scale. In C. M. Davis, W. L. Yaber, & S. L. Davis (Eds.), *Sexuality-related measures: A compendium*. Bloomington, IN.

Hatfield, E., & Sprecher, S. (1986). Measuring passionate love in intimate relations. *Journal of Adolescence, 9*, 383-410.

Hatfield, E., & Sprecher, S. (1986). *Mirror, mirror . . . .* New York: State University of New York Press.

Havas, D. A., Glenberg, A. M., Gutowski, K. A., Lucarelli, M. J., & Davidson, R. J. (2010). Cosmetic use of botulinum toxin-a affects processing of emotional language. *Psychological Science, 21*(7), 895-900.

Hays, R. B. (1985). A longitudinal study of friendship development. *Journal of Personality and Social Psychology, 48*, 909-924.

Hazan, C., & Shaver, P. (1987). Romantic love conceptualized as an attachment process. *Journal of Personality and Social Psychology, 52*(3), 511-524.

Heider, F. (1958). *The psychology of interpersonal relations*. Hillsdale, NJ: Erlbaum.

Heilman, M. E. (2001). Description and prescription: How gender stereotypes prevent women's ascent up the organizational ladder. *Journal of Social Issues, 57*(4), 657-674.

Heine, S. J., & Lehman, D. R. (1997). Culture, dissonance, and self-affirmation. *Personality and Social Psychology Bulletin, 23*, 389-400.

Henkel, L., & Mather, M. (2007). Memory attributions for choices: How beliefs shape our memories. *Journal of Memory and Language, 57*, 163-176.

Herek, G. M. (2009). Hate crimes and stigma-related experiences among sexual minority adults in the United States: Prevalence estimates from a national probability sample. *Journal of Interpersonal Violence, 24*, 54-74.

Higgins, E. T. (1987). Self-discrepancy: A theory relating self and affect. *Psychological Review, 94*, 319-340.

Higgins, E. T., & King, G. (1981). Accessibility of social constructs: Information-processing consequences of individual and contextual variability. In N. Cantor & J. Kihlstrom (Eds.), *Personality, cognition, and social interaction*. Hillsdale, NJ: Erlbaum.

Higgins, E. T., Rholes, W. S., & Jones, C. R. (1977). Category accessibility and impression formation. *Journal of Experimental Social Psychology, 13*, 141-154.

Hirono, N. (2000) Left frontotemporal hypoperfusion is associated with aggression in patients with dementia. *Arch Neurol, 57*(6), 861-866.

Hodson, G., Dovidio, J. R., & Esses, V. M. (2003). Ingroup identification as a moderator of positive-negative asymmetry in social discrimination. *European Journal of Social Psychology, 33*, 215-233.

Hoffman, C., & Hurst, N. (1990). Gender stereotypes: Perception or rationalization? *Journal of Personality and Social Psychology, 58*, 197-208.

Holland, R. W., Verplanken, B., & van Knippenberg, A. (2003). From repetition to conviction: Attitude accessibility as a determinant of attitude certainty. *Journal of Experimental Social Psychology, 39*(6), 594-601.

Holt-Lundstad, J., Birmingham, W., & Jones, B. Q. (2008). Is there something unique about marriage? The relative impact of marital status, relationship quality, and network social support on ambulatory blood pressure and mental health. *Annals of Behavioral Medicine, 35*(2), 239-244.

Holt-Lunstad J., Smith T. B., & Layton J. B. (2010). Social relationships and mortality risk: A meta-analytic review. *Public Library of Science Medicine, 7*(7).

Hoorens, V., Smits, T., & Sheppard, J. A. (2008). Comparative optimism in the spontaneous generation of future life events. *British Journal of Social Psychology, 47*(3), 441-451.

Hornstein, H. (1976). Cruelty and kindness: A new look at aggression and altruism. Englewood Cliffs, NJ: Prentice Hall.

Hovland, C. I., Irving, L. J., & Kelly, H. H. (1953). *Communication and Persuasion: Psychological Studies of Opinion Change*. New Haven, CT: Yale University Press.

Hovland, C. I., Lumsdale, A. A., & Sheffield, F. D. (1949). *Experiments on mass communication: Studies in social psychology in World War II: Volume III*. Princeton, NJ: Princeton University Press.

Hovland, C. I., & Weiss, W. (1951). The influence of source credibility on communication Effectiveness. *Public Opinion Quarterly, 15*, 635-650.

Huesmann, L. R., Moise-Titus, J., Podolski, C. L., & Eron, L. (2003). Longitudinal relations between children's exposure to TV violence and their aggressive and violent behavior in young adulthood: 1977-1992. *Developmental Psychology, 39*, 201-221.

Huffington Post. (2009, October 27). *Police: People watched gang rape of teen and did nothing to help*. Retrieved November 30, 2010, from http://www.huffingtonpost.com/2009/10/27/police-people-watched-gan_n_334975.html.

Hugenberg, K., & Bodenhausen, G. V. (2003). Facing prejudice: Implicit prejudice and the perception of facial threat. *Psychological Science, 14*, 640-643.

Hughes, S. M., Harrison, M. A., & Gallup Jr., G. G. (2002). The sound of symmetry: Voice as a marker of developmental stability. *Evolution and Human Behavior, 23*, 173-180.

Hull, J. G., & Young, R. D. (1983). The self-awareness-reducing effects of alcohol consumption: Evidence and implications. In J. Suls & A. G. Greenwald (Eds.), *Psychological Perspectives on the Self* (Vol. 2). Hillsdale, NJ: Erlbaum.

Husted, V., Madey, S. F., & Gilovich, T. (1995). When less is more: Counterfactual thinking and satisfaction among Olympic medalists. *Journal of Personality and Social Psychology, 69*(4), 603-610.

Huston, T. L., & Vangelisti, A. L. (1991). Socioemotional behavior and satisfaction in marital relationships: A longitudinal study. *Journal of Personality and Social Psychology, 61*, 721-733.

Hyde, J. S. (1984). How large are gender differences in aggression? A developmental meta-analysis. *Developmental Psychology, 20*(4), 722-736.

Hyman, H., & Sheatsley, P. (1956). Attitudes toward desegregation. *Scientific American, 195*, 35-39.

Iacoboni, M., Woods, R. P., Brass, M., Bekkering, H., Mazziotta, J. C., Rizzolatti, G. (1999). Cortical mechanisms of human imitation. *Science, 286*, 2526-2528.

Ickes, W. J., & Simpson, J. A. (2004). Motivational aspects of empathic accuracy. In M. B. Brewer & M. Hewstone (Eds.), *Emotion and Motivation: Perspectives on Social Psychology*. Malden, MA: Blackwell Publishing.

Imhoff, R. (2009) What motivates nonconformity? Uniqueness seeking blocks majority influence. *Personality and Social Psychology Bulletin, 35*(3), 309-320.

Ingham, A. G., Levinger, G., Graves, J., & Peckham, V. (1974). The Ringelmann effect: Studies of group size and group performance. *Journal of Experimental Social Psychology, 10*, 371-384.

Isen, A. M. (1970). Success, failure, attention, and reaction to others: The warm glow of success. *Journal of Personality and Social Psychology, 15*, 294-301.

Isen, A. M., Clark, M., & Schwartz, M. (1976). Duration of the effect of good mood on helping: "Footprints in the sands of time." *Journal of Personality and Social Psychology, 34*, 385-393.

Isen, A. M., & Levin, P. F. (1972). The effect of feeling good on helping: Cookies and kindness. *Journal of Personality and Social Psychology, 21*(3), 384-388.

Isen, A. M., Shalker, T. E., Clark, M., & Karp, L. (1978). Affect, accessibility of material in memory, and behavior. *Journal of Personality and Social Psychology, 36*, 1-12.

Isenberg, D. J. (1986). Group polarization: A critical review and meta-analysis. *Journal of Personality and Social Psychology, 50*, 1141-1151.

Ito, T. A., Larsen, J. T., Smith, N. K., & Cacioppo, J. T. (1998). Negative information weighs more heavily on the brain: The negativity bias in evaluative categorizations. *Journal of Personality and Social Psychology, 75*(4), 887-900.

Ito, T. A., Thompson, E., & Cacioppo, J. T. (2004). Tracking the timecourse of social perception: The effects of racial cues on event-related brain potentials. *Personality and Social Psychology Bulletin, 30*, 1267-1280.

Iyengar, S. S., & Lepper, M. R. (2000). When choice is demotivating: Can one desire too much of a good thing? *Journal of Personality and Social Psychology, 79*(6), 995–1006.

Izard, C. E. (1990). Facial expressions and the regulation of emotions. *Journal of Personality and Social Psychology, 58,* 487–498.

Jackman, M. R., & Jackman, R. (1983). *Class awareness in the United States.* Berkeley: University of California Press.

Jacobi, L., & Cash, T. F. (1994). In pursuit of the perfect appearance: Discrepancies among self-ideal percepts of multiple physical attributes. *Journal of Applied Social Psychology, 24*(5), 379–396.

Jacoby, J. (2008, April 6). Choosing to eliminate unwanted daughters. *The Boston Globe.* Retrieved August 17, 2010, from http://www.boston.com/bostonglobe/editorial_opinion/oped/articles/2008/04/06/choosing_to_eliminate_unwanted_daughters/.

Janis, I. L. (1982). *Groupthink* (2nd ed.). Boston: Houghton Mifflin.

Janis, I. L., & Feshbach, S. (1953). Effects of fear-arousing communications. *The Journal of Abnormal and Social Psychology, 48,* 78–92.

Jehl, D. (1999, June 20). For shame: A special report; Arab honor's price: A woman's blood. *The New York Times.* June 20, 1999.

Jiaquan, X., Kochanek, K. D., Murphy, S. L., & Tejada-Vera, B. (2010). Deaths: Final data for 2007. *National Vital Statistics Reports, 58*(19).

Johnson, D. E., Erez, A., Kiker, D. S., & Motowidlo, S. J. (2002). Liking and attributions of motives on relationship between a ratee's reputation and helpful behaviors. *Journal of Applied Psychology, 87,* 808–815.

Johnson, R. C., Danko, G. P. Darvill, T. J., Bochner, S., Bowers, J. K., Huang, Y. H., Park, J. Y., Pecjak, V., Rahim, A. R. A., & Pennington, D. (1989). Cross cultural assessment of altruism and its correlates. *Personality and Individual Differences, 10,* 855–868.

Johnson, R. D., & Downing, L. L. (1979). Deindividuation and valance of cues: Effects on prosocial and antisocial behavior. *Journal of Personality and Social Psychology, 37,* 1532–1538.

Jones, C. R., Olson, M. A., & Fazio, R. H. (2010). Evaluative conditioning: The "how" question. In M. P. Zanna & J. M. Olson (Eds.), *Advances in Experimental Social Psychology* (Vol. 43). San Diego: Academic Press.

Jones, E. E., & Davis, K. E. (1965). From acts to dispositions: The attribution process in social psychology. In L. Berkowitz (Ed.), *Advances in Experimental Social Psychology* (Volume 2, pp. 219–266). New York: Academic Press

Jones, E. E., & Harris, V. A. (1967). The attribution of attitudes. *Journal of Experimental Social Psychology, 3,* 1–24.

Jones, E. E., & Nisbett, R. E. (1971). *The actor and the observer: Divergent perceptions of the causes of behavior.* New York: General Learning Press.

Jones, E., & Sigall, H. (1971). The bogus pipeline: A new paradigm for measuring affect and attitude. *Psychological Bulletin, 76,* 349–364.

Jones, J. M. (2007). Some Americans reluctant to vote for Mormon, 72-year-old presidential candidates. *Gallup.* Retrieved August 17, 2010, from http://www.gallup.com/poll/26611/some-americans-reluctant-vote-mormon-72yearold-presidential-candidates.aspx.

Jones, J. T., & Cunningham, J. D. (1996). Attachment styles and other predictors of relationship satisfaction in dating couples. *Personal Relationships, 3,* 387–399.

Jones, J. T., Pelham, B. W., Carvallo, M., & Mirenberg, M. C. (2004). How do I love thee? Let me count the Js: Implicit egotism and interpersonal attraction. *Journal of Personality and Social Psychology, 87,* 665–683.

Judd, C. M., Blair, I. V., & Chapleau, K. M. (2004). Automatic stereotypes versus automatic prejudice: Sorting out the possibilities in the Payne (2002) weapon paradigm. *Journal of Experimental Social Psychology, 40,* 75–81.

Jussim, L. (1986). Self-fulfilling prophecies: A theoretical and integrative view. *Psychological Review, 93*(4), 429–445.

Jussim, L., & Harber, K. D. (2005). Teacher expectations and self-fulfilling prophecies: Knowns and unknowns, resolved and unresolved controversies. *Personality and Psychology Review, 9,* 131–155.

Kahneman, D., & Tversky, A. (1973). On the psychology of prediction. *Psychological Review, 80,* 237–251.

Kalven, H., & Zeisel, H. (1966). *The American jury.* Boston: Little, Brown.

Karau, S. J., & Williams, K. D. (1993). Social loafing: A meta-analytic review and theoretical integration. *Journal of Personality and Social Psychology, 65,* 681–706.

Katz, D. (1979). Floyd H. Allport (1890–1978). *American Psychologist, 34,* 351–353.

Katz, D., & Braly, K. (1933). Racial stereotypes of one hundred college students. *Journal of Abnormal and Social Psychology, 28,* 280–290.

Katz, P. A., Sohn, M., & Zalk, S. R. (1975). Perceptual concomitants of racial attitudes in urban grade-school children. *Developmental Psychology, 11,* 135–144.

Keelan, J. P. R., Dion, K. L., & Dion, K. K. (1994). Attachment style and heterosexual relationships among young adults: A short-term panel study. *Journal of Social and Personal Relationships, 11,* 201–214.

Kellerman, A. L. (1993). Gun ownership as a risk factor for homicide in the home. *New England Journal of Medicine, 329*(15), 1084–1091.

Kelley, H. H. (1950). The warm-cold variable in first impressions of persons. *Journal of Personality, 18,* 431–439.

Kelley, H. H. (1972) Attribution in social interaction. In E. E. Jones, D. E. Kanouse, H. H. Kelley, R. E. Nisbett, S. Valins, & B. Weiner (Eds.), *Attribution: Perceiving the causes of behavior* (pp. 1–26). Morristown, NJ: General Learning Press.

Kelley, H. H., & Michela, J. L. (1980). Attribution theory and research. *Annual Review of Psychology, 31,* 457–501.

Kelley, K., & Byrne, D. (1976). Attraction and altruism: With a little help from my friends. *Journal of Research in Personality, 10,* 59–68.

Kelly, D. J., Quinn, P. C., Slater, A. M., Lee, K., Ge, L., & Pascalis, O. (2007). The other-race effect develops during infancy: Evidence of perceptual narrowing. *Psychological Science, 18,* 1084–1089.

Kelman, H., & Hovland, C. (1953). Reinstatement of the communication in delayed measurement of attitude change. *Journal of Abnormal Social Psychology, 48,* 327–335.

Keltner, D., & Robinson, R. J. (1997). Defending the status quo: Power and bias in social conflict. *Personality and Social Psychology Bulletin, 23,* 1066–1077.

Kenny, D. A. (1994). *Interpersonal perception: A social relations analysis.* New York: Guilford.

Kenny, D. A. (2000). *PERSON: A general model for understanding interpersonal perception.* Unpublished manuscript, University of Connecticut.

Kenny, D. A., & Acitelli, L. K. (2001). Accuracy and bias in perceptions of the partner in close relationships. *Journal of Personality and Social Psychology, 80*(3), 438–439.

Kenrick, D. T., Neuberg, S. L., Zierk, K. L., & Krones, J. M. (1994). Evolution and social cognition: Contrast effects as a function of sex, dominance, and physical attractiveness. *Personality and Social Psychology Bulletin, 20,* 210–217.

Kenrick, D. T., Sadalla, E. K., Groth, G., & Trost, M. R. (1990). Evolution, traits, and the stages of human courtship: Qualifying the parental investment model [Special issue: Biological foundations of personality: Evolution, behavioral genetics, and psycho- physiology]. *Journal of Personality, 58,* 97–116.

Kernis, M. H. (2003). Toward a conceptualization of optimal self-esteem. *Psychological Inquiry, 14,* 1–26.

Key, J. P. (1997). Research design in occupational education. Oklahoma State University. Retrieved June 3, 2010, from http://www.okstate.edu/ag/agedcm4h/academic/aged5980a/5980/newpage110.htm.

Kiene, S. M., Barta, W. D., Zelenski, J. M., & Cothran, D. L. (2005). Why are you bringing up condoms *now?* The effect of message content on framing effects of condom use messages. *Health Psychology, 24,* 321–326.

Kim, H., & Markus, H. R. (1999). Deviance or uniqueness, harmony or conformity? A cultural analysis. *Journal of Personality and Social Psychology, 77*(4), 785–800.

King, G. (1995, September). Replication, replication. *PS: Political Science and Politics, 28*(3), 444–452.

Kitayama, S., & Markus, H. R. (1995). Construal of self as cultural frame: Implications for internationalizing psychology. In N. R. Goldberger & J. B. Veroff (Eds.), *The Culture and Psychology Reader* (pp. 366–383). New York: New York University Press.

Kitayama, S., Snibbe, A. C., Markus, H. R., & Suzuki, T. (2004). Is there any "free" choice? Self and dissonance in two cultures. *Psychological Science, 15*(8), 527–533.

Kleinke, C. L. (1977). Effects of dress on compliance to requests in a field setting. *Journal of Social Psychology, 101,* 223–224.

Klohnen, E. C. & Bera, S. (1998). Behavioral and experiential patterns of avoidantly and securely attachment women across adulthood: A 31-year longitudinal perspective. *Journal of Personality and Social Psychology, 74*(1), 211–223.

Klohnen, E. C., & Luo, S. (2003). Interpersonal attraction and personality: What is attractive—self similarity, ideal similarity, complementarity, or attachment security? *Journal of Personality and Social Psychology, 85,* 709–722.

Klucharev, V. A., Hytonen, K., Rijpkema, M., Smidts, A., & Fernandez, G. (2009). Reinforcement learning signal predicts social conformity. *Neuron, 61*, 140-151.

Ko, S. J., Judd, C. M., & Blair, I. (2006). What the voice reveals: Within- and between-category stereotyping on the basis of voice. *Personality and Social Psychology Bulletin, 32*(6), 806-819.

Kohler, P., Manhart, L., & Lafferty, W. (2008). Abstinence-only and comprehensive sex education and the initiation of sexual activity and teen pregnancy. *Journal of Adolescent Health, 42*(4), 344-351.

Köhnken, G., Milne, R., Memon, A., & Bull, R. (1999). The cognitive interview: A meta-analysis. *Psychology, Crime, & Law, 5*, 3-27.

Korchmaros, J. D., & Kenny, D. A. (2001). Emotional closeness as a mediator of the effect of genetic relatedness on altruism. *Psychological Science, 12,* 262-265.

Kowalczyk, L. (2009, February 25). Surgeon awarded $1.6 million in sex bias suit. *The Boston Globe.* Retrieved August 17, 2010, from http://www.boston.com/news/local/massachusetts/articles/2009/02/25/surgeon_awarded_16m_in_sex_bias_suit/.

Kozlowski, S. W. J., Kirsch, M. P., & Chao, G. T. (1986). Job knowledge, ratee familiarity, conceptual similarity, and halo error: An exploration. *Journal of Applied Psychology, 71,* 45-49.

Kraus, M. W., & Chen, S. (2009). Striving to be known by significant others: Automatic activation of self-verification goals in relationship contexts. *Journal of Personality and Social Psychology, 97*(1), 58-73.

Kriesberg, L. (2003, September). De-escalating gestures. Beyond Intractibility Version IV. Retrieved December 1, 2010, from http://www.beyond-intractability.org/essay/disarming_behavior.

Kristof, N., (2010). Celebrate: Save a mother. *The New York Times.* Retrieved July 17, 2010, from http://www.nytimes.com/2010/05/09/opinion/09kristof.html?_r=2.

Krosnick, J. A., & Alwin, D. F. (1989). Aging and susceptibility to attitude change. *Journal of Personality and Social Psychology,* 57, 416-425.

Krueger, J., & Clement, R. W. (1994). The truly false consensus effect: An ineradicable and egocentric bias in social perception. *Journal of Personality and Social Psychology, 67,* 596-610.

Kruglanski, A. W., & Webster, D. M. (1996). Motivated closing of the mind: "Seizing" and "freezing." *Psychological Review, 103*(2), 263-283.

Krupa, C. (2009). Biggest choke jobs in sports history. *FoxSports.* Retrieved August 5, 2010, from http://msn.foxsports.com/nhl/lists/Infamous-chokers-gallery#sport=NHL&photo=11204945.

Kuhn, M. H., & McPartland, T. S. (1954). An empirical investigation of self-attitude. *American Sociological Review, 19*(1), 68-76.

Kump, L. (2010, December 5). Teaching the teachers. *Forbes.* Retrieved July 17, 2010, from http://www.forbes.com/free_forbes/2005/1212/115.html.

Kunda, Z. (1999). *Social cognition: Making sense of people.* Cambridge, MA: The MIT Press.

Kurdek, L. A. (1991). Sexuality in homosexual and heterosexual couples. In K. McKinney & S. Sprecher (Eds.), *Sexuality in Close Relationships* (pp. 177-191). Hillsdale, NJ: Erlbaum.

Kurdek, L. A. (2004). Are gay and lesbian cohabiting couples really different from heterosexual married couples? *Journal of Marriage and Family, 66,* 880-900.

Laird, J. D. (1974). Self-attribution and emotion: The effects of expressive behavior on the quality of emotional experience. *Journal of Personality and Social Psychology, 29,* 475-486.

Laird, J. D. (2007). *Feelings: The perception of self. Series in affective science.* New York: Oxford University Press.

Langer, E. J. (1975). The illusion of control. *Journal of Personality and Social Psychology, 32*(2), 311-328.

Langer, E. J. (1982). The illusion of control. In D. Kahneman, P. Slovic, & A. Tversky (Eds.), *Judgment Under Uncertainty: Heuristics and Biases.* New York: Cambridge University Press.

Langer, E. J., Blank, A., & Chanowitz, B. (1978). The mindfulness of ostensibly thoughtful action. The role of "placebic" information in interpersonal interaction. *Journal of Personality and Social Psychology, 36*(6), 635-642.

Langlois, J. H., Ritter, J. M., Roggman, L. A., & Vaughn, L. S. (1991). Facial diversity and infant preferences for attractive faces. *Developmental Psychology, 27,* 79-84.

Langlois, J. H., & Roggman, L. A. (1990). Attractive faces are only average. *Psychological Science, 1,* 115-121.

LaPiere, R. T. (1934). Attitudes versus actions. *Social Forces, 13,* 230-237.

Larson, J. R. Jr., Foster-Fishman, P. G., & Keys, C. B. (1994). Information sharing in decision-making groups. *Journal of Personality and Social Psychology, 67,* 446-461.

Lashinsky, A. (2008). Google wins again. *Fortune Magazine.* Retrieved October 11, 2010, from http://money.cnn.com/2008/01/18/news/companies/google.fortune/index.htm.

Latane, B. (1981). The psychology of social impact. *American Psychologist, 36,* 343-356.

Latane, B., & Darley, J. M. (1968). Group inhibition of bystander intervention in emergencies. *Journal of Personality and Social Psychology, 10,* 215-221.

Latane, B., & Darley, J. (1969). Bystander "apathy." *American Scientist, 57,* 244-268.

Latane, B., Williams, K., & Harkins, S. (1979). Many hands make light the work: The causes and consequences of social loafing. *Journal of Personality and Social Psychology, 37,* 822-832.

Lawrence, E., Bunde, M., Barry, R. A., Brock, R. L., Sullivan, K. T., Pasch, L. A., . . . Adams, E. E. (2008). Partner support and marital satisfaction: Support amount, adequacy, provision, and solicitation. *Personal Relationships, 15*(4), 445-463.

Leach, C. W., Spears, R., Branscombe, N. R., & Doosje, B. (2003). Malicious pleasure: Schadenfreude at the suffering of another group. *Journal of Personality and Social Psychology, 84,* 932-943.

Leary, M. R. (1998). The social and psychological importance of self-esteem. In R. M. Kowalski & M. R. Leary (Eds.), *The Social Psychology of Emotional and Behavioral Problems: Interfaces of Social and Clinical Psychology* (pp. 197-221). Washington, DC: American Psychological Association.

Leary, M. R. (2004). *The Curse of the Self: Self-Awareness, Egotism, and the Quality of Human Life.* New York: Oxford University Press.

Leary, M. R. (2007). Motivational and emotional aspects of the self. *Annual Review of Psychology, 58,* 317-344.

LeDoux, J. (2002). *The synaptic self: How our brains become who we are.* New York: Penguin.

Lee, A., & Aaker, J. (2004). Bringing the grame into focus: The influence of regulatory fit on processing fluency and persuasion. *Journal of Personality and Social Psychology, 86,* 205-218.

Lee, C. M., Geisner, I. M., Lewis, M. A., Neighbors, C., & Larimer, M. E. (2007). Social motives and the interaction between descriptive and injunctive norms in college student drinking. *Journal of Studies on Alcohol and Drugs, 68*(5), 714-721.

Lent, R. W., Brown, S. D., & Larkin, K. C. (1984). Relation of self-efficacy expectations to academic achievement and persistence. *Journal of Counseling Psychology, 31,* 356-362.

Leonard, C. (2010, June 25). Panera Co. to open more pay-what-you-wish eateries. *Associated Press.* Retrieved August 16, 2010, from http://www.google.com/hostednews/ap/article/ALeqM5g__EQ-OG9DhU1YwC4Fo4s5QREdbgD9GIE6682.

Leonardi, A., & Gonida, E. (2007). Predicting academic self-handicapping in different age groups: The role of personal achievement goals and social goals. *British Journal of Educational Psychology, 77*(3), 595-611.

Lepper, M. R., Greene, D., & Nisbett, R. E. (1973). Undermining children's intrinsic interest with extrinsic rewards: A test of the "overjustification" hypothesis. *Journal of Personality and Social Psychology, 28,* 129-137.

Lerman, R. (2002). *Marriage and the economic well-being of families with children: A review of the literature.* Washington, DC: The Urban Institute and American University.

Lerner, J. S., Gonzalez, R. M., Small, D. A., & Fischhoff, B. (2003). Effects of fear and anger on perceived risks of terrorism. A national field experiment. *Psychological Science, 14,* 144-150.

Lerner, M. J. (1980). *The belief in a just world: A fundamental delusion.* New York: Plenum Press.

Leventhal, H., Singer, R., & Jones, S. (1965). Effects of fear and specificity of recommendation upon attitudes and behavior. *Journal of Personality and Social Psychology, 2,* 20-29.

Levin, I. P., & Gaeth, G. J. (1988). Framing of attribute information before and after consuming the product. *Journal of Consumer Research, 15,* 374-378.

Levine, M., Prosser, A., Evans, D., & Reicher, S. (2005). Identity and emergency intervention: How social group membership and inclusiveness of group boundaries shapes helping behavior. *Personality and Social Psychology Bulletin, 31*(4), 443-453.

Levine, R. (1997). *A Geography of Time.* New York: Basic Books.

Levine, R. V. (2003). Measuring helping behavior across cultures. In W. J. Lonner, D. L. Dinnel, S. A. Hayes, & D. N. Sattler (Eds.), *Online Readings in Psychology and Culture* (Unit 15, Chapter 9), (http://www.wwu.edu/~culture), Center for Cross-Cultural Research, Western Washington University, Bellingham, Washington.

Levine, R. V., Martinez, T. S., Brase, G., & Sorenson, K. (1994). Helping in 36 U.S. cities. *Journal of Personality and Social Psychology, 67*, 69-82.

Levine, R. V., & Norenzayan, A. (1999). The pace of life in 31 countries. *Journal of Cross Cultural Psychology, 30*, 178-205.

Lewin, K. (1948). *Resolving social conflicts: Selected papers on group dynamics*. New York: Harper.

Lewin, K., Lippitt, R., & White, R. W. (1939). Patterns of aggressive behavior in experimentally created "social climates." *The Journal of Social Psychology, 10*, 271-299.

Liberman, N., & Chaiken, S. (2009). When values matter: Expressing values in behavioral intentions for the near vs. distant future. *Journal of Experimental Social Psychology, 45*, 35-43.

Lieberman, J. D. (2002). Head over the heart or heart over the head CEST and extralegal heuristics in juror decision making. *Journal of Applied Social Psychology, 32*(12), 2526-2553.

Lieberman, M., Ochsner, K., Gilbert, D., & Schacter, D. (2001). Do amnesiacs exhibit cognitive dissonance reduction?: The role of explicit memory and attention in attitude change. *Psychological Science, 12*(2), 135-140.

Lightdale, J. R., & Prentice, D. A. (1994). Rethinking sex differences in aggression: Aggressive behavior in the absence of social roles. *Personality and Social Psychology Bulletin, 20*, 34-44.

Lilienfeld, S. O., Ammirati, R., & Landfield, K. (2009). Giving debiasing away: Can psychological research on correcting cognitive errors promote human welfare? *Perspectives on Psychological Science, 4*, 390-398.

Lindskold, S., & Han, G. (1988). GRIT as a foundation for integrative bargaining. *Personality and Social Psychology Bulletin, 14*, 335-345.

Livingston, I., Doyle, J., & Mangan, D. (2010, April 25). Stabbed hero dies as more than 20 people stroll past him. *The New York Post*. Retrieved from http://www.nypost.com/p/news/local/queens/passers_by_let_good_sam_die_5SGkf5XDP5oooudVuEd8fbI.

Lopez, R., & Marx, J. (2003). The money song. In *Avenue Q: The musical*. New York: RCA Victor.

Luszczynska, A., Cao, D. S., Mallach, N., Pietron, K., Mazurkiewicz, M., & Schwarzer, R. (2010). Intentions, planning, and self-efficacy predict physical activity in Chinese and Polish adolescents: Two moderated mediation analyses. *International Journal of Clinical and Health Psychology, 10*(2), 265-278.

Lyons, A., & Kashima, Y. (2003). How are stereotypes maintained through communication?: The influence of stereotype sharedness. *Journal of Personality and Social Psychology, 85*, 989-1005.

MacCoun, R. J., & Kerr, N. L. (1988). Asymmetric influence in mock jury deliberation: Jurors' bias for leniency. *Journal of Personality and Social Psychology, 54*, 21-33.

MacDonald, G., & Leary, M. R. (2005). Why does social exclusion hurt? The relationship between social and physical pain. *Psychological Bulletin, 131*, 202-223.

Mackay, N., & Barrowclough, C. (2005). Accident and emergency staff's perceptions of deliberate self-harm: Attributions, emotions and willingness to help. *British Journal of Clinical Psychology, 44*(2), 255-267.

Mackie, D. M., Worth, L. T., & Asuncion, A. G. (1990). Processing of persuasive in-group messages. *Journal of Personality and Social Psychology, 58*, 812-822.

Macrae, C. N., Bodenhausen, G. V., Milne, A. B., & Jetten, J. (1994). Out of mind but back in sight: Stereotypes on the rebound. *Journal of Personality and Social Psychology, 67*, 808-881.

Madell, D. E., & Muncer, S. J. (2007). Control over social interactions: An important reason for young people's use of the Internet and mobile phones for communication? *CyberPsychology & Behavior, 10*(1), 137-140.

Mann, S., Vrij, A., & Bull, R. (2004). Detecting true lies: Police officers' ability to detect suspects' lies. *Journal of Applied Psychology, 89*(1), 137-149.

Marangoni, C., Garcia, S., Ickes, W., & Teng, G. (1995). Empathic accuracy in a clinically relevant setting. *Journal of Personality and Social Psychology, 68*(5), 854-869.

Mares, M. L., & Woodard, E. (2005). Positive effects of television on children's social interactions: A meta-analysis. *Media Psychology, 7*, 301-322.

Marks, G., & Miller, N. (1987). Ten years of research on the false consensus effect: An empirical and theoretical review. *Psychological Bulletin, 102*, 72-90.

Markus, H. (1977). Self schemata and processing information about the self. *Journal of Personality and Social Psychology, 35*(2), 63-78.

Markus, H., & Kitayama, S. (1991). Culture and the self: Implications for cognition, emotion, and motivation. *Psychological Review, 98*, 224-253.

Markus, H., & Nurius, P. (1986). Possible selves. *American Psychologist, 41*, 954-969.

Marlow, L. A., Waller, J., & Wardle, J. (2010). Variation in blame attributions across different cancer types. *Cancer Epidemiology, Biomarkers, & Prevention, 19*(7), 1799-1805.

Marshall, G., & Zimbardo, P. G. (1979). The affective consequence of inadequately explained physiological arousal. *Journal of Personality and Social Psychology, 37*, 970-988.

Maslach, C. (1979). The emotional consequences of arousal without reason. In C. E. Izard (Ed.), *Emotions in Personality and Psychopathology* (pp. 565-590). New York: Plenum.

Mazur, A., & Booth, A. (1998). Testosterone and dominance in men. *Behavioral and Brain Sciences, 21*, 353-397.

Mather, M., & Johnson, M. K. (2000). Choice-supportive source monitoring: Do our decisions seem better to us as we age? *Psychology and Aging, 15*(4), 596-606.

Mather, M., Shafir, E., & Johnson, M. K. (2000). Remembering chosen and assigned options. *Memory & Cognition, 31*(3), 422-433.

McAdams, D. P. (1989). *Intimacy: The need to be close*. New York: Doubleday.

McArthur, L. Z. & Berry, D. S. (1987). Cross-cultural agreement in perceptions of babyfaced adults. *Journal of Cross-Cultural Psychology, 18*, 165-192.

McCauley, C. R., & Segal, M. E. (1987). Social psychology of terrorist groups. In C. Hendrick (Ed.), *Group Processes and Intergroup Relations: Review of Personality and Social Psychology* (Vol. 9, pp. 231-256). Newbury Park: Sage.

McConahay, J. B. (1986). Modern racism, ambivalence, and the Modern Racism Scale. In J. F. Dovidio & S. L. Gaertner (Eds.), *Prejudice, discrimination, and racism* (pp. 91-125). Orlando, FL: Academic Press.

McCrea, S. M. (2008). Self-handicapping, excuse making, and counterfactual thinking: Consequences for self-esteem and future motivation. *Journal of Personality and Social Psychology, 95*(2), 274-292.

McFadden, R. (1974). A model's dying screams are ignored at the site of Kitty Genovese's murder. *The New York Times*.

McGovern, L. P., Ditzian, J. L., & Taylor, S. P. (1975). The effect of one positive reinforcement on helping behavior. *Bulletin of the Psychonomics Society, 5*, 421-423.

McGuire, A. M. (1994). Helping behaviors in the natural environment: Dimensions and correlates of helping. *Personality and Social Psychology Bulletin, 20*, 45-56.

McGuire, W. J. (1964). Inducing resistance to persuasion, In L. Berkowitz (ed.) *Advances in experimental social psychology* (Volume 1, pp. 192-229), New York: McGraw-Hill.

McGuire, W. J., & Papageorgis, D. (1961). The relative efficacy of various types of prior belief-defense in producing immunity against persuasion. *The Journal of Abnormal and Social Psychology, 62*(2), 327-337.

McKenna, K. Y. A., Green, A., & Gleason, M. (2002). Relationship formation on the Internet: What's the big attraction? *Journal of Social Issues, 58*, 9-31.

McKinley, J. (2009, June 26). New border fear: Violence by a rogue militia. *The New York Times*. Retrieved December 1, 2010, from http://www.nytimes.com/2009/06/27/us/27arizona.html.

McNeill, D., Cassell, J., & McCullough, K. E. (1994). Communicative effects of speech-mismatched gestures. *Research on Language & Social Interaction, 27*(3), 223-237.

McPherson, M,. Smith-Lovin, L., & Cook, J. M. (2001). Birds of a feather: Homophily in social networks. *Annual Review of Sociology, 27*, 415-444.

Mead, G. H. (1934). *Mind, self, and society*. Chicago: University of Chicago Press.

Meagher, E. (2004, September 1). Are antidrug ads backfiring? *Psychology Today*. Retrieved July 15, 2010, from http://www.psychologytoday.com/articles/200411/are-antidrug-ads-backfiring.

Medvec, V. H., & Savitsky, K. (1997). When doing better means feeling worse: The effects of categorical cutoff points on counterfactual thinking and satisfaction. *Journal of Personality and Social Psychology, 72*, 1284-1296.

Meissner, C. A., & Brigham, J. C. (2001). Thirty years of investigating the own-race bias in memory for faces: A meta-analytic review. *Psychology, Public Policy, & Law, 7*, 3-35.

Melloy, K. (2010, June 29). Iceland's prime minister marries female partner. *Edge Boston*. Retrieved July 28, 2010, from http://www.edgeboston.com/index.php?ch=news&sc=&sc2=news&sc3=&id=107412.

Merton, R. K. (1948). The self-fulfilling prophecy. *Antioch Review, 8*, 193-210.

Merton, R. K., & Kitt, A. S. (1950). Contributions to the theory of reference group behaviour. In Merton, R. K., Lazarsfeld, P. F., eds., *Studies in the Scope and Method of 'The American Soldier'*. Glencoe, IL: The Free Press, pp. 40-106.

Meyerowitz, B. E., & Chaiken, S. (1987). The effect of message framing on breast self-examination attitudes, intentions, and behavior. *Journal of Personality and Social Psychology, 52*, 500-510.

Mickelson, K. D., Kessler, R. C., & Shaver, P. R. (1997). Adult attachment in a nationally representative sample. *Journal of Personality and Social Psychology, 73*, 1092-1106.

Midlarsky, E., & Midlarsky, M. (1973). Some determinants of aiding under experimentally-induced stress. *Journal of Personality, 41*, 305-327.

Milgram, S. (1963). Behavioral study of obedience. *Journal of Abnormal and Social Psychology, 67*, 371-378.

Miller, A. H. (2001). The Los Angeles riots: A study in crisis paralysis. *Journal of Contingencies and Crisis Management, 9*, 189-199.

Miller, C. (2009). Yes we did! Basking in reflected glory and cutting off reflected failure in the 2008 presidential election. *Analyses of Social Issues and Public Policy, 9*(1), 283-296.

Miller, J. G. (1984). Culture and the development of everyday social explanation. *Journal of Personality and Social Psychology, 46*(5), 961-978.

Miller, L. C., Putcha-Bhagavatula, A., & Pederson, W. C. (2002). Men's and women's mating preferences: Distinct evolutionary mechanisms? *Current Directions in Psychological Science, 11*(3), 88-93.

Miller, N., & Marks, G. (1982). Assumed similarity between self and other: Effect of expectation of future interaction with that other. *Social Psychology Quarterly, 45*, 100-105.

Miller, P. J. E., & Rempel, J. K. (2004). Trust and partner-enhancing attributions in close relationships. *Personality and Social Psychology Bulletin, 30*(6), 695-705.

Mishna, F., Saini, M., & Solomon, S. (2009). Ongoing and online: Children and youth's perceptions of cyber bullying. *Children and Youth Services Review, 31*, 1222-1228.

Mita, T. H., Dermer, M., & Knight, J. (1977). Reversed facial images and the mere-exposure hypothesis. *Journal of Personality and Social Psychology, 35*(8), 597-601.

Moll, J., Krueger, F., Zahn, R., Pardini, M., de Oliveira-Souza, R., & Grafman, J. (2006). Human fronto-mesolimbic networks guide decisions about charitable donation. *Proceedings of the National Academy of Sciences, 103*(42), 15623-15628.

Monin, B., & Norton, M. I. (2003). Perceptions of a fluid consensus: Uniqueness bias, false consensus, false polarization, and pluralistic ignorance in a water conservation crisis. *Personality and Social Psychology Bulletin, 29*(5), 559-567.

Monteith, M.J. (1993). Self-regulation of prejudiced responses: Implications for progress in prejudice reduction efforts. *Journal of Personality and Social Psychology, 65*, 469-485.

Moreland, R. L., & Beach, S. (1992) Exposure effects in the classroom: The development of affinity among students. *Journal of Experimental Social Psychology, 28*, 255-276.

Moreland, R. L., & Zajonc, R. B. (1982). Exposure effects in person perception: Familiarity, similarity, and attraction. *Journal of Experimental Social Psychology, 18*, 395-415.

Morell, V. (1993) Evidence found for a possible 'aggression gene.' *Science, 260*(5115), 1722-1723.

Morgan, G. S., Mullen, E., & Skitka, L. J. (in press). When values and attributions collide: Liberals' and conservatives' values motivate attributions for alleged misdeeds. *Personality and Social Psychology Bulletin.*

Moriarty, T. (1975). Crime, commitment, and the responsive bystander: Two field experiments. *Journal of Personality and Social Psychology, 59*, 50-60.

Morita, T., Itakura, S., Saito, D. N., Nakashita, S., Harada, T., Kochiyama, T., & Sadato, N. (2008). The role of the right prefrontal cortex in self-evaluation of the face: A functional magnetic resonance imaging study. *Journal of Cognitive Neuroscience, 20*(2), 342-355.

Morling, B., & Lamoreaux, M. (2008). Measuring culture outside the head: A meta-analysis of cultural products. *Personality and Social Psychology Review, 12*, 199-221.

Morris, M. W., & Peng, K. (1994). Culture and cause: American and Chinese attributions for social and physical events. *Journal of Personality and Social Psychology, 67*(6), 949-971.

Morrow-Howell, N., Lott, L., & Ozawa, M. (1990). The impact of race on volunteer helping relationships among the elderly. *Social Work, 35*(5), 395-402.

Morwitz, V. G., & Pluzinski, C. (1996). Do polls reflect opinion or do opinions reflect polls? The impact of political polling on voters' expectations, preferences, and behavior. *Journal of Consumer Research, 23*, 53-67.

Moscovici, S., & Zavalloni, M. (1969). The group as a polarizer of attitudes. *Journal of Personality and Social Psychology, 12*, 125-135.

Moskalenko, S., & Heine, S. J. (2003). Watching your troubles away: Television viewing as a stimulus for subjective self-awareness. *Personality and Social Psychology Bulletin, 29*, 76-85.

Mueller, C. M., & Dweck, C. S. (1998). Praise for intelligence can undermine children's motivation and performance. *Journal of Personality and Social Psychology, 75*(1), 33-52.

Mullen, B., Migdal, M. J., & Rozell, D. (2003). Self-awareness, deindividuation, and social identity: Unraveling theoretical paradoxes by filling empirical lacunae. *Personality and Social Psychology Bulletin, 29*, 1071-1081.

Munro, G. D., & Ditto, P. H. (1997). Biased assimilation, attitude polarization, and affect in the processing of stereotype-relevant scientific information. *Personality and Social Psychology Bulletin, 23*, 636-653.

Murdock, N., Edwards, C., & Murdock, T. B. (2010). Therapists' attributions for client premature termination: Are they self-serving? *Psychotherapy: Theory, Research and Practice, 47*(2), 221-234.

Murphy, K. R., & Balzer, W. K. (1986). Systematic distortions in memory-based behavior ratings and performance evaluation: Consequences for rating accuracy. *Journal of Applied Psychology, 71*, 39-44.

Murstein, B. & Christy, P. (1976). Physical attractiveness and marriage adjustment in middle-aged couples. *Journal of Personality and Social Psychology, 34*, 537-542.

Mustanski, B. (2010, March 22). New study suggests bans on gay marriage hurt mental health of LGB people. *Psychology Today*. Retrieved December 1, 2010, from http://www.psychologytoday.com/blog/the-sexual-continuum/201003/new-study-suggests-bans-gay-marriage-hurt-mental-health-lgb-people.

Myers, D. G. (2000). The funds, friends, and faith of happy people. *American Psychologist, 55*, 56-57.

Myers, J., Madathil, J., & Tingle, L. (2005). Marriage satisfaction and wellness in India and the United Status: A preliminary comparison of arranged marriage and marriages of choice. *Journal of Counseling and Development, 83*, 183-190.

Nadler, A., & Fisher, J. D. (1974). The effects of the level of the donor's resources on the recipient's perception of his subsequent self-help behavior. *Personality and Social Psychology Bulletin, 1*(1), 390-392.

Nadler, A., Fisher, J. D., & Itzhak, S. B. (1983). With a little help from my friend: Effect of single or multiple act aid as a function of donor and task characteristics. *Journal of Personality and Social Psychology, 44*(2), 310-321.

Nadler, A., Fisher, J. D., & Streufert, S. (1974). The donor's dilemma: Recipient's reactions to aid from friend or foe. *Journal of Applied Social Psychology, 4*(3), 275-285.

National Commission for the Protection of Human Subjects of Biomedical and Behavioral Research (1974). Ethical principles and guidelines for the protection of human subjects in research. *The Belmont Report*. Retrieved June 2, 2010, from http://ohsr.od.nih.gov/guidelines/belmont.html.

National Defense University (n.d.). *Strategic leadership and decision making: Strategic negotiations*. Retrieved August 1, 2010, from http://www.au.af.mil/au/awc/awcgate/ndu/strat-ldr-dm/pt3ch13.html.

National Fire Protection Association (2008). *The U.S. fire problem*. Retrieved May 4, 201, from http://www.nfpa.org/itemDetail.asp?categoryID=953&itemID=23071&URL=Research%20&%20Reports/Fire%20statistics/The%20U.S.%20fire%20problem&cookie%5Ftest=1.

Nauert, R. (2010, May 19). Good looks sway court decisions. *PsychCentral*. Retrieved October 11, 2010, from http://psychcentral.com/news/2010/05/18/good-looks-sway-court-decisions/13906.html.

Naumann, L. P., Vazire, S., Rentfrow, P. J., & Gosling, S. D. (2009). Personality judgments based on physical appearance. *Personality and Social Psychology Bulletin, 35,* 1661-1671.

The Negotiator Magazine (2005). Outstanding negotiation achievements. *The Negotiator Magazine.* Retrieved December 1, 2010, from http://www.negotiatormagazine.com/outstanding.shtml.

Nelson, J. (2003). Reality TV a mood lifter. *Chicago Tribune.* Retrieved July 13, 2010, from http://articles.chicagotribune.com/2003-09-17/features/0309170317_1_reality-television-writer-and-senior-editor-reality-tv.

Nelson, L. D., & Simmons, J. (2007). Moniker maladies: When names sabotage success. *Psychological Science, 18*(12), 1106-1112.

Newcomb, T. M. (1961). *The acquaintance process.* New York: Holt, Rinehart and Winston.

Newman, L. S. (1993). How individuals interpret behavior: Idiocentrism and spontaneous trait inference. *Social Cognition, 11,* 243-269.

Newsom, J. T. (1999). Another side to caregiving: Negative reactions to being helped. *Current Directions in Psychological Science, 8,* 183-187.

Nisbett, R. E., & Cohen, D. (1996). *Culture of honor: The psychology of violence in the South.* Denver, CO: Westview Press.

Nisbett, R. E., Fong, G. T., Lehman, D. R., & Cheng, P. W. (1987). Teaching reasoning. *Science, 238,* 625-631.

Nisbett, R. E., & Wilson, T. D. (1977). The halo effect: Evidence for unconscious alteration of judgments. *Journal of Personality and Social Psychology, 35*(4), 250-256.

Noel, J. G., Wann, D. L., & Branscombe, N. R. (1995). Peripheral ingroup membership status and public negativity toward outgroups. *Journal of Personality and Social Psychology, 68,* 127-137.

Noguchi, K., Gohm, C., Dalsky, D., & Sakamoto, S. (2006) Cultural differences related to positive and negative valence. *Asian Journal of Social Psychology, 10,* 68-76.

Norem, J. K., & Cantor, N. (1986). Defensive pessimism: Harnessing anxiety as motivation. *Journal of Personality and Social Psychology, 51*(6), 1208-1217.

North, A. C., Linley, A., & Hargreaves, D. J. (2000). Social loafing in a co-operative classroom task. *Educational Psychology, 20,* 389-392.

North, A. C., Tarrant, M., & Hargreaves, D. J. (2004). The effects of music on helping behavior: A field study. *Environment and Behavior, 36*(2), 266-275.

North, R. J., & Swann, W. B. (2009). Self-verification 360 degrees: Illuminating the light and dark sides. *Self and Identity, 8*(2-3), 131-146.

Nosek, B. A. (2007). Implicit-explicit reactions. *Current Directions in Psychological Science, 16,* 65-69.

Novotny, P., Colligan, R. C., Szydlo, D. W., Clark, M. M., Rausch, S., Wampfler, J., . . . Yang, P. (2010). A pessimistic explanatory style is prognostic for poor lung cancer survival. *Journal of Thoracic Oncology, 5*(3), 326-332.

Nuttin, J. M. (1987). Affective consequences of mere ownership: The name-letter effect in twelve European languages. *European Journal of Social Psychology, 15,* 381-402.

O'Connor, S. C., & Rosenblood, L. K. (1996). Affiliation motivation in everyday experience: A theoretical comparison. *Journal of Personality and Social Psychology, 70,* 513-522.

Ohman, A., Lundqvist, D., & Karolinska, F. E. (2001). The face in the crowd revisited: A threat advantage with schematic stimuli. *Journal of Personality and Social Psychology, 80*(3), 381-396.

O'Keefe, D. J., & Jensen, J. D. (2007). The relative persuasiveness of gain-framed and loss-framed messages for encouraging disease prevention behaviors: A meta-analytic review. *Journal of Health Communication, 12,* 623-644

Olson, I. R., & Marshuetz, C. (2005). Facial attractiveness is appraised in a glance. *Emotion, 5*(4), 498-502.

Olweus, R., Mattsson, A., Schalling, D., & Low, H. (1988). Circulating testosterone levels and aggression in adolescent males: A causal analysis. *Psychosomatic Medicine, 50*(3), 261-272.

Omoto, A. M., & Snyder, M. (1995). Sustained helping without obligation: Motivation, longevity of service, and perceived attitude change among AIDS volunteers. *Journal of Personality and Social Psychology, 68,* 671-686.

Osgood, C. E. (1962). *An alternative war or surrender.* Urbana, IL: University of Illinois Press.

Otten, S., & Wentura, D. (1999). About the impact of automaticity in the Minimal Group Paradigm: Evidence from an affective priming task. *European Journal of Social Psychology, 29,* 1049-1071.

Oyserman, D., Coon, H. M., & Kemmelmeier, M. (2002). Rethinking individualism and collectivism: Evaluation of theoretical assumptions and meta-analyses. *Psychological Bulletin, 128,* 3-72.

Pajares, F. (1996). Self-efficacy beliefs in achievement settings. *Review of Educational Research, 66,* 543-578.

Palmer, E., & McDowell, C. (1981). Children's understanding of nutritional information presented in breakfast cereal commercials. *Journal of Broadcasting, 25,* 295.

Parker, S. K., Bindel, U. K., & Strauss, K. (2010). Making things happen: A model of proactive motivation. *Journal of Management, 36*(4), 827-856.

Pavlov, I. P. (1927). *Conditioned reflexes: An investigation of the physiological activity of the cerebral cortex.* Oxford, UK: Oxford University Press.

Payne, B. K. (2001). Prejudice and perception: The role of automatic and controlled processes in misperceiving a weapon. *Journal of Personality and Social Psychology, 81,* 181-192.

Pechmann, C. & Shih, C. F. (1999), Smoking scenes in movies and antismoking advertisements before movies: Effects on youth. *Journal of Marketing, 63,* 1-13.

Pennebaker, J. W., Dyer, M. A., Caulkins, R. S., Litowitz, D. L., Ackerman, P. L., Anderson, D. B., & McGraw, K. M. (1979). Don't the girls get prettier at closing time: A country and western application to psychology. *Personality and Social Psychology Bulletin, 5,* 122-125.

Penner, L. A., Dertke, M. C., & Achenbach, C. J. (1973). The "flash" system: A field study of altruism. *Journal of Applied Social Psychology, 3,* 362-370.

Peplau, L. A., & Fingerhut, A. W. (2007). The close relationships of lesbians and gay men. *Annual Review of Psychology, 58,* 405-424.

Perlow, L., & Weeks, J. (2002). Who's helping whom? Layers of culture and workplace behavior. *Journal of Organizational Behavior, 23,* 345-361.

Peruche, B. M., & Plant, E. A. (2006). Racial bias in perceptions of athleticism: The role of motivation in the elimination of bias. *Social Cognition, 24*(4), 438-452.

Pettigrew, T. F. (1979). The ultimate attribution error: Extending Allport's cognitive analysis of prejudice. *Personality and Social Psychology Bulletin, 5*(4), 461-476.

Pettigrew, T. F. (1998). Intergroup contact theory. *Annual Review of Psychology, 49,* 65-85.

Pettigrew, T., & Tropp, L. (2006). A meta-analytic test of intergroup contact theory. *Journal of Personality and Social Psychology, 90,* 751-783.

Petty, R. E., & Cacioppo, J. T. (1977). Forewarning, cognitive responding, and resistance to persuasion. *Journal of Personality and Social Psychology, 35,* 645-655.

Petty, R. E., & Cacioppo, J. T. (1981). *Attitudes and persuasion: Classic and contemporary approaches.* Dubuque, IA: William C. Brown.

Petty, R. E., & Cacioppo, J. T. (1984). The effects of involvement on responses to argument quantity and quality: Central and peripheral routes to persuasion. *Journal of Personality and Social Psychology, 46,* 69-81.

Petty, R. E., & Cacioppo, J. T. (1986). *Communication and persuasion: Central and peripheral routes to attitude change.* New York: Springer-Verlag.

Petty, R. E., Cacioppo, J. T., & Goldman, R. (1981). Personal involvement as a determinant of argument-based persuasion. *Journal of Personality and Social Psychology, 41,* 847-885.

Petty, R. E., Wells, G. L., & Brock, T. C. (1976). Distraction can enhance or reduce yielding to propaganda: Thought disruption versus effort justification. *Journal of Personality and Social Psychology, 34,* 874-884.

Pew Research Center (2009, September 9). Muslims widely seen as facing discrimination: Views of religious similarities and differences. *Pew Research Center Publications.* Retrieved December 1, 2010, from http://pewresearch.org/pubs/1336/perceptions-of-islam-religious-similarities-differences.

Piliavin, J. A. (2003). Doing well by doing good: Benefits for the benefactor. In C. L. M. Keyes & J. Haidt (Eds.), *Flourishing: Positive Personality and the Life Well Lived* (pp. 227-247). Washington, DC: American Psychological Association.

Piliavin, J. A., Dovidio, J. F., Gaertner, S. L., & Clark, R. D., III. (1981). *Emergency intervention.* New York: Academic Press.

Piliavin, J. A., & Piliavin, I. M. (1972). The effects of blood on reactions to a film. *Journal of Personality and Social Psychology, 23,* 253-261.

Piliavin, J. A., & Unger, R. K. (1985) The helpful but helpless female: Myth or reality? In V. O'Leary, R. K. Unger, & B. S. Wallston (Eds.), *Women, Gender and Social Psychology,* 149-186.

Piwinger, M., & Ebert, H. (2001). Impression Management: Wie aus Niemand Jemand wird. In G. Bentele (Ed.), *Kommunikationsmanagement: Strategien, Wissen, Lösungen*. Neuwied, Germany: Luchterhand.

Plant, E. A., & Devine, P. G. (1998). Internal and external motivation to respond without prejudice. *Journal of Personality and Social Psychology, 75*, 811-832.

Plant, E. A., Peruche, B. M., & Butz, D. A. (2005). Eliminating automatic racial bias: Making race non-diagnostic for responses to criminal suspects. *Journal of Experimental Social Psychology, 41*, 141-156.

Pornpitakpan, C. (2004). The persuasiveness of source credibility: A critical review of five decades of evidence. *Journal of Applied Social Psychology, 34*, 243-281.

Porter, M., & Haslam, N. (2005). Predisplacement and postdisplacement factors associated with mental health of refugees and internally displaced persons: A meta-analysis. *JAMA: Journal of the American Medical Association, 294*, 602-612.

Postmes, T., Spears, R., & Cihangir, S. (2001). Quality of decision making and group norms. *Journal of Personality and Social Psychology, 80*, 918-930.

Postmes, T., Spears, R., & Lea, M. (1999). Social identity, group norms, and "deindividuation": Lessons from computer-mediated communication for social influence in the group. In N. Ellemers, R. Spears, & B. Doosje (Eds.), *Social Identity: Context, Commitment, Content*. Oxford: Blackwell.

Pratto, F., Sidanius, J., Stallworth, L. M., & Malle, B. F. (1994). Social dominance orientation: A personality variable predicting social and political attitudes. *Journal of Personality and Social Psychology, 67*, 741-763.

Provine, R. R. (2005). Yawning. *American Scientist, 93*, 532-539.

Rahim, S. (2010, June 21). "Finding the 'weapons' of persuasion to save energy," *The New York Times*. Retrieved July 15, 2010, from http://www.nytimes.com/cwire/2010/06/21/21climatewire-finding-the-weapons-of-persuasion-to-save-ene-8137.html.

Ramachandran, V. S. (2006). Mirror neurons and imitation learning as the driving force behind "the great leap forward" in human evolution. *The Third Culture*. Retrieved September 20, 2010, from http://www.edge.org/3rd_culture/ramachandran/ramachandran_p1.html.

Rapoport, A. (1960). *Fights, games, and debates*. Ann Arbor, MI: University of Michigan Press.

Reddy, R. D. (1980). Individual philanthropy and giving behavior. In D. H. Smith & J. Macaulay (Eds.), *Participation in social and political activities* (pp. 370-399). San Francisco, CA: Jossey-Bass.

Regan, D. T. (1971). Effects of a favor and liking on compliance. *Journal of Experimental Social Psychology, 7*, 627-639.

Reisenzein, R. (1983). The Schachter theory of emotion: Two decades later. *Psychological Bulletin, 94*, 239-264.

Rentfrow, P. J., & Gosling, S. D. (2006). Message in a ballad: The role of music preferences in interpersonal perception. *Psychological Science, 17*(3), 236-242.

Rhee, E., Uleman, J. S., Lee, H. K., & Roman, R. J. (1995). Spontaneous self-concepts and ethnic identities in individualistic and collectivistic cultures. *Journal of Personality and Social Psychology, 69*, 142-152.

Rhodes, G. (2006). The evolution of facial attractiveness. *Annual Review of Psychology, 57*, 199-266.

Ridge, S. R. & Feeney, J. A. (1998). Relationship history and relationship attitudes in gay males and lesbians: Attachment style and gender differences. *Australian & New Zealand Journal of Psychiatry, 32*(6), 848-860.

Ringelmann, M. (1913). Recherches sur les moteurs animes: Travail de l'homme. *Annales de l'Institut National Agronomique*, 2e serie, tom XIII, 1-40.

Rizzolatti, G., & Craighero, L. (2004). The mirror-neuron system. *Annual Review of Neuroscience, 27*, 169-192.

Robinson, L. A. (1999). The relationships between attachment style and romantic attachment, autonomy and equality in lesbian relationships. *Australian Journal of Psychology, 51*, 137-137.

Robinson, W. (2007). Operational definitions. *The University of Tennessee Knoxville*. Retrieved June 3, 2010 from http://web.utk.edu/~wrobinso/540_lec_opdefs.html.

Roese, N. J. (1997). Counterfactual thinking and marketing: Introduction to the special issue. *Psychology and Marketing, 17*, 277-280.

Ronquillo, J., Denson, T., Lickel, B., Lu, Z-L., Nandy, A., & Maddox, K. B. (2007). The effects of skin tone on race-related amygdala activity: An fMRI investigation. *Social Cognitive and Affective Neuroscience, 2*, 39-44.

Rosenbaum, M. E. (1986). The repulsion hypothesis: on the non-development of relationships. *Journal of Personality and Social Psychology, 50*, 29-36.

Rosenberg, M. (1965). *Society and adolescent self-image*. Princeton, NJ: Princeton University Press.

Rosenthal, R., & Jacobson, L. (1968). *Pygmalion in the classroom*. New York: Holt, Rinehart and Winston.

Rosenquist, J. N., Murabito, J., Fowler, J. H., & Christakis, N. A. (2010). The spread of alcohol consumption behavior in a large social network. *Annals of Internal Medicine, 152*(7), 426-433.

Ross, L. (1977). The intuitive psychologist and his shortcomings: Distortions in the attribution process. In L. Berkowitz (Ed.), *Advances in experimental social psychology* (vol. 10). New York: Academic Press.

Ross, L., Amabile, T. M., & Steinmetz, J. L. (1977). Social roles, social control, and biases in social perception. *Journal of Personality and Social Psychology, 35*, 485-494.

Ross, L., Greene, D., & House, P. (1977). The false consensus effect: An egocentric bias in social perception and attribution processes. *Journal of Experimental Social Psychology, 13*, 279-301.

Ross, L., Lepper, M. R., & Hubbard, M. (1975). Perseverance in self-perception and social perception: Biased attributional processes in the debriefing paradigm. *Journal of Personality and Social Psychology, 32*(5), 880-892.

Ross, L., & Nisbett, R. E. (1991) *The person and the situation*. New York: McGraw-Hill.

Rozin, P., & Royzman, E. B. (2001). Negativity bias, negativity dominance, and contagion. *Personality and Social Psychology Review, 5*, 296-320.

Ruder, M., & Bless, H. (2003). Mood and the reliance on the ease of retrieval heuristic. *Journal of Personality and Social Psychology, 85*, 20-32.

Rudman, L. A. (2004). Sources of implicit attitudes. *Current Directions in Psychological Science, 13*(2), 80-83.

Rudman, L. A., Ashmore, R. D., & Gary, M. L. (2001). "Unlearning" automatic biases: The malleability of implicit stereotypes and prejudice. *Journal of Personality and Social Psychology, 81*, 856-868.

Rudman, L. A., Phelan, J. E., & Heppen, J. (2007). Developmental sources of implicit attitudes. *Personality and Social Psychology Bulletin, 33*(12), 1700-1713.

Rusbult, C. (1983). A longitudinal test of the investment model: The development (and deterioration) of satisfaction and commitment in heterosexual involvements. *Journal of Personality and Social Psychology, 45*, 172-186.

Rusbult, C. E. (1991). Commentary on Johnson's "Commitment to personal relationships": What's interesting, and what's new? In W. H. Jones & D. W. Perlman (Eds.), *Advances in Personal Relationships* (Vol. 3, pp. 151-169). London: Kingsley.

Rusbult, C. E., & Zembrodt, I. M. (1983). Responses to dissatisfaction in romantic involvements: A multidimensional scaling analysis. *Journal of Experimental Social Psychology, 43*, 1230-1242.

Ruvolo, A. P., Fabin, L. A., & Ruvolo, C. M. (2001). Relationship experiences and change in attachment characteristics of young adults: The role of relationship breakups and conflict avoidance. *Personal Relationships, 8*(3), 265-281.

Ryan, C. S., & Bogart, L. M. (1997). Development of new group members' in-group and out-group stereotypes: Changes in perceived group variability and ethnocentrism. *Journal of Personality and Social Psychology, 73*, 719-732.

Sacks, O. (2007, September). The abyss: Music and amnesia. *The New Yorker*. Retrieved July 8, 2010, from http://www.newyorker.com/reporting/2007/09/24/070924fa_fact_sacks?currentPage=1.

Salwen, K., & Salwen, H. (2010). *The power of half: One family's decision to stop taking and start giving back*. Boston: Houghton Mifflin Harcourt.

Sangrigoli, S., Pallier, C., Argenti, A. M., Ventureyra, V. A. G., & de Schonen, S. (2005). Reversibility of the other-race effect in face recognition during childhood. *Psychological Science, 16*, 440-444.

Santos, A., Meyer-Lindenberg, A., Deruelle, C. (2010). Absence of racial, but not gender, stereotyping in Williams syndrome children. *Current Biology, 20*(7), R307-R308.

Saucier, D. A., Miller, C. T., & Doucet, N. (2005). Differences in helping whites and blacks: A meta-analysis. *Personality and Social Psychology Review, 9*(1), 2-16.

Sax, L. J., Lindholm, J. A., Astin, A. W., Korn, W. S., & Mahoney, K. M. (2002). *The American freshman: national norms for fall, 2002*. Los Angeles: Cooperative Institutional Research Program, UCLA.

Schachter, S., & Singer, J., (1962) Cognitive, social, and physiological determinants of emotional state. *Psychological Review, 69*, 379-399.

Schaller, M., & Cialdini, R. B. (1988). The economics of empathic helping: Support for a mood management motive. *Journal of Experimental Social Psychology, 24*, 163-181.

Scharfe, E., & Bartholomew, K. (1994). Reliability and stability of adult attachment patterns. *Personal Relationships, 1*, 2-43.

Schiller, D., Freeman, J. B., Mitchell, J. P., Uleman, J. S., & Phelps, E. A. (2009). A neural mechanism of first impressions. *Nature Neuroscience, 12*, 508-514.

Schnall, S., Roper, J., & Fessler, D. M. T. (2010). Elevation leads to altruistic behavior, above and beyond general positive affect. *Psychological Science, 21*, 315-320.

Schoenborn, C. A. (2004). Marital status and health: United States, 1999-2002. *Advance Data, 351*.

Schuman, H., Steeh, C., Bobo, L., & Kyrsan, M. (1997). *Racial attitudes in America: Trends and interpretations*. Cambridge, MA: Harvard University Press.

Schunk, D. H. (1995). Self-efficacy and education and instruction. In J. E. Maddux (Ed.), *Self-efficacy, adaptation, and adjustment: Theory, research, and application* (pp. 281-303). New York: Plenum Press.

Schwarz, N. (1990). Feelings as information: Informational and motivational functions of affective states. In E. T. Higgins & R. M. Sorrentino (Eds.), *Handbook of motivation and cognition* (pp. 527-561). New York: Guilford Press.

Schwarz, N., & Bohner, G. (2001). The construction of attitudes. In A. Tesser & N. Schwarz (Eds.), *Intrapersonal Processes (Blackwell Handbook of Social Psychology)* (pp. 436-457). Oxford, UK: Blackwell.

Sedikides, G., & Gregg, A. P. (2003). Portraits of the self. In M. A. Hogg & J. Cooper (Eds.), *Sage handbook of social psychology* (pp. 110-138). London: Sage.

Segerstrom S. C., & Sephton S. E. (2010). Optimistic expectancies and cell-mediated immunity: The role of positive affect. *Psychological Science, 21*(3), 448-455.

Seiter, J. S. (2007). Ingratiation and gratuity: The effect of complimenting customers on tipping behavior in restaurants. *Journal of Applied Social Psychology, 37*(3), 478-485.

Serbin, L. A., Poulin-Dubois, D., & Eichstedt, J. A. (2002). Infants' responses to gender-inconsistent events. *Infancy, 3*, 531-542.

Seyle, D. C., & Swann, W. B. (2007). Being oneself in the workplace: Self-verification and identity in organizational contexts. In C. A. Bartel, S. Blader, & A. Wrzesniewski (Eds.), *Identity and the modern organization* (pp. 201-222). Mahwah, NJ: Lawrence Erlbaum Associates.

Shaver, P. R., & Hazan, C. (1993). Adult romantic attachment: Theory and evidence. In D. Perlman & W. Jones (Eds.), *Advances in personal relationships* (Vol. 4, pp. 29-70). London: Kingsley.

Shaw, M. E. (1981). *Group Dynamics: The Psychology of Small Group Behavior*. New York: McGraw-Hill.

Sheeran, P., Abraham, C., & Orbell, S. (1999). Psychosocial correlates of heterosexual condom use: A meta-analysis. *Psychological Bulletin, 125*(1), 90-132.

Sheldon, K. M. (2005). Positive value change during college: Normative trends and individual differences. *Journal of Research in Personality, 39*(2), 209-223.

Shellenbarger, S. (2009). Father's day: Why men are hard-wired to cuddle their babies. *The Wall Street Journal Blogs*. Retrieved December 1, 2010, from http://blogs.wsj.com/juggle/2009/06/19/fathers-day-why-men-are-hard-wired-to-cuddle-their-babies/.

Sheridan, M. (2009, May 31). Kidnappers swoop on China's girls. *The Times*. Retrieved December 1, 2010, from http://www.timesonline.co.uk/tol/news/world/asia/article6396010.ece.

Sherif, M. (1936). *The psychology of social norms*. New York: Harper.

Sherif, M. (1937). An experimental approach to the study of attitudes. *Sociometry, 1*, 90-98.

Sherif, M. (1966). The psychology of social norms. Oxford, UK: Harper Torchbooks.

Sherif, M., Harvey, O. J., White, J., Hood, W. R., & Sherif, C. W. (1954). *Intergroup conflict and cooperation: The Robbers Cave experiment*. Norman, OK: University Book Exchange.

Sherif, M., & Sherif, C. W. (1956). *An outline of social psychology*. New York: Harper.

Sherman, J. W., Kruschke, J. K., Sherman, S. J., Percy, E. J., Petrocelli, J. V., & Conrey, F. R. (2009). Attentional processes in stereotype formation: A common model for category accentuation and illusory correlation. *Journal of Personality and Social Psychology, 96*, 305-323.

Shors, T. J., & Matzel, L. D. (1997). Long term potentiation (LTD): What's learning got to do with it? *Behavioral and Brain Sciences, 20*(4), 597-655.

Shotland, R. L., & Heinold, W. D. (1985). Bystander response to arterial bleeding: Helping skills, the decision-making process, and differentiating the helping response. *Journal of Personality and Social Psychology, 49*(2), 347-356.

Shotland, R. L., & Johnson, M. P. (1978). Bystander behavior and kinesics: The interaction between the helper and victim. *Environmental Psychology and Nonverbal Behavior, 2*, 181-190.

Shotland, R. L., & Stebbins, C. A. (1983). Emergency and cost as determinants of helping behavior and the slow accumulation of social psychological knowledge. *Social Psychology Quarterly, 46*, 36-46.

Shotland, R. L., & Straw, M. K. (1976). Bystander response to an assault: When a man attacks a woman. *Journal of Personality and Social Psychology, 34*, 990-999.

Shrout, P. E., Herman, C. M., & Bolger, N. (2006). The costs and benefits of practical and emotional support on adjustment: A daily diary study of couples experiencing acute stress. *Personal Relationships, 13*(1), 115-134.

Sidanius, J. & Pratto, F. (1999). *Social dominance: An intergroup theory of social hierarchy and oppression*. New York: Cambridge University Press.

Simpson, J. A., Campbell, B., & Berscheid, E. (1986). The association between romantic love and marriage: Kephart (1967). Twice revisited. *Personality and Social Psychology Bulletin, 12*, 363-372.

Simpson, J. A. Oriña, M. M., & Ickes, W. (2003). When accuracy hurts, and when it helps: A test of the empathic accuracy model in marital interactions. *Journal of Personality and Social Psychology, 85*(5), 881-893.

Singh, D. (1993). Adaptive significance of female physical attractiveness: Role of waist-to-hip ratio. *Journal of Personality and Social Psychology, 65*, 293-307.

Sintay, L., & Ibanga, I. (June 10, 2009). Recession causes increase in teen dating violence. *Good Morning America*. Retrieved June 3, 2010, from http://abcnews.go.com/GMA/story?id=7798098&page=1.

Sissons, M. (1981). Race, sex, and helping behavior. *British Journal of Social Psychology, 20*, 285-292.

Sistrunk, F., & McDavid, J. W. (1971). Sex variable in conforming behavior. *Journal of Personality and Social Psychology, 17*(2), 200-207.

Skinner, B.F. (1938). *The behavior of organisms: An experimental analysis*. Oxford, UK: Appleton-Century.

Skitka, L. J. (1999). Ideological and attributional boundaries on public compassion: Reactions to individuals and communities affected by a natural disaster. *Personality and Social Psychology Bulletin, 25*, 793-792.

Skitka, L. J., Mullen, E., Griffin, T., Hutchinson, S., & Chamberlin, B. (2002). Dispositions, ideological scripts, or motivated correction? Understanding ideological differences in attributions for social problems. *Journal of Personality and Social Psychology, 83*, 470-487.

Skitka, L. J., Saunders, B., Morgan, G. S., & Wisneski, D. (2009). Dark clouds and silver linings: Socio-psychological responses to September 11, 2001. In M. J. Morgan (Ed.), *The day that changed everything? Looking at the impact of 9-11*, Vol. 3 (pp. 63-80). New York: Palgrave MacMillan.

Slater, M. D. (1997). Persuasion processes across receiver goals and message genres. *Communication Theory, 7*(2), 125-148.

Slotter, E. B., Gardner, W. L., & Finkel, E. J. (2009). Who am I without you? The influence of romantic breakup on the self-concept. *Personality and Social Psychology Bulletin, 36*(2), 147.

Slovic, P., & Fischhoff, B. (1977). On the psychology of experimental surprises. *Journal of Experimental Psychology: Human Perception and Performance, 3*, 544-551.

Smeaton, G., Byrne, D., & Murnen, S. K. (1989). The repulsion hypothesis revisited: Similarity irrelevance or dissimilarity bias? *Journal of Personality and Social Psychology, 56*, 54-59.

Smith, B. N., Kerr, N. A., Markus, M. J., & Stasson, M. F. (2001). Individual differences in social loafing: Need for cognition as a motivator in collective performance. *Group Dynamics, 5*, 150-158.

Smith, K. D., Keating, J. P., & Stotland, E. (1989). Altruism reconsidered: The effect of denying feedback on a victim's status to empathic witnesses. *Journal of Personality and Social Psychology, 57*, 641-650.

Smith, P. B., & Bond, M. H. (1993). *Social psychology across cultures*. Hemel Hempstead: Harvester Wheatsheaf.

Smith, T. W. (2007). Job satisfaction in the United States. *NORC/University of Chicago*. Retrieved July 8, 2010 from http://www.norc.org/NR/rdonlyres/2874B40B-7C50-4F67-A6B2-26BD3B06EA04/0/JobSatisfactionintheUnitedStates.pdf.

Snyder, M. (1974). *Self-monitoring scale*. Retrieved August 13, 2010 from http://pubpages.unh.edu/~ckb/SELFMON2.html.

Snyder, M. (1979). Self-monitoring processes. In L. Berkowitz (Ed.), *Advances in experimental social psychology* (Vol. 12, 85–126). Orlando, FL: Academic Press.

Snyder, M., Berscheid, E., & Glick, P. (1985). Focusing on the exterior and the interior: Two investigations of the initiation of personal relationships. *Journal of Personality and Social Psychology, 48*, 1427–1439.

Snyder, M., Omoto, A. M., & Crain, A. L. (1999). Punished for their good deeds: Stigmatization of AIDS volunteers. *American Behavioral Scientist, 42,* 1175–1192.

Snyder, M., & Swann, W. B. (1978). Hypothesis-testing processes in social interaction. *Journal of Personality and Social Psychology, 36*(11), 1202–1212.

Social Psychology Network (2010). *2010 action teaching award winner*. Retrieved August 12, 2010, from http://www.socialpsychology.org/action/2010winner.html.

Society for the Psychological Study of Social Issues (2010). About SPSSI. *SPSSI*. Retrieved August 12, 2010, from http://www.spssi.org/index.cfm?fuseaction=Page.viewPage&pageId=479.

Solomon Asch Center for Study of Ethnopolitical Conflict (2000). *About Solomon Asch*. Retrieved May 2, 2010, from http://www.brynmawr.edu/aschcenter/about/solomon.htm.

Sommers, S. R., & Ellsworth, P. C. (2000). Race in the courtroom: Perceptions of guilt and dispositional attributions. *Personality and Social Psychology Bulletin, 26*, 1367–1379.

Sparrow, B., & Wegner, D. M. (2006). Unpriming: The deactivation of thoughts through expression. *Journal of Personality and Social Psychology, 91*(6), 1009–1019.

Spencer, S. J., Fein, S., Wolfe, C. T., Fong, C., & Dunn, M. A. (1998). Automatic activation of stereotypes: The role of self-image threat. *Personality and Social Psychology Bulletin, 24*, 1139–1152.

SPLC (2009). Active U.S. hate groups. *Southern Poverty Law Center*. Retrieved August 17, 2010, from http://www.splcenter.org/get-informed/hate-map.

Sprafkin, J. N., Liebert, R. M., & Poulos, R. W. (1975). Effects of a prosocial televised example on children's helping. *Journal of Experimental Child Psychology, 20,* 119–126.

Sprecher, S., & Schwartz, P. (1994). Equity balance in the exchange of contributions in close relationships. In M. L. Lerner and G. Mikula (Eds.), *Entitlement and the Affectional Bond: Justice in Close Relationships* (pp. 11–41). New York: Plenum Press.

Stasser, G., Kerr, N. L., & Bray, R. M. (1981). The social psychology of jury deliberations: Structure, process, and product. In N. L. Kerr & R. M. Bray (Eds.), *The Psychology of the Courtroom*. New York: Academic Press.

Staub, E. (1974). Helping a distressed person: Social, personality, and stimulus determinants. In L. Berkowitz (Ed.), *Advances in experimental social psychology* (Vol. 7, pp. 293–341). New York: Academic Press.

Staub, E. (1978). *Positive social behavior and morality: Social and personal influences* (Vol. 1). New York: Academic Press.

Steblay, N. M. (1987). Helping behavior in rural and urban environments: A meta-analysis. *Psychological Bulletin, 102,* 346–356.

Steele, C. M. (1988). The psychology of self-affirmation: Sustaining the integrity of the self. In L. Berkowitz (Ed.), *Advances in experimental social psychology, Vol. 21: Social psychological studies of the self: Perspectives and programs.* (pp. 261–302). San Diego, CA: Academic Press.

Steele, C. M., & Aronson, J. (1995). Stereotype threat and the intellectual test performance of African-Americans. *Journal of Personality and Social Psychology, 69,* 797–811.

Stel, M., van Baaren, R. B., & Vonk, R. (2007). Effects of mimicking: Acting prosocially by being emotionally moved. *European Journal of Social Psychology, 38*(6), 965–976.

Stel, M., & Vonk, R. (2010). Mimicry in social interaction: Benefits for mimickers, mimickees, and their interaction. *British Journal of Psychology, 101,* 311–323.

Stelzl, M., Janes, L., & Seligman, C. (2008). Champ or chump: Strategic utilization of dual social identities of others. *European Journal of Social Psychology, 38*(1), 128–138.

Sternberg, R. J. (1986). A triangular theory of love. *Psychological Review, 93*(2), 119–135.

Sternberg, R. J. (1987). Liking versus loving: A comparative evaluation of theories. *Psychological Bulletin, 102,* 331–345.

Sternberg, R. J. (1997). *Thinking styles*. New York: Cambridge University Press.

Stewart D. D. & Stasser G. (1995). Expert role assignment and information sampling during collective recall and decision making. *Journal of Personality and Social Psychology, 69*(4), 619–628.

Stewart, S., Stinnett, H., & Rosenfeld, L. B. (2000). Sex differences in desired characteristics of short-term and long-term relationship partners. *Journal of Social and Personal Relationships, 17,* 843–853.

Stewart-Williams, S. (2007). Altruism among kin vs. non kin: Effects of cost of help and reciprocal exchange. *Evolution and Human Behavior, 28,* 193–198.

Stice, E., Trost, A., & Chase, A. (2003). Healthy weight control and dissonance-based eating disorder prevention programs: Results from a controlled trial. *International Journal of Eating Disorders, 33,* 10–21.

Stinson, D. A., Cameron, J. J., Wood, J. V., Gaucher, D., & Holmes, J. G. (2009). Deconstructing the "reign of error": Interpersonal warmth explains the self-fulfilling prophecy of anticipated acceptance. *Personality and Social Psychology Bulletin, 35*(9), 1165–1178.

Stone, J., Aronson, E., Crain, A. L., Winslow, M. P., & Fried, C. B. (1994). Inducing hypocrisy as a means of encouraging young adults to use condoms. *Personality and Social Psychology Bulletin, 20*(1), 116–128.

Stoner, J. A. F. (1961). A comparison of individual and group decisions involving risk. Unpublished master's thesis. Massachusetts Institute of Technology.

Sullivan, P. (2010, September 10). Preparing children to be safe at college. *The New York Times*. Retrieved December 1, 2010, from http://www.nytimes.com/2010/09/11/your-money/11wealth.html.

Suls, J., Wan, C. K., & Sanders, G. S. (1998). False consensus and false uniqueness in estimating the prevalence of health-protective behaviors. *Journal of Applied Social Psychology, 18*(1), 66–79.

Sunstein, C. (2001). Echo chambers: Bush v. Gore, impeachment, and beyond. Princeton Digital Books Plus.

Swann, W. B., & Read, S. J. (1981). Self-verification processes: How we sustain our self-conceptions. *Journal of Experimental Social Psychology, 17*(4), 351–372.

Swann, W. B., Jr., Stein-Seroussi, A., & Giesler, B. (1992). Why people self-verify. *Journal of Personality and Social Psychology, 62,* 392–401.

Swim, J. K., Aikin, K. J., Hall, W. S., & Hunter, B. A. (1995). Sexism and racism: Old-fashioned and modern prejudices. *Journal of Personality and Social Psychology, 68,* 199–214.

Swim, J. K., & Sanna, L. J. (1996). He's skilled, she's lucky: A meta-analysis of observers' attributions for women's and men's successes and failures. *Personality and Social Psychology Bulletin, 22,* 507–519.

Tajfel, H., & Billig, M. (1974). Familiarity and categorization in intergroup behavior. *Journal of Experimental Social Psychology, 10,* 159–170.

Tajfel, H., & Turner, J. C. (1986). An integrative theory of intergroup conflict. In S. Worchel & W. Austin (Eds.), *Psychology of intergroup relations* (pp. 2–24). Chicago, IL: Nelson-Hall.

Tajfel, H., & Turner, J. C. (1986). The social identity theory of inter-group behavior. In S. Worchel & W. Austin (Eds.), *Psychology of intergroup relations*. Chigago, IL: Nelson-Hall.

Tan, D. T. Y., & Singh, R. (1995). Attitudes and attraction: A developmental study of the similarity–attraction and dissimilarity–repulsion hypotheses. *Personality and Social Psychology Bulletin, 21,* 975–986.

Tapper, K., & Boulton, M. J. (2004). Sex differences in levels of physical, verbal and indirect aggression amongst primary school children and their associations with beliefs about aggression. *Aggressive Behavior, 30,* 123–145.

Tapper, K., & Boulton, M. J. (2005). Victim and peer group responses to different forms of aggression among primary school children. *Aggressive Behavior, 31,* 238–253.

Tasso, A., Monaci, M. G., Trentin, R., & Rosabianca, A. (2005). Frame effects in persuasive messages against smoking. *Proceedings of the XXVII Annual Conference of the Cognitive Science Society*, Stresa, Italy, 2162–2165.

Tashiro, T., & Frazier, P. (2003). 'I'll never be in a relationship like that again': Personal growth following romantic relationship breakups. *Personal Relationships, 10,* 113–128.

Tavris, C., & Aronson, E. (2007). *Mistakes were made (but not by me): Why we justify foolish Beliefs, bad decisions, and hurtful acts*. New York: Houghton Mifflin Harcourt.

Taylor, S. E., & Brown, J. D. (1988). Illusion and well-being: A social psychological perspective on mental health. *Psychological Bulletin, 103,* 193–210.

Tennen, H., & Affleck, G. (1993). The puzzles of self-esteem: A clinical perspective. In R. F. Baumeister (Ed.), *Self-esteem: The puzzle of low self-regard* (pp. 241–262). New York: Plenum Press.

Tesser, A. (1988). Toward a self-evaluation maintenance model of social behavior. In L. Berkowitz (Ed.), *Advances in Experimental Social Psychology* (Vol. 21, pp. 181–227). New York: Academic Press.

Tetlock, P. E. (2005). *Expert political judgment: How good is it? How can we know?* Princeton, NJ: Princeton University Press.

Thaler, R. H., & Sunstein, C. R. (2008). *Nudge: Improving decisions about health, wealth, and happiness.* New Haven, CT: Yale University Press.

Thibaut, J. W., & Kelley, H. H. (1952). *The social psychology of groups.* New York: John Wiley & Sons.

Thibaut, J. W., & Kelley, H. H. (1959). *The social psychology of groups.* New York: John Wiley & Sons.

Thomasch, P., & Paul, F. (2008, October 3). Update 2-False web report plays havoc with Apple stock. *Reuters.com.* Retrieved August 16, 2010, from http://www.reuters.com/article/idUSN0333589620081003.

Thompson, L. (1998). *The mind and heart of the negotiator.* Upper Saddle River, NJ: Prentice-Hall.

Thompson, S. C. (1999). Illusions of control: How we overestimate our personal influence. *Current Directions in Psychological Science, 8*(6), 187–190.

Thorndike, E. L. (1935). Measurements of the influence of recency. *The American Journal of Psychology, 47,* 294–300.

Toi, M., & Batson, C. D. (1982). More evidence that empathy is a source of altruistic motivation. *Journal of Personality and Social Psychology, 43,* 281–292.

Toobin, J. (1996). *The run of his life: The people v. O. J. Simpson.* New York: Random House.

Tooby, J., & Cosmides, L. (1988). The evolution of war and its cognitive foundations. Technical report, Institute for Evolutionary Studies. Palo Alto, CA.

Towles-Schwen, T., & Fazio, R. H. (2001). On the origins of racial attitudes: Correlates of childhood experiences. *Personality and Social Psychology Bulletin, 27,* 162–175.

Tozer, S., Violas, P. C., & Senese, G. (1993). *School and society: Educational practice as social expression.* New York: McGraw-Hill.

Trafimow, D., Triandis, H. C., & Goto, S. G. (1991). Some tests of the distinction between the private self and the collective self. *Journal of Personality and Social Psychology, 60,* 649–655.

Trenholm, C., Devaney, B., Fortson, K., Quay, L., Wheeler, J., & Clark, M. (2007). *Impacts of four Title V, Section 510 abstinence education programs.* Princeton, NJ: Mathematica Policy Research.

Triandis, H. C. (1994). *Culture and social behavior.* New York: McGraw-Hill.

Triplett, N. (1898). The dynamogenic factors in pacemaking and competition. *American Journal of Psychology, 9,* 507–533.

Trope, Y., & Liberman, A. (1996). Social hypothesis testing: Cognitive and motivational mechanisms. In E. T. Higgins & A. W. Kruglanski (Eds.), *Social psychology: Handbook of basic principles.* New York: Guilford Press.

Tversky, A., & Kahneman, D. (1973). Availability: A heuristic for judging frequency and probability. *Cognitive Psychology, 5,* 207–232.

Tversky, A., & Kahneman, D. (1974). Judgment under uncertainty: Heuristics and biases. *Science, 185,* 1124–1131.

Tversky, A., & Kahneman, D. (1982). Evidential impact of base rates. In D. Kahneman, P. Slovic, & A. Tversky (Eds.), *Judgment under uncertainty: Heuristics and biases.* Cambridge, MA: Cambridge University Press.

Tynes, B., & Markoe, S. (2010). The role of color-blind racial attitudes in reactions to racial discrimination in social network sites. *Journal of Diversity in Higher Education, 3*(1), 1–13.

Uleman, J. S. (1989). A framework for thinking intentionally about unintended thoughts. In J. S. Uleman & J. A. Bargh (Eds.), *Unintended thought* (pp. 425–449). New York: Guilford Press.

Uleman, J. S., Newman, L. S., & Moskowitz, G. B. (1996). People as flexible interpreters: Evidence and issues from spontaneous trait inference. In M. P. Zanna (Ed.), *Advances in experimental social psychology* (Volume 28, pp. 211–279). San Diego, CA: Academic Press.

Uleman, J. S., Saribay, S. A., & Gonzalez, C. M. (2008). Spontaneous inferences, implicit impressions, and implicit theories. *Annual Review of Psychology, 59,* 329–360.

United Nations (2010). *Violence against women.* Retrieved July 28, 2010, from http://www.unifem.org/gender_issues/violence_against_women/.

University of Gothenburg (2010, February 22). Cyberbullying: A growing problem. *ScienceDaily.* Retrieved September 28, 2010, from http://www.sciencedaily.com/releases/2010/02/100222104939.htm.

Unkelbach, C., Forgas, J. P., & Denson, T. (2007). The turban effect: The influence of Muslim headgear and induced affect on aggressive responses in the shooter bias paradigm. *Journal of Experimental Social Psychology, 43,* 513–528.

Utne, M. K., & Kidd, R. F. (1980). Equity and attribution. In G. Mikula (Ed.), *Justice and social interaction* (pp. 63–93). New York: Springer-Verlag.

Valins, S. (1966). Cognitive effects of false heart-rate feedback. *Journal of Personality and Social Psychology, 4,* 400–408.

Vallone, R. P., Ross, L. & Lepper, M. R. (1985) The hostile media phenomenon: Biased perception and perceptions of media bias in coverage of the Beirut massacre. *Journal of Personality and Social Psychology, 49,* 577–585.

van Baaren, R. B., Holland, R. W., Kawakami, K., & van Knippenberg, A. (2004). Mimicry and prosocial behavior. *Psychological Science, 15*(1), 71–74.

van Baaren, E. R., Horgan, T. G., Chartrand, T. L., & Dijkmans, M. (2004). The forest, the trees, and the chameleon: Context dependence and mimicry. *Journal of Personality and Social Psychology, 86,* 453–459.

van Honk, J. & Schutter, D. (2007). Testosterone reduces conscious detection of signals serving social correction implications for antisocial behavior. *Psychological Science, 18*(8), 663–667.

Van Yperen, N., & Buunk, B. (1990). A longitudinal study of equity and satisfaction in intimate relationships. *European Journal of Social Psychology, 20,* 287–309.

Van Yperen, N. W., & Buunk, B. P. (1994). Social comparison and social exchange in marital relationships. In M. J. Lerner & G. Mikula (Eds.), *Entitlement and the Affectional Bond: Justice in Close Relationships* (pp. 89–115). New York: Plenum Press.

VanderStoep, S. W., & Shaughnessy, J. J. (1997, April). Taking a course in research methods improves reasoning about real-life events. *Teaching of Psychology, 24*(2), 122–124.

Vasey, P. L., & VanderLaan, D. P. (2010). An adaptive cognitive dissociation between willingness to help kin and nonkin in Samoan Fa'afafine. *Psychological Science, 21*(2), 292–97.

Vescio, T. K., Gervais, S., Snyder, M., & Hoover, A. (2005). Power and the creation of patronizing environments: The stereotype-based behaviors of the powerful and their effects on female performance in masculine domains. *Journal of Personality and Social Psychology, 88,* 658–672.

Visser, P. S., & Krosnick, J. A. (1998). Development of attitude strength over the life cycle: Surge and decline. *Journal of Personality and Social Psychology, 6*(75), 1389–1410.

Visser, P. S., Krosnick, J. A., & Simmons, J. P. (2003). Distinguishing the cognitive and behavioral consequences of attitude and certainty: A new approach to testing the common-factor hypothesis. *Journal of Experimental Social Psychology, 39*(2), 118–141.

Vittengl, J. R., & Holt, C. S. (2000). Getting acquainted: The relationship of self-disclosure and social attraction to positive affect. *Journal of Social and Personal Relationships, 17,* 53–66.

Vivian J. E., & Berkowitz N. H. (1992). Anticipated bias from an outgroup: An attributional analysis. *European Journal of Social Psychology, 22,* 414–424.

Volkman, K. (2010, May 20). Panera chairman: Pay-what-you-can cafe 'test of humanity.' *St. Louis Business Journal.* Retrieved December 1, 2010, from http://stlouis.bizjournals.com/stlouis/stories/2010/05/17/daily52.html.

von Schneidemesser, L. (1996). Soda or pop? *Journal of English Linguistics, 24*(4), 270–287.

Vonk, R. (2002). Self-serving interpretations of flattery: Why ingratiation works. *Journal of Personality and Social Psychology, 82*(4), 515–526.

Vrij, A., Evans, H., Akehurst, L., & Mann, S. (2004). Rapid judgments in assessing verbal and nonverbal cues: Their potential for deception researchers and lie detection. *Applied Cognitive Psychology, 18*(3), 283–296.

Wallace, H. M., Baumeister, R. F., & Vohs, K. D. (2005). Audience support and choking under pressure: A home disadvantage? *Journal of Sports Sciences, 23*(4), 429–438.

Wallach, M. A., Kogan, N., & Bem, D. J. (1962). Group influence on individual risk taking. *Journal of Abnormal and Social Psychology, 65,* 75–86.

Wallop, H., & Cockcroft, L. (2007, October 9). Oasis, Jamiroquai to follow Radiohead. *Telegraph.co.uk.* Retrieved December 1, 2010, from http://www.telegraph.co.uk/news/uknews/1565638/Oasis-Jamiroquai-to-follow-Radiohead.html.

Walster, E., Walster, G. W., Berscheid, E., & Dion, K. (1971). Physical attractiveness and dating choice: A test of the matching hypothesis. *Journal of Experimental Social Psychology, 7*(2), 173–189.

Walster, E. G., Walster, W., & Traupmann, J. (1978). Equity and premarital sex. *Journal of Personality and Social Psychology, 37*, 82–92.

Wang, A. (1994). Pride and prejudice in high school gang members. *Adolescence, 29*(114), 279–291.

Watkins, L. M. & Johnston, L. (2000). Screening job applicants: The impact of physical attractiveness and application quality. *International Journal of Selection and Assessment, 8*, 76–84.

Watt, S. E., & Larkin, C. (2010). Prejudiced people perceive more community support for their views: The role of own, media, and peer attitudes in perceived consensus. *Journal of Applied Social Psychology, 40*(3), 710–731.

Wayland, M. (2009). Today's swine flu headlines. *NBC San Diego*. Retrieved May 14, 2010, from http://www.nbcsandiego.com/news/localbeat/New-Today-on-Swine-Flu.html.

Webb, E. J., Campbell, D. T., Schwartz, R. D., & Sechrest, L. (1966). *Unobtrusive measures: Nonreactive measures in the social sciences*. Chicago: Rand McNally.

Weber, R., & Crocker, J. (1983). Cognitive processes in the revision of stereotypic beliefs. *Journal of Personality and Social Psychology, 45*, 961–977.

Wegener, D. T., & Petty, R. E. (1994). Mood management across affective states: The hedonic contingency hypothesis. *Journal of Personality and Social Psychology, 66*, 1034–1048.

Weinstein, N. D. (1982). Unrealistic optimism about susceptibility to health problems. *Journal of Behavioral Medicine, 5*(4), 441–460.

Wenzlaff, R. M., & Wegner, D. M. (2000). Thought suppression. *Annual Review of Psychology, 51*, 59–91.

Werner, C. M., Stoll, R., Birch, P., & White, P. H. (2002). Clinical validation and cognitive elaboration: Signs encourage sustained recycling. *Basic and Applied Social Psychology, 24*, 185–203.

Whitman, D. (1998). *The optimism gap: The I'm OK—they're not syndrome and the myth of American decline*. New York: Walker.

Widmeyer, W. N., & Loy, J. W. (1988). When you're hot, you're hot! Warm-cold effects in first impressions of persons and teaching effectiveness. *Journal of Educational Psychology, 80*(1), 118–121.

Wilbert, C. (2008, October 8). As economy worsens, so does stress. *WebMD*. Retrieved December 1, 2010 from http://www.webmd.com/balance/stress-management/news/20081008/as-economy-worsens-so-does-stress.

Wilder, D. A. (1993). The role of anxiety in facilitating stereotypic judgments of out-group behavior. In D. M. Mackie & D. L. Hamilton (Eds.), *Affect, cognition, and stereotyping* (pp. 87–109). San Diego, CA: Academic Press.

Wilke, H., & Lanzetta, J. T. (1970). The obligation to help: The effects of amount of prior help on subsequent helping behavior. *Journal of Experimental Social Psychology, 6*, 488–493.

Wilson, D. W., & Kahn, A. (1975). Rewards, costs, and sex differences in helping behavior. *Psychological Reports, 36*, 31–34.

Williams, K. D., Nida, S. A., Baca, L. D., & Latane, B. (1989). Social loafing and swimming: Effects of identifiability on individual and relay performance of intercollegiate swimmers. *Basic and Applied Social Psychology, 10*, 73–81.

Willis, J., & Todorov, A. (2006). First impressions: Making up your mind after a 100-ms exposure to a face. *Psychological Science, 17*(7), 592–598.

Wilson, S. J., & Lipsey, M. W. (2006). The effects of school-based social information processing interventions on aggressive behavior: Part I Universal Programs. *Campbell Systematic Reviews, 5*.

Wilson, T. D., & Schooler, J. W. (2008). Thinking too much: Introspection can reduce the quality of preferences and decisions. In R. H. Fazio & R. E. Petty (Eds.), *Attitudes: Their structure, function, and consequences* (pp. 299–317). New York: Psychology Press.

Wilson, T. D. (1990). Self-persuasion via self-reflection. In J. M. Olson & M. P. Zanna (Eds.), *Self-inference processes: The Ontario Symposium* (Vol. 6, pp. 43–67). Hillsdale, NJ: Erlbaum.

Wilson, T. D., & Gilbert, D. T. (2005). Affective forecasting: Knowing what to want. *Current Directions in Psychological Science, 14*(3), 131–134.

Winkielman, P., Halberstadt, J., Fazendeiro, T., & Catty, S. (2006). Prototypes are attractive because they are easy on the eye. *Psychological Science, 17*, 799–806.

Wispé, L. G., (1972). Positive forms of social behavior: An overview. *Journal of Social Issues, 28*(3), 1–19.

Wojcieszak, M. (2008). False consensus goes online: Impact of ideologically homogeneous groups on false consensus. *Public Opinion Quarterly, 72*(4), 781–791.

Wood, W. (1986). Access to attitude-relevant information in memory as a determinant of attitude-behavior consistency. *Journal of Experimental Social Psychology, 22*, 328–338.

Wood, W., Lundgren, S., Ouellette, J. A., Busceme, S., & Blackstone, T. (1994). *Psychological Bulletin, 115*(3), 323–345.

Wood, W., & Stagner, B. (1994). Why are some people easier to influence than others? In S. Shavitt & T. C. Brock (Eds.), *Persuasion* (pp. 149–174). Boston: Allyn & Bacon.

Worchel, S., Lee, J., & Adewole, A. (1975). Effects of supply and demand on ratings of object value. *Journal of Personality and Social Psychology, 32*, 906–914.

Word, C. O., Zanna, M. P., & Cooper, J. (1974). The nonverbal mediation of self-fulfilling prophecies in interracial interaction. *Journal of Experimental Social Psychology, 10*, 109–120.

Wu, S. (2007). The basics of the testable hypothesis. *Ohio State University Department of Agricultural, Environmental, and Development Economics*. Retrieved June 3, 2010, from http://aede.osu.edu/class/aede205/wu/Hypotheses.pdf.

Xiaohe, X., and Whyte, M. K. (1990). Love matches and arranged marriages: A Chinese replication. *Journal of Marriage and the Family, 52*, 709–722.

Young, R. K., Kennedy, A. H., Newhouse, A., Browne, P., & Theissen, D. (1993). The effects of names on perception of intelligence, popularity, and competence. *Journal of Applied Social Psychology, 23*, 21.

Yzerbyt, V., Corneille, O., & Estrada, C. (2001). The interplay of subjective essentialism and entitativity in the formation of stereotypes. *Personality and Social Psychology Review, 5*(2), 141–155.

Zaccaro, S. J. (2007). Trait-based perspectives of leadership. *American Psychologist, 62*, 6–16.

Zajonc, R. B. (1965). Social facilitation. *Science, 149*, 269–274.

Zajonc, R. B. (1968). Attitudinal effects of mere exposure. *Journal of Personality and Social Psychology, 9*, 1–27.

Zajonc, R. B. (1993). Brain temperature and subjective emotional experience. In M. Lewis & J. M. Haviland (Eds.), *Handbook of emotions* (pp. 209–220). New York: Guilford.

Zajonc, R. B., Heingartner, A., & Herman, E. M. (1969). Social enhancement and impairment of performance in the cockroach. *Journal of Personality and Social Psychology, 13*, 83–92.

Zajonc, R. B., & Rajecki, D. W. (1969). Exposure and affect: A field experiment. *Psychonomic Science, 17*(4), 216–217.

Zak, P. J., Kurzban, R., & Matzner, W. T. (2005). Oxytocin is associated with human trustworthiness. *Hormones and Behavior, 48*, 522–527. Retrieved June 4, 2010, from http://www.sas.upenn.edu/psych/PLEEP/pdfs/2005%20Zak%20Kurzban%20&%20Matzner%20H%20&%20B.pdf.

Zanna, M. P., & Pack, S. J. (1975). On the self-fulfilling nature of apparent sex differences in behavior. *Journal of Experimental Social Psychology, 11*(6), 583–591.

Zanna, M. P., & Rempel, J. K. (1988). Attitudes: A new look at an old concept. In D. Bartal & A. W. Kruglanski (Eds.), *The Social Psychology of Knowledge*, Cambridge, UK: Cambridge University Press, pp. 315–334.

Zárate, M. A., Garcia, B., Garza, A. A., & Hitlan, R. (2004). Cultural threat and perceived realistic group conflict as predictors of attitudes towards Mexican immigrants. *Journal of Experimental Social Psychology, 40*, 99–105.

Zillmann, D. (1971). Excitation transfer in communication-mediated aggressive behavior. *Journal of Experimental Social Psychology, 7*, 419–434.

Zillmann, D. (1983). Transfer of excitation in emotional behavior. In J. T. Cacipoppo & R. E. Petty (Eds.), *Social Psychophysiology: A Sourcebook*. New York: Guildford Press.

Zillmann, D. (1996). Sequential dependencies in emotional experience and behavior. In *Emotion: Interdisciplinary Perspectives*, eds. Robert D. Kavanaugh, Betty Zimmerberg, and Steven Fein. Mahwah, NJ: Lawrence Erlbaum.

Zimbardo, P. G. (1969). The human choice: Individuation, reason, and order versus deindividuation, impulse, and chaos. *Nebraska Symposium on Motivation, 17*, 237–307.

Zimbardo, P. G. (1970). The human choice: Individuation, reason, and order versus deindividuation, impulse, and chaos. In W. J. Arnold & D. Levine (Eds.), *1969 Nebraska Symposium on Motivation* (pp. 237–307). Lincoln, NE: University of Nebraska Press.

Zimbardo, P. G. (1971). One final act of rebellion. *The Stanford Prison Experiment*. Retrieved June 3, 2010, from http://www.prisonexp.org/psychology/36.

Zimbardo, P. G. (1971). The power and pathology of imprisonment. *Congressional Record*. (Serial No. 15, 1971-10-25). Hearings before Subcommittee No. 3, of the Committee on the Judiciary, House of Representatives, Ninety-Second Congress, *First Session on Corrections, Part II, Prisons, Prison Reform and Prisoner's Rights: California*. Washington, DC: U.S. Government Printing Office.

Zimmerman, B. J., Bandura, A., & Martinez-Pons, M. (1992). Self-motivation for academic attainment: The role of self-efficacy beliefs and personal goal setting. *American Educational Research Journal, 29*, 663–676.

Zuckerman, E., & Jost, J. T. (2001). What makes you think you're so popular? Self-evaluation maintenance and the subjective side of the "friendship paradox." *Social Psychology Quarterly, 64*, 207–233.

Zuwerink, J. R., & Devine, P. G. (1996). Attitude importance and resistance to persuasion: It's not just the thought that counts. *Journal of Personality and Social Psychology, 70*(5), 931–944.

CHAPTER 01 PAGE 2: Zefa/SuperStock; **4 (top to bottom):** NASA Langley Research Center; Kate Kunath/Getty Images; **5 (left to right):** Westend61/SuperStock; Mike Flippo/Shutterstock; Ariel Skelley/Getty Images; **6 (top to bottom):** Fuse/Getty Images; Jupiterimages/Thinkstock; **7 (top left):** Svemir/Shutterstock; **(top right):** ©Lbshooters/Dreamstime.com; **(bottom):** ©Bazuki Muhammad/Reuters/Corbis; **8:** AP Images; **10 (top to bottom):** wrangle/iStockphoto; Radius Images/Alamy; **11 (clockwise from top left):** LattaPictures/iStockphoto; Jason Stitt/Shutterstock; Comstock/Thinkstock; Supri Suharjoto/Shuttertock; **12:** Image Source/Getty Images; **13:** Tony Garcia/Getty Images

CHAPTER 02 PAGE 16: PhotoAlto/Alamy; **18 (top to bottom):** kated/Shutterstock; Steven Lewis/Newscom; **19 (top to bottom):** Ljupco Smokovski/Shutterstock; Dmitriy Shironosov/Shutterstock; **20 (top to bottom):** Michael Blann/Thinkstock; iStockphoto/Thinkstock; **21 (top to bottom):** Silver Pictures/The Kobal Collection; Loren Rodgers/Shutterstock; **22 (top to bottom):** oliveromg/Shutterstock; NemoImages/PhotoEdit; **23 (top to bottom):** Cusp/Shutterstock; iStockphoto/Thinkstock; **25:** Matt Grant/Shutterstock; **27:** Jupiterimages/Thinkstock; **29:** ©Gideon Mendel/In Pictures/Corbis; **30:** Itana/Shutterstock; **31:** Koksharov Dmitry/Shutterstock; **32:** iStockphoto/Thinkstock; **33:** iStockphoto/Thinkstock

READING 01 PAGES 36-37: Chad Baker/Thinkstock

CHAPTER 03 PAGE 38: Jupiterimages/Thinkstock; **41 (center):** AP Images/Ted S. Warren; **(cups):** Lenscap/Alamy; **42:** Gary Crabbe/Alamy; **43:** medicalpicture/Alamy; **44:** Steve Mason/Thinkstock; **45 (graph):** ©Yahia LOUKKAL/Fotolia; **(gun):** Romanchuck Dimitry/Shutterstock; **(bottom):** Steve Snowden/Shutterstock; **47 (top to bottom):** Peter Marshall/Alamy; Frederick M. Brown/Getty Images; **48:** Jonathan Nourok/PhotoEdit; **49:** ©Constantin Opris/Dreamstime.com; **50:** ©Monkey Business Images/Dreamstime.com; **51:** AP Images/Morry Gash; **52:** Tracy Whiteside/Shutterstock; **53 (monitor):** Kayros Studio "Be Happy!"/Shutterstock

CHAPTER 04 PAGE 56: Oleksiy Maksymenko/Photolibrary; **58:** Mat Szwajkos/Getty Images; **59 (top to bottom):** ©Archives du 7ème Art/Photo12 / The Image Works; ©Ellen Nolan; **60:** James Balog/Getty Images; **61 (left to right):** Edyta Pawlowska/Shutterstock; East/Shutterstock; **62 (top left):** Bloomberg/Getty Images; **(top right):** ©Ralf-Finn Hestoft/Corbis; **(bottom):** zhu difeng/Shutterstock; **63:** balaikin/Shutterstock; **64:** Corbis/Photolibrary; **65:** Imagesource/Photolibrary; **66:** ©Victor Fraile/Corbis; **67:** Eyecandy Images/Photolibrary; **69:** Granada/Fox TV/The Kobal Collection/Greg Gayne; **70:** Alex Segre/Alamy; **71:** ©The Image Works Archives

CHAPTER 05 PAGE 74: Hubert Boesl/dpa/Landov; **76:** Baevskiy Dmitry/Shutterstock; **78:** Moviestone Collection Ltd./Alamy; **79:** Commercial Eye/Getty Images; **80:** BananaStock/Thinkstock; **81:** Xandros/ iStockphoto; **82:** Aflo/Splash News/Newscom; **83:** Janine Wiedel Photolibrary/Alamy; **85:** Kzenon/Shutterstock; **86:** ©Flirt/SuperStock; **87 (center):** Alex Staroseltsev/Shutterstock; **(clockwise from top):** chang/iStockphoto; Jupiterimages/Thinkstock; Franck Camhi/Alamy; ©Stylephotographs/Dreamstime.com;OSTILL/iStockphoto; Gorich/ Shutterstock; **89:** Catchlight Visual Services/Alamy

APPLYING SOCIAL PSYCHOLOGY: BUSINESS PAGE 92: AP Images/John Cogill; **93:** Blend Images/SuperStock

CHAPTER 06 PAGE 94: ©U.S. Coast Guard/Corbis; **96:** Denkou Images/Alamy; **97:** Shutterstock; **98:** Jupiterimages/Photolibrary; **99 (top):** Denkou Images/Alamy; **(bottom left):** Radius/SuperStock; **(bottom right):** National Geographic Image Collection/Alamy; **100 (laptop):** Nadezda/Shutterstock; **(student):** East/Shutterstock; **101:** Lasse Kris-

tensen/Shutterstock; **103:** Green Stock Media/Alamy; **105:** gazmandhu/Shutterstock; **106 (top to bottom):** Mike Kemp/Photolibrary; Stockbyte/Photolibrary; **107:** The Granger Collection, NYC—All rights reserved; **109:** zentilia/Shutterstock

APPLYING SOCIAL PSYCHOLOGY: HEALTH PAGE 112: SOMOS/SuperStock; **113:** Alexandr Shevchenko/Shutterstock

CHAPTER 07 PAGE 114: ©Kati1313/Dreamstime.com; **116 (top to bottom):** Mike Clark/Getty Images; Matthew Peters/Getty Images; **117:** bumihills/Shutterstock; **118:** Maria R. T. Deseo/PhotoEdit; **119:** Artpose Adam Borkowski/Shutterstock; **120 (top to bottom):** Kevin Schafer/Peter Arnold/Getty Images; Bill Aron/PhotoEdit; **121:** Stephen Coburn/Shutterstock; **122 (top to bottom):** ©Radius/SuperStock; Jason Mitchell/Getty Images; **123 (fish):** Le Do/Shutterstock; **(plates):** oku/Shutterstock; **124:** AP Images/Chris O'Meara; **125 (top to bottom):** Andrew Bret Wallis/Getty Images; Maria R. T. Deseo/PhotoEdit; **126:** Vladimir Sazonov/Shutterstock; **127:** Alexandr Makarov/Shutterstock

READING 02 PAGES 132-135: George Doyle/Thinkstock

CHAPTER 08 PAGE 136: sébastien Baussais/Alamy; **138:** @erics/Shutterstock; **139 (top left):** Cynthia Farmer/Shutterstock; **(bottom left):** ©Syracuse Newspapers/Gary Walts/The Image Works; **(center):** Photodisc/Thinkstock; **(right):** Derek Gordon/Shutterstock; **140 (left to right):** ostill/Shutterstock; Fabio Lovino/Contrasto/Redux; **141 (top to bottom):** Science and Society/SuperStock; Stockbyte/ Thinkstock; **143 (left to right):** Photo Alto/Alamy; Corbis/ SuperStock; **145:** Bob Strong/Reuters/Landov; **147:** Mar Photographics/Alamy; **148:** c76/ZUMA Press/Newscom; **150:** Chepko Danil Vitalevich/Shutterstock; **151:** AP Images

CHAPTER 09 PAGE 154: AP Images/Al Behrman; **156 (top to bottom):** Sylvain Grandadam/Getty Images; Steve Skjold/Alamy; **157:** muzsy/Shutterstock; **158 (left to right):** Image Source/Alamy; Cliff Lipson/CBS/Landov; **159:** Claus Mikosch/Shutterstock; **160:** Ian Shaw/Alamy; **161:** Ryan McVay/Shutterstock; **162:** STILLFX/ Shutterstock; **163:** AP Images/Dana Edelson/NBC Universal; **164:** NASA; **165:** Steve Johnson/EPA/Landov; **166 (top to bottom):** b64/ZUMA Press/Newscom; mistydawnphoto/Shutterstock; **167:** Warner Bros./The Kobal Collection/Buitendijk, Jaap; **168:** PacificCoastNews/Newscom; **169:** Atta Kenare/AFP/Getty Images/Newscom

APPLYING SOCIAL PSYCHOLOGY: LAW PAGE 172: Corbis/SuperStock; **173:** AP Images/L.A. County Sheriff's Department

CHAPTER 10 PAGE 174: Aurora Open/Superstock; **176:** Panthera/Alamy; **178 (top to bottom):** ©Bettmann/Corbis; Olgysha/Shutterstock; **179 (left to right):** Michael Kappeler/AFP/Getty Images; Jewel Samad/AFP/Getty Images; **181 (top to bottom):** Digital Vision/Thinkstock; Ted Foxx/Alamy; **183:** age fotostock/SuperStock; **184:** Jupiterimages/Thinkstock; **185 (top to bottom):** Corbis/SuperStock; Cusp/SuperStock; **186:** ZOOM(189) Friends—Campus Life/Getty Images; **187:** Umit Erdem/Shutterstock; **188 (left to right):** Stock Connection Blue/Alamy; Andy Hayt/Getty Images; Umit Erdem/Shutterstock; **189 (top to bottom):** Blend Images/Alamy; Archive Holdings Inc./Getty Images

READING 03 PAGES 194-199: Comstock Images/Thinkstock

CHAPTER 11 PAGE 200: oliveromg/Shutterstock; **202:** Forward Pass/The Kobal Collection; **203 (clockwise from top left):** Zurijeta/Shutterstock; pzAxe/Shutterstock; PhotosIndia.com LLC/Alamy; prodakszyn/Shutterstock; **204:** ©Courtney Perry/Dallas Morning News/

291

PHOTO CREDITS

Swearing, persuasion and, 132–135
Swim, Janet, 180
Synaptic Self: How Our Brains Become Who We Are (LeDoux), 59

T
Tale-Yax, Hugo, 249
Tavris, Carol, 108
Thaler, Richard, 45, 48
That's-not-all technique, 147–148, 152
Thematic Apperception Test, 230
Theory, 20–21, 35
Theory of planned behavior, 103, 110
Third variable, 27, 35
Thorndike, Edward, 99
Thought suppression, 17
Three-stage model of attribution, 78–79, 91

Transactional leader, 164–166, 170
Transformational leader, 164–166, 170
Triangular theory of love, 230–231, 237
Triplett, Norman, 5, 157
Truth
    replication, 23
    research process steps, 21–22
TST. *See* Twenty Statements Test
Tuli, Sagan, 178
Tversky, Amos, 44, 47–48
Twelve Angry Men (movie), 172
Twenty Statements Test (TST), 60–61, 72
Tynes, Brendesha, 182, 197

U
UCR. *See* Unconditioned response
UCS. *See* Unconditioned stimulus

Ultimate attribution error, 184
Unconditioned response (UCR), 98, 110
Unconditioned stimulus (UCS), 98, 110
University of British Columbia, 32
University of Chicago, 65
Unrealistic optimism, 68, 72
Upward counterfactual, 50

V
Valence, 119–120, 130
Valid, 22, 35
Valins, Stuart, 108
Variables, 22, 35
Video games, aggression and, 213–214
Violence, aggression and, 206
Visual cleanliness, morality and, 263
Vittrup, Birgitte, 194–195

W
Ward, Deletha, 248
Washington, Steven Eugene, 181
Wearing, Clive, 58–59
Western, educated, industrialized, rich and democratic (WEIRD) societies, 36
What is beautiful is good effect, 83, 91
Williams syndrome (WS), 189
Woods, Tiger, 75
World War II, 8–10
WS. *See* Williams syndrome

Y
Yale Communication Model, 116

Z
Zahler, Sandra, 248
Zajonc, Robert, 157–158
Zak, Paul, 28
Zhong, Chen-Bo, 262–263